Bienvenue

ABOUT THE AUTHORS

Conrad J. Schmitt

Conrad J. Schmitt received his B.A. degree magna cum laude from Montclair State College, Upper Montclair, NJ. He received his M.A. from Middlebury College, Middlebury, VT. He did additional graduate work at Seton Hall University and New York University.

Mr. Schmitt has taught French and Spanish at the elementary, junior, and senior high school levels. He was Coordinator of Foreign Languages for the Hackensack, New Jersey, Public Schools. He also taught French at Upsala College, East Orange, NJ; Spanish at Montclair State College; and Methods of Teaching a Foreign Language at the Graduate School of Education, Rutgers University, New Brunswick, NJ. He was editor-in-chief of Foreign Languages and Bilingual Education for McGraw-Hill Book Company and Director of English Language Materials for McGraw-Hill International Book Company.

Mr. Schmitt has authored or co-authored more than eighty books, all published by Glencoe/McGraw-Hill or by McGraw-Hill. He has addressed teacher groups and given workshops in all states of the U.S. and has lectured and presented seminars throughout the Far East, Europe, Latin America, and Canada. In addition, Mr. Schmitt has travelled extensively throughout France, French-speaking Canada, North Africa, the French Antilles, and Haiti.

Katia Brillié Lutz

Ms. Lutz was Executive Editor of French at Macmillan Publishing Company. Prior to that, she taught French language and literature at Yale University and Southern Connecticut State College. Ms. Lutz also served as a senior editor at Harcourt Brace Jovanovich and Holt, Rinehart and Winston. She was a news translator and announcer for the BBC Overseas Language Services in London. Ms. Lutz has her *Baccalauréat* in Mathematics and Science from the Lycée Molière in Paris and her *Licence ès lettres* in Languages from the Sorbonne. She was a Fulbright Scholar at Mount Holyoke College. Ms. Lutz is the author of many foreign language textbooks at all levels of instruction. She presently devotes her time to teaching French at the United Nations and to writing.

Glencoe French 1

Bienvenue

Conrad J. Schmitt

Katia Brillié Lutz

Glencoe McGraw-Hill

New York, New York   Columbus, Ohio   Mission Hills, California   Peoria, Illinois

Send all inquiries to:
Glencoe/McGraw-Hill
15319 Chatsworth Street
P.O. Box 9609
Mission Hills, CA 91346-9609

ISBN 0-02-636679-7
ISBN 0-02-636682-7
ISBN 0-02-636684-3

Printed in the United States of America.

1 2 3 4 5 6 7 8 9   QPK   03 02 01 00 99 98 97

CONTENTS

INTRODUCTION

Welcome to **Glencoe French**, the junior high and high school French series from Glencoe/McGraw-Hill. Every element in this series has been designed to help you create an atmosphere of challenge, variety, cooperation, and enjoyment for your students. From the moment you begin to use **Glencoe French**, you will notice that not only is it packed with exciting, practical materials and features designed to stimulate young people to work together towards language proficiency, but that it goes beyond by urging students to use their new skills in other areas of the curriculum.

Glencoe French uses an integrated approach to language learning: from the introduction of new material, through reinforcement, evaluation and review, its presentations, exercises and activities are designed to span all four language skills. Another characteristic of this series is that students use and reinforce these new skills while developing a realistic, up-to-date awareness of French culture. **Glencoe French** also incorporates a new feature in which French is used as the medium of instruction for a series of interdisciplinary presentations in the areas of natural sciences, social sciences, and the arts and humanities.

The Teacher's Wraparound Edition you are reading has been developed based on the advice of experienced foreign language educators throughout the United States in order to meet your needs as a teacher both in and out of the foreign language classroom. Here are some of the features and benefits which make **Glencoe French** a powerful set of teaching tools:

- flexible format
- student-centered instruction
- balance among all four language skills
- contextualized vocabulary
- thorough, contextual presentation of grammar
- an integrated approach to culture

FEATURES AND BENEFITS

Flexible Format While we have taken every opportunity to use the latest in pedagogical developments in order to create a learning atmosphere of variety, vitality, communication and challenge, we have also made every effort to make the **Glencoe French** series "teacher-friendly." This is where flexibility comes in.

The Student Textbook and the Teacher's Wraparound Edition provide an instructional method. However, every minute of every class period is not laid out. Plenty of room has been built in for you the teacher to be flexible: to draw on your own education, experience and personality in order to tailor a language program that is suitable and rewarding for the individual "chemistry" of each class.

A closer look at the most basic component, the Student Textbook, serves as an example of this flexibility. Each chapter opens with two sections of vocabulary (*Vocabulaire: Mots 1* and *Mots 2*) each with its own set of exercises. *Vocabulaire* is followed by the *Structure* consisting of a series of grammar points, each with accompanying exercises. But, there is nothing which says that the material must be presented in this order. The items of vocabulary and grammar are so well integrated that you will find it easy, and perhaps preferable, to move back and forth between them. You may also wish to select from the third and fourth sections of each chapter (the *Conversation* and *Lecture et culture* sections) at an earlier point than that at which they are presented, as a means of challenging students to identify or use the chapter vocabulary and grammar to which they have already been introduced.

These options are left to you. The only requirement for moving successfully through the Student Textbook is that the vocabulary and grammar of each chapter eventually be presented in their entirety, since each succeeding chapter builds on what has come before.

In the Student Textbook, there is a marked difference between learning exercises (*Exercices*) and communication-based activities (*Activités de communication*), both of which are provided in each chapter. The former serve as their name implies, as exercises for the acquisition and practice of new vocabulary and structures, while the latter are designed to get students communicating in open-ended contexts using the French they have learned. You can be selective among these, depending on the needs of your students.

We have been looking only at the Student Textbook. The abundance of suggestions for techniques, strategies, additional practice, chapter projects, independent (homework) assignments, informal assessment, and more, which are provided in this Teacher's Wraparound Edition—as well as the veritable banquet of resources available in the wide array of ancillary materials provided in the series—are what make **Glencoe French** truly flexible and "teacher-friendly." They guarantee you a great pool of ideas and teaching tools from which to pick and choose in order to create an outstanding course.

Student-Centered Instruction Teaching a foreign language requires coping with different learning styles and special student needs. It

requires the ability to capitalize on the great cultural and economic diversity present in many classrooms and to turn this diversity into an engine for learning by putting students together in goal-oriented groups. It often requires effective techniques for managing large classes.

Glencoe French anticipates these requirements by offering ideas for setting up a cooperative learning environment for students. Useful suggestions to this end accompany each chapter, under the heading Cooperative Learning, in the bottom margin of the Teacher's Wraparound Edition. Additional paired and group activities occur in the Student Textbook (*Activités de communication*), and in headings such as Additional Practice in the Teacher's Wraparound Edition.

Besides cooperative learning strategies, **Glencoe French** contains many other student-centered elements that allow students to expand their learning experiences. Here are a few examples: suggestions are offered in the Teacher's Wraparound Edition for out-of-class projects on topics related to the chapter theme. There is a topic called "For the Younger Student," with activities aimed primarily at stimulating the middle school/junior high student. In the Student Textbook, new grammatical material is divided into "bite-sized" lessons, so as not to be intimidating. The Writing Activities Workbook provides a self-test after every fourth chapter, so that students can prepare alone or in study groups for teacher-administered quizzes and tests. The Audio Cassette Program allows students to work at their own pace, stopping the tape whenever necessary to make directed changes in the language or to refer to their activity sheets in the Student Tape Manual. The Computer Software element consists of not only a Test Generator for the teacher, but also a Practice Generator for students, with which they can practice vocabulary and grammar items at their own pace.

These and other features discussed elsewhere in this Teacher's Manual have been designed with the student in mind. They assure that each individual, regardless of learning style, special need, background, or age, will have the necessary resources for becoming proficient in French.

Balance Among All Four Language Skills

Glencoe French provides a balanced focus on the listening, speaking, reading, and writing skills throughout all phases of instruction. And since it is "teacher-friendly," it gives you leeway if you wish to adjust the integration of these skills to the needs of a particular individual, group or class. Several features of the series lend themselves to this: the overall flexibility of format, the abundance of suggested optional and additional activities and the design of the individual activities themselves. Flexibility was discussed above. Let's look at some sections of a typical chapter as examples of the other two characteristics mentioned.

If the suggested presentation is followed, students are introduced to new words and phrases in *Vocabulaire* by the teacher, and/or by the audio cassette presentation. The focus is on listening and speaking through modeling and repetition. The *Exercices* which accompany the *Vocabulaire* section can be done with books either closed (accentuating listening and speaking) or open (accentuating reading, listening and speaking). However, these *Exercices* can just as well be assigned or reassigned as written work if the teacher wishes to have the whole class or individuals begin to concentrate on reading and writing. Throughout the *Vocabulaire* section, optional and additional reinforcement activities are suggested in the Teacher's Wraparound Edition.

These suggestions address all four language skills. Later in each chapter, students are asked to combine the material learned in *Vocabulaire* with material from the grammar section (*Structure*) using a combination of listening, reading, writing and speaking skills in the process.

Reading and writing activities are brought into play early in the **Glencoe French** series. The authors realize that communication in French includes the use of reading and writing skills and that these skills are indispensable for the assimilation and retention of new language and the organization of thought. Students are launched into writing, for example, as early as Chapter 1, through the use of brief assignments such as lists, labeled diagrams, notetaking or short answers. Longer writing activities are added in later chapters. These textbook activities are further reinforced in the Writing Activities Workbook.

Let's take a closer look at how each of the four skills is woven into the Student Textbook, the Teacher's Wraparound Edition and the ancillary materials.

Listening You the teacher are the primary source for listening, as you model new vocabulary, dialogues, structure and pronunciation, share your knowledge of French culture, history and geography, talk to students about their lives and your own, or engage in culturally oriented activities, and projects. As always, it is your ability to use French as much as possible with your students, both in and outside of the classroom, which determines how relevant and dynamic their learning experience will be.

Glencoe French offers numerous ways in which to develop the listening skill. There are teacher-focused activities, which provide the consistent modeling that students need. Teachers who use the Audio Cassette Program will find that these recordings help students become accustomed to a variety of voices, as well as rates of speech. There are also activities in which students interact with each other to develop listening spontaneity and acuity.

In the Student Textbook, new vocabulary will be modeled by the teacher. Students' attention to the sounds of the new words can be maximized by presenting this material with books closed and using the Vocabulary Transparencies to convey meaning. Following each *Mots* segment are several *Exercices* for practicing the new vocabulary. These can also be done with books closed. After the two *Mots* segments come *Activités de communication*, in which students may work in pairs or groups and must listen to each other in order to find information, take notes or report to others on what was said in their group. In *Structure*, students listen as the teacher models new grammatical material and then are given a chance to practice each structure in several *exercices*. Once again, closing the book will provide increased focus on the listening skill. The next section of each chapter is *Conversation*, in which a real-life dialogue is modeled either by the teacher or by playing the recorded version from the Audio Cassette Program. The dialogue is followed by several communication-based activities, where students must listen to and interact with their peers. In *Bienvenue*

(Level 1), *Conversation* also contains a *Prononciation* segment, covering an aspect of pronunciation related to the chapter material. Here again, students will be listening either to the teacher or recorded models. The last section of each chapter, *Culmination*, offers more listening-intensive *Activités de communication orale*, where students must be able to understand what their partners say in order to play their role.

In addition to the Student Textbook, the Teacher's Wraparound Edition offers several other listening-based activities correlated to the chapters, the most intensive of which occur under the heading "Total Physical Response." Here students must perform an action after listening to a spoken command. There are further listening-based activities suggested under the heading "Cooperative Learning" and often under "Additional Practice," both of which occur in the bottom margins in each Teacher's Wraparound Edition chapter.

The Audio Cassette Program has two main listening components. The first is practice-oriented, wherein students further reinforce vocabulary and grammar, following directions and making changes in utterances. They can self-check their work by listening to the correctly modeled utterances, which are supplied after a pause.

The second part of the program places more attention on the receptive listening skills. Students listen to language in the form of dialogues, announcements, or advertisements—language delivered at a faster pace and in greater volume—and then are asked to demonstrate their understanding of the main ideas and important details of what they have heard. The Student Tape Manual contains activity sheets for doing this work, and the Teacher Edition contains the complete transcript of all audio materials to assist you in laying out listening tasks for your class.

More listening practice is offered through the Videocassette Program. This material corresponds to and enriches that in the Student Textbook, and gives students a chance to hear variations of the language elements they have been practicing, as spoken by a variety of native speakers from different parts of France and other francophone countries. Students'

listening comprehension can be checked and augmented by using the corresponding print activities in the Video Activities Booklet.

Speaking Most of the areas of the Student Textbook and the Teacher's Wraparound Edition mentioned above which develop listening skills simultaneously develop the speaking skill. After hearing a model in the *Vocabulaire* or *Structure* sections, students will repeat it, either as a whole class, in small groups, or as individuals. From these modeled cues, they will progress to visual ones, supplied by the Vocabulary Transparencies or the photos and graphics in the textbook. The real thrust in the *Exercices* accompanying these two sections is to get students to produce this new material actively. Then, in the *Activités de communication*, students have the opportunity to adapt what they have learned by asking for and giving information to their classmates on a given topic. Here, and in the *Conversation* sections, students are engaged in meaningful, interesting sessions of sharing information, all designed to make them want to speak and experiment with the language. The Student Textbook regularly enriches this by offering expressions and mannerisms of speech currently popular in French culture, especially among teenagers, so that from the start your students will be accustomed to speaking in a way that is reflective of contemporary French. In Chapter 2, for example, popular adjectives of pleasure or displeasure are taught, such as *chouette, moche, extra,* and *terrible.* Previously presented material is constantly recycled in the communication-based activities, so that students' speaking vocabularies and knowledge of structure are always increasing. For this purpose, beginning with Chapter 3, there is a *Réintroduction et recombinaison* segment in the *Culmination* section. Another feature of the Student Textbook is that the length of utterances is increased over time, so that when students complete Level 1 (*Bienvenue*) they will have acquired an appreciation of the intonation and inflection of longer streams of language. To assist you in fine-tuning your students' speech patterns, the *Prononciation* section occurs in each chapter of the Level 1 Student Textbook.

The speaking skill is stressed in the first part of each recorded chapter of the Audio Cassette Program, where pauses are provided for the student to produce directed, spoken changes in the language. This is an excellent opportunity for those students who are self-conscious about speaking out in class. The Audio Cassette Program gives these students a chance to work in isolation. The format of making a change in the language, uttering the change and then listening for the correct model may improve the speaking skill. Sensitively administered, the Audio Cassette Program can serve as a confidence-builder for such students, allowing them to work their way gradually into more spontaneous speech with their classmates.

The packet of Situation Cards provides students with yet another opportunity to produce spoken French. They put the student into a contextualized, real-world situation. Students must ask and/or answer questions in order to perform successfully.

Reading Each chapter of the Student Textbook has a *Lecture et culture* section containing two readings based on the chapter theme. The first reading is accompanied by a comprehension check and an exercise called *Étude de mots,* which focuses on useful strategies for vocabulary-building and recognizing word relationships, which students can carry over into other readings. The second reading, *Découverte culturelle,* is optional and is to be read for more specific and detailed information about the theme of the chapter and as a stimulus for discussion on this theme. In the next section of each chapter, *Réalités,* students again use their reading skills albeit to a lesser degree. While the *Réalités* section is primarily visual in nature, students nevertheless are referred to numbered captions to learn more about the photographs shown in this two-page spread.

After every four chapters of the Student Textbook, **Glencoe French** provides a unique section called *Lettres et sciences.* This presentation is designed to use reading as a means of bridging the gap between French and other areas of the curriculum. Three separate readings are offered, one in each of the three areas of natural sciences, social sciences, arts and humanities. Here students have a chance to stretch their reading abilities in French by reading basic information they may have already learned in other academic subjects. Although the material has been carefully written to include themes (as well as words

and structures) which students have learned in previous chapters, it contains the most challenging readings. The *Lettres et sciences* sections are optional.

The Writing Activities Workbook offers additional readings under the heading *Un Peu Plus*. These selections and the accompanying exercises focus on reading strategies such as cognate recognition, related word forms and the use of context clues.

In addition to the reading development above, students are constantly presented with authentic French texts such as announcements from periodicals, telephone listings, transportation schedules, labeled diagrams, floor plans, travel brochures, school progress reports and many others, as sources of information. Sometimes these documents serve as the bases for language activities, and other times they appear in order to round out a cultural presentation, but, in varying degrees, they all require students to apply their reading skills.

Writing Written work is interwoven throughout the language learning process in **Glencoe French**. The exercises, which occur throughout the *Vocabulaire* and *Structure* sections of each chapter in the Student Textbook, are designed in such a way that they can be completed in written form as well as orally. Frequently, you may wish to reassign (as written homework) exercises which you have gone through orally in class. The Teacher's Wraparound Edition makes special note of this under the topic "Independent Practice." At the end of each chapter of the Student Textbook, direct focus is placed on writing in the *Culmination* section, under the heading *Activités de communication écrite*. Here there are one or more activities that encourage students to use the new vocabulary and structures they have learned in the chapter to create their own writing samples. These are short, and may be descriptive, narrative, argumentative, analytical or in the form of dialogues or interviews. Often a context is set up and then students are asked to develop an appropriate written response.

The Writing Activities Workbook is the component in which writing skills receive the most overt attention. All of the exercises in it are writing-based, and they vary in length from one-word answers to short compositions. They are designed to focus on the same vocabulary and grammar presented in the corresponding chapter of the Student Textbook, but they are all new and all contextualized around fresh visual material or situational vignettes. Since they often have students making lists, adding to charts, and labeling, they provide an excellent means for them to organize the chapter material in their minds and make associations which will help them retain it. As students' knowledge of French increases, longer written pieces are required of them. One workbook section entitled *Mon Autobiographie* has students write installments of their own autobiographies. This is an effective way of stretching student writing skills. It also challenges students to personalize the French they have been studying.

Besides these major sources of writing, students are asked to make implicit use of writing almost everywhere in the series. They are constantly taking notes, listing, categorizing, labeling, summarizing, comparing or contrasting on paper. Even the Audio Cassette Program and the Videocassette Program involve students in writing through the use of activity sheets. By choosing among these options, you can be sure that your students will receive the practice they need to develop their writing skills successfully.

Contextualized Vocabulary

From the moment students see new words at the beginning of each chapter in **Glencoe French**, they see them within an identifiable context. So from the start, students learn to group words by association, thereby enhancing their ability to assimilate and store vocabulary for long-term retention. This contextualization remains consistent throughout the practice, testing and recycling phases of learning.

In the *Vocabulaire* section, each of the *Mots* segments contains a short exchange or a few lead-in sentences or phrases which, together with interesting, colorful visuals, establish the context. Other vocabulary items which occur naturally within this context are laid out among additional visuals, often as labels. The result is that students see at a glance the new language set into a real-life situation which provides "something to talk about"—a reason for using it. The accompanying exercises enrich this context. Each *exercice* practice item

is related to the others within the set, so that when taken together they form a meaningful vignette or story. In later sections of the chapter, i.e., *Structure, Conversation, Lecture et culture, Réalités* and *Culmination*, these words and phrases are reintroduced frequently.

Moreover, future chapters build on vocabulary and grammar from previous ones. Chapter themes introduced in Level 1 are reintroduced in Level 2 along with additional related vocabulary. Special attention has been given vocabulary in the reading sections of the series as well. For example, in *Lecture et culture*, students are encouraged to stretch their vocabularies in order to get as much meaning as possible from the selections. In addition to glossed words and frequent use of cognate recognition, the corresponding *Étude de mots* is there to help them with this. Another example is the *Lettres et sciences* section after every four chapters. The selections here include glossaries of the most important new vocabulary items, and the accompanying activities put implicit understanding of vocabulary to the test.

Thorough, Contextual Presentation of Grammar

A quick look through the chapters of *Bienvenue* will show the role grammar plays in the overall approach of the **Glencoe French** series. Although grammar is by no means the driving force behind the series, it is indeed an important aspect. In **Glencoe French**, grammar is presented as one of seven sections in each chapter. What makes this series particularly effective is that, as well as being thorough, the presentation of grammar runs concurrent with, and is embedded in, the chapter-long situational themes. Students are presented with French structure both directly, as grammar, and also as a set of useful functions that will aid them in communication, in expanding and improving their French across the four skills, and in learning about French culture as well as other areas of the school curriculum. Another important series characteristic is that the presentation of grammar has been divided into short, coherent "doses," which prevent grammar from becoming overwhelming to the student.

As you use this series, you will see as you teach the various grammar topics, student interest is kept high due to the presence of meaningful context and the diversity of the tasks that are given. As is the case with the vocabulary exercises, the individual practice items in the grammar section are related to each other contextually, in order to heighten student interest while assimilating and personalizing a new structure.

You will find that it is easy to move in and out of the teaching of grammar, dipping into the other sections of a chapter or other components as you see fit. This is true for several reasons: the grammar segments are short and intelligently divided, each one providing a good sense of closure; language elements (including grammar) taught in one section have been included as much as possible in the others; and again, there is a coherent contextual theme.

Aside from the Student Textbook and Teacher's Wraparound Edition, with their focus on grammar in the *Structure* section of each chapter and in the *Révision* after every four chapters, **Glencoe French** offers students opportunities to practice grammar in other components as well. Chapter by chapter, the Writing Activities Workbook provides ample tasks in which students must put into writing the new structures on which they have been working in class. The Audio Cassette Program includes recorded sections in every chapter of the Student Tape Manual which correspond directly to *Structure* in the Student Textbook. The Computer Software Program's Practice Generator contains additional grammar-based exercises. Of course students' knowledge of grammar is evaluated in the Chapter Quizzes and in the Testing Program, and each grammatical structure is practiced in other components, such as the Communication Activities Masters, Situation Cards and Videocassette Program.

An Integrated Approach to Culture

True competence in a foreign language cannot be attained without simultaneous development of the awareness of the culture in which the language is spoken. That is why **Glencoe French** places such great importance on culture. Accurate, up-to-date information on French culture is present either implicitly or explicitly throughout every phase of language

learning and in every component of the series.

The presentation of French in each chapter of the Student Textbook is embedded in running contextual themes, and these themes richly reflect the culture of France and areas of the world influenced by France. Even in chapter sections which focus primarily on vocabulary or grammar, the presence of culture comes through in the language used as examples or items in exercises, as well as in the content of the accompanying illustrations, photographs, charts, diagrams, maps or other reproductions of authentic, French documents. This constant, implicit inclusion of cultural information creates a format which not only aids in the learning of new words and structures, but piques student interest, invites questions, and stimulates discussion of the people behind the language.

Many culturally oriented questions raised by students may be answered in the two sections per chapter devoted to culture: *Lecture et culture* and *Réalités*. Through readings, captioned visuals and guided activities, these sections provide fundamental knowledge about such topics as French family life, school, restaurants, markets, sports, transportation, food, hotels, offices and hospitals, among many others. This information is presented with the idea that culture is a product of people—their attitudes, desires, preferences, differences, similarities, strengths and weaknesses—and that it is ever changing. Students are always encouraged to compare or contrast what they learn about French culture with their own, thereby learning to think critically and progress towards a more mature vision of the world. In addition to the presence of cultural material in each chapter of the Student Textbook, its importance is particularly apparent in the *Lettres et sciences* section which follows every four chapters. The readings here serve as valuable sources of information on the influence of the French people in the natural and social sciences and the arts and humanities. For more information on this unique feature, see the Teacher's Manual section immediately following, and also the section entitled ORGANIZATION OF THE STUDENT TEXTBOOK.

All of the cultural material described in the Student Textbook can be augmented by following a variety of suggestions in the Teacher's Wraparound Edition. There are guidelines for culturally rich instruction and activities, as well as useful, interesting facts for the teacher under headings such as Chapter Projects, Geography Connection, History Connection, Critical Thinking Activity, Did You Know? and others.

INTERDISCIPLINARY READINGS: LETTRES ET SCIENCES

This distinctive feature of **Glencoe French** allows students to use their French skills to expand their knowledge in other areas of the school curriculum. The interdisciplinary readings, called *Lettres et sciences*, occur in the Student Textbook after Chapters 4, 8, 12, and 16. They consist of three different readings on topics chosen from the Natural Sciences, the Social Sciences, the Arts and Humanities. Each reading topic is accompanied by pre- and post-reading activities. In the *Lettres et sciences* sections, students may read about important French explorers of the New World, for example, and begin to make associations between these men, their stories, and well-known names of cities or states in the United States. They may read and talk about the Impressionist movement in painting and a few of the great French artists who created it, as well as learn details which help to put the movement in perspective *vis à vis* other major events in world history. They may also learn about French scientists responsible for discoveries which are nowadays taken for granted.

Aside from providing basic information about the above topics—*[Pasteur] fonde une nouvelle science, la microbiologie,* for example—the readings have a French perspective. They include insights that students might not receive if they were reading about the same topic in an American textbook: *Au collège, [Pasteur] n'est pas très bon élève... il aime le dessin. On l'appelle «l'artiste»*. By using these interdisciplinary *Lettres et sciences* readings, you can open up two-way avenues of exchange between the French classroom and other subject areas in the school curriculum. These readings will also allow your students to exercise critical thinking skills, draw conclusions, and begin to interrelate in a mature way the knowledge coming to them from fields which they formerly considered unrelated to French. Perhaps the social studies, art, or science teachers in your school will have the pleasure of hearing from your students, "I learned in French class that ..." or conversely, students will have outside knowledge about a topic to bring to discussions in your class.

It is hoped that these readings with interdisciplinary content will make this kind of cognitive connection more common in the overall learning process. Of course, while learning about the other subject areas, students are building their French language skills. The selections in *Lettres et sciences* recycle as much as possible the structures and vocabulary from previous chapters. Glossaries contribute to vocabulary building, and the accompanying activities are designed to encourage discussion in French around the topic.

SERIES COMPONENTS

In order to take full advantage of the student-centered, "teacher-friendly" curriculum offered by **Glencoe French**, you may want to refer to this section to familiarize yourself with the various resources the series has to offer. Both Levels 1 and 2 of **Glencoe French** contain the following components:

- Student Edition
- Teacher's Wraparound Edition
- Writing Activities Workbook & Student Tape Manual, Student Edition
- Writing Activities Workbook, Teacher's Annotated Edition
- Student Tape Manual, Teacher's Edition (tapescript)
- Audio Program (Cassette or Compact Disc)
- Overhead Transparencies
- Video Program (Videocassette or Videodisc)
- Video Activities Booklet
- Interactive Conversation Video
- Computer Software: Practice and Test Generator
- Communication Activities Masters
- Lesson Plans with Block Scheduling
- Internet Activities Booklet
- Bell Ringer Review Blackline Masters
- Situation Cards
- Chapter Quizzes with Answer Key
- Testing Program with Answer Key
- Performance Assessment
- CD-ROM Interactive Textbook

LEVEL 1 **BIENVENUE** IN TWO VOLUMES

At the junior high and intermediate school levels, where the material in *Bienvenue* is normally presented in two years, a two-volume edition is available, consisting of *Bienvenue* **Part A** and *Bienvenue* **Part B**. This two-volume edition may also be more suitable for other types of language programs where students are studying French for limited periods of time, or where student aptitude varies from the norm or for those programs where the teacher chooses to modify the pacing for other reasons. In addition to the *Bienvenue* Student Edition, the components of Level 1 (which are also available in two volumes) are the Teacher's Wraparound Edition, and the Writing Activities Workbook and Student Tape Manual, Student Edition. All other Level 1 components are completely compatible with this "split" edition of *Bienvenue*.

Bienvenue **Part A** consists of Chapters 1 through 8. *Bienvenue* **Part B** opens with 33 pages of *Révision*, a review section containing new activities designed to reenter the material in **Part A**. It then continues with Chapters 9 through 18.

ORGANIZATION OF THE STUDENT TEXTBOOK

Bienvenue preliminary lessons Chapter 1 of the Level 1 textbook (*Bienvenue*) is preceded by a group of eight preliminary lessons which bear the same title as the Level 1 textbook. These short lessons, A through H, will help orient your students to some of the routines of the foreign language classroom at the beginning of the term. They prime students with a few essential question words and get them speaking high-frequency French phrases used in greetings and leave-takings as well as in moving about the classroom in French and identifying basic classroom objects. Each preliminary lesson contains exercises and activities to help students retain this introductory material. If you guide them through all of the preliminary lessons in the *Bienvenue* section before beginning Chapter 1, your students will be able to make a smooth transition into the regular chapter material, and you will be able to conduct more of the classroom activities, including giving directions, in French.

Following the eight preliminary lessons, each chapter of *Bienvenue* and *À bord* (Level 2) is divided into the following sections:

- *Vocabulaire (Mots 1 & Mots 2)*
- *Structure*
- *Conversation*
- *Lecture et Culture*
- *Réalités*
- *Culmination*

After every fourth chapter in Level 1, the following special sections appear:

- *Le Monde francophone*
- *Révision*
- *Lettres et sciences* (interdisciplinary readings)

Vocabulaire The new vocabulary is laid out in two segments, *Mots 1* and *Mots 2*. Each of these presents new words in a cultural context in keeping with the theme of the chapter. Ample use is made of labeled illustrations to convey meaning and to provide an interesting introduction to the new vocabulary. The contextual vignettes into which the vocabulary items are embedded make use of the same grammatical structures which will be formally addressed later in the chapter, and recycle words and structures from previous chapters. Accompanying each *Mots* segment are a series of *Exercices* requiring students to use the new words in context. These *Exercices* employ techniques such as short answer, matching, multiple choice and labeling. They are always contextual, forming coherent vignettes, and they lend themselves well to any variations you might wish to apply to their delivery (books open, books closed, done as a class, in groups or pairs, written for homework). Wrapping up the *Vocabulaire* section are the *Activités de communication*, a segment consisting of communication-based activities which combine the new words from both *Mots* sections. These are more open-ended activities, requiring students to personalize the new language by performing such tasks as gathering information from classmates, interviewing, taking notes, making charts or reporting to the class.

Structure This is the grammar section of each chapter. It is conveniently and logically divided into four or five segments to aid in student assimilation of the material. Each segment provides a step-by-step description in English of how the new grammatical structure is used in

French, accompanied by examples, tables and other visuals. Each segment's presentation is followed by a series of flexible *Exercices*, designed along the same lines as those which accompany the *Vocabulaire* section, but focusing on the grammar point. As in *Vocabulaire*, the presentation of the new structures and the subsequent exercises is contextualized: examples as well as items in the exercises are never separate and unrelated, but always fit together in vignettes to enhance meaning. These vignettes are always directly related to the overall chapter theme. The *Structure* section also makes regular use of the new vocabulary from *Mots 1* and *Mots 2*, allowing for free interplay between these two sections of the chapter. This thorough yet manageable layout allows you to adapt the teaching of grammar to your students' needs and to your own teaching personality.

Conversation   Now that students have had a chance to see and practice the new items of vocabulary and grammar for the chapter, this section provides a recombined version of the new language in the form of an authentic, culturally rich dialogue under the heading *Scènes de la vie*. This can be handled in a variety of ways, depending on the teacher and the class and as suggested by accompanying notes in the Teacher's Wraparound Edition. Teacher modeling, modeling from the recorded version, class or individual repetitions, reading aloud by students, role-playing or adaptation through substitution are some of the strategies suggested. The dialogue is accompanied by one or more exercises which check comprehension and allow for some personalization of the material. Then students are invited once again to recombine and use all the new language in a variety of group and paired activities via the *Activités de communication*. New vocabulary and expressions are sometimes offered here, but only for the sake of richness and variation, and not for testing purposes. Every chapter in Level 1 also contains a *Prononciation* segment, which appears in the *Conversation* section. It provides a guide to the pronunciation of one or more French phonemes, a series of words and phrases containing the key sound(s), and an illustration which cues a key word containing the sound(s). These pronunciation illustrations are part of the Overhead Transparency package

accompanying the series. *Prononciation* can serve both as a tool for practice as students perform the chapter tasks, and as a handy speaking-skills reference to be used at any time.

Lecture et culture   This is a reading about people and places from France and the francophonic world, offering further cultural input to the theme of the chapter and providing yet another *recombinaison* of the chapter vocabulary and grammar. As is always the case with **Glencoe French**, material from previous chapters is recycled. Following the reading and based on it is *Étude de mots*—an exercise that gives students a chance to experiment with and expand their French vocabularies by using strategies such as searching for synonyms, identifying cognates, completing cloze exercises, matching and others. Next comes a series of comprehension exercises based on the reading (*Compréhension*), and finally the *Découverte culturelle*, where more cultural information is offered in the form of a shorter reading. The *Découverte culturelle* is optional in each chapter.

Réalités   These pages are intended as brief but enjoyable visual insights into the French-speaking world. The two pages of this section are filled with photographs that are pertinent to the chapter theme. Each photograph is identified with a caption, thereby providing some additional reading practice. Students are encouraged to formulate questions about what they see, and to compare and contrast elements of French culture with their own. The *Réalités* section is optional in each chapter.

Culmination   This wrap-up section requires students to consolidate material from the present as well as from previous chapters in order to complete the tasks successfully. The *Culmination* provides an opportunity for students to assess themselves on their own and to spend time on areas in which they are weak. You the teacher can pick and choose from them as you see fit. The first segment of *Culmination* consists of *Activités de communication orale*, where students must use the French they have learned to talk about various aspects of themselves: likes, dislikes, favorite activities, hobbies or areas of expertise, among others. This is followed by *Activités de communication écrite*, which encourage students to apply their knowledge

of French in written form. The *Réintroduction et recombinaison* segment recalls selected items of vocabulary and grammar from previous chapters. It is short and not meant as a comprehensive review, but rather as a quick reminder of important words, expressions and structures. Finally, the vocabulary words and expressions taught in the current chapter are listed categorically under the heading *Vocabulaire*, serving as a handy reference resource for both the student and the teacher.

Le Monde francophone This section occurs after Chapters 4, 8, 12 and 16 in the Student Textbook. It is designed to make students aware that, in addition to France, the French language is spoken in many other countries around the world. Because French is the official or second language in numerous and diverse countries, knowledge of the French language and culture is an important tool for meeting the career demands of the 21st century.

Each francophone section illustrates a topic presented in one of the four preceding chapters. Through photos and text, students are able to appreciate the cultural diversity of the francophone world. Each section incorporates the active vocabulary from the four preceding chapters. These pages are optional.

Révision This review section, designed to coincide with the more comprehensive Review Tests in the Testing Program, occurs after Chapters 4, 8, 12, and 16 in the Student Textbook. In each *Révision*, the main vocabulary and grammar points from the previous four chapters are recycled through a variety of new exercises, activities and dialogues. While in the individual chapters new grammar was divided into smaller, "bite-sized" portions to aid in the planning of daily lessons and help students assimilate it, now it is reviewed in a more consolidated format. This allows students to see different grammatical points side by side for the first time, to make new connections between the different points, and to progress toward a generative, "whole grammar." For example, in the first *Révision* following Chapter 4 (Level 1), indefinite articles, definite articles and possessive adjectives are reviewed

together on two pages, accompanied by explanations and various exercises. From these pages, students are able to conclude, among other things, that all of these structures have something in common—namely that they are all noun determiners, whose changes in number and gender depend upon the noun with which they are associated. Previously, these concepts were distributed over Chapters 1 through 4, and this point may have been missed by some students. Of course every possible combination of vocabulary and grammar does not reappear in the *Révision*. However, by carefully going through these exercises and activities and referring to the preceding chapters, students will be encouraged to make necessary connections and extrapolations themselves and therefore develop a true, working knowledge of the French they have studied. *Révision* is designed to be used by students studying alone, in unguided study groups or as a whole class with teacher guidance.

Lettres et sciences This is a unique, interdisciplinary feature of **Glencoe French** which allows students to use their French language skills to obtain, reinforce, and further their knowledge of other subject areas, namely the natural sciences, social studies, arts and humanities. This material is presented in the form of three readings, one from each of the above areas, accompanied by photos and illustrations. To stimulate discussion and aid in comprehension, there are pre-reading and post-reading activities. The reading selections are more vocabulary intensive than those in the regular chapters, and a French–English glossary is provided for each one. The focus here, however, is on the interdisciplinary content rather than the language itself. By engaging your students in some or all of these readings, you will encourage them to stretch their French reading skills in order to obtain useful, interesting information which will be of great service to them in their other academic courses. Also, you will be giving students the opportunity to judge for themselves the added insight that the study of French offers to their overall education.

SUGGESTIONS FOR TEACHING THE STUDENT TEXTBOOK

Teaching the Preliminary Lessons A through H in *Bienvenue* (Level 1)

The first day of class, teachers may wish to give students a pep-talk concerning the importance of the language they have chosen to study. Some suggested activities are:

- Show students a map (the maps located in the back of the Student Textbook can be used) to give them an idea of the extent of the French-speaking world.
- Have students discuss the areas within North America in which there is a high percentage of French speakers.
- Make a list of place names such as Baton Rouge, Terre Haute, Des Moines, Vermont, or names in your locality that are of French origin.
- Explain to students the possibility of using French in numerous careers such as: government, teaching, business, (banking, import/export), tourism, translating.
- The first day teachers will also want to give each student a French name. In the cases of students with names such as Kevin and Erica, teachers may want to give them a French nickname.

The short Preliminary Lessons A through H in *Bienvenue* are designed to give students useful, everyday expressions that they can use immediately. Each lesson is designed to take one day. The topics present students with easily learned expressions such as *Salut, Bonjour, Ça va?, Au revoir, etc.*, but do not confuse the students by expecting them to make structural changes such as the manipulation of verb endings. Formal grammar begins with Chapter 1. No grammar is taught in the *Bienvenue* Preliminary Lessons.

Teaching Various Sections of the Chapter

One of the major objectives of the **Glencoe French** series is to enable teachers to adapt the material to their own philosophy, teaching style, and students' needs. As a result, a variety of suggestions are offered here for teaching each section of the chapter.

Vocabulaire

The *Vocabulaire* section always contains some words in isolation, accompanied by an illustration that depicts the meaning of the new word. In addition, new words are used in contextualized sentences. These appear in the following formats: l) one to three sentences accompanying an illustration, 2) a short conversation, 3) a short narrative or paragraph. In addition to teaching the new vocabulary, these contextualized sentences introduce, but do not teach, the new structure point of the chapter.

A vocabulary list appears at the end of each chapter in the Student Textbook.

General Techniques

- The Vocabulary Transparencies contain all illustrations necessary to teach the new words and phrases. With an overhead projector, they can easily be projected as large

visuals in the classroom for those teachers who prefer to introduce the vocabulary with books closed. The Vocabulary Transparencies contain no printed words.

- All the vocabulary in each chapter (*Mots 1* and *Mots 2*) is recorded on the Audio Cassette Program. Students are asked to repeat the isolated words after the model.

Specific Techniques

Option 1 Option 1 for the presentation of vocabulary best meets the needs of those teachers who consider the development of oral skills a prime objective.

- While students have their books closed, project the Vocabulary Transparencies. Point to the item being taught and have students repeat the word after you or the audio cassette several times. After presenting several words in this way, project the transparencies again and ask questions such as:

C'est une table libre?
Qu'est-ce que c'est?
C'est le serveur?
Qui est-ce? (Level 1, Chapter 5)

- To teach the contextualized segments in the *Mots*, project the Vocabulary Transparency in the same way. Point to the part of the illustration that depicts the meaning of any new word in the sentence, be it an isolated sentence or a sentence from a conversation or narrative. Immediately ask questions about the sentence. For example, the following sentence appears in Level 1, Chapter 6:

Jean fait les courses.
Il fait les courses le matin.

Questions to ask are:

Jean fait les courses?
Qui fait les courses?
Où est-ce que Jean fait les courses?
Est-ce qu'il fait les courses le matin?
Quand est-ce qu'il fait les courses?

- Dramatizations by the teacher, in addition to the illustrations, can also help convey the meaning of many words such as *chanter, danser,* etc.
- After this basic presentation of the *Mots* vocabulary, have students open their books and read the *Mots* section for additional reinforcement.

- Go over the exercises in the *Mots* section orally.
- Assign the exercises in the *Mots* section for homework. Also assign the corresponding vocabulary exercises in the Writing Activities Workbook. If the *Mots* section should take more than one day, assign only those exercises that correspond to the material you have presented.
- The following day, go over the exercises that were assigned for homework.

Option 2 Option 2 will meet the needs of those teachers who wish to teach the oral skills but consider reading and writing equally important.

- Project the Vocabulary Transparencies and have students repeat each word once or twice after you or the audio cassette.
- Have students repeat the contextualized sentences after you or the audio cassette as they look at the illustration.
- Ask students to open their books. Have them read the *Mots* section. Correct pronunciation errors as they are made.
- Go over the exercises in each *Mots* section.
- Assign the exercises of the *Mots* section for homework. Also assign the vocabulary exercises in the Writing Activities Workbook.
- The following day, go over the exercises that were assigned for homework.

Option 3 Option 3 will meet the needs of those teachers who consider the reading and writing skills of utmost importance.

- Have students open their books and read the *Mots* items as they look at the illustrations.
- Give students several minutes to look at the *Mots* words and vocabulary exercises. Then go over the exercises.
- Go over the exercises the following day.

Expansion activities

Teachers may use any one of the following activities from time to time. These can be done in conjunction with any of the options previously outlined.

- After the vocabulary has been presented, project the Vocabulary Transparencies or have students open their books and make up as many original sentences as they can, using

the new words. This can be done orally or in writing.

- Have students work in pairs or small groups. As they look at the illustrations in the textbook, have them make up as many questions as they can. They can direct their questions to their peers. It is often fun to make this a competitive activity. Individuals or teams can compete to make up the most questions in three minutes. This activity provides the students with an excellent opportunity to use interrogative words.
- Call on one student to read to the class one of the vocabulary exercises that tells a story. Then call on a more able student to retell the story in his/her own words.
- With slower groups you can have one student go to the front of the room. Have him or her think of one of the new words. Let classmates give the student the new words from the *Mots* until they guess the word the student in the front of the room has in mind. This is a very easy way to have the students recall the words they have just learned.

Structure

The *Structure* section of the chapter opens with a grammatical explanation in English. Each grammatical explanation is accompanied by many examples. With verbs, complete paradigms are given. In the case of other grammar concepts such as object pronouns, many examples are given with noun vs. pronoun objects. Irregular patterns are grouped together to make them appear more regular. For example, *sortir, partir, dormir,* and *servir* are taught together in Chapter 7, as are *pouvoir* and *vouloir* in Chapter 6. Whenever the contrast between English and French poses problems for students in the learning process, a contrastive analysis between the two languages is made. Two examples of this are the reflexive construction in Level 1 and the subjunctive in Level 2. Certain structure points are taught more effectively in their entirety and others are more easily acquired if they are taught in segments. An example of the latter is the direct and indirect object pronouns. In Chapter 15 *me, te, nous, vous* (as direct object pronouns) are presented, immediately followed by *le, la, l', les,* (Chapter 16), followed by *lui, leur* (Chapter 17).

Learning Exercises

The exercises that follow the grammatical explanation are plateaued or phased in to build from simple to more complex. In the case of verbs with an irregular form, for example, emphasis is placed on the irregular form, since it is the one students will most often confuse or forget. However, in all cases, students are given one or more exercises that force them to use all forms at random. The first few exercises that follow the grammatical explanation are considered **learning exercises** because they assist the students in grasping and internalizing the new grammar concept. These learning exercises are immediately followed by test exercises—exercises that make students use all aspects of the grammatical point they have just learned. This format greatly assists teachers in meeting the needs of the various ability levels of students in their classes. Every effort has been made to make the grammatical explanations as succinct and as complete as possible. We have purposely avoided extremely technical grammatical or linguistic terminology that most students would not understand. Nevertheless, it is necessary to use certain basic grammatical terms.

Certain grammar exercises from the Student Textbook are recorded on the Audio Cassette Program. Whenever an exercise is recorded, it is noted with an appropriate icon ( ) in the Teacher's Wraparound Edition.

The exercises in the Writing Activities Workbook also parallel the order of presentation in the Student Textbook. The Resource boxes and the Independent Practice topics in the Teacher's Wraparound Edition indicate when certain exercises from the Writing Activities Workbook can be assigned.

Specific Techniques for Presenting Grammar

Option 1 Some teachers prefer the deductive approach to the teaching of grammar. When this is the preferred method, teachers can begin the *Structure* section of the chapter by presenting the grammatical rule to students or by having them read the rule in their textbooks. After they have gone over the rule, have them read the examples in their textbooks or write the

examples on the chalkboard. Then proceed with the exercises that follow the grammatical explanation.

Option 2 Other teachers prefer the inductive approach to the teaching of grammar. If this is the case, begin the *Structure* section by writing the examples that accompany the rule on the chalkboard or by having students read them in their textbooks. Let us take, for example, the direct object pronouns *le, la, l', les*. The examples the students have in their books are:

Je sais le nom du film.	Je le sais.
Je vois le film.	Je le vois.
J'aime le film.	Je l'aime.
Je ne connais pas la vedette.	Je ne la connais pas.
Je lis les sous-titres.	Je les lis.
J'admire les costumes.	Je les admire.

In order to teach this concept inductively, teachers can ask students to do or answer the following:

- Have students find the object of each sentence in the first column. Say it or underline the object if it is written on the board.
- Have students notice that these words disappeared in the sentences in the second column. Have students give (or underline) the word that replaced each one.
- Ask students what word replaced *le nom du film, le film, la vedette, les sous-titres, les costumes*.
- Ask: What do we call a word that replaces a noun?
- Ask: What direct object pronoun replaces a masculine noun? A feminine noun, etc.?
- Have students look again. Ask: What word replaces *le film, la vedette*?
- Ask: Can *le* or *la* be used to replace a person or a thing?
- Ask: Where do the direct object pronouns *le, la, l', les* go, before or after the verb?

By answering these questions, students have induced, on their own, the rule from the examples. To further reinforce the rule, have students read the grammatical explanation and then continue with the grammar exercises that follow. Further suggestions for the inductive presentation of the grammatical points are given in the Teacher's Wraparound Edition.

Specific techniques for Teaching Grammar Exercises

In the development of the **Glencoe French** series, we have purposely provided a wide variety of exercises in the *Structure* section so that students can proceed from one exercise to another without becoming bored. The types of exercises they will encounter are: short conversations, answering questions, conducting or taking part in an interview, making up questions, describing an illustration, filling in the blanks, multiple choice, completing a conversation, completing a narrative, etc. In going over the exercises with students, teachers may want to conduct the exercises themselves or they may want students to work in pairs. The *Structure* exercises can be gone over in class before they are assigned for homework or they may be assigned before they are gone over. Many teachers may want to vary their approach.

All the *Exercices* and *Activités de communication* in the Student Textbook can be done with books open. Many of the exercises such as question-answer, interview, and transformation can also be done with books closed.

Types of Exercises

Question exercises The answers to many question exercises build to tell a complete story. Once you have gone over the exercise by calling on several students (Student 1 answers items numbered 1,2,3; Student 2 answers items numbered 4,5,6, etc.), you can call on one student to give the answers to the entire exercise. Now the entire class has heard an uninterrupted story. Students can ask one another questions about the story, give an oral synopsis of the story in their own words, or write a short paragraph about the story.

Personal questions or interview exercises Students can easily work in pairs or teachers can call a student moderator to the front of the room to ask questions of various class members. Two students can come to the front of the room and the exercise can be performed—one student takes the role of the interviewer and the other takes the role of the interviewee.

Completion of a conversation See Chapter 5, *Exercice D*, page 135, as an example. After students complete the exercise, they can be given time either in class or as an outside assignment to prepare a skit for the class based on the conversation.

Conversation

Specific Techniques Teachers may wish to vary the presentation of the *Conversation* from one chapter to another. In some chapters, the dialogue can be presented thoroughly and in other chapters it may be presented quickly as a reading exercise. Some possible options are:

- Have the class repeat the dialogue after you twice. Then have students work in pairs and present the dialogue to the class. The dialogue does not have to be memorized. If students change it a bit, all the better.
- Have students read the dialogue several times on their own. Then have them work in pairs and read the dialogue as a skit. Try to encourage them to be animated and to use proper intonation. This is a very important aspect of the *Conversation* section of the chapter.
- Rather than read the dialogue, students can work in pairs, having one make up as many questions as possible related to the topic of the dialogue. The other student can answer his/her questions.
- Once students can complete the exercise(s) that accompany the dialogue with relative ease, they know the dialogue sufficiently well without having to memorize it.
- Students can tell or write a synopsis of the dialogue.

Prononciation

Specific Techniques Have students read on their own or go over with them the short explanation in the book concerning the particular sound that is being presented. For the more difficult sounds such as *r, u, eu, en, in, un,* etc., teachers may wish to demonstrate the tongue and lip positions. Have students repeat the words after you or the model speaker on the audio cassette recording.

Activités de communication

Specific Techniques The *Activités de communication* presents activities that assist students in working with the language on their own. All the *Activités* are optional. In some cases, teachers may want the whole class to do them all. In other cases, teachers can decide which ones the whole class will do. Another possibility is to break the class into groups and have each one work on a different activity.

Lecture et culture

Specific Techniques: Option 1 Just as the presentation of the dialogue can vary from one chapter to the next, the same is true of the *Lecture.* In some chapters teachers may want students to go over the reading selection very thoroughly. In this case all or any combination of the following techniques can be used.

- Give students a brief synopsis of the story in French.
- Ask questions about the brief synopsis.
- Have students open their books and repeat several sentences after you or call on individuals to read.
- Ask questions about what was just read.
- Have students read the story at home and write the answers to the exercises that accompany the *Lecture.*
- Go over the *Étude de mots* and the *Compréhension* in class the next day.
- Call on a student to give a review of the story in his/her own words. If necessary, guide students to make up an oral review. Ask five or six questions, the answers to which review the salient points of the reading selection.
- After the oral review, the more able students can write a synopsis of the *Lecture* in their own words.

It should take less than one class period to present the *Lecture* in the early chapters. In later chapters, teachers may wish to spend two days on those reading selections they want students to know thoroughly.

Option 2 With those *Lectures* that teachers wish to present less thoroughly, the following techniques may be used:

- Call on an individual to read a paragraph.
- Ask questions about the paragraph read.

- Assign the *Lecture* to be read at home. Have students write the exercises that accompany the *Lecture*.
- Go over the *Etude de mots* and the *Compréhension* the following day.

Option 3 With some reading selections, teachers may wish merely to assign them to be read at home and then go over the exercises the following day. This is possible since the only new material in the *Lecture* consists of a few new vocabulary items that are always footnoted.

Découverte culturelle

The optional *Découverte culturelle* is a reading selection which is designed to give students an in-depth knowledge of many areas of the French-speaking world. You can omit any or all of this reading or they may choose certain selections that they would like the whole class to read. The same suggestions given for the *Lecture* of each chapter can be followed. Teachers may also assign the reading selections to different groups. Students can read the selection outside of class and prepare a report for those students who did not read that particular selection. This activity is very beneficial for slower students. Although they may not read the selection, they learn the material by listening to what their peers say about it. The *Découverte culturelle* can also be done by students on a voluntary basis for extra credit.

Réalités

Specific Techniques The purpose of the *Réalités* section is to permit students to look at photographs from the French-speaking world and to acquaint them with the many areas where French is spoken. The *Réalités* section contains no exercises. The purpose is for students to enjoy the material as if they were browsing through pages of a magazine. Items the students can think about are embedded in the commentary that accompanies the photographs. Teachers can either have students read the extended captions in class or students can read the captions on their own.

ORGANIZATION OF THE TEACHER'S WRAPAROUND EDITION

One important component, which is definitive of **Glencoe French** and adds to the series' flexible, "teacher-friendly" nature, is the Teacher's Wraparound Edition (TWE), of which this Teacher's Manual is a part. Each two-page spread of the TWE "wraps around" a slightly reduced reproduction of the corresponding pages of the Student Textbook and offers in the expanded margins a variety of specific, helpful suggestions for every phase in the learning process. A complete method for the presentation of all the material in the Student Textbook is provided—basically, a complete set of lesson plans—as well as techniques for background-building, additional reinforcement of new language skills, creative and communicative recycling of material from previous chapters and a host of other alternatives from which to choose. This banquet of ideas has been developed and conveniently laid out in order to save valuable teacher preparation time and to aid you in designing the richest, most varied language experience possible for you and your students. A closer look at the kinds of support in the TWE, and their locations, will help you decide which ones are right for your pace and style of teaching and the differing "chemistries" of your classes.

The notes in the Teacher's Wraparound Edition can be divided into two basic categories:

1. Core notes, appearing in the left- and right-hand margins, are those which most directly correspond to the material in the accompanying two-page spread of the Student Textbook.

2. Enrichment notes, in the bottom margin, are meant to be complementary to the material in the Student Textbook. They offer a wide range of options aimed at getting students to practice and use the French they are learning in diverse ways, individually and with their classmates, in the classroom and for homework. The enrichment notes also include tips to the teacher on clarifying and interconnecting elements in French language and culture—ideas that have proved useful to other teachers and which are offered for your consideration.

Description of Core Notes in the Teacher's Wraparound Edition

Chapter Overview At the beginning of each chapter a brief description is given of the language functions which students will be able to perform by chapter's end. Mention is made of any closely associated functions presented in other chapters. This allows for effective articulation between chapters and serves as a guide for more successful teaching.

Chapter Objectives This guide immediately follows the Chapter Overview and is closely related to it. Here the focus is on grammatical objectives for the chapter, which are stated in a concise list.

Chapter Resources The beginning of each chapter includes a reference list of all the ancillary components of the series that are applicable to what is being taught in the chapter, including the Writing Activities Workbook and

Student Tape Manual, Audio Cassette Program, Overhead Transparencies, Communication Activities Masters, Videocassette Program, Computer Software: Practice and Test Generator, Situation Cards, Chapter Quizzes and Test Booklets. A more precise version of this resource list will be repeated at the beginning of each section within the chapter, so that you always have a handy guide to the specific resources available to you for each and every point in the teaching process. Using these chapter and section resource references will make it easier for you to plan varied, stimulating lessons throughout the year.

Bell Ringer Reviews These short activities recycle vocabulary and grammar from previous chapters and sections. They serve as effective warm-ups, urging students to begin thinking in French, and helping them make the transition from their previous class to French. Minimal direction is required to get the Bell Ringer Review activity started, so students can begin meaningful, independent work in French as soon as the class hour begins, rather than wait for the teacher to finish administrative tasks, such as attendance, etc. Bell Ringer Reviews occur consistently throughout each chapter of Levels 1 and 2.

Presentation Step-by-step suggestions for the presentation of the material in all segments of the six main section headings in each chapter—*Vocabulaire*, *Structure*, *Conversation*, *Lecture et culture*, *Réalités*, and *Culmination* are presented in the left- and right-hand margins. They offer the teacher suggestions on what to say, whether to have books open or closed, whether to perform tasks individually, in pairs or in small groups, expand the material, reteach, and assign homework. These are indeed suggestions. You may wish to follow them as written or choose a more eclectic approach to suit time constraints, personal teaching style and class "chemistry." Please note however, that the central vocabulary and grammar included in each chapter's *Vocabulaire* and *Structure* sections is intended to be taught in its entirety, since this material is built into that which occurs in succeeding chapters. In addition, answers for all the *Exercices* in each segment are conveniently located near that exercise in the Student Textbook.

Because the answers will vary in the *Activités de communication*, they are usually not provided. However, the Presentation notes do offer other topics for enrichment, expansion and assessment. A brief discussion of these may help you incorporate them into your lesson plans.

Geography Connection These suggestions encourage students to use the maps provided in the Student Textbook as well as refer them to outside sources in order to familiarize them with the geography of France and the francophone world. These optional activities are another way in which **Glencoe French** crosses boundaries into other areas of the curriculum. Their use will instill in students the awareness that French Class is not just a study of language but an investigation into a powerful culture that has directly or indirectly affected the lives of millions of people all over the globe. Besides studying the geography within France itself, they will be urged to trace the presence of French culture throughout Europe, Africa, the Americas, Asia, and the Pacific. The notes also supply you the teacher with diverse bits of geographical and historical information which you might not have known, and you may decide to pass these on to your students.

Vocabulary Expansion These notes provide the teacher handy access to vocabulary items which are thematically related to those presented within the Student Textbook. They are offered to enrich classroom conversations, allowing students more varied and meaningful responses when talking about themselves, their classmates or the topic in question. Note that none of these items, or for that matter any information, in the TWE is included in the Chapter Quizzes, or in the Testing Program accompanying **Glencoe French**.

Cognate Recognition Since the lexical relationship between French and English is so rich, these notes have been provided to help you take full advantage of the vocabulary-building strategy of isolating them. The suggestions occur in the *Vocabulaire* section of each chapter and are particularly frequent in Level 1 in order to train students from the very beginning in the valuable strategy of recognizing cognates. Various methods of pointing out cognates are used, involving all four language skills, and the activities frequently encourage

students to personalize the new words by using them to talk about things and people they know. Pronunciation differences are stressed between the two languages. The teacher notes also call attention to false cognates when they occur in other chapter sections.

Informal Assessment Ideas are offered for making quick checks on how well students are assimilating new material. These checks are done in a variety of ways and provide a means whereby both teacher and students can monitor daily progress. By using the Informal Assessment topic, you will be able to ascertain (as you go along) the areas in which students are having trouble, adjust your pace accordingly, or provide extra help for individuals, either by making use of other activities offered in the TWE or devising your own. The assessment strategies are simple and designed to help you elicit from students the vocabulary word, grammatical structure, or other information you wish to check. Because they occur on the same page as the material to which they correspond, you may want to come back to them again when it is time to prepare students for tests or quizzes.

Reteaching These suggestions provided yet another approach to teaching a specific topic in the chapter. In the event some students were not successful in the initial presentation of the material the reteaching activity offers an alternate strategy. At the same time, they allow other students to further consolidate their learning.

History Connection Following these suggestions can be a very effective springboard from the French classroom into the history and social studies areas of the curriculum. Students are asked to focus their attention on the current world map, or historical ones, then they are invited to discuss the cultural, economic and political forces which shape the world with an eye on French influence. The notes will assist you in providing this type of information yourself or in creating projects in which students do their own research, perhaps with the aid of a history teacher. By making the history connection, students are encouraged to either import or export learning between the French classroom and the History or Social Studies realms.

Description of Enrichment Notes in the Teacher's Wraparound Edition

The notes in the bottom margin of the TWE enrich students' learning experiences by providing additional activities to those in the Student Textbook. These activities will be helpful in meeting each chapter's objectives, as well as in providing students with an atmosphere of variety, cooperation and enjoyment.

Chapter Projects Specific suggestions are given at the start of each chapter for launching individual students or groups into a research project in keeping with the chapter theme. Students are encouraged to gather information by using resources in school and public libraries, visiting local French institutions or interviewing French people or other persons knowledgeable in the area of French culture whom they may know. In Chapter 1, for example, they are asked to compare/contrast the French educational system with their own. These projects may serve as another excellent means for students to make connections between their learning in the French classroom and other areas of the curriculum.

Learning from Photos and Realia Each chapter of **Glencoe French** contains many colorful photographs and reproductions of authentic French documents, filled with valuable cultural information. In order to help you take advantage of this rich source of learning, notes of interesting information have been provided to assist you in highlighting the special features of these up-to-date realia. The questions that appear under this topic have been designed to enhance learners' reading, and critical thinking skills.

Total Physical Response (Level 1) At least one Total Physical Response (TPR) activity is provided with each *Mots* segment that makes up the *Vocabulaire* section of the chapter. The Total Physical Response approach to language instruction was developed by James J. Asher. Students must focus their attention on commands spoken by the teacher (or classmates) and demonstrate their comprehension by performing the physical task commanded. This strategy has proven highly successful for concentrating on the listening skill and assimilating new vocabulary. Students are relieved

momentarily of the need to speak—by which some may be intimidated—and yet challenged to show that they understand spoken French. The physical nature of these activities is another of their benefits, providing a favorable change of pace for students, who must move about the room and perhaps handle some props in order to perform the tasks. In addition, Total Physical Response is in keeping with cooperative learning principles, since many of the commands require students to interact and assist each other in accomplishing them.

Cooperative Learning At least one cooperative learning activity has been included in each chapter. These activities include guidelines both on the size of groups to be organized and on the tasks the groups will perform. They reflect two basic principles of cooperative learning: (a) that students work together, being responsible for their own learning, and (b) that they do so in an atmosphere of mutual respect and support, where the contributions of each peer are valued. For more information on this topic, please see the section in this Teacher's Manual entitled COOPERATIVE LEARNING.

Additional Practice There are a variety of Additional Practice activities to complement and follow up the presentation of material in the Student Textbook. Frequently the additional practice focuses on personalization of the new material and employs more than one language skill. Examples of Additional Practice activities include having students give oral or written descriptions of themselves or their classmates; asking students to conduct interviews around a topic and then report their findings to the class; using possessive forms to identify objects in the classroom and their owners. The additional practice will equip you with an ample, organized repertoire from which to pick and choose should you need extra practice beyond the Student Textbook.

Independent Practice Many of the exercises in each chapter lend themselves well to assignment or reassignment as homework. In addition to providing extra practice, reassigning on paper exercises that were performed orally in class makes use of additional language skills

and aids in informal assessment. The suggestions under the Independent Practice heading in the bottom margin of the TWE will call your attention to exercises that are particularly suited to this. In addition to reassigning exercises in the Student Textbook as independent practice, additional sources are suggested from the various ancillary components, specifically the Writing Activities Workbook and the Communication Activities Masters.

Critical Thinking Activities To broaden the scope of the foreign language classroom, suggestions are given that will encourage students to make inferences and organize their learning into a coherent "big picture" of today's world. These and other topics offered in the enrichment notes provide dynamic content areas to which students can apply their French language skills and their growing knowledge of French culture. The guided discussion suggestions derived from the chapter themes invite students to make connections between what they learn in the French program and other areas of the curriculum.

Did You Know? This is a teacher resource topic where you will find additional details relevant to the chapter theme. You might wish to add the information given under this topic to your own knowledge and share it with your students to spur their interest in research projects, enliven class discussions and round out their awareness of French culture, history or geography.

For the Younger Student Because Level 1 (*Bienvenue*) is designed for use at the junior high and intermediate level as well as the high school level, this topic pays special attention to the needs of younger students. Each chapter contains suggestions for meaningful language activities and tips to the teacher that cater to the physical and emotional needs of these youngsters. There are ideas for hands-on student projects, such as creating booklets or bringing and using their own props, as well as suggestions for devising games based on speed, using pantomime, show and tell, performing skits and more.

ADDITIONAL ANCILLARY COMPONENTS

All ancillary components are supplementary to the Student Textbook. Any or all parts of the following ancillaries can be used at the discretion of the teacher.

The Writing Activities Workbook and Student Tape Manual

The Writing Activities Workbook and Student Tape Manual is divided into two parts: all chapters of the Writing Activities Workbook appear in the first half of this ancillary component, followed by all chapters of the Student Tape Manual.

Writing Activities Workbook The consumable workbook offers additional writing practice to reinforce the vocabulary and grammatical structures in each chapter of the Student Textbook. Workbook exercises are presented in the same order as the material in the Student Textbook. The exercises are contextualized, often centering around line art illustrations. Workbook activities employ a variety of elicitation techniques, ranging from short answers, matching columns, and answering personalized questions, to writing paragraphs and brief compositions. To encourage personalized writing, there is a special section in each chapter entitled *Mon Autobiographie*. The workbook provides further reading skills development with the *Un Peu Plus* section, where students are introduced to a number of reading strategies such as scanning for information, distinguishing fact from opinion, drawing inferences and reaching conclusions, for the purpose of improving their reading comprehension and expanding their vocabulary. The *Un Peu Plus* section also extends the cultural themes presented in the corresponding Student Textbook chapter. The Writing Activities Workbook includes a Self-Test after Chapters 4, 8, 12, 16, and 18. The Writing Activities Workbook, Teacher Annotated Edition provides the teacher with all the material in the student edition plus the answers—wherever possible—to the activities.

Student Tape Manual The Student Tape Manual contains the activity sheets which students will use when listening to the audio recordings. The Teacher Edition of the Student Tape Manual contains, in addition, the answers to the recorded activities, plus the complete tapescript of all recorded material.

The Audio Program (Cassette or CD)

The recorded material for each chapter of **Glencoe French**, Levels 1 and 2 is divided into two parts—*Première partie* and *Deuxième partie*. The *Première partie* consists of additional listening and speaking practice for the *Vocabulaire (Mots 1 & 2)* and the *Structure* sections of each chapter. There is also a dramatization of the *Conversation* dialogue from the Student Textbook, and a pronunciation section. The *Première partie* concludes with a *dictée*.

The *Deuxième partie* contains a series of activities designed to further stretch students' receptive listening skills in more open-ended, real-life situations. Students indicate their understanding of brief conversations, advertisements, announcements, et cetera, by

making the appropriate response on their activity sheets located in the Student Tape Manual.

Overhead Transparencies

There are five categories in the package of Overhead Transparencies accompanying **Glencoe French**, Level 1. Each category of transparencies has its special purpose. Following is a description:

Vocabulary Transparencies These are full-color transparencies reproduced from each of the *Mots* presentations in the Student Textbook. In converting the *Mots* vocabulary pages to transparency format, all accompanying words and phrases on the *Mots* pages have been deleted to allow for greater flexibility in their use. The Vocabulary Transparencies can be used for the initial presentation of new words and phrases in each chapter. They can also be reprojected to review or reteach vocabulary during the course of teaching the chapter, or as a tool for giving quick vocabulary quizzes.

With more able groups, teachers can show the Vocabulary Transparencies from previous chapters and have students make up original sentences using a particular word. These sentences can be given orally or in writing.

Pronunciation Transparencies In the *Prononciation* section of each chapter of *Bienvenue* (Level 1), an illustration has been included to visually cue the key word or phrase containing the sound(s) being taught, e.g., Chapter 3, page 79. Each of these illustrations has been converted to transparency format. These Pronunciation Transparencies may be used to present the key sound(s) for a given chapter, or for periodic pronunciation reviews where several transparencies can be shown to the class in rapid order. Some teachers may wish to convert these Pronunciation Transparencies to black and white paper visuals by making a photocopy of each one.

Communication Transparencies For each chapter in Levels 1 and 2 of the series there is one original composite illustration which visually summarizes and reviews the vocabulary and grammar presented in that chapter. These transparencies may be used as cues for addi-

tional communicative practice in both oral and written formats. There are 18 Communication Transparencies for Level 1, and 16 for Level 2.

Map Transparencies The full-color maps located at the back of the Student Textbook have been converted to transparency format for the teacher's convenience. These can be used when there is a reference to them in the Student Textbook, or when there is a history or geography map reference in the Teacher's Wraparound Edition. The Map Transparencies can also be used for quiz purposes, or they may be photocopied in order to provide individual students with a black and white version for use with special projects.

Fine Art Transparencies These are full-color reproductions of works by well-known French artists including Matisse, Renoir, and others. Teachers may use these transparencies to reinforce specific culture topics in the *Réalités* sections as well as in the optional *Lettres et sciences* sections of the Student Textbook.

The Video Program (Cassette or Videodisc)

The video component for each level of **Glencoe French** consists of one hour-long video cassette and an accompanying Video Activities Booklet. Together, they are designed to reinforce the vocabulary, structures, and cultural themes presented in the corresponding Student Textbook. The **Glencoe French** Videocassette Program encourages students to be active listeners and viewers by asking them to respond to each video *Scène* through a variety of previewing, viewing and post-viewing activities. Students are asked to view the same video segment multiple times as they are led, via the activities in their Video Activities Booklet, to look and listen for more detailed information in the video segment they are viewing. The videocassette for each level of **Glencoe French** begins with an Introduction explaining why listening to natural, spoken French can be a difficult task and therefore why multiple viewings of each video *Scène* are required. The Introduction also points out the importance of using the print activities located in the Video Activities Booklet in order to use the Videocassette Program successfully.

Video Activities Booklet

The Video Activities Booklet is the vital companion piece to the hour-long video cassette for each level of **Glencoe French**. It consists of a series of pre-viewing, viewing, and post-viewing activities on Blackline Masters. These activities include specific instructions to students on what to watch and listen for as they view a given *Scène* on the videocassette. In addition to these student activities, the Video Activities Booklet also contains a Teacher's Manual, Culture Notes, and a complete transcript of the video soundtrack.

Computer Software: Practice and Test Generator

Available for Apple II, Macintosh and IBM-compatible machines, this software program provides materials for both students and teacher. The Practice Generator provides students with new, additional practice items for the vocabulary, grammar and culture topics in each chapter of the Student Textbook. All practice items are offered in a multiple choice format. The computer program includes a randomizer, so that each time a student calls up a set of exercises, the items are presented in a different order, thereby discouraging rote memorization of answers. Immediate feedback is given, along with the percent of correct answers, so that with repeated practice, students can track their performance. For vocabulary practice, illustrations from the *Vocabulaire* section of the Student Textbook have been scanned into the software to make practice more interesting and versatile.

The Test Generator allows the teacher to print out ready-made chapter tests, or customize a ready-made test by adding or deleting test items. The computer software comes with a Teacher's Manual as well as a printed transcript of all practice and test items.

Communication Activities Masters with Answer Key

This is a series of Blackline Masters, which provide further opportunities for students to practice their communication skills using the French they have learned. The contextualized, open-ended situations are designed to encourage students to communicate on a given topic, using specific vocabulary and grammatical structures from the corresponding chapter of the Student Textbook. The use of visual cues and interesting contexts will encourage students to ask questions and experiment with personalized responses. In the case of the paired communication activities, students actively work together as they share information provided on each partner's activity sheet. Answers to all activities are given in an Answer Key at the back of the Communication Activities Masters booklet.

Situation Cards

This is another component of **Glencoe French** aimed at developing listening and speaking skills through guided conversation. For each chapter of the Student Textbook, there is a corresponding set of guided conversational situations printed on hand-held cards. Working in pairs, students use appropriate vocabulary and grammar from the chapter to converse on the suggested topics. Although they are designed primarily for use in paired activities the Situation Cards may also be used in preparation for the speaking portion of the Testing Program or for informal assessment. Additional uses for the Situation Cards are described in the Situation Cards package, along with specific instructions and tips for their duplication and incorporation into your teaching plans. The cards are in Blackline Master form for easy duplication.

Bell Ringer Reviews on Blackline Masters

These are identical to the Bell Ringer Reviews found in each chapter of the Teacher's Wraparound Edition. For the teacher's convenience, they have been converted to this (optional) Blackline Master format. They may be either photocopied for distribution to students, or the teacher may convert them to overhead transparencies. The latter is accomplished by placing a blank acetate in the paper tray of your photocopy machine, then proceeding to make a copy of your Blackline Master (as though you were making a paper copy).

Interactive Conversation Video

An interactive video allows students to listen to and watch a real-life dramatization of each *Conversation* in the Student Textbook. Students may choose to participate in the video by taking the role of one of the characters.

Lesson Plans with Block Scheduling

Glencoe French offers flexible lesson plans for both 45- and 55-minute schedules. In addition, a separate set of lesson plans has been developed for those schools operating within a block scheduling arrangement.

The various **Glencoe French** support materials are incorporated into these lesson plans at their most logical point of use, depending on the nature of the presentation material on a given day. For example, the Vocabulary Transparencies and the Audio (Cassette or Compact Disc) Program can be used most effectively when presenting the chapter vocabulary. On the other hand, the corresponding Chapter Quiz is recommended for use one or two days after the initial presentation of vocabulary, or following a specific chapter structure point. Because student needs and teacher preferences vary, space has been provided on each lesson plan page for the teacher to write additional notes and comments, adjusting the day's activities as required.

Some Advantages of Block Scheduling

This type of scheduling differs from traditional scheduling in that fewer class sessions are scheduled for larger blocks of time over fewer days. For example, a course might meet for 90 minutes a day for 90 days, or half a school year.

For schools themselves, the greatest advantage of block scheduling is that there is a better use of resources. No additional teachers or classrooms may be needed, and more efficient use is made of those presently available in the school system. The need for summer school is greatly reduced because the students that do not pass a course one term can take it the next term. These advantages are accompanied by an increase in the quality of teacher instruction and student's time on-task.

There are many advantages for teachers who are in schools that use block scheduling. For example, teacher-student relationships are improved. With block scheduling, teachers have responsibility for a smaller number of students at a time, so students and teachers get to know each other better. With more time, teachers are better able to meet the individual needs of their students. Teachers can also be more focused on what they are teaching. Block scheduling may also result in changes in teaching approaches, classrooms that are more student-centered, improved teacher morale, increased teacher effectiveness, and decreased burn-out. Teachers feel free to venture away from discussion and lecture to use more productive models of teaching.

Block scheduling cuts in half the time needed for introducing and closing classes. It also eliminates half of the time needed for class changes, which results in fewer discipline problems. Flexibility is increased because less complex teaching schedules create more opportunities for cooperative teaching strategies such as team teaching and interdisciplinary studies.

Internet Activities Booklet

This booklet of blackline masters serves as a dynamic, real-world connection between cultural themes introduced in **Glencoe French**, and related topics available via the Internet. For example, **Bienvenue**, Chapter 2 is titled *Les copains et les cours*. The Internet activity for this chapter asks students to explore several WWW pages developed by French students, noting students' characteristics and interests. Using the vocabulary taught in Chapter 2, students are also asked to send a message to one of the student websites in France, describing himself/herself briefly, and mentioning a few personal interests.

In addition to serving as an innovative avenue for cultural reinforcement, the activities encourage both students and teachers to view the Internet as an engaging and valuable tool for learning the French language. Through this medium, students are able to further their knowledge of the French language, as well as increase their opportunities for participating in French-speaking communities around the world. The Internet activities encourage students to establish an ongoing keypal/pen pal relationship with French-speaking teenagers abroad.

The Internet Activities Booklet contains directions for the activities, student response sheets, and accompanying background teacher information, all on a chapter-by-chapter basis. Students will find the information required to complete each Internet activity by going to one or more of the websites whose addresses are provided on the Glencoe Foreign Language Home Page.

Chapter Quizzes with Answer Key

This component consists of short (5 to 10 minute) quizzes, designed to help both students and teachers evaluate quickly how well a specific vocabulary section or grammar topic has been mastered. For both Levels 1 and 2, there is a quiz for each *Mots* section (vocabulary) and one quiz for each grammar topic in the *Structure* section. The quizzes are on Blackline Masters. All answers are provided in an Answer Key at the end of the Chapter Quizzes booklet.

Testing Program with Answer Key

The Testing Program consists of three different types of Chapter Tests, two of which are bound into a testing booklet on Blackline Masters. The third type of test is available as part of the computer software component for **Glencoe French**.

1. The first type of test is discrete-point in nature, and uses evaluation techniques such as fill-in-the-blank, completion, short answers, true/false, matching, and multiple choice. Illustrations are frequently used as visual cues. The discrete-point tests measure vocabulary and grammar concepts via listening, speaking, reading, and writing formats. (As an option to the teacher, the listening section of each test has been recorded on cassette by native French speakers.) For testing cultural information, an optional section is included on each test corresponding to the *Lecture et Culture* section of the Student Textbook. For the teacher's convenience, the speaking portion of the tests has been physically separated from the listening, reading, and writing portions, and placed at the back of the testing booklet. These chapter tests can be administered upon the completion of each chapter. The Unit Tests can be administered upon the completion of each *Révision* (after every four chapters).

2. The Blackline Master testing booklet also contains a second type of test, namely the Chapter proficiency tests. These measure students' mastery of each chapter's vocabulary and grammar on a more global, whole-language level. For both types of tests above, there is an Answer Key at the back of the testing booklet.

3. In addition to the two types of tests described above, there is a third type which is part of the Computer Software: Practice and Test Generator Program (Macintosh; IBM; Apple versions). With this software, teachers have the option of simply printing out ready-made chapter tests, or customizing a ready-made test by selecting certain items, and/or adding original test items.

Performance Assessment

In addition to the tests described above, the Performance Assessment tasks provide an alternate approach to measuring student learning, compared to the more traditional paper and pencil tests. These tasks include individual student assignments, student interviews, and individual and small-group research projects with follow-up presentations. The Performance Assessment tasks can be administered following the completion of every fourth chapter in the Student Textbook.

GLENCOE FRENCH 1 CD-ROM INTERACTIVE TEXTBOOK

The **Glencoe French 1 CD-ROM Interactive Textbook** is a complete curriculum and instructional system for high school French students. The four-disc CD-ROM program contains all elements of the textbook plus photographs, videos, animations, a student portfolio feature, self-tests, and games, all designed to enhance and deepen students' understanding of the French language and culture. Although especially suited for individual or small-group use, it can be connected to a large monitor or LCD panel for whole-class instruction. With this flexible, interactive system, you can introduce, reinforce, or remediate any part of the French 1 curriculum at any time.

The CD-ROM program has four major sections: **Contents, Games, References**, and **Portfolio**. Of these four sections, the Games, Portfolio, and a special Contents feature—self-tests—are unique to the CD-ROM program.

Contents

The Contents section contains all the components of the French 1 *Bienvenue* textbook. The following selections can be found under Contents:

- **Vocabulaire** Vocabulary is introduced in thematic contexts. New words are introduced, and communication activities based on real-life situations are presented.

- **Structure** Students are given explanations of French structures. They then practice through contextualized exercises. One of the structure points in each chapter is enhanced with an electronic comic strip with which students can interact.

- **Conversation** Interactive videos, which were shot in France, enhance this feature comprised of real-life dialogues. Students may listen to and watch a conversation and then choose to participate as one of the two characters as they record their part of the dialogue.

- **Prononciation** Students are able to hear French pronunciation and then record the words and sentences themselves. They can then compare their pronunciation to that of native speakers.

- **Lecture et culture** Readings give students the opportunity to gain insight into French culture. They are also able to hear the readings in French. The similarities and differences between French and American culture are emphasized.

- **Réalités** In *Réalités*, students see glimpses of everyday life in France. The *Réalités* act as a starting point for discussions about similarities and differences that exist between life in France and in the United States.

- **Culmination** Chapter-end activities require students to integrate the concepts they have learned. There are oral and written activities as well as activities aimed at building skills, and a vocabulary review linked to the glossary.

- **Self-Test** The self-test, *Contrôle de révision*, provides a means for students to evaluate their own progress.

At the end of each four chapters are three features: *Le Monde francophone, Révision,* and *Lettres et sciences.* These selections may also be found in the Contents section.

- **Le Monde francophone** This section provides students with additional information about the various countries which comprise the francophone world. The text has been recorded to allow students to both read and hear authentic speech.

- **Révision** In the *Révision* section, students participate in a variety of review activities.

- **Lettres et sciences** This selection gives students the opportunity to practice their French reading skills through interdisciplinary readings that provide insights into French culture.

Games

The Games section gives users access to *Pour en savoir plus* (Discs 1 and 3) and to *Le Labyrinthe* (Discs 2 and 4). Each game reviews the vocabulary, structure, and culture topics that have been presented in the four chapters contained on that particular CD-ROM disc.

References

Maps, verb charts, and the French-English/ English-French glossaries can be selected from this tab. The maps include France, Paris, and a world map with the French-speaking countries highlighted.

Portfolio

The electronic portfolio feature may be accessed by clicking on this tab. Students can access a photo library, and choose from a variety of "stationery" templates to create original written work which they can then save on their portfolio document.

For more information, see the User's Guide accompanying the **Glencoe French 1 CD-ROM Interactive Textbook.**

COOPERATIVE LEARNING

Cooperative learning provides a structured, natural environment for student communication that is both motivating and meaningful. The affective filter that prevents many students from daring to risk a wrong answer when called upon to speak in front of a whole class can be minimized when students develop friendly relationships in their cooperative groups and when they become accustomed to multiple opportunities to hear and rehearse new communicative tasks.The goal of cooperative learning is not to abandon traditional methods of foreign language teaching, but rather to provide opportunities for learning in an environment where students contribute freely and responsibly to the success of the group. The key is to strike a balance between group goals and individual accountability. Group (team) members plan how to divide the activity among themselves, then each member of the group carries out his or her part of the assignment. Cooperative learning provides each student with a "safe," low-risk environment rather than a whole-class atmosphere. As you implement cooperative learning in your classroom, we urge you to take time to explain to students what will be expected of every group member—listening, participating, and respecting other opinions.

In the Teacher's Wraparound Edition, cooperative learning activities have been written to accompany each chapter of the Student Textbook. These activities have been created to assist both the teacher who wants to include cooperative learning for the first time, and for the experienced practitioner of cooperative learning as well.

Classroom Management: implementing Cooperative Learning activities

Many of the suggested cooperative learning activities are based on a four-member team structure in the classroom. Teams of four are recommended because there is a wide variety of possible interactions. At the same time the group is small enough that students can take turns quickly within the group. Pairs of students as teams may be too limited in terms of possible interactions, and trios frequently work out to be a pair with the third student left out. Teams of five may be unwieldy in that students begin to feel that no one will notice if they don't really participate.

If students sit in rows on a daily basis, desks can be pushed together to form teams of four. Teams of students who work together need to be balanced according to as many variables as possible: academic achievement in the course, personality, ethnicity, gender, attitude, etc. Teams that are as heterogeneous as possible will ensure that the class progresses quickly through the curriculum.

Following are descriptions of some of the most important cooperative learning structures, adapted from Spencer Kagan's Structural Approach to Cooperative Learning, as they apply to the content of *Bienvenue*.

Round-robin Each team member answers in turn a question, or shares an idea with teammates. Responses should be brief so that students do not have to wait too long for their turn.

Example from *Bienvenue*, Chapter 2, Days of the week:

Teams recite the days of the week in a round-robin fashion. Different students begin additional rounds so that everyone ends up needing to know all the names of the days. Variations include starting the list with a different day or using a race format, i.e., teams recite the list three times in a row and raise their hands when they have finished.

Roundtable Each student in turn writes his or her contribution to the group activity on a piece of paper that is passed around the team. If the individual student responses are longer than one or two words, there can be four pieces of paper with each student contributing to each paper as it is passed around the team.

A to Z Roundtable Using vocabulary from *Bienvenue*, Chapters 7 and 8, students take turns adding one word at a time to a list of words associated with plane or train travel in A to Z order. Students may help each other with what to write, and correct spelling. Encourage creativity when it comes to the few letters of the alphabet that don't begin a specific travel word from their chapter lists. Teams can compete in several ways: first to finish all 26 letters; longest word; shortest word; most creative response.

Numbered Heads Together Numbered Heads Together is a structure for review and practice of high consensus information. There are four steps:

Step 1: Students number off in their teams from 1 to 4.

Step 2: The teacher asks a question and gives the teams some time to make sure that everyone on the team knows the answer.

Step 3: The teacher calls a number.

Step 4: The appropriate student from each team is responsible to report the group response.

Answers can be reported simultaneously, i.e., all students with the appropriate number can stand by their seats and recite the answer together, or go to the chalkboard and write the answer at the same time. Answers can also be reported sequentially. Call on the first student to raise his or her hand or have all the students with the appropriate number stand. Select one student to give the answer. If the other students agree, they sit down; if not, they remain standing and offer a different response.

Example from *Bienvenue*, Chapter 2, Telling time:

Step 1: Using a blank clock face on the overhead transparency or chalkboard, the teacher adjusts the hands on the clock.

Step 2: Students put their heads together and answer the question: *Quelle heure est-il?*

Step 3: The teacher calls a number.

Step 4: The appropriate student from each team is responsible to report the group response.

Pantomimes Give each team one card. Have each team decide together how to pantomime for the class the action identified on the card. Each team presents the pantomime for ten seconds while the rest of the teams watch without talking. Then each of the other teams tries to guess the phrase and writes down their choice on a piece of paper. (This is a good way to accommodate kinesthetic learning styles as well as vary classroom activities.)

Example from *Bienvenue*, Chapter 3 vocabulary: The teacher writes the following sentences on slips of paper and places them in an envelope:

1. *Ils parlent.*
2. *Ils parlent au téléphone.*
3. *Ils écoutent des cassettes.*
4. *Ils écoutent des disques compacts.*
5. *Ils écoutent un walkman.*
6. *Ils écoutent la radio.*
7. *Ils regardent la télé.*
8. *Ils dansent.*
9. *Ils chantent.*
10. *Ils rigolent.*

Each team will draw one slip of paper from the envelope and decide together how to pantomime the action for the class. As one team pantomimes their action for 30 seconds, the other teams are silent. Then the students within each team discuss among themselves

what sentence was acted out for them. When they have decided on the sentence, each team sends one person to write it on the chalkboard.

Inside/Outside Circle Students form two concentric circles of equal number by counting off 1-2, 1-2 in their teams. The "ones" form a circle shoulder to shoulder and facing out. The "twos" form a circle outside the "ones" to make pairs. With an odd number of students, there can be one threesome. Students take turns sharing information, quizzing each other, or taking parts of a dialogue. After students finish with their first partners, rotate the inside circle to the left so that the students repeat the process with new partners. For following rounds, alternate rotating the inside and outside circles so that students get to repeat the identified tasks, but with new partners. This is an excellent way to structure 100% student participation combined with extensive practice of communication tasks.

Other suggested activities are similarly easy to follow and to implement in the classroom. Student enthusiasm for cooperative learning activities will reward the enterprising teacher. Teachers who are new to these concepts may want to refer to Dr. Spencer Kagan's book, Cooperative Learning, published by Resources for Teachers, Inc., Paseo Espada, Suite 622, San Juan Capistrano, CA 92675.

SUGGESTIONS FOR CORRECTING HOMEWORK

Correcting homework, or any tasks students have done on an independent basis, should be a positive learning experience rather than mechanical "busywork." Following are some suggestions for correcting homework. These ideas may be adapted as the teacher sees fit.

1. Put the answers on an overhead transparency. Have students correct their own answers.

2. Ask one or more of your better students to write their homework answers on the chalkboard at the beginning of the class hour. While the answers are being put on the chalkboard, the teacher involves the rest of the class in a non-related activity. At some point in the class hour, take a few minutes to go over the homework answers that have been written on the board, asking students to check their own work. You may then wish to have students hand in their homework so that they know this independent work is important to you.

3. Go over the homework assignment quickly in class. Write the key word(s) for each answer on the chalkboard so students can see the correct answer.

4. When there is no correct answer, e.g., "Answers will vary," give one or two of the most likely answers. Don't allow students to inquire about all other possibilities, however.

5. Have all students hand in their homework. After class, correct every other (every third, fourth, fifth, etc.) homework paper. Over several days, you will have checked every student's homework at least once.

6. Compile a list of the most common student errors. Then create a worksheet that explains the underlying grammar points and practices on these topics.

STUDENT PORTFOLIOS

The use of student portfolios to represent long-term individual accomplishments in learning French offers several benefits. With portfolios, students can keep a written record of their best work and thereby document their own progress as learners. For teachers, portfolios enable us to include our students in our evaluation and measurement process. For example, the content of any student's portfolio may offer an alternative to the standardized test as a way of measuring student writing achievement. Assessing the contents of a student's portfolio can be an option to testing the writing skill via the traditional writing section of the chapter or unit test.

There are as many kinds of portfolios as there are teachers working with them. Perhaps the most convenient as well as permanent portfolio consists of a three-ring binder which each student will add to over the school year and in which the student will place his or her best written work. In the **Glencoe French** series, selections for the portfolio may come from the Writing Activities Workbook; Communication Activities Masters; the more open-ended activities in the Student Tape Manual and the Video Activities Booklet, as well as from written assignments in the Student Textbook, including the *Activités de communication écrite* sections. The teacher is encouraged to refer actively to students' portfolios so that they are regarded as more than just a storage device. For example, over the course of the school year, the student may be asked to go back to earlier entries in his or her portfolio in order to revise certain assignments, or to develop an assignment further by writing in a new tense, e.g., the *passé composé*. In this way the student can appreciate the amount of learning that has occurred over several months' time.

Portfolios offer students a multidimensional look at themselves. A "best" paper might be the one with the least errors or one in which the student reached and synthesized a new idea, or went beyond the teacher's assignment. The Student Portfolio topic is included in each chapter of the Teacher's Wraparound Edition as a reminder that this is yet another approach the teacher may wish to use in the French classroom.

CD-ROM Electronic Portfolio

The Student Portfolio topic is a regular feature in each chapter of the Teacher's Wraparound Edition. In addition, the CD-ROM version of the student textbook (see page T37) includes an electronic portfolio feature. Students may access a photo library, and choose from a variety of stationery templates to create original written works which they can then store as a portfolio document. For more information, see the User's Guide accompanying the **Glencoe French 1 CD-ROM Interactive Textbook**.

PACING

Sample Lesson Plans

Level 1 (*Bienvenue*) has been developed so that it may be completed in one school year. However, it is up to the individual teacher to decide how many chapters will be covered. Although completion of the textbook by the end of the year is recommended, it is not necessary. Most of the important structures of Level 1 are reviewed in a different context in the early chapters of Level 2 (*À bord*). The establishment of lesson plans helps the teacher visualize how a chapter can be presented. However, by emphasizing certain aspects of the program and deemphasizing others, the teacher can change the focus and the approach of a chapter to meet students' needs and to suit his or her own teaching style and techniques. Sample lesson plans are provided below. They include some of the suggestions and techniques that have been described earlier in this Teacher's Manual.

STANDARD PACING

	Days	Total Days
(Preliminary Lessons A–H)	5 days	5
Chapitres 1–15	9 days per chapter	135
Testing	1 day per test	15
Révision (3)	3 days each	9
Lettres et sciences (3 [optional])	2 days each	6

	Class	Homework
Day 1	*Mots 1* (with transparencies) exercises (Student Textbook)	*Mots* exercises (written) Writing Activities Workbook: *Mots 1*
Day 2	*Mots 2* (with transparencies) exercises (Student Textbook)	*Mots* exercises (written) exercises from Student Textbook (written) prepare *Activités de communication* Writing Activities Workbook: *Mots 2*
Day 3	present *Activités de communication* one *Structure* topic exercises (Student Textbook)	exercises from Student Textbook (written) Writing Activities Workbook (written)

Day 4	two *Structure* topics exercises (Student Textbook)	exercises from Student Textbook (written) Student Tape Manual exercises
Day 5	one *Structure* topic exercises (Student Textbook)	exercises from Student Textbook (written) Writing Activities Workbook (written)
Day 6	*Conversation* (pronunciation) *Activités de communication* Audio Cassette Program	read *Lecture et culture* *Étude de mots*
Day 7	review *Lecture et culture* *Compréhension* questions Video Program	read *Découverte culturelle* and *Réalités*
Day 8	review homework *Activités de communication orale* Situation Cards	*Activités de communication écrite*
Day 9	Communication Activities Masters Communication transparency	review for test
Day 10	Test	after Chapters 4, 8, 12: *Révision* conversation

Révision (review) and *Lettres et sciences* (optional) sections

Day 1	grammar review	exercises in Student Textbook and Workbook
Day 2	correct homework *Activités de communication*	review for Test
Day 3	Unit Test	pre-read *Lettres et sciences*, first selection (optional)
Day 4	*Lettres et sciences*, first selection (optional)	*Lettres et sciences*, second selection (optional)
Day 5	*Lettres et sciences*, third selection (optional)	*Lettres et sciences*, second selection in-depth (optional)

ACCELERATED PACING

	Days	Total Days
(Preliminary Lessons A–H)	5 days	5
Chapters 1–8	8 days per chapter	64*
Chapters 9–18	7 days per chapter	70
Test	1 day per test	18
Révision (4)	2 days each	8
Lettres et Sciences (4 [optional])	2 days each	8

	Class	Homework
Day 1	*Mots 1* (with transparencies) exercises (Student Textbook)	*Mots* exercises (written) Writing Activities Workbook: *Mots 1*
Day 2	*Mots 2* (with transparencies) exercises (Student Textbook)	*Mots* exercises (written) exercises from Student Textbook (written) prepare *Activités de communication* Writing Activities Workbook: *Mots 2*
Day 3	present *Activités de communication* two *Structure* topics	exercises from Student Textbook (written) Writing Activities Workbook (written)
Day 4	two *Structure* topics	exercises from Student Textbook (written) Writing Activities Workbook (written)
Day 5	*Conversation* present *Activité de communication* Audio Cassette Program	read *Lecture et culture* *Étude de mots* and *Compréhension*
Day 6	*Découverte cultrelle* (optional) *Réalités* (optional) Videocassette Program Communication Activities Masters	*Culmination*
Day 7	review *Culmination* Situation Cards Communication transparency	review for test
Day 8	Test	After Chapters 4, 8, 12, 16: *Révision*

*Note: After Chapter 8, the teacher may choose among the *Culmination* activities on Days 6 and 7, thereby eliminating one day, or the teacher omits Chapter 18.

Révision (review) and *Lettres et sciences* (optional) sections

Day 1	*Révision* exercises	review for test
Day 2	Unit Test	
Day 3	*Lettres et sciences*, first selection (optional)	*Lettres et sciences,* second selection (optional)
Day 4	*Lettres et sciences*, third selection (optional)	

USEFUL CLASSROOM WORDS AND EXPRESSIONS

Below is a list of the most frequently used words and expressions needed in conducting a French class.

Words

le papier	paper
la feuille de papier	sheet of paper
le cahier	notebook
le cahier d'exercices	workbook
le stylo	pen
le stylo-bille	ballpoint pen
le crayon	pencil
la gomme	(pencil) eraser
la craie	chalk
le tableau noir	blackboard
la brosse	blackboard eraser
la corbeille	waste basket
le pupitre	desk
le rang	row
la chaise	chair
l'écran (m.)	screen
le projecteur	projector
la cassette	cassette
le livre	book
la règle	ruler

Commands

Both the singular and the plural command forms are provided.

Viens.	Venez.	Come.
Va.	Allez.	Go.
Entre.	Entrez.	Enter.
Sors.	Sortez.	Leave.
Attends.	Attendez.	Wait.

Mets.	Mettez.	Put.
Donne-moi.	Donnez-moi.	Give me.
Dis-moi.	Dites-moi.	Tell me.
Apporte-moi.	Apportez-moi.	Bring me.
Répète.	Répétez.	Repeat.
Pratique.	Pratiquez.	Practice.
Étudie.	Étudiez.	Study.
Réponds.	Répondez.	Answer.
Apprends.	Apprenez.	Learn.
Choisis.	Choisissez.	Choose.
Prépare.	Préparez.	Prepare.
Regarde.	Regardez.	Look at.
Décris.	Décrivez.	Describe.
Commence.	Commencez.	Begin.
Prononce.	Prononcez.	Pronounce.
Écoute.	Écoutez.	Listen.
Parle.	Parlez.	Speak.
Lis.	Lisez.	Read.
Écris.	Écrivez.	Write.
Demande.	Demandez.	Ask.
Suis le modèle.	Suivez le modèle.	Follow the model.
Joue le rôle de…	Jouez le rôle de…	Take the part of…
Prends.	Prenez.	Take.
Ouvre.	Ouvrez.	Open.
Ferme.	Fermez.	Close.
Tourne la page.	Tournez la page.	Turn the page.
Efface.	Effacez.	Erase.
Continue.	Continuez.	Continue.
Assieds-toi.	Asseyez-vous.	Sit down.
Lève-toi.	Levez-vous.	Get up.
Lève la main.	Levez la main.	Raise your hand.
Tais-toi.	Taisez-vous.	Be quiet.
Fais attention.	Faites attention.	Pay attention.
Attention.		Attention.
Attention, s'il vous plaît.		Your attention, please.
Silence.		Quiet.
Fais attention.	Faites attention.	Careful.
Encore.		Again.
Encore une fois.		Once again.
Un à un.		One at a time.
Tous ensemble.		All together.
À haute voix.		Out loud.
Plus haut, s'il vous plaît.		Louder, please.
En français.		In French.
En anglais.		In English.

ADDITIONAL FRENCH RESOURCES

Pen pal sources Following is a list of French and American organizations that assist in finding French pen pals:

1. American Association of Teachers of French
   Bureau de Correspondance Scolaire
   57 East Armory Avenue
   Champaign, IL 61820
   tel: (217) 333-2842
2. Fédération Internationale des Organisations de Correspondance et d'Échanges Scolaires (FIOCES)
   29, rue d'Ulm
   75230 Paris CEDEX 05
   France
3. Contacts
   55, rue Nationale
   37000 Tours
   France
4. Office National de la Coopération à l'École
   101 bis, rue du Ranelagh
   75016 Paris
   France
5. Mairie
   Maison des Sociétés
   Square Weingarten
   69500 Bron
   France

French Embassy and Consulates in the United States

French Embassy
Press and Information Service
4101 Reservoir Road, N.W.
Washington, DC 20007
tel: (202) 944-6060

French Consulates
Atlanta: (404) 522-4226
Boston: (617) 542-7374
Chicago: (312) 787-5359
Honolulu: (808) 599-4458
Houston: (713) 528-2181
Los Angeles: (310) 235-3200
Miami: (305) 372-9799
New York: (212) 606-3688
New Orleans: (504) 523-5772
San Francisco: (415) 397-4330
San Juan, Puerto Rico: (809) 753-1700

The Embassy of France distributes neither French flags nor posters. To purchase a flag contact one of the following manufacturers:

U.N. Association
Capital Area Division
1319 18th Street N.W.
Washington, DC 20036-1802
(202) 785-2640

Abacrome
1-B Quaker Ridge Rd.
New Rochelle, NY 10804
(914) 235-8152

Bienvenue

Bienvenue

Conrad J. Schmitt

Katia Brillié Lutz

Glencoe McGraw-Hill

New York, New York   Columbus, Ohio   Mission Hills, California   Peoria, Illinois

Glencoe/McGraw-Hill

A Division of The McGraw·Hill Companies

Copyright ©1998 by Glencoe/McGraw-Hill. All rights reserved. Except as permitted under the United States Copyright Act, no part of this publication may be reproduced or distributed in any form or by any means, or stored in a database or retrieval system, without prior permission of the publisher.

Printed in the United States of America.

Send all inquiries to:
    Glencoe/McGraw-Hill
    15319 Chatsworth Street
    P.O. Box 9609
    Mission Hills, CA 91346-9609

ISBN 0-02-636683-5 (Student Edition)
ISBN 0-02-636684-3 (Teacher's Wraparound Edition)

1 2 3 4 5 6 7 8 9 0 QPH 03 02 01 00 99 98 97

Photography
Front cover: ©Gridley, Peter, 1995/FPG International.
Allsport USA/Vandystadt: 252/2; Antman, M./Scribner: xM, xiT, 20B, 23, 243, 276/3, 289, 294, 295, 322/1/2/3, 323/5, 324, 350, 359/3, 374T, 389, 397, 428, 439, 486, 494, 499; Banahan, Lawrence/Allsport USA: xB, 300/3; Bayer, Carol/La Photothèque SDP: 381/6; Billow, Nathan/Allsport USA: 380/3; Blatty, Michael: 31; ©California Newsreel, San Francisco: 437/9, 437/10; Canedi, Daniel/La Photothèque SDP: 359/5; Carle, Eric/Bruce Coleman: 253/4; Chadefaux, A./Top Agence: 420; Château d'Agneaux Hôtel, Eliophot, Aix en Provence: 472BR; Cogan, Michel/Top Agence: 491; Collection Lausat/Explorer: 446L; Collection Violet/Roger Viollet/Gamma Liaison: 446R; Costa, S./Explorer: 250; Courlas, Tim/Horizons: 297, 312T, 355, 393; Cuny, C./Rapho/Gamma Liaison: 252/1; Damn, Fridmar/Leo de Wys Inc.: 463; Deschamps, Hervé/Gamma Liaison: 372; Ducasse, F./Rapho/Gamma Liaison: 404/1; Duomo: 300-301, 357, 359/4; Eschet, Zviki/La Photothèque SDP: 380/1; Fischer, Curt: ixT, xii, 2, 5, 9, 18, 20T, 21, 26, 28, 29T, 33, 256-257, 265, 275, 276/2, 277/4, 279, 293, 325, 352, 380, 406, 430-431/1, 470-471, 483, 502; Fleurent, C./Rapho/Gamma Liaison: 299; Ford, Matthew/FSP/Gamma Liaison: 329/7; FPG: 249; Foto World/The Image Bank: 436/7, Freed, Leonard/Magnum: 417; Gaveau, Alain: ix M, ixB, xT, xiii, 6, 13, 15, 17, 280-281, 316, 320, 321, 354, 400, 418, 429, 456, 472TR, 474-475, 487, 497/4; Geiersperger, W./Explorer: 335B; Gely/Imapress: 434/1; Gibson, Mark/Photo 20-20: 327/3; Giraudon/Art Resource: 444, 445L, 445R; Gossler/Schuster/ Explorer: 327/4; Gritscher, Helmut/Peter Arnold: 339; Gschiedle, Gerhard/Scribner: 238, 276-277; Guichaqua, Yann/Allsport USA/Vandystadt: viii; Gunn, F./Canapress: 348; Harlingue/Viollet/Gamma-Liaison: 337; Heaton, Dallas & John/Westlight: 460; Holmes, Robert/Photo 20-20: 377, 381/5; Hôtel de Paris, Cannes: 472L; Hôtel Idéal, Mont Blanc: 472M; Jalain, F./Explorer: 423; Jeffrey, David/The Image Bank: 3; Joana M./La Photothèque SDP: 253, 358-359, 379; Kent, Keith/Peter Arnold: 339T; Kirtley, M&A/ANA: 329/8; Lenfant, J.P./Vandystadt/Allsport USA: 251; Lessing, Eric/Art Resource, NY; Lisl, Dennis/The Image Bank: 436/8; Marché, Guy/La Photothèque: 332; Martin, Richard/Allsport USA: 300/1; Machatschek, Charles/La Photothèque SDP: 374, 382; McCurry, Steve/Magnum: 334; Menzel, Peter/Peter Menzel: 431/4, 470/2; Merlin/La Photothèque SDP: 416; Messerschmidt, Joachim/FPG: 501; Naci, Jean Paul/Leo de Wys Inc: 366; N'Diaye, Jean Claude/Imapress: 314; Neumiller, Roberto/ANA: 435/3; Paireault, J.P./ANA: 328/6; Parks, Claudia/The Stock Market: 326/1; Pelletier, M./Gamma Liaison: 434/2, Petit, Christian/Allsport USA/Vandystadt: 298; Photothèque de l'Institut Pasteur: 404/3L, 442, 443TL, 443TR; Pinheira/Option Photo: 30; Powell, Mike/Allsport USA: 348; Pronin, Anatoly/Art Resource, NY: 419; Radford, Ben/Allsport USA: 351; Rega/Rapho/Gamma Liaison: 322-323; Renard, Éric/Agence Temp Sport: 301/4; Renaudeau, M./Hoa-Qui: 326/2; 328/5, 358/2, 436/5; Romanelli, Marc/The Image Bank: 427; Rondeau, Pascal/Allsport USA: 380/4; Roux, Aimé/Explorer: 301/5; Rowe, Wayne: xiv-1, 10-11, 24-25, 234-235, 245, 248, 261, 266, 269, 270, 272T, 274, 288, 296T, 304-305, 312B, 313, 318, 319, 329/9, 340-341, 347, 353, 376, 384-385, 395, 396, 402, 403, 408-409, 416, 417, 425, 426, 430/2, 448-449, 466, 471/3, 478, 484, 487, 492, 496-497; Sallaz, William/Duomo: 438; Sanson, Nanette/Profolio: 362-363, 378; Scala/Art Resource, NY: 421; SNCF: 27, 29B; Streshinsky, Ted/Photo 20-20: 255; Suaiton, Ken/The Stock Market: 436/6; SuperStock: 254, 278T, 371, 457; Tauqueuer, Siegried/Leo de Wys, Inc.: 380-381/2; Testelin, X/Rapho/Gamma Liaison: 404-405/2; Thomas, Marc: xiM, xiB, 254/2, 272B, 291, 296B, 344, 360, 370, 388, 394, 458, 489; Tovy, Adina/Photo 20-20: 252-253; TPH/La Photothèque SDP: 278B; Walter/Rapho/Gamma Liaison: 7; Weiss, S/Rapho/Gamma Liaison: 277/5; Wolf, A./Explorer: 4043R, 443L; Wysocki, P./Explorer: 323/4, 335T, 405/4.

Illustration
Abadie, Stéphane: 464; Accardo, Anthony: 373, 461, 480, 481, 485; Collin, Marie Marthe: 309, 310, 342, 343, 364, 365, 450, 451, 454, 455, 462, 488; Gorde, Monique: 290, 368, 369, 452; Gregory, Lane: 16, 236, 237, 242, 258, 259, 260, 262, 263, 345, 346, 361, 367, 388; Kieffer, Christa: 19; 337; Metivet, Henry: 306, 307, 308, 324, Miller, Lyle: 32, 386, 387, Miyamoto, Masami: 393, 422;

Nicholson, Norman: 349, 410, 411, Spellman, Susan: 282, 283, 390, 391T, 416, Taber, Ed: 248, 264, 273, 289, 297, 302, 316, 318, 355, 376, 391, 401, 426, 467, 482, 493, 498; Thewlis, Diana: 12, 239, 240, 241, 286, 287, 414, 415; Watorek, Kena: 284, 476, 477.

Realia
A.N. Rafting, Le Grand Liou: 246; Air Afrique: 26; Banque Industrielle et Mobilière Privée: 497; Banque Nationale de Paris: 479L; Caisse d'Épargne Écureuil: 496B; Cartotec, illustration Yannick Intesse: 303; Christian Dior: 277; Collections de la Comédie-Française: 413; Crédit Agricole: 496T; Éditions Albert René, 1996. Goscinny/Uderzo. *Les Lauriers de César*, Dargaud Éditeur: 429T; Éditions Les Quatre Zéphires: 13; © Éditions S.A.E.P., 1993, Elle Magazine: 260; Espace Soleil: 244; France Télécom: 465; Galeries Lafayette, illustration Mats Gutafson: 267; Hachette-Gautier Languereau, illustration M. Boutet de Monvel: 14; Laboratoire Conseil Oberlin: 398, 399; Ligue Française pour les Auberges de la Jeunesse: 469; Locapark: 311, Michelin Red Guide France, 1992 Edition, Pneu Michelin, Services de Tourisme: 471; Monoprix: 271; Pariscope Magazine, Backdraft, © by Universal City Studios, Inc. courtesy of MCA Publishing Rights, a Division of MCA Inc: 424; Pomme de Pain: 9; La Poste: 479R; La Redoute Catalogue: 371; Rev'Vacances: 440; SNCF: 27, Societé IAG: 472; ©Télérama: 354; Vélo Sprint 2000 Magazine: 348

Fabric designs by *Les Olivades*.

Maps
Eureka Cartography, Berkeley, CA.

In appreciation
Special thanks to the following people in France for their cordial assistance and participation in the photo illustration:

M. le Maire d'Ansouis; M. le Proviseur, les professeurs et les élèves du Lycée Henri IV; M. le Proviseur, les professeurs et les élèves du Lycée Val de Durance; Mme le Principal, les professeurs, en particulier Mlle Marie-Claude Éberlé, et les élèves du Collège Mignet; M. le Principal, les professeurs et les élèves du Collège du Pays d'Aigues; M. Jacques Lefèbvre et les élèves du Lycée du Parc Impérial; Groupe Scolaire Sainte-Anne

Dr Christian Amat, Marie-Françoise, Camille, Emmanuel et Alexandre Amat/Jean-Pierre Antoine et Bébé le caniche/Helena Appel/La Famille Baud/Sonia Benaïs/La Famille Bérard/Jérôme Bernard/Sylvain Casteleiro/Adelaïde Chanal/Amy Chang/Andréa Clément/Émilie Cusset/La Famille Dandré et Josué/Michèle Descalis/Denise Deschamps/Mme Duclos/Élisabeth Éberlé/Jeanne Grisoli/Hélène Guion/David Hadida/Amelle Hafafsa, Amar et Riad/Thomas Hardy/Simone Kayem/Marie-France Lamy/Olivier Lucas/Harry Magdaléon/Dr Francis Maguet/Barbara Marone et Jessie le collie/Katy Martin/Jean Martinez/Dr Jean Mori/Claudette Mori/Elarif M'Ze/Magali Parola/Daniel Pauchon/Olivier Perrière/Élodie Perrin/Nelly Pouani/Estelle et Hélène Puigt/Claude Rivière/Nadège Rivière/Elzéar, Foulques et Amic de Sabran-Pontevès/Maître Frédéric Sanchez, avocat/Kalasea Sanchez/Martine Serbin/Michel Skwarczewski/Florence Vareilles/Maître Marie-Christine Viard-Vassiliev, avocate/Jonathan Viretto/Bernard et Jacqueline Vittorio

Air France (M. Philippe Boulze)/L'Art Glacier/Banque Marseillaise de Crédit/Boutique Frenchy's/Cabinet du Dr Amat/Cabinet du Dr Maguet/Charcuterie Guers/Compact Club/Complexe Sportif du Val de l'Arc/Fromagerie Gérard Paul/les Gendarmes de Beaumont/ Grand Café Thomas/Le Grand Véfour (M. Guy Martin)/Hôtel Le Moulin de Lourmarin/ Pâtisserie Chambost/Pharmacie de l'Europe/Restaurant La Récréation/Restaurant Le Viêt-Nam/Salon de Coiffure Sylvie

About the Cover

The Château Frontenac, a beautiful hotel, is located in the Old Town of Quebec overlooking the Saint Lawrence River. The hotel is named after Count Louis de Frontenac, the governor of New France in the 17th Century.

Acknowledgments

We wish to express our deep appreciation to the numerous individuals throughout the United States and France who have advised us in the development of these teaching materials. Special thanks are extended to the people whose names appear below.

Esther Bennett
Notre Dame High School
Sherman Oaks, California

Brillié Family
Paris, France

Kathryn Bryers
French teacher
Berlin, Connecticut

G. Gail Castaldo
The Pingry School
Martinsville, New Jersey

Veronica Dewey
Brother Rice High School
Birmingham, Massachusetts

Lyne Flaherty
Hingham High School
Hingham, Massachusetts

Marie-Jo Hoffmann
Poudre School District
Fort Collins, Colorado

Marcia Brown Karper
Fayetteville-Manlius Central Schools
Manlius, New York

Annette Lowry
Ft. Worth Independent School District
Ft. Worth, Texas

Fabienne Raab
Paris, France

Sally Schneider
Plano Independent School District
Plano, Texas

Faith Weldon
Schalmont Central School District
Schenectady, New York

TABLE DES MATIÈRES

PART B

RÉVISION

CHAPITRE 9

LES SPORTS ET LES ACTIVITÉS D'ÉTÉ

CHAPITRE 10

LES BOUTIQUES ET LES VÊTEMENTS

CHAPITRE 11

LA ROUTINE ET LA FORME PHYSIQUE

CHAPITRE 14

L'HIVER ET LES SPORTS D'HIVER

CHAPITRE 15

LA SANTÉ ET LA MÉDECINE

xi

CHAPITRE 16

LES LOISIRS CULTURELS

CHAPITRE 17

L'HÔTEL

CHAPITRE 18

L'ARGENT ET LA BANQUE

APPENDICES

RÉVISION A

RÉVISION
A

OVERVIEW

Review Chapters A–C cover the key grammatical points and vocabulary topics presented in *Bienvenue,* Part A. Additional review work can be found in the review chapters following Chapters 4 and 8 of *Bienvenue,* Part A, and in the *Réintroduction et recombinaison* section of each chapter. New material is presented starting in Chapter 1 of Part B.

This review chapter covers vocabulary needed to describe people, school, and home. These topics were first presented in *Bienvenue,* Part A, Chapters 1–4. The agreement of adjectives, the present tense of the verbs *être* and *aller,* and the contractions with *à* and *de* are also reviewed.

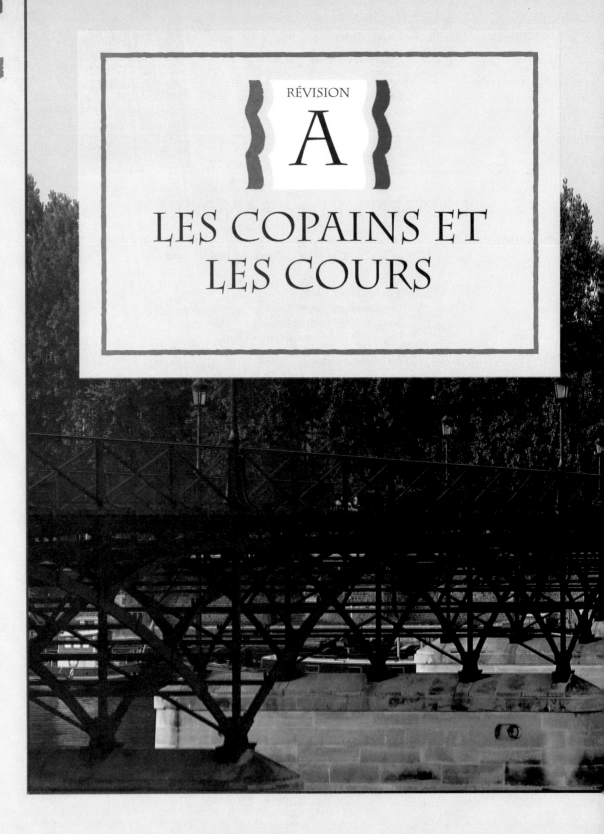

LES COPAINS ET LES COURS

1

Pacing

This review chapter should take two to three days depending on the length of the class and the age and aptitude of your students.

Note The Lesson Plans offer guidelines for 45- and 55-minute classes and **Block Scheduling**.

Exercices vs. *Activités*

The exercises and activities are color-coded. Exercises, which provide guided practice to prepare students for independent communication, are coded in blue. Communicative activities, which afford students the opportunity for creative, open-ended expression, are coded in red.

DID YOU KNOW?

The *Pont des Arts* faces the *Institut de France,* home of the *Académie française.* This bridge, which was built in 1803, was the first pedestrian bridge in Paris. From this bridge, there are panoramic views of the Île de la Cité and both the Right and Left Banks.

Vocabulary Teaching Resources

1. Bell Ringer Review Blackline Master: R-1, page 38
2. Workbook, *Mots et Conversation: A–C,* page R1

Bell Ringer Review

Put the following on the board or use BRR Blackline Master R-1: Make a list of expressions used for greeting people and saying good-bye to them.

Une Française

PRESENTATION *(page 2)*

A. Have students open their books and repeat the sentences about Nathalie after you.
B. Ask the questions that follow.

ANSWERS

Exercice A

1. C'est Nathalie.
2. Elle est française.
3. Elle est de Paris.
4. Elle est très intelligente.
5. Elle va au lycée Henri IV.

Deux Français

PRESENTATION *(page 2)*

A. Review the expressions used for greeting people and saying good-bye to them that students listed in the Bell Ringer Review. Then have the class repeat the conversation after you.
B. Call on two students to read the conversation to the class.

ANSWERS

Exercice B

1. Oui, il va bien.
2. Il va au cours de français.
3. M. Guillemette est le professeur de français.
4. Il est très chouette.

Une Française

Voici Nathalie.
Elle est française.
Nathalie est de Paris, la capitale.
Nathalie est très intelligente.
Elle est élève au lycée.
Elle va au Lycée Henri IV.

A **Nathalie.** Répondez.

1. Qui est la fille?
2. Elle est de quelle nationalité?
3. Elle est de quelle ville?
4. Nathalie est intelligente ou pas?
5. Elle va à quel lycée?

Deux Français

ÉRIC: Salut, Paul.
PAUL: Salut, Éric. Ça va?
ÉRIC: Oui, ça va bien, et toi?
PAUL: Pas mal.
ÉRIC: Où vas-tu maintenant?
PAUL: Je vais au cours de français.
ÉRIC: Qui est le prof?
PAUL: M. Guillemette. Il est très chouette.

B **Salut, Paul!** Répondez d'après la conversation.

1. Éric va bien ou pas?
2. Où est-ce que Paul va maintenant?
3. Qui est le professeur de français?
4. Comment est-il?

2 RÉVISION

ADDITIONAL PRACTICE

1. Have students make up questions about Nathalie to ask you or classmates.
2. Have students make up false statements about Éric and Paul. Their classmates will correct these statements.

PAIRED ACTIVITY

Have pairs of students change the conversations in any ways that make sense.

C **Les deux copains.** Répondez d'après la photo.

1. Qui sont les deux garçons?
2. Où sont-ils maintenant?
3. D'où sont les deux garçons?
4. Ils sont de quelle nationalité?
5. Comment sont les deux garçons?

Peter et Steve sont de New York.

D **Personnellement.** Donnez des réponses personnelles.

1. Salut!
2. Comment ça va?
3. Qui est ton/ta prof de français?
4. Comment est-il/elle?
5. Comment est le cours de français?

Exercices
PRESENTATION *(page 3)*
Exercices C and D
   These exercises can be done with books open or closed.

Extension of *Exercice C*
   After completing Exercise C, have a student retell the story in his/her own words.

ANSWERS
Exercice C
1. Ce sont Peter et Steve.
2. Ils sont à New York. (Ils sont dans le parc.)
3. Ils sont de New York.
4. Ils sont américains.
5. Answers will vary but may include: **Ils sont grands, intelligents et sympathiques.**

Exercice D
   Answers will vary.

LEARNING FROM PHOTOS

1. Ask students where they think the boys in the photo on page 3 might be going.
2. Have students give as thorough a description of the boys as possible.

INDEPENDENT PRACTICE

Assign any of the following:
1. Exercises, pages 2–3
2. Workbook, *Mots et Conversation: A–C,* page R1

3

STRUCTURE

Les articles définis et indéfinis

PRESENTATION *(page 4)*

As you go over the explanation, have students repeat the words and example sentences after you. Point to a specific person or object as you use the definite article.

Exercices

PRESENTATION *(pages 4–5)*

Extension of *Exercices* A and B

After completing each exercise, call on a student to read the entire exercise as a story.

ANSWERS

Exercice A

1. la
2. l'
3. le
4. Le
5. La
6. la
7. le
8. Les
9. le

Les articles définis et indéfinis

1. In French, you use the definite articles *le, la, l'* to express "the." Note that these articles change to *les* in the plural. Remember that before a vowel or a silent *h*, *le* and *la* change to *l'* and there is a liaison between *les* and the following word.

SINGULIER	PLURIEL
le garçon	les garçons
la fille	les filles
l'ami	les amis
l'école	les écoles

Qui est le garçon? C'est Paul Gallimard.
Qui est la fille? C'est sa cousine.

2. In French, you use the indefinite articles *un, une* to express "a" or "an." Note that these articles change to *des* in the plural.

SINGULIER	PLURIEL
un garçon	des garçons
un immeuble	des immeubles
une fille	des filles
une école	des écoles

François est un ami sympathique.
Carole est une amie sincère.
François et Carole sont des amis très chouettes.

A **La fille est à l'école.**   Complétez avec «le», «la», «l'» ou «les».

Qui est ___ fille là-bas? C'est Pauline. Pauline est ___ amie de Guy Laserre.
₁   ₂
Pauline et Guy sont élèves dans ___ même lycée à Paris. ___ professeur de
₃   ₄
français est M. Ettori. ___ classe de français est assez grande. Il y a vingt-huit
₅
élèves dans ___ classe. Mais ___ professeur de français est très content. ___
₆   ₇   ₈
élèves sont très intelligents. Et ___ cours de français est très intéressant.
₉

ADDITIONAL PRACTICE

You may wish to review the names and genders of classroom objects by asking students *Qu'est-ce que c'est?*

B **Un garçon et une fille.** Complétez avec «un», «une» ou «des».

1. Patrick est ___ beau garçon.
2. Et Corinne est ___ jolie fille.
3. Patrick est ___ ami sincère.
4. Et Corinne est ___ amie sincère aussi.
5. Corinne et Patrick sont élèves dans ___ lycée excellent à Paris.
6. Ils ont ___ cours et ___ professeurs très intéressants.
7. Corinne habite dans ___ bel appartement à Paris.
8. L'appartement de la famille de Patrick est dans ___ très joli immeuble dans ___ très beau quartier de Paris.
9. La famille de Patrick a ___ voisins très sympathiques.
10. Les voisins ont ___ belle maison en Bretagne.

L'accord des adjectifs

1. Adjectives agree with the nouns they describe. If the noun is feminine, the adjective must be in the feminine form. If the noun is plural, the adjective must be in the plural form. Review the following.

	FÉMININ	MASCULIN
SINGULIER	une fille intelligente une amie sincère	un garçon intelligent un ami sincère
PLURIEL	des filles intelligentes des amies sincères	des garçons intelligents des amis sincères

2. Note that adjectives that end in a consonant in the masculine form (*intelligent*) change pronunciation in the feminine form. Adjectives that end in -*e* (*sincère*) do not change pronunciation.

C **Qui est-ce?**
Décrivez un ami.

D **Les amies.**
Décrivez les filles.

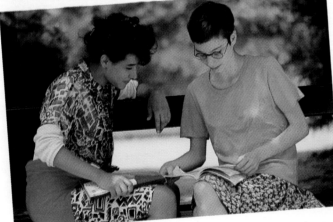

Exercice B
  1. un
  2. une
  3. un
  4. une
  5. un
  6. des, des
  7. un
  8. un, un
  9. des
10. une

L'accord des adjectifs
PRESENTATION *(page 5)*

A. Read step 1 to the class.
B. Write the adjectives in the chart on the board. Cross out the -*e* at the end of *intelligente* and remind students that the pronunciation changes. Have them repeat *intelligente/intelligent* after you. Then ask them what the difference is in pronunciation.
C. Explain to students that adjectives that end in a consonant have four forms and those that end in -*e* have two forms.

Exercices
PRESENTATION *(page 5)*
Exercices C and D
   Encourage students to say as much as they can when doing these exercises. After students do them orally, you may wish to have them write them.

ANSWERS
Exercices C and D
   Answers will vary.

PRESENTATION *(page 6)*

A. Have students repeat the verb forms after you.
B. Remind students to make the liaison in *vous êtes, nous allons, vous allez.*
C. Have students read the example sentences after you.

Exercices

PRESENTATION *(pages 6–7)*

Exercice E

Call on two students with good pronunciation to read the conversation in this exercise to the class.

Extension of *Exercice E*

Call on a student to retell the story of the conversation in his/her own words.

ANSWERS

Exercice E

1. Non, il n'est pas français. (Non, il est américain.)
2. Il est américain.
3. Il est de New York.
4. Non, il ne va pas à l'université.
5. Il va à l'école secondaire à New York.

Les verbes *être* et *aller*

1. Review the forms of the important irregular verbs *être,* "to be," and *aller,* "to go."

ÊTRE	ALLER
je suis	je vais
tu es	tu vas
il	il
elle } est	elle } va
on	on
nous sommes	nous allons
vous êtes	vous allez
ils } sont	ils } vont
elles	elles

2. Note that to make a sentence negative, you put *ne… pas* (or *n'… pas*) around the verb.

| Je suis française. | Je *ne* suis *pas* américaine. |
| Jeanne est élève dans un lycée français. | Elle *n'est pas* élève dans une école américaine. |

3. Remember that you also use *aller* to express how someone feels.

Comment vas-tu?
Comment allez-vous? } Je vais bien, merci.

E **Charles est de New York.** Répétez la conversation.

ANNICK: Bonjour, Charles. Ça va?
CHARLES: Oui, ça va bien, et toi?
ANNICK: Bien, merci. Tu es français, Charles, n'est-ce pas?
CHARLES: Mais non, je ne suis pas français. Je suis américain.
ANNICK: Sans blague! Tu es de quelle ville?
CHARLES: Je suis de New York.
ANNICK: Tu vas à l'université à New York?
CHARLES: Non, non. Je ne vais pas à l'université. Je vais à l'école secondaire.

6 RÉVISION

ADDITIONAL PRACTICE

Read the following to the class or write it on the board or on a transparency:
Faites une liste des caractéristiques que vous cherchez dans un(e) ami(e) et que vous considérez comme importantes.

LEARNING FROM PHOTOS

1. Have students describe the people in the photo.
2. Have them make up a conversation between the two people.

Répondez d'après la conversation.

1. Charles est français?
2. Il est de quelle nationalité?
3. Il est de quelle ville?
4. Il va à l'université?
5. Où est-ce qu'il va à l'école?

 Moi! Donnez des réponses personnelles.

1. Qui es-tu?
2. D'où es-tu?
3. Tu es de quelle nationalité?
4. Tu vas à quelle école?
5. Tu vas à l'école avec des copains?
6. Tes copains et toi, vous allez à l'école à pied ou en bus?
7. Où est l'école?
8. Comment sont les professeurs?

G Au restaurant. Complétez avec «être» ou «aller».

1. Ce soir la famille de Françoise Carron ___ au restaurant.
2. C'___ un petit restaurant. Il ___ vraiment très bon.
3. Tous les serveurs ___ vietnamiens.
4. La cuisine vietnamienne ___ délicieuse.
5. Le copain de Françoise y ___ aussi.
6. Françoise et son copain ___ commander un plat végétarien.
7. Ta famille et toi, vous ___ dîner au restaurant ce soir ou vous ___ dîner chez vous?
8. Au restaurant, qui ___ demander l'addition?
9. Qui ___ payer?
10. Vous ___ laisser un pourboire?

PRESENTATION (continued)

Exercice F
   It is recommended that you do Exercise F once orally with books closed.

Extension of *Exercice F*
   Call on a student to say as much as possible about his or her school.

Exercice G
   This exercise is more difficult than Exercises E and F because students must determine which verb to use in addition to using the correct form.

ANSWERS
Exercice F
   Answers will vary.

Exercice G
   1. va
   2. est, est
   3. sont
   4. est
   5. va
   6. vont
   7. allez, allez
   8. va
   9. va
   10. allez

PAIRED ACTIVITY

   Have students work in pairs. One student describes a famous person and the other tries to guess who it is.

LEARNING FROM PHOTOS

   Ask students the following questions about the photo on page 7: *C'est quelle sorte de restaurant? Ce restaurant accepte les cartes de crédit? Ce restaurant est en France? Il y a des restaurants vietnamiens dans votre ville? Vous aimez la cuisine vietnamienne? Quelle sorte de cuisine préférez-vous?*

Les contractions avec *à* et *de*

1. The preposition *à* can mean "to," "in," or "at." It remains unchanged with the articles *la* and *l'*, but it contracts with *le* to form one word, *au,* and with *les* to form one word, *aux*. Note the liaison with *aux* and a word that begins with a vowel or silent *h*. The *x* is pronounced like a *z*. Review the following.

à + la	= à la	Je vais *à la* boulangerie.
à + l'	= à l'	Je vais *à l'*école.
à + le	= au	Je vais *au* restaurant.
à + les	= aux	Je parle *aux* élèves.

2. The preposition *de,* meaning "of" or "from," also contracts with *le* and *les* to form one word, *du* or *des*. Note that *de* is also a part of many longer prepositions such as *près de, loin de,* etc.

de + la	= de la	Il habite près *de la* cathédrale.
de + l'	= de l'	Il habite près *de l'*école.
de + le	= du	Elle habite loin *du* parc.
de + les	= des	Elle habite loin *des* magasins.

 On y va ou pas?   Complétez avec «à».

Aujourd'hui on ne va pas ___ parc, on ne va pas ___ restaurant, on ne va pas
               1   2
___ maison, on ne va pas ___ pâtisserie. Où est-ce qu'on va alors? On va ___
 3   4   5
école. On va ___ cours de français. On va parler ___ professeur et ___ élèves.
             6   7   8

I   **Où habites-tu?**   Donnez des réponses personnelles.

1. Tu habites près ou loin de l'aéroport?
2. Tu vas souvent à l'aéroport?
3. Tu habites près ou loin de la gare?
4. Tu vas souvent à la gare?
5. Tu habites près ou loin de l'école?
6. Tu quittes l'école à quelle heure?
7. Tu habites près ou loin des magasins?
8. Tu vas souvent au magasin?

Les contractions avec à et de

PRESENTATION *(page 8)*

A. Write the contractions on the board.

B. Have students read the example sentences aloud.

C. Since the *au* and *du* forms present the greatest problem, you may wish to start by asking the following simple questions: *Tu vas au parc? Tu vas au restaurant? Tu vas au lycée? Tu vas au magasin? Tu vas au marché? Tu habites près du parc? Tu habites près du restaurant? Tu habites près du lycée? Tu habites près du magasin? Tu habites près du marché?*

Exercices

PRESENTATION *(page 8)*
Exercices H and I

It is recommended that you go over the exercises in class before assigning them for homework.

ANSWERS
Exercice H

1. au
2. au
3. à la
4. à la
5. à l'
6. au
7. au
8. aux

Exercice I
Answers will vary.

STUDENT PORTFOLIO

Written assignments which may be included in students' portfolios are *Activités de communication écrite A–B* on page R6 of the Workbook.

Activités de communication orale

A **Des copains.** Imagine you are walking down the street in Aix-en-Provence and run into one of your French friends (your partner). Say hello to each other and find out how things are going before you go on your way.

B **L'amie(e) idéal(e).** Make a list of qualities you look for in a friend. Then ask your partner if he or she likes the same things in a friend.

> Élève 1: Pour moi, l'ami(e) idéal(e) est très sympathique. Tu es d'accord?
> Élève 2: Oui, je suis d'accord. Pour moi, l'ami(e) idéal(e) est aussi très patient(e).

C **Au restaurant.** Work with a classmate and make up a conversation between a waiter or waitress and a customer at a restaurant. The following are some words and expressions you may want to use.

la carte	saignant
le service	à point
un hamburger	bien cuit
une pizza	l'addition
un coca	

Activités de communication orale

PRESENTATION (*page 9*)

These activities encourage students to use the language on their own. You may wish to let them choose the activities they would like to do.

Note Activity A reviews material from "Bienvenue," the preliminary chapter of *Bienvenue*, Part A; Activity B, Chapters 1 and 2; and Activity C, Chapter 5.

Extension of *Activité C*

After completing Activity C, have students present their conversation to the class.

ANSWERS

Activités A, B, and C

Answers will vary.

LEARNING FROM REALIA

Have students make up a conversation between a waiter and a customer using the menu from Le Restaurant Pomme de Pain.

INDEPENDENT PRACTICE

Assign any of the following:
1. Exercises and activities, pages 4–9
2. Workbook, *Structure: A–J,* pages R2–R5

OVERVIEW

This chapter reviews vocabulary related to home and family activities, after-school activities, dining out, and shopping at a market. These topics were first presented in *Bienvenue,* Part A, Chapters 3–6.

The structures reviewed are the present tense of regular *-er* verbs, the infinitive, the irregular verbs *avoir* and *faire*, the partitive, and possessive adjectives.

RÉVISION

B

DES ACTIVITÉS AMUSANTES

11

REVIEW RESOURCES

1. Bell Ringer Review
   Blackline Masters
2. Workbook
3. Lesson Plans
4. Testing Program

Pacing

This review chapter should take two to three days depending on the length of the class and the age and aptitude of your students.

Note The Lesson Plans offer guidelines for 45- and 55-minute classes and **Block Scheduling**.

Exercices vs. *Activités*

The exercises and activities are color-coded. Exercises, which provide guided practice to prepare students for independent communication, are coded in blue. Communicative activities, which afford students the opportunity for creative, open-ended expression, are coded in red.

LEARNING FROM PHOTOS

You may wish to ask students the following questions about the photo and about themselves: *Où sont les filles? Elles ont faim ou soif? Qu'est-ce qu'elles commandent au café? Allez-vous souvent au café ou au restaurant fast-food? Vous y allez après les cours ou avant les cours? Qu'est-ce que vous commandez quand vous avez soif? Et quand vous avez faim?*

Vocabulary Teaching Resources

1. Bell Ringer Review Blackline Masters: R-2 & R-3, page 39
2. Workbook, *Mots et Conversation: A–C*, pages R7–R8

Bell Ringer Review

Put the following on the board or use BRR Blackline Master R-2:
Make a list of party activities: *Dans une fête, on…*

La fête de Caroline

PRESENTATION *(page 12)*

Have students repeat the sentences after you. Intersperse your presentation with questions from Exercises A and B.

Exercices

PRESENTATION *(page 12)*

Go over the exercises orally first with books closed. Have students write the exercises for homework and go over them the next day with books open.

ANSWERS

Exercice A

1. Oui, elle donne une fête.
2. Oui, elle invite des copains.
3. Oui, ils arrivent chez Caroline à sept heures.
4. Oui, ils parlent à Caroline. Ils parlent français.
5. Oui, ils dansent pendant la fête.
6. Oui, ils écoutent des cassettes.

La fête de Caroline

Caroline donne une fête.
Elle invite des copains.

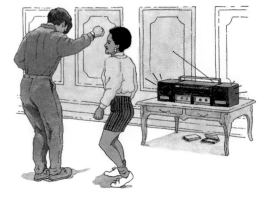

Les copains arrivent chez Caroline à sept heures.
Ils parlent à Caroline.

Pendant la fête, les copains dansent.
Ils écoutent des cassettes.

A Chez Caroline. Répondez.

1. Caroline donne une fête?
2. Elle invite des copains?
3. Les copains arrivent chez Caroline à sept heures?
4. Ils parlent à Caroline? Ils parlent français ou anglais?
5. Pendant la fête, les copains dansent?
6. Ils écoutent des cassettes?

B Qui? Répondez.

1. Qui donne la fête?
2. Qui arrive chez Caroline?
3. Quand est-ce qu'ils arrivent?
4. Qui parle?
5. À qui est-ce qu'ils parlent?
6. Qui écoute des cassettes?
7. Qui danse?

ADDITIONAL PRACTICE

To reinforce the review material, you may wish to ask students the following questions: *Donnez-vous souvent des fêtes? Qui invitez-vous? À quelle heure arrivent-ils? Qu'est-ce que vous faites dans une fête? Vous dansez? Vous écoutez des cassettes? Vous chantez?*

C **La maison de Caroline.** Lisez le paragraphe.

La maison de Caroline est jolie.
Au rez-de-chaussée il y a quatre pièces.
Au premier étage il y a les chambres à coucher.
Caroline a une très jolie chambre.
Elle fait ses devoirs dans sa chambre.

D **Comment est sa maison?** Décrivez la maison de Caroline.

E **Qu'est-ce que les amis de Caroline font?** Choisissez la bonne réponse.

1. Les amis écoutent des cassettes?
   a. Oui, ils détestent la musique.
   b. Oui, ils adorent le rock.
   c. Oui, ils vont au théâtre.

2. Quand est-ce qu'ils dansent?
   a. Le samedi soir à la fête.
   b. Quand je vais à l'école.
   c. Quand nous réservons une table au restaurant.

3. Ils parlent français à Caroline?
   a. Oui, je téléphone à mon amie.
   b. Oui, ils sont français.
   c. Oui, nous parlons français.

4. La maison de Caroline est grande?
   a. Oui, il y a deux étages.
   b. Oui, il y a trois pièces.
   c. Oui, il y a deux immeubles.

RÉVISION **13**

Exercice B
1. Caroline donne la fête.
2. Les copains arrivent chez Caroline.
3. Ils arrivent à sept heures.
4. Les copains parlent.
5. Ils parlent à Caroline.
6. Les copains écoutent des cassettes.
7. Les copains dansent.

Bell Ringer Review
Put the following on the board or use BRR Blackline Master R-3: Make a list of the rooms of a house.

PRESENTATION *(page 13)*
Exercice C
Call on a student to read the sentences in Exercise C.

Exercice D
Call on another student to say as much as possible about the photo in Exercise D.

ANSWERS
Exercice C
Students read the paragraph in the text.

Exercice D
Answers will vary but may include: **La maison est grande et jolie. Il y a un grand jardin avec une table et des chaises. Dans la maison il y a quatre pièces au rez-de-chaussée et il y a des chambres à coucher au premier étage.**

Exercice E
1. b
2. a
3. b
4. a

STRUCTURE

Structure Teaching Resources

1. Bell Ringer Review Blackline Masters: R-4 & R-5, page 39
2. Workbook, *Structure: A–N*, pages R9–R12

Les verbes réguliers en -er

PRESENTATION *(page 14)*

A. Write the forms of *parler* and *aimer* on the board and underline the endings.

B. Have students read the forms aloud. Point to the ones that are pronounced the same even though they are written differently.

Exercices

PRESENTATION *(pages 14–15)*

Exercices A, B, and C

Exercises A and B can be done with books open or closed. Exercise C can be done with books open. After completing each of these exercises, call on a student to give the information in the exercise in his/her own words.

ANSWERS

Exercice A

Answers will vary.

Les verbes réguliers en *-er*

The infinitive of many regular French verbs ends in *-er.* Review the following present tense forms of regular *-er* verbs. Note that before a verb beginning with a vowel or silent *h, je* becomes *j'* and there is a liaison between *nous, vous, ils,* or *elles* and the following word.

INFINITIVE	PARLER	AIMER	
STEM	parl-	aim-	ENDINGS
je parle		j' aime	-e
tu parles		tu aimes	-es
il elle on } parle		il elle on } aime	-e
nous parlons		nous aimons	-ons
vous parlez		vous aimez	-ez
ils elles } parlent		ils aiment elles aiment	-ent

A **Moi!** Donnez des réponses personnelles.

1. Tu habites quelle ville?
2. Tu habites une petite ville ou une grande ville?
3. Tu arrives à l'école à quelle heure le matin?
4. Tu parles à tes copains?
5. Tes copains et toi, vous étudiez le français?
6. Vous aimez le cours de français?
7. Vous chantez en français?

14   RÉVISION

B Une fête. Donnez des réponses personnelles.

1. Tu aimes donner des fêtes?
2. Tu donnes des fêtes?
3. Qui invites-tu?
4. Tu téléphones à tes copains?
5. Ils acceptent toujours ton invitation?
6. Quel soir est-ce que tu donnes la fête?
7. Tes amis arrivent à quelle heure?
8. Tes copains et toi, vous dansez pendant la fête?

C On dîne au restaurant. Complétez.

1. Ce soir Angélique ne ___ pas le dîner. (préparer)
2. Elle ___ d'aller dîner au restaurant. (décider)
3. Elle ___ à sa copine. (téléphoner)
4. Elle ___ sa copine au restaurant. (inviter)
5. Elles ___ dans un restaurant italien. (aller)
6. Les deux amies ___ au restaurant à sept heures. (arriver)
7. Le serveur ___ à leur table. (arriver)
8. Les deux amies ___ une pizza. (commander)
9. Angélique ___ l'addition. (demander)
10. Tu ___ la pizza? (aimer)
11. Quand tes copains et toi ___ dans un restaurant italien, qu'est-ce que vous ___? (aller, commander)

Exercice B
    Answers will vary.

Exercice C
1. prépare
2. décide
3. téléphone
4. invite
5. vont
6. arrivent
7. arrive
8. commandent
9. demande
10. aimes
11. allez, commandez

L'infinitif

PRESENTATION (*page 16*)

Have students read the example sentences.

Exercices

ANSWERS

Exercice D

Answers will vary but may include the following:

1. Oui (Non), j'aime (je n'aime pas) manger.
2. Je préfère manger dans un restaurant italien (chinois).
3. Oui (Non), je (ne) vais (pas) dîner au restaurant ce soir.
4. Oui (Non), j'aime (je n'aime pas) donner des (de) fêtes.
5. Oui (Non), je (ne) vais (pas) inviter mes amis à la fête.
6. Je préfère donner (aller à) des fêtes.

Exercice E

1. Non, mais je vais écouter la radio ce soir.
2. Non, mais je vais travailler ce soir.
3. Non, mais il va téléphoner ce soir.
4. Non, mais il va arriver ce soir.

Exercice F

1. Ils aiment écouter la radio.
2. Ils aiment écouter des compact discs.
3. Ils aiment lire des magazines.
4. Ils aiment étudier (travailler, faire leurs devoirs).
5. Ils aiment donner des fêtes.

L'infinitif

1. The infinitive form follows verbs such as *aimer*, *détester*, *adorer*, and *préférer*.

   J'aime danser mais je déteste chanter.
   Je n'aime pas du tout chanter.

2. You also use the infinitive after the verb *aller* to tell what you or others are going to do.

   Ce soir je vais regarder la télé.
   Demain nous allons donner une fête.

D **Mes préférences.** Donnez des réponses personnelles.

1. Tu aimes manger?
2. Tu préfères manger dans un restaurant italien ou dans un restaurant chinois?
3. Tu vas dîner au restaurant ce soir?
4. Tu aimes donner des fêtes?
5. Tu vas inviter tes amis à la fête?
6. Tu préfères donner des fêtes ou aller à des fêtes?

E **Pas maintenant.** Répondez d'après le modèle.

   Tu regardes la télé maintenant?
   Non, mais je vais regarder la télé ce soir.

1. Tu écoutes la radio maintenant?
2. Tu travailles maintenant?
3. Ton copain téléphone maintenant?
4. Ton copain arrive maintenant?

F **Qu'est-ce qu'ils aiment faire?** Répondez d'après les dessins.

1.
2.
3.
4.
5.

16   RÉVISION

Les verbes *avoir* et *faire*

1. Review the forms of the irregular verbs *avoir,* "to have," and *faire,* "to do," "to make."

AVOIR	FAIRE
j' ai	je fais
tu as	tu fais
il	il
elle } a	elle } fait
on	on
nous avons	nous faisons
vous avez	vous faites
ils ont	ils
elles ont	elles } font

2. You use the verb *avoir* to express age.

   Tu as quel âge? Moi, j'ai quatorze ans.

3. The verb *faire* is used in many expressions:

faire du français	**faire la cuisine**
faire de la gymnastique	**faire un pique-nique**
faire les courses	

4. Remember that in negative sentences *un, une,* and *des* change to *de (d').*

J'ai un frère.	Je *n'*ai *pas de* sœur.
Elle fait du français.	Elle *ne* fait *pas* d'espagnol.
Tu as des livres.	Tu *n'*as *pas de* cahiers.

G Les Dejarnac. Complétez avec «avoir».

1. La famille Dejarnac ___ une maison dans la banlieue parisienne.
2. La maison des Dejarnac ___ sept pièces.
3. M. et Mme Dejarnac ___ deux enfants.
4. Pierre ___ cinq ans et Michèle ___ douze ans.
5. Les Dejarnac ___ un chien?
6. Vous ___ un chien?
7. Non, nous n'___ pas de chien mais nous ___ un chat.

PRESENTATION *(page 18)*

Exercice I

Have two students read the conversation to the class. After completing the comprehension questions that follow, have a student retell the story of the conversation in his/her own words.

ANSWERS

Exercice H

Answers will vary.

Exercice I

1. Oui, elle va bien.
2. Oui, elle va faire les courses.
3. Oui, elle va au marché de la rue Mouffetard.
4. Oui, elle a beaucoup de choses à acheter.

H Moi! Donnez des réponses personnelles.

1. Tu as une grande ou une petite famille?
2. Tu as combien de frères?
3. Tu as combien de sœurs?
4. Ta famille et toi, vous avez un chat ou un chien?
5. Tu as une voiture?

I On fait les courses. Répétez la conversation.

CHRISTINE: Salut, Michèle. Comment vas-tu?
MICHÈLE: Bien, merci. Et toi?
CHRISTINE: Pas mal. Où vas-tu maintenant?
MICHÈLE: Je vais faire les courses.
CHRISTINE: Tu fais les courses où?
MICHÈLE: Au marché de la rue Mouffetard. Et aujourd'hui j'ai beaucoup de choses à acheter.

Répondez d'après la conversation.

1. Michèle va bien?
2. Est-ce qu'elle va faire les courses?
3. Elle va au marché de la rue Mouffetard?
4. Elle a beaucoup de choses à acheter?

18   RÉVISION

LEARNING FROM PHOTOS

After completing the exercises on the partitive on pages 19 and 20, you may wish to come back to this photo and have the students say as much as they can about it.

INDEPENDENT PRACTICE

Assign any of the following:

1. Exercises on pages 17–18
2. Workbook, *Structure: G–I*, pages R10–R11
3. Bell Ringer Review Blackline Masters R-4 and R-5, page 39

Le partitif

1. In French, you use the definite article when talking about a specific item.

   La salade est sur *la* table dans *la* cuisine.

2. You also use the definite article when talking about a noun in the general sense.

   Moi, j'aime beaucoup *le* chocolat.

3. However, when you refer to only a part or a certain quantity of something, the partitive construction is used. The partitive is expressed in French by *de* + the definite article.

de + le = du	J'ai *du* pain.
de + la = de la	J'ai *de la* crème.
de + l' = de l'	J'ai *de l'*argent.
de + les = des	J'ai *des* gâteaux.

4. When the partitive follows a verb in the negative, all forms change to *de* or *d'*.

J'ai du pain.	Je n'ai pas *de* pain.
J'ai de la viande.	Je n'ai pas *de* viande.
J'ai de l'argent.	Je n'ai pas *d'*argent.
J'ai des fruits.	Je n'ai pas *de* fruits.

J Qu'est-ce qu'on peut acheter à l'épicerie?   Répondez.

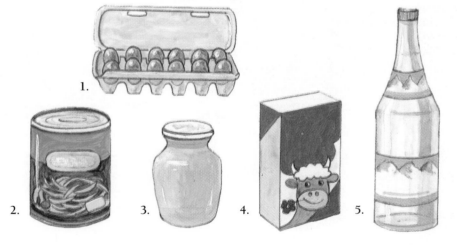

1. 2. 3. 4. 5.

Le partitif
PRESENTATION *(page 19)*
A. When explaining step 1, you may wish to point to some specific items in class: *Le livre est sur la table. Le crayon est sur le livre.*
B. When going over step 2, mention some other things people may like: *J'aime le lait. J'aime les légumes. J'aime les sports.*
C. When going over step 3, put some objects on a table and point to them from a distance. To demonstrate the use of the partitive, say, for example: *Il y a des livres sur la table. Il y a des crayons sur la table. Il y a de l'argent.*
D. Then take the items off the table to demonstrate the negative: *Il n'y a pas de livres sur la table. Il n'y a pas de crayons sur la table. Il n'y a pas d'argent.*

Exercices
ANSWERS
Exercice J
1. On peut acheter des œufs à l'épicerie.
2. ... des boîtes de conserve...
3. ... de la moutarde...
4. ... du lait...
5. ... de l'eau minérale...

ADDITIONAL PRACTICE

1. Write the names of the following stores on the board: *l'épicerie, la crémerie, la poissonnerie, la boulangerie-pâtisserie, la charcuterie, le supermarché, la boucherie.* Have students say what they can buy there: *À la boucherie, on peut acheter...*
2. Have students name several foods they don't have in their refrigerator at home.

K **Pas aujourd'hui.** Répondez d'après le modèle.

l'eau minérale

J'aime l'eau minérale.
J'achète souvent de l'eau minérale.
Mais aujourd'hui je n'achète pas d'eau minérale.

1. le poisson
2. la viande
3. le bœuf
4. les fruits
5. le pain français
6. les pâtisseries

L **Georges fait les courses.** Complétez.

Georges fait les courses. Il va à la boulangerie où il achète ___(1) pain. Georges achète ___(2) pain tous les jours. Mais il n'achete pas toujours ___(3) viande. Aujourd'hui il n'achète pas ___(4) viande. Il ne va pas à la boucherie. Il achète ___(5) poisson. Pour acheter ___(6) poisson il va à la poissonnerie. Ensuite il va à l'épicerie du coin où il achète ___(7) eau minérale et ___(8) boîtes de conserve. Il n'achète pas ___(9) lait aujourd'hui.

M **Mes possessions.** Donnez des réponses personnelles.

1. Tu as un crayon?
2. Tu as un stylo?
3. Tu as un cahier?
4. Tu as un sac à dos?
5. Tu as un chat?
6. Tu as un ordinateur?
7. Tu as une sœur?
8. Tu as un frère?

Les adjectifs possessifs

1. Like all other French adjectives, the possessive adjectives must agree with the noun they modify. Remember that *son, sa,* and *ses* can mean either "his" or "her." The agreement is with the item owned, not the owner.

la voiture de Marc ⟶ sa voiture
le livre de Marie ⟶ son livre

MASCULIN SINGULIER	FÉMININ SINGULIER	PLURIEL
mon père	ma mère	mes parents
ton père	ta mère	tes parents
son père	sa mère	ses parents

2. Remember that the masculine singular form is used before feminine singular nouns that begin with a vowel and that there is a liaison.

mon amie   ton amie   son amie

3. The adjectives *notre, votre,* and *leur* have only two forms, singular and plural.

MASCULIN SINGULIER	FÉMININ SINGULIER	PLURIEL
notre cousin	notre cousine	nos cousin(e)s
votre cousin	votre cousine	vos cousin(e)s
leur cousin	leur cousine	leurs cousin(e)s

N **Moi!** Donnez des réponses personnelles.

1. Tu as des oncles et des tantes?
2. Tu as une grande ou une petite famille? Tu as combien de cousins?
3. Tes parents ont une voiture?
4. Leur voiture est dans le garage le soir?
5. Ta mère travaille?
6. Ton père travaille?
7. Où est votre maison ou appartement?
8. Votre maison ou appartement a combien de pièces?

Les adjectifs possessifs
PRESENTATION *(page 21)*

A. Explain to students that the adjectives *mon, ton,* and *son* have three forms. The adjectives *notre, votre,* and *leur* have two forms.
B. Call students to the front of the room. Have them point to indicate the meaning of the possessive adjectives: to themselves *(mon)*, to someone they are talking to *(ton)*, to a boy or girl in the distance *(son)*.

ANSWERS
Exercice N
Answers will vary.

Activités de communication orale et écrite

PRESENTATION (page 22)

These activities recycle material from *Bienvenue,* Part A, Chapters 2, 3, and 4.

Extension of *Activité A*

After completing Activity A, call on volunteers to give the same information about themselves as they did for Alain.

ANSWERS

Activités A and B

Answers will vary.

A **La chambre d'Alain.** Look at the picture of Alain Legrand's room. Based on what you see, ask your partner questions about Alain, his possessions, his likes and dislikes.

B **J'aime…** Work with a partner. Find out what food he or she likes or doesn't like to eat. Then tell the class your common likes and dislikes.

> Élève 1: Robert, tu aimes les haricots verts?
> Élève 2: Oui, j'aime les haricots verts. (Non, je déteste les haricots verts.) Et toi?
> Élève 1: Moi, j'aime les haricots verts aussi.
> Élève 1 (*à la classe*): Robert et moi, nous aimons les haricots verts. (Robert et moi, nous détestons les haricots verts. / Moi, j'aime les haricots verts, mais Robert déteste les haricots verts.)

 STUDENT PORTFOLIO

Written assignments which may be included in students' portfolios are *Activités de communication C–D* on page 23 and *Activité de communication écrite A* on page R13 of the Workbook.

C **Ma famille.** Imagine you're a French exchange student. One of your classmates wants to find out more about you and your family. He or she asks you the following questions.

> Où est-ce que tu habites?
> Comment est ta maison ou ton appartement?
> Il y a combien de personnes dans ta famille?
> Tu as combien de frères et combien de sœurs?
> Tu as quel âge?
> Tu vas à quelle école?
> Tu aimes quels cours?
> Tu n'aimes pas quels cours?
> Qu'est-ce que tu fais après les cours?

D **Ma maison et ma chambre.** Write a short paragraph describing your house or apartment and your room.

E **Aujourd'hui.** Work with a classmate. Find out the following information from him or her.

1. what day is it
2. what the date is today
3. what time it is
4. what time his or her English class is
5. what time he or she is leaving school today

Activités C et D
   Answers will vary.

Activité E
   Answers will vary, but É1's questions may include the following:
1. C'est quel jour?
2. Quelle est la date aujourd'hui?
3. Quelle heure est-il?
4. Ton cours d'anglais est à quelle heure?
5. Tu quittes l'école à quelle heure aujourd'hui?

LEARNING FROM PHOTOS

Have students identify as many items as they can in the photos on page 23. You may wish to teach them the words: *une trousse, une lampe, un feutre, un bloc-notes.*

RÉVISION C

OVERVIEW

This chapter reviews vocabulary dealing with train and plane travel that was first presented in *Bienvenue*, Part A, Chapters 7 and 8.

The structure points reviewed are the present tense of regular *-ir* and *-re* verbs, verbs like *partir* and *dormir*, and the verbs *pouvoir* and *vouloir*.

RÉVISION C

ON VOYAGE

25

25

REVIEW RESOURCES

1. Bell Ringer Review Blackline Masters
2. Workbook
3. Lesson Plans
4. Testing Program
5. Map Transparencies

Pacing

This review chapter should take two to three days depending on the length of the class and the age and aptitude of your students.

Note The Lesson Plans offer guidelines for 45- and 55-minute classes and **Block Scheduling**.

Exercices vs. *Activités*

The exercises and activities are color-coded. Exercises, which provide guided practice to prepare students for independent communication, are coded in blue. Communicative activities, which afford students the opportunity for creative, open-ended expression, are coded in red.

LEARNING FROM PHOTOS

You may wish to ask students the following questions about the photo: *C'est une petite ou une grande gare? Où sont les voyageurs? Qu'est-ce qu'ils attendent? Il y a combien de voyageurs sur le quai?*

Vocabulary Teaching Resources

1. Bell Ringer Review Blackline Masters: R-6 & R-7, page 40
2. Workbook, *Mots et Conversation: A–C,* page R14

Bell Ringer Review

Put the following on the board or use BRR Blackline Master R-6: Write down as many words and expressions as you can think of having to do with airports.

À l'aéroport

PRESENTATION *(page 26)*

A. Have students share the words they wrote down for the Bell Ringer Review.
B. Have students repeat each sentence of the conversation once after you.
C. Call on a pair of students to read the conversation with as much expression as possible.

Exercices

PRESENTATION *(page 26)*

Extension of *Exercice A*

After completing Exercise A, have one student retell the story of the conversation in his/her own words.

ANSWERS

Exercice A

1. Elle est à l'aéroport.
2. Elle va au Sénégal.
3. Ahmed parle à Thérèse.
4. Il part pour Dakar.
5. Elle part pour le Sénégal.
6. Oui, elle a sa carte d'embarquement.
7. Elle a la place 22A.
8. Ils entendent l'annonce du départ d'un avion.
9. C'est le 214.
10. Il part de la porte 25.

MOTS ET CONVERSATION

À l'aéroport

AHMED: Salut, Thérèse. Qu'est-ce que tu fais ici à l'aéroport?
THÉRÈSE: Je vais au Sénégal.
AHMED: Pas possible! Moi aussi, je pars pour Dakar. Tu as ta carte d'embarquement?
THÉRÈSE: Bien sûr.
AHMED: Tu as quelle place?
THÉRÈSE: 22A. On annonce le départ d'un avion. C'est quel numéro de vol?
AHMED: Le 214. C'est notre vol. L'avion part de quelle porte?
THÉRÈSE: De la porte 25.

A **On part pour Dakar.** Répondez d'après la conversation.

1. Où est Thérèse?
2. Où va-t-elle?
3. Qui parle à Thérèse à l'aéroport?
4. Ahmed part pour quelle ville?
5. Et Thérèse part pour quel pays?
6. Elle a sa carte d'embarquement?
7. Thérèse a quelle place?
8. Qu'est-ce qu'ils entendent?
9. Quel est le numéro de leur vol?
10. Leur avion part de quelle porte?

26   RÉVISION

PAIRED ACTIVITY

Have students work in pairs and make up a conversation about a trip to a French-speaking destination that interests them. Then ask for volunteers to present their conversations to the class.

À la gare

Alain est dans la gare de Deauville. Il a de la chance. Il n'y a pas de queue devant le guichet. Il va au guichet. Il achète un billet aller-retour en seconde pour Paris. Il composte le billet et va sur le quai où il attend le train. Le train part exactement à 14h10. Alain monte dans une voiture non-fumeurs.

B **Un voyage en train.** Répondez par «oui» ou «non».

1. Alain est dans la salle d'attente de la gare?
2. Il est dans la gare à Paris?
3. Il y a une queue devant le guichet?
4. Alain achète un aller simple?
5. Il voyage en première classe?
6. Alain va sur le quai?
7. Le train part en retard?
8. Alain choisit une voiture fumeurs?

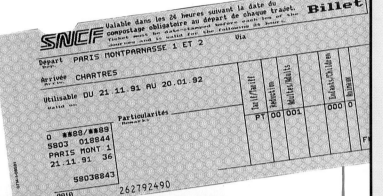

Bell Ringer Review

Put the following on the board or use BRR Blackline Master R-7: Write down as many words related to train travel as you can.

À la gare
PRESENTATION *(page 27)*

Call on a student with good pronunciation to read the paragraph to the class.

Exercice
PRESENTATION *(page 27)*
Exercice B

Do Exercice B orally with books closed.

ANSWERS
Exercice B
1. Oui, il est dans la salle d'attente de la gare.
2. Non, il est dans la gare à Deauville.
3. Non, il n'y a pas de queue devant le guichet.
4. Non, il achète un (billet) aller-retour.
5. Non, il voyage en seconde.
6. Oui, il va sur le quai.
7. Non, il part à l'heure.
8. Non, il choisit une voiture non-fumeurs.

ADDITIONAL PRACTICE

After completing Exercice B with the students, you may wish to ask the following questions about it in order to practice question words: *Qui est dans la gare? Où est Alain? Qu'est-ce qu'il a? Où va-t-il? Qu'est-ce qu'il achète? Où est-ce qu'il attend le train? Le train part à quelle heure?*

LEARNING FROM REALIA AND PHOTOS

1. You may wish to ask the following questions about Alain's ticket: *Le train va partir de quelle gare? Il va arriver où? Quel est le prix du billet? Alain voyage en quelle classe?*
2. Have students say as much as they can about the photo of the train station.

STRUCTURE

Structure Teaching Resources

Workbook, *Structure: A–L,* pages R15–R18

Les verbes en -ir et -re

PRESENTATION (*page 28*)

Write the verb forms on the board and have students repeat them aloud.

Note Other common *-ir* verbs the students know are *choisir, obéir à, réussir à, atterrir.* Other *-re* verbs the students know are *entendre, répondre, perdre, descendre, vendre.*

Exercices

PRESENTATION (*pages 28–29*)

Exercice A

Go over the exercise once in class before assigning it for homework.

ANSWERS

Exercice A

Answers will vary but may include the following:

1. Oui (Non), je (ne) choisis (pas) un vol Air France.
2. Je choisis une place côté fenêtre (couloir).
3. Oui (Non), beaucoup de passagers choisissent des places côté couloir (fenêtre).
4. Oui (Non), je (ne) réussis (pas) à avoir toujours les places que je désire.
5. Oui (Non), mon avion (n') atterrit (pas) généralement à l'heure.

STRUCTURE

Les verbes en *-ir* et *-re*

Review the following forms of regular *-ir* and *-re* verbs.

INFINITIVE	FINIR	
STEM	**fin-**	ENDINGS
je finis		-is
tu finis		-is
il elle on } finit		-it
nous finissons		-issons
vous finissez		-issez
ils elles } finissent		-issent

INFINITIVE	ATTENDRE	
STEM	**attend-**	ENDINGS
j' attends		-s
tu attends		-s
il elle on } attend		—
nous attendons		-ons
vous attendez		-ez
ils attendent elles attendent		-ent

A **Un voyage en avion.**   Répondez.

1. Quand tu voyages, tu choisis un vol Air France?
2. Tu choisis une place côté fenêtre ou côté couloir?
3. Beaucoup de passagers choisissent des places côté couloir?
4. Vous réussissez à avoir toujours les places que vous désirez?
5. Votre avion atterrit généralement à l'heure?

28   RÉVISION

INDEPENDENT PRACTICE

Assign any of the following:
1. Exercises, pages 28–29
2. Workbook, *Structure: A–E,* pages R15–R16

B Un voyage en train. Complétez.

B Un voyage en train. Complétez.

1. On ___ les billets au guichet. (vendre)
2. On ___ des magazines et des journaux au kiosque. (vendre)
3. Les passagers ___ le train. (attendre)
4. Nous aussi, nous ___. (attendre)
5. Vous ___ le train dans la salle d'attente. (attendre)
6. J'___ l'annonce du départ de notre train. (entendre)
7. Marie aussi ___ l'annonce au haut-parleur. (entendre)

Les verbes *partir, sortir, servir* et *dormir*

Study the irregular *-ir* verbs which also end in *-ir* in the infinitive.

PARTIR	SORTIR	SERVIR	DORMIR
je pars	je sors	je sers	je dors
tu pars	tu sors	tu sers	tu dors
il	il	il	il
elle } part	elle } sort	elle } sert	elle } dort
on	on	on	on
nous partons	nous sortons	nous servons	nous dormons
vous partez	vous sortez	vous servez	vous dormez
ils	ils	ils	ils
elles } partent	elles } sortent	elles } servent	elles } dorment

C En voiture! Répondez d'après les indications.

1. Le train part de quelle voie? (numéro deux)
2. Il part à quelle heure? (18h16)
3. On sert des repas dans le train? (oui)
4. Qui sert les repas? (les serveurs)
5. Les passagers dorment? (oui, dans une voiture-lit)
6. Le contrôleur arrive. Tu sors ton billet? (oui)

D Carole fait un voyage. Complétez.

Carole est à la Gare du Nord. Où est-ce qu'on ___
(vendre) les billets? Ah, voilà le guichet. Carole achète son billet. Elle ___
(sortir) de l'argent de son sac à dos et paie. Son train ___ (partir) de la voie
numéro quatre. Tous les trains ___ (partir) à l'heure. Beaucoup de passagers
___ (dormir) dans le train. Mais Carole ne ___ (dormir) pas. Elle aime bien
voyager en train.

PRESENTATION (*continued*)
Exercice B
Go over the exercise once
in class before assigning it for
homework.

ANSWERS
Exercice B
1. vend
2. vend
3. attendent
4. attendons
5. attendez
6. entends
7. entend

Les verbes partir, sortir, servir *et* dormir
PRESENTATION (*page 29*)
Have students repeat the verb
forms after you.

Exercices
PRESENTATION (*page 29*)
Exercice C
This exercise can be done with
books open or closed.

Exercice D
This exercise can be done with
books open.

ANSWERS
Exercice C
1. Il part de la voie numéro deux.
2. Il part à 18h16.
3. Oui, on sert des repas dans le
   train.
4. Les serveurs servent les repas.
5. Oui, ils dorment dans une
   voiture-lit.
6. Oui, je sors mon billet.

Exercice D
1. vend
2. sort
3. part
4. partent
5. dorment
6. dort

LEARNING FROM PHOTOS

1. You may wish to ask the following
   questions about the photo at the top of
   the page: *C'est un kiosque? Où est le
   kiosque? Qu'est-ce qu'on vend au kiosque?
   Qu'est-ce que les clients regardent?*
2. Ask the following questions about the
   other photo: *Où sont les voyageurs? Ils
   achètent des billets? Ils font la queue? Ils ont
   des sacs à dos?*

Les adjectifs *ce, quel et tout*

PRESENTATION *(page 30)*

Write the forms of the adjectives on the board and have students repeat them after you.

Exercices

PRESENTATION *(page 30)*

Exercices E and F

These exercises can be done with books open.

ANSWERS

Exercice E

1. Tous (Toutes), ce
2. Ce
3. quel, quel
4. quel, quel
5. quelle

Exercice F

1. tous
2. tous, cette, ce
3. ce, quelle
4. ce
5. Quelles
6. Ces

HISTORY CONNECTION

Have students find Avignon on the map of France on page 504 or use the Map Transparency. You may wish to tell them that during the 14th century Pope Clement V established the papacy at Avignon to escape unrest in Italy. Avignon was the home of the popes for over 70 years. The *Palais des Papes* looks like a fortress because it was. The popes of that time had to defend themselves against roving bands of mercenaries.

Les adjectifs *ce, quel et tout*

Review the forms of the adjectives *ce* (this, that), *quel* (which), and *tout* (the whole, all, every). Remember that you use the definite article with *tout*.

ce train	cette voiture	ces billets	ces places
quel train	quelle voiture	quels billets	quelles places
tout le train	toute la voiture	tous les billets	toutes les places

E **Tous les élèves aiment ce professeur.** Complétez d'après les indications.

1. ___ les élèves aiment ___ cours. (tout, ce)
2. ___ professeur est très intéressant. (ce)
3. Mais tu parles de ___ cours et de ___ professeur? (quel, quel)
4. De ___ cours? Du cours d'histoire! Et de ___ professeur? De Madame Rambouillet, bien sûr. (quel, quel)
5. Le cours d'histoire est dans ___ salle de classe? (quel)

F **Quel train va à Avignon?** Complétez avec «tout», «ce» ou «quel».

1. Est-ce que ___ les trains vont à Avignon?
2. Non, ___ les trains qui partent de ___ gare ne vont pas nécessairement à Avignon. Mais le prochain train qui part de ___ quai va à Avignon.
3. Il va partir de ___ quai à ___ heure? Il va partir à dix heures.
4. Il est nécessaire de payer un supplément pour ___ train? Non.
5. ___ voitures sont non-fumeurs?
6. ___ voitures sont non-fumeurs.

Le Palais des Papes à Avignon

Les verbes *pouvoir et vouloir*

1. Review the forms of the verbs *pouvoir,* "to be able," "can," and *vouloir,* "to want."

POUVOIR	VOULOIR
je peux	je veux
tu peux	tu veux
il	il
elle } peut	elle } veut
on	on
nous pouvons	nous voulons
vous pouvez	vous voulez
ils } peuvent	ils } veulent
elles	elles

2. These verbs are frequently followed by the infinitive.

> Je peux sortir et je veux sortir.
> Tu veux sortir avec moi?
> Elle ne veut pas sortir avec Gilles.

G Un petit voyage à Nice. Répondez par «oui».

1. Marie-Claire veut aller à Nice?
2. Elle peut partir demain?
3. Son frère veut aller à Nice aussi?
4. Ils peuvent faire le voyage ensemble?
5. Ils veulent aller à Nice en train?
6. Ils peuvent aller à Nice en train? En avion?
7. Ils veulent regarder la mer Méditerranée?
8. Tu veux regarder la mer Méditerranée?
9. Tu peux regarder la mer Méditerranée?

Vues de la côte et de la mer Méditerranée

Les verbes pouvoir *et* vouloir

PRESENTATION *(page 31)*

A. Have students read the verb forms and the example sentences aloud.

B. **Extension** Call on students to tell what they can do this weekend: *Ce week-end je peux…*

Exercices

ANSWERS

Exercice G

1. Oui, elle veut aller à Nice.
2. Oui, elle peut partir demain.
3. Oui, il veut aller à Nice aussi.
4. Oui, ils peuvent faire le voyage ensemble.
5. Oui, ils veulent aller à Nice en train.
6. Oui, ils peuvent aller à Nice en train. Ils peuvent aller à Nice en avion aussi.
7. Oui, ils veulent regarder la mer Méditerranée.
8. Oui, je veux regarder la mer Méditerranée.
9. Oui, je peux regarder la mer Méditerranée.

PAIRED ACTIVITY

Have students work in pairs. One student makes a statement about what he/she wants to do tomorrow but can't. The other reports to the class about what his/her partner has just said. For example:

É1: Je veux aller au cinéma, mais je ne peux pas.

É2: Kelly veut aller au cinéma demain, mais elle ne peut pas.

INDEPENDENT PRACTICE

Assign any of the following:
1. Exercises on pages 29–31
2. Workbook, *Structure: F–L,* pages R16–R18

Activités de communication orale et écrite

PRESENTATION (*pages 32–33*)

Activités A, B, C, D, and E

These activities recycle material from *Bienvenue*, Part A, Chapters 7 and 8.

Extension of *Activité C*

After completing Activity C, you may wish to have the students present the conversation to the class.

Extension of *Activité D*

You may wish to have the students write Activity D.

ANSWERS

Activités A, B, C, and D

Answers will vary.

Activités de communication orale et écrite

A   On fait les courses.   You and two classmates are planning a picnic in Évian-les-Bains, a town on Lake Geneva. First, make a list of what you need. Then take turns asking one another where you would buy these items.

> du pain
>
> Élève 1: Où est-ce qu'on achète du pain?
> Élève 2: On achète du pain à la boulangerie.

B   En avion.   Make a list of words associated with airline travel. Write a short paragraph using these words to describe a plane trip you plan to make (or would like to make).

C   À la gare.   Work with a classmate and prepare a conversation between a passenger who wants to buy a ticket and a ticket agent in a train station. You may want to use some of the following words and expressions.

un aller-retour	en première/en seconde
un aller simple	à quelle heure
un billet	le quai
combien	la voie

D   La gare.   Describe the illustration in your own words.

E **Des photos.** Make up as many questions as you can about each photo, and then ask a classmate your questions. Take turns asking the questions and responding.

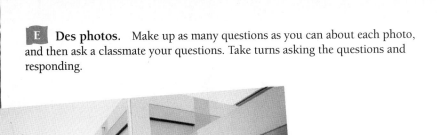

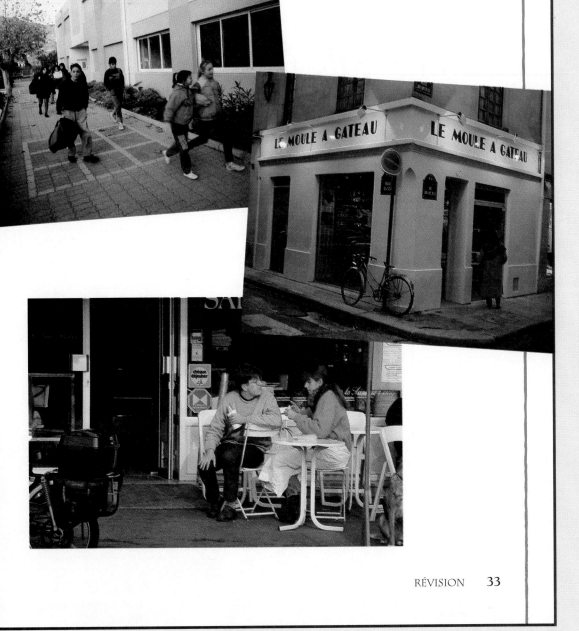

RÉVISION **33**

Activité E
Answers will vary.

STUDENT PORTFOLIO

Written assignments which may be included in students' portfolios are *Activité de communication B* on page 32 and *Activité de communication écrite A* on page R18 of the Workbook.

CHAPTER OVERVIEW

Students will learn vocabulary associated with summer weather and sports. They will also learn *prendre* and similar verbs, stress pronouns, and adjectives with a double consonant.

The cultural focus is on French summer vacations and resorts.

CHAPTER OBJECTIVES

By the end of this chapter, students will know:

1. summer weather, beach, and summer sports vocabulary
2. the verbs *prendre, apprendre,* and *comprendre*
3. the *pronoms accentués,* or stress pronouns
4. adjectives with a double consonant in the feminine

CHAPTER 9 RESOURCES

1. Workbook
2. Student Tape Manual
3. Audio Cassette 6A/CD-6
4. Bell Ringer Review Blackline Masters
5. Vocabulary Transparencies
6. Pronunciation Transparency P-9
7. Communication Transparency C-9
8. Communication Activities Masters
9. Map Transparencies
10. Situation Cards
11. Conversation Video
12. Videocassette/Videodisc, Unit 3
13. Video Activities Booklet, Unit 3
14. Lesson Plans
15. Computer Software: Practice/Test Generator
16. Chapter Quizzes
17. Testing Program
18. Internet Activities Booklet
19. CD-ROM Interactive Textbook

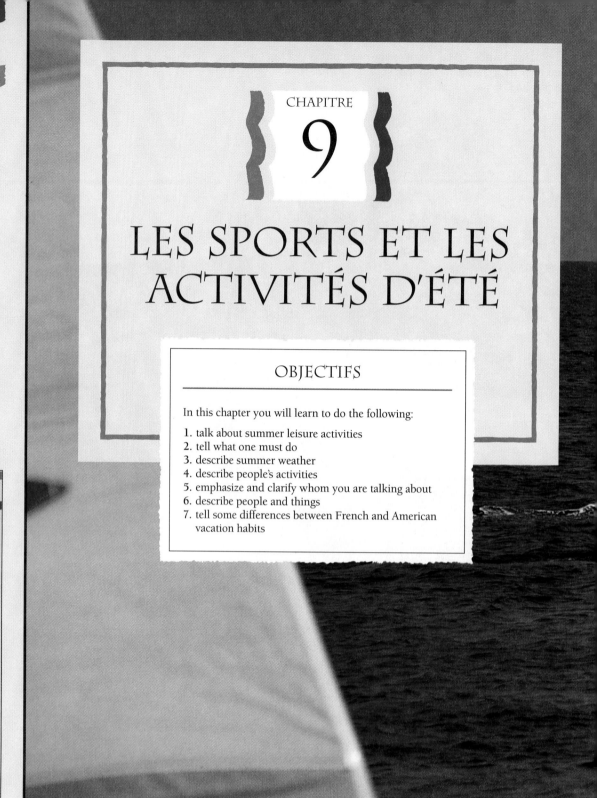

CHAPITRE 9

LES SPORTS ET LES ACTIVITÉS D'ÉTÉ

OBJECTIFS

In this chapter you will learn to do the following:

1. talk about summer leisure activities
2. tell what one must do
3. describe summer weather
4. describe people's activities
5. emphasize and clarify whom you are talking about
6. describe people and things
7. tell some differences between French and American vacation habits

CHAPTER PROJECTS

(optional)

1. Have students share their family's vacation habits by bringing in photos and vacation paraphernalia. You may wish to group them according to the kinds of vacations they are accustomed to (mountains, seaside, camping, visiting a city, etc.) and have each group tell as much as they can in French about their type of vacation.

2. Have groups plan the ideal five-week vacation in France. The description should be in French and should include information about transportation, meals, and leisure activities. They may do a poster or collage to illustrate it. Students can then choose the trip they would most like to take.

Pacing

This chapter requires eight to ten class sessions. Pacing will vary according to class length and the age and aptitude of the students.

Note The Lesson Plans offer guidelines for 45- and 55-minute classes and **Block Scheduling.**

NOTE ON DIRECTIONS TO STUDENT EXERCISES AND ACTIVITIES

Beginning in Chapter 9, the English translations of the exercise directions have been dropped in order to increase the amount of authentic communication in French in the classroom and to provide students with further practice in the language. You may wish to avoid even mentioning this change and see if students notice it.

Exercices vs. *Activités*

All exercises (which provide guided practice) are coded in blue. All communicative activities are coded in red.

INTERNET ACTIVITIES

(optional)

You will find these activities, student worksheets, and related teacher information in the *Bienvenue* Internet Activities Booklet and on the Glencoe Foreign Language Home Page at:

http://www.glencoe.com/secondary/fl

DID YOU KNOW?

You may wish to tell students that windsurfing *(la planche à voile)* is a popular sport along France's Atlantic coast. The 1988 windsurfing championships were held at Les Sables d'Olonne, a town on the Atlantic coast, south of the Loire.

VOCABULAIRE

MOTS 1

Bell Ringer Review

Write the following on the board or use BRR Blackline Master 9-1: Change the underlined words to a word or phrase with the same meaning.

1. un vol <u>d'un pays à l'autre</u>
2. un vol <u>qui arrive de</u> Paris
3. un vol <u>dans le même pays</u>
4. un vol <u>qui va à</u> Tahiti

PRESENTATION *(pages 236–237)*

A. Show Vocabulary Transparencies 9.1. Point to individual items and have the class repeat the words after you or Cassette 6A/CD-6.
B. As an alternative, you may wish to bring in some props such as sunglasses, suntan lotion, and so on.
C. During your presentation, ask: *C'est la plage? C'est le sable ou la mer? Il y a du sable sur la plage? C'est une vague? Il y a des vagues dans la mer? C'est une station balnéaire? Il y a des stations balnéaires au bord de la mer? Où est-ce qu'il y a des stations*

EN ÉTÉ

la mer

une station balnéaire au bord de la mer

une vague

des lunettes de soleil

le sable

un maillot (de bain)

la plage

À la plage il faut faire attention.
Il faut mettre de la crème solaire.
André met de la crème solaire.
Il prend un bain de soleil.
Il bronze.

Christine met des lunettes de soleil.
Mais elle attrape un coup de soleil.
Pourquoi? Parce qu'elle ne fait pas attention.
Elle ne met pas de crème solaire.

Note: The impersonal expression *il faut,* "one must," is used often in French. It is followed by the infinitive.

faire de la planche à voile

faire de la plongée sous-marine

faire du ski nautique

TOTAL PHYSICAL RESPONSE

(following the Vocabulary presentation)

TPR 1
____, levez-vous et venez ici, s'il vous plaît.
Vous allez mimer les activités suivantes.
Nagez.
Faites du ski nautique.
Faites de la planche à voile.
Faites de la plongée sous-marine.

Plongez.
Prenez un bain de soleil.
Merci, ____. Retournez à votre place, s'il vous plaît.

faire du surf

faire une promenade

aller à la pêche

nager
une piscine
plonger
un moniteur

Robert aime nager.
Il nage dans la piscine.
Et Caroline plonge dans la piscine.

Laure prend des leçons de natation.
Elle apprend à nager.
Elle comprend les instructions du moniteur.

CHAPITRE 9   **237**

Note *Pourquoi* questions (with *parce que* responses) are the most challenging to answer. The following are some questions you may wish to ask more able students while presenting words in this section: *Pourquoi faut-il mettre de la crème solaire à la plage? Pourquoi faut-il faire attention à la plage? André bronze. Pourquoi? Christine ne bronze pas. Elle attrape un coup de soleil. Pourquoi?*

RECYCLING

In this section, the concept of *-er* verbs is reinforced with the new verbs *bronzer, attraper, nager,* and *plonger.* In addition, the verbs *aller, faire,* and *mettre* are reintroduced. You may wish to explain that *nager* and *plonger* have the same spelling change as *manger: nous mangeons, nous nageons, nous plongeons.*

RETEACHING (*Mots 1*)

Refer students back to the party in Chapter 3, *Mots 2.* You may wish to use Vocabulary Transparencies 3.2 (A & B). Then have students imagine they are having a party at the beach. Have them make up a story combining the party vocabulary with the new beach vocabulary.

DRAMATIZATION

You may wish to have students dramatize the following words or expressions: *mettre de la crème solaire, nager, plonger, faire de la planche à voile, faire du ski nautique, aller à la pêche, mettre des lunettes de soleil.* As one student does the dramatization, another student can describe what he/she is doing.

TPR 2

___, venez ici, s'il vous plaît.

Vous allez à la pêche. Prenez la ligne ou la canne à pêche. Tenez!

Mettez la ligne dans l'eau.

Soyez patient(e). Asseyez-vous. Attendez quelques instants.

Ah, voilà! Vous avez attrapé un poisson.

Sortez votre ligne de l'eau. Allez-y doucement.

Regardez le poisson. Oh, qu'il est grand, votre poisson!

Tout le monde est d'accord?

Retirez le poisson de la ligne.

Mettez le poisson sur la table.

Vous allez préparer le poisson? Oui? Non?

Vous voulez manger le poisson?

Merci, ___. Vous avez très bien fait. Vous êtes un(e) très bon(ne) pêcheur/pêcheuse.

Et maintenant vous pouvez retourner à votre place.

Exercices

PRESENTATION (page 238)

Extension of *Exercice A*:
Speaking

After completing Exercise A, focus on the speaking skill by making the exercise a TV interview show. One student is the MC who interviews two other students using the questions in the exercise.

Exercice B

Exercise B can be done with books closed, open, or both ways. You may wish to call on one individual to answer two or three items.

Extension of *Exercice B*

After completing the exercise, call on one student to give the information in his/her own words.

Extension of *Exercice C*

In the *Mots 1* section, students only encountered the *il/elle* forms of the new verbs *prendre, apprendre,* and *comprendre.* Since there is no difference in sound in the singular forms of these verbs, you may wish to go over Exercise C again orally. Change *Jeanne* to *tu.* The students respond with *je.*

ANSWERS

Exercices A and B

Answers will vary.

Exercice C

1. Oui, Jeanne apprend à nager.
2. Oui, elle prend des leçons de natation.
3. Elle apprend à nager dans une piscine.
4. Oui, elle comprend bien les instructions de la monitrice.

INFORMAL ASSESSMENT
(*Mots 1*)

Check for understanding by mixing true and false statements about Vocabulary Transparencies 9.1. Students either agree by saying *Je suis d'accord* or they correct the statement.

A **Tu aimes les activités d'été?** Donnez des réponses personnelles.

1. Tu aimes nager quand il y a de grandes vagues?
2. Tu aimes plonger dans une piscine?
3. Tu aimes faire de la planche à voile?
4. Tu aimes faire de la plongée sous-marine?
5. Tu aimes faire du ski nautique?
6. Tu aimes faire du surf?
7. Tu aimes aller à la pêche?
8. Tu aimes prendre des bains de soleil sur le sable?
9. Tu aimes faire des promenades sur la plage?

B **Qu'est-ce qu'on fait en été?** Donnez des réponses personnelles.

1. En été, tu aimes aller à la plage?
2. Tu vas à quelle station balnéaire?
3. Tu préfères nager dans la mer ou dans une piscine?
4. Quand tu vas à la plage, tu mets un beau maillot?
5. À ton avis, est-ce qu'il faut mettre de la crème solaire?
6. Est-ce que tu mets de la crème solaire?
7. Tu bronzes facilement ou tu attrapes des coups de soleil?
8. Tu mets des lunettes de soleil quand tu vas à la plage?

C **Qu'est-ce qu'elle apprend à faire?** Répondez d'après la photo.

1. Jeanne apprend à nager?
2. Elle prend des leçons de natation?
3. Elle apprend à nager dans la mer ou dans une piscine?
4. Elle comprend bien les instructions de la monitrice?

NATATION – SKI NAUTIQUE

POUR ÉVITER DE MULTIPLES DANGERS:
courants, trous d'eau, épaves, vents, marées, barres, sables mouvants, tourbillons, etc.

CHOISISSEZ UNE PLAGE SURVEILLÉE.

Baignade interdite

Baignade dangereuse

Baignade autorisée

LA BAIGNADE
La natation est un **sport**; n'allez pas au-delà de vos possibilités.

L'hydrocution est un **accident** qui survient le plus souvent après:
• un repas copieux
• un bain de soleil prolongé

238

Assign any of the following:
1. Exercises, page 238
2. Workbook, *Mots 1: A–D,* pages 83–84
3. Communication Activities Masters, *Mots 1: A,* page 43
4. CD-ROM, Disc 3, pages 236–238

Ask students to look at the flyer. Ask them what it's about. What do the red, yellow (amber), and green flags indicate? Have them look at the flyer again and find any cognates. Now, have them find the French words for the following:

swimming	quicksand
bathing	don't overdo it
currents	

VOCABULAIRE

MOTS 2

LE TENNIS

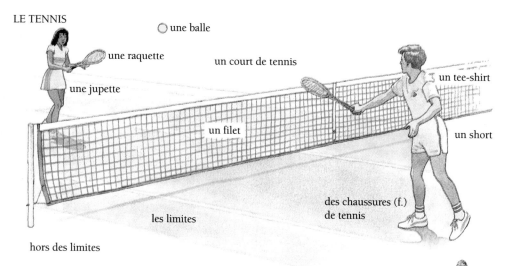

une balle

une raquette

un court de tennis

un tee-shirt

une jupette

un filet

un short

des chaussures (f.)
de tennis

les limites

hors des limites

On joue au tennis.
C'est un match de tennis.
Un des joueurs sert.

L'autre joueur renvoie la balle.
Il frappe fort.
Le score est de quinze à zéro.

Vocabulary Teaching Resources

1. Vocabulary Transparencies 9.2 (A & B)
2. Audio Cassette 6A/CD-6
3. Student Tape Manual, Teacher's Edition, *Mots 2: D–F,* pages 101–102
4. Workbook, *Mots 2: E–G,* page 85
5. Communication Activities Masters, *Mots 2: B,* page 44
6. Chapter Quizzes, *Mots 2: Quiz 2,* page 49
7. Computer Software, *Vocabulaire*
8. CD-ROM, Disc 3, *Mots 2:* pages 239–242

Bell Ringer Review

Write the following on the board or use BRR Blackline Master 9-2: Sketch people engaged in five sports associated with the beach. Label each sketch.

PRESENTATION (*pages 239–240*)

A. Model the new words using Vocabulary Transparencies 9.2 (A & B). Have students repeat after you or Cassette 6A/CD-6.

B. Using Vocabulary Transparencies 9.2 (A & B), say the words and phrases in random order and have volunteers stand at the screen and point to the appropriate illustrations.

C. Continue this process, expanding your statements about the illustrations in order to recombine the new material and recycle vocabulary from previous chapters. For example: *Elle sert. Il renvoie la balle. Il attend la balle. Elle attend la balle. Il a un microphone. La balle n'est pas hors des limites.*

ADDITIONAL PRACTICE

(*After completing Exercises A–C, page 238*)
1. Have students list things they can do at the beach, using *pouvoir.* Then have them organize their lists in order of preference and report to the class. For example: *À la plage, on peut nager. On peut bronzer. On peut faire du surf.* Students can do the same task with swimming pools and *aimer.* For example: *À la piscine, j'aime nager. J'aime plonger.*
2. Student Tape Manual, Teacher's Edition, *Activités B–C,* pages 100–101

On joue une partie en double.
Elle fait une promenade sur la plage quand il fait beau.

D. Ask students for the opposites of the following: *servir (renvoyer la balle);* (mime this one) *frapper doucement (frapper fort); une partie en simple (une partie en double); perdre le match (gagner le match); une jupette (un short); Il fait beau. (Il fait mauvais.) Il fait chaud. (Il fait froid.) Il fait du soleil. (Il y a des nuages.)*

Vocabulary Expansion

1. The following are some additional weather expressions you may wish to give students. These expressions are often used for the *météo* both on TV and in the newspaper. (See the weather map in *Météorologie: La Prévision du Temps* in *Lettres et sciences,* page 338.)
   Le temps est ensoleillé.
   Il est nuageux.
   Le ciel est couvert.
   Il y a des averses.
   Il y a des éclaircies.
2. If you present the above expressions, you may wish to have the students do the following exercise.
   Exprimez d'une autre façon:
   1. Il fait du soleil.
   2. Il y a des nuages.
   3. Il pleut.
   4. Le temps est nuageux.
   5. Le ciel n'est pas couvert.
3. With more able groups, do some additional word study. Show students the verb and noun forms of the following words.

jouer	le joueur
	la joueuse
nager	le nageur
	la nageuse
plonger	le plongeur
	la plongeuse
pêcher	le pêcheur
	la pêcheuse
skier	le skieur
	la skieuse

une partie en simple
un match entre deux joueurs

une partie en double
un match entre quatre joueurs

gagner le match

Note: The verb *jouer* takes the preposition *à* when followed by a sport.

On joue au tennis.   On joue au volley.   On joue au foot.

LE TEMPS EN ÉTÉ

Quel temps fait-il?   Il fait du soleil.   Il fait beau.

Il fait chaud.

Il y a des nuages.   Il pleut.   Il fait mauvais.

Il fait du vent.

Il fait froid.

ADDITIONAL PRACTICE

2. Student Tape Manual, Teacher's Edition, *Activités E–F,* page 102

1. Have students compile a calendar using photographs, magazine pictures, postcards or other illustrations of summer weather conditions. For each month of summer, they should write a sample date, a weather description, and a sentence about the illustration they have chosen. For example: *C'est aujourd'hui le 7 juillet. Il fait très chaud. Nous allons à la plage pour faire du surf.*

Exercices

A Un match de tennis.   Donnez des réponses personnelles.

1. Tu aimes le tennis?
2. Tu joues au tennis?
3. Si tu ne joues pas au tennis, tu veux apprendre à jouer au tennis?
4. Tu as une raquette?
5. Il y a un court de tennis près de ta maison ou ton appartement?
6. Ton école a des courts de tennis?

B Le tennis.   Complétez.

1. Quand un garçon ou un homme joue au tennis, il met un ___, un ___ et des ___.
2. Quand une fille ou une femme joue au tennis, elle met un ___, une ___ et des ___.
3. ___ est un match entre deux joueurs.
4. ___ est un match entre quatre personnes.
5. Quand on joue au tennis, on a une ___ et des ___.
6. 15–"love" est un ___ de quinze à zéro.
7. On ___ ou ___ la balle avec la raquette.
8. Un joueur sert, mais la balle va dans le ___. Quand il sert encore la balle est ___! Il n'a pas de chance!
9. Un des joueurs ___ très fort. Il ___ le match.

C Le temps.   Répondez.

1. En été, il fait beau ou il fait mauvais dans ta ville?
2. Il fait du soleil?
3. Il pleut souvent?
4. Il fait du vent à la plage?
5. Quel temps fait-il aujourd'hui?

D Quel temps fait-il?   Répondez d'après les dessins.

1.

2.

3.

4.

5.

6.

INDEPENDENT PRACTICE

Assign any of the following:
1. Exercises, page 241
2. Workbook, *Mots 2: E–G,* page 85
3. Communication Activities Masters, *Mots 2: B,* page 44
4. CD-ROM, Disc 3, pages 239–241

Exercices

PRESENTATION *(page 241)*

Exercice A

This exercise may be done with books open or closed.

Exercice B

Exercise B must be done with books open. Call on an individual to say as much about tennis as he/she can.

Extension of *Exercices C* and *D*

After completing the exercises, make statements about the weather and have students say the same thing using a negative form. For example: *Il fait froid. (Il ne fait pas chaud.)*

Extension of *Exercice D*

After completing Exercise D, have students say all they can about each illustration.

ANSWERS

Exercice A

Answers will vary.

Exercice B

1. tee-shirt, short, chaussures de tennis
2. tee-shirt, jupette, chaussures de tennis
3. Une partie en simple
4. Une partie en double
5. raquette, balles
6. score
7. sert, renvoie
8. filet, hors des limites
9. frappe, gagne

Exercice C

Answers will vary.

Exercice D

1. Il fait chaud. (Il fait du soleil. Il fait beau.)
2. Il y a des nuages. (Il ne fait pas de soleil.)
3. Il pleut. (Il fait mauvais. Il y a des nuages.)
4. Il fait du vent.
5. Il fait beau. (Il fait du soleil. Il fait chaud.)
6. Il fait froid.

INFORMAL ASSESSMENT
(*Mots 2*)

Show magazine pictures that depict different types of weather. Have students say what the weather is in each one.

PRESENTATION *(page 242)*

Activités A, B, C, and D

It is not necessary to do all the
activities. You may select those
that are most appropriate for your
students, or you may permit the
students to select the activity or
activities they would like to take
part in.

Extension of *Activité D*

All of us have a lot of things we
have to do in life. Have students
tell some of these things using
Il faut…

ANSWERS

Activités A, B, C, and D

Answers will vary.

Activités de communication orale
Mots 1 et 2

A **À la plage.** Work with a classmate. One of you describes the weather (sunny, rainy, windy, etc.) on a day at the beach and the other says what he or she likes (or doesn't like) to do there on that kind of day. Take turns.

> Élève 1: **Il fait du vent.**
> Élève 2: **Quand il fait du vent, j'aime faire de la planche à voile.**

B **Les vacances parfaites.** Plan a great summer vacation at the beach. Tell your classmate where you want to go and why, and what you like to do there. Then find out your partner's plans.

> Élève 1: **Je voudrais aller à Hawaii parce qu'il fait toujours du soleil là-bas. J'aime nager. Et toi?**
> Élève 2: **Moi aussi, j'aime Hawaii. Je voudrais faire de la plongée sous-marine et du surf.**

C **Un match de tennis entre Guy et Nadine.** You're a sports announcer for a local radio station. Describe the tennis match in the illustration below. Don't forget to tell your listeners what the players are wearing.

D **Il faut…** Work with a classmate. One of you chooses a place or a situation from the list below and the other has to name two things that should or shouldn't be done at that place or in that situation. Take turns until all the items on the list have been used.

> à l'école
> Élève 1: **À l'école, qu'est-ce qu'il faut faire?**
> Élève 2: **À l'école, il faut étudier et faire ses devoirs.**

à la plage	au cours de français
après un dîner au restaurant	pour gagner un match
avant un examen	pour organiser une fête
avant un voyage	

ADDITIONAL PRACTICE

Have students role-play in pairs: A French student (your partner) asks you for the following information: (1) what the weather is like in summer in your town, (2) if you go to the beach, (3) if you like to swim, (4) if you prefer to swim in the ocean or in a pool, (5) which sports you engage in at the beach. Answer, then reverse roles.

INDEPENDENT PRACTICE

Assign any of the following:
1. Activities, page 242
2. CD-ROM, Disc 3, page 242

STRUCTURE

Les verbes *prendre, apprendre* et *comprendre* au présent

Describing People's Activities

1. The verb *prendre*, "to take," is irregular. Study the following forms.

PRENDRE	
je prends	nous prenons
tu prends	vous prenez
il	ils
elle } prend	elles } prennent
on	

Je prends mes livres quand je quitte la classe.
Vous prenez l'avion pour aller à Boston mais Julie et Marc prennent le train.

Note that the singular forms of *prendre* are the same as those of any regular *-re* verb, but the plural forms are irregular.

2. The verb *prendre* has a number of additional meanings. Here are a few of them.

a. Used with food or beverages, *prendre* means either "to eat" or "to drink."

Au restaurant Marie-Lise prend toujours du poulet.
Au café les enfants prennent toujours de l'eau minérale.

b. *Prendre le petit déjeuner* means "to eat breakfast." Note, however, that you do not use *prendre* with other meals in French. "To eat lunch" is *déjeuner* and "to eat dinner" is *dîner*.

Gérard prend son petit déjeuner à la maison mais il déjeune à la cafétéria.

c. *Prendre les billets* means "to buy tickets."

Je prends mon billet au guichet et j'attends le train.

3. Two other verbs that are conjugated like *prendre* are *apprendre*, "to learn," and *comprendre*, "to understand." You use the preposition *à* after *apprendre* when it is followed by an infinitive.

Ma sœur et mon frère apprennent à jouer au tennis.
Vous comprenez le français, n'est-ce pas?

CHAPITRE 9   **243**

LEARNING FROM PHOTOS

You may wish to ask the following questions about the photo: *C'est un joueur de tennis? Qu'est-ce qu'il a à la main? Il a aussi une raquette? Il a la main sur le filet?*

Structure Teaching Resources

1. Workbook, *Structure: A–E,* pages 86–87
2. Student Tape Manual, Teacher's Edition, *Structure: A–D,* pages 103–104
3. Audio Cassette 6A/CD-6
4. Communication Activities Masters, *Structure: A–C,* pages 45–46
5. Computer Software, *Structure*
6. Chapter Quizzes, *Structure: Quizzes 3–5,* pages 50–52
7. CD-ROM, Disc 3, pages 243–247

Bell Ringer Review

Write the following on the board or use BRR Blackline Master 9-4: Match the word or phrase on the left with the related word or phrase on the right.

1. nager	a. au bord de la mer
2. le sable	b. le match
3. la balle	c. faire du surf
4. la station balnéaire	d. la plage
5. les vagues	e. la piscine
6. le score	f. la raquette
7. bronzer	g. il pleut
8. des nuages	h. prendre un bain de soleil

Les verbes prendre, apprendre *et* comprendre au présent

PRESENTATION *(page 243)*

Model the pronunciation of the forms of *prendre* and have students repeat them in unison. Pay attention to the pronunciation. The *n* of the root is nasal in the singular forms, but not in the plural forms.

Exercices

Exercices A–F

All exercises may be done with books open or closed.

Exercices A, B, and C

These exercises use forms that have no pronunciation change. The remainder require sound and spelling changes.

ANSWERS

Exercice A

1. Oui, on prend un bain de soleil à la plage.
2. Non, on ne prend pas de bain de soleil quand il y a des nuages.
3. Oui, on met de la crème solaire quand on prend un bain de soleil.
4. Oui, on bronze quand on prend un bain de soleil.

Exercice B

Answers will vary.

Exercice C

É1 will use **Tu prends...** and É2 will respond with **Oui (Non), je (ne) prends (pas)...**

Exercice D

Answers will employ **Nous (ne) prenons (pas)...**

Exercice E

1. Il prend un crème et ses copains prennent un express.
2. Il prend une salade et ses copains prennent une soupe à l'oignon.
3. Il prend un sandwich au pâté et ses copains prennent un croque-monsieur.
4. Il prend une glace au chocolat et ses copains prennent une glace à la vanille.
5. Il prend de l'eau minérale et ses copains prennent du thé.

Exercices

A **On prend un bain de soleil.** Répondez.

1. On prend un bain de soleil à la plage?
2. On prend un bain de soleil quand il y a des nuages?
3. On met de la crème solaire quand on prend un bain de soleil?
4. On bronze quand on prend un bain de soleil?

B **Moi, en été.** Donnez des réponses personnelles.

1. En été, tu prends des bains de soleil sur le sable?
2. Tu bronzes ou tu attrapes des coups de soleil?
3. Tu préfères nager dans une piscine, dans la mer ou dans un lac?
4. Tu prends des leçons de surf?
5. Tu apprends à faire de la planche à voile?
6. Tu apprends à faire du ski nautique?
7. Tu comprends le moniteur?

C **Qu'est-ce que tu prends?** Posez des questions à un copain ou à une copine d'après le modèle.

> le train
> Élève 1: Tu prends le train?
> Élève 2: Non, je ne prends pas le train. (Oui, je prends le train.)

1. ton billet au guichet à la gare
2. le bus pour aller à l'école
3. l'avion pour aller à New York
4. l'avion pour aller en France

D **Le petit déjeuner.** Répondez en utilisant «nous».

1. Vous prenez votre petit déjeuner à la maison?
2. Vous prenez votre petit déjeuner à quelle heure?
3. Vous prenez votre petit déjeuner quand vous êtes en retard?
4. Vous prenez votre petit déjeuner dans la cuisine ou dans la salle à manger?
5. Vous prenez du lait au petit déjeuner?

E **Qu'est-ce qu'ils prennent au café?** Changez d'après le modèle.

> Il prend un coca. (un citron pressé)
> *Il prend un coca et ses copains prennent un citron pressé.*

1. Il prend un crème. (un express)
2. Il prend une salade. (une soupe à l'oignon)
3. Il prend un sandwich au pâté. (un croque-monsieur)
4. Il prend une glace au chocolat. (une glace à la vanille)
5. Il prend de l'eau minérale. (du thé)

244 CHAPITRE 9

ADDITIONAL PRACTICE

3. Student Tape Manual, Teacher's Edition, *Activités A–B,* page 103

(*After completing Exercises A–F*)

1. Have students introduce each of the following words or phrases with *j'apprends, je comprends,* or both: *le prof, la leçon, l'article du journal, le français.*
2. Have students make up a list of things they learn and a list of things they learn to do (*J'apprends... , J'apprends à...*).

F Au cours de français.   Répondez.

1. Au cours de français, les élèves apprennent beaucoup de mots?
2. Ils apprennent le vocabulaire?
3. Ils apprennent des règles de grammaire?
4. Ils apprennent la civilisation française?
5. Et toi, tu apprends à parler français?
6. Tes copains et toi, vous comprenez bien quand le professeur parle français?

Le pronoms accentués

Emphasizing and Clarifying Whom You Are Talking About

1. Compare the subject pronouns below with the corresponding stress pronouns.

STRESS PRONOUNS	SUBJECT PRONOUNS
moi	je
toi	tu
lui	il
elle	elle
nous	nous
vous	vous
eux	ils
elles	elles

La Côte d'Azur: Villefranche-sur-Mer

2. You use stress pronouns in several ways in French.

   a. to reinforce or stress the subject

      Moi, je vais au bord de la mer en été.
      Lui, il reste à la maison.

   b. after a preposition such as *avec, pour, chez,* etc.

      David veut jouer avec nous.
      Les filles rentrent chez elles après la fête.

   c. alone or in a phrase without a verb

      Qui fait du ski nautique? Moi!
      Et eux? Est-ce qu'ils prennent des leçons?

   d. before and after *et* or *ou*

      Marie et moi, nous allons à la plage.
      Qui va faire les courses ce soir? Lui ou elle?

CHAPITRE 9   **245**

Exercices

ANSWERS

Exercice A

Moi
Lui
elle
elle
moi
Moi, eux

Exercice B

1. Moi? Oui, j'adore aller au bord de la mer.
2. Lui? Oui, il adore faire du ski nautique.
3. Elles? Oui, elles adorent faire de la plongée sous-marine.
4. Nous? Oui, nous adorons nager.
5. Eux? Oui, ils adorent faire du surf.

Exercice C

1. lui
2. moi
3. elle, moi
4. moi, eux

INFORMAL ASSESSMENT

Show students magazine pictures of people and ask them to compare personality traits or physical characteristics (*petit, grand, beau,* etc.) using stress pronouns. Cue the trait or characteristic you wish compared, if necessary.

---

e. after *c'est* or *ce n'est* pas

> C'est toi, Yvonne?
> Oui, c'est moi.
> C'est Jean-Luc?
> Non, ce n'est pas lui.

f. with *-même(s)* to express "myself," "herself," and so forth

> Je vais faire les valises moi-même.
> Ils font la cuisine eux-mêmes.

Exercices

A **Moi, toi et les autres.** Complétez.

DAVID: ___, j'adore nager.
CÉLINE: Et ton frère? Il aime nager?
DAVID: ___? Il aime faire du ski nautique.
CÉLINE: Et ta sœur, ___, elle aime faire du ski nautique aussi?
DAVID: Non, mais ___, elle aime faire de la planche à voile.
CÉLINE: Sans blague! Ma copine et ___, nous aimons faire de la planche à voile aussi.
DAVID: ___ aussi, j'aime faire de la planche à voile. Mais mes copains, ___, ils n'aiment pas ça.

B **Tu aimes les sports d'été?** Répondez d'après le modèle.

> Tu aimes nager?
> *Moi? Oui, j'adore nager.*

1. Tu aimes aller au bord de la mer?
2. Et ton frère, il aime faire du ski nautique?
3. Et tes sœurs, elles aiment faire de la plongée sous-marine?
4. Et vous, vous aimez nager?
5. Et tes copains, ils aiment faire du surf?

C **Une fête.** Complétez.

1. Tu vas donner une fête pour Jean? Oui, je vais donner une fête pour ___.
2. Qui va organiser la fête? Toi? Oui, c'est ___.
3. Et qui va faire les courses? Ta mère? Pas ___! Moi, je vais aller au marché ___-même!
4. Jean va arriver chez toi avec ses copains? Oui, il va arriver chez ___ avec ___.

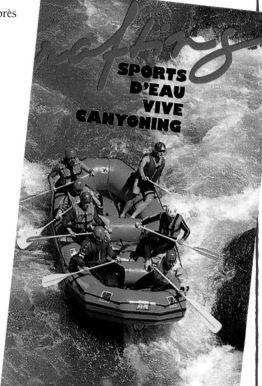

SPORTS D'EAU VIVE CANYONING

ADDITIONAL PRACTICE

1. Write a paragraph describing at least five differences between you and another person. Use the stress pronouns. For example: *Moi, je suis petit. Lui, il est très grand.*
2. Have students circulate in the room, pointing to classmates and telling what they do. For example: *Lui, il joue au foot. Elle, elle joue au tennis. Et toi, tu…*
3. Student Tape Manual, Teacher's Edition, *Activités A–D,* pages 103–104

Les adjectifs avec une double consonne

Describing People and Things

1. Note that certain adjectives double their final consonant in the feminine forms. Study the following.

	FÉMININ	MASCULIN
SINGULIER	une compagnie aérienne une voiture européenne	un vol aérien une café européen
PLURIEL	des compagnies aériennes des voitures européennes	des vols aériens des cafés européens

2. Here are some other adjectives that follow the same pattern.

    canadien(ne)   italien(ne)   parisien(ne)

3. The adjective *bon*, which precedes the noun, also doubles its final consonant. Study these forms.

    C'est une très **bonne** idée.   Robert est un très **bon** élève.
    Il a de **bonnes** notes.   Et il a de **bons** profs.

4. The adjective *gentil*, "nice," also doubles its final consonant.

    une fille **gentille**   un garçon **gentil**

Exercices

A **D'après vous.** Répondez.

1. C'est une bonne idée de voyager avec une bonne compagnie aérienne canadienne?
2. C'est une bonne idée de passer une bonne journée sur une belle plage?
3. Est-ce que la compagnie aérienne italienne sert des spécialités italiennes pendant ses vols?
4. Est-ce que les femmes parisiennes font leurs courses dans les beaux magasins parisiens?

B **Une compagnie canadienne.** Complétez.

La compagnie ___(1)___ (aérien) ___(2)___ (canadien) offre des vols vers des destinations ___(3)___ (européen). Le service est très ___(4)___ (bon). À bord les stewards sont très ___(5)___ (gentil) et les hôtesses de l'air aussi sont très ___(6)___ (gentil). Il est agréable d'avoir une ___(7)___ (bon) place dans un avion ___(8)___ (canadien) et de faire un ___(9)___ (bon) voyage ___(10)___ (européen).

CHAPITRE 9   **247**

INDEPENDENT PRACTICE

Assign any of the following:
1. Exercises, pages 246–247
2. Workbook, *Structure: D–E*, page 87
3. Communication Activities Masters, *Structure: B–C*, pages 45–46
4. Computer Software, *Structure*
5. CD-ROM, Disc 3, pages 245–247

LEARNING FROM REALIA

Have students look at the ad on page 246. Ask them how you say "rafting" in French (*le rafting*). This is a fine example of the wholesale takeover of English words into French, an increasingly common phenomenon. Ask them what they think *canyoning* is: does the word exist in English or is it a French invention? How does one say "whitewater" in French? (*eaux vives*).

Les adjectifs avec une double consonne

PRESENTATION (*page 247*)

A. It is recommended that you not spend a great deal of time on this point. Students will need reinforcement of the spelling of these adjectives throughout their study of French.

B. Lead students through steps 1–4 on page 247, modeling the pronunciation of the feminine versus the masculine forms of the adjectives and having students repeat in unison.

Exercices

PRESENTATION (*page 247*)

Exercice B

After going over this exercise, calling on several students to complete the sentences, have one student reread the entire exercise.

ANSWERS

Exercice A

Answers will vary.

Exercice B

1. aérienne
2. canadienne
3. européennes
4. bon
5. gentils
6. gentilles
7. bonne
8. canadien
9. bon
10. européen

DICTATION

You may wish to give the following dictation:

Les filles canadiennes sont gentilles. Elles portent de bonnes lunettes italiennes.

PRESENTATION (*page 248*)

A. Have students close their books and watch the Conversation Video or listen as you either read the conversation to them or play Cassette 6A/CD-6.

B. Have them repeat the conversation once or twice in unison.

C. Call on pairs to read the conversation with as much expression as possible.

D. Have pairs act out the conversation, allowing them to make any changes that make sense.

Note In the CD-ROM version, students can play the role of either one of the characters and record the conversation.

ANSWERS

Exercice A

1. Oui, il fait chaud.
2. Oui, Nathalie veut aller à la plage.
3. Françoise va chercher son maillot de bain.
4. Nathalie n'a pas de crème solaire.
5. Nathalie va prendre un bain de soleil.
6. Oui, elle aime bronzer.
7. Elle va nager et faire du ski nautique.

Prononciation

PRESENTATION (*page 248*)

A. Model the key phrase *un vieux soleil en maillot* and have students repeat chorally after you. Then model the other words and phrases in similar fashion.

B. For additional practice, use: Cassette 6A/CD-6: *Prononciation;* Pronunciation Transparency P-9; and the Student Tape Manual, Teacher's Edition, *Activités G–I,* page 106.

C. Give the following *dictée:*
La gentille fille a un billet. Le soleil brille. La fille ne travaille pas en maillot.

Scènes de la vie *Une belle journée d'été*

NATHALIE: Il fait terriblement chaud!
FRANÇOISE: C'est vrai, c'est horrible!
NATHALIE: Tu veux aller à la plage?
FRANÇOISE: D'accord. Je vais chercher mon maillot de bain.
NATHALIE: Tu as de la crème solaire?
FRANÇOISE: Oui. Pourquoi? Tu vas prendre un bain de soleil?
NATHALIE: Mais bien sûr!
FRANÇOISE: Pas moi.
NATHALIE: Pas toi? Qu'est-ce que tu vas faire alors?
FRANÇOISE: Je vais nager et faire du ski nautique.

A **La plage.** Répondez d'après la conversation.

1. Il fait chaud?
2. Nathalie veut aller à la plage?
3. Qu'est-ce que Françoise va chercher?
4. Qui n'a pas de crème solaire?
5. Qui va prendre un bain de soleil?
6. Elle aime bronzer?
7. Et Françoise, qu'est-ce qu'elle va faire?

Prononciation *Les sons /y/ et /y/ + voyelle*

The sound /y/ occurs in three positions: final, between two vowel sounds, and in combination with another vowel sound. Repeat the following.

fille	soleil	gentille
maillot	travailler	billet
canadien	aérien	vieux

Now repeat the following sentences.

J'ai un vieux maillot.
On ne travaille pas bien au soleil.
C'est un avion canadien.

un vieux soleil en maillot

LEARNING FROM PHOTOS

Ask the following questions about the photo: *La fille à la bicyclette, c'est Nathalie ou Françoise? Quelle fille sur la photo prend un bain de soleil? Elle va prendre un bain de soleil à la plage aussi? À ton avis c'est la maison de Françoise ou de Nathalie?*

Activités de communication orale

A **Qu'est-ce que vous prenez au snack bar?** Divide into small groups and choose a leader. The leader asks the others what they usually buy to eat or drink at the beach snack bar. He or she takes notes, then reports to the class.

> Élève 1: Qu'est-ce que tu prends quand tu as soif (faim)?
> Élève 2: Moi, je prends de l'eau minérale (un sandwich au jambon).
> Élève 1 (*à la classe*): Marc prend de l'eau minérale. Anne et Paul prennent…

B **Moi, je veux apprendre à…** Take turns with a classmate and find out what each of you would like to learn to do and why.

> Élève 1: Qu'est-ce que tu veux apprendre à faire?
> Élève 2: Moi, je voudrais apprendre à bien parler français.
> Élève 1: Pourquoi?
> Élève 2: Parce que je voudrais aller en France.

C **En été.** Tell a classmate some things you do in the summer, then find out what your partner likes to do.

> Élève 1: En été je vais à la plage, je fais du surf et de la planche à voile. Et toi, qu'est-ce que tu aimes faire en été?
> Élève 2: Moi, j'aime aller à la plage aussi, mais je ne fais pas de surf. J'aime nager et j'aime aller à la pêche.

Les chutes de Montmorency à dix kilomètres de Québec

Bell Ringer Review

Write the following on the board or use BRR Blackline Master 9-6: Describe the following, using the adjectives given in parentheses. Follow the model:
La tour Eiffel (parisien)
La tour Eiffel est un monument parisien.
1. Marie (gentil)
2. Montréal (canadien)
3. Patrick (bon)
4. la Porsche (européen)
5. Air France (aérien)

Activités de communication orale

PRESENTATION (*page 249*)

Activités A, B, and C
Let students choose the activity they want to work with.

ANSWERS

Activités A, B, and C
Answers will vary.

CROSS-CULTURAL COMPARISON

Very few teenagers in France work during summer vacation. That time is primarily devoted to relaxation and being with their families.

Vocabulary Expansion

Students may ask why the title of the *Conversation* uses the word *journée,* not *jour.* For English speakers the distinction may be a bit subtle. Explain that *la journée* usually refers to a duration of time, a whole day, a more subjective notion of time than that connoted by *le jour,* which is just a simple measure of time. (The same applies to *l'an* and *l'année.*) *La journée* and *l'année* as a result are often qualified with adjectives (as in *Une belle journée d'été*).

INDEPENDENT PRACTICE

Assign any of the following:
1. Exercises and activities, pages 248–249
2. Workbook, *Un Peu Plus,* pages 88–90
3. CD-ROM, Disc 3, pages 248–249

DID YOU KNOW?

At 83 meters high (270 feet), the Montmorency Falls are one-and-a-half times higher than Niagara Falls. A cable car takes visitors to the top of the falls, where they can view an impressive panorama. In winter, at the foot of the falls, a strange natural phenomenon known as the "sugar loaf" (*pain de sucre*) can be observed.

LECTURE ET CULTURE

READING STRATEGIES
(page 250)

Pre-reading

Have students scan the reading for cognates.

Reading

A. Have the class read the selection once silently.

B. Call on individuals to read one paragraph each.

C. Ask comprehension questions based on each paragraph.

Post-reading

If possible, bring in pictures or slides of popular French beach or mountain vacation areas and share them with your students. Some sources for these materials might be your own collection, that of an acquaintance, your library or a local travel agency.

Note Point out to students that in informal conversational French, people say *Qu'est-ce qu'elles sont belles* or *Ce qu'elles sont belles* for *Qu'elles sont belles.*

Note Students may listen to a recorded version of the *Lecture* on the CD-ROM.

Étude de mots

ANSWERS

Exercice A

1. d	4. e
2. c	5. a
3. b	6. f

Exercice B

1. mois	4. montagnes
2. vacances	5. ouest
3. côtes, belles	

LES VACANCES D'ÉTÉ

C'est le premier août. Tout le monde prend la route pour aller au bord de la mer. Les vacances d'été commencent. En France le mois d'août, c'est le mois des vacances. On ne travaille pas. On passe le mois entier au bord de la mer ou à la montagne.

Qu'elles sont belles[1], les plages en France! Il y a des stations balnéaires le long des côtes[2]: sur la Manche au nord, sur l'océan Atlantique à l'ouest, et sur la Côte d'Azur au sud, au bord de la mer Méditerranée.

Qu'est-ce qu'on fait au bord de la mer? On va à la plage, bien sûr. À la plage on prend des bains de soleil. Tout le monde veut rentrer chez soi[3] bien bronzé. Les

Une belle plage bretonne

gens[4] sportifs nagent ou font de la planche à voile. Moi, je fais du ski nautique. Qu'est-ce que tu fais en été?

Vers deux heures on a faim. Après une belle journée à la plage on a une faim de loup. L'air de la mer donne faim. On fait un pique-nique sur la plage ou on va dans un petit restaurant en plein air[5] où on commande des fruits de mer[6].

[1] Qu'elles sont belles   *How beautiful they are*
[2] le long des côtes   *along the coasts*
[3] chez soi   *home*
[4] gens   *people*
[5] en plein air   *outdoor*
[6] fruits de mer   *seafood*

Étude de mots

A   Quel est le mot?   Trouvez une expression équivalente.

1. sportif	a. dans toutes les régions
2. une faim de loup	b. tout le mois
3. le mois entier	c. très faim
4. en plein air	d. qui aime les sports
5. partout	e. à l'extérieur, dehors
6. commencer	f. le contraire de *finir*

CRITICAL THINKING ACTIVITY

(Thinking skills: decision making, evaluating consequences.)

Put the following on the board or on a transparency:

1. Christine va à la plage. Mais elle ne bronze pas. Elle attrape toujours des coups de soleil. Elle doit (*must*) acheter de la crème solaire. Elle a 80 francs. Elle veut acheter des lunettes de soleil qui coûtent 70 francs. Les lunettes sont très jolies. Mais si elle achète les lunettes, elle ne va pas avoir d'argent pour acheter la crème solaire. Qu'est-ce qu'elle doit faire?

2. Christine succombe à la tentation! Elle achète les lunettes de soleil et elle va à la plage. Quelles sont les conséquences de sa décision?

B Des faits. Complétez les phrases d'après la lecture.

1. Le ___ d'août a trente et un jours.
2. Le mois d'août est le mois des ___ parce que les gens ne travaillent pas.
3. Le long des ___ de la France, il y a de très ___ plages.
4. Les Pyrénées et les Alpes sont des ___.
5. L'océan Atlantique est à l'___ de la France.

Compréhension

C Au bord de la mer. Répondez d'après la lecture.

1. Quelle est la date?
2. Tout le monde prend la route pour aller où?
3. On passe combien de temps au bord de la mer?
4. Il y a des plages partout en France?
5. Qu'est-ce qu'on fait à la plage?
6. Que font les gens sportifs?
7. Tout le monde veut rentrer chez soi comment?
8. Quelle est l'heure du déjeuner?
9. Où est-ce qu'on va manger?
10. Qu'est-ce qu'on commande au bord de la mer?

D Les vacances. Trouvez les renseignements suivants dans la lecture.

1. Quel est le mois des vacances, le mois où très peu de gens travaillent?
2. Où est-ce que les Français aiment passer leurs vacances?
3. Les Français passent combien de temps au bord de la mer ou à la montagne?

DÉCOUVERTE CULTURELLE

*L*es Français sont très travailleurs. Mais les vacances sont très importantes pour eux. Le Français typique a à peu près cinq semaines de vacances par an. Le mois favori pour les vacances d'été, c'est le mois d'août. Le premier août il y a des bouchons et des embouteillages[1] partout. Tout le monde est pressé[2] d'arriver au bord de la mer pour commencer les vacances.

Tes parents ont combien de semaines de vacances? Ta famille et toi, où passez-vous les vacances? Quand est-ce que vous y allez? Vous y passez combien de temps?

[1] des bouchons et des embouteillages *traffic jams*
[2] est pressé *is in a hurry*

Compréhension
ANSWERS
Exercice C

1. C'est le premier août.
2. Tout le monde prend la route pour aller au bord de la mer.
3. On passe le mois entier au bord de la mer.
4. Il y a des plages le long des côtes, à l'ouest, au nord et au sud.
5. À la plage, on prend des bains de soleil.
6. Les gens sportifs nagent ou font de la planche à voile ou du ski nautique.
7. Tout le monde veut rentrer chez soi bien bronzé.
8. Deux heures est l'heure du déjeuner.
9. On va manger dans un petit restaurant en plein air ou on va faire un pique-nique sur la plage.
10. On commande des fruits de mer.

Exercice D

1. C'est le mois d'août.
2. Ils aiment passer leurs vacances au bord de la mer ou à la montagne.
3. Ils passent le mois entier au bord de la mer ou à la montagne.

OPTIONAL MATERIAL

Découverte culturelle

PRESENTATION *(page 251)*

Before reading the selection, have students discuss vacations in the U.S.: How long do Americans usually get for their vacation? Do they usually take their vacation in summer? Is one month more popular than the other for summer vacations? How do most American families travel in the summer—by car, plane or train?

Note Students may listen to a recorded version of the *Découverte culturelle* on the CD-ROM.

DID YOU KNOW?

The beautiful beach pictured in the photo on page 250 is just one of many on the coast of Brittany. The clean, sandy beaches are all popular vacation spots in the summer. Dinard, Perros-Guirec, Trégastel-Plage, Douarnenez, Carnac, and La Baule are among the best.

LEARNING FROM PHOTOS

Ask students the following questions about the photo: *Cette fille fait de la planche à voile ou du surf? Est-ce qu'elle fait bien du surf ou est-ce qu'elle apprend à faire du surf? Qui est-ce, derrière elle sur la photo?*

PRESENTATION (*pages 252–253*)

Have the students sit back and enjoy the beautiful photographs as they read the information about them.

Note In the CD-ROM version, students can listen to the recorded captions and discover a hidden video behind one of the photos.

Culture Note In regard to **Photo 2**, you may wish to tell students that in 1991 France won the Davis Cup when Guy Forget defeated the American, Pete Sampras. It was France's first Davis Cup since 1932.

RÉALITÉS

C'est une colonie de vacances en montagne **1**. Les enfants jouent avec les monitrices. Tout le monde adore l'été. C'est la belle saison.

Voici Yannick Noah **2**. C'est un champion de tennis célèbre. Tu voudrais jouer contre lui?

Voici la plage de Nice, une ville sur la Côte d'Azur **3**. Sur la plage à Nice, il y a du sable ou des galets?

Voici Audierne, un joli port de pêche en Bretagne **4**. Il y a beaucoup de bateaux dans le port?

La jeune femme fait une promenade en vélo en montagne **5**. C'est un vélo tout terrain (VTT).

252

DID YOU KNOW?

Nice is a resort city on the French Riviera. It lies at the foot of the Alps near Italy. The Alps protect the city from cold northern winds and give it a mild winter climate. Most tourists visit Nice during the winter or from July to September. Nice has a famous Mardi Gras celebration, *le Carnaval*, which lasts for two weeks.

CROSS-CULTURAL COMPARISON

You may wish to tell students that American tourists on the French Riviera are often intrigued by the stones on the beach at Nice. The word for these stones is *les galets*.

GEOGRAPHY CONNECTION

Tell students that due to its location, France has many wonderful beach resorts. Call on students to go to the wall map of France (or use the Map Transparency) and locate the following general areas.

la côte bretonne
    (la côte de la Bretagne)
la côte normande
    (la côte de la Normandie)
la côte de l'Atlantique
la côte de la mer
    Méditerranée

Then have them locate the following popular resort areas:

La Baule (Bretagne)
Arcachon
    (Côte de l'Atlantique)
le Cap d'Agde
    (la Méditerranée)

ADDITIONAL PRACTICE

Assign any of the following:
1. Student Tape Manual, Teacher's Edition, *Deuxième Partie*, pages 107–109
2. Situation Cards, Chapter 9

RECYCLING

The *Activités de communication orale* and *Activités de communication écrite* focus on situations within the contexts of the seaside and sports in order to recycle the words and structures from this chapter and previous ones. Recycled language includes food vocabulary, time expressions, the *futur proche*, the verbs *faire, aller, partir, avoir,* and regular verbs.

INFORMAL ASSESSMENT

Oral Activities A and B may serve as a speaking evaluation. They are both guided activities, yet they provide an opportunity for students to come up with their own utterances within the given situations. Use the evaluation criteria on page 34 of this Teacher's Wraparound Edition.

Activités de communication orale

PRESENTATION (*page 254*)

Activité A

In the CD-ROM version of this activity, students can interact with an on-screen native speaker.

ANSWERS

Activités A and B

Answers will vary.

Activité de communication écrite

ANSWERS

Activité A

Answers will vary.

Activités de communication orale

A   Une nouvelle amie.   At the beach in Saint-Tropez you have just met Danielle Lacroix, a French teen around the same age as you. She wants to find out more about you. Answer her questions.

1. Alors tu es comme moi—tu adores la plage! Qu'est-ce que tu aimes faire à la plage?
2. À quelle heure est-ce que tu arrives à la plage?
3. Où est-ce que tu déjeunes?
4. Tu veux déjeuner avec moi demain?

B   Tu veux jouer au tennis avec moi?   The new French exchange student (your partner) wants to know if you play tennis (or would like to learn to play), if you have a racket, and if you'd like to play tennis with him or her tomorrow. Answer, then reverse roles.

Activité de communication écrite

A   Une carte postale.   You're spending two weeks at the beach resort of your choice. Write a postcard to a friend about your vacation. Tell him or her where you are and what the place is like; what the weather's like; what you do every day; a new sport you're learning, and what you think of the instructor; and when you're going to return home.

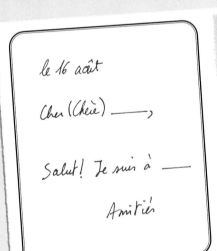

le 16 août

Cher (Chère) ———,

Salut! Je suis à ———

Amitiés

FOR THE YOUNGER STUDENT

1. Have students draw a map of France. On the coastal areas have them write the names of famous beaches. They should highlight these locations by drawing in figures of people engaged in various aquatic sports. When finished, students can write a paragraph explaining what is on their map.

2. Have students draw a beach scene on a piece of paper the size of a postcard. They should include figures to represent themselves. On the back of the paper have them write to a friend telling about their vacation at the beach.

3. Using a large map of France or of the U.S., have students play the role of a TV weather forecaster giving the forecast for a typical summer day.

Réintroduction et recombinaison

A On prend le train. Complétez.

1. Jacques _____ le train. (prendre)
2. Jacques et ses copains _____ le train. (prendre)
3. Ils _____ au bord de la mer. (aller)
4. Ils _____ le train dans la salle d'attente. (attendre)
5. Jacques _____ au guichet. (aller)
6. Au guichet il _____ les billets pour tous ses copains. (prendre)
7. Les copains _____ l'annonce du départ du train. (entendre)
8. Ils _____ l'annonce. (comprendre)
9. Ils _____ sur le quai. (aller)
10. Ils _____ dans le train. (monter)
11. Ils _____ à la prochaine gare. (descendre)
12. Ils _____ à Deauville à quatorze heures dix-huit. (arriver)

La plage de Deauville en Normandie

Vocabulaire

NOMS
l'été (m.)
la station balnéaire
le bord de la mer
la plage
le sable
la mer
la vague
la crème solaire
les lunettes (f.) de soleil
le maillot (de bain)
la natation
la piscine
la leçon
le moniteur

le tennis
le court de tennis
la balle
le filet
la raquette
le match
le joueur
la partie (en simple, en double)
les limites (f.)
le score
les chaussures (f.) de tennis
le tee-shirt

le short
la jupette

ADJECTIFS
aérien(ne)
bon(ne)
canadien(ne)
européen(ne)
gentil(le)
italien(ne)
parisien(ne)

VERBES
bronzer
frapper
gagner
jouer à
nager
plonger
renvoyer
apprendre (à)
comprendre
prendre

AUTRES MOTS ET EXPRESSIONS
faire de la planche à voile
faire de la plongée sous-marine
faire du ski nautique

faire du surf
faire une promenade
aller à la pêche
attraper un coup de soleil
prendre le petit déjeuner
prendre un bain de soleil
prendre un billet
Il faut + infinitif
entre
fort
hors des limites

pourquoi
parce que

Quel temps fait-il?
Il fait beau.
Il fait chaud.
Il fait du soleil.
Il fait froid.
Il fait mauvais.
Il fait du vent.
Il pleut.
Il y a des nuages.

OPTIONAL MATERIAL

Réintroduction et recombinaison

PRESENTATION *(page 255)*

Exercise A recycles the forms of the regular -re verbs and the three irregular ones introduced in this chapter. It also recycles *aller* and regular -er verbs. You may wish to refer students to appropriate pages in their book to look for sample answers to items with which they have trouble.

ANSWERS
Exercice A
1. prend
2. prennent
3. vont
4. attendent
5. va
6. prend
7. entendent
8. comprennent
9. vont
10. montent
11. descendent
12. arrivent

ASSESSMENT RESOURCES

1. Chapter Quizzes
2. Testing Program
3. Situation Cards
4. Communication Transparency C-9
5. Computer Software: Practice/Test Generator

VIDEO PROGRAM

INTRODUCTION   (29:08)

C'EST CHOUETTE,   (29:51)
SAINT-MALO!

LEARNING FROM PHOTOS

You may wish to give the students the words for "beach (or deck) chair" and "beach umbrella": *un transat, un parasol.*

STUDENT PORTFOLIO

Written assignments that may be included in students' portfolios are *Activité de communication écrite A* on page 254 and the *Mon Autobiographie* section of the Workbook on page 91.

Note Students may create and save both oral and written work using the Electronic Portfolio feature on the CD-ROM.

CHAPTER OVERVIEW

In this chapter students will learn to identify and describe articles of clothing, to talk about what they and others wear for different occasions, and to communicate in various situations that arise when shopping for clothes. They will learn to make observations and express opinions using comparative and superlative statements about people and things. In addition, students will learn to use and conjugate verbs such as *croire* and *voir*.

The cultural focus of Chapter 10 is on clothing stores in France, ranging from the boutiques of the *hauts couturiers* to the stalls at the flea markets (*marchés aux puces*).

CHAPTER OBJECTIVES

By the end of this chapter, students will know:

1. vocabulary associated with clothing and its description, including size and color
2. some basic vocabulary and structures necessary for locating items and speaking with salespeople in various types of apparel stores
3. the use of the adverb *trop* in qualitative constructions
4. the present indicative forms of the verbs *croire* and *voir*
5. some adjectives with irregular forms
6. the formation and use of the comparative
7. the formation and use of the superlative

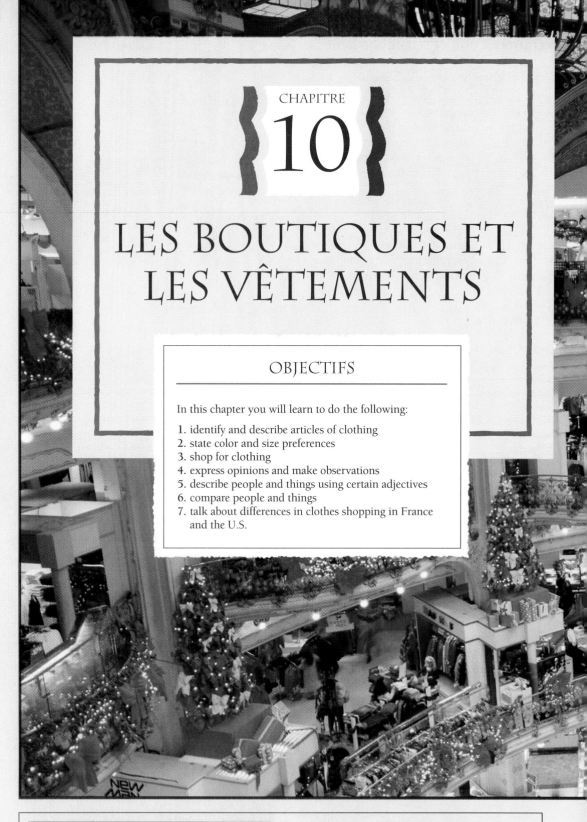

CHAPITRE

{ **10** }

LES BOUTIQUES ET LES VÊTEMENTS

OBJECTIFS

In this chapter you will learn to do the following:

1. identify and describe articles of clothing
2. state color and size preferences
3. shop for clothing
4. express opinions and make observations
5. describe people and things using certain adjectives
6. compare people and things
7. talk about differences in clothes shopping in France and the U.S.

CHAPTER PROJECTS

(optional)

1. Encourage students to watch any fashion-oriented television shows that are aired in your area. Have them write down any French words they hear to share with the class.
2. Do a group research project on fashion designers, with each group studying a different designer. Students can focus on such information as when and how the designer started in the industry; if he/she is alive today; what defines the particular label of the designer; what each house is most famous for; if the house designs anything besides clothing. You may want to include American designers as well as European ones.

257

Pacing

This chapter requires eight to ten class sessions. Pacing will depend on class length and the age and aptitude of the students.

Note The Lesson Plans offer guidelines for 45- and 55-minute classes and **Block Scheduling**.

Exercices vs. Activités

All exercises (which provide guided practice) are coded in blue. All communicative activities are coded in red.

INTERNET ACTIVITIES

(optional)

These activities, student worksheets, and related teacher information are in the *Bienvenue* Internet Activities Booklet and on the Glencoe Foreign Language Home Page at http://www.glencoe.com/secondary/fl

LEARNING FROM PHOTOS

Tell students: *C'est un grand magasin à Paris, les Galeries Lafayette. Le magasin est très joli, n'est-ce pas? Il est décoré pour Noël. Ça, c'est un arbre de Noël. C'est quel mois?*

Bell Ringer Review

Write the following on the board or use BRR Blackline Master 10-1: Make a list in French of as many articles of clothing as you know.

PRESENTATION *(pages 258–259)*

A. Identify items of clothing students are actually wearing. Have the class repeat each item after you once or twice. Ask *Qu'est-ce que c'est?* and have a student respond.

B. Show Vocabulary Transparencies 10.1 (A & B). Have students repeat each item after you or Cassette 6B/CD-6.

C. Ask questions about the material on page 259, referring to the Vocabulary Transparencies. For example: *Lise est une cliente ou une vendeuse? Elle est à quel rayon? Qu'est-ce qu'elle regarde? Qu'est-ce que le garçon regarde? Où est-ce que Madame Laval paie? Combien coûtent les chaussettes? Et le chemisier?*

VOCABULAIRE

MOTS 1

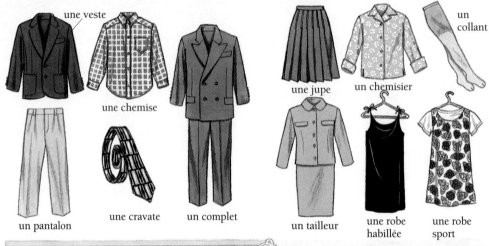

LES VÊTEMENTS POUR HOMMES

une veste
une chemise
un pantalon
une cravate
un complet

LES VÊTEMENTS POUR FEMMES

une jupe
un chemisier
un collant
un tailleur
une robe habillée
une robe sport

un blouson
un pull
une chaussette
un jean
une paire de chaussures

Marc porte un sweat-shirt.

LAURENT

la boutique d'un grand couturier

TOTAL PHYSICAL RESPONSE

(following the Vocabulary presentation)

Getting Ready

Dramatize the meaning of *enlevez*.

TPR 1
(Student 1), **venez ici, s'il vous plaît.**
Vous êtes au rayon des blousons.
Cherchez un joli blouson.
Prenez le blouson.

Essayez le blouson. Mettez le blouson.
Allez au miroir.
Regardez-vous dans le miroir.
Admirez-vous.
Indiquez que vous aimez le blouson.
Et maintenant, enlevez le blouson.
(Student 2), **venez ici, s'il vous plaît.**
Vous êtes le caissier/la caissière.
Allez à la caisse.
Et (Student 1), allez à la caisse aussi.
(continued on next page)

AU GRAND MAGASIN

des soldes

un vendeur

une vendeuse

~~350F~~
SOLDES
270F

un rayon prêt-à-porter

un client

Lise voit beaucoup de chemisiers.
Elle voit les chemisiers au rayon
prêt-à-porter.
Elle va faire ses achats au rayon
prêt-à-porter.

une cliente

le prix

moins
cher

100F

1000F

plus cher

bon marché

25F

240F

cher

Mme Laval paie à la caisse.
Elle dépense* de l'argent.

* dépenser: employer de l'argent pour
faire des achats

D. Play a game using the new vocabulary. One student describes what someone in the class is wearing and calls on classmates to guess who is being described.

Extension of D Recycle earlier vocabulary by having students describe the person as well as what that person is wearing.

E. Ask personal questions about yourself and students such as: *Qui porte une jupe aujourd'hui? Je porte une cravate? Marie porte un pantalon ou une robe?* After a few such examples, see if volunteers can come up with similar questions.

CROSS-CULTURAL COMPARISON

Note the invariable adjective *sport (une robe sport)* and the adjective *habillée (une robe habillée)*. There is no precise French word that conveys the English "formal" or "dressy" in regard to clothing. *Habillé* is the closest approximation to "formal." Another word students will encounter frequently, if they peruse magazines, is *décontracté,* which conveys the English "casual," "informal."

Vocabulary Expansion

Many other articles of clothing will be presented in later chapters as they are needed. It is therefore recommended that you not give students an extensive list of additional vocabulary now. You may, however, wish to give them the names of a few accessories.
une ceinture
une montre
un bracelet
une bague
une boucle d'oreille

TPR (continued)
Sortez de l'argent de votre poche.
Donnez de l'argent au caissier/à la caissière.
(Student 2), mettez le blouson dans un sac.
Donnez le sac au client/à la cliente.
(Student 1), prenez le sac.
Merci (Student 1) et (Student 2). Retournez
à vos places, s'il vous plaît.

Exercices

PRESENTATION (pages 260–261)

Extension of *Exercice A*

After completing Exercise A, have students say what Albert is wearing now. Have students name articles of clothing that Christine is not wearing now.

***Exercice B*: Paired Activity**

Have students practice both listening and speaking by doing Exercise B in pairs. One partner reads the questions in random order while the other listens and answers with his/her book closed. Then partners switch roles. Or you can have one student read the questions to the entire class and then call on individuals to respond.

ANSWERS

Exercice A

1. Albert va mettre une cravate, une veste, un pantalon, une chemise, des chaussettes et des (une paire de) chaussures.
2. Christine porte un jean, un pull, un blouson, des chaussettes et des (une paire de) chaussures (de tennis).

Exercice B

Answers will vary.

Exercices

A **Albert et Christine.** Répondez d'après les dessins.

1. Qu'est-ce qu'Albert va mettre?
2. Qu'est-ce que Christine porte?

B **Qu'est-ce qu'on met?** Répondez.

1. Ce soir M. Ben-Azar va aller dans un restaurant élégant. Qu'est-ce qu'il va porter?
2. Qu'est-ce que sa femme va mettre?
3. Qu'est-ce que tu portes à l'école?
4. Qu'est-ce que tu portes quand il n'y a pas de cours?
5. Qu'est-ce que tu mets quand il fait froid?
6. Qu'est-ce qu'une femme met quand elle va au travail?
7. Qu'est-ce qu'un homme met quand il va au travail?

REVUE DE DÉTAILS

NEWS MODE REPÉRÉ AUX QUATRE COIN DE LA MODE, TOUT CE QU PLAÎT. DE LA TÊTE AUX PIED

STRETCH (1) Robe en panne de velours (Capucine Puerari, 1 360 F, 5 tailles, 8 coloris, rens. 45 49 26 90).
SOIR CHIC (2) Veste croisée, en drap de laine, sur jupe en taffetas de soie (Corinne Sarrut, 1 900 F, 3 tailles, 5 coloris (veste) et 900 F, du 36 au 42, en noir ou bronze (jupe), rens. 42 61 71 60). Gilet en satin (Chacok).
INTÉRIEUR (3) Robe de chambre en soie (Claudie Pierlot, 800 F, 2 tailles, 3 coloris, rens. 42 36 69 93).

COL HIRONDELLE Très 70, des chemises bicolo (Agnès B., 490 F, 3 tailles, 3 coloris, rens. 45

COLORISSIMO (1) Chemise en satin de soie

LEARNING FROM REALIA	ADDITIONAL PRACTICE
1. Ask students to look at the advertisement. Ask them to find as many English words as they can. 2. Have students find as many cognates as they can.	Student Tape Manual, Teacher's Edition, *Activités B–C*, pages 111–112.

C Une boutique ou un grand magasin? Répondez.

1. On vend beaucoup de marchandises différentes dans la boutique d'un grand couturier ou dans un grand magasin?
2. Il y a beaucoup de rayons dans une boutique ou dans un grand magasin?
3. Qui vend des marchandises dans les boutiques et les grands magasins?
4. Et qui fait des achats?
5. Où est-ce qu'on paie dans les boutiques et les grands magasins?
6. Est-ce que les femmes riches achètent leurs vêtements au rayon prêt-à-porter ou chez les grands couturiers?
7. Est-ce qu'on peut acheter des vêtements sport et habillés dans un grand magasin?
8. Est-ce que les gens riches dépensent beaucoup d'argent pour leurs vêtements?

D On va acheter des vêtements. Complétez.

1. Il y a beaucoup de réductions pendant les ___. Les prix sont plus bas, moins élevés.
2. Je préfère faire mes achats quand il y a des ___ parce que je ___ moins d'argent.
3. Le jean est une sorte de ___ sport, pas habillé.
4. Quel est le ___ de ce blouson? 800 francs?
5. Oh là là! Ce blouson n'est pas bon marché! Il est très ___.

AN LACROIX

LEARNING FROM PHOTOS

You may wish to ask: *C'est une boutique élégante? C'est la boutique de quel grand couturier? On vend quelle sorte de vêtements ici? Est-ce que les vêtements sont en solde? Ils sont chers ou bon marché?*

INDEPENDENT PRACTICE

Assign any of the following:
1. Exercises, pages 260–261
2. Workbook, *Mots 1: A–C,* pages 92–93
3. Communication Activities Masters, *Mots 1: A,* page 47
4. CD-ROM, Disc 3, pages 258–261

PRESENTATION *(page 261)*
Exercice C

You may wish to go over Exercise C orally first and then reinforce it as a reading activity with books open.

ANSWERS
Exercice C

1. On vend beaucoup de marchandises différentes dans un grand magasin.
2. Il y a beaucoup de rayons dans un grand magasin.
3. Les vendeurs et les vendeuses vendent des marchandises.
4. Les client(e)s font des achats.
5. On paie à la caisse.
6. Les femmes riches achètent leurs vêtements chez les grands couturiers.
7. Oui, on peut acheter des vêtements sport et habillés dans un grand magasin.
8. Oui, les gens riches dépensent beaucoup d'argent pour leurs vêtements.

Exercice D

1. soldes
2. soldes, dépense
3. pantalon (vêtement)
4. prix
5. cher

INFORMAL ASSESSMENT
(Mots 1)

Check for comprehension by using Vocabulary Transparencies 10.1. Call individuals to the screen. As classmates say words or expressions from *Mots 1,* the student at the screen points to the appropriate image.

RETEACHING *(Mots 1)*

Have students open their books to page 258 and write down what they wear when they do the following things.
dîner en ville
jouer au tennis
aller au café
aller à l'école
travailler à plein temps

MOTS 2

Bell Ringer Review

Write the following on the board or use BRR Blackline Master 10-2: Name five articles of clothing a boy and girl would wear for a job interview.

PRESENTATION *(pages 262–263)*

A. For an activity that's fun, you may wish to bring articles of old clothing to class, or have students bring in articles of old clothing. Have students put on the wrong sizes to convey *large, serré, étroit, long, court, haut, bas.* They should say the appropriate phrase: *Je voudrais la taille au-dessus* or *Je voudrais la taille au-dessous.*

B. Have students open their books and repeat the vocabulary after you or Cassette 6B/CD-6.

C. Model the conversation at the top of page 262. Then have volunteers perform it as a demonstration of *trop* and the various adjectives, substituting different articles of clothing and sizes. Use American sizes here.

MOTS 2

Ce pantalon est trop grand. Il est trop large. Je voudrais la taille au-dessous.

Ce pantalon est trop petit. Il est trop serré. Je voudrais la taille au-dessus.

un talon bas

un talon haut

des chaussures étroites

des chaussures larges

Vous faites quelle pointure?

Je fais du 38.

Vous faites quelle taille?

Je fais du 40.

262   CHAPITRE 10

TOTAL PHYSICAL RESPONSE

(following the Vocabulary presentation)

Note You may vary the articles of clothing below and their colors according to what the students are wearing.

TPR
Attention, tout le monde. Si vous portez le vêtement que je mentionne, levez-vous.
Je vois un pantalon blanc.

Je vois un sweat-shirt noir.
Je vois une chemise bleue.
Je vois un tee-shirt rouge.
Je vois une jupe verte.
Je vois un short beige.
Je vois un jean noir.
Merci bien, tout le monde! Asseyez-vous.

un cadeau

une manche longue

un chemisier
à manches
longues

une manche courte

Martine voit des chemisiers.
Elle trouve les chemisiers merveilleux, vraiment fantastiques!
Elle pense: «Tiens! Je vais acheter un cadeau.»

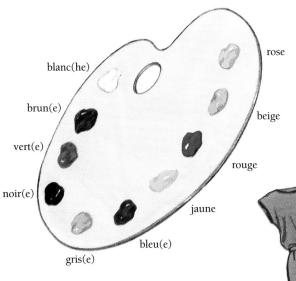

blanc(he)

rose

brun(e)

beige

vert(e)

rouge

noir(e)

jaune

bleu(e)

gris(e)

À mon avis cette couleur est plue jolie que l'autre.
Je trouve que cette couleur est plus jolie que l'autre.
Et je crois que Catherine préfère cette couleur aussi.

Elle est très contente (heureuse).
Pourquoi? Parce qu'elle voit que les chemisiers sont en solde.

De quelle couleur est le chemisier?
Il est vert.

Note: The colors below are invariable. They do not change to agree with the noun they describe.

**bleu marine
marron
orange**

une robe orange

un pantalon
bleu marine

des chaussures marron

100 F

Quelle taille de chemise fais-tu, Marc? (Je fais du 14.) Voici la taille 16. Tu veux acheter cette chemise? (Non. Elle est trop grande.)

D. Go around the room and describe some of the articles of clothing students are wearing: *des chaussures à talons bas (hauts), une chemise à manches longues (courtes).*

E. Ask the following questions about the sentences on page 263: *Qu'est-ce que Martine voit? Elle porte un chemisier à manches longues ou courtes? Elle aime les chemisiers? Elle trouve les chemisiers fantastiques? Qu'est-ce qu'elle va acheter? Les chemisiers sont en solde? Martine est contente? Pourquoi?*

F. Use the overhead transparency to teach the colors. Have the students repeat each color twice.

G. Then go around the room and have students tell the color of articles of clothing other students are wearing: *De quelle couleur est le chemisier de ___?*

Note Emphasize that the following colors, which are often used to describe clothes, are invariable: *bleu marine, marron, orange.* They do not agree with the feminine or plural noun they describe.

Vocabulary Expansion

1. Students tend to enjoy the sound of the popular French word *moche.* Make a face as you say *moche, pas chouette.* Have students tell you things they think are *moche* and things they think are *chouette.*

2. You may wish to give students the following additional vocabulary to allow them to talk about colors. Note that all of these adjectives are invariable.

crème	**sable**
bordeaux	**olive**
café	**kaki**
écru	**saumon**

COOPERATIVE LEARNING

Have students work in groups. Each group makes a list of several people that everyone in the group knows. The people can be celebrities or classmates who are not in the room. Then each student chooses one of the people and describes what that person is probably wearing today. The other students try to guess who it is, choosing from the list.

Exercices

PRESENTATION (*pages 264–265*)

Extension of *Exercice A*

After completing Exercise A, have students write three questions about the *Mots 2* vocabulary that require negative answers. Then they ask their questions of a partner.

Extension of *Exercice B*

With more able groups you may wish to present the noun forms of colors: *Tu préfères quelle couleur? Moi, je préfère le bleu. Pour une chemise, je préfère le blanc.*

Extension of *Exercice C*

After completing Exercise C, have students quickly write a description of a really ridiculous outfit. Call on volunteers to read their description to the class.

ANSWERS

Exercice A

1. Martine veut acheter un chemisier.
2. Oui, elle aime les chemisiers.
3. Oui, elle trouve que les chemisiers sont merveilleux, vraiment fantastiques.
4. Oui, Martine voit que les chemisiers sont en solde.

Exercice B

Answers will vary.

Exercice C

1. Ces chaussures sont trop étroites.
2. Cette jupe est trop courte.
3. Cette chemise a des manches longues.
4. Ce pantalon est large.

Exercices

A **Qu'est-ce que Martine voit?** Répondez.

1. Qu'est-ce que Martine veut acheter?
2. Elle aime les chemisiers?
3. Elle trouve que les chemisiers sont merveilleux, vraiment fantastiques?
4. Est-ce que Martine voit que les chemisiers sont en solde?

B **De quelle couleur… ?** Donnez des réponses personnelles.

1. De quelle couleur est ton blouson favori?
2. De quelle couleur est ton jean favori?
3. De quelle couleur est ta chemise favorite ou ton chemisier favori?
4. Qu'est-ce que tu portes aujourd'hui? De quelle couleur sont tes vêtements?

C **De petits problèmes.** Répondez d'après les dessins.

1. Ces chaussures sont trop larges ou trop étroites?

2. Cette jupe est trop longue ou trop courte?

3. Cette chemise a des manches longues ou courtes?

4. Ce pantalon est serré ou large?

ADDITIONAL PRACTICE

Student Tape Manual, Teacher's Edition, *Activités E–G*, pages 113–114.

PAIRED ACTIVITIES

1. Each student describes the color of his or her clothing. If they are both wearing the same thing, they will say, *Nous deux, nous portons…*
2. Each student makes a list of articles of clothing. Then they combine their lists. Working together, they categorize the clothing under the headings *Sport* and *Habillé*.

D **Mes préférences.** Donnez des réponses personnelles.

1. Tu préfères des vêtements sport ou habillés?
2. Tu préfères des chaussures à talons bas ou hauts? Tu fais quelle pointure?
3. Tu préfères une chemise ou un chemisier à manches longues ou courtes?
4. Tu préfères tes vêtements un peu serrés ou larges?
5. Tu préfères un pantalon plus large? Tu voudrais la taille au-dessus?
6. Tu préfères un pantalon plus serré? Tu voudrais la taille au-dessous?
7. Tu préfères faire des achats quand il y a des soldes ou pas?
8. Tu aimes dépenser beaucoup d'argent pour tes vêtements?
9. Tu aimes acheter des cadeaux pour tes copains ou tes copines? Qu'est-ce que tu achètes?

Activités de communication orale
Mots 1 et 2

A **Qui est-ce?** Work with a classmate. One of you describes what someone in the class is wearing and the other has to guess who it is. Take turns.

B **Une paire de chaussures.** You're in a shoe store in Montreal. Tell the salesperson (your partner) what kind of shoes you want and what size you wear. You try on several pairs before you find the right shoes in the right size at the right price, but the salesperson is very patient.

C **Qui porte… ?** Work with a classmate. One of you names an article of clothing and the other has to say who wears it (men, women, or both) and when or where they wear it. Take turns.

> Élève 1: un blouson
> Élève 2: Les hommes et les femmes portent un blouson quand il fait froid.

D **Les grands couturiers.** Imagine you and your classmates are costume designers working on a new movie starring two of your favorite actors. You need to create outfits for the stars to wear in various scenes. One person suggests an article of clothing in a certain color, and the next person repeats the item and adds another. Take turns until you have a complete outfit for each star.

Exercice D
Answers will vary.

Activités de communication orale
Mots 1 et 2
PRESENTATION *(page 265)*
Activités A, B, C, and D

The *Activités de communication orale* allow students to use the chapter vocabulary and grammar in open-ended situations. It is not necessary to do all the activities. You may select those that are most appropriate for your students.

ANSWERS
Activité A
Answers will vary.

Activité B
Answers will vary, but may include the following:

É1: Bonjour, Monsieur (Mademoiselle, Madame). Je voudrais des (une paire de) chaussures noires très habillées. Je fais du 38.

É2: Voici une paire de chaussures très élégantes en 38.

É1: Elles sont trop étroites. Je voudrais la pointure au-dessus.

É2: Voilà la pointure au-dessus.

É1: Elles coûtent combien, ces chaussures? Elles sont en solde?

É2: Elles coûtent 500F. Elles ne sont pas en solde.

É1: C'est trop cher. Je voudrais voir une autre paire de chaussures. (Etc.)

Activités C and D
Answers will vary.

LEARNING FROM REALIA

Tell the students to study the shirt carefully. It contains some cute statements. Have the students find them. For example: **J'aime jouer au grand air. Un sportif reste toujours jeune! Excellente idée, allons faire une course de natation. Voilà l'été qui approche. Vive le sport!**

INDEPENDENT PRACTICE

Assign any of the following:
1. Exercises and activities, pages 264–265
2. Workbook, *Mots 2: D–H*, pages 93–95
3. Communication Activities Masters, *Mots 2: B*, page 48
4. Computer Software, *Vocabulaire*
5. CD-ROM, Disc 3, pages 262–265

Structure Teaching Resources

1. Workbook, *Structure: A-K*, pages 96–101
2. Student Tape Manual, Teacher's Edition, *Structure: A–C*, page 115
3. Audio Cassette 6B/CD-6
4. Communication Activities Masters, *Structure: A–D*, pages 49–53
5. Computer Software, *Structure*
6. Chapter Quizzes, *Structure:* Quizzes 3–6, pages 55–58
7. CD-ROM, Disc 3, pages 266–271

Bell Ringer Review

Write the following on the board or use BRR Blackline Master 10-3: Give the opposite of each word:

1. **serré**
2. **étroit**
3. **long**
4. **petit**
5. **cher**
6. **au-dessous**

Les verbes croire *et* voir *au présent*

PRESENTATION *(page 266)*

A. *Croire* and *voir* can be done quickly since there are only three oral forms.

B. Lead students through steps 1–2. Write a few examples on the board and explain: *Une proposition, c'est un groupe de mots qui a un sujet et un verbe.* Ask volunteers for other examples, first of clauses, then of sentences with *croire* or *voir* + a clause.

Exercices

ANSWERS

Exercice A

Answers will vary but will begin with *Elles voient.*

STRUCTURE

Les verbes *croire* et *voir* au présent

Expressing Opinions and Making Observations

1. Study the following forms of the irregular verbs *croire*, "to think," "to believe," and *voir*, "to see."

CROIRE		VOIR	
je	crois	je	vois
tu	crois	tu	vois
il / elle / on	croit	il / elle / on	voit
nous	croyons	nous	voyons
vous	croyez	vous	voyez
ils / elles	croient	ils / elles	voient

2. The verbs *croire* and *voir* are often followed by a clause. The clause is introduced by *que* which is shortened to *qu'* before a vowel or a silent *h*. In French you must use *que* even though its equivalent, "that," is often omitted in English.

Je crois que c'est une bonne idée.
Je vois qu'elle aime cette boutique.

Exercices

A Qu'est-ce qu'elles voient?
Qu'est-ce qu'Annick et Claire voient dans la vitrine de la boutique?

ADDITIONAL PRACTICE

After completing Exercises A–E, reinforce the lesson with the following: Have students use the following cues to write sentences with *croire*. For example: *un chanteur/une chanteuse chouette (Je crois qu' Alanis Morrissette est une chanteuse chouette!)*

1. **un cours intéressant**
2. **un film horrible**
3. **un livre intéressant**
4. **un chanteur chouette**
5. **une actrice extraordinaire**
6. **un bel acteur**
7. **une belle actrice**

B La fête. Répondez d'après le modèle.

> Il va faire beau demain soir?
> *Oui, je crois. Toi, tu ne crois pas?*

1. Il faut porter une robe habillée à la fête?
2. David va inviter Sylvie à la fête?
3. La fête va être amusante?
4. On va servir un gâteau énorme?
5. L'appartement de David est assez grand pour la fête?

C Tu vois des films? Donnez des réponses personnelles.

1. Tu vois beaucoup de films?
2. Tu vois des films au cinéma ou à la télé?
3. En général, tu vois des films d'horreur, des films d'aventures ou des films d'amour?
4. Tes parents voient souvent des films?
5. Tu vois tes copains pendant le week-end? Qu'est-ce que tu fais avec eux?

D Les opinions. Répondez par «oui».

> Tes copains et toi, vous croyez que le tennis est un sport merveilleux?
> *Oui, nous croyons que le tennis est un sport merveilleux.*

1. Vous croyez que Paris est une belle ville?
2. Vos parents croient que vous êtes intelligents?
3. Votre professeur de français croit que vous travaillez bien?
4. Vos amis croient que vous êtes sympathiques?
5. Vous croyez que les jeans sont chic?
6. Vos grands-parents croient que vous êtes adorables?

E Des opinions différentes! Complétez avec «croire».

1. Moi, je ___ que la cousine de Sandra est française mais mes copains ___ qu'elle est italienne.
2. Le professeur ___ que l'examen va être facile mais les élèves ___ que l'examen va être difficile.
3. Tu ___ que les chats sont plus intelligents que les chiens mais ton frère ___ que les chiens sont plus intelligents que les chats.
4. Hélène ___ que Paris est près de Nice mais nous ___ que c'est assez loin de Nice.
5. Tu ___ qu'il va pleuvoir mais je ___ qu'il va faire beau.

GALERIES Lafayette

Le Grand Magasin Capitale de la Mode.

267

D'autres adjectifs irréguliers

PRESENTATION *(page 268)*

A. Have students close their books and repeat after you only the singular forms of the adjectives in the chart. Start with the feminine forms since students tend to have an easier time dropping the final sound. Then have students open their books and read aloud the four forms of each adjective.

B. Now lead students through step 2 on page 268, modeling the pronunciation and having students repeat chorally.

C. Demonstrate some of the adjectives by using them in questions. For example: *Marie, tu es sérieuse? Henri, tu es sérieux? Isabelle, qui est le premier garçon dans ce rang? Et qui est la première fille?*

Exercices

ANSWERS

Exercice A

Students use the correct pronunciation.

Exercice B

1. Oui, Nathalie est sportive.
2. Oui, son frère est sportif.
3. Oui, Nathalie est active.
4. Oui, il est actif.
5. Oui, le rouge est la couleur favorite de Nathalie.
6. Oui, la planche à voile est son sport favori.
7. Oui, Nathalie est sérieuse.
8. Oui, son frère est un garçon sérieux.
9. Oui, elle est souvent heureuse.
10. Oui, il est souvent heureux.

1. In spoken French the feminine forms of the adjective end in a consonant sound. This consonant sound is dropped in the masculine forms. Here are some irregular adjectives that follow this pattern. Note their spelling changes.

FÉMININ PLURIEL	FÉMININ SINGULIER	MASCULIN PLURIEL	MASCULIN SINGULIER
sérieuses	sérieuse	sérieux	sérieux
délicieuses	délicieuse	délicieux	délicieux
heureuses	heureuse	heureux	heureux
merveilleuses	merveilleuse	merveilleux	merveilleux
basses	basse	bas	bas
favorites	favorite	favoris	favori
longues	longue	longs	long
premières	première	premiers	premier
dernières	dernière	derniers	dernier
entières	entière	entiers	entier
chères*	chère	chers	cher

*All forms of *cher* are pronounced the same way.

2. Here are two adjectives whose endings are pronounced in both the feminine and masculine forms. Note that the feminine ending has a softer sound than the masculine one.

sportives	**sportive**	**sportifs**	**sportif**
actives	**active**	**actifs**	**actif**

Exercices

A **La prononciation.** Prononcez.

1. active / actif
2. favorite / favori
3. longue / long
4. basse / bas
5. merveilleuse / merveilleux
6. délicieuse / délicieux
7. généreuse / généreux
8. première / premier

B **Nathalie et son frère.** Répondez par «oui».

1. Nathalie est sportive?
2. Son frère est sportif?
3. Nathalie est active?
4. Et lui, il est actif?
5. Le rouge est la couleur favorite de Nathalie?
6. La planche à voile est son sport favori?
7. Nathalie est sérieuse?
8. Et son frère est un garçon sérieux?
9. Elle est souvent heureuse?
10. Et lui, il est souvent heureux?

268 CHAPITRE 10

C **La famille Beauchamp.** Complétez.

La famille Beauchamp est très ___(1)___ (sportif). Les parents sont très ___(2)___ (actif) et les deux enfants, Véronique et Nicole, sont ___(3)___ (actif) aussi. Aujourd'hui, les deux filles sont très ___(4)___ (heureux) parce qu'elles partent pour Biarritz, leur station balnéaire ___(5)___ (favori), où chaque année la famille passe des vacances ___(6)___ (merveilleux). À Biarritz, les filles et les parents vont pratiquer leurs sports ___(7)___ (favori), la planche à voile et la natation. Après de ___(8)___ (long) journées à la plage, tout le monde est content de manger des fruits de mer ___(9)___ (délicieux) à la terrasse d'un restaurant.

Le comparatif des adjectifs — *Comparing People and Things*

1. You use the comparative to compare two or more people or things. The following words are used to express comparisons.

> (+) *plus... que*
> (−) *moins... que*
> (=) *aussi... que*

Study the following sentences.

> Cette vendeuse est plus sympathique que l'autre vendeuse.
> Ce blouson est moins cher que la veste.
> Les chaussures américaines sont aussi chères que les chaussures françaises.

2. Note the liaison after *plus* and *moins* when they are followed by a vowel.

> plus intéressant
> moins élégant

3. If you are comparing people, you use the stress pronouns after *que*.

> Il est plus jeune que son ami.   Il est plus jeune que *lui*.
> Elle est plus âgée que ses amis.   Elle est plus âgée qu'*eux*.

4. Note that the adjective *bon* has an irregular form in the comparative, *meilleur*.

> Ils trouvent que le pain français est meilleur que le pain américain.
> La robe rose est meilleur marché que la robe blanche.

INDEPENDENT PRACTICE

Assign any of the following:
1. Exercises, pages 268–269
2. Workbook, *Structure: D–G*, pages 97–98
3. Communication Activities Masters, *Structure: B*, page 51
4. CD-ROM, Disc 3, pages 268–269

LEARNING FROM PHOTOS

Ask students: *C'est une robe habillée ou sport? De quelles couleurs est la robe? La robe est belle, à votre avis? Vous aimez cette sorte de robe? À votre avis, elle coûte cher?*

PRESENTATION (*page 269*)
Exercice C
Call on several students or just one student to do Exercise C. Then call on another student to tell the story in his or her own words.

ANSWERS
Exercice C
1. sportive
2. actifs
3. actives
4. heureuses
5. favorite
6. merveilleuses
7. favoris
8. longues
9. délicieux

RETEACHING
Using the list of adjectives on page 268, have students give nouns that can be used with each adjective. Then have them make up original sentences using the adjectives and the nouns.

> **Bell Ringer Review**
> *Write the following on the board or use BRR Blackline Master 10-5:* Give two nouns that can be used with each adjective.
> 1. première   3. actif
> 2. basse   4. délicieux

Le comparatif des adjectifs

PRESENTATION (*page 269*)
A. Lead students through steps 1–4 and the examples.
B. Now have students make a list of words they know that can be used to describe people.
C. Draw two stick figures on the board and name them. Using their list of adjectives, have students make up sentences comparing the two stick figures.
D. Provide additional examples by comparing objects or students in the room. For example: *Regardez. Roland est plus grand que Pierre ou pas? (Oui, Roland est plus grand que Pierre.)*

Exercices

Exercices

A **Plus ou moins que l'autre.** Répondez d'après les dessins. Suivez le modèle.

Le blouson bleu est aussi long que le blouson noir?
Oui, le blouson bleu est aussi long que le blouson noir.

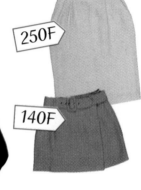

450F

250F

140F

400F

1. Le blouson bleu est plus cher que le blouson noir?
2. Le blouson bleu est moins joli que le blouson noir?
3. La jupe jaune est moins chère que la jupe grise?
4. La jupe grise est plus courte que la jupe jaune?
5. La robe verte est aussi élégante que la robe rouge?
6. La robe verte est moins habillée que la robe rouge?

B **Non, pas plus.** Répondez d'après le modèle.

Cette chemise est plus chère que l'autre?
Non, elle n'est pas plus chère. Mais elle est aussi chère que l'autre.

1. Cette cravate est plus chère que l'autre?
2. Cette robe est plus habillée que l'autre?
3. Ce pull est plus cher que l'autre?
4. Ce chemisier est plus serré que l'autre?
5. Ces chaussures sont plus larges que les autres?
6. Ces manches sont plus courtes que les autres?

C **À mon avis.** Donnez des réponses personnelles.

1. Le cours de français est plus difficile ou plus facile que le cours de maths?
2. Le professeur de français est plus sévère, moins sévère ou aussi sévère que les autres professeurs?
3. Le football américain est plus intéressant ou moins intéressant que le basket-ball?
4. Une Volkswagen est moins chère ou plus chère qu'une Porsche?
5. Le coca est meilleur que le lait ou le lait est meilleur que le coca?
6. Les fruits et les légumes sont meilleurs pour la santé *(health)* que les pâtisseries?

270   CHAPITRE 10

270

Le superlatif — *Comparing People and Things*

1. You use the superlative to single out one item from the group and compare it to all the others. You form the superlative in French by using *le, la,* or *les* and *plus* or *moins* with the adjective.

> Cette robe est *la plus jolie* de la boutique.
> Cette robe est *la moins chère* de la boutique.

2. Note that the superlative is followed by *de* + a noun.

> Robert est le plus intelligent de la classe.
> Carole est la meilleure en maths du lycée.
> Les frères Dumas sont les plus amusants de tous les élèves.

Exercices

A   La plus chère et la plus grande. Répondez d'après les indications.

1. Quelle boutique est la plus chère de toute la ville? (cette boutique)
2. Quelle ville est la plus grande de tout le pays? (Paris)
3. Quel magasin est le plus grand du centre commercial? (Monoprix)
4. Quel marché est le moins cher de tous les marchés? (le Village Suisse)
5. Quel couturier est le plus célèbre? (Yves Saint-Laurent)

B   Ma famille. Donnez des réponses personnelles.

1. Qui est le plus jeune ou la plus jeune de ta famille?
2. Qui est le plus âgé ou la plus âgée de ta famille?
3. Qui est le plus amusant ou la plus amusante de ta famille?
4. Qui est le plus intelligent ou la plus intelligente de ta famille?
5. Qui est le plus beau ou la plus belle de ta famille?
6. Qui est le plus timide ou la plus timide de ta famille?
7. Qui est le plus sportif ou la plus sportive de ta famille?
8. Qui est le plus heureux ou la plus heureuse de ta famille?

MONOPRIX
UNIPRIX
On pense à vous tous les jours.

Bell Ringer Review

Write the following on the board or use BRR Blackline Master 10-6: Using the vocabulary you now have for colors and clothes, write four sentences about the people in the Chapter 2, *Mots 1* illustration at the bottom of page 38.

Le superlatif

PRESENTATION (*page 271*)

A. Follow the same suggestions given for presenting the comparative on page 269 of this Teacher's Wraparound Edition.

B. Have students open their books to page 271. Lead them through steps 1 and 2.

C. Tell students that the superlative is followed by *de* in French. Do not explain that it is *de* in French and "in" in English. When this comparison is not made, students tend not to use *dans.*

Note In the CD-ROM version, this structure point is presented via an interactive electronic comic strip.

Exercices

ANSWERS

Exercice A

1. Cette boutique est la plus chère de toute la ville.
2. Paris est la plus grande de tout le pays.
3. Monoprix est le plus grand du centre commercial.
4. Le Village Suisse est le moins cher de tous les marchés.
5. Yves Saint-Laurent est le plus célèbre.

Exercice B
Answers will vary.

ADDITIONAL PRACTICE

1. After completing Exercises A and B on page 271, have students make exaggerated statements using comparative and superlative constructions. They should stick to topics they know in French.
2. Student Tape Manual, Teacher's Edition, *Activités A–C,* page 115

CRITICAL THINKING ACTIVITY

(*Thinking skills: making inferences*)
Tell students to look at the advertisement on this page and answer these questions in French.
1. What do you think Monoprix is? (*un grand magasin*)
2. What do you think the ducks represent? (*une famille*)

Bell Ringer Review

Write the following on the board or use BRR Blackline Master 10-7: Make at least four comparisons between various members of your family.

PRESENTATION *(page 272)*

A. Have students open their books to page 272. Have them look at the photo and guess what the conversation is about.

B. Have them watch the Conversation Video or listen to Cassette 6B/CD-6. Then have the class repeat the conversation after you or the cassette/CD. Call on two individuals to read it aloud with as much expression as possible.

C. Now do the comprehension exercise on this page.

Note In the CD-ROM version, students can play the role of either one of the characters and record the conversation.

ANSWERS

Exercice A

1. Oui, Sandrine est dans un grand magasin.
2. Elle est au rayon chemises.
3. Elle est au rayon hommes.
4. Oui, elle veut acheter un cadeau.
5. Le cadeau est pour son père.
6. La vendeuse propose une chemise.
7. Il fait du quarante.
8. Elle préfère le bleu marine ou le blanc.
9. Oui, les chemises sont en solde.
10. La chemise va être moins chère.

Scènes de la vie   *Un petit cadeau pour Papa*

LA VENDEUSE: Vous désirez, Mademoiselle?

SANDRINE: Je voudrais un petit cadeau pour mon père.

LA VENDEUSE: Pour la Fête des Pères?

SANDRINE: Non, c'est pour son anniversaire.

LA VENDEUSE: Une chemise, peut-être?

SANDRINE: Oui. Pourquoi pas?

LA VENDEUSE: Il fait quelle taille, votre père?

SANDRINE: Il fait du quarante, je crois. Oui, c'est ça, quarante.

LA VENDEUSE: Vous préférez quelle couleur?

SANDRINE: Bleu marine ou blanc. Il aime le look conservateur.

LA VENDEUSE: Bien, Mademoiselle. Et vous avez de la chance. Toutes les chemises sont en solde aujourd'hui.

A   **Un cadeau d'anniversaire.**   Répondez d'après la conversation.

1. Sandrine est dans un grand magasin?
2. Elle est au rayon chemises ou complets?
3. Elle est au rayon hommes ou femmes?
4. Elle veut acheter un cadeau?
5. C'est pour qui, le cadeau?
6. Qu'est-ce que la vendeuse propose?
7. Le père de Sandrine fait quelle taille?
8. Sandrine préfère quelle couleur?
9. Les chemises sont en solde?
10. La chemise va être plus chère ou moins chère?

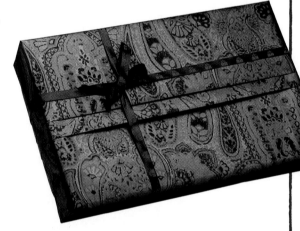

PAIRED ACTIVITY

Have students work in pairs and prepare a skit based on purchasing any item of clothing.

LEARNING FROM PHOTOS

Have students say as much as they can about the *Conversation* photo.

Prononciation   *Les sons /sh/ et /zh/*

It is important to make a distinction between the sound /sh/ as in *chat* and /zh/ as in *joli*. Put your fingers on your throat. When you say the sound /zh/ as in *joli* you should feel a vibration, but not when you say /sh/ as in *chat*. Repeat the following words with the sounds /sh/ and /zh/.

a*ch*eter	lar*ge*
*ch*aussure	*j*upe
*ch*emise	oran*ge*
a*ch*ats	bei*ge*
*sh*ort	*j*eune

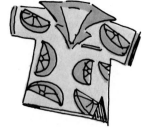

Now repeat the following sentences that combine both sounds.

J'achète toujours des chaussures bon marché.
Je cherche un joli tee-shirt jaune et un short orange.

chemise orange

Activités de communication orale

A **Une boutique chic.**   You're in a boutique on the chic Rue du Faubourg Saint-Honoré in Paris. A salesperson (your partner) greets you. Tell the salesperson what you're looking for. You're a very demanding customer, but after some trial and error the salesperson manages to find something terrific in your size and at a price you can afford.

B **Comparaisons.**   Work in small groups. Use the adjectives below on the right to make as many comparisons as you can about each pair on the left. Compare your results with other groups'.

les chiens et les chats

Les chiens sont plus intelligents (moins calmes, aussi beaux, etc.) que les chats.

l'anglais et les maths	meilleur	intelligent
les avions et les trains	difficile	sympathique
une Rolls-Royce et une Toyota	rapide	actif
notre école et une autre école	cher	sportif
les filles et les garçons	heureux	facile

LECTURE ET CULTURE

LECTURE ET CULTURE

Bell Ringer Review

Write the following on the board or use BRR Blackline Master 10-9: Name the colors associated with each topic.

1. les couleurs de l'automne
2. les couleurs du bord de la mer
3. les couleurs de l'école
4. les couleurs que tu aimes porter

READING STRATEGIES
(page 274)

Pre-reading

A. Ask students whether they spend their own money for clothes. Do they like malls? Why or why not?

B. Share clothing ads from French magazines (*Elle, Marie-Claire, Homme,* etc.) with students.

Reading

A. Have students read the selection once silently.

Teaching Tip Adherence to pre-set time limits will encourage students to read all the material and not get "bogged down" and stop every time they think they don't know something. Encourage students to read for ideas, rather than word by word.

B. Call on a student to read half a paragraph aloud. Ask some comprehension questions.

Post-reading

Call on volunteers to summarize what they've read.

Note Students may listen to a recorded version of the *Lecture* on the CD-ROM.

Étude de mots

ANSWERS

Exercice A

1. b	4. g	6. f
2. c	5. d	7. e
3. a		

274

LES ACHATS

Si la France est un pays de gastronomie, c'est aussi un pays de haute couture. Les noms des grands couturiers sont célèbres dans le monde entier—Yves Saint-Laurent, Dior, Courrèges, Cardin, Givenchy, Lacroix. Ces couturiers dictent la mode non seulement à Paris, mais à Tokyo, New York et Rio. À Paris on vend les vêtements et accessoires de ces couturiers dans des boutiques Place Vendôme, rue du Faubourg Saint-Honoré ou rue François Ier.

Mais attention[1]! La plupart des Français ne font pas leurs achats chez les grands couturiers. Il y a des grands magasins de toutes les catégories, des plus luxueuses aux plus modestes—les Galeries Lafayette, La Samaritaine, Monoprix, Prisunic, etc. Dans les grands magasins on peut aller d'un rayon à l'autre et acheter toutes sortes de choses dans le même magasin. Beaucoup de gens profitent des soldes quand on vend les marchandises avec d'importantes réductions.

À Paris les jeunes—garçons et filles—achètent leurs vêtements dans les mêmes boutiques unisexe du Quartier Latin. Dans ces boutiques on trouve du prêt-à-porter original et à la mode[2]. Mais si on a très peu d'argent à dépenser on peut aller aux Puces[3] ou au Village Suisse. Nicole adore aller aux Puces ou au Village Suisse où elle trouve presque[4] toujours un chemisier ou un accessoire avec la griffe[5] célèbre d'un grand couturier—et à un prix très bas.

[1] Mais attention!   *Careful! Watch out!*
[2] à la mode   *in style*
[3] aux Puces   *to the flea market*
[4] presque   *almost*
[5] griffe   *label*

Étude de mots

A **Cherchez les mots.** Choisissez la définition.

1. le créateur de modèles
2. fameux
3. en vogue, populaire
4. fantastique
5. les produits commerciaux
6. profiter
7. presque toujours

a. à la mode
b. le couturier
c. célèbre
d. les marchandises
e. fréquemment
f. bénéficier
g. merveilleux

274   CHAPITRE 10

ADDITIONAL PRACTICE

After completing the *Étude de mots*, reinforce the lesson with the following:

Have students match each numbered item with its lettered opposite.

1. l'achat
2. bon marché
3. bas
4. vendre
5. différent
6. dépenser

a. haut
b. la vente
c. acheter
d. gagner
e. cher
f. même

Compréhension

B **Boutiques et magasins.** Complétez.

1. La France est un pays de gastronomie et de ___.
2. Deux ___ célèbres sont Pierre Cardin et Yves Saint-Laurent.
3. Les vêtements faits par un couturier portent la ___ du couturier.
4. Les Galeries Lafayette et La Samaritaine sont des ___, pas des boutiques.
5. Les clients dans un grand magasin peuvent aller d'un ___ à l'autre et ils peuvent acheter toutes sortes de choses dans le même magasin.
6. Pendant les ___ il y a d'importantes réductions.
7. Une boutique ___ vend des vêtements pour garçons et filles.

C **Le shopping.** Répondez.

1. On vend les vêtements et les accessoires des grands couturiers au Prisunic?
2. Il y a beaucoup de différents grands magasins en France?
3. Tous les grands magasins sont plus ou moins de la même catégorie?
4. Pendant les soldes, tout est plus cher ou meilleur marché?
5. Qu'est-ce qu'une boutique unisexe?
6. Qui aime les boutiques unisexe?
7. Les marchandises sont chères aux Puces?

D **Les achats.** Trouvez les renseignements suivants dans la lecture.

1. trois couturiers français
2. deux grands magasins français
3. deux marchés parisiens qui ont des prix très bas

DÉCOUVERTE CULTURELLE

En France et en Europe en général les pointures et les tailles ne sont pas les mêmes qu'aux États-Unis. Voici les tailles des vêtements et les pointures des chaussures.

Si vous voulez acheter des chaussures en France, vous demandez quelle pointure? Si vous voulez acheter une chemise ou un chemisier, vous demandez quelle taille?

FEMMES				
CHAUSSURES				
États-Unis	6	7	8	9
France	36	37	38	39
ROBES, TAILLEURS, PULLS, CHEMISIERS				
États-Unis	6	8	10	12	14
France	38	40	42	44	46

HOMMES				
CHEMISES				
États-Unis	14½	15	15½	16	16½
France	37	38	39	40	41
CHAUSSURES				
États-Unis	9	10	11	12
France	40	41	42	43

CRITICAL THINKING ACTIVITY

(Thinking skills: supporting statements with reasons)

Put the following on the board or on a transparency:
1. À votre avis, il faut dépenser beaucoup d'argent pour acheter des vêtements ou pas? Justifiez vos idées.
2. Il faut porter un uniforme à l'école. Discutez des avantages et des inconvénients.

INDEPENDENT PRACTICE

Assign any of the following:
1. *Étude de mots* and *Compréhension* exercises, pages 274–275
2. Workbook, *Un Peu Plus,* pages 102–103
3. CD-ROM, Disc 3, pages 274–275

Compréhension

PRESENTATION *(page 275)*

Exercice B

Have students find the answers to Exercise B in the reading. Call on volunteers to read the completed statements.

ANSWERS

Exercice B

1. haute couture
2. couturiers
3. griffe
4. grands magasins
5. rayon
6. soldes
7. unisexe

Exercice C

1. Non.
2. Oui.
3. Non.
4. Meilleur marché.
5. Une boutique où on vend des vêtements pour garçons et filles.
6. Les jeunes.
7. Non.

Exercice D

Answers will vary but may include the following:

1. Yves Saint-Laurent, Dior, Courrèges, Cardin, Givenchy, Lacroix.
2. Les Galeries Lafayette, la Samaritaine, Monoprix, Prisunic.
3. Le Village Suisse, les Puces.

OPTIONAL MATERIAL

Découverte culturelle

PRESENTATION *(page 275)*

A. Before doing the reading, have students make up a chart of their clothing and shoe sizes using the American system. Tell them to leave space between items—they'll be making additions.

B. Have students read the selection silently and study the chart. Beside each of their American sizes, have them write the equivalent European size. If their size isn't in the chart, they should extrapolate.

Note Students may listen to a recorded version of the *Découverte culturelle* on the CD-ROM.

Bell Ringer Review

Write the following on the board or use BRR Blackline Master 10-10: In what kind of store would the following people shop for clothes?

1. Elizabeth Taylor
2. a university student
3. a lawyer
4. Michael Jordan
5. you and your friends

PRESENTATION *(pages 276–277)*

The main objective of this section is to have students enjoy the photographs and absorb some French culture. However, if you would like to do more, do some of the following activities.

A. Ask students to comment on the French shopping scenes depicted in the photos. Are there any differences between these scenes and students' personal shopping experiences?

B. Call on volunteers to read the captions aloud. Then discuss the information as a class.

C. Ask the class these questions: From what you know about young French people, what are some advantages they have when it comes to money and clothes shopping? Some disadvantages? Do any of you shop with credit cards? What are the advantages or disadvantages? Do any of you have your own credit cards? Do you think young French people do? Why or why not?

D. You may wish to explain to students that there is very little difference in the way French and U.S. students dress.

Note In the CD-ROM version, students can listen to the recorded captions and discover a hidden video behind one of the photos.

RÉALITÉS

ADDITIONAL PRACTICE

1. Student Tape Manual, Teacher's Edition, *Deuxième Partie,* pages 118–120
2. Situation Cards, Chapter 10

Voici une boutique au Quartier Latin. Les deux copines regardent des vêtements ensemble. Tu aimes ces pulls? Tu veux acheter un pull dans cette boutique 1?

C'est un groupe de jeunes Français 2. Vous trouvez qu'il y a une grande différence entre les vêtements que vous portez et les vêtements que portent les jeunes Français?

C'est le marché aux puces à Lyon 3.

On est aux Galeries Lafayette à Noël 4. À la caisse on paie avec une carte de crédit, un chèque ou en espèces.

Les grands couturiers vendent aussi des articles de luxe comme les foulards en soie dans leurs boutiques 5.

277

Note Chapter 5 of *À bord* deals with the related topic of hairstyles and beauty products.

HISTORY CONNECTION

In 1852, Aristide Boucicaut opened Au Bon Marché in Paris—the first department store in the world. Boucicaut wanted to offer his customers a large selection of high-quality merchandise as well as inexpensive items, under one roof. Soon other department stores, le Printemps, la Samaritaine, and les Galeries Lafayette, opened in Paris. Today these department stores attract millions of customers every year. More economy-minded French shoppers will be found at Au Bon Marché and la Samaritaine. Monoprix and Prisunic also offer inexpensive merchandise.

Throughout Europe one can see narrow shopping streets in the older sections of cities and towns closed to vehicles and open only to pedestrians. Shopping malls *(centres commerciaux)* are also becoming more popular. They are most frequently found on the outskirts of cities or towns. Today there is a very modern "mall" type of development in the heart of Paris. Called Le Forum, it stands where the famous old food market, Les Halles, once stood before it was moved to the outskirts of Paris.

THE FRANCOPHONE WORLD

Students may be interested in viewing clothing and clothing store windows in other French-speaking countries. See the section entitled *La Mode* in *Le Monde francophone,* pages 326–329.

INDEPENDENT PRACTICE

Have groups create a poster advertising a sale, a special designer collection, or a fashion show. They should use shopping vocabulary, colors, and the comparative and superlative of adjectives.

COOPERATIVE LEARNING

Display Communication Transparency C-10. Have students work in groups of five to create the conversations illustrated on the transparency. Have groups present their conversations to the class.

INFORMAL ASSESSMENT

Oral Activities A and B may serve as a means to evaluate students' speaking ability.

Teaching Tip For students who are uncomfortable speaking in public, try working with a "cassette mail" system. Students record the assigned task in a private setting and give you the cassette. You can then record your evaluative comments and return the cassette to them. Use the evaluation criteria given on page 34 of this Teacher's Wraparound Edition.

Activités de communication orale

PRESENTATION (*page 278*)

Activité A

In the CD-ROM version of this activity, students can interact with an on-screen native speaker.

ANSWERS

Activités A and B

Answers will vary.

Activités de communication écrite

ANSWERS

Activités A and B

Answers will vary.

Réintroduction et recombinaison

PRESENTATION (*page 279*)

Exercices A and B

Exercise A recycles stress pronouns. Exercise B recombines clothing vocabulary with Chapter 9's seaside setting. It also contrasts *mettre* (meaning "to put on") with *porter*.

Activités de communication orale

A **Un sondage: Le shopping.** You're in a department store in France and have agreed to answer a few questions for a shopping survey.

1. Quel est votre magasin favori? Pourquoi?
2. Que préférez-vous: les grands magasins ou les boutiques?
3. Quelle sorte de vêtements achetez-vous le plus souvent? Des vêtements habillés ou des vêtements sport?
4. Quand vous achetez des vêtements, préférez-vous aller dans les magasins seul(e) ou avec des amis?

B **Jeu de mémoire.** Study the clothing of all the students in the next row for several minutes. Then turn your back to that row and see if you can answer classmates' questions about what the people in the row are wearing. (*Qui porte un tee-shirt rouge? un jean noir?*, etc.) If you can't answer, the people in the row may help out by giving hints such as *La personne est blonde* or *Elle est assise derrière Suzanne.*

Activités de communication écrite

A **Le catalogue.** Write five descriptions for a clothing catalogue. Using the vocabulary in this chapter, describe the items. Tell the sizes they come in, the colors, the occasions they could be worn for, and the prices.

> **Voici une belle robe longue, très habillée, rouge et noire, parfaite pour les fêtes. Tailles: du 36 au 44. Prix: 1.200F**

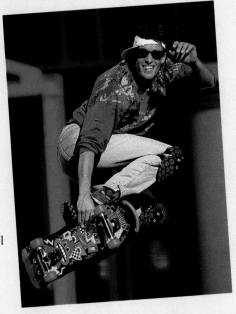

B **Le look de ton école.** Write a note to your French friend describing *le look* at your school. Tell him or her what boys and girls usually wear to school and what types of clothing and colors are "in" (*à la mode*).

FOR THE YOUNGER STUDENT

1. Set up a clothing store in the room, using items of clothing or pictures from magazines. Have pairs of students make up skits between a salesperson and a customer buying a gift.
2. Have students make collages using magazine photos, advertisements, fabrics, etc. Then have them describe their collages.

LEARNING FROM PHOTOS

1. Have students identify as many colors as they can find in the photos on this page.
2. Ask students: What dates are on the photo on page 279? What will customers get? What do they have to have?

Réintroduction et recombinaison

A **Des préférences.** Complétez.

1. ___, je préfère un look sportif.
2. Mais ___, il préfère un look conservateur.
3. Les autres, ___, ils font toujours leurs achats dans les boutiques chères.
4. Et ___? Où est-ce que tu fais tes achats?

B **En été.** Donnez des réponses personnelles.

1. Quand est-ce que tu mets un maillot?
2. Qu'est-ce que tu portes quand il fait chaud?
3. Tu vas dans quelle sorte de magasin pour acheter un maillot?
4. Tu voudrais un maillot de quelle couleur?
5. Est-ce qu'on met des lunettes de soleil quand il pleut?
6. Qu'est-ce qu'une femme porte quand elle joue au tennis?

Vocabulaire

NOMS
les vêtements (m.)
le blouson
la chaussette
la chaussure
la paire
le talon
le jean
le pantalon
le pull
le sweat-shirt
le chemisier
la manche
le collant
la jupe
la robe
le tailleur
la chemise
le complet
la cravate
la veste
le cadeau
la couleur
la taille
   au-dessus
   au-dessous
la pointure

le grand magasin
la boutique
le rayon (prêt-à-porter)
le/la client(e)
le vendeur
la vendeuse
le prix
les soldes (f.)
le grand couturier

ADJECTIFS
bon marché (inv.)
cher, chère
bas(se)
haut(e)
long(ue)
court(e)
étroit(e)
serré(e)
large
habillé(e)
sport (inv.)
sportif, sportive
actif, active
favori(te)
heureux, heureuse
merveilleux, merveilleuse

sérieux, sérieuse
délicieux, délicieuse
dernier, dernière
entier, entière
meilleur(e)
beige
bleu(e)
bleu marine (inv.)
blanc, blanche
brun(e)
gris(e)
jaune
marron (inv.)
noir(e)
orange (inv.)
rose
rouge
vert(e)

VERBES
croire
dépenser
penser
porter
voir

AUTRES MOTS ET EXPRESSIONS
à mon avis
beaucoup de
faire des achats
trop
vraiment

CHAPITRE 11

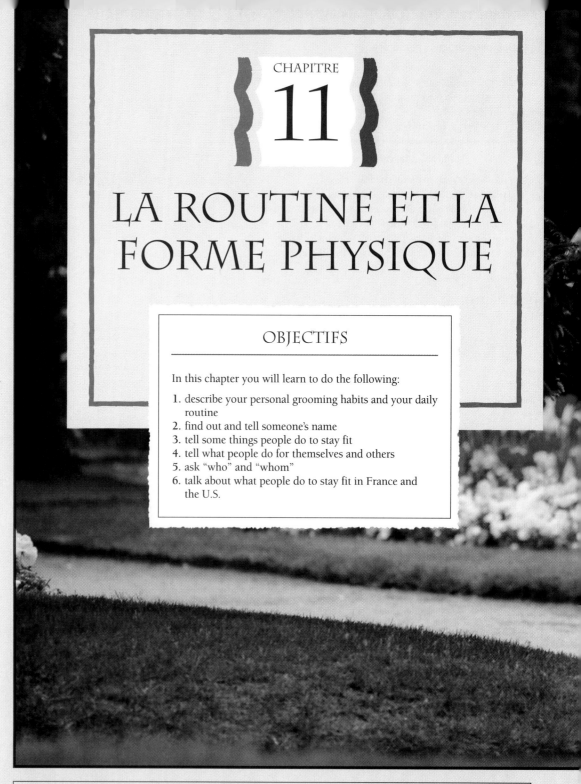

CHAPITRE
{ 11 }

LA ROUTINE ET LA FORME PHYSIQUE

OBJECTIFS

In this chapter you will learn to do the following:

1. describe your personal grooming habits and your daily routine
2. find out and tell someone's name
3. tell some things people do to stay fit
4. tell what people do for themselves and others
5. ask "who" and "whom"
6. talk about what people do to stay fit in France and the U.S.

CHAPTER OVERVIEW

In this chapter students will learn to discuss some aspects of their daily routine, personal hygiene, and keeping in shape. In order to do this they will learn the reflexive verbs, certain verbs with orthographic changes, and the pronoun *qui*.

The cultural focus of Chapter 11 is on French attitudes and activities related to fitness.

CHAPTER OBJECTIVES

By the end of this chapter, students will know:

1. vocabulary associated with morning and evening personal routines and hygiene
2. vocabulary associated with physical fitness and exercise
3. the construction *avoir besoin de*
4. the present indicative forms of reflexive verbs
5. the reflexive pronouns
6. orthographic changes in verbs like *acheter*, verbs that end in *-cer*, verbs like *manger*, and the verb *s'appeler*
7. question formation with *qui* as subject and as object

CHAPTER PROJECTS

(optional)
Do some aerobics with the class in French, using the Total Physical Response approach.

COMMUNITIES

1. Try to obtain video recordings of French sporting events, such as the Tour de France or a Quebec soccer match, and view them with your students.
2. If a French person is available, have students question him/her on the physical education system in French schools, the Tour de France, and so on.

281

Pacing

This chapter requires eight to ten class sessions. Pacing will vary according to class length and the age and aptitude of the students.

Note The Lesson Plans offer guidelines for 45- and 55-minute classes and **Block Scheduling.**

Exercices vs. *Activités*

All exercises (which provide guided practice) are coded in blue. All communicative activities are coded in red.

INTERNET ACTIVITIES

(optional)

These activities, student worksheets, and related teacher information are in the *Bienvenue* Internet Activities Booklet and on the Glencoe Foreign Language Home Page at: http://www.glencoe.com/secondary/fl

LEARNING FROM PHOTOS

After teaching the vocabulary, ask the following questions: *Il y a combien de jeunes gens? Ils sont au parc? Ils font du jogging ou ils se promènent? Qu'est-ce qu'ils portent? Ils veulent rester en forme?*

VOCABULAIRE

MOTS 1

LA ROUTINE

les cheveux (m.)

la figure

les dents (f.)

la main

se réveiller

se lever

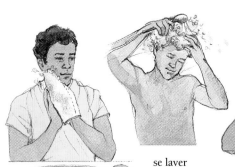

se laver

se laver
les cheveux

se brosser les dents

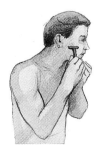

se raser

se peigner

se maquiller

s'habiller

282 CHAPITRE 11

Vocabulary Teaching Resources

1. Vocabulary Transparencies 11.1 (A & B)
2. Audio Cassette 7A/CD-7
3. Student Tape Manual, Teacher's Edition, *Mots 1: A–C,* pages 121–122
4. Workbook, *Mots 1: A–D,* pages 105–107
5. Communication Activities Masters, *Mots 1: A,* page 54
6. Chapter Quizzes, *Mots 1:* Quiz 1, page 59
7. CD-ROM, Disc 3, *Mots 1:* pages 282–285

Bell Ringer Review

Write the following on the board or use BRR Blackline Master 11-1: Use these cues to write a conversation that might take place in a department store.

1. greet the salesperson
2. say what you are looking for
3. give the size, the color, and the style of an article of clothing
4. say how much you would like to spend
5. ask if there is a sale

PRESENTATION (*pages 282–283*)

A. Model the new words using Vocabulary Transparencies 11.1 (A & B). Point to each illustration and have the class repeat after you or Cassette 7A/CD-7.

B. Act out the new words: *se réveiller, se lever, se laver, se laver les cheveux, se brosser les dents, se raser.*

282

TOTAL PHYSICAL RESPONSE

(following the Vocabulary presentation)

Getting Ready

You may wish to use a chair for a bed and bring in an alarm clock as a prop.

TPR 1

_____, venez ici, s'il vous plaît.

Il est sept heures du matin. Vous dormez encore.

Vous entendez le réveil.
Vous vous réveillez.
Vous regardez le réveil.
Vous arrêtez le réveil.
Vous vous levez.
Vous allez dans la salle de bains.
Vous vous lavez.
Vous vous brossez les dents.
Vous vous regardez dans la glace.
Vous vous brossez les cheveux.

(continued on next page)

se coucher

s'endormir

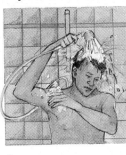

prendre un bain

une glace

prendre une douche

du savon

du déodorant
du dentifrice

1. Elle s'appelle Nathalie.
Nathalie se réveille.
Elle se lève tout de suite.

André va faire sa toilette.
Il a besoin de savon.
Il a besoin de dentifrice.
Il a besoin d'une glace.

2. D'abord elle se lave.

3. Ensuite elle se brosse les dents.

4. Enfin elle prend son petit déjeuner.

> Bonjour!
> Je m'appelle Christian.
> Comment vous appelez-vous?

CHAPITRE 11 **283**

C. As you present the new vocabulary, ask: *La fille se réveille le matin ou le soir? Ensuite, elle se lève ou elle se couche? Elle se lave la figure et les mains? Elle se brosse les dents? Elle se lave les cheveux tous les matins? Elle s'habille vite? Elle s'habille dans la salle de bains ou dans la chambre à coucher? Elle se lève ou se couche à dix heures et demie du soir? Quand elle se couche, elle s'endort tout de suite?*

D. Call out the following verbs and have students pantomime each one: *se réveiller, se lever, se laver, se laver les cheveux, se brosser les cheveux (les dents), se peigner, s'habiller, se regarder dans la glace, se maquiller.*

E. Demonstrate the meaning of *avoir besoin de* by miming looking for something you need. For example: *Je veux écrire quelque chose. J'ai besoin d'un stylo. Je n'ai pas de stylo. Je ne peux pas écrire.*

F. When you teach *Elle s'appelle Nathalie*, continue down the left column of the page so the meaning of *d'abord* and *ensuite* is clear.

G. **Chain drill** Have one student ask his or her neighbor's name. (*Comment t'appelles-tu?*) The student who responds then asks the next student and so on.

Vocabulary Expansion

You may give students the following additional vocabulary in order to talk about personal grooming:
du shampooing
un peigne
une brosse à dents
des ciseaux
un rasoir
du maquillage

TPR *(continued)*
Vous vous habillez vite.
Vous partez pour l'école. Au revoir et bonne journée!
Merci, ___. Vous pouvez retourner à votre place.

TPR 2
Attention, tout le monde. Levez-vous. Nous allons mimer des actions.
Réveillez-vous.

Lavez-vous la figure et les mains.
Lavez-vous les cheveux.
Rasez-vous.
Brossez-vous les dents.
Brossez-vous les cheveux.
Habillez-vous.
Couchez-vous.
Endormez-vous. Bonne nuit!
Merci, tout le monde. Asseyez-vous.

PRESENTATION (pages 284–285)

Exercice A

Exercise A can be done with books either closed or open.

Extension of *Exercice A*: Paired Activity

After completing Exercise A, have pairs of students say or write negative sentences explaining what Nathalie *doesn't* do in her routine.

Extension of *Exercice B*: Paired Activity

Have pairs of students create a morning routine for Gérard. One or both of them can explain the routine to the class.

ANSWERS

Exercice A

1. Oui, le matin Nathalie se réveille à six heures et demie.
2. Oui, elle se lève tout de suite.
3. Oui, d'abord elle va dans la salle de bains pour faire sa toilette.
4. Oui, ensuite elle se lave les mains et la figure avec du savon.
5. Oui, elle se brosse les dents avec du dentifrice et une brosse à dents.
6. À mon avis, elle prend une douche (elle prend un bain).
7. À mon avis, elle se maquille, elle se peigne, elle se regarde dans la glace et elle s'habille.
8. Oui, elle prend son petit déjeuner.

Exercice B

1. Oui, Gérard rentre chez lui vers cinq heures.
2. Oui, il se lave les mains avant le dîner.
3. Il dîne dans la cuisine.
4. Oui, il se brosse les dents après le dîner.
5. Oui, à dix heures il se déshabille.
6. Il prend un bain le soir.
7. Oui, quand il se couche, il s'endort tout de suite.

Exercices

A La routine de Nathalie. *Répondez.*

1. Le matin Nathalie se réveille à six heures et demie?
2. Elle se lève tout de suite?
3. D'abord elle va dans la salle de bains pour faire sa toilette?
4. Ensuite elle se lave les mains et la figure avec du savon?
5. Elle se brosse les dents avec du dentifrice et une brosse à dents?
6. À ton avis, elle prend une douche ou un bain?
7. À ton avis, elle se maquille? Elle se peigne? Elle se regarde dans la glace? Elle s'habille?
8. Elle prend son petit déjeuner?

B La routine de Gérard. *Répondez d'après les dessins.*

1. Gérard rentre chez lui vers cinq heures?
2. Il se lave les mains avant le dîner?
3. Il dîne dans la cuisine ou dans la salle à manger?
4. Il se brosse les dents après le dîner?
5. À dix heures il se déshabille?
6. Il prend un bain le soir ou le matin?
7. Quand il se couche, il s'endort tout de suite?

284   CHAPITRE 11

LEARNING FROM ILLUSTRATIONS

Have students say as much as they can about *le petit chat de Gérard.* You may wish to give them the word for "bathtub," *la baignoire.*

ADDITIONAL PRACTICE

Student Tape Manual, Teacher's Edition, *Activités B–C,* page 122.

C **Dans quelle pièce?** Complétez.

1. On se brosse les dents dans ___.
2. On s'endort dans ___.
3. On prend une douche dans ___.
4. On se regarde dans la glace dans ___.
5. On se couche dans ___.
6. On prend son petit déjeuner dans ___.
7. La douche est dans ___.
8. Le lit est dans ___.

D **Il a besoin de...** Choisissez la bonne réponse.

1. Il va se brosser les dents. Il a besoin de ___.
   a. crème   **b.** dentifrice

2. Il va prendre une douche. Il a besoin de ___.
   a. savon   **b.** dentifrice

3. Il va se raser. Il a besoin d'un ___.
   a. peigne   **b.** rasoir

4. Il veut se peigner. Il a besoin d'un ___.
   a. peigne   **b.** rasoir

5. Il veut se laver les cheveux. Il a besoin de ___.
   a. déodorant   **b.** shampooing

6 F 90 Bain crème, parfums au choix, 1 litre

4 F 90 Gel douche, parfums au choix, 300 ml (le litre : 16,34 F)

20 F 00 Lot de 3 brosses à dents GIBBS Intégral

35 F 00 1 brosse + 1 froufrou + 1 peigne + 1 miroir, coloris divers

CHAPITRE 11   **285**

PRESENTATION *(continued)*

***Exercices C and D:* Listening**

Focus on the listening skill by having students do Exercises C and D in pairs. One partner reads the sentences in random order and the other partner, with his/her book closed, completes the sentences. Then partners switch roles.

Exercice C

1. la salle de bains
2. la chambre à coucher
3. la salle de bains
4. la salle de bains (la chambre à coucher)
5. la chambre à coucher
6. la cuisine (la salle à manger)
7. la salle de bains
8. la chambre à coucher

Exercice D

1. b
2. a
3. b
4. a
5. b

INFORMAL ASSESSMENT
(Mots 1)

Check for comprehension of the expression *avoir besoin de* by making statements about what people want to do and having students say what is needed to do it. For example: *Elle veut se peigner.* (*Elle a besoin d'un peigne.*) *Ils veulent se raser.* (*Ils ont besoin d'un rasoir.*)

RETEACHING *(Mots 1)*

Show Vocabulary Transparencies 11.1 and let students say as much as they can about them in their own words.

LEARNING FROM REALIA

Have students look at the ads and their copy. They will understand almost all the words. The students will probably enjoy the word *froufrou*.

INDEPENDENT PRACTICE

Assign any of the following:
1. Exercises, pages 284–285
2. Workbook, *Mots 1: A–D*, pages 105–107
3. Communication Activities Masters, *Mots 1: A*, page 54
4. CD-ROM, Disc 3, pages 282–285

Vocabulary Teaching Resources

1. Vocabulary Transparencies 11.2 (A & B)
2. Audio Cassette 7A/CD-7
3. Student Tape Manual, Teacher's Edition, *Mots 2: D–F,* pages 123–124
4. Workbook, *Mots 2: E–G,* page 108
5. Communication Activities Masters, *Mots 2: B,* page 55
6. Chapter Quizzes, *Mots 2: Quiz 2,* page 49
7. Computer Software, *Vocabulaire*
8. CD-ROM, Disc 3, *Mots 2:* pages 286–289

Bell Ringer Review

Write the following on the board or use BRR Blackline Master 11-2: Which reflexive verb(s) do you associate with these nouns?

1. les cheveux   3. la figure
2. les dents   4. les mains

PRESENTATION (*pages 286–287*)

A. Have students close their books. Show Vocabulary Transparencies 11.2 (A & B). Have students repeat each word after you or Cassette 7A/CD-7 as you point to each item.
B. Ask questions about the statements on page 287: *Robert veut se mettre en forme? Qu'est-ce qu'il fait pour se mettre en forme? Où est-ce qu'il se promène?*

Teaching Tip To demonstrate the meaning of *toujours,* say: *le lundi, le mardi, le mercredi, tous les jours de la semaine—toujours. En décembre, en janvier, en février, etc.—toujours.*

286

VOCABULAIRE

MOTS 2

LA FORME PHYSIQUE

grossir

maigrir

un gymnase

faire de la gymnastique

un club de forme

faire de l'exercice

faire de l'aérobic

TOTAL PHYSICAL RESPONSE

(*following the Vocabulary presentation*)

TPR
___, levez-vous et venez ici, s'il vous plaît.
Vous êtes au club de forme.
Mettez un short.
Mettez un tee-shirt.
Mettez des tennis.
Montrez que vous avez grossi.

Montrez que vous voulez **maigrir.**
Faites de l'exercice vigoureux.
Vous êtes très fatigué(e).
Merci. Retournez à votre place et asseyez-vous.

pratiquer un sport

mettre un survêtement

Robert veut se mettre en forme.
Pour se mettre en forme il se
promène.
Il se promène dans le parc.

Robert veut rester en forme.
C'est toujours le problème.
Pour rester en forme il fait de
l'exercice.

Il fait du jogging.

Les copains s'amusent.
Ils s'amusent bien.

C. After presenting the vocabulary with the transparencies, have students open their books and read the words and sentences.
D. After each student reads a sentence, call on a more able student to ask a question about the sentence. He/She calls on another student to answer the question.

Vocabulary Expansion

You may wish to give the students the following expressions when teaching *grossir* and *maigrir: prendre des kilos, perdre des kilos.*

Activity: Have students respond with *On prend des kilos* or *On perd des kilos:*
On mange beaucoup de glace.
On fait du jogging.
On est toujours assis.
On fait beaucoup d'exercice.
On mange beaucoup.
On dort toujours.

ADDITIONAL PRACTICE

As a receptive activity, you may tell students to do the following:
Levez la main si vous aimez aller au
  gymnase.
Levez la main si vous aimez faire de
  l'aérobic.
Levez la main si vous faites de l'aérobic.
Levez la main si vous faites de l'exercice.

Levez la main si vous faites de l'exercice au
  gymnase de l'école.
Levez la main si vous pratiquez un sport.
Levez la main si vous pratiquez un sport
  après les cours.
Levez la main si vous faites du jogging.
Levez la main si vous habitez près d'un parc.

Exercices

PRESENTATION (*page 288*)

ANSWERS

Exercice A

 You may wish to use to recorded version of this exercise.

1. Bien manger, c'est bon pour la santé.
2. Manger beaucoup de pâtisseries, c'est mauvais pour la santé.
3. Prendre du lait, c'est bon pour la santé.
4. Prendre du coca au petit déjeuner, c'est mauvais pour la santé.
5. Ne pas faire d'exercice, c'est mauvais pour la santé.
6. Faire de l'aérobic, c'est bon pour la santé.
7. Prendre des vitamines, c'est bon pour la santé.
8. Fumer, c'est mauvais pour la santé.
9. Pratiquer un sport, c'est bon pour la santé.
10. Grossir, c'est mauvais pour la santé.
11. Se promener tous les jours, c'est bon pour la santé.
12. Se mettre en forme, c'est bon pour la santé.

Exercice B

Answers will vary.

Exercice C

1. a
2. b
3. b
4. b
5. a
6. a

Activités de communication orale

Mots 1 et 2

ANSWERS

Activité A

Answers will vary.

Exercices

A **Pour rester en forme.** C'est bon ou mauvais pour la santé (*health*)?

manger beaucoup de chocolat
Manger beaucoup de chocolat, c'est mauvais pour la santé.

1. bien manger
2. manger beaucoup de pâtisseries
3. prendre du lait
4. prendre du coca au petit déjeuner
5. ne pas faire d'exercice
6. faire de l'aérobic
7. prendre des vitamines
8. fumer
9. pratiquer un sport
10. grossir
11. se promener tous les jours
12. se mettre en forme

B **En forme.** Donnez des réponses personnelles.

1. Tu aimes être en forme?
2. Tu fais de l'exercice pour rester en forme?
3. Tu fais du jogging? Tu mets un survêtement?
4. Tu pratiques un sport?
5. Tu pratiques quel sport?
6. Tu es membre d'un club de forme?
7. Tu fais de la gymnastique à l'école ou au gymnase?
8. Tu grossis quand tu manges beaucoup?
9. Rester en forme, c'est un problème pour toi?

C **Quel est le mot?** Choisissez.

1. Il prend des kilos. Il ___.
   a. grossit   b. maigrit
2. Il perd des kilos. Il ___.
   a. grossit   b. maigrit
3. Il va faire du jogging. Il met ___.
   a. une chemise   b. un survêtement
4. Il va faire du jogging. Il met ___.
   a. un complet   b. des tennis
5. Il va au parc. Il va ___.
   a. se promener   b. se raser
6. Il va ___ avec ses copains dans le parc.
   a. s'amuser   b. se réveiller

Activités de communication orale

Mots 1 et 2

A **La routine.** Tell your French-Canadian friend (your partner) about a member of your family. Include the information below. Then reverse roles.

1. his or her name
2. what time he or she gets up
3. some of his or her grooming habits
4. what he or she does to stay in shape
5. what sports he or she participates in

COOPERATIVE LEARNING

Have each team of four assemble a composite list of activities from *Mots 1* and 2 that they like or don't like to do when they are on vacation. The list is started by one member and passed on until each member has contributed at least three activities, for a total of twelve. Encourage students to help each other with their contributions.

LEARNING FROM PHOTOS

Have students tell whether you're describing the photo on page 288 or the one on page 289:
La danseuse est en forme.
C'est un sport nautique.
Ils font du kayak.
Elle danse bien.

B **Les sportifs.** Work with a classmate. Ask each other the following questions.

1. Qu'est-ce que tu fais pour rester en forme?
2. Où… ?
3. Avec qui… ?
4. Quand… ?

C **Tu as besoin de…** Play this game in small groups. One person states that he or she wants to do one of the activities listed below. The others have 20 seconds to write down as many things as they can think of that the first student needs in order to do the activity. Players receive one point per correct item.

> Élève 1: Je veux jouer au tennis.
> Élève 2: Tu as besoin d'une raquette, d'une balle, d'un court, d'un short…

aller à la plage	faire un voyage
faire du jogging	jouer au tennis
faire les courses	prendre un bain de soleil
faire les devoirs de…	préparer le dîner

D **Madame Nette.** Madame Nette is a very organized woman whose daily routine is always the same. With your classmates, take turns describing Madame Nette's day from morning to night. The first student suggests her first activity of the day. The next student repeats that activity and adds another.

> Élève 1: Madame Nette se réveille à six heures.
> Élève 2: Madame Nette se réveille à six heures.
>   Elle se lève tout de suite.

CHAPITRE 11   **289**

PRESENTATION (*page 289*)

Extension of *Activité B*

Call on a student to retell in his/her own words what he/she does to stay in shape, based on the answers to Activity B.

ANSWERS

Activité B

Answers will vary.

Activité C

Answers will vary, but may include the following (all **É1** answers begin with *Je veux* and all **É2** answers begin with *Tu as besoin de [d']*):

É1: Je veux aller à la plage.
É2: Tu as besoin d'un maillot, (de crème solaire, de lunettes de soleil…).
É1: … faire du jogging.
É2: … d'un survêtement (de tennis, d'un sweat-shirt…).
É1: … faire les courses.
É2: … d'un filet (d'un sac, d'argent, d'une liste…).
É1: … faire les devoirs d'histoire (de biologie…).
É2: … d'un livre d'histoire (d'un livre de biologie…).
É1: … faire un voyage.
É2: … d'une valise (d'un passeport…).
É1: … jouer au tennis.
É2: … de chaussures de tennis (d'une balle…).
É1: … prendre un bain de soleil.
É2: … de crème solaire (de lunettes de soleil, de soleil…).
É1: … préparer le dîner.
É2: … d'un steak (de pommes de terre, d'une cuisine…).

Activité D

Answers will vary.

ADDITIONAL PRACTICE

1. Elicit *Mots 1* and *2* vocabulary by saying days/times of day (especially before and after school and around bedtime) and having individuals say what they're usually doing then. For example: *Le mercredi, 7h30 du matin. Patrick? (Je me brosse les dents.) Georges? (Je prends mon petit déjeuner.)*, etc.
2. Student Tape Manual, Teacher's Edition, *Activité F*, page 124.

INDEPENDENT PRACTICE

Assign any of the following:
1. Exercises and activities, pages 288–289
2. Workbook, *Mots 2: E–G*, page 108
3. Communication Activities Masters, *Mots 2: B*, page 55
4. Computer Software, *Vocabulaire*
5. CD-ROM, Disc 3, pages 286–289

STRUCTURE

Structure Teaching Resources

1. Workbook, *Structure: A–H*, pages 109–112
2. Student Tape Manual, Teacher's Edition, *Structure: A–D*, pages 124–125
3. Audio Cassette 7A/CD-7
4. Grammar Transparency G-11
5. Communication Activities Masters, *Structure: A–C*, pages 56–58
6. Computer Software, *Structure*
7. Chapter Quizzes, *Structure: Quizzes 3–5*, pages 61–63
8. CD-ROM, Disc 3, pages 290–295

Bell Ringer Review

Write the following on the board or use BRR Blackline Master 11-3: Correct the following sentences.

1. Je prends mon petit déjeuner dans la salle de bains.
2. Je me brosse les dents avec du savon.
3. Je me maquille les mains.
4. Je me regarde dans la figure.

Les verbes réfléchis

PRESENTATION *(pages 290–291)*

A. Have students make a list of the verbs learned in this chapter that describe what they do almost every morning.
B. Write the model verbs shown on page 290 on the board. Underline the reflexive pronouns.
C. Lead students through steps 1–3, calling on volunteers to read the material.

Les verbes réfléchis

Telling What People Do for Themselves

1. Compare the following pairs of sentences.

Chantal lave le bébé.

Chantal se lave.

Chantal regarde le bébé.

Chantal se regarde.

Chantal couche le bébé.

Chantal se couche.

In the sentences on the left Chantal performs the action and the baby receives it. In the sentences on the right Chantal herself is the receiver of the action. In these sentences Chantal both performs and receives the action of the verb. For this reason the pronoun *se* must be used. *Se* refers to Chantal and is called a reflexive pronoun. It indicates that the action of the verb is reflected back to the subject.

290 CHAPITRE 11

2. Each subject pronoun has its corresponding reflexive pronoun. Study the following.

SE LAVER	S'HABILLER
je me lave	je m'habille
tu te laves	tu t'habilles
il se lave	il s'habille
elle se lave	elle s'habille
on se lave	on s'habille
nous nous lavons	nous nous habillons
vous vous lavez	vous vous habillez
ils se lavent	ils s'habillent
elles se lavent	elles s'habillent

Note that *me, te,* and *se* become *m', t',* and *s'* before a vowel or silent *h*.

3. In the negative form of a reflexive verb, *ne* is placed before the reflexive pronoun. *Pas* follows the verb.

Je me réveille mais je *ne* me lève *pas* tout de suite.
On *ne* se brosse *pas* les dents avant le dîner.
Je me couche mais je *ne* m'endors *pas* tout de suite.
Nous *ne* nous rasons *pas* tous les jours.

Exercices

A **La routine de Charles.** Répétez la conversation.

ROGER: Tu te lèves à quelle heure, Charles?
CHARLES: À quelle heure est-ce que je me lève ou je me réveille?
ROGER: Tu te lèves.
CHARLES: Je me lève à six heures et demie.
ROGER: Et tu quittes la maison à quelle heure?
CHARLES: À sept heures. Je me lave, je me brosse les dents, je me rase et je prends mon petit déjeuner en une demi-heure.
ROGER: Et tu t'habilles aussi?
CHARLES: Bien sûr que je m'habille!

Répondez d'après la conversation.

1. Charles se lève à quelle heure?
2. Il se lave?
3. Il se brosse les dents dans la salle de bains?
4. Il se rase?
5. Il quitte la maison à quelle heure?

Note Point out to students that the forms of these verbs are the same as those of any other *-er* verb. The only addition is the pronoun.

D. Have students refer to the list of verbs they made for Presentation step A. For each verb they wrote down, have them make up sentences with *je*.

E. Ask questions using the reflexive verbs and call on volunteers to respond. For example: *À quelle heure est-ce que tu te réveilles? Tu te couches avant minuit? Tu te brosses les dents trois fois par jour?*, etc.

Note In the CD-ROM version, this structure point is presented via an interactive electronic comic strip.

Exercices

PRESENTATION (*page 291*)

Exercice A

Have a pair of students read the conversation aloud with as much expression as possible. Then call on individuals to answer the questions that follow.

Extension of *Exercice A*

Have students work in pairs. Have them change the information in the conversation in Exercise A to relate to themselves.

ANSWERS
Exercice A
1. Il se lève à six heures et demie.
2. Oui, il se lave.
3. Oui, il se brosse les dents dans la salle de bains.
4. Oui, il se rase.
5. Il quitte la maison à sept heures.

ADDITIONAL PRACTICE

1. Have pairs of students redo the conversation in Exercise A, changing *Charles* to *Charles et Robert* in order to practice the *nous* and *vous* forms.
2. Student Tape Manual, Teacher's Edition, *Activités B–D*, pages 124–125

Bell Ringer Review

Write the following on the board or use BRR Blackline Master 11-4: Fill in the blanks with a reflexive pronoun or an X if no pronoun is needed.

Ma mère ___ réveille à six heures. Ensuite elle ___ réveille mon frère. Ils ___ préparent le petit déjeuner. Moi, je ___ prépare dans ma chambre et ensuite, je ___ pré-pare nos sandwichs pour le déjeuner.

Verbes avec changements d'orthographe

PRESENTATION *(pages 292–293)*

A. Go over this topic rather quickly and continue to rein-force good spelling habits throughout your students' study of French.
B. Lead students through steps 1–4 on pages 292–293.

292

B **Jacqueline et Véronique.** Changez *Jacqueline* en *Jacqueline et Véronique.*

1. Jacqueline se réveille à sept heures.
2. Jacqueline se lève tout de suite.
3. Jacqueline se brosse les dents.
4. Jacqueline se lave les mains et la figure.
5. Jacqueline se brosse les cheveux.
6. Jacqueline se maquille.

C **Je fais ma toilette.** Donnez des réponses personnelles.

1. Tu te lèves à quelle heure?
2. Tu vas dans la salle de bains?
3. Tu fais ta toilette?
4. Tu te laves les mains et la figure?
5. Tu prends une douche ou un bain?
6. Tu te laves les cheveux avec du shampooing?
7. Tu te brosses les dents?
8. Tu te peignes?
9. Tu t'habilles vite (rapidement)?

D **Marc répond.** Complétez.

1. Marc, tu ___? (se raser)
2. Oui, je ___. (se raser)
3. Tu ___ tous les jours? (se raser)
4. Oui, malheureusement il faut ___ tous les jours. (se raser)
5. Tu ___ les cheveux ou tu ___? (se brosser, se peigner)
6. Moi, je ___. Je ne ___ pas les cheveux. (se peigner, se brosser)
7. Tu ___ avant ou après le petit déjeuner? (s'habiller)
8. Je ___ avant le petit déjeuner. (s'habiller)

Verbes avec changements d'orthographe
Verbs with Spelling Changes

1. The verbs *se promener* and *se lever,* like *acheter,* take an *accent grave* in all forms except the infinitive, *nous,* and *vous.*

SE PROMENER	
je me promène	nous nous promenons
tu te promènes	vous vous promenez
il/elle/on se promène	ils/elles se promènent

SE LEVER	
je me lève	nous nous levons
tu te lèves	vous vous levez
il/elle/on se lève	ils/elles se lèvent

292   CHAPITRE 11

ADDITIONAL PRACTICE

1. Have pairs of students make sentences with the following verbs, taking turns and alternating between reflexive and transitive constructions. For example: É1: *Je me promène.* É2: *Je promène mon chien.*

amuser	promener	peigner
laver	brosser	réveiller

2. You might wish to play the following game for more practice with reflexive verbs. Write the reflexive verbs on index cards, one to a card. Put the cards in a deck. A student picks a card and pantomimes the action of the verb. Another student tells him/her what he/she is doing, using the *tu* form.

2. The verb *s'appeler* doubles the *l* in all forms except the infinitive, *nous*, and *vous*.

S'APPELER	
je m'appelle	nous nous appelons
tu t'appelles	vous vous appelez
il/elle/on s'appelle	ils/elles s'appellent

3. Verbs that end in *-ger* such as *manger, nager,* and *voyager* add an *e* in the *nous* form in order to maintain the soft consonant sound.

nous mangeons   **nous nageons**   **nous voyageons**

4. Verbs that end in *-cer*, such as *commencer*, take a cedilla on the *c* in the *nous* form in order to maintain the soft consonant sound.

nous commençons

Exercices

A **Moi et toi.**   Mettez au pluriel.

Je me lève à sept heures et tu te lèves à neuf heures.
Nous nous levons à sept heures et vous vous levez à neuf heures.

1. Je me lève à 8 heures.
2. Je vais au magasin où j'achète un short.
3. Je me promène dans le parc.
4. Ensuite je nage dans la piscine.
5. Je commence à avoir faim.
6. Je rentre chez moi et je mange une pomme.
7. Et toi, tu te lèves à quelle heure?
8. Qu'est-ce que tu achètes au magasin?
9. Tu te promènes dans le parc aussi?
10. Ensuite tu nages dans la piscine?

B **Je m'appelle…**   Complétez avec «s'appeler».

1. Bonjour, je ____ …
2. Mon frère ____ …
3. Et ma sœur ____ …
4. Mon père ____ …
5. Ma mère ____ …
6. Mes meilleurs amis ____ …
7. Et comment ____-vous?
8. Nous ____ Dupont.

CHAPITRE 11   **293**

INDEPENDENT PRACTICE

Assign any of the following:
1. Exercises, pages 292–293
2. Workbook, *Structure: A–F,* pages 109–111
3. Communication Activities Masters, *Structure: A–B,* pages 56–57
4. CD-ROM, Disc 3, pages 290–293

LEARNING FROM PHOTOS

You may wish to ask students: *C'est une piscine? La piscine est grande ou petite? C'est une piscine en plein air ou une piscine couverte? C'est une piscine olympique? La jeune fille aime nager? Et vous, vous aimez nager? Est-ce qu'il y a une piscine couverte dans votre école?*

PRESENTATION *(page 293)*

Exercices A and B

Since the major difficulty with these verbs involves their spelling, you may wish to have students prepare these exercises first in writing. Then call on individuals to read them aloud.

ANSWERS

Exercice A

1. Nous nous levons à 8 heures.
2. Nous allons au magasin où nous achetons un short.
3. Nous nous promenons dans le parc.
4. Ensuite nous nageons dans la piscine.
5. Nous commençons à avoir faim.
6. Nous rentrons chez nous et nous mangeons une pomme.
7. Et vous, vous vous levez à quelle heure?
8. Qu'est-ce que vous achetez au magasin?
9. Vous vous promenez dans le parc aussi?
10. Ensuite vous nagez dans la piscine?

Exercice B

1. m'appelle
2. s'appelle
3. s'appelle
4. s'appelle
5. s'appelle
6. s'appellent
7. vous appelez
8. nous appelons

INFORMAL ASSESSMENT

Have students study the verbs presented on pages 292–293 for homework. Give a spelling quiz on selected forms the following day.

RETEACHING

Give the correct form of the verb in parentheses.
1. tu (se promener)
2. vous (manger)
3. ils (acheter)
4. nous (nager)
5. elle (commencer)

Le pronom interrogatif qui

PRESENTATION *(page 294)*

A. Have students close their books. Ask volunteers to supply examples of questions using *qui*. Write them on the board.

B. Now have students open their books. Lead them through steps 1–3 and the accompanying examples on page 294.

1. You have been using the pronoun *qui* to form a question.

> Qui est là?
> Qui parle?
> Qui se lève?

2. You can also use *qui* as the object of the verb or as the object of a preposition. In this case *qui* means "whom."

> Tu vois qui?
> Vous invitez qui?
>
> Vous parlez à qui?
> Vous allez au cinéma avec qui?

3. Note that in the above questions *qui* is at the end of the sentence. In informal French, people put the question word at the end of the sentence and raise the tone of their voice. However, in formal or written French, the pronoun *qui* is placed at the beginning of the question and the subject and verb are inverted. Observe the following differences.

INFORMAL	FORMAL / WRITTEN
Tu vois qui?	Qui vois-tu?
Vous invitez qui?	Qui invitez-vous?
Vous parlez à qui?	À qui parlez-vous?
Vous allez au cinéma avec qui?	Avec qui allez-vous au cinéma?

294   CHAPITRE 11

Exercices

A   **Pardon? Qui ça?**   Posez des questions d'après le modèle.

> **Marie parle.**
> *Pardon? Qui parle?*

1. Son frère arrive.
2. Sa mère va à la porte.
3. Sa mère est très contente.
4. Le frère de Marie s'appelle David.
5. David a un cadeau.

B   **Qui?**   Posez des questions d'après le modèle.

> **Je regarde Suzanne.**
> *Tu regardes qui?*

1. Je téléphone à Robert.
2. Je parle à Robert.
3. J'invite Alice.
4. Je vois mon ami.
5. Je danse avec Isabelle.

C   **Parlons bien.**   Récrivez les questions d'après le modèle.

> **Vous ressemblez à qui?**
> *À qui ressemblez-vous?*

1. Vous téléphonez à qui?
2. Vous parlez à qui?
3. Vous invitez qui à la fête?
4. Vous achetez un cadeau pour qui?
5. Vous allez au restaurant avec qui?
6. Vous êtes derrière qui dans la queue?

ADDITIONAL PRACTICE

Have students work in pairs. Each partner makes a list of the things he/she does to stay in shape. Partners then compare and contrast their lists and report to the class. For example: *Moi, je me promène dans le parc mais* (partner) *ne se promène pas dans le parc. Il/Elle… Moi, je fais de l'aérobic et* (partner) *aussi fait de l'aérobic. Nous faisons de l'aérobic.*

INDEPENDENT PRACTICE

Assign any of the following:
1. Exercises, page 295
2. Workbook, *Structure: G–H,* pages 111–112
3. Communication Activities Masters, *Structure: C,* page 58
4. Computer Software, *Structure*
5. CD-ROM, Disc 3, pages 294–295

Exercices

ANSWERS

Exercice A

1. Pardon? Qui arrive?
2. Pardon? Qui va à la porte?
3. Pardon? Qui est très contente?
4. Pardon? Qui s'appelle David?
5. Pardon? Qui a un cadeau?

Exercice B

1. Tu téléphones à qui?
2. Tu parles à qui?
3. Tu invites qui?
4. Tu vois qui?
5. Tu danses avec qui?

Exercice C

1. À qui téléphonez-vous?
2. À qui parlez-vous?
3. Qui invitez-vous à la fête?
4. Pour qui achetez-vous un cadeau?
5. Avec qui allez-vous au restaurant?
6. Derrière qui êtes-vous dans la queue?

INFORMAL ASSESSMENT

Have students make up as many original sentences with *qui* as they can. For example: *Qui est le prof de… ? Qui est le meilleur élève de la classe?*

RECYCLING

Ask the following questions with *qui* to recycle previously learned vocabulary: *Qui travaille au restaurant? Qui paie à la caisse? Qui travaille à l'aéroport? Qui parle aux passagers à bord de l'avion? Qui vend des billets au guichet à la gare? Qui vérifie les billets dans le train? Qui donne des leçons de natation? Qui travaille dans une boutique?*

CONVERSATION

CONVERSATION

Bell Ringer Review

Write the following on the board or use BRR Blackline Master 11-6: Use each of the following words or expressions in a logical sentence:

faire de	s'endormir
l'aérobic	se peigner
maigrir	

PRESENTATION *(page 296)*

A. Tell students they will hear a conversation between André and Richard.

B. Have them close their books and watch the Conversation Video or listen as you read the conversation or play Cassette 7A/CD-7.

C. Now have them open their books and read the conversation silently.

D. Call on pairs to act out the conversation.

E. Now do Exercise A. Call on individuals to answer each question or call on one student to give all the answers.

Note In the CD-ROM version, students can play the role of either one of the characters and record the conversation.

ANSWERS

Exercice A

1. Il parle à Richard.
2. Il se réveille à six heures et demie.
3. Il reste au lit jusqu'à sept heures.
4. Oui, il aime rester au lit.
5. Il peut vite faire sa toilette et s'habiller.
6. Oui, il va faire du jogging cet après-midi.
7. Richard veut rester en forme.

Scènes de la vie   *Qui est en forme?*

ANDRÉ: Tu te lèves à quelle heure, Richard?
RICHARD: Moi, je me lève à sept heures. Mais je me réveille à six heures et demie.
ANDRÉ: Ah, tu aimes rester un peu au lit.
RICHARD: Oui, mais je peux faire ma toilette, m'habiller et être prêt à quitter la maison en cinq minutes.
ANDRÉ: Tu vas faire du jogging cet après-midi?
RICHARD: Bien sûr. Il faut rester en forme.
ANDRÉ: Rester en forme? Il faut d'abord se mettre en forme!

A **La forme.** Répondez d'après la conversation.

1. André parle à qui?
2. Richard se réveille à quelle heure?
3. Mais il reste au lit jusqu'à quelle heure?
4. Il aime rester au lit?
5. Qu'est-ce qu'il peut vite faire?
6. Richard va faire du jogging cet après-midi?
7. Qui veut rester en forme?

296   CHAPITRE 11

Prononciation *Les sons /s/ et /z/*

It is important to make a distinction between the sounds /s/ and /z/. You would not want to confuse *poisson* with *poison*! Repeat the following words with the sound /s/ as in *assez* and /z/ as in *raser*.

assez	dessert	cassette	boisson	classe
raser	désert	magasin	prise	valise

Now repeat the following sentences. Pay attention to which sounds occur.

Ils s'appellent Dumas.	Ils appellent leur chien.
Elles s'habillent vite.	Elles habillent les bébés.
Ils sont sympathiques.	Ils ont faim.

poisson/poison

Activités de communication orale

A **L'horaire du matin.**   Your French friend Sylvie wants to know about your morning routine. Answer her questions.

1. Tu te réveilles à quelle heure?
2. Tu te lèves tout de suite?
3. Tu pars à quelle heure le matin?
4. Tu prends ton petit déjeuner avant de partir?

B **L'horaire du soir.**   Find out about a classmate's evening routine: when he or she comes home from school, eats, does homework, goes to bed, etc. Then answer his or her questions about your evening routine.

Sylvie

C **La révolte du samedi et du dimanche.**   When the weekend comes, everybody wants a change of pace. In small groups, discuss some of things you do on weekends that are different from the things you do during the week. Then compare results with those of other groups.

Le samedi et le dimanche, on ne se lève pas à sept heures. On se lève à neuf heures.
On ne prend pas son petit déjeuner à huit heures mais à 11 heures.
On se promène dans le parc…

CHAPITRE 11 **297**

LECTURE ET CULTURE

LA FORME PHYSIQUE

Dans beaucoup de pays, la forme physique et la santé sont en ce moment une obsession. La forme physique et la santé intéressent bien sûr les Français mais peut-être pas au même point ou degré qu'aux États-Unis.

Que font les Français pour rester en forme? Les Français estiment qu'il faut faire de l'exercice. On voit des gens qui font du jogging dans les parcs et le long des fleuves[1]. Il y a maintenant de plus en plus de clubs de forme avec tout l'équipement nécessaire pour se mettre en forme. Il y a des classes pour faire de l'aérobic et pour les jeunes il y a des soirées aérobic. Dans les villes, il y a de plus en plus de piscines couvertes[2] pour faire de la natation toute l'année. Le cyclisme est très populaire en France. Le cyclisme est sans aucun doute[3] une excellente forme d'exercice. Le Tour de France est une course[4] cycliste internationale qui a lieu[5] en juillet. Et le tennis? Le tennis est un autre sport qui a de plus en plus de «disciples» en France. On parle toujours des marathons qui ont lieu dans les grandes villes des États-Unis. Il y a aussi un très grand marathon à Paris au mois d'octobre. Beaucoup de coureurs[6] participent au marathon de Paris.

[1] fleuves *rivers*
[2] piscines couvertes *indoor pools*
[3] sans aucun doute *without a doubt*
[4] course *race*
[5] a lieu *takes place*
[6] coureurs *runners*

Le marathon de Paris

Étude de mots

A **Le français, c'est facile.** Trouvez quatre mots apparentés dans la lecture.

B **Les noms et les verbes.** Trouvez le verbe qui correspond au nom.

1. l'équipement
2. une obsession
3. la participation
4. l'intérêt
5. le coureur, la course

a. intéresser
b. participer
c. obséder
d. équiper
e. courir

298 CHAPITRE 11

Compréhension

C Oui ou non? Corrigez les phrases fausses.

1. La forme physique intéresse beaucoup plus les Français que les Américains.
2. Les Français ne font pas d'exercice.
3. Il y a des clubs de forme en France.
4. L'aérobic n'est pas du tout populaire en France.
5. Le cyclisme n'est pas populaire chez les Français.
6. Le Tour de France est une course cycliste internationale qui a lieu en France.
7. Le marathon de Paris est une autre course cycliste.
8. Très peu de gens font du tennis en France.

D La forme physique en France. Répondez.

1. Qu'est-ce que les Français font pour rester en forme?
2. Qu'est-ce qu'il y a dans les clubs de forme?
3. Où peut-on nager toute l'année?
4. Quel sport a de plus en plus de «disciples»?
5. Il y a un grand marathon dans quelle ville?
6. Le marathon de Paris a lieu quand?
7. Le Tour de France a lieu quand?

E L'essentiel. Quelle est l'idée principale de cette lecture?

DÉCOUVERTE CULTURELLE

PETIT DÉJEUNER FRANÇAIS
Croissant au Beurre
Pain, Beurre, Confiture,
Café ou Thé ou Chocolat,
35,00

AMERICAN BREAKFAST
3 Œufs sur le plat, Pain, Beurre,
Jus d'Orange,
Café ou Thé ou Chocolat,
56,00

*A*vant de quitter la maison, André prend son petit déjeuner. Mais qu'est-ce qu'un petit déjeuner typiquement français? C'est du pain, des croissants ou des brioches avec une tasse de café au lait pour les adultes et une tasse de chocolat chaud pour les enfants. Mais des œufs, du bacon, des pommes de terre, absolument pas! Même les céréales ne sont pas très populaires chez les Français.

Comparez les deux petits déjeuners sur la carte d'un café parisien. Qui prend des œufs sur le plat, les Français ou les Américains? Qui prend des croissants?

CHAPITRE 11   **299**

RÉALITÉS

OPTIONAL MATERIAL

PRESENTATION *(pages 300–301)*

Have students look at the photographs for enjoyment. If they would like to talk about them, let them say anything they can.

Note In the CD-ROM version, students can listen to the recorded captions and discover a hidden video behind one of the photos.

Ce nageur français nage la brasse papillon **1**. Il porte des lunettes. À ton avis, c'est un nageur sérieux?

Cette jeune femme fait de l'aérobic **2**. À ton avis, est-elle en bonne forme?

Voici des cyclistes dans le Tour de France **3**. Ils traversent tout le pays—la campagne et les villes.

Ces deux hommes sont au gymnase **4**. Ils jouent au racquetball. Le racquetball ressemble à quels autres sports? Est-ce que le racquetball est un sport populaire aux États-Unis?

Voici des coureurs dans la course de 20 kilomètres à Paris **5**. Est-ce que tu aimes participer à des courses à pied?

300

DID YOU KNOW?

Interest in physical fitness has led to an increased interest in sports among the French. For example, the municipal office for each *arrondissement* of Paris provides a list of addresses where various sports can be practiced. A recent brochure for the 16ème offered the following activities. Share them with the students and have them try to guess the meanings of new words.

Aérobic	Arts martiaux
Gymnastique	Pelote basque
Danse	Pétanque
Tennis	Jogging
Équitation	Boxe
Golf	Plongée sous-marine
Spéléologie	Natation
Judo	Squash
Escrime	Tennis de table
Patinage	Basket-ball

(continued on next page)

4

5

301

GEOGRAPHY CONNECTION

Have students compare the map on page 356 showing the Tour de France with the map of France on page 504, or use the Map Transparency. Point out how much of the route passes through mountainous terrain. The cyclists must cross the Pyrenees, the Alps, and the Massif Central. These sections of the race are particularly grueling.

The Tour de France route is changed every year, but there are always several *étapes* in the mountains, and the finish line is always in Paris. In recent years the race always goes through one or more neighboring countries, and *étapes* going through Belgium, Germany, and Spain are typical.

Note There is a Tour de France game on the *À bord* CD-ROM. Students compete against each other to win the famous *maillot jaune* by answering vocabulary, structure, and culture questions.

HISTORY CONNECTION

The first Tour de France took place in 1904. Since then it has become the most famous bicycle race in the world. It is a grueling race that lasts about 24 days and covers about 2,000 miles. The distance is divided into stages. Cyclists are timed for each stage, and the one with the lowest total time for all the stages wins. There is also a women's Tour de France, which began in 1984.

(continued)

Ski	Athlétisme
Cyclotourisme	Randonnée
Football	Rugby
Hand-ball	Volley-ball
Hockey sur gazon	Tir

ADDITIONAL PRACTICE

1. Student Tape Manual, Teacher's Edition, *Deuxième Partie*, pages 128–130
2. Situation Cards, Chapter 11
3. Workbook, *Un Peu Plus*, pages 113–114
4. Communication Transparency C-11
5. Communication Activities Masters, pages 54–58

RECYCLING

These *Activités de communication orale* and *Activités de communication écrite* are designed to aid students in personalizing the vocabulary and structures learned in Chapter 11 and recombine them with material from previous chapters. Recycled language includes food and clothing vocabulary, time expressions, and prepositions of time and location.

INFORMAL ASSESSMENT

Oral Activity B is well suited for evaluating speaking skills. Assign less able students the role of asking the guided questions, perhaps with help from their partner in the construction of the questions. Better students have free rein in creating the answers to the questions. Use the evaluation criteria given on page 34 of this Teacher's Wraparound Edition.

Activités de communication orale

PRESENTATION *(page 302)*

Activité A

Activity A is designed as a whole-class activity that provides fun and physical action in the classroom as well as practice with *qui* and prepositions of location.

ANSWERS

Activités A and B

Answers will vary.

Activités de communication écrite

ANSWERS

Activité A

Answers will vary but may include the following: du café au lait, du thé, du chocolat, du pain, des croissants, da la confiture, des brioches

Activité B

Answers will vary.

302

Activités de communication orale

A **Qui est devant qui?** Play this game with your classmates. Each student takes a turn going to the front of the class. With his or her back to the class, the student has to answer classmates' questions about where various students are seated. The words below can be used in your questions.

> à côté de   à gauche de   derrière   à droite de   devant
>
> Élève 1: Isabelle est devant qui?
> Élève 2: Elle est devant Paul.

B **Une interview.** You're interviewing the new French exchange student (your partner) for the school newspaper. Find out the following: his or her name, where he or she's from, what he or she does after school, his or her friends' names, what he or she does to stay in shape, and what he or she likes to eat.

Activités de communication écrite

A **Qu'est-ce qu'un petit déjeuner typiquement français?** You're living with a French family for the summer. Write a note to one of your friends describing a typical French breakfast. Tell him or her if you like it or not.

> En France au petit déjeuner, on mange…

B **Monsieur Dodu veut se mettre en forme.** Monsieur Dodu would like to lose some weight and get in shape. As his personal trainer, write out a daily routine for him telling him what time to get up, when to exercise, and what type of exercise to do. Plan his meals for him, too, and suggest what time he should eat them.

> La routine de M. Dodu
>
> | 6h | Il se réveille et il se lève tout de suite. |
> | 6h15 à 7h | Il fait de l'exercice avec moi. |
> | 7h à 7h05 | Il prend une douche froide. |

302   CHAPITRE 11

Réintroduction et recombinaison

A **À votre tour.** Répondez.

1. Quand tu t'habilles le matin, qu'est-ce que tu mets?
2. Qu'est-ce que tu prends au petit déjeuner?
3. Tu vas à l'école comment? En bus, en voiture ou à pied?
4. Tu fais des achats après les cours?
5. Tu aimes faire des achats dans un grand magasin ou dans une boutique?
6. Tu achètes des cadeaux pour tes copains?
7. De quelle couleur est ton pantalon ou ton tee-shirt favori?
8. Pour les chaussures tu fais quelle pointure?
9. Tu demandes la pointure au-dessus ou au-dessous quand les chaussures sont trop larges?

B **L'anniversaire de mon frère.** Complétez.

Je ___ (aller) aux Galeries Lafayette. Je ___ (vouloir)
        1   2
acheter un cadeau pour mon frère. C'est son anniversaire.
Qu'est-ce que je ___ (pouvoir) acheter? Qu'est-ce qu'il
                     3
___ (aimer)? Je ___ (aller) au rayon articles de sport. Je
  4   5
___ (voir) une raquette de tennis. Voilà! C'est une bonne
  6
idée. Mon frère ___ (aimer) bien le tennis. Ses copains
                   7
et lui ___ (jouer) souvent au tennis mais mon frère ___
        8   9
(avoir) une vieille raquette. J'___ (acheter) la raquette
                                   10
et je ___ (payer) à la caisse.
        11

Vocabulaire

NOMS
les cheveux (m.)
les dents (f.)
la figure
la main

le dentifrice
le savon
le déodorant
la glace

le club de forme
le gymnase
le parc
le survêtement

le lit
le problème

VERBES
s'amuser
s'appeler
se réveiller
se lever
se brosser
se laver
se peigner
s'habiller
se maquiller
se raser
se promener

se coucher
s'endormir
maigrir
grossir

ADVERBES
d'abord
enfin
ensuite
tout de suite

AUTRES MOTS
ET EXPRESSIONS
avoir besoin de
faire de l'exercice

faire de l'aérobic
faire de la gymnastique
faire du jogging
pratiquer un sport
se mettre en forme
rester en forme
faire sa toilette
prendre un bain (une douche)

CHAPITRE 11   303

OPTIONAL MATERIAL

Réintroduction et recombinaison
ANSWERS
Exercice A
  Answers will vary.

Exercice B
1. vais
2. veux
3. peux
4. aime
5. vais
6. vois
7. aime
8. jouent
9. a
10. achète
11. paie

ASSESSMENT RESOURCES
1. Chapter Quizzes
2. Testing Program
3. Situation Cards
4. Communication Transparency C-11
5. Computer Software: Practice/Test Generator

VIDEO PROGRAM

INTRODUCTION   (36:09)

TU ES EN FORME?   (37:20)

LEARNING FROM REALIA
Ask students to give more correct ways of expressing the statements in the realia on page 303.

STUDENT PORTFOLIO
Written assignments that may be included in students' portfolios are the *Activités de communication écrite* on page 302 and the *Mon Autobiographie* section of the Workbook on page 115.

Note Students may create and save both oral and written work using the Electronic Portfolio feature on the CD-ROM.

CHAPTER OVERVIEW

In this chapter students will learn to talk about cars and good driving habits. They will also learn expressions needed to communicate with a gas station attendant. In order to do this, students will learn vocabulary associated with cars, verbs conjugated like *conduire*, and negative constructions.

The cultural focus of Chapter 12 is on French driving customs and the highways of France.

CHAPTER OBJECTIVES

By the end of this chapter, students will know:

1. vocabulary associated with automobile types, features, and basic servicing
2. vocabulary associated with driver's education, driver's licenses, parking, and traffic regulations.
3. the present indicative forms of the verbs *conduire, lire, écrire,* and *dire*
4. the negative constructions *ne… rien, ne… personne,* and *ne… jamais*
5. the formation of questions with inverted word order

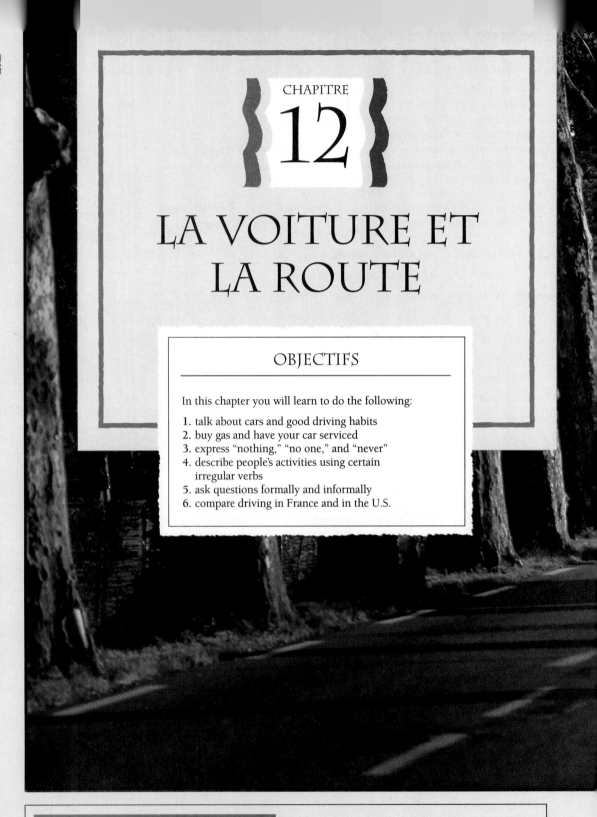

CHAPITRE 12

LA VOITURE ET LA ROUTE

OBJECTIFS

In this chapter you will learn to do the following:

1. talk about cars and good driving habits
2. buy gas and have your car serviced
3. express "nothing," "no one," and "never"
4. describe people's activities using certain irregular verbs
5. ask questions formally and informally
6. compare driving in France and in the U.S.

INTERDISCIPLINARY CONNECTIONS

Borrow a driver's education film from the Driver's Ed. class at your school. Have students view it and have them discuss it in French to the best of their ability. Then have them make a poster illustrating good driving tips and label it in French. Have them share the poster with the Driver's Ed. class.

305

Pacing

This chapter requires eight to ten class sessions. Pacing will vary according to class length and the age and aptitude of the students.

Note The Lesson Plans offer guidelines for 45- and 55-minute classes and **Block Scheduling.**

Exercices vs. *Activités*

All exercises (which provide guided practice) are coded in blue. All communicative activities are coded in red.

INTERNET ACTIVITIES

(optional)
These activities, student worksheets, and related teacher information are in the *Bienvenue* Internet Activities Booklet and on the Glencoe Foreign Language Home Page at: **http://www.glencoe.com/secondary/fl**

DID YOU KNOW?

Tell students that the beautiful tree-lined road in the photo is very typical of France. Plane trees (*les platanes*) often form an arch over the road. The trees grow in temperate regions of the northern hemisphere but are cultivated particularly in Europe because of their rapid growth and attractive bark. The species that grows in North America is called the buttonwood or sycamore tree.

VOCABULAIRE

MOTS 1

Vocabulary Teaching Resources

1. Vocabulary Transparencies 12.1 (A & B)
2. Audio Cassette 7B/CD-7
3. Student Tape Manual, Teacher's Edition, *Mots 1: A–C,* pages 131–133
4. Workbook, *Mots 1: A–C,* pages 116–117
5. Communication Activities Masters, *Mots 1: A,* page 59
6. Chapter Quizzes, *Mots 1:* Quiz 1, page 64
7. CD-ROM, Disc 3, *Mots 1:* pages 306–308

Bell Ringer Review

Write the following on the board or use BRR Blackline Master 12-1: Write three things you do in the morning and three things you do in the evening.

PRESENTATION (pages 306–307)

A. Using Vocabulary Transparencies 12.1 (A & B), point to each illustration and have students repeat the corresponding word two or three times after you or Cassette 7B/CD-7. Dramatize *freiner* and *s'arrêter* to clarify the meaning.

B. Point to items at random and ask *Qu'est-ce que c'est?* Have students identify each item with the appropriate word or expression.

C. Ask students to open their books to pages 306–307 and read the new words and sentences. Call on individuals to read or have students repeat in unison.

LA VOITURE

les deux roues

une moto

un vélomoteur

un break

une voiture de sport

PEUGEOT

une marque française

une décapotable

une clé

accélérer

mettre le contact

une conductrice

rouler vite

un conducteur

La voiture s'arrête.

La conductrice freine.

TOTAL PHYSICAL RESPONSE

(following the Vocabulary presentation)

Getting Ready

Set up a chair as a driver's seat. Pieces of paper can serve as accelerator and brake pedals. One student plays the part of a driver, the other a service station attendant. Demonstrate the terms *le capot, le pied,* and *tourner.*

TPR 1

___, levez-vous, s'il vous plaît. Venez ici. C'est votre voiture.
Montez dans votre voiture.
Asseyez-vous.
Fermez la portière.
Mettez votre ceinture de sécurité.
Regardez la carte routière.
Mettez le contact.
Mettez le pied sur l'accélérateur. Accélérez.

(continued on next page)

À LA STATION-SERVICE

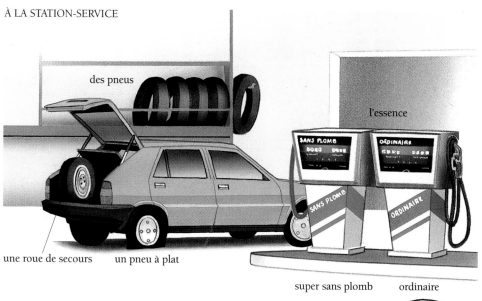

des pneus

l'essence

une roue de secours   un pneu à plat

super sans plomb   ordinaire

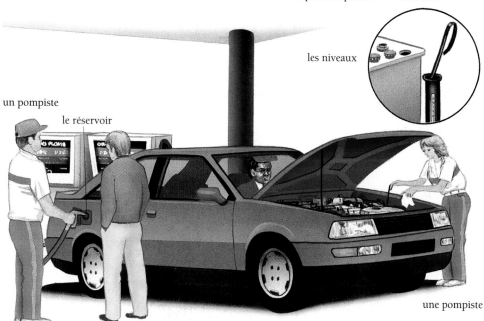

les niveaux

un pompiste

le réservoir

une pompiste

Le pompiste fait le plein.
Il met trente litres de super sans plomb dans le réservoir.
Quelqu'un parle au pompiste.
Une autre pompiste vérifie les niveaux.

Exercices

Exercices

A Qu'est-ce que c'est?
Répondez d'après les dessins.

1. C'est une voiture de sport ou un break?
2. C'est un vélomoteur ou une moto?
3. La moto a deux roues ou quatre roues?
4. La décapotable, c'est la voiture de sport ou le break?

B Tu as une voiture? Donnez des réponses personnelles.

1. Tu as une voiture? Tu as quelle marque de voiture?
2. Tu veux une voiture? De quelle marque?
3. Tu préfères les breaks ou les voitures de sport?
4. Tu aimes les décapotables?
5. Tu préfères les voitures ou les motos?
6. Ta mère roule vite? Et ton père?

C Les voitures. Choisissez la bonne réponse.

1. À la station-service le pompiste fait le plein. Il met de l'essence dans ___.
   a. le radiateur   b. le réservoir
2. Il vérifie les niveaux. Il met de l'eau dans ___.
   a. le moteur   b. le radiateur
3. Il met de l'air dans ___.
   a. les roues   b. les pneus
4. Le conducteur veut rouler plus vite. Il ___.
   a. freine   b. accélère
5. La conductrice veut s'arrêter. Elle ___.
   a. freine   b. accélère
6. Quand quelqu'un a un pneu à plat, il ou elle a besoin d'___.
   a. une roue de secours   b. une clé
7. Pour mettre le contact, on a besoin d'___.
   a. une clé   b. un réservoir
8. En général, dans les voitures de sport on met de l'essence ___.
   a. super   b. ordinaire
9. Aux États-Unis les nouvelles voitures consomment de l'essence ___.
   a. avec plomb   b. sans plomb

Exercices

PRESENTATION (page 308)

You may do the exercises while still working with the overhead transparencies since the exercises help the students learn the new words depicted on the transparencies.

Extension of *Exercice B*: Listening

After doing Exercise B as a whole-class activity, have students work in pairs. One partner reads the questions in random order. The second partner listens and answers with book closed. Then they reverse roles.

Extension of *Exercice C*

After completing Exercise C, ask questions such as the following: *Le pompiste ne met pas d'essence dans le radiateur. Qu'est-ce qu'il met dans le radiateur? (de l'eau) Il ne met pas d'eau dans le moteur. Qu'est-ce qu'il met dans le moteur? (de l'huile) Le conducteur ne veut pas rouler plus vite. Il veut rouler moins vite. Qu'est-ce qu'il fait? (Il freine.)*, etc.

ANSWERS

Exercice A

1. C'est une voiture de sport.
2. C'est un vélomoteur.
3. La moto a deux roues.
4. La décapotable, c'est la voiture de sport.

Exercice B

Answers will vary.

Exercice C

1. b	4. b	7. a
2. b	5. a	8. a
3. b	6. a	9. b

INFORMAL ASSESSMENT (Mots 1)

Check for comprehension by having one student read vocabulary items at random from pages 306–307 while another points to the appropriate illustrations on the overhead transparencies.

COOPERATIVE LEARNING

Ask students to write in English four or five characteristics of their car or their family car (model, make, color, year). They then use their prepared lists of features to follow your example and describe their cars to each other in small groups, using the *Mots 1* vocabulary. Do this with books closed. Group members can ask each other for words they can't remember.

INDEPENDENT PRACTICE

Assign any of the following:
1. Exercises, page 308
2. Workbook, *Mots 1: A–C*, pages 116–117
3. Communication Activities Masters, *Mots 1: A*, page 59
4. CD-ROM, Disc 3, pages 306–308

VOCABULAIRE

MOTS 2

LA ROUTE

un permis de conduire

l'auto-école (f.)

prendre des leçons de conduite

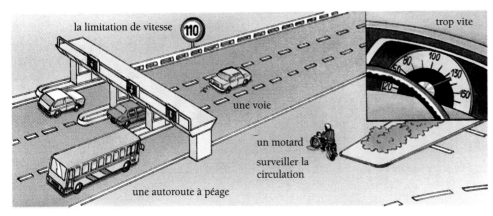

la limitation de vitesse

trop vite

une voie

un motard

surveiller la circulation

une autoroute à péage

un croisement

un carrefour

CHAPITRE 12   309

TOTAL PHYSICAL RESPONSE

(following the Vocabulary presentation)

Getting Ready

Set up a chair as a driver's seat. One student plays the part of a driver and the other a parking enforcement officer.

TPR

(Student 1), venez ici, s'il vous plaît. Vous êtes le conducteur/la conductrice.

Montez dans la voiture.
Mettez le contact.
Roulez, mais pas trop vite.
Maintenant, accélérez.
Vous arrivez en ville. Freinez.
Vous voulez garer la voiture.
Cherchez une place.
Voilà une place. Garez la voiture.
Ouvrez la portière.
Descendez.

(continued on page 310)

Vocabulary Teaching Resources

1. Vocabulary Transparencies 12.2 (A & B)
2. Audio Cassette 7B/CD-7
3. Student Tape Manual, Teacher's Edition, *Mots 2: D–F,* pages 133–134
4. Workbook, *Mots 2: D–G,* pages 117–118
5. Communication Activities Masters, *Mots 2: B,* page 60
6. Computer Software, *Vocabulaire*
7. Chapter Quizzes, *Mots 2: Quiz 2,* page 65
8. CD-ROM, Disc 3, *Mots 2:* pages 309–312

Bell Ringer Review

Write the following on the board or use BRR Blackline Master 12-2: Write the identity of each thing:

1. **Elle a deux roues et un moteur mais pas de pédales.**
2. **On met le contact avec cet objet.**
3. **Elle a quatre roues et un moteur. Elle roule très vite et elle est souvent belle.**

PRESENTATION *(pages 309–310)*

A. Have students close their books. Show Vocabulary Transparencies 12.2 (A & B). Have students repeat each word several times after you or Cassette 7B/CD-7.

B. Ask questions such as: *Il y a combien de personnes dans la voiture? Qui conduit? Qu'est-ce qu'elle prend? Elle a son permis de conduire? Elle va avoir son permis de conduire? L'autoroute a combien de voies? Qui surveille la circulation? Quelle est la limitation de vitesse? Il faut payer un*

péage sur l'autoroute? Les con-
ducteurs s'arrêtent pour payer le
péage? Où s'arrêtent-ils?

C. Ask the following questions
that can be answered with one
word. These give excellent
practice for oral comprehension: *Qui prend la leçon de*
conduite, le conducteur ou le
moniteur? Qui paie le péage, le
motard ou le conducteur? Qui
surveille la circulation, le motard
ou le conducteur? Qui obéit à la
limitation de vitesse, le motard
ou le conducteur? Qui traverse la
rue, le piéton ou le conducteur?
Qui gare la voiture, le piéton
ou le conducteur? Qui met la
ceinture de sécurité, le piéton
ou le conducteur? Qui surveille
le stationnement, le motard ou
la contractuelle? Qui écrit des
contraventions, les piétons ou
les contractuelles?

D. Ask students personalized
questions. For example: *Tu as*
ton permis de conduire, Jessica?
Benjamin, tu prends des leçons
de conduite? Où? Qui va à
l'auto-école? Devant le lycée,
quelle est la limitation de vitesse?
Sara, tu mets ta ceinture de
sécurité? Marc, que fait ta
mère à un feu rouge? Qui a des
contraventions?, etc.

Vocabulary Expansion

You may wish to give stu-
dents the following additional
vocabulary in order to talk
about driving.
la carte routière
un panneau
une rue à sens unique
la flèche
un agent de police
un parcmètre
doubler

un feu rouge
(orange)
(vert)

un piéton

une piétonne

les clous (m.)

un trottoir

traverser la rue dans les clous

garer la voiture

une place

une ceinture
de sécurité

Carole conduit la voiture.
Elle conduit prudemment.
Didier met sa ceinture de sécurité.
Il lit le Guide Michelin.

une contractuelle

Il est interdit de stationner ici.

ZUT!

une contravention

La contractuelle écrit une contravention.
La contractuelle ne dit rien.
Elle ne parle à personne.

Camille lit la contravention.
Elle est fâchée.
Elle dit: «Zut!»

310 CHAPITRE 12

TPR *(continued from page 309)*
Fermez la portière à clé.
Allez faire ce que vous voulez faire.
(Student 2), levez-vous, s'il vous plaît. Vous
êtes la contractuelle.
Regardez. Le stationnement est interdit.
Écrivez une contravention.
Mettez la contravention ici, sur le pare-
brise. *(Indicate.)*

Et (Student 1), venez ici, s'il vous plaît. Vous
revenez à votre voiture. Regardez. Prenez
la contravention.
Lisez-la.
Qu'est-ce que vous êtes fâché(e)! Dites
quelque chose.
Merci, (Student 1) et (Student 2). Vous avez
très bien fait. Asseyez-vous, s'il vous
plaît.

Exercices

A **En voiture.** Répondez par «oui» ou «non».

1. Il faut payer quand on roule sur une autoroute à péage?
2. Les autoroutes ont souvent quatre ou six voies?
3. À un carrefour il faut faire attention aux piétons?
4. Il faut mettre sa ceinture de sécurité quand on conduit?
5. On peut conduire sans avoir de permis de conduire?
6. Il faut conduire prudemment à un croisement?
7. Il faut respecter la limitation de vitesse?
8. Il faut rouler vite quand le feu est rouge?
9. Il faut s'arrêter quand le feu est vert?
10. Il faut accélérer pour s'arrêter?
11. Il est interdit de garer sa voiture sur le trottoir?

B **À vous de choisir.** Choisissez la bonne réponse.

1. Les ___ traversent la rue dans les clous quand le feu est vert.
   a. motards   b. piétons
2. Les motards surveillent ___.
   a. la circulation   b. le stationnement
3. Les contractuelles surveillent ___.
   a. le stationnement   b. la circulation
4. Les motards donnent des contraventions aux ___ qui roulent trop vite.
   a. conducteurs   b. contractuelles
5. Quand on veut garer sa voiture, on cherche ___.
   a. une place   b. le trottoir

C **Tu conduis ou pas?** Donnez des réponses personnelles.

1. Tu as ton permis de conduire?
2. Tu vas passer ton permis de conduire?
3. Tu as quel âge maintenant?
4. On passe le permis de conduire à quel âge?
5. Tu vas prendre des leçons de conduite?
6. Tu vas prendre des leçons de conduite à l'école ou à une auto-école?

D **Que font-ils?** Complétez en utilisant «conduit», «lit», «dit» ou «écrit».

1. Carole ___ la voiture.
2. Didier ne ___ pas la voiture.
3. Didier ___ le Guide Michelin.
4. Carole ne ___ pas le guide parce qu'elle ___.
5. La contractuelle ___ une contravention.
6. Carole est fâchée. Elle ___: «Zut!»
7. La contractuelle ne ___ rien. Elle ne parle à personne.

COOPERATIVE LEARNING

Working in teams of three, students make up a list of activities related to the road. They then separate the activities according to who does them: *le conducteur, le motard, le piéton.* Then each team member plays one of the above roles. For example: *Moi, je suis la conductrice/le conducteur. Je roule dans ma voiture…*

Exercices

PRESENTATION (*page 311*)

Exercices A and C: Listening

After doing Exercises A and C as a whole-class activity, focus on the listening skill by having students do them in pairs, one partner reading the questions in random order while the other answers with book closed.

Exercices B and D

After doing Exercises B and D, call on a student to review the information in his or her own words.

ANSWERS

Exercice A

1. Oui.	7. Oui.
2. Oui.	8. Non.
3. Oui.	9. Non.
4. Oui.	10. Non.
5. Non.	11. Oui.
6. Oui.	

Exercice B

1. b
2. a
3. a
4. a
5. a

Exercice C

Answers will vary.

Exercice D

1. conduit
2. conduit
3. lit
4. lit, conduit
5. écrit
6. dit
7. dit

INFORMAL ASSESSMENT
(*Mots 2*)

Have students close their books. Check for comprehension by indicating pictures on Vocabulary Transparencies 12.2 and giving students two minutes to note down everything they can remember to say about them. Call on individuals to report orally from their notes.

Activités de communication orale

Mots 1 et 2

> **Bell Ringer Review**
>
> *Write the following on the board or use BRR Blackline Master 12-3:* Make two lists: one of good driving habits, the other of bad ones.

PRESENTATION *(page 312)*

Activité C

In the CD-ROM version of this activity, students can interact with an on-screen native speaker.

ANSWERS

Activité A

Questions will begin with *C'est une bonne idée de… ?* Answers will begin with *Non, ce n'est pas une bonne idée de…* and end with the cues in the text.

Activités B and C

Answers will vary.

Activités de communication orale

Mots 1 et 2

A **C'est une bonne idée?**   Ask a classmate if it's a good idea to do the following things when driving.

> conduire sans avoir de permis de conduire
>
> Élève 1: C'est une bonne idée de conduire sans avoir de permis de conduire?
>
> Élève 2: Non, ce n'est pas une bonne idée de conduire sans avoir de permis de conduire.

1. traverser la rue quand le feu est rouge
2. rouler avec un pneu à plat
3. rouler sans avoir beaucoup d'essence dans le réservoir
4. se maquiller quand on conduit
5. lire le Guide Michelin quand on conduit

B **On conduit bien ou mal?** Ask the Driver's Ed. instructor in your school for a booklet on driving techniques. Work with a classmate and make a list of five good driving habits that you know how to express in French. Make a second list of five things that a good driver shouldn't do. Present your lists to the class in random order and ask your classmates to decide whether the people being described drive well or not.

> Élève 1: On ne respecte pas la limitation de vitesse.
>
> La classe: On conduit mal.

C **Le permis de conduire.**   Your French friend Alain wants to know about driving in the U.S. Answer his questions.

1. Tu as ton permis de conduire?
2. On peut avoir son permis de conduire à quel âge aux États-Unis?
3. Quelle est la limitation de vitesse sur les autoroutes?
4. Les motards donnent beaucoup de contraventions?

Alain

ADDITIONAL PRACTICE	**INDEPENDENT PRACTICE**

ADDITIONAL PRACTICE

1. Have students pretend they had a minor accident. They fill out an accident report including the following details:

Nom	Heure	Marque de
Âge	Lieu	voiture
Sexe	Vitesse	Accidentés
Date		*(victims)*

2. Student Tape Manual, Teacher's Edition, *Activité F,* page 134.

INDEPENDENT PRACTICE

Assign any of the following:

1. Exercises and activities, pages 311–312
2. Workbook, *Mots 2: D–G,* pages 117–118
3. Communication Activities Masters, *Mots 2: B,* page 60
4. Computer Software, *Vocabulaire*
5. CD-ROM, Disc 3, pages 309–312

STRUCTURE

Les verbes *conduire, lire, écrire* et *dire* au présent

Describing People's Activities

1. Study the following forms of the verbs *conduire,* "to drive," *lire,* "to read," *écrire,* "to write," and *dire,* "to say." Note how similar they are to one another in the present tense.

2. Note the irregular verb form of *dire: vous dites.*

CONDUIRE	LIRE	ÉCRIRE	DIRE
je conduis	je lis	j' écris	je dis
tu conduis	tu lis	tu écris	tu dis
il	il	il	il
elle } conduit	elle } lit	elle } écrit	elle } dit
on	on	on	on
nous conduisons	nous lisons	nous écrivons	nous disons
vous conduisez	vous lisez	vous écrivez	vous dites
ils	ils	ils	ils
elles } conduisent	elles } lisent	elles } écrivent	elles } disent

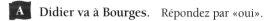

Exercices

A **Didier va à Bourges.** Répondez par «oui».

1. Didier va à Bourges?
2. Didier conduit prudemment?
3. Avant le voyage Didier lit le Guide Michelin?
4. Didier dit que Bourges est loin?
5. Didier écrit une lettre à son copain Guillaume?
6. Dans sa lettre il dit que Bourges est une jolie ville?
7. Guillaume lit la lettre de Didier?

B **Je lis et j'écris.** Donnez des réponses personnelles.

1. Tu aimes lire?
2. Tu lis beaucoup?
3. Tu lis le journal tous les jours?
4. Tu lis des magazines?
5. Tu lis quels magazines?
6. Tu écris des lettres à tes amis?
7. Tu écris à tes grands-parents ou tu téléphones à tes grands-parents?

CHAPITRE 12 **313**

314

C Une question, mon ami. Posez des questions à un copain ou une copine d'après le modèle.

> écrire beaucoup de lettres
> Élève 1: Tu écris beaucoup de lettres?
> Élève 2: Oui, j'écris beaucoup de lettres. (Non, je n'écris pas beaucoup de lettres.)

1. écrire des poèmes
2. écrire des compositions au cours d'anglais
3. lire le journal
4. lire des magazines
5. conduire une nouvelle voiture
6. dire que les voitures de sport sont chouettes

D Ses amis et lui. Complétez.

1. Lui, il dit des choses stupides, des bêtises, et ses amis ___ des bêtises aussi.
2. Lui, il conduit une vieille voiture et ses amis ___ de vieilles voitures aussi.
3. Lui, il conduit prudemment et ses amis ___ prudemment aussi.
4. Lui, il écrit une lettre et ses amis ___ une lettre aussi.
5. Lui, il lit un magazine et ses amis ___ un magazine aussi.

E Oui ou non? Répondez en utilisant «nous».

1. Vous dites des bêtises?
2. Vous dites des choses sérieuses?
3. Vous dites des choses intéressantes?
4. Vous dites des choses amusantes?
5. Vous conduisez beaucoup?
6. Vous lisez beaucoup?
7. Vous écrivez souvent à vos amis?

F Qui dit ça? Complétez avec «dire».

1. On ____ que les autoroutes sont bonnes en France.
2. Je ____ que les autoroutes françaises sont bonnes mais je ____ aussi qu'il y a trop de circulation.
3. Jean ____ que la plupart des autoroutes sont à péage.
4. Tu ____ qu'il faut payer sur les autoroutes à péage?
5. Paul et Monique, qu'est-ce que vous ____? Vous ____ qu'il faut payer sur les autoroutes américaines aussi? Vous ____ que la plupart des autoroutes aux États-Unis sont à péage?
6. Nos amis américains ____ qu'il y a beaucoup d'autoroutes à huit voies, c'est-à-dire quatre voies dans chaque sens (direction).

Les mots négatifs

Expressing "Nothing," "No One," and "Never"

1. You have already learned the negative expression *ne... pas*. Study the following negative expressions that function the same way as *ne... pas*.

AFFIRMATIF	NÉGATIF
Il dit quelque chose.	Il ne dit rien.
Il écrit quelque chose.	Il n'écrit rien.
Il voit quelqu'un.	Il ne voit personne.
Il parle à quelqu'un.	Il ne parle à personne.
Il voyage toujours.	Il ne voyage jamais.
Il lit souvent.	Il ne lit jamais.
Il écrit quelquefois.	Il n'écrit jamais.

2. As with *ne... pas*, when *ne... jamais* is followed by *un, une, des*, or *de la, de l', du*, and *des*, these words change to *de*.

Il fait souvent une promenade.   Il ne fait jamais de promenade.
Elle fait toujours du sport.   Elle ne fait jamais de sport.

Exercices

A **Non, au contraire.** Répondez par «non».

Il voit quelque chose?
Non, il ne voit rien.

1. Il dit quelque chose?
2. Il écrit quelque chose?
3. Il entend quelque chose?
4. Il lit quelque chose?
5. Il vend quelque chose?
6. Il regarde quelque chose?
7. Il voit quelqu'un?
8. Il regarde quelqu'un?
9. Il parle à quelqu'un?
10. Il écrit à quelqu'un?

B **Elle ne voyage jamais.** Répondez d'après le modèle.

Pascale adore nager.
Tu crois? Elle dit ça, mais elle ne nage jamais.

1. Pascale adore conduire.
2. Pascale adore lire.
3. Pascale adore voyager.
4. Pascale adore faire du sport.
5. Pascale adore jouer au tennis.
6. Pascale adore faire du ski nautique.

ADDITIONAL PRACTICE

After completing Exercises A and B, write the following verbs on the board:

Je vois	J'achète	J'attends
Je veux	J'entends	J'écris
J'ai	Je dis	J'apprends

Have students use either *quelque chose* or *quelqu'un* with each verb. Then have them put the sentences in the negative with *ne... rien* or *ne... personne*.

INDEPENDENT PRACTICE

Assign any of the following:
1. Exercises, pages 313–315
2. Workbook, *Structure: A–E*, pages 119–121
3. Communication Activities Masters, *Structure: A–C*, pages 61–62
4. CD-ROM, Disc 3, pages 313–315

Les mots négatifs

PRESENTATION (page 315)

A. Present negative expressions by holding up an object (pencil, book, etc.) as you say: *J'ai quelque chose (Je vois quelque chose)*. Then put the object away and say: *Je n'ai rien (Je ne vois rien)*.

B. Have a student stand by you as you say: *Je vois quelqu'un. J'entends quelqu'un*. Then have the person go away as you say: *Je ne vois personne. Je n'entends personne*.

C. Lead students through steps 1 and 2 on page 315.

Note In the CD-ROM version, this structure point is presented via an interactive electronic comic strip.

Note Point out that the words *rien, personne*, and *jamais* can stand alone as short answers. For example: *Qu'est-ce que tu as? Rien! Qui parle? Personne. Tu y vas souvent? Non, jamais.*

Exercices

PRESENTATION (page 315)

Exercices A and B

You may wish to use the recorded version of these exercises.

ANSWERS

Exercice A

1. Non, il ne dit rien.
2. Non, il n'écrit rien.
3. Non, il n'entend rien.
4. Non, il ne lit rien.
5. Non, il ne vend rien.
6. Non, il ne regarde rien.
7. Non, il ne voit personne.
8. Non, il ne regarde personne.
9. Non, il ne parle à personne.
10. Non, il n'écrit à personne.

Exercice B

1. Tu crois? Elle dit ça, mais elle ne conduit jamais.
2. ... elle ne lit jamais.
3. ... elle ne voyage jamais.
4. ... elle ne fait jamais de sport.
5. ... elle ne joue jamais au tennis.
6. ... elle ne fait jamais de ski nautique.

Les questions et les mots interrogatifs

You may wish to refer to the **Note on Interrogatives** in Chapter 1, page 13, of this Teacher's Wrap-around Edition. Students have now had a great deal of exposure to the various question forms, including both inverted and normal word order. It is suggested that when students actively formulate their own questions, you allow them to use whichever word order they select.

Teaching Tip You can get students started by asking them the three ways they already know to formulate questions in French (rising intonation, *est-ce que,* and inversion). Then ask them what question (interrogative) words they know.

PRESENTATION *(page 316)*

A. Lead students through steps 1–5 on page 316.
B. Have students read aloud all the example questions that appear in the explanation.

Les questions et les mots interrogatifs

Asking Questions Formally and Informally

1. Review the following ways in which questions can be formed in French.

> Vous parlez français?
> Est-ce que vous parlez français?
> Parlez-vous français?

2. Review the following question words you have already learned.

> à quelle heure   comment   où   quand
> combien de   pourquoi   qui

3. Note that you can use these question words in three ways.

   a. In informal, spoken French the question word is often placed at the end of the sentence.

   > Tu vas où?
   > Tu vas au cinéma avec qui?
   > Vous allez arriver au cinéma à quelle heure?

   b. The question word can also be used with *est-ce que.*

   > Où est-ce que tu vas?
   > Avec qui est-ce que tu vas au cinéma?
   > Quand est-ce que vous allez arriver au cinéma?

   c. In more formal conversation and in written French the subject and verb are inverted after a question word.

   > Où vas-tu?
   > Avec qui vas-tu au cinéma?
   > Quand allez-vous arriver au cinéma?

4. With a noun subject, both the noun and *il(s)* or *elle(s)* are used in the inverted question form.

   > Où *les copains* dînent-*ils*?
   > Comment *Marie* conduit-*elle*?
   > Combien de roues *les motos* ont-*elles*?
   > Pourquoi *Jean* vend-*il** la voiture?

   * The final **d** is pronounced as a /t/.

5. In the inverted question form you insert a *t* between *il, elle,* or *on* and any verb that does not end in a *t* or a *d.*

   > Où Béatrice déjeune-t-elle?
   > Comment va-t-on à la rue Racine?
   > Pourquoi gare-t-elle la voiture sur le trottoir?

LEARNING FROM PHOTOS

Have students make up questions about the car. Encourage them to give the same question in various forms. For example: *La voiture est garée sur le trottoir? Est-ce que la voiture est garée sur le trottoir? La voiture est-elle garée sur le trottoir? La voiture est garée où? Où est-ce que la voiture est garée? Où la voiture est-elle garée?*

ADDITIONAL PRACTICE

1. Using question words, students write out dialogues for this situation: Pretend you're the nervous parents of a teenager who's going out with a friend who has recently gotten his/her license. Find out how he/she drives, where they are going, when they are going to return, and so on.
2. Student Tape Manual, Teacher's Edition, *Activité E,* page 137.

Exercices

A **Tu vas où?** Transposez les questions d'après le modèle.

> **Arlette, où vas-tu?**
> *Tu vas où, Arlette?*

1. Où vas-tu?
2. Comment vas-tu au restaurant?
3. À quelle heure arrives-tu au restaurant?
4. Avec qui dînes-tu?
5. Où es-tu maintenant?

B **Où allez-vous?** Transposez les questions d'après le modèle.

> **Où est-ce que vous allez?**
> *Où allez-vous?*

1. Où est-ce que vous allez dîner?
2. Comment est-ce que vous allez au restaurant?
3. Est-ce que vous conduisez?
4. Est-ce que vous prenez l'autoroute à péage?
5. Avec qui est-ce que vous allez au restaurant?
6. Est-ce que vous parlez français au serveur?

C **Encore des questions!** Écrivez des questions d'après le modèle.

> **Marie lit la carte.**
> *Marie lit-elle la carte?*

1. Marie va au restaurant.
2. Marie conduit.
3. Marie gare sa voiture devant le restaurant.
4. Marie regarde la carte.
5. Marie parle au serveur.
6. Marie commande un sandwich au jambon.
7. Le serveur sert le sandwich.
8. Marie mange le sandwich.
9. Le sandwich est bon.
10. Marie paie.
11. Marie laisse un pourboire pour le serveur.

D **À qui Jean parle-t-il?** Écrivez des questions d'après le modèle.

> **Jean parle à sa copine. (à qui)**
> *À qui Jean parle-t-il?*

1. Jean parle à sa copine au téléphone. (à qui)
2. Il invite sa copine au cinéma. (qui)
3. Ils vont aller au cinéma ce soir. (quand)
4. Jean arrive chez sa copine à sept heures. (à quelle heure)
5. Ils voient le film «Au revoir, les enfants». (quel film)
6. Après le cinéma ils vont au café. (quand)

CHAPITRE 12   **317**

CONVERSATION

PRESENTATION (page 318)

A. Tell students they will hear a conversation between Francine and Philippe.

B. Have them close their books and watch the Conversation Video or listen as you read the conversation or play Cassette 7B/CD-7.

C. Have pairs of students play the roles of Francine and Philippe. Have the student taking the part of Francine look puzzled.

D. Call on some students to do the conversation orally without looking at their books. They may ad lib. They do not have to know the conversation verbatim.

Note In the CD-ROM version, students can play the role of either one of the characters and record the conversation.

ANSWERS
Exercice A

1. Non, il n'a pas son permis de conduire.
2. Il a seulement quinze ans.
3. Oui, elle croit que Philippe conduit.
4. Oui, il conduit.
5. Elle voit Alain, le frère de Philippe.
6. Elle croit que c'est Philippe.

Prononciation

PRESENTATION (page 318)

A. Model the key word *trottoir* and have students repeat chorally.

B. Now model the other words and sentences in similar fashion.

C. For additional practice, use Pronunciation Transparency P-12, the *Prononciation* section on Cassette 7B/CD-7, and the Student Tape Manual, Teacher's Edition, *Activités H–J*, page 139.

Scènes de la vie *Tu as ton permis de conduire?*

FRANCINE: Tu as ton permis de conduire?
PHILIPPE: Non, je n'ai pas mon permis. J'ai seulement quinze ans.
FRANCINE: Mais tu conduis, n'est-ce pas?
PHILIPPE: Tu veux rigoler! Je ne conduis jamais!
FRANCINE: C'est bizarre. Je suis sûre que…
PHILIPPE: Ah… Je comprends! Tu vois mon frère Alain qui conduit et tu crois que c'est moi.

A **Qui conduit?** Répondez d'après la conversation.

1. Philippe a son permis de conduire?
2. Pourquoi pas?
3. Francine croit que Philippe conduit?
4. Le frère de Philippe conduit?
5. Francine voit qui?
6. Elle croit que c'est qui?

Prononciation *Le son /wa/*

Repeat the following words with the sound /wa/ as in *moi*:

toi	voie	réservoir
croisement	trottoir	pouvoir

Now repeat the following sentences:

Tu ne vois pas le croisement devant toi!
Il va pouvoir partir à trois heures.
Moi, je ne crois pas Antoine!

trottoir

318   CHAPITRE 12

CRITICAL THINKING ACTIVITY

(Thinking skills: drawing conclusions and problem solving)

Read the following to the class or put it on the board or on a transparency:

1. Faut-il toujours respecter la limitation de vitesse? Si l'on ne respecte pas la limitation de vitesse, quelles peuvent être les conséquences?

2. Robert veut aller quelque part. Il veut prendre la voiture. Mais il y a très peu d'essence dans le réservoir. Le réservoir est presque vide. Robert compte son argent. Il n'a pas assez d'argent pour faire le plein. Qu'est-ce qu'il peut faire?

Activités de communication orale

A **Une enquête.** Divide into small groups and choose a leader. The leader interviews the others to find out how often (*souvent, quelquefois, jamais*) they do the activities listed below. The leader takes notes and reports to the class.

Activité	souvent	quelquefois	jamais
Jouer au tennis			✗

jouer au tennis

Élève 1: Tu joues au tennis?
Élève 2: Non, je ne joue jamais au tennis.
Élève 1 (*à la classe*): Patrick ne joue jamais au tennis.

acheter beaucoup de cadeaux	faire des voyages
aller au bord de la mer	faire du jogging
chanter sous la douche	faire les courses
conduire	lire le journal
écouter du jazz	manger des fruits de mer
écrire des lettres	prendre des bains de soleil
faire de la planche à voile	regarder la télé

B **Qu'est-ce que tu dis?** Divide into small groups. Write down several statements that would make your classmates respond with one of the expressions below, then exchange papers with another group member. Take turns reading and responding to the statements.

Absolument pas!	C'est un miracle!	Quelle surprise!
C'est chouette, ça!	Jamais!	Tu veux rigoler!
C'est impossible!	Quelle chance!	Zut!

Élève 1: Suzanne a son permis de conduire!
Élève 2: Je dis: «C'est chouette, ça!» (Je dis: «Quelle surprise!»)

Bonne route.
Soyez prudent !
Le prochain Relais
vous accueillera
à 75 KM (A7)
à 125 KM (A9).

Bell Ringer Review

Write the following on the board or use BRR Blackline Master 12-6: Say the opposite. *For example:* Marie-Jo achète trois robes. Et vous? (*Nous n'achetons rien.*)

1. Mathieu lit quelque chose. Et Juliette?
2. La sœur de Carine parle à quelqu'un. Et Raoul?
3. Laure chante quelquefois. Et Jérôme?

Activités de communication orale

ANSWERS

Activité A
Questions follow the model provided. Answers will vary.

Activité B
Answers will vary.

READING STRATEGIES
(page 320)

Reading

A. Read the *Lecture* to the students a paragraph at a time as they follow along in their books.

B. Now call on a student to read. After he/she has read several sentences, ask questions of other students.

Teaching Tip Use other students to answer questions since the student who read aloud was probably concentrating on his/her pronunciation and comprehended little.

C. Allow the class five minutes to reread the *Lecture*.

Post-reading

Have students mention some things they think are different about driving in France.

Note Students may listen to a recorded version of the *Lecture* on the CD-ROM.

Étude de mots

ANSWERS

Exercice A

Answers may include any five: **populaires, japonaises, parkings, américaines, direction, routes, nationales, départementales, pittoresques, attention, dangereux, respecter, limitation, surveillent, vigilantes, strictes, circulation, places.**

Exercice B

1. a   3. e   5. c
2. d   4. b

320

LECTURE ET CULTURE

ON VA CONDUIRE EN FRANCE?

En France presque[1] tout le monde a une voiture. Les Français conduisent quelles marques de voiture? Il y a deux marques françaises qui sont très populaires, Renault et Peugeot. On voit aussi beaucoup de voitures japonaises sur les autoroutes françaises, mais très peu de voitures américaines.

Les autoroutes en France sont très bonnes. Elles ont trois ou quatre voies dans chaque sens (direction). La plupart des autoroutes sont à péage. Il y a aussi des routes nationales qui sont des routes à grande circulation. Les routes départementales sont plus pittoresques mais il faut faire attention aux croisements, qui peuvent être dangereux.

Si vous conduisez en France, il faut respecter la limitation de vitesse sur les routes et dans les agglomérations[2]. Les motards surveillent la circulation. Si vous roulez trop vite, vous allez avoir une contravention.

Et le stationnement! Il n'y a jamais assez de[3] parkings ou de places pour garer les voitures. Si vous garez votre voiture là où le stationnement est interdit, vous allez trouver une contravention sur le parebrise[4] à votre retour[5]. Les contractuelles sont très vigilantes et très strictes.

[1] presque   *almost*
[2] agglomérations   *populated areas*
[3] assez de   *enough*
[4] parebrise   *windshield*
[5] à votre retour   *upon your return*

Étude de mots

A   **Le français, c'est facile.**   Trouvez cinq mots apparentés dans la lecture.

B   **Synonymes.**   Trouvez les expressions équivalentes.

1. vite
2. la direction
3. surveiller
4. l'agglomération
5. garer

a. rapidement
b. une zone développée
c. stationner
d. le sens
e. contrôler, observer attentivement

ADDITIONAL PRACTICE

After completing Exercises A and B, write the following on the board: Find the noun that corresponds to the verb.

1. conduire
2. circuler
3. limiter
4. surveiller
5. stationner
6. retourner

a. la limitation
b. la surveillance
c. la conduite
d. le stationnement
e. la circulation
f. le retour

LEARNING FROM PHOTOS

You may wish to ask students: *Qu'est-ce que c'est?* (un parcmètre) *C'est pour quoi faire? (On met une pièce dedans et on achète un ticket qui est valable pour un certain nombre de minutes [heures] de stationnement.)*

Compréhension

C **Sur la route en France.** Corrigez les phrases.

1. Il y a plus de voitures américaines que de voitures japonaises en France.
2. Il n'y a pas de voitures françaises. L'industrie automobile n'existe pas en France.
3. Beaucoup d'autoroutes en France ne sont pas bonnes.
4. On ne paie jamais sur les autoroutes à péage françaises.
5. La plus grande route c'est la route départementale.
6. Il y a des croisements dangereux sur les autoroutes.
7. Il n'y a pas de limitation de vitesse dans les agglomérations.
8. Les conducteurs aiment avoir des contraventions.

D **En route.** Répondez.

1. Les grandes autoroutes en France ont combien de voies dans chaque sens?
2. Qu'est-ce qu'il faut payer sur la plupart des autoroutes?
3. Il y a une limitation de vitesse sur les routes en France?
4. Qui surveille les autoroutes?
5. Il y a toujours assez de places pour stationner?
6. Qui a la responsabilité de surveiller le stationnement?
7. Quelles sont deux marques françaises de voiture?

DÉCOUVERTE CULTURELLE

Voici un vélomoteur. Il faut avoir plus de seize ans et un permis spécial pour conduire un vélomoteur.

Le rêve[1] de beaucoup de jeunes, c'est une moto. On peut conduire une moto à partir de seize ans[2] avec un permis spécial moto. Et le casque[3] est obligatoire! Si vous êtes en France, vous pouvez conduire une moto? Pourquoi?

Et pour conduire une voiture il faut avoir dix-huit ans en France. Là où vous habitez, il faut avoir quel âge pour obtenir un permis de conduire?

[1] rêve *dream*
[2] à partir de seize ans *from age 16 on*
[3] casque *helmet*

Compréhension

ANSWERS

Exercice C

1. Il y a plus de voitures japonaises que de voitures américaines en France. (Il y a moins de voitures américaines que…)
2. Il y a beaucoup de voitures françaises. L'industrie automobile existe en France.
3. Les autoroutes en France sont très bonnes.
4. On paie toujours sur les autoroutes à péage françaises.
5. La plus grande route c'est l'autoroute.
6. Il y a des croisements dangereux sur les routes départementales. (Il n'y a pas de croisements dangereux sur les autoroutes.)
7. Il y a une limitation de vitesse dans les agglomérations.
8. Les conducteurs n'aiment pas avoir de contraventions.

Exercice D

1. Les grandes autoroutes en France ont trois ou quatre voies dans chaque sens.
2. Il faut payer un péage sur la plupart des autoroutes.
3. Oui, il y a une limitation de vitesse sur les routes en France.
4. Les motards surveillent les autoroutes.
5. Non, il n'y a jamais assez de places pour stationner.
6. Les contractuelles ont la responsabilité de surveiller le stationnement.
7. Peugeot et Renault sont deux marques françaises de voiture.

OPTIONAL MATERIAL

Découverte culturelle

PRESENTATION *(page 321)*

After students have read the selection, discuss similarities and differences between French and American driving requirements.

Note Students may listen to a recorded version of the *Découverte culturelle* on the CD-ROM.

DID YOU KNOW?

Mopeds, scooters, and motorcycles are very popular in France among young people because cars (even used ones) are expensive to buy and maintain, and gasoline costs more than twice what it does in the United States. Anyone driving or riding on a motorbike is required to wear a helmet.

LEARNING FROM PHOTOS

You may wish to ask students: *Ce n'est pas une moto. C'est un vélomoteur? Qu'est-ce que le jeune homme conduit? Qu'est-ce qu'il porte? Porter un casque est obligatoire? Est-ce que le jeune homme roule vite? Il est en ville ou sur l'autoroute?*

RÉALITÉS

322

Bell Ringer Review

Write the following on the board or use BRR Blackline Master 12-8: Write as many words as you can having to do with cars and driving.

OPTIONAL MATERIAL

PRESENTATION (*pages 322–323*)

The main objective of this section is to allow students to enjoy the photographs. However, if you would like to do more with it, you might wish to do the following activities.

Pre-reading

Before reading the captions, have students cover them and look only at the photos. Ask them to describe in as much detail as possible what they see. Use questions as a guide, if necessary.

Reading

Have students read the captions on page 323 silently and be prepared to answer the questions in captions 2 and 5.

Post-reading

Discuss the captions as a class and answer the questions.

Ask students (drivers if possible) what problems they might encounter when driving a car in France for the first time.

Note In the CD-ROM version, students can listen to the recorded captions and discover a hidden video behind one of the photos.

DID YOU KNOW?

Most drivers fear the *motards*, motorcycle police officers. The *motards* mean business when they stop speeding motorists. They ride powerful motorcycles and dress to allow minimum friction while on a speed chase. Some *motards* wear egg-shaped helmets to reduce air drag.

L'agent de police est dans les villes **1**. Les agents de police règlent la circulation.

Voici trois panneaux routiers **2**. Quel panneau indique une autoroute à péage, à ton avis?

Pour traverser la rue, les piétons appuient sur le bouton **3**.

Voici des gendarmes français **4**. Eux, ils sont toujours sur la route, souvent à moto. Ils portent toujours un casque s'ils sont à moto.

Voici quelques signaux importants qu'il faut comprendre pour conduire en France **5**. Quelle est la limitation de vitesse sur cette route?

VOUS N'AVEZ PAS LA PRIORITÉ

45

RAPPEL

323

CULMINATION

RECYCLING

The *Activités de communication orale* and *Activités de communication écrite* provide a forum for students to create and answer their own questions and come up with their own dialogues while working within the automobile context of Chapter 12.

INFORMAL ASSESSMENT

Oral Activities A and B may serve as a means to evaluate students' speaking skills. Activity A is effective as a one-on-one check of spontaneous question-creating abilities. You can designate one part of the illustration at a time to focus attention on the vocabulary and structure necessary to ask a question about that part.

Activity B can be used as a guide for interviews conducted either before the class, or alone with the teacher, or recorded on cassette for an oral grade. Use the evaluation criteria given on page 34 of this Teacher's Wraparound Edition.

Activités de communication orale

ANSWERS

Activités A and B
Answers will vary.

Activités de communication orale

A À la station-service.

1. Make up as many questions about this illustration as you can.
2. Work with a classmate and have him or her answer your questions.

B La route. The new French exchange student (your partner) asks you a lot of questions about driving in the U.S. Answer his or her questions and then reverse roles. You can use the list below for suggestions.

beaucoup de circulation

Élève 1: Quand est-ce qu'il y a beaucoup de circulation?
Élève 2: Il y a beaucoup de circulation le matin de huit heures à neuf heures et le soir de cinq heures à six heures.

des autoroutes à péage
la limitation de vitesse
assez de parkings dans la ville
des vélomoteurs
beaucoup de stations-service
de l'essence sans plomb
des motards
des contraventions

324   CHAPITRE 12

Activités de communication écrite

A **Mon permis de conduire.** Write a letter to your French friend. Tell him or her how old you are and whether you have your driver's license yet. Tell your friend what you have to do to get a license and find out what people in France have to do to get one.

B **Zut!** A *contractuelle* is writing a parking ticket when the owner of the car comes running up. Write down what they say to each other.

Réintroduction et recombinaison

A **Personnellement.** Donnez des réponses personnelles.

1. Comment t'appelles-tu?
2. Tu es d'où?
3. Tu es de quelle nationalité?
4. Tu vas à quelle école?
5. Qui est ton professeur de français?
6. Qu'est-ce que tu fais au cours de français?
7. Tu aimes être en forme?
8. Qu'est-ce que tu fais pour rester en forme?

B **Jamais!** Répondez en utilisant «ne… jamais».

1. Tes parents se lèvent à midi en semaine?
2. Les élèves se couchent à six heures du soir?
3. Le professeur s'endort en classe?
4. Les garçons se rasent en classe?

Vocabulaire

NOMS
la voiture
la voiture de sport
le break
la décapotable
la marque
les deux roues (f.)
la moto
le vélomoteur
la roue de secours
le pneu (à plat)
le réservoir
la clé
la ceinture de sécurité
le conducteur
la conductrice
l'auto-école (f.)
la leçon de conduite

le permis de conduire
le guide
la route
l'autoroute (f.) à péage
la voie
la limitation de vitesse
le motard
la circulation
le croisement
le carrefour
le trottoir
le piéton
la piétonne
les clous (m.)
le feu
le stationnement
la place
la contractuelle
la contravention

la station-service
le/la pompiste
l'essence (f.)
　super
　ordinaire
　sans plomb
les niveaux (m.)

VERBES
rouler
accélérer
freiner
s'arrêter
traverser
surveiller
conduire
dire
écrire
lire

AUTRES MOTS ET EXPRESSIONS
garer la voiture
faire le plein
vérifier les niveaux
mettre le contact

quelqu'un
ne… jamais
ne… personne
ne… rien

fâché(e)
il est interdit
prudemment
sans
trop
vite
Zut!

Activités de communication écrite

ANSWERS

Activités A and B
　Answers will vary.

OPTIONAL MATERIAL

Réintroduction et recombinaison

ANSWERS

Exercice A
1. Answers will vary.

Exercice B
1. Mes parents ne se lèvent jamais à midi en semaine.
2. Les élèves ne se couchent jamais à six heures du soir.
3. Le professeur ne s'endort jamais en classe.
4. Les garçons ne se rasent jamais en classe.

ASSESSMENT RESOURCES

1. Chapter Quizzes
2. Testing Program
3. Situation Cards
4. Communication Transparency C-12
5. Performance Assessment
6. Computer Software: Practice/Test Generator

VIDEO PROGRAM

INTRODUCTION　　(38:40)

EN ROUTE!　　(39:17)

STUDENT PORTFOLIO

Written assignments which may be included in students' portfolios are the *Activités de communication écrite* on page 325 and the *Mon Autobiographie* section of the Workbook on page 125.

Note Students may create and save both oral and written work using the Electronic Portfolio feature on the CD-ROM.

INDEPENDENT PRACTICE

1. Activities and exercises, pages 324–325
2. CD-ROM, Disc 3, pages 324–325
3. Communication Activities Masters, pages 59–63

La Mode

PRESENTATION *(pages 326–329)*

This cultural material is presented for students to enjoy and to help them gain an appreciation of the francophone world. Since the material is *optional*, you may wish to have students read it on their own as they look at the colorful photographs that accompany it. They can read it at home, or you may wish to give them a few minutes in class to read it.

If you prefer to present some of the information in greater depth, you may follow the suggestions given for other reading selections throughout the book. Students can read aloud, answer questions asked by the teacher, ask questions of one another in small groups and, finally, give a synopsis of the information in their own words in French.

MORE ABOUT THE PHOTOS

Photo 2 Jewelry is important to both men and women in Africa. There is a great variety of jewelry in Africa. In the Sahara and North Africa, the preferred metal for jewelry is silver. Elsewhere in Africa, the preferred metal for jewelry is gold.

Beads and amulets are popular jewelry forms. In areas where there are animistic religious beliefs, these beads and amulets have a religious significance and they can play a role in community rituals. The charms worn around the neck are called *grisgris*.

LA MODE

Aujourd'hui, dans la plupart des grandes villes du monde, on s'habille plus ou moins de la même façon, mais les vêtements traditionnels existent toujours parce qu'ils sont parfaitement adaptés au climat et à la géographie. On s'habille d'une façon en Suisse où il fait froid et d'une autre façon au Sénégal où il fait toujours chaud.

1, 2 La petite fille qui habite à la montagne en Suisse ne porte pas les mêmes vêtements que cette belle Sénégalaise qui habite dans un pays tropical.

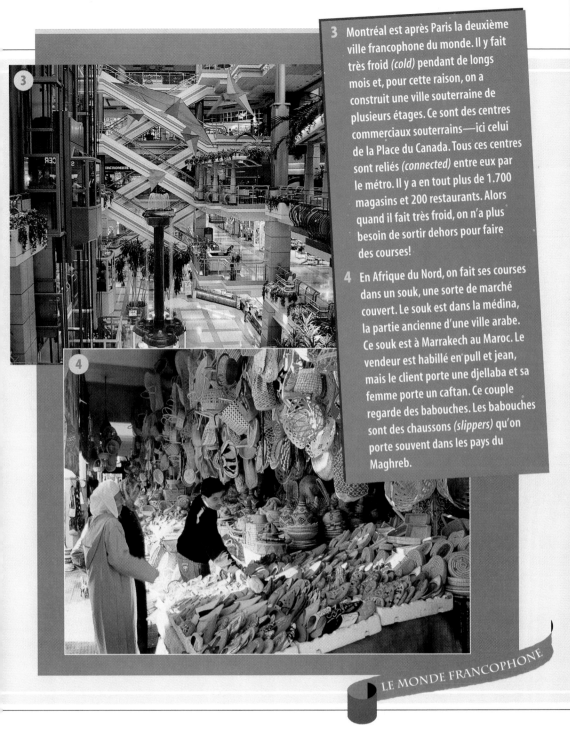

3. Montréal est après Paris la deuxième ville francophone du monde. Il y fait très froid *(cold)* pendant de longs mois et, pour cette raison, on a construit une ville souterraine de plusieurs étages. Ce sont des centres commerciaux souterrains—ici celui de la Place du Canada. Tous ces centres sont reliés *(connected)* entre eux par le métro. Il y a en tout plus de 1.700 magasins et 200 restaurants. Alors quand il fait très froid, on n'a plus besoin de sortir dehors pour faire des courses!

4. En Afrique du Nord, on fait ses courses dans un souk, une sorte de marché couvert. Le souk est dans la médina, la partie ancienne d'une ville arabe. Ce souk est à Marrakech au Maroc. Le vendeur est habillé en pull et jean, mais le client porte une djellaba et sa femme porte un caftan. Ce couple regarde des babouches. Les babouches sont des chaussons *(slippers)* qu'on porte souvent dans les pays du Maghreb.

LE MONDE FRANCOPHONE

Photo 4 The *djellaba* is an extremely practical garment. It is very loose and does not hinder movement. It protects the garments worn underneath from rain as well as from the dust that blows in from the Sahara. *Djellabas* are made from all types of fabrics, but particularly gabardine. There are other fancy fabrics woven in the small villages. The *djellaba* has no religious significance.

The veil worn by women in many of the Islamic countries is rarely worn by young urban women of the Maghreb. With the spread of Islamic fundamentalism, however, the veil is becoming more common, particularly in Algeria.

In Tunisia, women wear the *sifsari* everywhere. A *sifsari* resembles a "cloak-shawl." Its loose folds wrap around the woman's head and shoulders. The *sifsari* is extremely practical as it can be pulled across the face to protect the wearer from wind or the sand of the desert. The *sifsari* has no religious significance.

Shoes are taken off when entering a house in the Maghreb. People will often put on a pair of *babouches* to wear in the house or they will go barefoot. Both men and women wear *babouches*. Men's *babouches* are usually white or a light color and they are very simple. There is little or no ornamentation. Women's *babouches* are decorated with gold or silver embroidery.

Photo 5 The beautiful designs on the fabrics of the clothing in this market are distinctively African. Many of the designs are indigo wood-block prints and batiks.

The technique for making a batik fabric is very interesting. It is done by hand, and wax is used as a dye repellent to cover parts of a design while the uncovered fabric is being dyed with one or more colors. After the dyeing process, the wax is dissolved in boiling water.

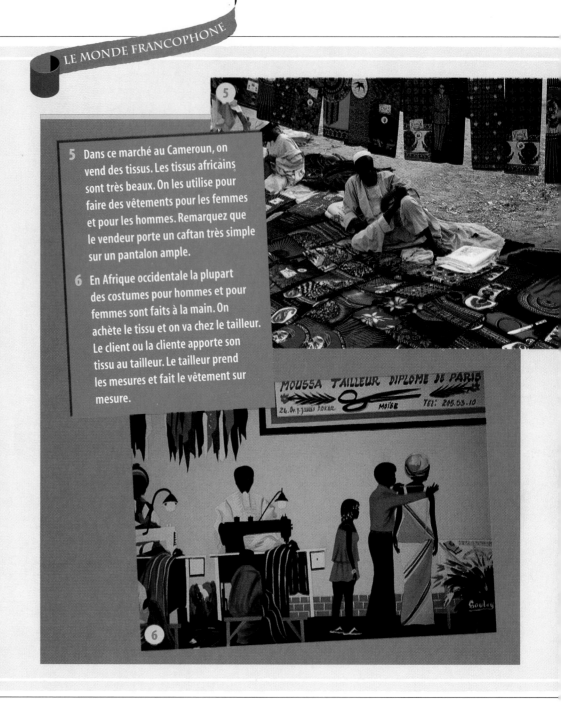

LE MONDE FRANCOPHONE

5 Dans ce marché au Cameroun, on vend des tissus. Les tissus africains sont très beaux. On les utilise pour faire des vêtements pour les femmes et pour les hommes. Remarquez que le vendeur porte un caftan très simple sur un pantalon ample.

6 En Afrique occidentale la plupart des costumes pour hommes et pour femmes sont faits à la main. On achète le tissu et on va chez le tailleur. Le client ou la cliente apporte son tissu au tailleur. Le tailleur prend les mesures et fait le vêtement sur mesure.

7 Cette boutique chic est à Monaco, un petit pays indépendant situé sur la Côte d'Azur. C'est une principauté, c'est-à-dire que c'est un pays dirigé (*ruled*) par un prince. Monaco attire les gens riches et célèbres du monde entier.

8 Cette boutique est à Dakar au Sénégal. Les deux femmes regardent des robes européennes prêt-à-porter dans la vitrine. Mais elles portent des robes traditionnelles faites à la main. Dans beaucoup de pays de l'Afrique occidentale les hommes et les femmes portent une robe longue. Comme vous le voyez, ces robes sont très élégantes. Une robe très élégante s'appelle un grand *boubou*. Les hommes mettent un grand *boubou* sur un pantalon et une chemise.

9 Ces poupées portent le costume traditionnel des *doudous*—«jeunes filles» en créole, le dialecte qu'on parle à la Martinique. On voit la forte influence africaine sur ces costumes martiniquais.

LE MONDE FRANCOPHONE

Photo 7 The principality of Monaco has been under the rule of the Grimaldi family since 1297. Monaco is a very short distance from the Riviera city of Nice. The citizens of Monaco are called *Monégasques*. Monaco has a population of some 30,000 but only slightly more than 5,000 are *Monégasques*. Citizenship in Monaco is very difficult to obtain. It is not even granted automatically to a person born in Monaco.

The belief that citizens of Monaco pay no personal income taxes because all government expenses are financed by casino revenues is not completely true, but it is true that they are far less burdened with taxes than are outsiders. Non-citizens residing in Monaco pay high taxes.

The official language of the principality is French and the currency is the French franc.

Photo 8 In general, Africans place much importance on dress. They spend a large portion of their after-food budget on clothing.

The *boubou* is worn by both men and women. A woman's elegant *grand boubou* is a long, regal floor-length embroidered dress, while a man's *grand boubou* is an embroidered robe-like garment that reaches the ground.

For everyday dress, women wear a loose top and wrap a length of cloth, called *un pagne*, around themselves as a skirt.

OVERVIEW

This section reviews key grammatical structures and vocabulary from Chapters 9–12. The structure topics were first presented on the following pages: reflexive verbs, page 290; verbs like *prendre*, page 243; *croire* and *voir*, page 266; *lire*, *dire*, *écrire*, and *conduire*, page 313; stress pronouns, page 245; the comparative and the superlative, pages 269 and 271.

REVIEW RESOURCES

1. Workbook, Self-Test 3, pages 126–129
2. Videocassette/Videodisc, Unit 3
3. Video Activities Booklet, Unit 3: Chapters 9–12, pages 34–49
4. Computer Software, Chapters 9–12
5. Testing Program, Unit Test: Chapters 9–12, pages 73–78
6. Performance Assessment
7. CD-ROM, Disc 3, *Révision: Chapters 9–12*, pages 330–333
8. CD-ROM, Disc 3, Self-Tests 9–12
9. CD-ROM, Disc 3, Game: *Pour en savoir plus*
10. Lesson Plans

Conversation

PRESENTATION *(page 330)*

Have students repeat each sentence after you. Then call on individuals to dramatize the conversation for the class.

ANSWERS

Exercice A

1. Il voit Stéphanie en robe.
2. La robe est rose.

330

Conversation   *Stéphanie en robe!*

ANTOINE: Qu'est-ce que je vois! Stéphanie en robe!
STÉPHANIE: Euh… tu crois que la robe bleue est plus jolie que la robe rose?
ANTOINE: Mais non. Tu es très jolie en rose.
STÉPHANIE: Je préfère vraiment les pantalons!
ANTOINE: Tu sors avec qui?
STÉPHANIE: Avec Jérôme. On va au restaurant.
ANTOINE: Ah oui, avec lui, c'est toujours les restaurants chic.
STÉPHANIE: Oui, mais on s'amuse bien ensemble.
ANTOINE: Tu pars à quelle heure?
STÉPHANIE: Dans cinq minutes. Je me peigne, je me maquille et je pars.

A   **Stéphanie et son frère.**   Répondez.

1. Qu'est-ce qu'Antoine voit?
2. De quelle couleur est la robe de Stéphanie?
3. D'après Antoine, la robe bleue est plus jolie que la robe rose?
4. Qu'est-ce que Stéphanie préfère, les robes ou les pantalons?
5. À ton avis, est-ce qu'Antoine aime Jérôme?
6. Est-ce que Stéphanie aime sortir avec Jérôme? Pourquoi?
7. Est-ce que Stéphanie va partir dans quelques minutes?
8. Qu'est-ce qu'elle va faire avant de partir?

Structure

Les verbes réfléchis

Review the present tense forms of reflexive verbs.

1. Remember that in reflexive constructions, the subject and the reflexive pronoun refer to the same person.

SE LEVER	
je me **lève**	*nous nous* **levons**
tu te **lèves**	*vous vous* **levez**
il/elle/on se **lève**	*ils/elles se* **lèvent**

LEARNING FROM PHOTOS

Give students the words for the cosmetics pictured: *du rouge à lèvres, un poudrier, de la poudre, de l'ombre à paupières, un flacon de parfum.* Now ask them questions using these words: *Tu mets du rouge à lèvres tous les jours? Quelles couleurs préfères-tu? Tu as un poudrier dans ton sac? Qu'est-ce qu'il y a à l'intérieur d'un poudrier? Tu mets souvent de l'ombre à paupières? Tu aimes le parfum? Quels parfums?*

2. Review the placement of *ne... pas, ne... plus, ne... jamais.*

> Vous *ne* vous levez *pas?*
> Il *ne* s'endort *jamais* tout de suite.

A On sort. Complétez.

Ma sœur et moi, nous ___ (s'amuser) bien quand nous sortons. Mais elle ___
          1   2

(se préparer) pendant des heures, et moi, je ___ (se laver) et je ___ (s'habiller)
                                            3   4

en deux minutes. D'abord, elle, elle ___ (se brosser) les dents pendant cinq
                                            5

minutes! Puis elle ___ (s'habiller), mais elle ___ (se changer) trois fois (*times*)
                    6   7

avant de se décider. Puis, elle ___ (se maquiller) pendant une demi-heure.
                                          8

Enfin, elle ___ (se peigner). Pendant ce temps, moi, je lis un livre. Quelquefois,
                  9

je ___ (s'endormir)!
    10

Les verbes *prendre, croire, voir, lire, dire, écrire* et *conduire*

Review the following forms of some irregular verbs you have learned.

PRENDRE	je prends, tu prends, il/elle/on prend nous prenons, vous prenez, ils/elles prennent
COMPRENDRE	je comprends, tu comprends, il/elle/on comprend nous comprenons, vous comprenez, ils/elles comprennent
CROIRE	je crois, tu crois, il/elle/on croit nous croyons, vous croyez, ils/elles croient
VOIR	je vois, tu vois, il/elle/on voit nous voyons, vous voyez, ils/elles voient
LIRE	je lis, tu lis, il/elle/on lit nous lisons, vous lisez, ils/elles lisent
DIRE	je dis, tu dis, il/elle/on dit nous disons, vous dites, ils/elles disent
ÉCRIRE	j'écris, tu écris, il/elle/on écrit nous écrivons, vous écrivez, ils/elles écrivent
CONDUIRE	je conduis, tu conduis, il/elle/on conduit nous conduisons, vous conduisez, ils/elles conduisent

---

3. Non, il préfère la robe rose.
4. Elle préfère les pantalons.
5. Answers will vary.
6. Elle aime sortir avec lui parce qu'ils s'amusent bien ensemble.
7. Oui, elle va partir dans cinq minutes.
8. Elle va se peigner et se maquiller.

Structure
Les verbes réfléchis
PRESENTATION (*pages 330–331*)

A. Write the forms of *se lever* on the board.
B. Point out the pronunciation change in the stem of *se lever* and the written accent in the forms where it appears.
C. Have students give you other reflexive verbs they know. Select one and write its forms on the board.
D. Have students repeat the forms of *se lever* and the other verb you wrote on the board.

Exercice
PRESENTATION (*page 331*)

Exercice A
  Call on several individuals to complete the exercise with books open. Then call on one individual to read the entire exercise.

ANSWERS
Exercice A
  1. nous amusons
  2. se prépare
  3. me lave
  4. m'habille
  5. se brosse
  6. s'habille
  7. se change
  8. se maquille
  9. se peigne
  10. m'endors

INFORMAL ASSESSMENT
  Have students tell you anything they can about their daily routine.

Les verbes prendre, croire, voir, lire, dire, écrire et conduire
PRESENTATION (*page 331*)

  Have students read the verb forms aloud in chorus with you.

COOPERATIVE LEARNING

  Have students work in teams of three. One student asks another about his/her routine. The student responds, and the third reports what was said. For example:
É1: Tu te lèves à quelle heure?
É2: Moi, je me lève à sept heures.
É3: ___ se lève à sept heures.

PAIRED ACTIVITY

  Students work in pairs and list as many daily activities as they can, classifying them as to the time they occur: *le matin/l'après-midi/le soir.* Then they ask each other how often they do these things at those times.
É1: Tu te maquilles toujours le matin?
É2: Non, je ne me maquille pas toujours le matin. Souvent, quand je vais sortir, je me maquille le soir.

B **Qu'est-ce qu'on fait?** Remplacez les mots en italique et faites les changements nécessaires.

1. *Vous* écrivez beaucoup? (elles)
2. *Moi, je* lis beaucoup. (elles)
3. *Ils* écrivent souvent à leurs parents? (tu)
4. *Ils* voient leurs parents toutes les semaines. (je)
5. *Amélie* conduit bien? (tes frères)
6. Non, *elle* apprend à conduire. (ils)
7. *Tu* dis déjà «au revoir»? (vous)
8. Oui, *je* prends l'avion dans une heure. (nous)
9. *Tu* conduis beaucoup? (elles)
10. Non, *je* vois mal. (elles)
11. *Robert* lit le journal tous les matins? (ils)
12. *Je* crois qu'*il* lit le journal. (nous, ils)

Les pronoms accentués

1. Review the stress pronouns and the corresponding subject pronouns.

STRESS PRONOUNS	SUBJECT PRONOUNS
moi	je
toi	tu
lui	il
elle	elle
nous	nous
vous	vous
eux	ils
elles	elles

2. Remember that you use stress pronouns:

   a. to emphasize the subject   Moi, j'ai faim!
   b. after a preposition   C'est pour moi?
   c. when there is no verb in the sentence   Qui? Moi?
   d. after *c'est* or *ce sont*   C'est lui qui n'écrit jamais.
   e. after *que* in comparisons   Anne est plus grande que toi.

C **En vacances.** Répondez d'après le modèle.

> Sa mère joue au tennis. Et son père?
> *Lui aussi, il joue au tennis.*

1. Son frère fait de la plongée sous-marine. Et ses cousins?
2. Je fais de la planche à voile. Et toi?
3. Nous bronzons facilement. Et vous deux?
4. Il plonge bien. Et ses sœurs?
5. Vous sortez ce soir. Et nous?
6. Tu vas au restaurant. Et moi?
7. Ils aiment les fruits de mer. Et elle?
8. J'aime le soleil. Et vous?

Le comparatif et le superlatif

1. You use the comparative to compare two people or two items.

> **Nathalie est plus (moins, aussi) sportive que son frère.**

2. You use the superlative to single out one person or one item from the group and compare it to all the others.

> **Nathalie est la plus (la moins) sportive de la famille.**
> **Serge est le plus (le moins) sportif de la famille.**
> **Ils sont les plus (les moins) sportifs de la famille.**

3. Remember that the adjective *bon* has an irregular form in the comparative and the superlative: *meilleur(e)*.

> **Mon idée est meilleure que ton idée.**
> **Jean-Claude est le meilleur de la classe.**

D **Bernard et moi.** Répondez d'après le modèle.

> Élève 1: Bernard est très sérieux.
> Élève 2: Il est plus sérieux que moi?
> Élève 1: Non, mais il est aussi sérieux que toi.

1. Bernard est très timide.
2. Bernard est très sportif.
3. Bernard est très généreux.
4. Bernard est très actif.
5. Bernard est très nerveux.
6. Bernard est très grand.
7. Bernard est très patient.
8. Bernard est très intelligent.

E **Nathalie et moi.** Changez *Bernard* en *Nathalie* dans l'Exercice D.

F **Les élèves de Mme Leblond.** Répondez d'après le modèle.

> Véronique est très amusante.
> *Véronique est la plus amusante de la classe.*

1. Alain est très timide.
2. Catherine et Émilie sont très intelligentes.
3. Louise est très jolie.
4. Les frères Gautier sont très désagréables.
5. Les sœurs Duhamel sont très gentilles.
6. Olivier est très aimable.
7. Valérie est très réservée.
8. Martine est très bonne.

Activité de communication orale

A **Au Club Med.** Imagine that you're a group leader (*un gentil organisateur* or *un G.O.*) at Club Med. Tell about your daily routine: what time you get up, what you wear, what sports you play, what you eat, and what you do at night.

ADDITIONAL PRACTICE

Have students bring in some Club Med ads or brochures from travel magazines or a travel agency. Have them write a short description of one of the photos—what the weather's like, what the people are doing, etc. You could post these paragraphs on your bulletin board or have the students add them to their **Student Portfolio**.

INDEPENDENT PRACTICE

Assign any of the following:
1. Exercises and activity, pages 330–333
2. Workbook, Self-Test 3, pages 126–129
3. CD-ROM, Disc 3, pages 330–333
4. CD-ROM, Disc 3, Self-Tests 9–12
5. CD-ROM, Disc 3, Game: *Pour en savoir plus*

Le comparatif et le superlatif

PRESENTATION (*page 333*)

Go over steps 1–3. Have students give additional examples.

ANSWERS

Exercice D

1. É2: Il est plus timide que moi?
   É1: Non, mais il est aussi timide que toi.
2. … plus sportif que moi?
   … aussi sportif que toi.
3. … plus généreux que moi?
   … aussi généreux que toi.
4. … plus actif que moi?
   … aussi actif que toi.
5. … plus nerveux que moi?
   … aussi nerveux que toi.
6. … plus grand que moi?
   … aussi grand que toi.
7. …plus patient que moi?
   … aussi patient que toi.
8. … plus intelligent que moi?
   … aussi intelligent que toi.

Exercice E

1. É2: Elle est plus timide que moi?
   É1: Non, mais elle est aussi timide que toi.
2. … plus sportive… aussi…
3. … plus généreuse… aussi …
4. … plus active… aussi…
5. … plus nerveuse… aussi…
6. … plus grande… aussi…
7. … plus patiente… aussi…
8. … plus intelligente… aussi…

Exercice F

1. … le plus timide…
2. … les plus intelligentes…
3. … la plus jolie…
4. … les plus désagréables…
5. … les plus gentilles…
6. … le plus aimable…
7. … la plus réservée…
8. … la meilleure…

Activité de communication orale

PRESENTATION (*page 333*)

Activité A

This activity can be done either orally or in writing.

ANSWERS

Activité A

Answers will vary.

LETTRES ET SCIENCES

Écologie: La Pollution de l'eau

OVERVIEW

The readings in this *Lettres et sciences* section are related topically to material in Chapters 9 and 10. See page 228 in this Teacher's Wraparound Edition for suggestions on presenting the readings.

Avant la lecture

PRESENTATION *(page 334)*

A. Have students do the *Avant la lecture* activities. Activity 2 asks them to do some scanning.

B. You may wish to give the students the cognates that appear in this reading, or you may prefer to have them scan the passage and look for cognates.

C. Call on a student who has studied biology to describe the water cycle, or draw a diagram of the water cycle on the board and label the following in French: *l'océan, l'eau, les nuages, la pluie, le sol, un arbre, une feuille.* (Water from the oceans evaporates and forms clouds. The clouds produce rain that soaks the ground. Ground water is taken up by the roots of plants. The plants then lose water to the atmosphere through transpiration. This moisture also forms clouds.)

D. Have the students look at the photos to get an idea of what they will be reading about.

Lecture

PRESENTATION *(pages 334–335)*

A. Give students a couple of minutes to read each paragraph. Then ask what the paragraph was about. They can answer in English.

ÉCOLOGIE: LA POLLUTION DE L'EAU

Avant la lecture

1. Is water scarce or abundant where you live? Think about the role that water plays in your town. Are there any regulations concerning the watering of lawns, the washing of cars, the amount of certain substances that can be present in the town water?

2. Here are four titles. Scan the text and see if you can match these titles with the four paragraphs in the text.

   La répartition de l'eau
   Sauvons l'eau!
   La circulation de l'eau
   Les différents genres de pollution

Lecture

L'eau, tu es
la plus grande richesse
qui soit° au monde,   *exists*
et tu es la plus délicate,
toi, si pure
au ventre° de la terre.   *in the depths of*

Antoine de Saint-Exupéry

Nous «sommes» de l'eau. Notre corps est composé de 65% d'eau. On trouve l'eau partout: 96% dans les mers et les océans, 3% dans les glaciers et 1% qui prend part au «cycle de l'eau».

L'eau des lacs et des mers s'évapore. Ensuite elle retombe en pluie et s'infiltre dans le sol. Du sol, elle est absorbée par les arbres où elle arrive dans les feuilles et s'évapore encore, etc.

On ne peut pas vivre (exister) sans eau, mais malheureusement, l'eau est mal distribuée: par exemple, en Afrique certaines régions n'ont pas assez d'eau[1],

Le Gange déborde et cause des inondations.

mais en Inde, quand le Gange, le grand fleuve, déborde, il y a trop d'eau[2]. Aux États-Unis, nous avons quelquefois des périodes de sécheresse quand il n'y a pas de pluie ou, au contraire, des inondations, quand il y a trop de pluie. Mais en général, nous n'avons ni trop, ni trop peu[3] d'eau. Notre problème, c'est la pollution.

La pollution peut prendre plusieurs formes.

1. Les pluies acides

Quand les nuages passent au-dessus des zones industrielles, ils absorbent tous les gaz qui s'échappent (sortent) des cheminées et des voitures. Les nuages transportent ces gaz et les pluies qui tombent un peu plus loin sont des «pluies acides». Ces pluies acides causent la destruction des forêts et contaminent les lacs.

INTERDISCIPLINARY CONNECTIONS

Students form a research partnership with the biology class to find out what people can do to conserve water, prevent pollution, and protect the environment. Then they design posters illustrating these issues and they label them in French.

2. Les engrais[4]

Les agriculteurs utilisent beaucoup d'engrais, en général des phosphates, pour maintenir la fertilité du sol. Ces engrais chimiques sont entraînés[5] par les pluies jusque dans les lacs et les rivières. Ils polluent les rivières et les lacs parce qu'ils font pousser les plantes aquatiques[6]. Ces plantes prennent tout l'oxygène de l'eau. Sans oxygène, les poissons ne peuvent pas vivre et disparaissent. Les engrais polluent aussi les mers. Ils sont entraînés dans les mers par les rivières où ils nourrissent les algues. Ces algues se transforment en véritables «marées[7] rouges» et tuent[8] les poissons.

3. La marée noire

La marée noire est causée par le mazout[9] qui est jeté dans la mer par des pétroliers.

4. Les déchets[10] radioactifs

Il y a à notre époque plus de 100.000 tonnes de déchets radioactifs au fond de l'océan Atlantique et de l'océan Pacifique!

Il faut sauver l'eau. Il faut apprendre à conserver les réserves. Et surtout il faut apprendre à ne pas polluer, à ne pas verser les déchets toxiques dans l'eau. C'est le but[11] de beaucoup d'écologistes qui veulent protéger et sauver notre environnement.

[1] assez d'eau   *enough water*
[2] trop d'eau   *too much water*
[3] nous n'avons ni trop, ni trop peu   *we have neither too much nor too little*
[4] engrais   *fertilizers*
[5] entraînés   *carried*
[6] ils font pousser les plantes aquatiques   *they make aquatic vegetation grow*
[7] marées   *tides*
[8] tuent   *kill*
[9] mazout   *fuel oil*
[10] déchets   *waste*
[11] but   *the goal*

Quelques formes de pollution

Après la lecture

A **La pollution.**   Vrai ou faux?

1. 65% de l'eau prend part au «cycle de l'eau».
2. On ne peut pas vivre sans eau.
3. Les marées rouges font disparaître les poissons.
4. La marée noire est causée par des algues.
5. Il y a des déchets radioactifs dans l'océan Pacifique.
6. Il faut apprendre à conserver les réserves d'eau.

B **Il faut sauver l'eau.**   Répondez.

1. Quels sont les risques de pollution de l'eau là où vous habitez?
2. Quelles sont les mesures adoptées par votre ville pour ne pas polluer l'eau ou pour la conserver? S'il n'y a pas de mesures adoptées, faites des recommandations.

LETTRES ET SCIENCES   **335**

B. Have students form four groups. Each group reads and discusses a separate topic within the reading and then presents its findings to the rest of the class. The reading can be divided into the following sections: (1) introduction, (2) acid rain, (3) fertilizers, (4) oil spills and radioactive waste.

Après la lecture

PRESENTATION *(page 335)*

A. Go over the *Après la lecture* exercises.

B You may wish to have the students discuss the following question: *Comment utilisez-vous de l'eau?* Prompt them with questions if they cannot come up with the information on their own: *Vous prenez souvent un verre d'eau? Vous vous lavez? Vous vous brossez les dents? Vous vous lavez les cheveux? Vous lavez vos vêtements? Vous lavez la voiture? Vous lavez votre chien? Vous nagez dans une piscine? Vous arrosez vos plantes?*

Exercices

PRESENTATION *(page 335)*

Students can prepare the exercises on their own. You may then go over them in class after completing the reading.

ANSWERS

Exercice A

1. faux
2. vrai
3. vrai
4. faux
5. vrai
6. vrai

Exercice B

Answers will vary.

LETTRES ET SCIENCES

Littérature: Apollinaire (1880–1918)

PRESENTATION *(page 336)*

A. Tell students they are going to read about a famous poet who had a very interesting life. His name is Apollinaire.

B. Go over the many cognates that appear in the biographical introduction.

C. Have students read the biography silently.

D. Tell students to look for the following information in the biography: *les villes qu'Apollinaire visite, l'époque où il écrit ses poèmes, des amis d'Apollinaire.*

«La Cravate»
Avant la lecture

PRESENTATION *(page 336)*

A. Have students discuss the *Avant la lecture* activities.

B. Have them look at the poem and figure out the order in which the words should be read.

Lecture

PRESENTATION *(page 336)*

A. Read the poem to the class.

B. Have students read it silently.

C. Have students tell you the message they get from the poem.

D. Ask students if they agree with the sentiments of the poet.

Après la lecture

ANSWERS

Exercices A and B
   Answers will vary.

LITTÉRATURE: APOLLINAIRE (1880–1918)

Guillaume Apollinaire a une vie très fantaisiste et mouvementée. Sa poésie reflète sa vie. Il voyage dans toute l'Europe—à Munich, Berlin, Prague, Vienne. Il s'intéresse à tous les mouvements intellectuels et artistiques de son époque. C'est la période avant la guerre de 1914, une période très riche en idées en tous genres. C'est le début du cubisme, par exemple. Les poètes et les artistes peintres *(painters)* discutent ensemble ces nouvelles idées. Apollinaire est l'ami des peintres Picasso, Vlaminck et Marie Laurencin. Apollinaire est un des premiers grands poètes français modernes. Il annonce les grands mouvements artistiques des années 20 *(1920's)*.

   Certains des poèmes d'Apollinaire sont des «caligrammes»: le poème est écrit en forme d'objet. *La cravate* est un exemple de ce genre de poème.

Avant la lecture

1. The poem is written in the shape of a tie. When do men or women wear ties? What impression does a tie convey?

2. What could a tie represent in terms of freedom and society?

Lecture

Après la lecture

A **Les vêtements.**   Répondez.

1. Qu'est-ce que vous mettez quand vous vous habillez «bien»?

2. Est-ce que vous jugez les gens d'après leurs vêtements?

3. D'après vous, est-ce qu'une école doit *(must)* imposer certaines normes vestimentaires?

B **Êtes-vous poète?**

Avec des amis «poètes», écrivez un calligramme.

INTERDISCIPLINARY CONNECTIONS

1. Bring in a copy of *Calligrammes* and share some of the other poems, such as *"Le jet d'eau,"* with your students.

2. Refer students to page 368 of the Level 4 textbook, *Trésors du temps,* for an example of the cubist art that was popular at the time of Apollinaire. (Picasso's *Les Trois musiciens*). Then, with the help of the art teacher and other samples of cubist art he/she may be able to provide, students do a drawing in the cubist style based on either of the Apollinaire poems on these pages.

SCIENCES

En 1901–1902 Apollinaire est en Allemagne et rencontre une jeune Anglaise, Annie Playden. Mais Annie qui est mennonite émigre aux États-Unis.

Avant la lecture

1. Find out about the Mennonites.
2. In French, the word *bouton* means both button (for clothes) and bud (for flowers). In the last stanza of the poem, the poet makes a joke. See if you can explain what the joke is.

Lecture

ANNIE

Sur la côte du Texas
Entre Mobile et Galveston il y a
Un grand jardin tout plein de roses
Il contient aussi une villa
Qui est une grande rose

Une femme se promène souvent
Dans le jardin toute seule
Et quand je passe sur la route
   bordée de tilleuls°   *linden trees*
Nous nous regardons

Comme cette femme est mennonite
Ses rosiers et ses vêtements n'ont
   pas de boutons
Il en manque deux° à mon veston   *two are*
La dame et moi suivons le même rite   *missing*

Apollinaire, blessé à la tête pendant la guerre de 1914

Après la lecture

A **Discutons du poème.** Répondez.

1. The poet imagines his lost love in America. Find examples in the poem that show that this is just a fantasy.
2. In a typically French way, Apollinaire makes light of his emotion and sadness with a "joke." What is the only remaining link between the couple?

DID YOU KNOW?

You may wish to give students some background on the Mennonites. You might ask them to pretend they are listening to a lecture and have them take some notes.

Les mennonites sont membres d'un secte religieux. La plupart des mennonites sont aux États-Unis. Ils ont une vie très, très simple. Ils portent toujours des vêtements simples. Leurs vêtements sont toujours en noir ou en gris. Ils préfèrent les couleurs sombres pour leurs vêtements. Tout le monde porte les mêmes vêtements ou presque. Leurs enfants ne vont pas à l'école. Les parents instruisent eux-mêmes leurs enfants. Les mennonites sont contre la guerre. Ils ne portent pas d'armes. Les mennonites sont des pacifistes. Et ils sont très religieux.

Météorologie: La Prévision du temps
Avant la lecture

PRESENTATION *(page 338)*

A. Call on science fans to explain briefly the following:
  1. a high-pressure area
  2. a low-pressure area
  3. an air mass
  4. wind
  5. clouds

  These explanations will assist non-science-oriented students in understanding the reading.
B. Do the *Avant la lecture* activities in the textbook.
C. Have students scan the selection for cognates.

Lecture

PRESENTATION *(pages 338–339)*

A. Have the students read the selection silently.
B. Have them prepare a list of weather terms they remember.

MÉTÉOROLOGIE: LA PRÉVISION DU TEMPS

Avant la lecture

1. Find a weather map in one of your newspapers.
2. Match the French and English terms for weather expressions by comparing the legend of your weather map with that of the French weather map below.

Lecture

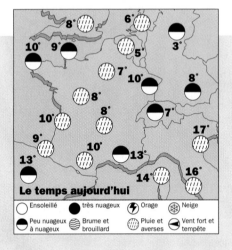

Le matin, beaucoup de gens écoutent le bulletin météorologique à la radio ou le regardent à la télévision pour décider comment s'habiller.

La météo est la science qui étudie l'atmosphère: les vents, les pluies, les dépressions ou zones de basses pressions, et les anticyclones ou zones de hautes pressions. Pour prévoir le temps, les météorologistes doivent savoir[1] le temps qu'il fait sur tout le globe. Il y a trois centres météorologiques dans le monde qui rassemblent toutes les informations météorologiques; ils sont situés à Washington aux États-Unis, à Moscou en Russie et à Melbourne en Australie.

Le soleil chauffe la Terre[2]; la Terre à son tour chauffe l'air et forme l'atmosphère. Mais l'atmosphère n'est pas la même partout: il y a des masses d'air froid au-dessus des pôles, et des masses d'air chaud au-dessus de l'équateur. Quand les masses d'air passent au-dessus des mers ou des océans, elles absorbent de la vapeur d'eau. Il y a donc plusieurs catégories de masses d'air: froides et humides, froides et sèches, chaudes et humides, chaudes et sèches. Ces masses d'air pèsent de manière différente

sur le sol[3]. Dans un anticyclone, elles pèsent lourd[4]: c'est donc une zone de hautes pressions. Dans une dépression, elles ne pèsent pas lourd: c'est donc une zone de basses pressions. Dans un anticyclone, les masses d'air sont trop lourdes et ne peuvent s'affronter[5]. Le temps reste stable. Dans une dépression, les différentes masses d'air s'affrontent si elles sont différentes—une masse d'air froid va contre une masse d'air chaud, par exemple. Le front est la zone où les deux masses s'affrontent; il apporte de la pluie ou du vent.

Les vents sont des mouvements d'air entre les anticyclones (zones de hautes pressions) et les dépressions (zones de

INTERDISCIPLINARY CONNECTIONS

With the help of the science class, students consult the weather map in the newspaper for their own state or for the United States as a whole. They then make a weather map for one of these using the map on page 338 as a model. Be sure that they use the French weather symbols and key.

SCIENCES

Les cumulo-nimbus annoncent souvent un orage.

basses pressions). L'air est repoussé[6] par les anticyclones, mais il est aspiré[7] par les dépressions. Ce mouvement d'air est le vent.

Les nuages sont l'ensemble de particules d'eau très fines. Elles sont maintenues en suspension par les mouvements verticaux de l'air.

On peut souvent prévoir le temps d'après les nuages. La forme, la couleur et l'altitude donnent des renseignements relativement précis sur le temps.

[1] doivent savoir   *must know*
[2] chauffe la Terre   *heats the Earth*
[3] pèsent…sol   *exert varying amounts of pressure on the surface of the Earth*
[4] lourd   *heavily*
[5] s'affronter   *collide*
[6] repoussé   *pushed back*
[7] aspiré   *pulled in*

Après la lecture

A Le bulletin météorologique.
Donnez une définition en français pour les mots suivants.

1. la météorologie
2. les dépressions
3. les anticyclones
4. le front
5. le vent

B La météorologie.   Répondez aux questions.

1. Qu'est-ce que la météorologie étudie?
2. Comment est-ce qu'on obtient les informations nécessaires?
3. Où sont les trois centres météorologiques?
4. Qu'est-ce qui arrive (*happens*) quand les masses d'air passent au-dessus des mers?
5. Quand est-ce que le temps reste stable? Quand est-ce qu'il pleut ou qu'il y a du vent?
6. De quelle autre manière est-ce qu'on peut prévoir le temps?

C La carte du temps.   Faites la carte du temps pour les États-Unis pour la journée de demain (en français, bien sûr).

D Savez-vous que…   Dans le système Celsius, 0° est la température où l'eau gèle, et 100° est la température où l'eau bout. Si vous voulez passer de degrés Celsius en degrés Fahrenheit ou vice versa, voici deux formules qui peuvent vous aider.

$9/5°C + 32 = °F$	Ex: $(9/5 \times 20°C) + 32 = 68°F$
$(°F - 32) \times 5/9 = °C$	Ex: $(86°F - 32) \times 5/9 = 30°C$

Faites les calculs suivants.

1. 98.6° F = ___° C
2. 32° F = ___° C
3. 17° C = ___° F
4. 25° C = ___° F

LETTRES ET SCIENCES   **339**

Après la lecture

PRESENTATION   (*page 339*)

Ask students the following questions: *Quel temps fait-il aujourd'hui? Décrivez-le. Donnez tous les détails possibles. Est-ce qu'il y a des nuages? Décrivez-les. Il y a du vent? Il va faire quel temps plus tard aujourd'hui? Et il va faire quel temps demain?*

ANSWERS

Exercice A

Answers will vary but may include the following:

1. **La météorologie est la science qui étudie l'atmosphère.**
2. **Les dépressions sont des zones de basses pressions.**
3. **Les anticyclones sont des zones de hautes pressions.**
4. **Le front est la zone où deux masses d'air s'affrontent.**
5. **Le vent est un mouvement d'air entre les anticyclones et les dépressions.**

Exercice B

1. **La météorologie étudie l'atmosphère.**
2. **On obtient les informations nécessaires des trois centres météorologiques.**
3. **Ils sont à Washington aux États-Unis, à Moscou en Russie et à Melbourne en Australie.**
4. **Les masses d'air absorbent de la vapeur d'eau.**
5. **Le temps reste stable dans un anticyclone. Il pleut ou il y a du vent quand il y a un front.**
6. **On peut prévoir le temps d'après les nuages.**

Exercice C

Answers will vary.

Exercice D

1. 37
2. 0
3. 62,2
4. 77

CHAPTER OVERVIEW

In this chapter students will expand their sports vocabulary. They will learn to talk about cycling as well as team sports such as soccer, basketball, and volleyball. They will also learn to describe the equipment needed for each sport and the seasons in which various sporting events take place. To do this, students will learn the *passé composé* of regular verbs conjugated with *avoir* and the interrogative phrase *qu'est-ce que*.

The cultural focus of Chapter 13 is on soccer and other sports which the French either play or enjoy as fans.

CHAPTER OBJECTIVES

By the end of this chapter, students will know:

1. vocabulary associated with soccer
2. vocabulary associated with basketball, volleyball, cycling, running, football, and baseball
3. the formation and use of the *passé composé* of regular verbs conjugated with *avoir* in the affirmative and negative
4. time expressions frequently used with the *passé composé*
5. interrogative sentence structure using *qu'est-ce que* and *que*

CHAPITRE

13

LES SPORTS

OBJECTIFS

In this chapter you will learn to do the following:

1. talk about soccer and other sports
2. describe past actions
3. ask questions with "what"
4. express reactions
5. discuss some differences between sports in the U.S. and in France

CHAPTER PROJECTS

(*optional*)
1. Try to get a video of a sporting event in French. Have students watch about five minutes of it. Then have them say as much about it as they can.
2. Have students prepare a TV description of a sporting event.

COMMUNITIES

Attend a soccer match or a basketball game with your students. Comment on the action in French and encourage them to do the same.

341

Pacing

This chapter requires eight to ten class sessions. Pacing will vary according to class length and the age and aptitude of the students.

Note The Lesson Plans offer guidelines for 45- and 55-minute classes and **Block Scheduling.**

Exercices vs. *Activités*

All exercises (which provide guided practice) are coded in blue. All communicative activities are coded in red.

INTERNET ACTIVITIES

(*optional*)

These activities, student worksheets, and related teacher information are in the *Bienvenue* Internet Activities Booklet and on the Glencoe Foreign Language Home Page at: http://www.glencoe.com/secondary/fl

LEARNING FROM PHOTOS

After presenting the *Mots 1* vocabulary, ask students: *C'est quel sport? Dans quelle ville est-ce que ces joueurs jouent? Ils jouent sous quel monument célèbre?*

VOCABULAIRE

MOTS 1

Bell Ringer Review

Write the following on the board or use BRR Blackline Master 13-1: Complete the sentences logically with the correct form of *prendre, comprendre,* or *apprendre.*

1. Au lycée nous ___ le français.
2. Mais moi, je ne ___ pas toujours le professeur.
3. Vous ___ un coca?
4. Non, nous ___ du thé.

PRESENTATION (*pages 342–343*)

A. Tell students that the names of many sports are cognates, but don't allow them to anglicize their pronunciation.

B. Using Vocabulary Transparencies 13.1 (A & B), have students repeat the new words after you or Cassette 8A/CD-8.

Note Many masculine nouns ending in *-eur* that formerly did not have a feminine form are now being heard with the *-euse* (or-*rice*) ending. See **CROSS-CULTURAL COMPARISON** on page 359 of this Teacher's Wraparound Edition.

VOCABULAIRE

MOTS 1

LE FOOT(BALL)

le but

siffler

un gardien de but

un arbitre

un terrain de foot(ball)

un ballon

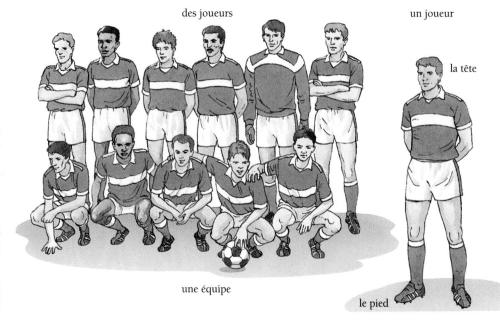

des joueurs

un joueur

la tête

une équipe

le pied

TOTAL PHYSICAL RESPONSE

(following the Vocabulary presentation)

Getting Ready

You will need a lightweight ball, such as one made of foam, or something to serve as an imaginary soccer ball.

TPR 1

(Student 1), **venez ici, s'il vous plaît.**
Montrez-moi la tête. Et le pied.

Voici un ballon. Prenez le ballon.
Donnez un coup de pied dans le ballon.
(Student 2), allez chercher le ballon.
Renvoyez le ballon à (Student 1).
(Student 3), venez ici, s'il vous plaît.
Vous êtes l'arbitre. Prenez le sifflet.
Sifflez.
Merci, ___. Vous avez tous très bien fait.
Asseyez-vous, s'il vous plaît.

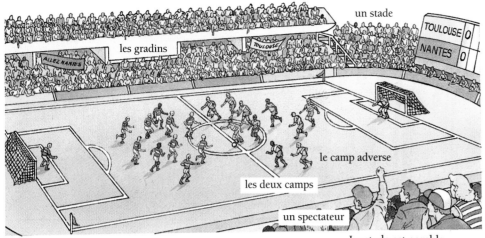

les gradins   un stade

le camp adverse

les deux camps

un spectateur

Le stade est comble.
Il y a beaucoup de monde.
Les gradins sont pleins.

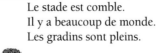

hier   aujourd'hui

Hier Nantes a joué contre Toulouse.
Le match a opposé Toulouse à Nantes.

Peyre a donné un coup de pied dans le ballon.

Roland a envoyé le ballon dans le but.
Il a marqué un but.

C. Ask questions to elicit the vocabulary. Begin with yes/no and either/or questions and progress to question-word questions. Encourage full-sentence responses. For example: *C'est un terrain de football? C'est un arbitre ou un joueur? Qui siffle?*

Teaching Tip For the last three illustrations on page 343, make it clear that the Nantes/Toulouse match took place yesterday and the actions described are in the past. First demonstrate the meaning of *hier* by constrasting it with *aujourd'hui* and the current date or day. For example: *Aujourd'hui—mardi. Hier—lundi. Aujourd'hui—le 28. Hier—le 27.* Point a thumb back over one shoulder to indicate *hier* and the past in general. Use this gesture from now on to indicate or elicit past structures.

Note The *passé composé* is presented in the *il/elle* form so you can immediately ask questions using it while presenting the new words. Students can respond to the questions without having to manipulate forms of the *passé composé*. They will learn the forms in this chapter.

D. As you go over the sentences on page 343, you may wish to ask questions such as: *Nantes a joué contre qui? Contre quelle équipe? Quand ça? Le match a opposé quelles équipes? Qui a donné un coup de pied dans le ballon? Qui a envoyé le ballon dans le but? Il a marqué un but? Qu'est-ce qu'il a marqué? Qui a marqué le but?*

TPR 2

___, venez ici. Vous êtes un spectateur/une spectatrice. Cherchez une place dans les gradins.
Prenez votre place. Regardez le match. Quelqu'un va marquer un but. Levez-vous. Regardez bien.
Ah oui, il a marqué un but. Applaudissez.
Merci, ___. Et maintenant, retournez à votre place, s'il vous plaît.

ADDITIONAL PRACTICE

Student Tape Manual, Teacher's Edition, *Activités B–C,* pages 143–144

Exercices

Exercices

A **Le stade est comble.** Répondez.

1. Il y a beaucoup de spectateurs dans le stade?
2. Les gradins sont pleins de spectateurs ou il y a beaucoup de places libres?
3. Le stade est comble?
4. Il y a beaucoup de monde dans le stade?
5. Le foot est un sport d'équipe. C'est un sport individuel ou collectif?

B **Un match de foot.** Répondez d'après les indications.

1. Dans un match de foot, il y a combien d'équipes? (deux)
2. Chaque équipe a combien de joueurs? (onze)
3. Il y a combien de joueurs sur le terrain? (vingt-deux)
4. Dans un match il y a combien de camps? (deux)
5. Le match est divisé en quoi? (mi-temps)
6. Il y a combien de mi-temps? (deux)
7. Chaque mi-temps dure combien de minutes? (quarante-cinq)
8. Qui garde le but? (le gardien de but)
9. Qu'est-ce que chaque équipe veut faire? (marquer un but)
10. Qui bloque ou arrête le ballon? (le gardien de but)

C **Toulouse contre Nantes.** Répondez par «oui».

1. Toulouse a joué contre Nantes?
2. Peyre a donné un coup de pied dans le ballon?
3. Peyre a passé le ballon à Roland?
4. Roland a envoyé le ballon dans le but?
5. Roland a marqué un but?
6. Le gardien n'a pas arrêté le ballon?
7. Roland a égalisé le score?
8. L'arbitre a sifflé?
9. Il a déclaré un penalty contre Toulouse?
10. Nantes a gagné le match?
11. Toulouse a perdu le match?

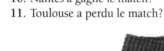

Exercice C

This exercise allows students to practice using past participles without having to manipulate forms.

ANSWERS

Exercice A

1. Oui, il y a beaucoup de spectateurs dans le stade.
2. Les gradins sont pleins de spectateurs.
3. Oui, le stade est comble.
4. Oui, il y a beaucoup de monde dans le stade.
5. C'est un sport collectif.

Exercice B

1. Dans un match de foot, il y a deux équipes.
2. Chaque équipe a onze joueurs.
3. Il y a vingt-deux joueurs sur le terrain.
4. Dans un match il y a deux camps.
5. Le match est divisé en mi-temps.
6. Il y a deux mi-temps.
7. Chaque mi-temps dure quarante-cinq minutes.
8. Le gardien de but garde le but.
9. Chaque équipe veut marquer un but.
10. Le gardien de but bloque ou arrête le ballon.

Exercice C

1. Oui, Toulouse a joué contre Nantes.
2. Oui, Peyre a donné un coup de pied dans le ballon.
3. Oui, Peyre a passé le ballon à Roland.
4. Oui, Roland a envoyé le ballon dans le but.
5. Oui, Roland a marqué un but.
6. Oui (Non), le gardien n'a pas arrêté le ballon.
7. Oui, il a égalisé le score.
8. Oui, l'arbitre a sifflé.
9. Oui, il a déclaré un penalty contre Toulouse.
10. Oui, Nantes a gagné le match.
11. Oui, Toulouse a perdu le match.

ADDITIONAL PRACTICE

After completing Exercises A–C, reinforce the lesson with the following: Have students bring in action photographs from sports magazines and describe them in as much detail as possible.

INDEPENDENT PRACTICE

Assign any of the following:

1. Exercises, page 344
2. Workbook, *Mots 1: A–C,* page 130
3. Communication Activities Masters, *Mots 1: A,* page 64
4. CD-ROM, Disc 4, pages 342–344

VOCABULAIRE

MOTS 2

D'AUTRES SPORTS

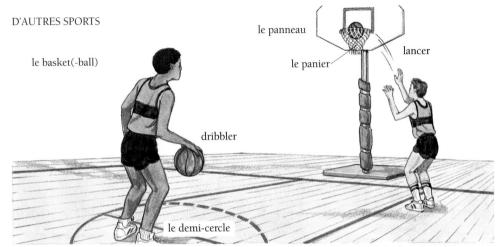

le basket(-ball)

le panneau

le panier

lancer

dribbler

le demi-cercle

Un joueur a dribblé le ballon.
Il a dribblé le ballon jusqu'au demi-cercle.

Un autre joueur a lancé le ballon dans le panier.

le volley(-ball)

le filet

le sol

Un joueur a servi.

par dessus le filet

Un autre joueur a renvoyé le ballon.

CHAPITRE 13   **345**

COOPERATIVE LEARNING

Each group chooses a leader, who asks the others what their favorite sports are and whether they prefer to play the sports, watch them on TV, or go to games. The leader takes notes and reports to the class. You can follow up with a class survey, grouping names of students on the board according to their preferences and discussing the results.

TOTAL PHYSICAL RESPONSE

(following the Vocabulary presentation)

Getting Ready

If you wish, set up part of a mock basketball court on the floor with tape and use a toy basketball and hoop. Demonstrate the meaning of *lentement*.

(continued on page 346)

Vocabulary Teaching Resources

1. Vocabulary Transparencies 13.2 (A & B)
2. Audio Cassette 8A/CD-8
3. Student Tape Manual, Teacher's Edition, *Mots 2: D–F,* pages 145–147
4. Workbook, *Mots 2: D–F,* page 131
5. Communication Activities Masters, *Mots 2: B,* page 65
6. Computer Software, *Vocabulaire*
7. Chapter Quizzes, *Mots 2: Quiz 2,* page 70
8. CD-ROM, Disc 4, *Mots 2:* pages 345–349

Bell Ringer Review

Write the following on the board or use BRR Blackline Master 13-2: Make a list of six articles of clothing you would like for your birthday.

PRESENTATION *(pages 345–346)*

A. Using Vocabulary Transparencies 13.2 (A & B) and realia, have students repeat after you or Cassette 8A/CD-8. Stress the correct French pronunciation of words borrowed from English.

B. Have students close their books. Make negative statements about the illustrations on Vocabulary Transparencies 13.2. Ask individuals to respond with an appropriate affirmative statement. For example: *Le joueur n'a pas lancé le ballon. (Le joueur a dribblé le ballon.) Le joueur n'a pas renvoyé le ballon. (Le joueur a servi.)*

C. Have students prepare questions to ask you about which sports you prefer, whether you participate in or watch them, what your favorite teams are, and so on. Hold a question-and-answer session using this material.

le cyclisme

une course cycliste

des coureurs cyclistes

un vélo

un gagnant

un coureur

une piste

Leblanc (27) a gagné la course.
Boulet (28) a perdu la course.

une coupe

Aux États-Unis le football américain est un sport d'automne.

Le base-ball est un sport de printemps.

346 CHAPITRE 13

TPR 1 *(continued from page 345)*

___, venez ici, s'il vous plaît.
Vous allez jouer au basket-ball.
Dribblez le ballon lentement.
Dribblez le ballon vite.
Allez au demi-cercle.
Lancez le ballon dans le panier. Bravo! Vous avez lancé le ballon dans le panier.
Merci, ___. Vous avez très bien joué.
  Retournez à votre place, s'il vous plaît.

TPR 2

___, venez ici, s'il vous plaît.
Vous allez jouer au volley-ball.
Prenez le ballon.
Voici le filet. Servez.
Sautez. (Dramatize *sauter.)*
Renvoyez le ballon par-dessus le filet.
Merci, ___. Vous avez très bien joué.
  Retournez à votre place, s'il vous plaît.

Exercices

A Un match de basket. Répondez.

1. On joue au basket-ball sur une piste ou sur un terrain?
2. Le basket-ball est un sport individuel ou un sport d'équipe?
3. Il y a cinq ou onze joueurs dans une équipe de basket-ball?
4. Pendant un match de basket les joueurs dribblent le ballon ou donnent un coup de pied dans le ballon?
5. Un joueur a dribblé le ballon jusqu'au panneau ou jusqu'au demi-cercle?
6. Un autre joueur a lancé le ballon dans le panier ou dans le but?

B Le volley-ball. Répondez par «oui» ou «non».

1. Une équipe de volley-ball a six joueurs?
2. Un joueur sert?
3. Un joueur du camp adverse renvoie le ballon?
4. Quand il renvoie le ballon, le ballon peut toucher le filet?
5. On renvoie le ballon par dessus le filet?
6. Le ballon peut toucher le sol?

C C'est quel sport? Identifiez.

le base-ball
le basket-ball
le football
le football américain
le volley-ball

1. Aux États-Unis c'est un sport d'automne.
2. Aux États-Unis c'est un sport de printemps.
3. Le ballon ne peut pas toucher le sol.
4. Il y a cinq joueurs dans l'équipe.
5. Le joueur a donné un coup de pied dans le ballon.
6. Le joueur a renvoyé le ballon par dessus le filet.
7. Le gardien de but a bloqué le ballon.
8. Le joueur a servi.
9. Le joueur a lancé le ballon dans le panier.
10. Le joueur a marqué un but.

Ces jeunes pratiquent des arts martiaux.

CHAPITRE 13 **347**

Exercices

PRESENTATION (pages 347–348)

Exercices A and B: Listening

After doing Exercises A and B as a whole-class activity, focus on the listening skill by having students do them again in pairs, with one partner reading the questions in random order while the other listens and answers with his/her book closed.

Extension of Exercice B

After completing Exercise B, have students use it as a model to make up six new questions about the game of soccer. Then, in pairs, they take turns asking the questions and answering.

Exercice C

You may wish to use the recorded version of this exercise.

ANSWERS

Exercice A

1. On joue au basket-ball sur un terrain.
2. Le basket-ball est un sport d'équipe.
3. Il y a cinq joueurs dans une équipe de basket-ball.
4. Pendant un match de basket les joueurs dribblent le ballon.
5. Un joueur a dribblé le ballon jusqu'au demi-cercle.
6. Un autre joueur a lancé le ballon dans le panier.

Exercice B

1. Oui. 4. Non.
2. Oui. 5. Oui.
3. Oui. 6. Non.

Exercice C

1. le football américain
2. le base-ball
3. le volley-ball
4. le basket-ball
5. le football, le football américain
6. le volley-ball
7. le football
8. le volley-ball
9. le basket-ball
10. le football, le football américain

COOPERATIVE LEARNING

Have students work in teams of three. The first team member gives the name of a student on one of the school sports teams. The second student makes a statement about the team this person plays on. The third student says whether he or she likes or dislikes that particular sport and whether or not he or she attends the games.

DID YOU KNOW?

Tell students that the martial arts practiced in France are the same as those practiced in the U.S.; they are mainly Asian in origin. The vocabulary is therefore very similar: *le jiu-jitsu, le judo, le karaté, l'aikido.* A black belt is *une ceinture noire.* A person who practices judo is *un(e) judoka* and one who practices karate is *un(e) karatéka.*

347

Des coureurs cyclistes aux Jeux Paraolympiques

D **Une course cycliste.** Choisissez.

1. Un vélo est ___.
   a. une bicyclette   b. une voiture   c. un stade

2. ___ roule à vélo.
   a. Une bicyclette   b. Un coureur cycliste   c. Un spectateur

3. Dans une course internationale, chaque équipe ___.
   a. gagne un trophée   b. gagne la coupe   c. représente son pays

4. Le gagnant de la course est ___.
   a. la coupe   b. le champion   c. le coureur

5. ___ gagnent de l'argent.
   a. Les professionnels   b. Les amateurs
         c. Les spectateurs

6. ___ gagne.
   a. Le premier   b. Le dernier
   c. Chaque équipe

7. On donne ___ au gagnant.
   a. la course   b. la coupe
   c. la bicyclette

8. Dans une course cycliste les coureurs roulent sur ___.
   a. des gradins   b. un terrain
   c. une piste

ABONNEZ - VOUS A
VÉLO
SPRINT 2000

UN AN
11 numéros
dont 3 numéros
spéciaux

27% de remise !

et recevez en cadeau
ce chronomètre
multifonctions

Ce chronomètre sera pour vous un instrument indispensable pour mesurer vos performances !
De plus, il pourra vous servir de montre, en affichant l'heure et la date du jour, mais aussi de réveil, puisqu'il possède une alarme en continu ou avec pause.

348   CHAPITRE 13

Activités de communication orale
Mots 1 et 2

A **C'est quel sport?** Give a classmate several details about a sport without mentioning the name of the sport. Your partner has to guess what sport you're describing. Then reverse roles.

> Élève 1: Il y a cinq joueurs dans l'équipe. Les joueurs dribblent le ballon. Les meilleurs joueurs sont souvent très grands. Ils lancent le ballon dans le panier.
> Élève 2: C'est le basket-ball.

B **Ton équipe favorite.** Ask a classmate what his or her favorite team is and why. Then reverse roles and report to the class.

> Élève 1: Quelle est ton équipe favorite? Pourquoi?
> Élève 2: Mon équipe favorite de base-ball, c'est les Expos parce que je suis de Montréal. (Je n'ai pas d'équipe favorite de basket-ball.)

C **Un match de football.** Ask a classmate several questions about the illustration using *qui, quel(le), est-ce que, combien,* and *où.* Then reverse roles.

Bell Ringer Review
Write the following on the board or use BRR Blackline Master 13-3: Sketch the following:
le ballon
la tête
le filet
une coupe

Activités de communication orale
Mots 1 et 2

ANSWERS

Activités A and B
Answers will vary.

Activité C
Note Stress to students that all their questions need not have a definite answer. The answer to some of their questions may be *Je ne sais pas.* For example: *Quel joueur marque un but?* is a good question, but the answer is not readily apparent from the illustration.
Questions will vary.

RETEACHING (*Mots 1* and 2)
Have students write three sentences describing the sporting activities from *Mots 1* and *2* that can be mimed. Then they choose a partner who must correctly mime the activity in front of the class when it is read only once or twice.

INDEPENDENT PRACTICE

Assign any of the following:
1. Exercises and activities, pages 347–349
2. Workbook, *Mots 2: D–F,* page 131
3. Communication Activities Masters, *Mots 2: B,* page 65
4. Computer Software, *Vocabulaire*
5. CD-ROM, Disc 4, pages 345–349

Le passé composé des verbes réguliers

Describing Past Actions

1. You use the *passé composé* to express actions completed in the past. The *passé composé* is made up of the present tense of *avoir* and the past participle of the verb. Review the present tense of the verb *avoir*.

AVOIR	
j'ai	nous avons
tu as	vous avez
il/elle/on a	ils/elles ont

2. Study the following forms of the past participle of regular French verbs.

-er ⟶ -é	-ir ⟶ -i	-re ⟶ -u
regarder regardé	choisir choisi	perdre perdu
parler parlé	réussir réussi	vendre vendu

Almost all past participles of French verbs end in the sound /é/, /i/, or /ü/.

PARLER	FINIR	PERDRE
j'ai parlé	j'ai fini	j'ai perdu
tu as parlé	tu as fini	tu as perdu
il/elle/on a parlé	il/elle/on a fini	il/elle/on a perdu
nous avons parlé	nous avons fini	nous avons perdu
vous avez parlé	vous avez fini	vous avez perdu
ils/elles ont parlé	ils/elles ont fini	ils/elles ont perdu

3. The *passé composé* is often used with time expressions such as:

> avant-hier
> hier
> hier matin
> hier soir
> l'année dernière
> la semaine dernière

VISITEURS 0
F.C. St LEU 1

Structure Teaching Resources

1. Workbook, *Structure: A–H,* pages 132–135
2. Student Tape Manual, Teacher's Edition, *Structure: A–B,* page 148
3. Audio Cassette 8A/CD-8
4. Communication Activities Masters, *Structure: A–B,* pages 66–67
5. Computer Software, *Structure*
6. Chapter Quizzes, *Structure:* Quizzes 3–4, pages 71–72
7. CD-ROM, Disc 4, pages 350–353

Le passé composé des verbes réguliers

PRESENTATION *(pages 350–351)*

A. Quickly review the forms of *avoir* in the chart on page 350. Students have used this verb many times by now.

B. Show students how the past participle of regular verbs is formed. The more past participles students can repeat the better. Ear training is extremely important. The following are regular verbs they have already learned in the present tense: *chanter, danser, donner, écouter, étudier, gagner, habiter, inviter, parler, regarder, quitter, rigoler, travailler, bavarder, dîner, préparer, chercher, commander, déjeuner, trouver, acheter, payer, laisser, bronzer, jouer, nager, plonger, renvoyer, dépenser, porter, accélérer, freiner, garer, traverser, vérifier, dribbler, envoyer, lancer, opposer, siffler; choisir, finir, remplir, réussir, obéir, punir, atterrir, dormir, servir, maigrir, grossir; attendre, entendre, perdre, vendre, répondre.*

C. Guide students through steps 1–4 on pages 350–351.

ADDITIONAL PRACTICE

After completing Exercises A and B on page 351, you may wish to ask students additional personalized questions to further reinforce the *tu/je* questions and answers in the *passé composé: Jeanne, tu as téléphoné à des amis hier soir? Tu as parlé avec qui? Tu as écouté des cassettes? Tu as étudié? Qu'est-ce que tu as étudié hier soir? Tu as dîné à quelle heure? Qu'est-ce que tu as mangé? Tu as regardé la télé? Qu'est-ce que tu as regardé? À quelle heure?,* etc.

Note When formulating your own questions, be sure to use only regular verbs conjugated with *avoir.*

Study the following examples of the *passé composé*.

J'ai regardé le match à la télé hier soir.
Nantes a joué contre Toulouse.
L'année dernière Toulouse a gagné la coupe.
Mais hier soir Toulouse a perdu le match.
L'arbitre a puni Toulouse.
Il a déclaré un penalty contre Toulouse.
Les spectateurs ont applaudi.

4. Note the placement of *ne… pas* in negative sentences with the *passé composé*. *Ne… pas* goes around the verb *avoir*.

Je *n'*ai *pas* parlé à Suzanne.
Tu *n'*as *pas* regardé la télé?
Il *n'*a *pas* entendu le téléphone.

Le Niger joue contre l'Argentine pour la Coupe du Monde.

Exercices

A **Quel est le participe passé?** Donnez le participe passé.

1. habiter
2. quitter
3. parler
4. écouter
5. travailler
6. remplir
7. obéir
8. réussir
9. servir
10. dormir
11. perdre
12. vendre
13. attendre
14. répondre

B **Hier ou la semaine dernière.**
Donnez des réponses personnelles.

1. Hier matin tu as quitté la maison à quelle heure?
2. Avant les cours tu as rigolé avec tes copains?
3. Tu as parlé au prof de français?
4. La semaine dernière tu as passé un examen? Tu as réussi à l'examen?
5. Tu as répondu à toutes les questions?
6. Tu as quitté l'école à quelle heure hier?
7. Tu as attendu le bus devant l'école?

Le forcing

Encore une victoire pour l'équipe de Strasbourg. Les Niçois ont perdu leur troisième match.

STRASBOURG ET NICE 6–3

Après l'échec total de Lyon et le demi-échec face à Bourges, Nice a commis une troisième erreur en trois matchs. Les Strasbourgeois ont pratiqué un football collectif de qualité, se montrant patients et prudents pendant la première mi-temps. Le jeu niçois manquait de mouvement et de vitesse. Dortez se pose en rival sérieux de Peyre. Au début du match il a fait le forcing pour égaliser le score.
Ce n'est qu'après la mi-temps qu'il a marqué trois buts de suite. Et quels buts! On n'a jamais vu ça depuis le match légendaire qui

a opposé Toulouse et Nantes l'année dernière. Dortez avait du mal à croire ce qu'il venait de faire. Lors d'une interview après le match il a dit: «Je dois être un peu fou. C'est sûrement pour cela que j'intéresse tout le monde». lui est difficile de faire le humbl quand son talent saute aux yeu Peyre, par contre, n'essaie mêm pas de cacher son ego. «Je su plus fort que jamais,» a-t-il pr cisé l'autre jour. «Il est vrai q nous avons perdu trois matc mais cela n'a pas d'importanc ou si peu. La semaine procha je vais pouvoir montrer de quo

---

Note In the CD-ROM version, this structure point is presented via an interactive electronic comic strip.

Exercices

PRESENTATION *(pages 351–352)*

Extension of *Exercice B*

After doing Exercise B, call on a student to tell the story in his/her own words.

ANSWERS

Exercice A

1. habité
2. quitté
3. parlé
4. écouté
5. travaillé
6. rempli
7. obéi
8. réussi
9. servi
10. dormi
11. perdu
12. vendu
13. attendu
14. répondu

Exercice B

Answers will vary, but may include the following constructions:

1. J'ai quitté…
2. J'ai rigolé… (Je n'ai pas rigolé…)
3. J'ai parlé… (Je n'ai pas parlé…)
4. J'ai passé… (Je n'ai pas passé…) J'ai réussi… (Je n'ai pas réussi…)
5. J'ai répondu… (Je n'ai pas répondu…)
6. J'ai quitté…
7. J'ai attendu… (Je n'ai pas attendu…)

LEARNING FROM PHOTOS

Have students say as much as they can about the photo using the vocabulary from this chapter.

ADDITIONAL PRACTICE

Student Tape Manual, Teacher's Edition, *Activité A*, page 148

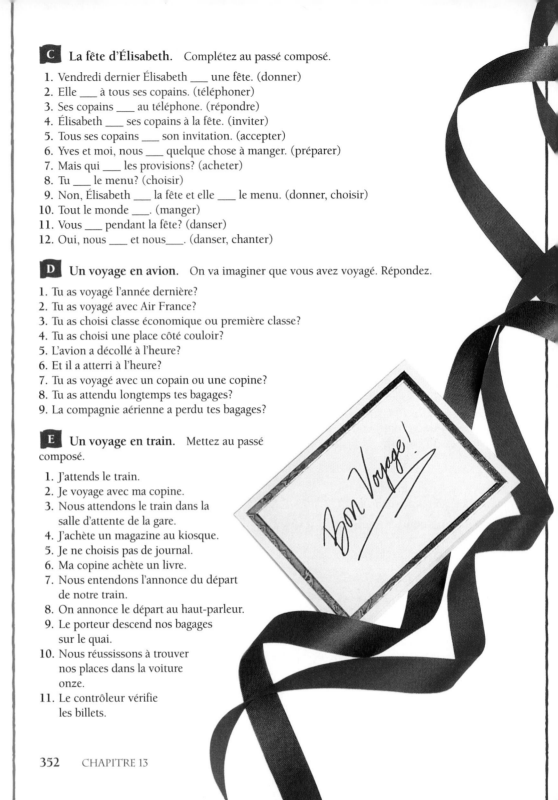

C La fête d'Élisabeth.   Complétez au passé composé.

1. Vendredi dernier Élisabeth ___ une fête. (donner)
2. Elle ___ à tous ses copains. (téléphoner)
3. Ses copains ___ au téléphone. (répondre)
4. Élisabeth ___ ses copains à la fête. (inviter)
5. Tous ses copains ___ son invitation. (accepter)
6. Yves et moi, nous ___ quelque chose à manger. (préparer)
7. Mais qui ___ les provisions? (acheter)
8. Tu ___ le menu? (choisir)
9. Non, Élisabeth ___ la fête et elle ___ le menu. (donner, choisir)
10. Tout le monde ___. (manger)
11. Vous ___ pendant la fête? (danser)
12. Oui, nous ___ et nous___. (danser, chanter)

D Un voyage en avion.   On va imaginer que vous avez voyagé. Répondez.

1. Tu as voyagé l'année dernière?
2. Tu as voyagé avec Air France?
3. Tu as choisi classe économique ou première classe?
4. Tu as choisi une place côté couloir?
5. L'avion a décollé à l'heure?
6. Et il a atterri à l'heure?
7. Tu as voyagé avec un copain ou une copine?
8. Tu as attendu longtemps tes bagages?
9. La compagnie aérienne a perdu tes bagages?

E Un voyage en train.   Mettez au passé composé.

1. J'attends le train.
2. Je voyage avec ma copine.
3. Nous attendons le train dans la salle d'attente de la gare.
4. J'achète un magazine au kiosque.
5. Je ne choisis pas de journal.
6. Ma copine achète un livre.
7. Nous entendons l'annonce du départ de notre train.
8. On annonce le départ au haut-parleur.
9. Le porteur descend nos bagages sur le quai.
10. Nous réussissons à trouver nos places dans la voiture onze.
11. Le contrôleur vérifie les billets.

Qu'est-ce que — Asking "What?"; Expressing Reactions

1. *Qu'est-ce que* is another question or interrogative expression. It means "what" and refers to a thing.

> **Qu'est-ce que vous voyez?**
> **Qu'est-ce qu'il regarde?**
> **Qu'est-ce que vous avez?**

Note that *Qu'est-ce que vous avez?* also means "What's the matter?"

2. To ask "what?" in formal or written French you use *que* and invert the subject and verb.

> **Que voyez-vous?**
> **Que regarde-t-il?**
> **Qu'avez-vous?**

3. In informal French *qu'est-ce que* is used in exclamations.

> **Qu'est-ce qu'il est beau ce garçon!**   *How handsome that boy is!*
> **Qu'est-ce qu'elle est belle!**   *How beautiful she is!*
> **Qu'est-ce que je suis fatigué!**   *How tired I am!*

Exercices

A   **Comment? Qu'est-ce que tu fais?**   Posez des questions d'après le modèle.

> **J'écoute la radio.**
> *Comment? Qu'est-ce que tu écoutes?*

1. Je lis le journal.
2. Je regarde la télé.
3. Je fais des exercices.
4. Je fais les courses.
5. J'achète un cadeau.
6. Je lave la voiture.
7. Nous écrivons un poème.
8. Nous préparons le petit déjeuner.
9. Nous commandons une boisson.

B   **Des mini-conversations.**   Posez des questions et répondez d'après le modèle.

> **marquer/un but**
> Élève 1: Qu'est-ce que les joueurs ont marqué?
> Élève 2: Ils ont marqué un but.

1. lancer/le ballon
2. dribbler/le ballon
3. envoyer/le ballon
4. perdre/le match
5. gagner/la coupe
6. égaliser/le score
7. gagner/de l'argent

VAINQUEUR DE LA COUPE DE FRANCE 1987

CHAPITRE 13   **353**

Qu'est-ce que
PRESENTATION *(page 353)*

A. Students have been using *qu'est-ce que* for some time. The purpose of this presentation is to have students actively use and produce this interrogative phrase on their own.
B. Lead students through steps 1–3 on page 353.

Note In spoken French one hears both *Qu'est-ce qu'il est beau!* and *Qu'il est beau!* in exclamations.

Exercices
ANSWERS

Exercice A

1. Comment? Qu'est-ce que tu lis?
2. … tu regardes?
3. … tu fais?
4. … tu fais?
5. … tu achètes?
6. … tu laves?
7. … vous écrivez?
8. … vous préparez?
9. … vous commandez?

Exercice B

1. É1: Qu'est-ce que les joueurs ont lancé? É2: Ils ont lancé le ballon.
2. … ont dribblé? … le ballon.
3. … ont envoyé? … le ballon.
4. … ont perdu? … le match.
5. … ont gagné? … la coupe.
6. … ont égalisé? … le score.
7. … ont gagné? … de l'argent.

ADDITIONAL PRACTICE

Show students photographs with prominent features (big mountains, tall buildings or people, fast cars, hot weather, etc.), which will, as much as possible, elicit spontaneous exclamations from students. If necessary, cue an adjective or adverb orally.

Note You can use these same pictures as cues for practicing *que* and/or *qu'est-ce que* as question words.

INDEPENDENT PRACTICE

Assign any of the following:
1. Exercises, pages 351–353
2. Workbook, *Structure: A–H*, pages 132–135
3. Communication Activities Masters, *Structure: A–B*, pages 66–67
4. Computer Software, *Structure*
5. CD-ROM, Disc 4, pages 350–353

CONVERSATION

PRESENTATION *(page 354)*

A. Tell students they will hear Romain and Corinne discussing a recent international soccer match.

B. Have them watch the Conversation Video or listen as you read the conversation or play Cassette 8A/CD-8.

C. Have pairs of students present the conversation to the class.

D. You may have a more able student retell the conversation in narrative form in his/her own words.

Note In the CD-ROM version, students can play the role of either one of the characters and record the conversation.

ANSWERS

Exercice A

1. Corinne a regardé la télé hier soir.
2. Elle a regardé le match France-Brésil.
3. Le Brésil a joué contre la France.
4. La France a gagné le match.
5. Le Brésil a perdu le match.
6. Non, le Brésil n'a pas réussi à égaliser le score parce que le gardien français a bloqué le ballon.
7. Le gardien de but français s'appelle Peyre.
8. Roland a marqué le but pour la France.
9. Romain a oublié son nom.

CONVERSATION

Scènes de la vie   *Une retransmission sportive*

ROMAIN: Tu as regardé la télé hier soir?
CORINNE: Oui, j'ai regardé la retransmission du match France–Brésil.
ROMAIN: Tu parles de la victoire de la France sur le Brésil?
CORINNE: Voilà! La France a gagné un à zéro.
ROMAIN: Le Brésil a fait le forcing pour égaliser le score.
CORINNE: Oui, mais sans succès. À chaque fois Peyre a bloqué le ballon. Ce type est un gardien vachement fort.
ROMAIN: Qui a marqué le but pour la France? J'ai oublié.
CORINNE: Tu as oublié? Tu n'as pas de mémoire! Moi, je ne vais jamais oublier ça! Roland. C'est Roland qui a marqué le but.

A **Quel match alors!** Répondez d'après la conversation.

1. Qui a regardé la télé hier soir?
2. Qu'est-ce qu'elle a regardé à la télé?
3. Qui a joué contre la France?
4. Qui a gagné le match?
5. Quelle équipe a perdu le match?
6. Le Brésil a réussi à égaliser le score? Pourquoi pas?
7. Comment s'appelle le gardien de but français?
8. Qui a marqué le but pour la France?
9. Qui a oublié son nom?

20.30

20.25 TF1 22.35

Football
En direct de Rotterdam. Commentaires : Thierry Roland et Jean-Michel Larqué.

Feyenoord/AS Monaco
Demi-finale retour de la **Coupe d'Europe des vainqueurs de Coupes.**
•Je crois sincèrement que l'on forme un groupe de joueurs très unis. Quand l'un est en difficulté, l'autre a la volonté de venir l'aider. C'est important comme état d'esprit, car cela veut dire qu'en Coupe d'Europe, où le mental compte énormément, on peut avoir confiance en la solidarité. Je pense qu'on a une équipe capable d'embêter beaucoup de monde.»
Rob Witschge, qui prononce ces paroles pleines de bon sens, sait de quoi il parle. Il connaît aussi bien le football néerlandais que le football français, pour avoir joué pendant deux ans à Saint-Etienne.

Désormais attaqua: l'ancien Stéphanois ment adapté au st: son équipe, qui re: mément à celui de tous les défenseurs les attaquants défe tat : les défenses ad vent confrontées à de lantes bien difficile Arsène Wenger, l'e: Monégasques, craint du rouleau compres: cache pas : «Feyen forte impression. Ce est très disciplinée. d'elle une grande for:

En cas d'égalité à la fin c mentaire, il sera procédé tions et éventuellement a:

20.30 C++ 21.00
Journal du c:
Présentation : Michel

20.30 M6 20.40
Surprise-part:

DID YOU KNOW?

Soccer is the most important team sport in France. Almost every city has its own team, and competition is fierce for the national title. Soccer fans pack the stadiums on Sundays.

During qualifying games for the Coupe de France, in which the best French teams play for the national title, people are glued to their TV sets or radios. When France plays against other European teams, fans travel in large groups to neighboring countries to watch the games and support their teams. When France wins, French fans throughout the country drive their cars on the main streets of their city, honking their horns, yelling, singing, and waving the French flag. This goes on until the early hours of the morning.

Prononciation   *Liaison et élision*

l'arbitre

1. You have already seen that in French certain words are pronounced differently depending on whether they are followed by a vowel or a consonant. There is either liaison or elision. Compare the following.

   les copains / les‿amis   je regarde / j'écoute

2. Liaison is the linking of a usually silent consonant to the following word when the word begins with a vowel or silent *h*. Liaison occurs with plural subject pronouns, plural articles, and plural possessive adjectives. Repeat the following.

   ils‿ont gagné   les‿équipes   des‿arbitres   mes‿amis

3. Elision is the linking of a consonant and a vowel sound. It is made by dropping the vowel at the end of a word before a vowel at the beginning of the next. Elision occurs with the articles *le* and *la*, with the pronoun *je*, and with the negative word *ne*. Repeat the following.

   l'arbitre   l'équipe   j'attends   j'ai gagné   Tu n'écoutes pas!

   Now repeat and compare the following pairs of sentences.

   Vous‿avez perdu. / Vous n'avez pas perdu.
   J'ai fini. / Je n'ai pas fini.

les‿arbitres

Activités de communication orale

A   Le week-end dernier.   Your classmate wants to know what you did last weekend. Tell him or her several things you did or didn't do, using the verbs below. Then reverse roles.

acheter	dîner	jouer	regarder	téléphoner
attendre	dormir	manger	rigoler	travailler

B   Ton sport d'équipe favori.   Your French friend Nathalie wants to know about your sports interests. Answer her questions.

1. Quelle est ton équipe préférée?
2. C'est une équipe de football?
3. Tu joues à ce sport ou tu préfères regarder les matchs à la télé?
4. Ton équipe préférée a gagné beaucoup de matchs cette année?

Nathalie

355

Prononciation

PRESENTATION *(page 355)*

A. Model the key words *l'arbitre/les arbitres* and have students repeat chorally.
B. Now lead students through steps 1–3 on page 355 and model the other words, phrases, and sentences.
C. You may wish to give the students the following *dictée:* **Mes amis ont joué. Ils ont gagné. L'arbitre a sifflé. L'équipe a marqué un but.**
D. For additional practice, you may wish to use Pronunciation Transparency P-13, the *Prononciation* section on Cassette 8A/CD-8, and the Student Tape Manual, Teacher's Edition, *Activités E–G,* pages 150–151.

Activités de communication orale

PRESENTATION *(page 355)*

Activité B

In the CD-ROM version of this activity, students can interact with an on-screen native speaker.

ANSWERS

Activité A
Answers will vary.

Activité B

1. Answers will vary.
2. Oui (Non), c'est (ce n'est pas) une équipe de football. (C'est une équipe de basket [baseball, etc.])
3. Je joue à ce sport. (Je préfère regarder les matchs à la télé.)
4. Oui (Non), mon équipe préférée (n') a (pas) gagné beaucoup de matchs cette année.

LECTURE ET CULTURE

READING STRATEGIES
(page 356)

Note If your students aren't interested in sports, go over the *Lecture* quickly. If they're sports-minded, you can do the reading thoroughly.

Pre-reading
Give students a brief oral synopsis of the reading in French.

Reading
A. Call on individuals to read 2–3 sentences at a time. After each one reads, ask others follow-up questions.
B. Ask 5–6 questions that review the main points. The answers will give a coherent oral review of the *Lecture*.
C. Have a more able student summarize the *Lecture*. Call on slower students to answer questions about the summary. Then have a slower student orally summarize the reading based on the more able student's review.
D. **Writing** Have students in more able classes write their own summary of the *Lecture* in 6–7 minutes.

Post-reading
Have students work in groups to write brief news announcements for three different types of sports and present them to the class.

Note Students may listen to a recorded version of the *Lecture* on the CD-ROM.

Étude de mots

ANSWERS

Exercice A

1. f	4. e
2. d	5. c
3. a	6. b

356

LES SPORTS EN FRANCE

*E*st-ce que les Français sont des sportifs sérieux? On peut dire que les sports collectifs intéressent les Français moins que les Américains ou les Russes, par exemple. Mais de nos jours, de plus en plus de Français pratiquent un sport. Le sport d'équipe le plus populaire en France, c'est le football ou, comme on dit souvent, le foot. Chaque grande ville a son équipe de foot. Des championnats nationaux et internationaux attirent[1] des fanas du monde entier. Mais le football en France, et en Europe en général, n'est pas le même que le football américain. D'abord le ballon est rond et les joueurs ne peuvent pas toucher le ballon avec les mains. Ils donnent un coup de tête ou un coup de pied dans le ballon pour envoyer le ballon dans le but de l'équipe adverse.

En France on pratique presque[2] tous les sports—le basket-ball, le volley-ball et le hand-ball. Mais il y a un sport qu'on ne pratique jamais: c'est le base-ball. Le base-ball n'est pas du tout populaire.

La France est le pays du cyclisme. Les courses dans les vélodromes attirent toujours beaucoup de monde. En juillet le célèbre Tour de France a lieu[3]. C'est une course internationale tout autour du[4] pays. Les coureurs cyclistes professionnels de tous les pays du monde participent au Tour de France. On donne au gagnant un trophée. On donne aussi une somme d'argent au nouveau héros international.

[1] attirent *attract*
[2] presque *almost*
[3] a lieu *takes place*
[4] tout autour du *all around*

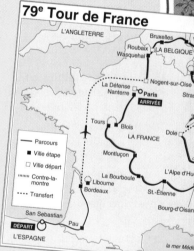

79e Tour de France

Étude de mots

A **Quelle est la définition?** Trouvez les mots qui correspondent.

1. un sport collectif	a. le contraire de «différent»
2. un sport individuel	b. faire du sport, jouer
3. le même	c. l'opposition
4. un joueur	d. un sport qu'on pratique seul
5. le camp adverse	e. une personne qui pratique un sport
6. pratiquer un sport	f. un sport d'équipe

356   CHAPITRE 13

CRITICAL THINKING ACTIVITY

(Thinking skills: supporting statements with reasons)

Read the following to the class or put it on the board or on a transparency.

1. **Vous préférez les sports d'équipe ou les sports individuels? Pourquoi?**
2. **Toutes les écoles aux États-Unis ont des équipes de sport. Dans beaucoup d'écoles les sports sont considérés comme très** importants. Il y a beaucoup de compétition. Qu'est-ce que vous en pensez? Cette compétition sportive est bonne ou pas? Justifiez vos arguments.
3. **Le base-ball n'est pas populaire en France. Pourquoi? Qu'en pensez-vous?**

Compréhension

B **Les sports.** Répondez par «oui» ou «non».

1. Les sports collectifs sont plus populaires en France qu'aux États-Unis.
2. Le sport d'équipe le plus populaire en France, c'est le football.
3. Le football est un sport collectif qu'on pratique en compétition.
4. Quand on joue au football américain on peut toucher le ballon avec les mains.
5. Le ballon de football en France est ovale.
6. Le base-ball est assez populaire en France.
7. Le cyclisme est plus populaire aux États-Unis qu'en France.
8. Le Tour de France a lieu au mois de septembre.

C **Les Français aiment les sports.** Répondez.

1. On pratique quels sports d'équipe en France?
2. Quel sport est-ce qu'on ne pratique jamais en France?
3. Quel sport est plus populaire en France qu'aux États-Unis?
4. Qu'est-ce que c'est, le Tour de France?
5. Qui participe au Tour de France?
6. Qu'est-ce qu'on donne au gagnant du Tour de France?

DÉCOUVERTE CULTURELLE

*I*l y a un sport qu'on pratique en France qui ressemble au football américain? Oui, mais ce n'est pas le foot. C'est le rugby. Le football américain ressemble au rugby.

Aux États-Unis toutes les écoles secondaires ont toujours des équipes de football américain et d'autres sports. En France, ce n'est pas le cas. Les sports ne sont pas très importants dans les lycées français. Il n'y a pas d'équipes organisées. Mais les élèves secondaires en France ont le mercredi après-midi libre et, grâce aux¹ associations sportives scolaires, ils peuvent profiter de leur temps libre pour faire du sport.

Les Françaises et les Français font de la gymnastique, du tennis et du jogging. Mais ce sont surtout les hommes qui jouent au foot.

¹ grâce aux   *thanks to*

CHAPITRE 13   **357**

Compréhension

ANSWERS

Exercice B

1. Non.	5. Non.
2. Oui.	6. Non.
3. Oui.	7. Non.
4. Oui.	8. Non.

Exercice C

1. On pratique le football, le basket-ball, et le volley-ball en France.
2. On ne pratique jamais le base-ball en France.
3. Le cyclisme (Le football) est plus populaire en France qu'aux États-Unis.
4. C'est une course cycliste internationale.
5. Les coureurs cyclistes professionnels de tous les pays du monde participent au Tour de France.
6. On donne un trophée et une somme d'argent au gagnant du Tour de France.

OPTIONAL MATERIAL

Découverte culturelle

PRESENTATION *(page 357)*

A. Before reading the selection, focus on the topics by asking students from which game American football is adapted. Also ask them to name in French all of the extracurricular and intramural sports available at your school. Which is the most popular?

B. Have students read the selection silently and restate its three main ideas in their own words.

Note Students may listen to a recorded version of the *Découverte culturelle* on the CD-ROM.

OPTIONAL MATERIAL

PRESENTATION *(pages 358–359)*

The purpose of this section is to have students enjoy the photographs and gain an appreciation of French culture. If you'd like to do something more, you may do some of the following activities.

A. Have students open their books to pages 358–359 and cover the captions on page 359. For each photo, allow them one minute to come up with one statement about it.

B. Call on volunteers to read the captions on page 359 and answer the questions in numbers 2, 4, and 5.

C. Challenge students to find at least five cognates in the captions and give their English equivalents.

D. Ask personal questions related to the activities shown in the pictures. For example: *Tu fais du cyclisme? Où? Il y a beaucoup de vélodromes aux États-Unis? Qui fait de l'alpinisme? Où? C'est un sport difficile? Dangereux?*

Note In the CD-ROM version, students can listen to the recorded captions and discover a hidden video behind one of the photos.

R É A L I T É S

358

COOPERATIVE LEARNING

Display Communication Transparency C-13. Have students work in groups to make up as many questions as they can about the illustration. Have groups take turns asking and answering the questions.

INDEPENDENT PRACTICE

Assign any of the following:
1. *Étude de mots* and *Compréhension* exercises, pages 356–357
2. Situation Cards, Chapter 13
3. CD-ROM, Disc 4, pages 356–357

L'alpinisme est un sport très pratiqué en France **1**.

Voici des joueuses de volley-ball. Est-ce que l'arbitre regarde attentivement le match **2**?

En France aussi on aime faire du patin à roulettes sur les rampes **3**.

Le Tour de France finit à Paris. Quel monument parisien célèbre est sur la photo **4**?

C'est un match de football à Mulhouse **5**. On joue la nuit. Les gradins sont pleins?

CROSS-CULTURAL COMPARISON

Sports are taking on more importance as people become more and more interested in fitness. There are many new words being used for those who participate in sports:

le footballeur
la footballeuse
le basketballeur
la basketballeuse
le volleyballeur
la volleyballeuse
le joueur de tennis
la joueuse de tennis
le coureur
la coureuse

Until recently, the word *coureuse* had quite another meaning, but today it is used for a female runner.

There is a difference between *un tennisman* and *un joueur de tennis (une tenniswoman* and *une joueuse de tennis)*. The *joueur/joueuse* is a player and the *tennisman/ tenniswoman* is a professional.

GEOGRAPHY CONNECTION

Have students locate Chamonix on the map of France on page 504 or use the Map Transparency. Chamonix is the oldest and largest French winter sports resort. It is very close to Mont Blanc, the highest peak in the Alps. In the summer, Chamonix is a center for mountain climbers who want to scale Mont Blanc. For the less experienced there are other peaks in the area that can be climbed without ropes or other special equipment.

(See page 374 for further information on Chamonix.)

DID YOU KNOW?

The Tour de France, an international bicycle race with competitors from all over the world, lasts for many days and covers several *étapes,* or stages. Each stage lasts one day, at the end of which the winner is awarded the coveted *maillot jaune* (yellow jersey), which he or she can wear the next day. The course is torturous, and many cyclists are eliminated because of heat and fatigue. The final victor carries off the *maillot jaune* and considerable financial winnings as well.

RECYCLING

The *Activités de communication orale* allow students to use the *passé composé* and practice the forms within meaningful contexts. The *Activité de communication écrite* recombines vocabulary and structures from earlier chapters with the sports context of Chapter 13.

INFORMAL ASSESSMENT

The highly guided nature of Oral Activities A and B make them suitable for evaluating the speaking skill. Use either or both as a speaking test. Use the evaluation criteria given on page 34 of this Teacher's Wraparound Edition.

Activités de communication orale

ANSWERS

Activité A

É2 answers will vary. É1 questions will vary, but may include the following:

Qu'est-ce que tu as étudié l'année dernière?

As-tu joué au tennis hier?, etc.

Activité B

Answers will vary.

Activité de communication écrite

ANSWERS

Activité A

Answers will vary, but may include the following:

1. C'est un match de foot (basket, etc.)/une course (à pied, cycliste).
2. Le match (La course) a lieu à ___ (place) le ___ (day of week) à ___ h.
3. L'équipe (de) ___ joue contre l'équipe (de) ___.
4. Nous pouvons y aller à pied (en voiture, en bus, etc.).

360

Activités de communication orale

A **Le temps passé.** Ask a classmate several questions about his or her activities, using the verbs and the time expressions below. Then reverse roles and answer your partner's questions.

> quitter/hier
>
> Élève 1: À quelle heure as-tu quitté l'école hier?
>
> Élève 2: J'ai quitté l'école à quatre heures hier.

VERBES	EXPRESSIONS DE TEMPS
étudier	ce matin
jouer	hier
perdre	hier soir
quitter	l'année dernière
regarder	la semaine dernière
téléphoner	pendant le week-end
travailler	avant-hier
attendre	

B **Une enquête.** Divide into small groups and choose a leader. Using the list below, the leader asks the others what they did last summer, takes notes, and reports to the class.

> Élève 1: Qui a voyagé en Europe l'été dernier?
>
> Élève 2: Moi, j'ai voyagé en Europe l'été dernier.

étudier le français	gagner beaucoup d'argent
jouer au tennis	voyager en avion / train / voiture
travailler	passer quelques semaines à la plage

Activité de communication écrite

A **Une invitation.** Your parents gave you two tickets to a sports event you want to see. Write a short note inviting a friend to go with you. Don't forget to tell your friend:

1. what the event is
2. when and where it's going to be
3. which teams are playing
4. how you plan to get there

360 CHAPITRE 13

FOR THE YOUNGER STUDENT

1. Have groups make posters for a sports day at your school. They should include the date, events, team names, times, etc.
2. Have students pick their favorite athlete and say as much as they can about him or her.

Réintroduction et recombinaison

A **Mes vêtements.** Donnez des réponses personnelles.

1. Quelle est la couleur de ta chemise préférée ou de ton chemisier préféré?
2. Quand tu achètes des chaussures, tu fais quelle pointure?
3. Tu achètes des vêtements prêt-à-porter ou sur mesure?
4. Si ton pantalon est trop large, tu as besoin de la taille au-dessus ou de la taille au-dessous?
5. Et s'il est trop serré, tu as besoin de quelle taille?

B **Raoul.** Répondez d'après le dessin.

1. Raoul est où?
2. Il parle à qui?
3. Que veut Raoul?
4. Qui met de l'essence dans le réservoir?
5. Qu'est-ce que la pompiste vérifie?

C **Serge roule en voiture.** Complétez.

1. Serge ___ bien. (conduire)
2. Il ___ le code de la route. (lire)
3. Il ___ que St.-Brieuc est assez loin d'ici. (dire)
4. Il ___ une carte postale de St.-Brieuc. (écrire)

D **Et vous aussi!** Récrivez les phrases de l'Exercice C en utilisant «vous».

Vocabulaire

NOMS
le foot(ball)
le terrain de football
l'équipe (f.)
le camp
le joueur
le gardien de but
le ballon
le but
l'arbitre (m.)
la tête
le pied
le basket(-ball)
le panier
le panneau
le demi-cercle

le base-ball
le volley-ball
le sol
le vélo
le cyclisme
le coureur cycliste
le coureur
la course
la piste
le stade
le gradin
le spectateur
le gagnant
la coupe
l'automne (m.)
le printemps

ADJECTIFS
adverse
comble
plein(e)

VERBES
dribbler
envoyer
lancer
opposer
siffler

AUTRES MOTS ET EXPRESSIONS
donner un coup de pied
marquer un but
contre
par dessus
jusqu'à
beaucoup de monde
hier
hier matin
hier soir
avant-hier
l'année dernière

CHAPITRE 13 **361**

OPTIONAL MATERIAL

Réintroduction et recombinaison

RECYCLING

These exercises review question words and the irregular verbs *conduire, lire, écrire,* and *dire.* They also review vocabulary related to clothing and cars.

ANSWERS
Exercice A
Answers will vary.

Exercice B
1. Raoul est à la station-service.
2. Il parle au pompiste.
3. Il veut faire le plein.
4. Le pompiste met de l'essence dans le réservoir.
5. La pompiste vérifie les niveaux.

Exercice C
1. conduit   3. dit
2. lit   4. écrit

Exercice D
1. Vous conduisez bien.
2. Vous lisez le code de la route.
3. Vous dites que St.-Brieuc est assez loin d'ici.
4. Vous écrivez une carte postale de St.-Brieuc.

ASSESSMENT RESOURCES

1. Chapter Quizzes
2. Testing Program
3. Situation Cards
4. Communication Transparency C-13
5. Computer Software: Practice/Test Generator

VIDEO PROGRAM

INTRODUCTION   (41:44)

QU'EST-CE QU'ON A BIEN JOUÉ!   (42:42)

STUDENT PORTFOLIO

Written assignments that may be included in students' portfolios include *Activité de communication écrite A* on page 360 and the *Mon Autobiographie* section of the Workbook on page 137.

Note Students may create and save both oral and written work using the Electronic Portfolio feature on the CD-ROM.

INDEPENDENT PRACTICE

1. Activities and exercises, pages 360–361
2. Communication Activities Masters, pages 64–67
3. CD-ROM, Disc 4, pages 360–361

CHAPTER OVERVIEW

In this chapter students will learn to discuss winter sports: the activities themselves, some of the clothing and equipment needed for them, and some information about winter resorts in the French-speaking world. They will also learn to talk about winter weather. They will increase their ability to talk about actions using the *passé composé* of many irregular verbs that are conjugated with *avoir.* Students will also learn the question words *qui* and *quoi*.

The cultural focus of Chapter 14 is on winter sports facilities and traditions in France, Canada, and Switzerland.

CHAPTER OBJECTIVES

By the end of this chapter, students will know:

1. vocabulary associated with different types of skiing, ski equipment and clothing, and some ski resort personnel and procedures
2. vocabulary associated with ice skating
3. vocabulary associated with winter weather and weather reports in general
4. construction of the *passé composé* of irregular verbs that take *avoir*
5. the interrogative words *qui* and *quoi*

CHAPITRE

{ 14 }

L'HIVER ET LES SPORTS D'HIVER

OBJECTIFS

In this chapter you will learn to do the following:

1. talk about skiing and ice skating
2. describe winter weather
3. describe past actions
4. ask "whom" or "what"
5. describe French and Canadian ski resorts

CHAPTER PROJECTS

(optional)

1. Have groups or individuals research the winter carnival in Quebec, including such things as dates, events, and the mascot, *Bonhomme Carnaval.*
2. Put on your own class version of a winter carnival, using information gathered from researching the one in Quebec, complete with snow queen, *Bonhomme Carnaval,* etc.
3. Using the formulas on page 339 of *Lettres et sciences* (*La Météorologie: La Prévision du Temps*), have students convert Fahrenheit temperatures to Celsius and vice versa. Apply Celsius to some familiar temperature ranges in order to give students a "feel" for it. For example, water freezes at 0°C and boils at 100°C. A comfortable Celsius ambient temperature is 24°.

363

CHAPTER 14 RESOURCES

1. Workbook
2. Student Tape Manual
3. Audio Cassette 8B/CD-8
4. Bell Ringer Review Blackline Masters
5. Vocabulary Transparencies
6. Pronunciation Transparency P-14
7. Communication Transparency C-14
8. Communication Activities Masters
9. Map Transparencies
10. Situation Cards
11. Conversation Video
12. Videocassette/Videodisc, Unit 4
13. Video Activities Booklet, Unit 4
14. Lesson Plans
15. Computer Software: Practice/Test Generator
16. Chapter Quizzes
17. Testing Program
18. Internet Activities Booklet
19. CD-ROM Interactive Textbook

Pacing

This chapter requires eight to ten class sessions. Pacing will vary according to class length and the age and aptitude of the students.

Note The Lesson Plans offer guidelines for 45- and 55-minute classes and **Block Scheduling.**

Exercices vs. *Activités*

All exercises (which provide guided practice) are coded in blue. All communicative activities are coded in red.

INTERNET ACTIVITIES

(*optional*)

These activities, student worksheets, and related teacher information are in the *Bienvenue* Internet Activities Booklet and on the Glencoe Foreign Language Home Page at: **http://www.glencoe.com/secondary/fl**

LEARNING FROM PHOTOS

After presenting the chapter vocabulary, you may wish to ask questions about the photo: *C'est la ville de Québec? C'est quelle saison? C'est le Palais de Glace? Le Palais est beau? Est-ce que vous faites des sculptures de neige ou de glace en hiver? Vous faites des bonhommes de neige (snowmen)?*

VOCABULAIRE

MOTS 1

UNE STATION DE SPORTS D'HIVER

un sommet

une montagne

une piste très raide

une vallée

des bosses (f.)

un télésiège

un chalet

une skieuse

un skieur — un bonnet

des lunettes (f.)

une écharpe

un anorak

un gant

un bâton

un ski

une chaussure de ski

364 CHAPITRE 14

Vocabulary Teaching Resources

1. Vocabulary Transparencies 14.1 (A & B)
2. Audio Cassette 8B/CD-8
3. Student Tape Manual, Teacher's Edition, *Mots 1: A–C*, pages 155–157
4. Workbook, *Mots 1: A–D*, pages 138–139
5. Communication Activities Masters, *Mots 1: A*, page 68
6. Chapter Quizzes, *Mots 1:* Quiz 1, page 73
7. CD-ROM, Disc 4, *Mots 1:* pages 364–367

Bell Ringer Review

Write the following on the board or use BRR Blackline Master 14-1: Make two lists in French: one of summer sports and one of any weather expressions you remember.

PRESENTATION *(pages 364–365)*

A. To vary the procedure for presenting the vocabulary, you may wish to ask students to open their books to pages 364–365. Have them look at the illustrations as you play Cassette 8B/CD-8 once.

B. Show Vocabulary Transparencies 14.1 (A & B). Have students close their books and repeat the new words after you two or three times.

C. Call a student to the front of the room. As you say a new word or phrase, have the student point to the appropriate item on the transparency.

TOTAL PHYSICAL RESPONSE

(following the Vocabulary presentation)

Getting Ready

Demonstrate *faire une chute.*

TPR 1

___, venez ici, s'il vous plaît.

Asseyez-vous ici, s'il vous plaît.

Mettez vos chaussures de ski.

Et maintenant, levez-vous.

Mettez votre anorak.

Mettez votre bonnet.

Mettez vos lunettes et vos gants.

Mettez les skis.

Prenez les bâtons.

Prenez un bâton dans la main droite.

Prenez l'autre bâton dans la main gauche.

Et maintenant, allez faire du ski!

Merci, ___. Vous pouvez retourner à votre place.

le ski de fond

le ski alpin

une piste de slalom

un moniteur   une monitrice

Marie est débutante.
L'hiver dernier elle a pris des leçons de ski.
Elle a appris à faire du ski.
Elle a eu un très bon moniteur.
Le moniteur a appris à faire du ski à Marie.
Elle a compris les instructions du moniteur.

Marie a mis son anorak.
Elle a mis ses gants, son écharpe
    et son bonnet.
Elle a mis ses skis.

Marie a descendu la piste.
Elle a descendu la piste verte.
La piste verte est pour les débutants.

CHAPITRE 14   365

TPR 2

___, venez ici, s'il vous plaît.
Vous êtes dans une station de sports d'hiver.
Faites la queue.
Attendez le télésiège.
Le voilà, il arrive. Asseyez-vous sur le
    télésiège.
Prenez les bâtons dans votre main gauche.

À tout à l'heure, ___!
Maintenant vous êtes au sommet de la
    montagne.
Descendez du télésiège.
Prenez un bâton dans chaque main.
Descendez. Faites une chute!
Regardez la jambe.
Non, il n'y a pas de problème. Levez-vous et
    skiez encore.
Merci, ___. Retournez à votre place.

PRESENTATION (*page 366*)

Exercice B: Speaking

After doing Exercise B as a whole-class activity, focus on the speaking skill by having students work in pairs. One partner reads the questions to the other in random order. The second partner listens and answers with his/her book closed. Partners then reverse roles.

ANSWERS

Exercice A

1. Oui, Marie a appris à faire du ski.
2. Le moniteur a appris à Marie à faire du ski.
3. Oui, elle a eu un très bon moniteur.
4. Oui, elle a compris les instructions du moniteur.
5. Oui, Marie a mis son anorak.
6. Oui, elle a mis ses gants, son écharpe et son bonnet.
7. Oui, elle a mis ses chaussures de ski et ses skis.
8. Elle a descendu la piste verte.
9. Oui, la piste verte est pour les débutants.

Exercice B

1. Non. (Le ski est un sport d'hiver.)
2. Oui.
3. Non. (Ce n'est pas une piste avec des bosses.)
4. Oui.
5. Non. (Les skieurs prennent le télésiège pour monter.)
6. Oui.
7. Oui.
8. Non. (Les débutants descendent la piste verte.)
9. Oui.
10. Oui.

Exercices

A **Marie a appris à faire du ski.**   Répondez.

1. Marie a appris à faire du ski?
2. Qui a appris à Marie à faire du ski?
3. Elle a eu un très bon moniteur?
4. Elle a compris les instructions du moniteur?
5. Marie a mis son anorak?
6. Elle a mis ses gants, son écharpe et son bonnet?
7. Elle a mis ses chaussures de ski et ses skis?
8. Elle a descendu quelle piste?
9. La piste verte est pour les débutants?

B **Un sport fabuleux.**   Répondez par «oui» ou «non».

1. Le ski est un sport d'été.
2. Les débutants ne font pas bien de ski.
3. Une piste très raide, c'est une piste avec des bosses.
4. Le moniteur ou la monitrice apprend à faire du ski aux débutants.
5. Les skieurs prennent le télésiège pour descendre la piste.
6. Les skieurs prennent le télésiège pour monter au sommet de la montagne.
7. On n'a pas vraiment besoin de pistes pour faire du ski de fond.
8. Les débutants descendent la piste de slalom.
9. Les skieurs portent souvent des lunettes.
10. Après le ski on va dans le chalet.

Méribel: Des skieurs déjeunent à la terrasse d'un restaurant.

366   CHAPITRE 14

ADDITIONAL PRACTICE

1. Show a video about skiing to the class. Stop the video when the scene changes and ask students to describe in French what they have seen. Guide them with your own questions and comments.
2. Student Tape Manual, Teacher's Edition, *Activité B,* page 156

C On fait du ski. Répondez d'après les dessins.

1. C'est une station balnéaire ou une station de sports d'hiver?
2. C'est une plage ou une montagne?
3. C'est une piste ou une piscine?
4. C'est un skieur ou un nageur?
5. C'est un ski nautique ou un bâton?
6. C'est un maillot ou un anorak?
7. Elle fait du ski alpin ou du ski nautique?
8. Il fait du ski de fond ou du ski alpin?
9. C'est le sommet de la montagne ou la vallée?
10. C'est un gant ou une écharpe?

PRESENTATION (*page 367*)

Extension of *Exercice C*: Speaking

After completing Exercise C, have students make at least one additional statement about each of the illustrations. Statements can be affirmative or negative.

ANSWERS

Exercice C
1. C'est une station de sports d'hiver.
2. C'est une montagne.
3. C'est une piste.
4. C'est un skieur.
5. C'est un bâton.
6. C'est un anorak.
7. Elle fait du ski alpin.
8. Il fait du ski de fond.
9. C'est le sommet de la montagne.
10. C'est un gant.

INFORMAL ASSESSMENT
(*Mots 1*)

Check for comprehension by reading sentences, words, or expressions from *Mots 1* in random order and having individuals point to the corresponding illustration on Vocabulary Transparencies 14.1 (A & B).

COOPERATIVE LEARNING

Have teams create composite stories about a ski trip. Start them off with one sentence, such as *Les Dupont arrivent à la station de sports d'hiver.* The team copies the sentence and then passes it around, each member adding a sentence until a story emerges. Teams can pass the story around as many times as they wish. Call on volunteers to read the finished stories.

INDEPENDENT PRACTICE

Assign any of the following:
1. Exercises, pages 366–367
2. Workbook, *Mots 1: A–D,* pages 138–139
3. Communication Activities Masters, *Mots 1: A,* page 68
4. CD-ROM, Disc 4, pages 364–367

Bell Ringer Review

Write the following on the board or use BRR Blackline Master 14-2: Write down these two categories: *faire du ski nautique, faire du ski alpin.* What words do you associate with each?

PRESENTATION *(pages 368–369)*

A. Have students close their books. Briefly review seasons and weather-related vocabulary from Chapter 9.
B. Using an appropriate illustration from a wall calendar, magazine, or ski poster, show a winter scene and introduce as much of the *Mots 2* vocabulary as possible from pages 368–369. Have students repeat the new vocabulary after you.
C. Introduce the temperature vocabulary by drawing a thermometer on the board and asking *Quelle est la température aujourd'hui?* Repeat this a few times, changing the temperature each time.

VOCABULAIRE

MOTS 2

EN HIVER

Il fait froid.
Le ciel est couvert.
Il neige.
Il gèle.
Le vent est très froid.

Quelle est la température aujourd'hui?
Il fait deux (degrés Celsius).

TOTAL PHYSICAL RESPONSE

TPR

____, venez ici, s'il vous plaît.
Vous allez faire le mime.
Il fait très froid et vous avez froid.
Mettez votre anorak.
Mettez vos patins.
Faites du patin.
Tournez à gauche.
Tournez à droite.
Faites une chute.
Levez-vous.
Vous êtes fatigué(e).
Vous voyez un ami.
Saluez votre ami.
Faites une boule de neige. Lancez la boule de neige à votre ami.
Très bien, ____. Merci. Maintenant, retournez à votre place.

jouer dans la neige

lancer une
boule de neige

une patinoire

une patineuse

un patineur

le patinage

la glace

un patin à glace

Hier Robert a fait du patin.
Il a eu un petit accident.
Il a fait une chute.

CHAPITRE 14   **369**

D. Referring to Vocabulary Transparencies 14.2 (A & B), have students keep their books closed as they repeat the vocabulary chorally after you or Cassette 8B/CD-8. Then repeat the procedure with books open.

E. Ask yes/no and either/or questions to elicit the vocabulary, referring to the Vocabulary Transparencies. For example: *Il fait chaud ou il gèle? Il fait du soleil ou le ciel est couvert? Est-ce qu'elle lance une boule de neige? C'est de la glace ou de la neige?*

F. Now ask interrogative-word questions. For example: *Quel temps fait-il? Qu'est-ce qu'elle lance? Et lui, qu'est-ce qu'il fait? Qu'est-ce qu'il va faire? Que fait cette patineuse?*, etc.

G. Include some or all of the exercises on page 370 as you present the *Mots 2* vocabulary. These exercises help students learn the new words in *Mots 2*.

COOPERATIVE LEARNING

Have students form teams and write two lists, one of summer and one of winter activities. Each team exchanges lists with another team. Teams then divide the activities on the lists they have received among their members, who write down what gear and clothing are needed for each of the activities as well as short descriptions of locations where each activity can take place. When finished, have teams share all the information. If you wish, have the teams create composite class lists for each activity on the board.

Exercices A, B, C, and D

You may want to have students write the answers to all of these exercises or just some of them, after you have gone over them in class.

Extension of Exercices A, B, and C

Call on a student to retell the story in Exercises A, B, and C in his/her own words.

Exercice D

You may wish to use the recorded version of this exercise.

ANSWERS

Exercice A

1. Robert a fait du patin.
2. Il a mis ses patins.
3. Il a fait une chute sur la patinoire.
4. Il a eu un petit accident.

Exercice B

1. En hiver il fait froid.
2. Il neige en hiver.
3. Quand il neige, le ciel est couvert.
4. Quand il neige, il fait froid.
5. Oui, il gèle quelquefois en hiver.
6. Oui, le vent est froid.
7. En général, il fait entre ___ degrés et ___ degrés en hiver dans ma ville.
8. Les températures en hiver sont basses.

Exercice C

Answers will vary.

Exercice D

1. le patinage
2. le ski
3. le ski
4. le ski
5. le patinage
6. le ski
7. le patinage

Exercices

A Le petit accident de Robert.   Répondez.

1. Robert a fait du patin ou du ski?
2. Il a mis ses patins ou ses skis?
3. Il a fait une chute sur la patinoire ou sur la piste de slalom?
4. Il a eu un petit accident ou un accident grave?

B Le temps en hiver.   Répondez.

1. En hiver il fait froid ou il fait chaud?
2. Il neige en hiver ou en été?
3. Quand il neige, le ciel est couvert ou il fait du soleil?
4. Quand il neige, il fait chaud ou il fait froid?
5. Il gèle quelquefois en hiver?
6. Le vent est froid?
7. En général, quelle est la température dans ta ville en hiver?
8. Les températures en hiver sont basses ou élevées?

C Les sports d'hiver et d'été.   Donnez des réponses personnelles.

1. Tu préfères l'été ou l'hiver?
2. Quelle est ta saison favorite?
3. Tu préfères les sports d'hiver ou les sports d'été?
4. Qu'est-ce que tu mets quand il fait très froid?
5. Tu as fait du ski? Où?
6. Tu aimes faire du ski?
7. Il y a une station de sports d'hiver près de chez toi?
8. Tu aimes jouer dans la neige?
9. Tu aimes lancer des boules de neige?
10. Tu aimes faire du patin?
11. Tu es bon patineur ou bonne patineuse?
12. Tu as des patins à glace?

D C'est le ski ou le patinage?   Choisissez.

1. On pratique ce sport sur la glace.
2. On pratique ce sport sur la neige.
3. On descend une piste.
4. Les champions font du slalom.
5. On met des patins à glace.
6. On utilise des bâtons.
7. On pratique ce sport sur une patinoire.

ADDITIONAL PRACTICE

After completing Exercises A–D, tell students they have just won an all-expenses-paid vacation to the ski area of their choice, and they may take along a friend. They should write a note to their friend in which they:

1. explain that they have won a trip to a ski resort
2. say where they want to go and why
3. invite their friend to go along
4. say what the weather is going to be like
5. tell what clothing and equipment their friend will need.

Activités de communication orale
Mots 1 et 2

A **À quels sports joue-t-on?** A French exchange student (your partner) asks you what the weather is like in your town in summer and winter and what people do during these seasons. Give him or her as much information as you can.

B **La météo: Il va faire quel temps demain?** Tomorrow is Saturday, and you'd like to make some plans. Find out if a classmate has heard the weather report (*la météo*) and, if so, what the weather's going to be like. Based on what your partner says about the weather, make some plans with him or her for either an indoor or an outdoor activity.

C **Dans les Alpes.** While skiing at a resort in the French Alps, you meet Jacques Monnier. Answer his questions.

1. Bonjour. Tu es des États-Unis?
2. Tu fais souvent du ski?
3. Tu fais aussi du ski de fond?
4. Tu aimes mieux le ski de fond ou le ski alpin?

Jacques Monnier

INDEPENDENT PRACTICE

Assign any of the following:
1. Exercises and activities, pages 370–371
2. Workbook, *Mots 2: E–G,* pages 139–140
3. Communication Activities Masters, *Mots 2: B,* page 68
4. Computer Software, *Vocabulaire*
5. CD-ROM, Disc 4, pages 368–371

LEARNING FROM PHOTOS

Have students identify as many items as they can in the top photo.

Bell Ringer Review
Write the following on the board or use BRR Blackline Master 14-3: You are going on a ski trip for two days. Make a list of the things you will take with you. Include clothing, personal care items, ski equipment, and anything else you may need.

PRESENTATION (*page 371*)

Activité C

In the CD-ROM version of this activity, students can interact with an on-screen native speaker.

ANSWERS

Activité A
Answers will vary.

Activité B
É2 answers will vary. É1 questions will vary but may include the following:
1. Tu as entendu la météo pour demain?
2. Il va faire quel temps demain? (Il va neiger/faire froid?, etc.)
3. Tu voudrais faire du ski (jouer dans la neige/faire du patin/te promener, etc.) avec moi demain?

Activité C
Answers will vary but may include the following:
1. Bonjour. Oui, je suis des États-Unis.
2. Oui (Non), je (ne) fais (pas) souvent du (de) ski.
3. Oui, je fais aussi du ski de fond. (Non, je ne fais pas de ski de fond.)
4. J'aime mieux le ski de fond (alpin).

RETEACHING (*Mots 1 and 2*)
Have students take turns pantomiming words and expressions from *Mots 1* and 2 while the rest of the class guesses.

STRUCTURE

Le passé composé des verbes irréguliers

Describing Past Actions

---

1. You have already learned the past participles of regular verbs in French which end with an /é/, /i/, or /ü/ sound. Note the past participles of the following irregular verbs which also end with an /i/ or /ü/ sound.

INFINITIF ⟶	PARTICIPE PASSÉ
mettre	mis
permettre	permis
prendre	pris
comprendre	compris
apprendre	appris
dire	dit
écrire	écrit
conduire	conduit
avoir	eu
croire	cru
voir	vu
pouvoir	pu
vouloir	voulu
lire	lu

Un skieur sur les pistes de La Plagne

J'ai pris des leçons de ski.
J'ai appris à faire du ski.
J'ai compris toutes les instructions de la monitrice.
Elle a dit: «Bravo! Vous faites très bien du ski!»
J'ai eu de la chance. J'ai eu une très bonne monitrice.
Elle a écrit un livre sur le ski alpin. J'ai lu son livre.

2. The commonly used verbs *être* and *faire* also have irregular past participles.

être	été
faire	fait

J'ai fait un voyage à Megève l'année dernière.
J'ai été très content de pouvoir faire du ski.

Bell Ringer Review

Write the following on the board or use BRR Blackline Master 14-4: Write sentences in the *passé composé* using each of the following verbs.

faire du ski	jouer
faire du patin	lancer

Le passé composé des verbes irréguliers

PRESENTATION *(pages 372–373)*

A. Explain step 1 quickly to students. Have them repeat the /i/ and /ü/ sounds in isolation. Then have them repeat after you the past participles in the list.

B. Write the infinitives from the chart on the board. As you write each one, have the class give you the appropriate past participle. Write it alongside the infinitive.

C. In the case of the /i/ verbs, underline the *-s* and *-t*. Tell students to remember the difference in spelling.

D. Have students read the sentences in unison or call on individuals to read.

DID YOU KNOW?

You may wish to tell students that the skier pictured above is Denis Lechaplain, who began skiing at age 25, seven years after a terrible car accident in which he lost the use of his legs. He now slides down all types of slopes on a "ski-chair" and has been actively involved in ski competitions and in promoting mountain sports among the disabled.

In the photo, he is skiing the slopes of the La Plagne ski resort in the French Alps, site of the 1992 Albertville Olympic luge and bobsled events. La Plagne is actually a conglomeration of 10 villages, each with its own hotels, chalets, restaurants, etc. It is a favorite spot for families because of its child care centers and children's ski schools.

3. Note the position of short adverbs such as *déjà, bien, trop,* and *vite* with the *passé composé.* They are placed between *avoir* and the past participle.

J'ai *déjà* mangé.	*I have already eaten.*
Il a *vite* fini son sandwich.	*He quickly finished his sandwich.*
Il a *bien* choisi son moniteur.	*He chose his instructor well.*

Adverbs of time such as *hier* and *aujourd'hui* follow the past participle.

Il a fait du ski *hier*.
Mais il n'a pas fait de ski *aujourd'hui*.

Exercices

A **Gilles a fait du ski.** Répondez d'après les dessins.

Bonne chance, Gilles!

LE SKI

1. Gilles a mis son anorak?
2. Il a dit «Bonne chance» à son ami?
3. Son ami a déjà fait du ski aujourd'hui?
4. Gilles a bien fait du ski?
5. Il a eu un accident?
6. Après l'accident Gilles a lu un livre pour les débutants?

E. Lead students through steps 2 and 3.

Note In the CD-ROM version, this structure point is presented via an interactive electronic comic strip.

Exercices

PRESENTATION *(page 373)*

Extension of *Exercice A*
   Call on students to give a summary of the story after doing Exercise A.

ANSWERS

Exercice A

1. Oui, Gilles a mis son anorak.
2. Non, son ami a dit «bonne chance» à Gilles.
3. Oui, son ami a déjà fait du ski aujourd'hui.
4. Non, Gilles n'a pas bien fait de ski.
5. Oui, il a eu an accident.
6. Oui, après l'accident Gilles a lu un livre pour les débutants.

ADDITIONAL PRACTICE

1. Have students refer to the illustrations that accompany Exercise A and make up their own story based on them. This can be done orally or in writing.
2. Student Tape Manual, Teacher's Edition, *Activités A–B,* pages 159–160

INDEPENDENT PRACTICE

Assign any of the following:
1. Exercises, pages 373–374
2. Workbook, *Structure: A–C,* pages 141–142
3. Communication Activities Masters, *Structure: A,* page 69
4. Computer Software, *Structure*
5. CD-ROM, Disc 4, pages 372–374

ANSWERS

Exercice B

1. a dit, a lu, a écrit
2. avons dit, avons lu, avons écrit
3. as dit, as lu, as écrit
4. avez dit, avez lu, avez écrit
5. ont dit, ont lu, ont écrit

Exercice C

Answers will vary but may include the following:

1. Oui (Non), j'ai (je n'ai pas) lu… Mes parents (n') ont (pas) lu…
2. Oui (Non), les élèves (n') ont (pas) lu…
3. Oui (Non), j'ai (je n'ai pas) dit…
4. Oui (Non), nous (n') avons (pas) dit…
5. Oui, la femme a dit «Zut!» quand elle a trouvé…
6. Oui (Non), les élèves (n') ont (pas) écrit des (de)…
7. Oui (Non), ils (n') ont (pas) écrit une (de)…
8. Oui (Non), j'ai bien (je n'ai pas bien) écrit…

Exercice D

1. a dit
2. a lu
3. a vu
4. a voulu
5. ont permis
6. a pris
7. a conduit
8. a fait
9. a été
10. ont mis
11. ont pris
12. ont, eu

RETEACHING

Have students write a sentence in the *passé composé* using each of the following verbs. They should change the subject each time. For further practice, have them exchange sentences with a partner and change the partner's sentences to the negative.

dire	lire
prendre	croire
pouvoir	mettre
avoir	faire

374

B **Tu as dit quoi?** Complétez d'après le modèle avec «dire», «lire» ou «écrire».

> J'___ que j'___ ce que j'___.
> *J'ai dit que j'ai lu ce que j'ai écrit.*

1. Il ___ qu'il ___ ce qu'il ___.
2. Nous ___ que nous ___ ce que nous ___.
3. Tu ___ que tu ___ ce que tu ___.
4. Vous ___ que vous ___ ce que vous ___.
5. Elles ___ qu'elles ___ ce qu'elles ___.

C **Qu'est-ce qu'on a fait?** Répondez.

1. Est-ce que tu as lu le journal ce matin? Et tes parents?
2. Les élèves ont lu leur livre de français avant l'examen?
3. Est-ce que tu as dit «Salut!» à tes copains ce matin?
4. Tes amis et toi, vous avez dit «Au revoir!» à votre professeur de français hier?
5. La femme a dit «Zut!» quand elle a trouvé une contravention sur le parebrise de sa voiture?
6. Les élèves ont écrit des lettres à leurs grands-parents?
7. Ils ont écrit une composition au cours d'anglais?
8. Est-ce que tu as bien écrit cet exercice?

D **En route!** Complétez au passé composé.

Mon ami Laurent ___ (dire) que $\frac{}{1}$ Chamonix est une belle station de sports d'hiver. Il ___ (lire) le Guide Michelin et $\frac{}{2}$ il ___ (voir) que Chamonix est loin de $\frac{}{3}$ Paris. Mais il ___ (vouloir) y aller. Ses $\frac{}{4}$ parents ___ (permettre) à Laurent $\frac{}{5}$ de prendre leur voiture. Il ___ (prendre) $\frac{}{6}$ leur voiture et il ___ (conduire) jusqu'à $\frac{}{7}$ Chamonix. Il ___ (faire) le voyage avec $\frac{}{8}$ son copain Alain qui ___ (être) très $\frac{}{9}$ content de partir avec lui. Ils ___ (mettre) $\frac{}{10}$ leurs skis sur la voiture. Ils ___ (prendre) $\frac{}{11}$ l'autoroute. Ils n'___ pas ___ (avoir) de $\frac{}{12}$ problème.

La Mer de Glace près de Chamonix

ADDITIONAL PRACTICE

You may wish to ask the following questions to practice the *passé composé* while reviewing previously learned vocabulary: *Gilles a mis son maillot? Il a mis de la crème solaire? Il a pris un bain de soleil à la plage? Il a pris des leçons de natation? Il a eu un bon moniteur? Il a appris à faire du ski nautique? Il a fait du ski nautique? Il a compris tout ce que le moniteur a dit?*

DID YOU KNOW?

At Chamonix (see GEOGRAPHY CONNECTION, page 359) one can board a two-car train that climbs up to La Mer de Glace, a glacier offering dramatic views. Its unusual caves are filled with ice sculptures. Some visitors returning from the top of *l'Aiguille du Midi* (see DID YOU KNOW?, page 376), get off the gondola halfway down and hike along a scenic, winding trail to La Mer de Glace.

Les pronoms *qui* et *quoi* — Asking "Whom" or "What"

1. You use the pronouns *qui*, "whom," and *quoi*, "what," with prepositions such as *à*, *de*, *avec*, and *chez* to ask questions in French. *Qui* refers to a person and *quoi* refers to a thing. Study the following examples.

> **Tu parles à qui?**
> **Tu vas chez qui?**
> **Tu parles de quoi?**

2. Note the inversion in formal or written French.

INFORMAL	FORMAL
Vous parlez à qui?	**À qui parlez-vous?**
Vous allez chez qui?	**Chez qui allez-vous?**
Vous avez besoin de quoi?	**De quoi avez-vous besoin?**

Exercices

A **Comment? Je n'ai pas entendu.**   Répondez d'après le modèle.

> **Elle parle de sa sœur.**
> *Comment? Je n'ai pas entendu. Elle parle de qui?*

1. Elle parle de sa tante.
2. Elle parle de son prof.
3. Elle parle au moniteur.
4. Elle parle à son amie.
5. Elle est chez ses parents.
6. Elle va chez son copain.
7. Elle travaille avec sa cousine.
8. Elle parle de son travail.
9. Elle parle de ses vacances à la montagne.
10. Elle a besoin d'argent.
11. Elle a besoin de skis.

B **Au téléphone.**   Posez une question d'après le modèle.

> **Vous allez au cinéma avec votre amie.**
> *Avec qui allez-vous au cinéma?*

1. Vous téléphonez à votre amie.
2. Vous parlez à votre amie.
3. Vous parlez de choses sérieuses.
4. Vous laissez un message pour le frère de votre amie.

Un forfait-journée

Les pronoms *qui* et *quoi*

PRESENTATION *(page 375)*

A. To show that *qui* is for a person and *quoi* is for a thing, draw a stick figure on the board and ask: *Qui?* Then draw a box and ask: *Quoi?*

B. Lead students through steps 1–2 on page 375. Explain the use of *qui* versus *quoi* with prepositions.

Teaching Tip Explain the term "object of a preposition" and provide examples in both French and English.

Exercices

PRESENTATION *(page 375)*

Extension of *Exercice A*

You may want to do this exercise again, this time with formal word order.

ANSWERS

Exercice A

1. Comment? Je n'ai pas entendu. Elle parle de qui?
2. … Elle parle de qui?
3. … Elle parle à qui?
4. … Elle parle à qui?
5. … Elle est chez qui?
6. … Elle va chez qui?
7. … Elle travaille avec qui?
8. … Elle parle de quoi?
9. … Elle parle de quoi?
10. … Elle a besoin de quoi?
11. … Elle a besoin de quoi?

Exercice B

1. À qui téléphonez-vous?
2. À qui parlez-vous?
3. De quoi parlez-vous?
4. Pour qui laissez-vous un message?

ADDITIONAL PRACTICE

Have students write questions with *qui* or *quoi* that would elicit the following answers:
1. **Hélène va au cinéma avec son amie.**
2. **Elle a besoin d'argent.**
3. **Max achète un cadeau pour sa mère.**
4. **Les amis vont chez Luc après les cours.**
5. **Madame Martin téléphone à sa fille.**

INDEPENDENT PRACTICE

Assign any of the following:
1. Exercises, page 375
2. Workbook, *Structure: D–E,* page 143
3. Communication Activities Masters, *Structure: B–C,* page 70
4. Computer Software, *Structure*
5. CD-ROM, Disc 4, pages 372– 375

CONVERSATION

Bell Ringer Review

Write the following on the board or use BRR Blackline Master 14-5: It is January. You are in the French Alps and your friend is in Martinique in the Caribbean. Describe the weather in both places.

PRESENTATION (page 376)

A. Tell students they will hear a conversation between Lisette and Michel who are at a ski resort.

B. Have them close their books and watch the Conversation Video, then have them repeat after you or Cassette 8B/CD-8.

C. Call on students to read and dramatize the conversation.

D. Have pairs make up a similar conversation about skiing or skating.

Note In the CD-ROM version, students can play the role of either one of the characters and record the conversation.

ANSWERS

Exercice A

1. Michel a fait du ski hier.
2. Il a descendu la piste noire.
3. La piste noire est difficile.
4. Oui, les pistes noires sont des pistes très raides.
5. Oui, Michel a eu un problème.
6. Oui, il a fait une chute.

Prononciation

PRESENTATION (page 376)

A. Model the key word *une radio* and have students repeat chorally.

B. Now model the other words and sentences in similar fashion.

376

CONVERSATION

Scènes de la vie *Tu as fait du ski?*

LISETTE: Michel, tu as fait du ski hier?
MICHEL: Oui. J'ai descendu la piste noire.
LISETTE: La piste noire? Mais tu es fou! C'est dangereux.
MICHEL: Oui, mais je n'ai pas eu de problème.
LISETTE: Tu n'as pas fait de chute?
MICHEL: Si, une petite chute, rien de grave!

A **La piste noire.** Répondez d'après la conversation.

1. Qui a fait du ski hier?
2. Il a descendu quelle piste?
3. La piste noire est facile ou difficile?
4. Les pistes noires sont des pistes très raides?
5. Michel a eu un problème?
6. Il a fait une chute?

Prononciation *Le son /r/ initial*

You have already practiced saying the /r/ sound in the middle or at the end of a word. You will now practice saying it at the beginning of a word. Repeat the following pairs of words.

opéra / radio	mari / restaurant
favori / rigoler	adoré / rez-de-chaussée

Now repeat the following sentences.

C'est la radio qui réveille Richard.
Pour rester en forme, Raoul ne regarde pas trop la télévison.
Robert roule très vite dans sa Renault rouge.

une radio

376 CHAPITRE 14

DID YOU KNOW?

Although the French like to ski in the Pyrenees, the Vosges, and the Jura, the slopes of the Alps are their favorite places to ski. The Alps offer long ski runs and breathtaking views.

One of the most spectacular and popular ski lifts in all of Europe is *l'Aiguille du Midi*, next to Mont Blanc. To get to the top of the 12,600-foot-high rock needle, skiers take two different gondolas. As they get off the second gondola, they proceed through an ice tunnel to reach the top of the slope. From there, the view is magnificent and the descent exhilarating.

Activités de communication orale

A **Au téléphone.** Find out if a classmate talked on the phone last night. If he or she did, find out who your partner spoke to (*à qui*) and what they talked about (*de quoi*). Then reverse roles.

B **Le week-end dernier.** You want to know if a classmate did one of the activities listed below last weekend. If the answer is "yes," try to get some details. Then reverse roles.

    voir un film
    Élève 1: Tu as vu un film le week-end dernier?
    Élève 2: Oui, j'ai vu *Independence Day*.
    Élève 1: C'est un bon film?

    avoir un accident   inviter un copain ou une copine au cinéma
    écrire une composition   jouer au football / base-ball / basket-ball, etc.
    étudier   lire un journal / un magazine / un livre
    faire ses devoirs   parler au téléphone
    faire du ski   regarder la télé
    faire du patin

C **J'ai appris à…** Tell a classmate something you learned to do recently (last week, last winter, last summer, etc.). Your partner asks you for the information below. Answer, then reverse roles.

1. when you learned to do the activity
2. where you learned
3. who taught you
4. if you took lessons
5. if you had a good instructor
6. if you understood the instructions

On fait beaucoup de ski au Canada.

INDEPENDENT PRACTICE

Assign any of the following:
1. Exercise and activities, pages 376–377
2. CD-ROM, Disc 4, pages 376–377

LEARNING FROM PHOTOS

Have students say as much about the photo as they can.

C. You may wish to give students the following *dictée*:
Robert regarde la route. Carole écoute une opéra à la radio. Le mari de Carole adore ce restaurant. René roule vite sur la route.

D. For additional practice, use Pronunciation Transparency P-14, the *Prononciation* section on Cassette 8B/CD-8 and *Activité E*, page 161 in the Student Tape Manual, Teacher's Edition.

Bell Ringer Review
Write the following on the board or use BRR Blackline Master 14-6: You are taking your driving exam. The exam asks you for instances when you should slow down instead of accelerating. Write down as many as you can.

Activités de communication orale

ANSWERS

Activité A
É2 answers will vary. É1 questions will vary but may include the following:
Tu as parlé au téléphone hier soir?
Tu as parlé à qui?
Vous avez parlé de quoi?

Activité B
É1 initial questions will follow the model. É2 answers will vary.

Activité C
É2 answers will vary. É1 questions may include:
1. **Quand est-ce que tu as appris à…?**
2. **Où est-ce que tu as appris à…?**
3. **Qui t'a appris à…?**
4. **Tu as pris des leçons de…?**
5. **Tu as eu un bon moniteur/une bonne monitrice?**
6. **Tu as (bien) compris les instructions?**

READING STRATEGIES
(page 378)

Note Find out which members
of the class are skiers. If your
students do not ski because of
geographical or socio-economic
reasons, you may wish to go over
this *Lecture* very quickly.

Pre-reading

A. Using a wall map, point out the
geographic locations mentioned
in the reading.

B. There are many instances of the
passé composé in the *Lecture*.
Have students find several.

Reading

Have students open their books
to page 378 and follow along as
you read the first paragraph. Then
have students read the rest of the
Lecture silently.

Post-reading

Lead students through the
exercises that follow the *Lecture*.

Note Students may listen to a
recorded version of the
Lecture on the CD-ROM.

Étude de mots

ANSWERS

Exercice A

1. a
2. b
3. a
4. b
5. b

378

LECTURE ET CULTURE

ON VA AUX SPORTS D'HIVER

En février dernier la classe de Madame
Carrigan a fait un voyage au Canada.
Les élèves ont eu une semaine de
vacances. Ils ont pris le train de New
York pour aller à Montréal. Ils ont passé
trois jours à Montréal où ils ont parlé
français. Montréal est la deuxième ville
francophone[1] du monde, après Paris.

Après deux jours à Montréal ils ont pris
le car[2] jusqu'au Parc du Mont-Sainte-
Anne. Le Mont-Sainte-Anne est une
station de sports d'hiver tout près de la
jolie ville de Québec. Après leur arrivée
à Sainte-Anne ils ont tous mis leur
anorak et leurs chaussures de ski. Ils ont
acheté leur ticket de télésiège. Ils ont
pris le télésiège jusqu'au sommet de la
montagne. Du sommet ils ont eu une
vue splendide sur les montagnes et les
vallées couvertes de neige. As-tu jamais[3]
vu les montagnes couvertes de neige?
C'est vraiment superbe!

Les bâtons à la main et les skis aux pieds,
ils ont commencé à descendre une piste.
Mais ils ont choisi la mauvaise[4] piste, une
piste très raide, trop difficile pour des
débutants. Qui a eu un accident? Le
casse-cou[5] Michel? Mais oui, c'est lui! Il a
fait une chute. Il a glissé jusqu'en bas[6] de
la piste. Tous ses copains ont rigolé. Ils
ont dit: «Michel, tu es une vraie boule de
neige qui roule, roule, roule!»

[1] francophone   *French-speaking*
[2] car   *bus*
[3] jamais   *ever*
[4] mauvaise   *wrong*
[5] casse-cou   *daredevil*
[6] a glissé jusqu'en bas   *slid to the bottom*

Le Mont-Sainte-Anne

Étude de mots

A **Quel est le mot?** Choisissez.

1. Février est ____.
   a. un mois   b. une saison

2. Février est en ____.
   a. été   b. hiver

3. Montréal est une ville ____.
   a. francophone   b. française

4. Les chaussures de ski sont des ____.
   a. tennis   b. bottes

5. On met ____ quand il fait très froid.
   a. un maillot   b. un anorak

DID YOU KNOW?

Quebec City is the oldest city in Canada
and the only walled city in North America.
Most of the present-day city lies outside
the walls. Every February Quebec City holds
its *Carnaval de Québec.* Attended by 500,000
tourists, it lasts two weeks and includes costume balls, dog-sled and ice-canoe races, snow
and ice sculpture contests, a ski triathlon, and
much more, all presided over by a Snow Queen.

Mont-Sainte-Anne, a ski resort of international stature in Quebec province, has the
highest drop east of the Rockies, excellent ski
jumps, and a gondola lift. The region known
as Mont Tremblant in the Laurentians is a
well-known ski resort area in Quebec, as
is Lac Beauport, which features a beautiful
descente aux flambeaux (skiers with lighted
torches going down the slopes at night)
during carnival season.

Compréhension

B **Une excursion.** Corrigez les phrases.

1. Les élèves de Madame Carrigan ont fait un voyage en France.
2. Ils ont pris l'avion.
3. Ils ont passé trois jours à Québec.
4. Québec est la deuxième ville francophone du monde.
5. Le Parc du Mont-Sainte-Anne est une station balnéaire.
6. Les élèves de Madame Carrigan font tous très bien du ski.

C **Un fait important.** Vous avez appris quelque chose d'important au sujet de Montréal. Qu'est-ce que c'est?

DÉCOUVERTE CULTURELLE

Quelques pays francophones ont des stations de sports d'hiver fabuleuses. En France, par exemple, il y a beaucoup de stations de sports d'hiver dans les Alpes et les Pyrénées. La Suisse est un pays célèbre pour le ski. Et n'oubliez pas que le français est une des langues officielles de la Suisse. En Suisse on parle français, allemand et italien. Et au Québec, la province francophone du Canada, il y a des stations de sports d'hiver superbes.

En France les écoles primaires ont des classes de neige. Les élèves vont dans une station de sports d'hiver. Le matin ils ont des cours. Ils étudient les maths, l'anglais, etc. L'après-midi, des moniteurs apprennent à faire du ski aux élèves. Il y a des classes de neige aux États-Unis? Vous croyez que c'est une bonne idée?

Dans les stations de sports d'hiver en France les pistes sont classées selon leur difficulté. Les couleurs indiquent le niveau, ou le degré, de difficulté.

PISTE	NIVEAU	TYPE DE SKIEURS
	facile	débutants
	moyen	bons skieurs
	difficile	très bons skieurs
	très difficile	très, très bons skieurs

CHAPITRE 14   379

CRITICAL THINKING ACTIVITY

(Thinking skill: making inferences)
Read the following to the class or put it on the board or on a transparency.

1. C'est la première fois que Christophe fait du ski. Qu'est-ce qu'il doit *(must)* faire?
2. Mais Christophe est toujours très impatient. La piste verte pour les débutants, ce n'est pas pour lui. Il va descendre la piste rouge. Le panneau indique que c'est une piste pour les très bons skieurs. Quelles peuvent être les conséquences de la décision de Christophe?

Compréhension

PRESENTATION *(page 379)*

Extension of *Exercices B* and *C*
Ask students: *Après leur arrivée à Sainte-Anne, qu'est-ce que les élèves ont mis? Qu'est-ce qu'ils ont acheté? Qu'est-ce qu'ils ont pris pour aller au sommet de la montagne? Qu'est-ce qu'ils ont vu du sommet? Qui a eu un accident? Qu'est-ce qu'il a fait? Il a glissé jusqu'où?*

ANSWERS

Exercice B

1. … au Canada.
2. … le train.
3. … à Montréal.
4. Montréal…
5. … de sports d'hiver.
6. … ne font pas tous très bien de ski.

Exercice C

Montréal est la deuxième ville francophone du monde, après Paris.

OPTIONAL MATERIAL

Découverte culturelle

PRESENTATION *(page 379)*

A. Before reading the selection, point out the Vosges, the Alps, the Jura, the Massif Central, and the Pyrenees, as well as Switzerland and Quebec, on the maps on pages 504 and 506.
B. Have students read silently, then ask these *vrai/faux* questions: *La Suisse a trois langues officielles. On ne fait pas de ski dans les Pyrénées. En France, les écoles primaires ont des classes de neige dans les villes. Dans les classes de neige, les élèves apprennent à faire du ski le matin. Une piste rouge est plus facile qu'une piste bleue.*

Note Students may listen to a recorded version of the *Découverte culturelle* on the CD-ROM.

RÉALITÉS

PRESENTATION *(pages 380–381)*

The main objective of this section is to have the students enjoy the photographs and absorb some French culture. However, if you would like to do more, you may wish to do some of the following activities.

A. Before reading the captions, ask students to name as many winter sports as they can think of. How many of these make up part of the Winter Olympics?

B. Have student volunteers read the captions on page 380 and answer any questions they find.

Note In the CD-ROM version, students can listen to the recorded captions and discover a hidden video behind one of the photos.

THE FRANCOPHONE WORLD

Photos of Quebec and additional information about it may be found in *Le Monde francophone*, pages 112, 223, 327, and 436.

RÉALITÉS

1

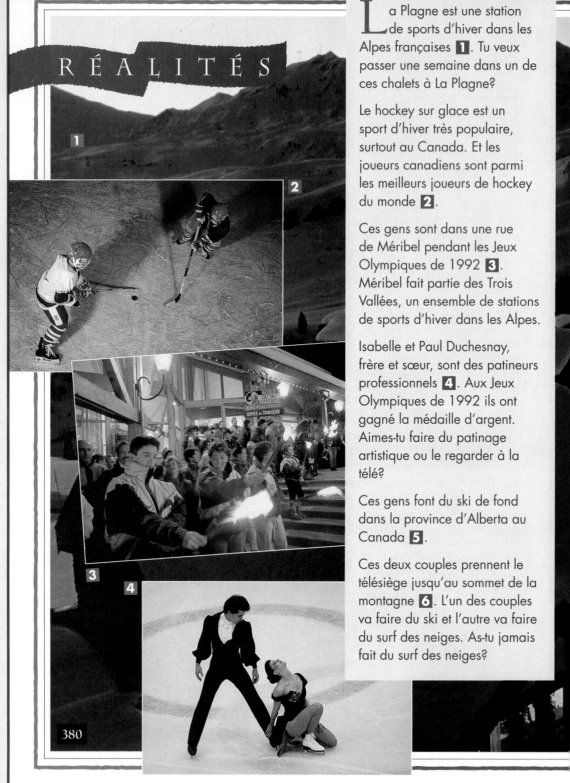

380

La Plagne est une station de sports d'hiver dans les Alpes françaises **1**. Tu veux passer une semaine dans un de ces chalets à La Plagne?

Le hockey sur glace est un sport d'hiver très populaire, surtout au Canada. Et les joueurs canadiens sont parmi les meilleurs joueurs de hockey du monde **2**.

Ces gens sont dans une rue de Méribel pendant les Jeux Olympiques de 1992 **3**. Méribel fait partie des Trois Vallées, un ensemble de stations de sports d'hiver dans les Alpes.

Isabelle et Paul Duchesnay, frère et sœur, sont des patineurs professionnels **4**. Aux Jeux Olympiques de 1992 ils ont gagné la médaille d'argent. Aimes-tu faire du patinage artistique ou le regarder à la télé?

Ces gens font du ski de fond dans la province d'Alberta au Canada **5**.

Ces deux couples prennent le télésiège jusqu'au sommet de la montagne **6**. L'un des couples va faire du ski et l'autre va faire du surf des neiges. As-tu jamais fait du surf des neiges?

DID YOU KNOW?

Megève, an elite resort in the Alps, offers skiers a choice of three mountains and 124 slopes, served by 81 lifts. (For information on Méribel and La Plagne, see DID YOU KNOW?, pages 366 and 372, respectively.) In all these resorts *après-ski* activities abound: shopping, restaurants (many serving gourmet-quality food), and night entertainment galore.

COOPERATIVE LEARNING

Display Communication Transparency C-14. Have students work in groups to make up as many questions as they can about the illustration. Have groups take turns asking and answering the questions.

René Martin est un élève de Tours. En ce moment il est avec sa classe dans la région des Alpes. Il y a quelque chose qui surprend René. Il remarque qu'il y a beaucoup de chalets en bois *(wood)* dans cette région. C'est assez rare en France. La plupart des maisons en France sont en brique ou en pierre, mais dans la région des Alpes il y a beaucoup de maisons en bois.

381

ADDITIONAL PRACTICE

1. Student Tape Manual, Teacher's Edition, *Deuxième Partie*, pages 162–163
2. Situation Cards, Chapter 14

INDEPENDENT PRACTICE

Assign any of the following:
1. *Étude de mots* and *Compréhension* exercises, pages 378–379
2. Workbook, *Un peu plus*, pages 144–146
3. CD-ROM, Disc 4, pages 378–381

RECYCLING

The *Activités de communication orale* and *Activités de communication écrite* provide various ways for students to recycle and recombine structures and vocabulary associated with clothing, travel, sports activities, food and restaurants, weather, making plans, and expressing opinions, preferences, and needs.

INFORMAL ASSESSMENT

Oral Activities A and D may serve as a means to evaluate the speaking skill.

Use the evaluation criteria given on page 34 of this Teacher's Wraparound Edition.

Activités de communication orale

ANSWERS

Activité A

Answers will vary but may include the following:

Tu préfères les sports d'été ou les sports d'hiver? Quels sports (en particulier) est-ce que tu aimes? Pourquoi?

Activités B and C

Answers will vary.

Activité D

É1 answers will follow the model. É2 answers will vary but will always begin with *On a besoin de (d')* and may include the following items:

1. une voiture/un permis de conduire/essence/la clé de la voiture
2. un stylo/papier/une bonne idée/instructions
3. skis/bâtons/chaussures de ski/neige
4. billets/une valise/copains/un itinéraire
5. une raquette/un filet/un court/une balle
6. pain/viande/un couteau/beurre

382

Activités de communication orale

A **Sports d'hiver ou sports d'été.** Find out if a classmate prefers winter or summer sports. Then ask which ones he or she likes and why. Reverse roles.

B **Nord et Sud.** Imagine that you're from a city in the South and a classmate is from a city in the North. Contrast the two places you choose in winter. Talk about the weather, clothing, activities, and so on.

> Élève 1: À (*ville du Sud*) il fait chaud en hiver.
> Élève 2: À (*ville du Nord*) il fait froid en hiver.

C **La location de skis.** You need to rent some ski equipment from the attendant (your partner) at a ski resort. Tell your partner what equipment you need and for how long. Your partner will help you find the right equipment for a skier at your level and the right size boots. Discuss price and method of payment.

D **De quoi a-t-on besoin pour… ?** Ask a classmate what people need in order to do one of the activities in the list below. Your partner gets one point for each thing he or she can name. Then reverse roles.

> Élève 1: De quoi a-t-on besoin pour apprendre le français?
> Élève 2: On a besoin d'un bon professeur, d'un livre et de beaucoup de patience!

conduire une voiture	faire un voyage
écrire une composition	jouer au tennis
faire du ski	préparer un sandwich

Le Mont d'Arbois à Megève

Activités de communication écrite

A **Au Canada.** Your Canadian pen pal has invited you to spend a week in Québec during the winter. Write back accepting or declining the invitation. Give several reasons why you can or cannot accept.

382 CHAPITRE 14

B **Une station de sports d'hiver idéale.** Write a paragraph describing an ideal winter resort (real or imaginary). Be sure to include the following information.

1. where it's located and how to get there
2. what the weather's generally like
3. what facilities there are (lifts, skating rinks, restaurants, etc.)
4. what else you can do there besides ski

Réintroduction et recombinaison

A **Un match de foot.** Mettez au passé composé.

1. Je joue au foot.
2. Je passe le ballon à Charles.
3. Il renvoie le ballon.
4. Le gardien bloque le ballon.
5. Nous ne marquons pas de but.
6. L'arbitre déclare un penalty.
7. L'équipe adverse marque un but.
8. Nous faisons le forcing pour égaliser le score.

B **La télé.** Complétez au passé composé.

1. Hier soir j'___ la télé. (regarder)
2. J'___ un film intéressant. (voir)
3. J'___ la météo: demain, neige et froid, températures basses. (entendre)
4. À neuf heures mon copain Éric m'___. (téléphoner)
5. Il n'___ pas ___ de bonnes nouvelles. (avoir)
6. Il ___ un examen et il n'___ pas ___ à l'examen. (passer, réussir)

Vocabulaire

NOMS
l'hiver (m.)
le vent
le ski (*skiing*)
le ski alpin
le ski de fond
le skieur
la skieuse
le/la débutant(e)
le moniteur
la monitrice
la piste (raide)
la piste de slalom
la bosse

la station de sports
  d'hiver
le chalet
le télésiège
la montagne
le sommet
la vallée

le ski (*ski*)
le bâton
la chaussure de ski
l'anorak (m.)
le bonnet
l'écharpe (f.)
le gant
les lunettes (f.)

le patinage
le patin à glace
le patineur
la patineuse
la patinoire
la glace
l'accident (m.)
la chute

VERBES
apprendre à quelqu'un
  à faire quelque chose
descendre

**AUTRES MOTS
ET EXPRESSIONS**
faire du ski
faire du patin
faire une chute
il fait ___ degrés Celsius
il fait froid
il gèle
il neige

CHAPITRE 14 **383**

INDEPENDENT PRACTICE

1. Activities and exercises, pages 382–383
2. Communication Activities Masters, pages 68–70
3. CD-ROM, Disc 4, pages 382–383

CHAPTER OVERVIEW

In this chapter, students will learn to talk about routine illnesses and to describe their symptoms to a doctor. They will learn vocabulary associated with medical exams, prescriptions, and minor ailments such as colds, flu, and headache. Students will learn to talk about themselves and others using the object pronouns *me, te, nous, vous;* the present and *passé composé* of verbs like *ouvrir* and *souffrir;* and the imperative forms of verbs.

The cultural focus of Chapter 15 is on French medical services and facilities, social security, and attitudes towards minor illnesses.

CHAPTER OBJECTIVES

By the end of this chapter, students will know:

1. vocabulary associated with headaches, colds, fevers, and flu
2. body parts associated with various ailments
3. vocabulary associated with a visit to a doctor or a pharmacy
4. informal expressions used to comment on one's own health and that of others
5. the pronouns *me, te, nous,* and *vous* used as direct and indirect objects
6. negative constructions using the object pronouns *me, te, nous,* and *vous*
7. the present tense of verbs like *ouvrir*
8. the past participles of verbs like *ouvrir*
9. the formation of formal and informal imperatives as well as the *nous* imperative
10. negative imperative constructions

CHAPITRE {15}

LA SANTÉ ET LA MÉDECINE

OBJECTIFS

In this chapter you will learn to do the following:

1. describe symptoms of a minor illness such as a cold, the flu, or an upset stomach
2. have a prescription filled at a pharmacy
3. give formal and informal commands
4. tell what you do for others and what others do for you
5. describe more activities
6. compare American and French medical services
7. compare some American and French attitudes toward health

CHAPTER PROJECTS

(optional)

1. Obtain a first-aid film from the health department in your school and use it as a springboard for discussing health and illness using new vocabulary from this chapter. You may also wish to use the film to review the parts of the body in French.
2. Have students create a poster of a man or woman like the kind in doctors' offices, labeling in French as many external and internal body parts as they can. This poster can be displayed in your classroom.

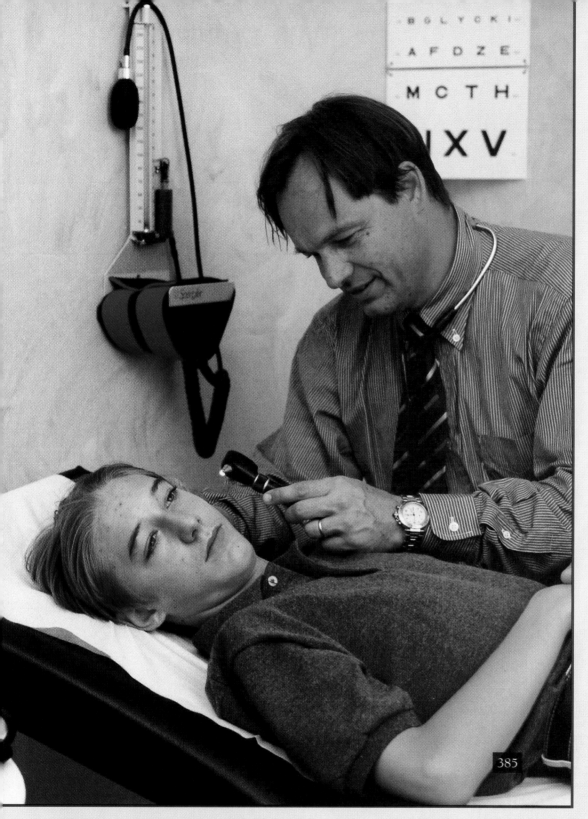

385

Pacing

This chapter requires eight to ten class sessions. Pacing will vary according to class length and the age and aptitude of the students.

Note The Lesson Plans offer guidelines for 45- and 55-minute classes and **Block Scheduling.**

Exercices vs. *Activités*

All exercises (which provide guided practice) are coded in blue. All communicative activities are coded in red.

INTERNET ACTIVITIES

(*optional*)

These activities, student worksheets, and related teacher information are in the *Bienvenue* Internet Activities Booklet and on the Glencoe Foreign Language Home Page at: **http://www.glencoe.com/secondary/fl**

LEARNING FROM PHOTOS

After students have learned the vocabulary of this chapter, you may wish to ask the following questions about the photo: *Le médecin examine le malade? Il l'ausculte? Il regarde sa bouche? Qu'est-ce qu'il examine? Le malade souffre? Il a mal? Il se sent bien? Il a de la fièvre, à ton avis? Qu'est-ce qu'il a, à ton avis? Le médecin va faire un diagnostic au malade? Il va faire une ordonnance au malade?*

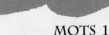

Bell Ringer Review

Write the following on the board or use BRR Blackline Master 15-1: Last weekend Maurice had a party at his house. Write sentences explaining at least two things he probably did before the party, two things he or his guests probably did during it, and two things he probably did after it.

PRESENTATION (pages 386–387)

Teaching Tip You may wish to bring a handkerchief, tissues, and throat lozenges to class to make the presentation of the *Mots 1* vocabulary more lively for the students.

A. Have students make a list of the parts of the body they already know in French.
B. Point to yourself to model the following parts of the body: *la bouche, le nez, la gorge, l'oreille, les yeux, le ventre.*
C. Use gestures to teach the following expressions: *avoir de la fièvre; avoir des frissons; il est très malade; il n'est pas en bonne*

VOCABULAIRE

MOTS 1

ON EST MALADE

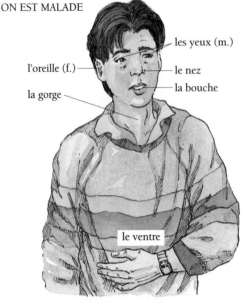

les yeux (m.)
l'oreille (f.)
le nez
la bouche
la gorge
le ventre

avoir de la fièvre

Paul a un rhume.
Il est enrhumé.
Il éternue.

Atchoum!

un kleenex

Il tousse.

un mouchoir

Martin n'est pas en bonne santé.
Il est en mauvaise santé.
Il est très malade, le pauvre.
Il ne se sent pas bien.
Qu'est-ce qu'il a, le pauvre garçon?

Note: The expression *Qu'est-ce qu'il a?* means "What's wrong with him?"

TOTAL PHYSICAL RESPONSE

(following the Vocabulary presentation)

TPR

____, venez ici, s'il vous plaît.
Montrez-moi la bouche.
Montrez-moi la main.
Montrez-moi le nez.
Montrez-moi le pied.
Montrez-moi le ventre.
Montrez-moi la gorge.
Montrez-moi les yeux.
Levez la main.
Ouvrez la bouche.
Fermez les yeux.
Mettez la main sur la tête.
Touchez les pieds avec les mains.
Merci, ____. Retournez à votre place et asseyez-vous, s'il vous plaît.

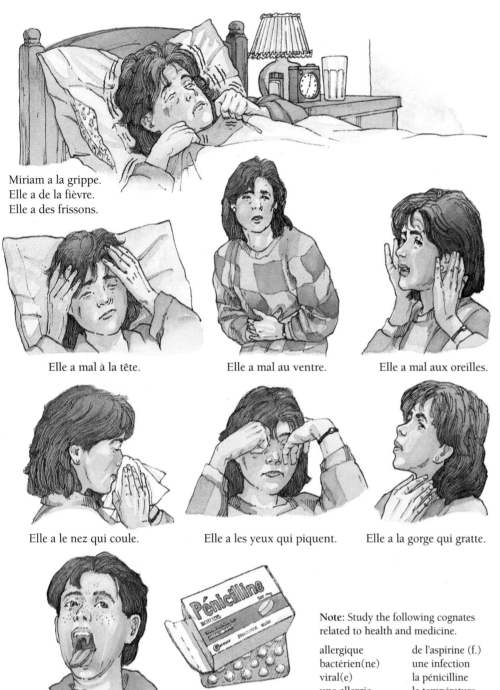

Miriam a la grippe.
Elle a de la fièvre.
Elle a des frissons.

Elle a mal à la tête.

Elle a mal au ventre.

Elle a mal aux oreilles.

Elle a le nez qui coule.

Elle a les yeux qui piquent.

Elle a la gorge qui gratte.

Christophe a très mal à la gorge. Il a une angine.

Note: Study the following cognates related to health and medicine.

allergique	de l'aspirine (f.)
bactérien(ne)	une infection
viral(e)	la pénicilline
une allergie	la température
un antibiotique	

santé; il a mal au ventre; il tousse; il éternue; il a mal à la tête; il a mal aux oreilles; elle a le nez qui coule; elle a les yeux qui piquent; elle a la gorge qui gratte.

D. Have students repeat the cognates carefully after you or Cassette 9A/CD-9. These are the words they are most likely to anglicize.

Note Remind students that in French the definite article is usually used when talking about parts of the body. Introduce the singular of *les yeux* (*un œil*).

E. Ask several volunteers to come to the front of the room. Have each one mime a different ailment. The rest of the class describes the symptoms and suggests what he/she needs. Use as many props as possible. Guide the class with questions when necessary. For example: *Pauvre Isabelle! Elle a un rhume. (Elle a le nez qui coule.) (Elle a mal à la gorge.) (Elle a un peu de fièvre.) De quoi est-ce qu'elle a besoin? (Elle a besoin de beaucoup de kleenex.) (Elle a besoin d'aspirine.),* etc.

F. Ask each volunteer to recapitulate his/her illness, symptoms, and needs. Cue key words or ask the class for help as necessary. For example: *J'ai un rhume. J'ai le nez qui coule. J'ai besoin d'aspirine.,* etc.

Vocabulary Expansion

Tourists often experience stomach problems. If you wish, you may give the students the following useful words and expressions.
Vous avez des nausées?
Vous avez de la diarrhée?
Vous êtes constipé(e)?
Vous avez de la constipation?
Vous vomissez?
Vous avez des vomissements?
Vous avez des crampes?

DID YOU KNOW?

You may wish to introduce the colloquial expression *Mon œil!* to students. It means, "Come on, do you think I'm going to believe that?" When people say it they usually put their finger up to their eye.

ADDITIONAL PRACTICE

Play a game of *Jacques a dit.* Call the first round yourself and have students act out the following:
Jacques a dit: Vous avez mal à la tête.
Jacques a dit: Mettez les mains sur la tête.
Jacques a dit: Toussez.
Jacques a dit: Éternuez.
Then call on students to lead the game.

Exercices

Extension of *Exercice B*

After doing Exercise B, call on a student to give a summary of the story in his or her own words.

ANSWERS

Exercice A

1. la gorge
2. l'oreille
3. la tête
4. les yeux
5. le nez
6. la bouche
7. le ventre
8. la main
9. le pied

Exercice B

1. Oui, Miriam est très malade.
2. Non, elle ne se sent pas bien.
3. Elle a la grippe.
4. Oui, elle a de la fièvre et des frissons.
5. Oui, elle a la gorge qui gratte.
6. Oui, elle a les yeux qui piquent et le nez qui coule.
7. Oui, elle a mal à la tête.
8. Oui, elle a mal au ventre.
9. Oui, elle a mal aux oreilles.

388

Exercices

A Qu'est-ce que c'est? Identifiez.

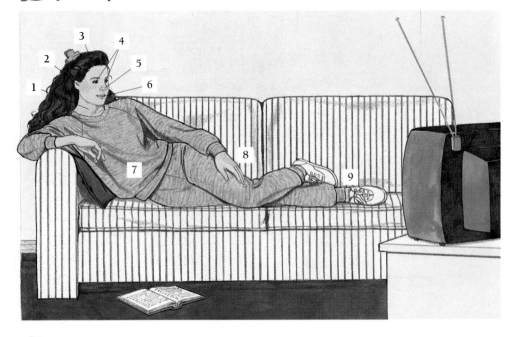

B Qu'est-ce qu'elle a, la pauvre Miriam? Répondez.

1. Miriam est très malade?
2. Elle ne se sent pas bien?
3. Qu'est-ce qu'elle a?
4. Elle a de la fièvre et des frissons?
5. Elle a la gorge qui gratte?
6. Elle a les yeux qui piquent et le nez qui coule?
7. Elle a mal à la tête?
8. Elle a mal au ventre?
9. Elle a mal aux oreilles?

388 CHAPITRE 15

LEARNING FROM ILLUSTRATIONS

Have students say anything they can about the illustration that accompanies Exercise A. Tell students the word "sofa" is the same in French: *un sofa*, but one also frequently hears *un canapé* or *un divan*.

LEARNING FROM REALIA

Have students look at the realia. Tell them to give you the brand name of the medication. Then have them find what it is for. They should be able to guess when they see the word *gorge*. Then ask them for the singular form of the word *maux (mal)*. Ask in what form the medicine is (*comprimés*). If they are *comprimés*, what does *sucer* mean? What does one do with these *comprimés*?

ASSURANCES GENERALES DE FRANCE
Jean MOUREY
ASSUREUR CONSEIL
ACCIDENTS – INCENDIE – VIE
RETRAITE – MALADIE – CHIRURGIE
BUREAUX OUVERTS: 8h30 – 12h et 14h – 18h30
BUREAUX FERMES LUNDI MATIN et SAMEDI APRES – MIDI
2ᵉ ETAGE

Docteur Anne-Marie BOUCHER
ANCIENNE EXTERNE DES HOPITAUX DE PARIS
CES NATIONAL D' HEPATO-GASTRO-ENTEROLOGIE
ESTOMAC-FOIE-INTESTIN
ENDOSCOPIE ET RADIOLOGIE DIGESTIVES
SUR RENDEZ-VOUS   Tél.45.32.20

DOCTEUR M. ALACOQUE
Diplômé de la Faculté de Médecine de Lyon
MEDECINE GENERALE
HOMEOPATHIE
TEL: 85-20-33

C La santé. Donnez des réponses personnelles.

1. Tu es en bonne santé ou en mauvaise santé?
2. Quand tu es enrhumé(e), tu as le nez qui coule?
3. Tu as les yeux qui piquent?
4. Tu as la gorge qui gratte?
5. Tu tousses?
6. Tu éternues?
7. Tu as mal à la tête?
8. Tu ne te sens pas bien?
9. Tu as de la fièvre quand tu as un rhume ou la grippe?
10. Quand tu as de la fièvre, tu as quelquefois des frissons?
11. Quand tu as mal à la tête, tu prends de l'aspirine?

D On a mal. Complétez.

1. On prend de l'aspirine. On a mal à la ___.
2. On a très mal à la gorge. On a une ___.
3. La ___ est un antibiotique.
4. On ne peut pas prendre de pénicilline quand on est ___ à la pénicilline.
5. On a une température de 40°C. On a de la ___.
6. Quand on est toujours malade, on est en ___.
7. Les ___ accompagnent souvent la fièvre.
8. On donne des antibiotiques comme la pénicilline pour combattre des infections bactériennes, pas ___.
9. Quand on a le nez qui coule, on a toujours besoin d'un ___ ou d'un ___.
10. Quand on a un rhume, on ___ et on ___.
11. Quand on a de la fièvre, on prend de l'___.
12. Quand on est enrhumé ou quand on écoute trop la musique, on a mal aux ___.

CHAPITRE 15   **389**

Bell Ringer Review

Write the following on the board or use BRR Blackline Master 15-2: Write down what part(s) of the body you associate with the following.

1. des lunettes
2. un bonnet de ski
3. un thermomètre
4. un kleenex

PRESENTATION *(pages 390–391)*

A. Have students close their books. Use TPR, a few props and student volunteers to demonstrate the *Mots 2* vocabulary and act out the sequences as much as possible. Props might include a red cross labeled with a doctor's name for *chez le médecin,* a labeled sign with a green cross for *la pharmacie,* a plastic stethoscope, empty medicine bottles, etc.

B. Have students keep their books closed. Dramatize the following expressions from *Mots 2: ouvrir la bouche; examiner la gorge;*

VOCABULAIRE

~~~~~~

MOTS 2

CHEZ LE MÉDECIN

Le médecin examine le malade.
Le malade ouvre la bouche.
Le médecin examine la gorge du malade.

Elle ausculte le malade.
Il souffre, le pauvre.

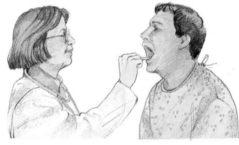

Le médecin parle.

TOTAL PHYSICAL RESPONSE

(following the Vocabulary presentation)

TPR 1

——, levez-vous et venez ici, s'il vous plaît.
Vous allez chez le médecin. Moi, je suis le médecin. Je vais vous examiner.
——, asseyez-vous, s'il vous plaît.
Ouvrez la bouche.
Dites «Ah».
Ouvrez les yeux.
Et maintenant, fermez les yeux.
Levez-vous, s'il vous plaît.
Je vais vous ausculter. Respirez à fond.
Encore une fois.
Merci, ——. Vous avez très bien fait. Vous êtes un(e) bon(ne) patient(e). Retournez à votre place, s'il vous plaît.

une ordonnance

des comprimés (m.)

le pharmacien

la pharmacienne

Le médecin me fait un diagnostic.
Elle me prescrit des antibiotiques.
Elle me fait une ordonnance.

Je suis à la pharmacie.
Qu'est-ce que la pharmacienne te donne?
Elle me donne des médicaments.

Note: You may use the following informal expressions to talk about health.

1. When you are not feeling well, you can say:

Je ne suis pas dans mon assiette aujourd hui.

2. To tell someone he or she will soon be better, you can say:

Tu vas être vite sur pied.

3. When someone has a high fever, you can say:

Il a une fièvre de cheval.

4. To say "It hurts," you say:

Ça fait mal!

5. When you have a "frog in your throat," you can say:

J'ai un chat dans la gorge.

CHAPITRE 15 **391**

souffrir; tousser; respirer à fond.
Ask students to imitate each of your dramatizations and repeat each corresponding word.

C. **Recycling** Bring back previously learned vocabulary by asking *Où avez-vous mal?* and pointing to your hand, foot, eyes, ear, nose, stomach, head, or throat. Have students respond using the correct word.

D. Ask students to open their books to pages 390–391. Have them read along and repeat the new material after you or Cassette 9A/CD-9.

E. Have students close their books. Use Vocabulary Transparencies 15.2 to review all the words and expressions from *Mots 2,* including the informal expressions on page 391. Point to each illustration and have students say as much as they can about it.

F. Practice the expressions on page 391 by miming or supplying the literal statement and having students supply the informal expression. For example: *Je ne peux pas parler. (Vous avez un chat dans la gorge.) Je ne me sens pas bien. (Vous n'êtes pas dans votre assiette.)* Clutch your arm and say «*Aïe!*» (*Ça fait mal.*)

Vocabulary Expansion

You may wish to give students the following expressions related to physical exams.
prendre la tension artérielle
prendre le pouls
faire une piqûre
faire une prise de sang
faire un électrocardiogramme

TPR 2
___, venez ici, s'il vous plaît.
Vous allez faire le mime.
Respirez à fond.
Toussez.
Éternuez.
Vous avez mal à la tête.
Vous avez de la fièvre.
Vous avez des frissons.
Vous avez les yeux qui piquent.
Vous avez le nez qui coule.

Prenez un kleenex.
Prenez un comprimé.
Merci, ___. Très bien. Retournez à votre place, s'il vous plaît.

Exercices

A **Chez le médecin.** Choisissez.

1. Où est le malade?
   a. À l'hôpital. b. Chez lui. c. Chez le médecin.
2. Qui souffre?
   a. Le médecin. b. Le malade. c. Le pharmacien.
3. Qu'est-ce que le médecin examine?
   a. La bouche. b. La gorge. c. Le ventre.
4. Qu'est-ce que le malade ouvre?
   a. La bouche. b. La gorge. c. L'oreille.
5. Le médecin ausculte le malade. Comment respire-t-il?
   a. Il éternue. b. À fond. c. Bien.
6. Qui est-ce que le médecin ausculte?
   a. Le malade. b. Le pharmacien. c. La pharmacienne.
7. Que fait le médecin?
   a. Un diagnostic. b. Des comprimés. c. Des médicaments.
8. Qu'est-ce qu'il a, le pauvre malade?
   a. Une angine. b. Mal au ventre. c. Mal aux yeux.
9. Que fait le médecin?
   a. Un pharmacien. b. Une ordonnance. c. Un comprimé.
10. Qu'est-ce qu'elle prescrit?
    a. La pharmacie. b. Des ordonnances. c. Des antibiotiques.
11. Où va le malade pour acheter des médicaments?
    a. Chez le médecin. b. À la pharmacie. c. À l'ordinateur.

B **Le médecin m'examine.** Donnez des réponses personnelles.

1. Tu vas chez le médecin quand tu es très malade?
2. Le médecin te demande: «Où avez-vous mal?»
3. Quand tu as une angine, ça fait très mal?
4. Le médecin te dit: «Ouvrez la bouche»?
5. Il t'ausculte?
6. Il te dit: «Respirez à fond»?
7. Le médecin te fait un diagnostic?
8. Il te prescrit des comprimés?
9. Tu vas à la pharmacie pour acheter les médicaments?
10. Tu prends quelquefois des antibiotiques?

C **Plus familier, s'il te plaît.** Dites d'une manière familière.

1. Je ne vais pas très bien aujourd'hui.
2. Tu vas bientôt te sentir mieux.
3. J'ai beaucoup de fièvre!
4. Je ne peux pas parler facilement.

PAIRED ACTIVITY

After completing Exercises A, B, and C, have students work in pairs. Have them take turns telling each other that they think they have the flu or a bad cold. They should explain why they think they are sick by explaining their symptoms. The partner should respond by giving advice.

Activités de communication orale
Mots 1 et 2

Josiane Briand

A **Qu'est-ce que tu as?** You were absent from school today because you had the flu. Josiane Briand, the French exchange student, calls to find out how you are feeling.

1. Alors, tu as la grippe? Qu'est-ce que tu as? Tu as de la fièvre… euh…
2. Tu prends des médicaments?
3. Tu vas aller chez le médecin?
4. Tu vas encore rester à la maison demain?

B **Je ne suis pas dans mon assiette!** Yesterday you did something that made you feel ill today. Using List 1 below, tell a classmate what you did. He or she has to guess what's wrong with you, choosing from List 2.

> trop regarder la télé
> Élève 1: Hier j'ai trop regardé la télé.
> Élève 2: Tu as mal aux yeux.

1	2
lire pendant six heures	être enrhumé(e)
manger trop de chocolat	avoir mal aux yeux
passer beaucoup d'examens	avoir la gorge qui gratte
trop crier au match	avoir mal aux pieds
faire une longue promenade	être fatigué(e)
étudier jusqu'à 3h du matin	avoir mal aux oreilles
trop écouter de la musique	avoir mal à la tête
jouer dans la neige en tee-shirt	avoir mal au ventre

C **Quel médecin?** While on a trip to France, you get sick. Describe your symptoms. A classmate will look at the list of doctors at the Hôpital Saint-Pierre and tell you which one to call and what the phone number is.

> Élève 1: J'ai mal au ventre.
> Élève 2: Appelle le docteur Simonet au 43.89.39.25.

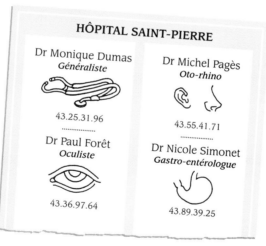

HÔPITAL SAINT-PIERRE

Dr Monique Dumas
Généraliste
43.25.31.96

Dr Michel Pagès
Oto-rhino
43.55.41.71

Dr Paul Forêt
Oculiste
43.36.97.64

Dr Nicole Simonet
Gastro-entérologue
43.89.39.25

Activités de communication orale
Mots 1 et 2

PRESENTATION *(page 393)*

Activité A

In the CD-ROM version, students can interact with an on-screen native speaker.

ANSWERS

Activité A
Answers will vary, but may include the following:
1. J'ai mal à la tête (à la gorge, etc.). Oui, j'ai de la fièvre.
2. Oui, je prends des médicaments.
3. Oui (Non), je (ne) vais (pas) aller chez le médecin.
4. Oui (Non), je vais encore rester (je ne vais pas rester) à la maison demain.

Activité B
Answers will vary.

Activité C
Answers will vary, but some possible symptoms are listed under the appropriate doctor.

Dr Dumas
J'ai mal au (aux, à la)…
J'ai la grippe.
J'ai une angine, etc.

Dr Forêt
J'ai mal aux yeux.
J'ai les yeux qui piquent.
Je ne vois pas bien.

Dr Pagès
J'ai mal à la gorge (le nez qui coule; une angine; un rhume).
J'éternue.
J'ai mal à l'oreille.
Je n'entends pas bien.

Dr Simonet
J'ai mal au ventre.

STRUCTURE

Les pronoms *me, te, nous, vous*

Telling What You Do for Others and What Others Do for You

1. You have already seen the pronouns *me, te, nous,* and *vous* with reflexive verbs. These same pronouns function as objects of the verb.

Le médecin *te* voit?	Oui, il *me* voit.
Le médecin *t'*examine?	Oui, il *m'*examine.
Le médecin *vous* regarde?	Oui, il *me* regarde.
	Oui, il *nous* regarde.
Le médecin *te* fait une ordonnance?	Oui, il *me* fait une ordonnance.
Il *vous* parle?	Oui, il *me* parle.
	Oui, il *nous* parle.

2. Note that the object pronoun comes right before the verb of which it is the object. This is true even when there is a helping verb, such as *pouvoir, vouloir,* or *aller* in the sentence.

> Il *m'*examine.
> Il va *m'*examiner.
> Il peut *m'*examiner.

3. The object pronoun cannot be separated from the verb by a negative word.

> Il ne *vous fait* pas d'ordonnance.
> Il ne *nous examine* pas.
> Il ne *m'ausculte* jamais.

Exercices

A **Chez le médecin.** Donnez des réponses personnelles.

1. Quand tu vas chez le médecin, il te parle?
2. Il te regarde?
3. Il t'examine?
4. Il t'ausculte?
5. Il te fait un diagnostic?
6. Il te fait une ordonnance?
7. Il te prescrit des médicaments?
8. Il te prescrit des antibiotiques?
9. Le pharmacien te donne des médicaments?

Structure Teaching Resources

1. Workbook, *Structure: A–H,* pages 150–152
2. Student Tape Manual, Teacher's Edition, *Structure: A–C,* pages 168–169
3. Audio Cassette 9A / CD-9
4. Communication Activities Masters, *Structure: A–C,* pages 73–74
5. Computer Software, *Structure*
6. Chapter Quizzes, *Structure: Quizzes 3–5,* pages 79–81
7. CD-ROM, Disc 4, pages 394–399

Bell Ringer Review

Write the following on the board or use BRR Blackline Master 15-4: Make a list of health tips. For example, *Il faut faire de l'exercice.*

Les pronoms me, te, nous, vous

Note The object pronouns *me, te, nous, vous* are introduced before the third-person pronouns for two reasons. First, they are less complicated than the third-person pronouns since they are both direct and indirect objects. Second, they are the only object pronouns that are truly necessary for communication. For example, if asked a question with *te* or *vous,* one must answer with *me* or *nous.* When speaking in the third person, however, one could respond with a noun instead of a pronoun: *Non, je n'ai pas invité Jean, mais j'ai téléphoné à Marie.* Third-person pronouns will be presented in Chapters 16 and 17.

PRESENTATION (pages 394–395)

Lead students through steps 1–3.

ADDITIONAL PRACTICE

1. Have students ask each other for something. For example:
   Robert, tu me donnes ton crayon?
   Oui, je te donne mon crayon.
2. Then have two students ask two others for something.
   Robert et Louise, vous nous donnez ce livre?
   Oui, nous vous donnons ce livre.

PAIRED ACTIVITY

After completing Exercise D on page 395, have students work in pairs and prepare a short skit at a clothing store.

B **Elle nous invite à la fête.** Répondez d'après le modèle.

> **Suzanne vous parle de sa fête?**
> *Oui, elle nous parle de sa fête.*

1. Elle vous téléphone?
2. Elle vous parle au téléphone?
3. Elle vous invite à la fête?
4. Elle vous dit l'heure de la fête?
5. Elle vous dit où elle habite?
6. Elle vous donne son adresse?

C **Elle ne nous invite pas à la fête.** Répondez par «non» aux questions de l'Exercice B.

D **Au rayon prêt-à-porter.** Complétez avec «vous» ou «me».

Je suis au rayon prêt-à-porter des Galeries Lafayette. La vendeuse ___ parle.

$\underset{1}{}$

Elle ___ demande:

$\underset{2}{}$

—Vous désirez?

—Je voudrais un chemisier, s'il ___ plaît. Je fais du 40.

$\underset{3}{}$

—D'accord. Je peux ___ proposer ces deux types de chemisiers.

$\underset{4}{}$

—Ce chemisier bleu marine à manches longues ___ intéresse beaucoup.

$\underset{5}{}$

—Je ___ suggère la taille au-dessous alors. Ces chemisiers sont très grands.

$\underset{6}{}$

—D'accord. Je peux ___ payer avec une carte de crédit?

$\underset{7}{}$

—Mais bien sûr!

E **Pourquoi ça?** Répondez d'après le modèle.

> **Élève 1: Il me regarde.**
> **Élève 2: Il te regarde? Pourquoi?**

1. Il me pose des questions.
2. Il me parle.
3. Il me téléphone.
4. Il me dit son numéro de téléphone.
5. Il me donne son adresse.

F **C'est ton anniversaire.** Donnez des réponses personnelles.

1. Tes copains vont te téléphoner le jour de ton anniversaire?
2. Ils vont te voir?
3. Ils vont t'inviter au cinéma ou au concert?
4. Ils vont te dire: «Joyeux anniversaire»?
5. Pour ton anniversaire, ils vont te faire un gâteau?

Note In the CD-ROM version, this structure point is presented via an interactive electronic comic strip.

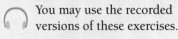

Exercices

PRESENTATION (*pages 394–395*)

Exercices B and E
You may use the recorded versions of these exercises.

Extension of *Exercice B*
After finishing Exercise B, have students say as much as they can about a party.

ANSWERS

Exercice A
Answers will vary.

Exercice B
1. Oui, elle nous téléphone.
2. Oui, elle nous parle au téléphone.
3. Oui, elle nous invite à la fête.
4. Oui, elle nous dit l'heure de la fête.
5. Oui, elle nous dit où elle habite.
6. Oui, elle nous donne son adresse.

Exercice C
1. Non, elle ne nous téléphone pas.
2. Non, elle ne nous parle pas au téléphone.
3. Non, elle ne nous invite pas à la fête.
4. Non, elle ne nous dit pas l'heure de la fête.
5. Non, elle ne nous dit pas où elle habite.
6. Non, elle ne nous donne pas son adresse.

Exercice D
1. me   4. vous   6. vous
2. me   5. m'   7. vous
3. vous

Exercice E
1. Il te pose des questions? Pourquoi?
2. Il te parle? Pourquoi?
3. Il te téléphone? Pourquoi?
4. Il te dit son numéro de téléphone? Pourquoi?
5. Il te donne son adresse? Pourquoi?

Exercice F
Answers will vary.

ADDITIONAL PRACTICE

Student Tape Manual, Teacher's Edition, *Activité C*, page 169

INDEPENDENT PRACTICE

Assign any of the following:
1. Exercises, pages 394–395
2. Workbook, *Structure: A–B*, page 150
3. Communication Activities Masters, *Structure: A*, page 73
4. CD-ROM, Disc 4, pages 394–395

Les verbes comme ouvrir au présent et au passé composé

PRESENTATION *(page 396)*

Note The material on page 396
should be rather easy since students
have already had a great deal of
practice with the *-er* verbs. Since
all of these verbs, except for *ouvrir*,
are of fairly low frequency, it is suggested that you cover them quickly.

Have students open their books to
page 396. Lead them through steps
1–2. Have students repeat the forms
after you, one verb at a time.

Exercices

ANSWERS

Exercice A
Answers will vary.

---

1. Although the verbs *ouvrir, souffrir, couvrir,* and *découvrir* have infinitives
   that end in *-ir,* they follow the same pattern as *-er* verbs in the present tense.

OUVRIR	SOUFFRIR
j' ouvre	je souffre
tu ouvres	tu souffres
il	il
elle } ouvre	elle } souffre
on	on
nous ouvrons	nous souffrons
vous ouvrez	vous souffrez
ils ouvrent	ils
elles ouvrent	elles } souffrent

2. The past participles of these verbs are irregular.

INFINITIF ⟶	PARTICIPE PASSÉ
ouvrir	ouvert
couvrir	couvert
découvrir	découvert
souffrir	souffert
offrir	offert

Pendant la nuit il a ouvert la fenêtre.
Hier le médecin a découvert la cause
   de la maladie.

Exercices

A **Tu souffres?**   Donnez des réponses personnelles.

1. Tu souffres quand tu es enrhumé(e)?
2. Tu souffres plus quand tu as un rhume ou quand tu as la grippe?
3. Tu prends de l'aspirine quand tu souffres d'une allergie?
4. Tu ouvres la bouche quand le médecin t'examine la gorge?
5. Tu ouvres les yeux quand le médecin t'examine les yeux?
6. Tu offres un bouquet de roses à ton amie malade?

INDEPENDENT PRACTICE

Assign any of the following:
1. Exercises, pages 396–397
2. Workbook, *Structure: C–E,* pages 150–151
3. Communication Activities Masters
   Structure: B, page 74
4. CD-ROM, Disc 4, pages 396–397

B Qu'est-ce qu'on fait? Complétez avec «ouvrir» ou «offrir».

1. Nous ___ les yeux quand nous nous réveillons.
2. Elle ___ un livre à sa mère pour la Fête des Mères.
3. Vous ___ le magazine pour regarder les photos qui vous intéressent?
4. Vous ___ la bouche quand le médecin vous examine la gorge?
5. Ils ___ la bouche pour chanter.
6. J'___ le livre et je commence à lire.
7. J'___ la fenêtre quand il fait chaud.
8. Tu ___ les cadeaux que tes amis t'___ pour ton anniversaire?

C Il a été malade. Répondez par «oui».

1. Charles a été malade?
2. Il a été à l'hôpital?
3. Le médecin a examiné Charles?
4. Charles a ouvert la bouche?
5. Le médecin a découvert la cause de sa maladie?
6. Il a couvert le pauvre Charles?
7. Le médecin a fait un diagnostic?
8. Charles a compris le diagnostic?
9. Le médecin a prescrit des médicaments?
10. Charles a pris les médicaments?
11. Il a pris trois comprimés par jour?
12. Il a beaucoup souffert?
13. Ses amis ont offert un petit cadeau à Charles?

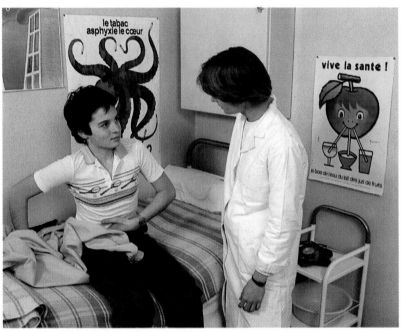

Une femme médecin parle à son jeune patient.

PRESENTATION (*continued*)

Extension of *Exercice C*

After going over Exercise C, have a student retell the story in his/her own words. As a further extension, have other students make up questions based on the student's story.

ANSWERS

Exercice B

1. ouvrons
2. offre
3. ouvrez
4. ouvrez
5. ouvrent
6. ouvre
7. ouvre
8. ouvres, offrent

Exercice C

1. Oui, il a été malade.
2. Oui, il a été à l'hôpital.
3. Oui, il a examiné Charles.
4. Oui, il a ouvert la bouche.
5. Oui, il a découvert la cause de sa maladie.
6. Oui, il a couvert le pauvre Charles.
7. Oui, il a fait un diagnostic.
8. Oui, il a compris le diagnostic.
9. Oui, il a prescrit des médicaments.
10. Oui, il a pris les médicaments.
11. Oui, il a pris trois comprimés par jour.
12. Oui, il a beaucoup souffert.
13. Oui, ils ont offert un petit cadeau à Charles.

LEARNING FROM PHOTOS

1. Ask questions about the photo: *Quel âge a le malade? Où est-il? À qui parle-t-il? Qu'est-ce qu'il a? Quel sport aime-t-il? Pourquoi dites-vous ça?*
2. Have students look at the posters on the walls of the doctor's office. Ask what they are about. What three drinks are being promoted in the poster on the right? Have students give you the French terms from the poster.

Bell Ringer Review

Write the following on the board or use BRR Blackline Master 15-6: Complete the sentences with the correct form of *ouvrir, souffrir, couvrir,* or *offrir.*

1. Tu ＿＿ un cadeau à ta mère?
2. La mère ＿＿ le bébé.
3. Elle ＿＿ le livre à la page 12.
4. Ils ＿＿ beaucoup.

L'impératif

PRESENTATION *(page 398)*

Note Students should have little trouble learning the imperative since they are already familiar with the verb forms. The only thing that will be new to them is the dropping of the *-s* in the spelling of the *tu* form of *-er* verbs.

A. Have students open their books to page 398. Lead them through steps 1–3.

B. Illustrate the difference between singular and plural imperatives by giving commands to one student and to groups or pairs of students. For example: *Yvonne, prends ton livre de français. Va au tableau. Ouvre le livre à la page 15. Guillaume et Martine, allez à la porte. Ouvrez la porte. Asseyez-vous.*

C. Practice the negative forms by calling out TPR commands and having students change them to the negative. Then reverse the procedure.

L'impératif

Giving Formal and Informal Commands

1. You use the imperative to give commands and make suggestions. The forms are usually the same as the *tu, vous,* or *nous* form of the present tense. Note, however, that you drop the final *s* of the *tu* form of verbs ending in *-er,* including *aller.* The same is true for verbs like *ouvrir* and *souffrir,* which are conjugated like *-er* verbs. In commands the subject is omitted.

INFINITIF	TU	VOUS
regarder	regarde	regardez
aller	va	allez
ouvrir	ouvre	ouvrez
finir	finis	finissez
attendre	attends	attendez
prendre	prends	prenez
faire	fais	faites
dire	dis	dites

Marie, regarde le tableau! Va au tableau!
Madame, prenez des vitamines!
Roger et Vincent, faites attention!

2. To express "Let's…," you use the *nous* form of the verb without the subject.

> Dansons!
> Choisissons le menu touristique.

3. With commands, negative expressions go around the verb.

> Ne parle pas en classe.
> N'écoutez jamais ce disque.
> Ne disons rien.

Les vitamines

Laboratoire Conseil Oberlin

Exercices

A **La loi, c'est moi!** Donnez un ordre à un copain ou à une copine d'après le modèle.

> **chanter**
> *Chante!*

1. danser
2. écouter la musique
3. parler français
4. travailler plus
5. préparer le dîner
6. commander un sandwich
7. ouvrir la porte

B **Et vous aussi!** Refaites l'Exercice A d'après le modèle.

> **chanter**
> *Chantez!*

C **Ne fais pas ça!** Donnez un ordre à un copain ou à une copine d'après le modèle.

> **regarder**
> *Ne regarde pas!*

1. lire le journal
2. écrire une lettre
3. prendre le métro
4. attendre dans la gare
5. descendre
6. aller vite
7. faire attention
8. entrer

D **Ne faites pas ça!** Refaites l'Exercice C d'après le modèle.

> **regarder**
> *Ne regardez pas!*

E **Allons-y!** Répondez d'après le modèle.

> **Vous voulez inviter Marie?**
> *Oui, invitons Marie!*

1. Vous voulez aller à la plage?
2. Vous voulez nager?
3. Vous voulez faire du ski nautique?
4. Vous voulez prendre le petit déjeuner?
5. Vous voulez aller au restaurant?
6. Vous voulez manger des fruits?

le stress

Laboratoire Conseil Oberlin

Stressé? N'oubliez pas de vous relaxer!

CHAPITRE 15   **399**

Exercices
ANSWERS

Exercice A
1. Danse.
2. Écoute la musique.
3. Parle français.
4. Travaille plus.
5. Prépare le dîner.
6. Commande un sandwich.
7. Ouvre la porte.

Exercice B
1. Dansez.
2. Écoutez la musique.
3. Parlez français.
4. Travaillez plus.
5. Préparez le dîner.
6. Commandez un sandwich.
7. Ouvrez la porte.

Exercice C
1. Ne lis pas le journal.
2. N'écris pas de lettre.
3. Ne prends pas le métro.
4. N'attends pas dans la gare.
5. Ne descends pas.
6. Ne va pas vite.
7. Ne fais pas attention.
8. N'entre pas.

Exercice D
1. Ne lisez pas le journal.
2. N'écrivez pas de lettre.
3. Ne prenez pas le métro.
4. N'attendez pas dans la gare.
5. Ne descendez pas.
6. N'allez pas vite.
7. Ne faites pas attention.
8. N'entrez pas.

Exercice E
1. Oui, allons à la plage.
2. Oui, nageons.
3. Oui, faisons du ski nautique.
4. Oui, prenons le petit déjeuner.
5. Oui, allons au restaurant.
6. Oui, mangeons des fruits.

INFORMAL ASSESSMENT

Have students quickly make up as many commands as they can.

LEARNING FROM REALIA

Have students look at the cards on pages 398 and 399. Explain that these types of cards are provided by drug companies and distributed free at pharmacies. Have students pick out all the cognates and make up sentences using *les vitamines, stressé(e), se relaxer.*

INDEPENDENT PRACTICE

Assign any of the following:
1. Exercises, page 399
2. Workbook, *Structure: F–H,* page 152
3. Communication Activities Masters, *Structure: C,* page 74
4. Computer Software, *Structure*
5. CD-ROM, Disc 4, pages 398–399

CONVERSATION

CONVERSATION

Bell Ringer Review

Write the following on the board or use BRR Blackline Master 15-7: Write several pieces of advice to a friend who is about to go skiing for the first time.

PRESENTATION *(page 400)*

A. Tell students they will hear a conversation between Charlotte and a doctor.

B. Have students close their books and watch the Conversation Video or listen as you read the conversation or play Cassette 9A/CD-9.

C. Now reread the conversation or replay the cassette or CD, stopping after each of the three sections to ask simple comprehension questions.

D. Have students dramatize the conversation.

E. Have a student summarize the conversation in his or her own words.

Note In the CD-ROM version, students can play the role of either one of the characters and record the conversation.

ANSWERS

Exercice A

1. Oui, elle souffre beaucoup.
2. Oui, elle a les yeux qui piquent.
3. Oui, elle a la gorge qui gratte.
4. Oui, elle a mal à la tête.
5. Elle a mal partout.
6. Oui, elle a de la fièvre et des frissons.
7. Il va prendre sa température.
8. Elle ouvre la bouche.
9. Elle a la gorge très rouge.
10. Elle a une angine.
11. Il prescrit des antibiotiques.
12. Oui, elle va être vite sur pied.

Scènes de la vie   *Charlotte souffre*

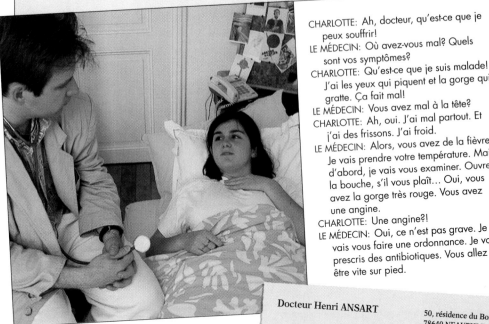

CHARLOTTE: Ah, docteur, qu'est-ce que je peux souffrir!
LE MÉDECIN: Où avez-vous mal? Quels sont vos symptômes?
CHARLOTTE: Qu'est-ce que je suis malade! J'ai les yeux qui piquent et la gorge qui gratte. Ça fait mal!
LE MÉDECIN: Vous avez mal à la tête?
CHARLOTTE: Ah, oui. J'ai mal partout. Et j'ai des frissons. J'ai froid.
LE MÉDECIN: Alors, vous avez de la fièvre. Je vais prendre votre température. Mais d'abord, je vais vous examiner. Ouvrez la bouche, s'il vous plaît… Oui, vous avez la gorge très rouge. Vous avez une angine.
CHARLOTTE: Une angine?!
LE MÉDECIN: Oui, ce n'est pas grave. Je vais vous faire une ordonnance. Je vous prescris des antibiotiques. Vous allez être vite sur pied.

A **Une angine.** Répondez d'après la conversation.

1. Charlotte souffre beaucoup?
2. Elle a les yeux qui piquent?
3. Elle a la gorge qui gratte?
4. Elle a mal à la tête?
5. Où a-t-elle mal?
6. Elle a de la fièvre et des frissons?
7. Qu'est-ce que le médecin va prendre?
8. Qu'est-ce que Charlotte ouvre?
9. Elle a la gorge comment?
10. Qu'est-ce qu'elle a?
11. Qu'est-ce que le médecin prescrit?
12. Charlotte va être vite sur pied?

Docteur Henri ANSART

50, résidence du Bois du Four
78640 NEAUPHLE-LE-CHÂTEAU
(Yvelines)
Tél. 36.89.00.07   36.89.08.95

DUROSEL Charlotte

Hyconcil :

2 gélules matin et soir pendant 5 jours.

Locabiotal :

3 pulvérisations par jour.

400   CHAPITRE 15

CRITICAL THINKING ACTIVITY

(Thinking skills: locating causes)

Put the following on the board or on an overhead transparency:

1. **Tout le monde parle du stress. Il y a beaucoup de stress dans la société moderne. Quelles sont les causes du stress?**

2. **Si l'on se sent stressé(e), qu'est-ce qu'on peut faire pour se relaxer?**

LEARNING FROM REALIA

You may wish to ask questions about the prescription: *Qu'est-ce que c'est? Comment s'appelle le médecin? Quelle est son adresse? Quel est le nom de la malade? L'ordonnance est pour quels médicaments? Quand la malade va-t-elle prendre l'Hyconcil? Combien de fois par jour? Et pendant combien de jours? Comment dit-on en français* two capsules *et* three sprays?

Prononciation   *Le son /ü/*

1. To say the sound /ü/, first say the sound /i/ but round your lips. Repeat the following words.

température	enrhumé	chaussure
voiture	descendu	

2. The sound /ü/ also occurs in combination with other vowels.

éternuer	lui	depuis
aujourd'hui	je suis	

Now repeat the following words and sentences.

Quelle est la température aujourd'hui?
Luc conduit depuis huit ans.
Il a mis ses chaussures dans la voiture.

température

Activités de communication orale

A   Ah docteur, je suis très malade!   Imagine you're sick with a cold, the flu, or a throat infection. Tell the doctor (your partner) what your symptoms are. Your partner makes a diagnosis and tells you what to do to get better.

Élève 1: J'ai mal à la tête et j'éternue tout le temps.
Élève 2: Vous avez un rhume. Prenez de l'aspirine et du bouillon de poulet.

B   Je déteste ce cadeau!   In your worst nightmare, what did the following people give you for your birthday? Your partner will ask you about each person. Answer, then reverse roles.

Élève 1: Qu'est-ce que ta grand-mère t'a offert pour ton anniversaire?
Élève 2: Elle m'a offert des cassettes de Frank Sinatra.

tes parents	tes grands-parents
ton meilleur ami	ton frère
ta meilleure amie	ta sœur

CHAPITRE 15   **401**

Prononciation

PRESENTATION   *(page 401)*

A. Model the key word *température* and have students repeat chorally.
B. Now model the other words and sentences in similar fashion.
C. You may wish to give students the following *dictée:*
Il est descendu à l'avenue Victor-Hugo. Je suis enrhumé(e). Lui, il éternue. Zut! Mes chaussures sont dans la voiture.
D. For additional practice, use Pronunciation Transparency P-15, the *Prononciation* section on Cassette 9A/CD-9 and the Student Tape Manual, Teacher's Edition, *Activités F–H*, pages 170–171.

Bell Ringer Review

Write the following on the board or use BRR Blackline Master 15-8: You have just visited the doctor's office. How would you fill out the following insurance form?

Nom de famille _____
Prénom _____
Maladie _____
Symptômes _____
Médicaments _____
Signature _____

Activités de communication orale

ANSWERS

Activités A and B
Answers will vary.

INDEPENDENT PRACTICE

Assign any of the following:
1. Exercise and activities, pages 400–401
2. CD-ROM, Disc 4, pages 400–401

READING STRATEGIES
(page 402)

Reading

A. Briefly synopsize the *Lecture* in French. Ask a few questions about it.

B. Have a student read 3–4 sentences. Ask a few questions to check comprehension, then have another student read. Continue this way for the rest of the reading.

C. **Finding information:** Have students scan the last paragraph and find the French word for "doctor's fee."

Post-reading

Assign the reading and the exercises that follow as homework. Go over these exercises the next day in class.

Note Students may listen to a recorded version of the *Lecture* on the CD-ROM.

Étude de mots

ANSWERS

Exercice A

1. … une fièvre de cheval.
2. Il n'est pas dans son assiette.
3. … prendre rendez-vous chez le médecin.
4. … ne donne pas de consultations…
5. … à domicile.
6. … ausculte Richard.
7. … grave.
8. … va être vite sur pied.

UNE CONSULTATION OU UNE VISITE

*L*e pauvre Richard! Qu'est-ce qu'il est malade! Il tousse. Il éternue. Il a mal à la tête. Il a une fièvre de cheval. Il a des frissons. Il n'est pas du tout dans son assiette. Il n'est pas très courageux, notre Richard. Il veut prendre rendez-vous[1] chez le médecin, mais c'est le week-end. Son médecin ne donne pas de consultations.

Alors que faire? Pas de problème! Appelons S.O.S Médecins, un service qui envoie des médecins à domicile. Un médecin arrive chez Richard. Il examine Richard. Il ausculte le malade. Il prend sa température. Le médecin dit que Richard a la grippe. Mais ce n'est pas grave. Il va vite se sentir mieux. Le médecin fait une ordonnance à Richard. Il prescrit des antibiotiques: trois comprimés par jour, un à chaque repas[2].

Richard paie le médecin. Mais en France la Sécurité Sociale rembourse les honoraires des médecins, c'est-à-dire l'argent qu'on donne aux médecins. Les honoraires et tous les frais[3] médicaux sont remboursés de 80 à 100% (pour cent) par la Sécurité Sociale.

[1] prendre rendez-vous   *make an appointment*
[2] repas   *meal*
[3] frais   *expenses*

Étude de mots

A **Autrement dit.**   Dites d'une autre manière.

1. Richard a *beaucoup de fièvre.*
2. Il *ne se sent pas bien.*
3. Il veut *aller voir* le médecin.
4. Le médecin *ne voit pas de malades* pendant le week-end.
5. S.O.S Médecins envoie des médecins *chez les malades.*
6. Le médecin *écoute la respiration de* Richard.
7. La grippe n'est pas une maladie *sérieuse.*
8. Richard va vite *se sentir mieux.*

DID YOU KNOW?

In France many drugs can be obtained over the counter at the pharmacy without a prescription. The only medications that cannot be dispensed without a prescription are those that contain a controlled substance.

INDEPENDENT PRACTICE

Assign any of the following:
1. *Étude de mots* and *Compréhension* exercises, pages 402–403
2. Workbook, *Un Peu Plus*, page 153
3. CD-ROM, Disc 4, pages 402–403

Compréhension

B **Vous avez compris?** Répondez par «oui» ou «non».

1. Richard est très courageux quand il est malade.
2. Il a beaucoup de fièvre.
3. Il a mal au ventre.
4. Richard veut aller chez le médecin.
5. Son médecin donne des consultations tous les jours.
6. Richard prend rendez-vous chez le médecin de S.O.S Médecins.
7. Le médecin prescrit des comprimés d'aspirine.
8. Les frais médicaux ne sont pas remboursés en France.

C **En France.** Qu'est-ce que vous avez appris sur les médecins et les services médicaux en France?

DÉCOUVERTE CULTURELLE

*L*a culture influence la médecine? Certainement. Par exemple, en France tout le monde parle de son foie[1]. Les Français disent souvent, «J'ai mal au foie». En Amérique on n'entend jamais «J'ai mal au foie». Pourquoi pas? Parce que, pour les Américains, une maladie du foie est quelque chose de grave. Mais quand un Français dit qu'il a mal au foie, il veut dire tout simplement qu'il a un trouble digestif. Ce n'est rien de grave. Il n'est peut-être pas dans son assiette aujourd'hui mais il va être vite sur pied.

Aux États-Unis on parle d'allergies. Beaucoup d'Américains souffrent d'une petite allergie. Les symptômes d'une allergie ressemblent aux symptômes d'un rhume. On éternue et on a souvent mal à la tête. Une allergie est désagréable, mais pas grave. En France, on parle moins souvent d'allergies. Vive la différence!

[1] foie *liver*

Les troubles digestifs

Compréhension

ANSWERS

Exercice B

1. Non.   5. Non.
2. Oui.   6. Non.
3. Non.   7. Non.
4. Oui.   8. Non.

Exercice C

Answers will vary but may include the following:

En France la Sécurité Sociale rembourse les honoraires des médecins et tous les frais médicaux de 80% à 100%.

En France il y a un service qui envoie des médecins à domicile.

OPTIONAL MATERIAL

Découverte culturelle

PRESENTATION *(page 403)*

Before reading the selection, focus on the topic by asking students what minor ailments Americans frequently complain about. They might mention hay fever, migraines, indigestion, back pain, etc.

Note Students may listen to a recorded version of the *Découverte culturelle* on the CD-ROM.

LEARNING FROM REALIA

(Bottom) Point to the rabbit and say: C'est un lapin. Qu'est-ce qu'il a, le lapin? Qu'est-ce qu'il a mangé? Il a mangé trop de carottes? Tu aimes les carottes? Tu manges beaucoup de carottes? Est-ce qu'on dit que les carottes sont bonnes pour les yeux?

ADDITIONAL PRACTICE

After reading the *Découverte culturelle,* ask students the following questions.
La culture a une influence sur la médecine?
Que disent souvent les Français?
Que veut dire un Français qui dit: «J'ai mal au foie»?
Quels sont les symptômes d'une allergie?
Qui parle plus d'allergies, les Français ou les Américains?

RÉALITÉS

Bell Ringer Review

Write the following on the board or use BRR Blackline Master 15-10: Rewrite the following sentences in the passé composé.

1. Nous choisissons un film intéressant.
2. On passe *La Belle et la Bête.*
3. J'aime ce film.
4. On vend les billets au cinéma.
5. Nous achetons et mangeons du maïs grillé (*popcorn*).

OPTIONAL MATERIAL

PRESENTATION (*pages 404–405*)

The main objective of this section is to have students enjoy the photographs and gain an appreciation of France, its people, and its culture. However, if you would like to do more with it, you might want to do some of the following activities.

A. Have students cover the captions. Call on volunteers to say as much as they can about each photo. Encourage them to use *Je pense que* or *Je crois que* to indicate that they are guessing.

B. Call on volunteers to read the captions aloud. What information do students now have that they didn't have before? Which new words can they guess the meaning of from the reading?

C. You may wish to explain to students what the acronym *SIDA* means (*syndrome immuno-déficitaire acquis*).

Note In the CD-ROM version, students can listen to the recorded captions and discover a hidden video behind one of the photos.

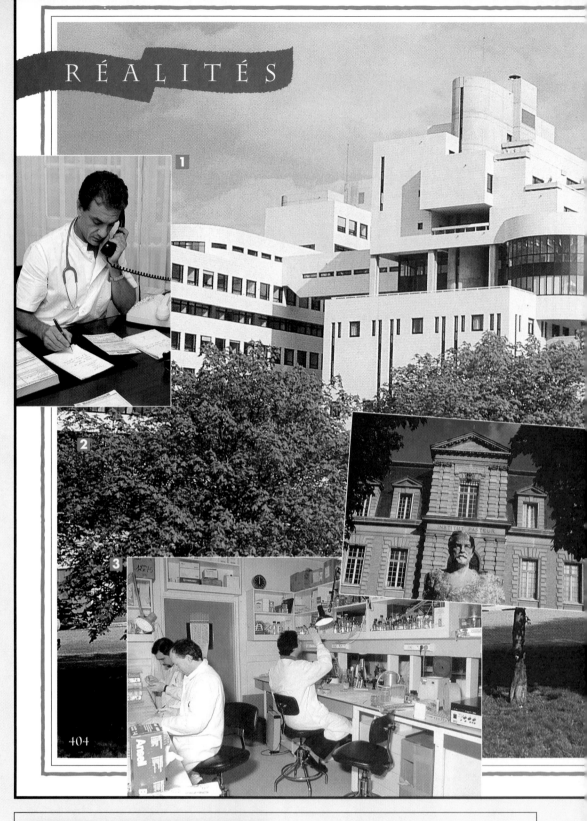

404

DID YOU KNOW?

1. In addition to some 12 medical schools in the Paris region, there are also *Centres hospitaliers universitaires* in the following cities: Brest, Rennes, Caen, Rouen, Angers, Nantes, Lille, Amiens, Reims, Strasbourg, Nancy, Dijon, Besançon, Tours, Poitiers, Lyon, Limoges, Clermont-Ferrand, Grenoble, Bordeaux, Montpellier, Toulouse, Marseille.

2. In France, students who want to pursue a career in medicine can do so at minimum expense. Tuition at French universities is low, but competition in medical school is fierce. Many students drop out before completing the seven years of study required to become a general practitioner.

Voici un médecin généraliste dans son cabinet 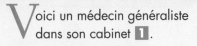.

Voici un grand hôpital pédiatrique à Paris **2**. Les grands hôpitaux ont l'équipement le plus moderne et le plus avancé technologiquement. Les services médicaux en France sont généralement excellents.

En France on fait beaucoup de recherches médicales et pharmaceutiques. À l'Insititut Pasteur de Paris, on fait des recherches continues pour trouver des médicaments ou des vaccins pour traiter ou combattre le SIDA, la maladie la plus grave de notre époque **3**.

Voici une ambulance du SAMU (le Service d'Aide Médicale d'Urgence). On appelle le SAMU en cas d'urgence **4**.

405

Note Information follows in the *Lettres et sciences* section, page 442, about Louis Pasteur and the Pasteur Institute.

CRITICAL THINKING ACTIVITY

(*Thinking skill: supporting arguments with reasons*)

Put the following on the board or on a transparency:

Faites une liste des caractéristiques que vous considérez comme importantes pour un médecin. Essayez de dire pourquoi vous les trouvez important.

ADDITIONAL PRACTICE

1. Student Tape Manual, Teacher's Edition, *Deuxième Partie*, pages 172–173
2. Situation Cards, Chapter 15
3. Communication Transparency C-15

RECYCLING

The *Activités de communication orale* and *Activité de communication écrite* provide a forum for students to create and answer their own questions and come up with their own dialogues while working within the health context of Chapter 15.

INFORMAL ASSESSMENT

The guided nature of Oral Activity B, with its numbered cues, makes it more suitable for use as a speaking evaluation, especially for less able students. Use the evaluation criteria given on page 34 of this Teacher's Wraparound Edition.

Activités de communication orale

ANSWERS

Activité A

Answers will be either **C'est bon** or **C'est mauvais pour la santé.**

Activité B

É2 answers will vary. É1 questions may include:

1. **Je te téléphone à minuit. Qu'est-ce que tu me dis?**
2. **Je te propose de sortir ensemble. …**
3. **Je te dis que j'ai besoin d'argent. …**
4. **Je te demande de faire mes devoirs pour moi. …**
5. **Je te donne un sandwich au pâté. …**
6. **Je te dis que je ne suis pas dans mon assiette. …**

Activité de communication écrite

ANSWERS

Activité A

Answers will vary.

Activités de communication orale

A **C'est bon ou mauvais pour la santé?**   Ask students in the health class for a list of health tips. Then, with a partner, make a list in French of things that people should do to stay healthy. Make a second list of things people should avoid doing. Present your lists to the class in random order and ask your classmates to decide whether the suggestion is good or bad for your health.

B **Qu'est-ce que tu me dis?**   Suggest the following situations to your partner and ask what he or she would say in each case.

> **t'offrir un bouquet de roses**
> **Élève 1: Je t'offre un bouquet de roses. Qu'est-ce que tu me dis?**
> **Élève 2: Je te dis: «Merci beaucoup, les roses sont magnifiques!»**

1. te téléphoner à minuit
2. te proposer de sortir ensemble
3. te dire que j'ai besoin d'argent
4. te demander de faire mes devoirs pour moi
5. te donner un sandwich au pâté
6. te dire que je ne suis pas dans mon assiette

Activité de communication écrite

A **Excusez-moi…**   You're supposed to take a French test today but you're not feeling well. Write a note to your French teacher explaining why you can't take the test, and mention some symptoms you have. Give the date and time you'd like to take the test.

FOR THE YOUNGER STUDENT

1. Have students make colorful get-well cards using some of the expressions they have learned. If someone they know is ill, they can send him or her the cards.
2. Have students draw their own cartoons to illustrate the following expressions: *Je ne suis pas dans mon assiette aujourd'hui. Il a une fièvre de cheval. Elle a un chat dans la gorge.*
3. Students work in teams to create a composite "monster." They cut out scrap paper and use markers to make body parts, one per member, including facial features as well as limbs, torsos, hair, etc. They should label the back of each cut-out in French. Collect the cut-outs and put them in a bag. Call on students one at a time to draw out one body part and pin it to the bulletin board to create a "monster."

Réintroduction et recombinaison

A **Isabelle se sent très bien aujourd'hui!** Complétez au présent.

Qui ___ (dire) qu'Isabelle n'___ (être) pas dans son assiette aujourd'hui? Ce
₁$$₂
n'___ (être) pas du tout vrai. Elle ___ (aller) très bien. Elle ___ (se lever) de
₃$$₄$$₅
bonne heure, ___ (prendre) son petit déjeuner et ___ (quitter) la maison. Elle
₆$$₇
___ (vouloir) rester en forme. Elle ___ (aller) au gymnase où elle ___ (faire)
₈$$₉$$₁₀
de l'aérobic. Elle ___ (avoir) beaucoup de copains au gymnase. Ils ___ (mettre)
₁₁$$₁₂
un survêtement et ils ___ (faire) de l'exercice ensemble.
₁₃

B **Aux sports d'hiver.** Complétez au passé.

1. L'hiver dernier Sylvie et Maryse ___ (passer) une semaine à Val d'Isère dans les Alpes françaises.
2. Le premier jour elles ___ (mettre) leur anorak, leurs gants et leurs skis.
3. Elles ___ (prendre) le télésiège jusqu'au sommet de la montagne.
4. Malheureusement elles ___ (choisir) la mauvaise piste—une piste noire, très difficile.
5. Sylvie ___ (glisser) et ___ (faire) une chute.
6. Elle ___ (perdre) ses bâtons qui ___ (glisser) jusqu'en bas de la piste.
7. Deux garçons très sympa ___ (trouver) les bâtons et ils ___ (donner) les bâtons à Sylvie.
8. Les deux filles ___ (dire) «merci» aux garçons et ils ___ (faire) du ski ensemble toute la journée.

Vocabulaire

NOMS			
la santé	l'aspirine (f.)	bactérien(ne)	se sentir
la médecine	l'antibiotique (m.)	enrhumé(e)	prescrire
le médecin	la pénicilline	malade	
le/la malade	le comprimé	viral(e)	AUTRES MOTS ET EXPRESSIONS
le/la pauvre	la pharmacie		avoir mal à
l'allergie (f.)	le/la pharmacien(ne)	VERBES	avoir un chat dans la gorge
l'angine (f.)	le kleenex	examiner	avoir de la fièvre
la température	le mouchoir	ausculter	avoir une fièvre de cheval
la fièvre		respirer (à fond)	avoir les yeux qui piquent
les frissons (m.)	les yeux (m.)	éternuer	avoir le nez qui coule
la grippe	le nez	tousser	avoir la gorge qui gratte
le rhume	la bouche	couvrir	ne pas être dans son assiette
l'infection (f.)	l'oreille (f.)	découvrir	être en bonne (mauvaise) santé
	la gorge	offrir	être vite sur pied
le médicament	le ventre	ouvrir	faire un diagnostic
l'ordonnance (f.)		souffrir	faire une ordonnance
	ADJECTIFS		Ça fait mal.
	allergique		

Réintroduction et recombinaison
PRESENTATION *(page 407)*

Exercice A

Exercise A provides practice with many of the irregular verbs students have studied.

Exercice B

Exercise B provides practice in the formation of the *passé composé* of regular and irregular verbs.

ANSWERS
Exercice A

1. dit	8. veut
2. est	9. va
3. est	10. fait
4. va	11. a
5. se lève	12. mettent
6. prend	13. font
7. quitte	

Exercice B

1. ont passé
2. ont mis
3. ont pris
4. ont choisi
5. a glissé, a fait
6. a perdu, ont glissé
7. ont trouvé, ont donné
8. ont dit, ont fait

ASSESSMENT RESOURCES

1. Chapter Quizzes
2. Testing Program
3. Situation Cards
4. Communication Transparency C-15
5. Computer Software: Practice/Test Generator

VIDEO PROGRAM

INTRODUCTION (46:35)

QU'EST-CE QU'IL A, ÉTIENNE? (47:07)

STUDENT PORTFOLIO

Have students add the *Mon Autobiographie* section of the Workbook on page 154 to their portfolios.

Note Students may create and save both oral and written work using the Electronic Portfolio feature on the CD-ROM.

INDEPENDENT PRACTICE

1. Activities and exercises, pages 406–407
2. CD-ROM, Disc 4, pages 406–407
3. Communication Activities Masters, pages 71–74

CHAPTER OVERVIEW

In this chapter students will learn how to discuss cultural events and express their cultural likes and dislikes. In order to do this, they will learn vocabulary associated with films, museums, the theater, etc. They will also learn to use the verbs *savoir* and *connaître*, the object pronouns *le, la,* and *les*, prepositions with geographical terms, and the verb *venir*.

The cultural focus of this chapter is on French attitudes and preferences with regard to cultural events.

CHAPTER OBJECTIVES

By the end of this chapter, students will know:

1. vocabulary associated with the theater and movies, including some genres of films and plays
2. vocabulary associated with museums and art, including painting and sculpture
3. the present indicative forms of *savoir* and *connaître* and the difference in meaning between the two verbs
4. the use of the direct object pronouns *le, la,* and *les*
5. the names and genders of countries
6. the use of *en, à*, or contractions with *à* to express "to" or "in" a country, city, or continent
7. the use of *de* or contractions with *de* to express "from" a country, city, or continent
8. the present indicative forms of verbs like *venir*

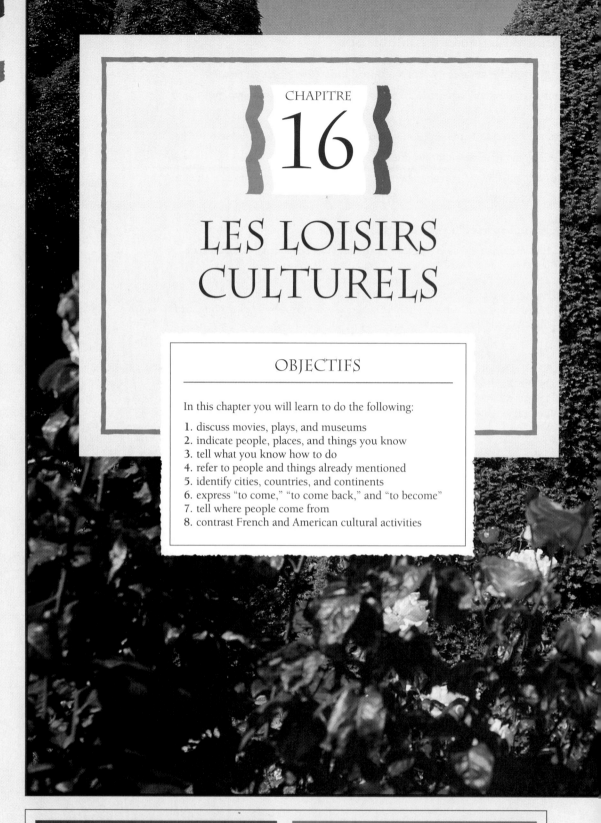

CHAPITRE

16

LES LOISIRS CULTURELS

OBJECTIFS

In this chapter you will learn to do the following:

1. discuss movies, plays, and museums
2. indicate people, places, and things you know
3. tell what you know how to do
4. refer to people and things already mentioned
5. identify cities, countries, and continents
6. express "to come," "to come back," and "to become"
7. tell where people come from
8. contrast French and American cultural activities

CHAPTER PROJECTS

1. Have students visit a local art museum to see different styles of art and the works of French artists.
2. Let students leaf through some French comic books (*Astérix, Tintin,* etc.). Describe a certain character to them or have them focus on French words for noises (*toc toc* = knock, knock; *aïe* = ouch, etc.).

INTERDISCIPLINARY CONNECTIONS

Divide the class into small groups and have them ask students in the art class to help them research several French painters and sculptors. Later, invite the art students to the French class, where each group puts on an "art show" with prints of their artist's most famous works.

409

Pacing

This chapter requires eight to ten class sessions. Pacing will vary according to class length and the age and aptitude of the students.

Note The Lesson Plans offer guidelines for 45- and 55-minute classes and **Block Scheduling**.

Exercices vs. *Activités*

All exercises (which provide guided practice) are coded in blue. All communicative activities are coded in red.

INTERNET ACTIVITIES

(optional)

These activities, student worksheets, and related teacher information are in the *Bienvenue* Internet Activities Booklet and on the Glencoe Foreign Language Home Page at: http://www.glencoe.com/secondary/fl

DID YOU KNOW?

The Musée Rodin, in the 7th *arrondissement*, is housed in a beautiful 18th-century mansion that was once Rodin's studio. *Le Penseur*, pictured above (with the dome of Napoleon's Tomb behind it), is located in the garden along with many other of Rodin's sculptures, including *Les Bourgeois de Calais*, a photo of which can be found on page 419.

Vocabulary Teaching Resources

1. Vocabulary Transparencies 16.1 (A & B)
2. Audio Cassette 9B/CD-10
3. Student Tape Manual, Teacher's Edition, *Mots 1: A–C*, pages 174–176
4. Workbook, *Mots 1: A–E*, pages 155–157
5. Communication Activities Masters, *Mots 1: A*, page 75
6. Chapter Quizzes, *Mots 1: Quiz 1*, page 82
7. CD-ROM, Disc 4, *Mots 1:* pages 410–413

Bell Ringer Review

Write the following on the board or use BRR Blackline Master 16-1: Make a list of activities you like to do in your free time.

PRESENTATION (pages 410–411)

A. Using Vocabulary Transparencies 16.1 (A & B), play the *Mots 1* presentation on Cassette 9B/CD-10. Point to the appropriate illustration as you play the cassette or CD.

B. Have students repeat each word or expression after you or the cassette two or three times as you point to the corresponding item on the transparency.

C. Call on individual students to point to the corresponding illustration on the transparency as you say the word or expression.

Teaching Tip Ask questions about students' personal preferences when practicing the vocabulary. For example: *Jacques, tu préfères les drames ou les documentaires? Qui aime les films policiers?*

VOCABULAIRE

MOTS 1

AU CINÉMA

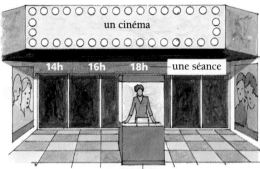

un cinéma
14h 16h 18h une séance
le guichet

Qui joue dans ce film?

l'écran
une salle de cinéma
un dessin animé

les vedettes (f.)
un acteur
une actrice

un film étranger

Qu'est-ce que tu vas faire?

les sous-titres (m.)

On passe un film étranger à Paris.
On passe le film en V.O., c'est-à-dire en version originale.
On le voit en version originale avec des sous-titres français.

Le film est doublé.
La version originale est en anglais.
La version doublée est en français.

410 CHAPITRE 16

TOTAL PHYSICAL RESPONSE

(following the Vocabulary presentation)

Getting Ready

Demonstrate the terms *parmi* and *serrer la main à…*

TPR

___, levez-vous et venez-ici, s'il vous plaît.
Vous êtes un acteur/une actrice célèbre.

Habillez-vous.
Mettez votre costume.
Le rideau se lève. Entrez en scène.
Dites «bonjour» aux spectateurs.
Chantez.
Dansez.
Marchez parmi les spectateurs.
Serrez la main à quelqu'un.
Merci, ___. C'est bien. Retournez à votre place, s'il vous plaît.

Tu préfères quels genres de films?

un documentaire   un film policier   un film d'horreur   un film de science-fiction

un film d'aventures   un film d'amour   une comédie   un drame

AU THÉÂTRE

une pièce de théâtre

le rideau

le décor

On monte une pièce.
C'est une comédie.

Comédie-Française
1680

Comédie-Française

**Molière
Le Tartuffe**

Acte 1 Scène 1
        Scène 2

Entracte
Acte 2 Scène 1
        Scène 2

Acte 3 Scène 1
        Scène 2

un costume

la scène

La pièce a trois actes.
Chaque acte a deux scènes.
Entre deux actes il y a un entracte.

Voici quelques genres de pièces:

    une tragédie
    un opéra
    une comédie musicale

l'entracte (m.)

CHAPITRE 16   411

411

D. Mention some well-known films and ask students to classify them and name their stars. For example: **Frankenstein**—*C'est un très vieux film d'horreur avec Boris Karloff.* **Dead Poets' Society** (*Le Cercle des Poètes disparus*)—*C'est un drame avec Robin Williams.*

E. Ask film trivia questions, incorporating a variety of questioning techniques. For example: **Out of Africa**—*c'est un documentaire? Qui joue dans ce film? C'est un film américain ou un film africain? C'est un film de quelle année?*, etc.

F. Read the following movie summaries to the students and ask them to identify the type of film: *Les acteurs et les actrices habitent sur une autre planète et voyagent dans l'espace. La police recherche un criminel. On étudie la vie des animaux dans leurs milieux. Un couple décide de traverser l'océan Atlantique tout seul dans un canoë.*

Vocabulary Expansion

You may wish to give students the following additional words.
**le fauteuil
l'orchestre
le balcon
le rang
le lever du rideau**

PAIRED ACTIVITY

Have students work in pairs to prepare a skit. One plays the part of a box office clerk at a movie theater; the other plays the part of a ticket buyer.

COOPERATIVE LEARNING

Students work in groups of four. Each person writes down the title of a movie he/she has seen recently. They put their titles together and scramble them. Each person in turn picks one and asks: *Qui a vu ce film?* and then makes up as many present-tense questions about it as possible. The student who saw the film answers. If anyone picks his/her own film, he/she tells the others about it.

Exercices

A **Fana de cinéma ou pas?**   Donnez des réponses personnelles.

1. Tu es fana de cinéma? C'est-à-dire, tu aimes beaucoup voir des films?
2. Tu vas souvent au cinéma?
3. Il y a un cinéma près de chez toi?
4. La première séance est à quelle heure?
5. Il y a toujours un dessin animé avant le film?
6. Tu fais la queue devant le cinéma? Quels soirs spécialement?
7. Où est-ce que tu prends les billets?
8. Dans la salle de cinéma, tu préfères une place près de l'écran ou loin de l'écran?
9. Quel est ton acteur préféré ou ton actrice préférée?
10. Quelle est la vedette de ton film préféré?
11. Si tu vois un film étranger, tu préfères voir la version originale avec des sous-titres ou une version doublée?

B **Au cinéma.**   Complétez.

1. Ce soir on ___ un très bon film au cinéma Rex.
2. C'est un film étranger. Il n'est pas doublé, il a des ___.
3. On ne passe pas le film en ___ originale.
4. La prochaine ___ commence à quelle heure?
5. Combien coûte le ___?

C **Tu aimes quels genres de films?**   Donnez des réponses personnelles.

1. Tu préfères les documentaires ou les dessins animés?
2. Tu préfères les films policiers ou les films d'horreur?
3. Tu préfères les films d'aventures ou les films de science-fiction?
4. Tu préfères les comédies ou les drames?
5. Quand tu vas au magasin de vidéos, tu choisis généralement quel genre de films?

D **Des pièces et des films.**   Complétez.

1. Au théâtre on ___ une pièce.
2. On voit un film au cinéma et on voit une pièce au ___.
3. Une pièce a des ___ et les ___ ont des ___.
4. Entre deux actes il y a un ___.
5. Un ___ joue le rôle de Roméo.
6. Une ___ joue le rôle de Juliette.
7. Le balcon de Juliette est le ___ d'une scène d'amour célèbre.
8. Les acteurs et les actrices portent des ___.
9. Le mot ___ en français signifie (veut dire) *scene* et *stage* en anglais.
10. Le ___ se lève à 20 heures.

E Au théâtre. Donnez des réponses personnelles.

1. Tu es fana de théâtre?
2. Tu vas souvent au théâtre?
3. Il y a un théâtre dans ta ville?
4. Ton école a un club d'art dramatique?
5. Tu es membre du club d'art dramatique?
6. Le club monte combien de pièces par an?
7. Cette année le club va monter quelle pièce?

F Mes préférences. Donnez des réponses personnelles.

1. Tu préfères les comédies ou les tragédies?
2. Tu aimes l'opéra?
3. Tu aimes les comédies musicales?
4. Tu as déjà joué dans une pièce?
5. Quel rôle as-tu joué?

Collections de la Comédie-Française

CHAPITRE 16 **413**

Exercices E and F
Answers will vary.

LITERATURE CONNECTION

Molière wrote his major works between 1661 and 1673. Like Shakespeare, he wrote, directed and acted in his own plays. In 1673 Molière was taken ill on stage during a performance of *Le Malade imaginaire* and died several hours later.

LEARNING FROM REALIA

Have students look at the theater listings above to see if they have heard of any of the plays. Have them look at the ticket. Ask: *Comment s'appelle le théâtre?* (Le Théâtre Français = La Comédie-Française.) *Quel est le titre de la pièce? À quelle heure commence la pièce? Combien coûte le billet?*

Note Students will read an excerpt from *Le Malade imaginaire* in *En voyage.*

INDEPENDENT PRACTICE

Assign any of the following:
1. Exercises, pages 412–413
2. Workbook, *Mots 1: A–E,* pages 155–157
3. Communication Activities Masters, *Mots 1: A,* page 75
4. CD-ROM, Disc 4, pages 410–413

VOCABULAIRE

MOTS 2

AU MUSÉE
une exposition d'art

la peinture

un tableau

une statue

la sculpture

une peintre

un peintre

414 CHAPITRE 16

Vocabulary Teaching Resources

1. Vocabulary Transparencies 16.2 (A & B)
2. Audio Cassette 9B/CD-10
3. Student Tape Manual, Teacher's Edition, *Mots 2: D–E*, page 177
4. Workbook, *Mots 2: F–H*, pages 157–158
5. Communication Activities Masters, *Mots 2: B*, pages 76–77
6. Computer Software, *Vocabulaire*
7. Chapter Quizzes, *Mots 2: Quiz 2*, page 83
8. CD-ROM, Disc 4, *Mots 2:* pages 414–417
9. Art Transparencies F-5 and F-6

Bell Ringer Review

Write the following on the board or use BRR Blackline Master 16-2: Write the titles of the last five movies you saw or the last five books you read. Classify them (comedy, science-fiction, etc.) in French and write one sentence about each one.

PRESENTATION (pages 414–415)

A. Introduce the new words by showing French paintings on slides from an art book, or use Art Transparencies F-5 and F-6.
B. Have students close their books. Model the *Mots 2* vocabulary, using Vocabulary Transparencies 16.2 (A & B). Have them repeat the new vocabulary after you or Cassette 9B/CD-10. Repeat the procedure with books open.
C. Ask questions using *Qu'est-ce que c'est?* If a student fails to

---

TOTAL PHYSICAL RESPONSE

Getting Ready
    Demonstrate the term *l'escalier.*

TPR
(Student 1) et (Student 2), **levez-vous et venez ici, s'il vous plaît.**
Vous êtes devant le Musée d'Art Moderne.
Entrez dans le musée.
Allez à l'ascenseur.

(Student 1), **appuyez sur le bouton.**
Montez dans l'ascenseur.
(Student 2), **appuyez sur le bouton du quatrième étage.**
Attendez.
Voilà le quatrième étage.
Sortez de l'ascenseur.
Vous êtes dans une exposition de peinture abstraite.

(continued on the next page)

des sculpteurs (m.)

une œuvre

Je sais le nom du peintre.
C'est Duval.
Je ne connais pas ce peintre
personnellement.
Je connais son œuvre, c'est-à-dire
ses tableaux.

Musée d'Art Moderne
Ouvert : du mardi au dimanche
de 9h à 18h
Fermé : le lundi

Moi, je connais bien le Musée d'Art
Moderne.
Je le visite souvent.
Je sais que le musée est fermé le
lundi.
Il est ouvert tous les jours sauf le
lundi.

CHAPITRE 16   **415**

answer, rephrase the question
as an either/or question. For
example: *C'est un tableau ou une
sculpture?*

COGNATE RECOGNITION

Ask students to identify as
many cognates as they can in *Mots
2*. Pay particular attention to their
pronunciation of these cognates.

Vocabulary Expansion

You may wish to give stu-
dents the following additional
vocabulary in order to talk
about art.
une gravure
une lithographie
de la poterie
une aquarelle
un portrait
une peinture à l'huile

Information about culture
and cultural institutions in
other francophone countries
can be found in the *Les Arts*
section of *Le Monde francophone* on pages 434–437.

TPR (*continued*)
Promenez-vous.
Regardez les tableaux.
(Student 1), montrez un tableau que vous
    aimez à (Student 2).
Promenez-vous encore.
Arrêtez-vous devant un grand tableau.
Regardez le tableau ensemble.
Qu'est-ce qu'il est énorme, ce tableau!
Regardez très haut.

Regardez à gauche. Regardez à droite.
C'est un tableau très bizarre. Vous ne le
    comprenez pas.
(Student 2), montrez en gesticulant que
    vous aimez le tableau.
(Student 1), montrez en gesticulant que
    vous ne l'aimez pas du tout.
Merci, (Student 1) et (Student 2). Vous avez
    très bien fait.
Retournez à vos places et asseyez-vous.

Exercices

PRESENTATION *(page 416)*

Extension of *Exercice B*

Since the *je* and *tu* forms of *savoir* and *connaître* sound the same as the il/*elle* forms, you may wish to personalize Exercise B by asking: *Tu sais le nom d'un artiste? Qu'est-ce que c'est? Tu connais l'artiste? Tu sais sa nationalité? Tu connais l'œuvre de cet artiste? Tu connais un musée? Quel musée connais-tu? Tu sais où est le musée? Tu sais l'adresse du musée?*

ANSWERS

Exercice A

1. C'est un musée.
2. Le musée est ouvert.
3. C'est une exposition de peinture.
4. Elle est sculpteur.
5. C'est une statue.

Exercice B

1. Oui, il sait le nom du peintre.
2. Non, il ne connaît pas le peintre.
3. Oui, il connaît l'œuvre du peintre.
4. Oui, elle sait le nom du musée.
5. Oui, elle connaît le musée.
6. Oui, elle connaît le Musée d'Art Moderne.
7. Oui, elle le visite souvent.
8. Oui, elle sait que le musée est fermé le lundi.
9. Oui, il est ouvert tous les jours sauf le lundi.

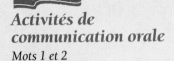

Activités de communication orale
Mots 1 et 2

PRESENTATION *(pages 416–417)*

Activité B

In the CD-ROM version of this activity, students can interact with an on-screen native speaker.

Activité F

Your students might enjoy the following movies: *Au revoir les enfants, Les Quatre Cents Coups, L'Enfant sauvage, Le Ballon rouge, Jean de Florette, La Gloire de mon père, Cyrano de Bergerac.*

Exercices

A **Un peu de culture.** Répondez d'après les dessins.

1. C'est un musée ou un théâtre?
2. Le musée est ouvert ou fermé?
3. C'est une exposition de peinture ou une exposition de sculpture?

4. Elle est peintre ou sculpteur?
5. C'est un tableau ou une statue?

B **Qui le sait?** Répondez.

1. Robert sait le nom du peintre?
2. Il connaît le peintre?
3. Il connaît l'œuvre du peintre?
4. Annick sait le nom du musée?
5. Elle connaît le musée?

6. Elle connaît le Musée d'Art Moderne?
7. Elle le visite souvent?
8. Elle sait que le musée est fermé le lundi?
9. Le Musée d'Art Moderne est ouvert tous les jours sauf le lundi?

Activités de communication orale
Mots 1 et 2

A **Le théâtre.** A French exchange student at your school (your partner) is interested in theater. He or she wants to know if you like to go to the theater and what kinds of plays you like; if there are theaters in your town; if your school has a drama club and, if so, what play(s) the club is putting on or has put on this year.

B **Tu aimes le cinéma?** You're talking to a French teenager, Hélène Bouvier, in a café in Cannes during the movie festival. You're talking about the movies. Answer her questions.

1. Tu aimes aller au cinéma?
2. Tu y vas souvent?
3. Quels sont tes acteurs préférés?
4. Tu préfères quels genres de films?
5. Ça coûte combien, un billet de cinéma aux États-Unis?

Hélène Bouvier

C **Mon film préféré.** Find out what a classmate's favorite movies are and why. Then find out which movies he or she hates and why. Reverse roles.

D **Au musée.** The French tourist office has sent you the brochure below describing Paris museums. Find out which museum a classmate would like to visit and why. (If he or she doesn't want to visit any of them, find out why.) Then reverse roles.

> Élève 1: Tu veux visiter quel musée?
> Élève 2: Je veux visiter le Centre Pompidou parce que j'aime l'art moderne.

E **Renseignements.** You're in Paris and you'd like to visit one of the museums listed in the brochure on the right. Call the museum and find out from the museum employee (your partner) where it's located, when it opens and closes, what day it's closed, and how much a ticket costs. Your partner can use the information in the brochure to answer your questions.

F **Allons au cinéma!** With your classmates, see a French film that is playing at a local movie theater. Afterwards, go out for a snack together and discuss the movie in French. If there are no French movies playing in your community, ask your teacher to rent a French video that you can watch and discuss in class.

LES MUSÉES

MUSÉE DE L'ARMÉE
Esplanade des Invalides. 45.55.37.70. Tous les jours de 10h à 18h. Entrée: 27F, Tarif réduit: 14F. (Musée accessible aux handicapés physiques).

CENTRE POMPIDOU (BEAUBOURG)
Rue Rambuteau. 42.77.12.33. Semaine de 12h à 22h. Samedi, dimanche et fêtes de 10h à 22h. Fermé le mardi. Tarif musée: 27F. Tarif réduit: 18F. *Le Musée National d'Art Moderne de l'après-impressionnisme à nos jours, plus des expositions temporaires, concerts, ballets, cinémathèque.*

MUSÉE DU LOUVRE
Rue de Rivoli. Ouvert tous les jours sauf le mardi de 9h à 18h. Entrée: 30F. Tarif réduit: 15F. *Six musées en un seul: antiquités gréco-romaines, égyptiennes, orientales, beaux-arts français, italiens et d'autres encore. En vedette, «la Vénus de Milo», et «la Joconde».*

MUSÉE DU SPORT
24, rue du Commandant Guilbaud. 40.45.99.12. Entrée: 20F. Tarif réduit: 10F. Ouvert tous les jours de 9h30 à 12h30 et de 14h à 17h. Fermé mercredi, samedi et fêtes. *Exposition permanente: Trésors et curiosités du sport.*

MUSÉE DU CINÉMA-HENRI LANGLOIS
Palais de Chaillot. 45.53.74.39. Tous les jours sauf mardi et fêtes. Visites guidées à 10h, 11h, 14h, 15h, et 16h. Entrée: 22F. Tarif réduit: 14F. *Documents sur le cinéma de 1895 à nos jours.*

LEARNING FROM REALIA

Ask students to look at the museum listings. Ask: *Où est le Musée de l'Armée? Il est ouvert quels jours? Il est ouvert quelles heures? Combien coûte l'entrée? Il y a un tarif réduit? C'est combien le tarif réduit? À qui le musée est-il accessible?* Ask students which museum they would like to visit.

INDEPENDENT PRACTICE

Assign any of the following:
1. Exercises and activities, pages 416–417
2. Workbook, *Mots 2: F–H*, pages 157–158
3. Communication Activities Masters *Mots 2: B*, pages 76–77
4. Computer Software, *Vocabulaire*
5. CD-ROM, Disc 4, pages 414–417

STRUCTURE

Structure Teaching Resources

1. Workbook, *Structure: A–J,* pages 159–162
2. Student Tape Manual, Teacher's Edition, *Structure: A–G,* pages 178–181
3. Audio Cassette 9B/CD-10
4. Communication Activities Masters, *Structure: A–F,* pages 78–81
5. Computer Software, *Structure*
6. Chapter Quizzes, *Structure:* Quizzes 3–7, pages 84–88
7. CD-ROM, Disc 4, pages 418–425

Les verbes connaître et savoir *au présent*

PRESENTATION *(page 418)*

A. Write the plural forms of *savoir* and *connaître* on the board and have students repeat after you.
B. Lead students through steps 1–4 and the examples.
C. Make two lists on the board, one of information that follows *connaître* (names of people, cities and other places, artistic and literary works), and the other with facts that follow *savoir* (dates, times, telephone numbers, addresses, infinitives, clauses).
D. Give students the following words or expressions and have them say whether they would use *savoir* or *connaître*: *André, sa famille, son adresse, son numéro de téléphone, le nom de son école, ses professeurs, son quartier.*

Les verbes *connaître* et *savoir* au présent

Indicating People, Places, and Things You Know and What You Know How to Do

1. Study the following forms of the irregular verbs *connaître* and *savoir,* both of which mean "to know."

CONNAÎTRE	SAVOIR
je connais	je sais
tu connais	tu sais
il	il
elle } connaît	elle } sait
on	on
nous connaissons	nous savons
vous connaissez	vous savez
ils	ils
elles } connaissent	elles } savent

2. You use *savoir* to indicate that you know a fact.

> Je sais le numéro de téléphone et l'adresse du cinéma.
> Je sais que le cinéma n'est pas loin d'ici.
> Il sait à quelle heure la séance commence.

3. You use *savoir* + infinitive to indicate that you know how to do something.

> Elle sait conduire.
> Tu sais danser?

4. *Connaître* means "to know" in the sense of "to be acquainted with." You use it with people, places, and things. Compare the meanings of *savoir* and *connaître* in the sentences below.

> Je sais son nom. C'est Nathalie. Je connais bien Nathalie.
> Je sais où elle habite. Elle habite à Grenoble. Je connais Grenoble.
> Je sais le nom de l'auteur. C'est Victor Hugo. Je connais son œuvre.

LEARNING FROM REALIA

Have students read the information on the sign. Emphasize pronunciation since this is a rather difficult street name for Americans to pronounce. Ask: *L'avenue Victor Hugo est dans quel arrondissement? Victor Hugo est né en quelle année? Il est mort en quelle année? Il a eu beaucoup de professions? Quelles professions?*

COOPERATIVE LEARNING

Have students write five things they know how to do using *savoir* + the infinitive. Team members interview each other, compile a team report, and present it to the class. Students might then practice questioning techniques. For example: *Qui sait nager? Qui ne sait pas nager? Qu'est-ce que Carole sait faire? Tous les membres de l'équipe C savent faire quoi?*

Exercices

A **Qu'est-ce que tu sais?** Donnez des réponses personnelles.

1. Tu sais l'adresse de ton ami(e)? Il/Elle habite quelle ville?
2. Tu connais la ville?
3. Tu sais le nom d'un bon restaurant? Quel est son nom?
4. Tu connais le restaurant?
5. Tu sais le nom de l'auteur de la tragédie de *Macbeth*? Quel est son nom?
6. Tu connais les pièces de Shakespeare?
7. Tu connais *Macbeth*?

B **On sait tout.** Complétez avec «savoir».

1. Moi, je ___ le nom du théâtre.
2. Et Paul ___ le numéro de téléphone du théâtre.
3. Paul et moi, nous ___ l'adresse du théâtre.
4. Mais nous ne ___ pas l'heure du lever de rideau.
5. Voilà Guy et Monique. Ils ___ à quelle heure la pièce commence.
6. Je ___ que le théâtre est fermé le dimanche.
7. Vous ___ quelle pièce on monte maintenant à la Comédie-Française?
8. Et toi, tu ___ qui joue le rôle principal dans cette pièce?

C **Qu'est-ce que tu sais faire?** Donnez des réponses personnelles.

1. Tu sais jouer au tennis?
2. Tu sais faire de l'aérobic?
3. Tu sais faire des costumes?
4. Tu sais organiser une très bonne fête?
5. Tu sais parler français?

D **Qui connaît quoi?** Complétez avec «connaître».

1. Je ___ bien la France.
2. Les élèves de Madame Benoît ___ la peinture française.
3. Mais ils ne ___ pas très bien la littérature française.
4. Tu ___ la culture française?
5. Et Paul, il ___ la culture française contemporaine?
6. Vous ___ l'art français?
7. Nous ___ les Impressionnistes comme Monet, Manet et Renoir.
8. Tu ___ l'œuvre du peintre Degas?
9. Ah, oui. Je ___ son œuvre. J'adore ses danseuses de ballet.

Auguste Rodin: «Les Bourgeois de Calais»

INDEPENDENT PRACTICE

Assign any of the following:
1. Exercises, page 419
2. Workbook, *Structure: A–D*, pages 159–160
3. Communication Activities Masters, *Structure: A–B*, page 78
4. CD-ROM, Disc 4, pages 418–419

Exercices

PRESENTATION *(page 419)*

Extension of *Exercice D*: Higher Skills

After completing the exercise, ask students for some names: *des noms d'artistes, d'auteurs, de poètes, de musiciens, de compositeurs.*

ANSWERS

Exercice A

Answers will vary, but should include **Je (ne) sais (pas)** or **Je (ne) connais (pas)**.

Exercice B

1. sais	5. savent
2. sait	6. sais
3. savons	7. savez
4. savons	8. sais

Exercice C

All answers include **Je (ne) sais (pas)**.

Exercice D

1. connais	6. connaissez
2. connaissent	7. connaissons
3. connaissent	8. connais
4. connais	9. connais
5. connaît	

RETEACHING

Ask students to give a name that they know for each category: *un restaurant que je connais; une famille; un film; un(e) artiste; un médecin; une compagnie aérienne; une école; un professeur.*

HISTORY CONNECTION

Have students find Calais on the map on page 504 or use the Map Transparency. Rodin's sculpture, pictured on this page, commemorates an event of 1347. The English had just captured Calais, and the king of England promised to spare the town if six prominent citizens would give up their lives. The mayor and five other *bourgeois* volunteered. Fortunately, the king relented.

Note You may wish to refer students to the photo of *Le Penseur* on page 409.

Les pronoms le, la, les

PRESENTATION *(page 420)*

Write a few example sentences from step 1 on the board. Put a box around the noun object. Circle the object pronoun. Draw a line from the box to the circle. This helps students grasp the concept.

Exercices

PRESENTATION *(pages 420–421)*

Exercice C

 You may use the recorded version of this exercise.

ANSWERS

Exercice A

1. Les gâteaux? Je les aime beaucoup. (Je ne les aime pas. Je les déteste!)
2. … Je l'aime beaucoup. (Je ne l'aime pas. Je la déteste!)
3. … Je l'aime beaucoup. (Je ne l'aime pas. Je la déteste!)
4. … Je l'aime beaucoup. (Je ne l'aime pas. Je le déteste!)
5. … Je l'aime beaucoup. (Je ne l'aime pas. Je le déteste!)
6. … Je l'aime beaucoup. (Je ne l'aime pas. Je la déteste!)
7. … Je les aime beaucoup. (Je ne les aime pas. Je les déteste!)
8. … Je les aime beaucoup. (Je ne les aime pas. Je les déteste!)
9. … Je l'aime beaucoup. (Je ne l'aime pas. Je le déteste!)
10. … Je les aime beaucoup. (Je ne les aime pas. Je les déteste!)

Les pronoms *le, la, les*   *Referring to People and Things Already Mentioned*

---

1. You have already learned to use *le, la, l',* and *les* as definite articles. These same words are also used as direct object pronouns. A direct object pronoun can replace either a person or a thing. Note that the direct object pronoun in French comes right before the verb.

Je sais le nom du film.	**Je *le* sais.**
Je vois le film.	**Je *le* vois.**
J'aime le film.	**Je *l'*aime.**
Je ne connais pas la vedette.	**Je ne *la* connais pas.**
Je lis les sous-titres.	**Je *les* lis.**
J'admire les costumes.	**Je *les* admire.**

2. Note the placement of the direct object pronoun in negative sentences. It cannot be separated from the verb by the negative word.

Tu connais l'auteur?	**Non, je ne *le* connais pas.**
Tu regardes la télé?	**Je ne *la* regarde jamais.**
Tu aimes les tragédies?	**Je ne *les* aime pas du tout.**

3. Remember that in sentences with a verb + infinitive, the pronoun comes right before the infinitive.

Nous pouvons lire les sous-titres.	**Nous pouvons *les* lire.**
Il ne peut pas comprendre le film.	**Il ne peut pas *le* comprendre.**

Exercices

A   **Tu aimes les pâtisseries?**   Donnez des réponses personnelles d'après le modèle.

> **les pâtisseries**
> ***Les pâtisseries? Je les aime beaucoup.***
>   (*Je ne les aime pas. Je les déteste!*)

1. les gâteaux
2. l'eau minérale
3. la viande
4. le bœuf
5. le poisson
6. la glace
7. les fruits
8. les crevettes
9. le poulet
10. les haricots verts

Paul Cézanne: «L'Assiette bleue—Abricots et cerises»

DID YOU KNOW?

You may wish to give students some information about Cézanne: *Paul Cézanne est un peintre français du 19ème siècle. Comme les autres Impressionnistes, Cézanne aime pratiquer la peinture en plein air. Il peint des portraits, des natures mortes et des paysages. Ce tableau, L'Assiette bleue—Abricots et cerises, est une nature morte. Qu'est-ce qu'une nature morte en anglais?* (still life)

ADDITIONAL PRACTICE

Student Tape Manual, Teacher's Edition, *Activités A–B,* page 178

B On voit le film en version originale. Complétez.

1. — On voit le film doublé ou en version originale?
   — On ___ voit en version originale.
2. — Tu sais le nom de la vedette?
   — Oui, je ___ sais.
3. — Tu connais la vedette?
   — Tu veux rigoler! Mais non, je ne ___ connais pas.
4. — Tu comprends le français?
   — Oui, je ___ comprends.
5. — Tu ___ comprends assez bien pour comprendre le film?
   — Non, mais il n'y a pas de problème. Il y a des sous-titres et je ___ lis quand je ne comprends pas le dialogue.

C Qu'est-ce qu'il est beau! Répondez d'après le modèle.

Tu vois la statue?
Oui, je la vois. Qu'est-ce qu'elle est belle!

1. Tu vois le théâtre?
2. Tu aimes la pièce?
3. Tu vois le tableau?
4. Tu entends le concert?
5. Tu vois le ballet?
6. Tu vois le film?
7. Tu lis le poème?
8. Tu vois le décor?
9. Tu regardes les costumes?
10. Tu vois la vedette?
11. Tu vois l'actrice?
12. Tu regardes les tableaux?

D Qu'est-ce qu'on va faire?
Répondez en utilisant «le», «la» ou «les».

1. Après les cours tu vas prendre le bus?
2. Tu vas écouter la radio?
3. Tu vas faire les devoirs de français ce soir?
4. Tu vas regarder la télé?
5. Ton père ou ta mère va préparer le dîner?
6. Tes parents vont lire le journal?

Edgar Degas: «Deux Danseuses en scène»

---

1. le   4. le
2. le   5. le, les
3. la

Exercice C

1. Oui, je le vois. Qu'est-ce qu'il est beau!
2. Oui, je l'aime. Qu'est-ce qu'elle est belle!
3. Oui, je le vois. Qu'est-ce qu'il est beau!
4. Oui, je l'entends. Qu'est-ce qu'il est beau!
5. Oui, je le vois. Qu'est-ce qu'il est beau!
6. Oui, je le vois. Qu'est-ce qu'il est beau!
7. Oui, je le lis. Qu'est-ce qu'il est beau!
8. Oui, je le vois. Qu'est-ce qu'il est beau!
9. Oui, je les regarde. Qu'est-ce qu'ils sont beaux!
10. Oui, je la vois. Qu'est-ce qu'elle est belle!
11. Oui, je la vois. Qu'est-ce qu'elle est belle!
12. Oui, je les regarde. Qu'est-ce qu'ils sont beaux!

Exercice D

Answers will vary, but may include the following constructions:

1. Je vais le prendre. (Je ne vais pas le prendre.)
2. Je vais l'écouter. (Je ne vais pas l'écouter.)
3. Je vais les faire. (Je ne vais pas les faire.)
4. Je vais la regarder. (Je ne vais pas la regarder.)
5. Mon père (Ma mère) va le préparer.
6. Ils vont le lire. (Ils ne vont pas le lire.)

ART CONNECTION

Use Fine Art Transparencies F-5 and F-6 to view the Cézanne and Degas works on pages 420–421.

DID YOU KNOW?

Students can read about Degas, Renoir, and Monet in the *Lettres et sciences* section, pages 444–445.

INDEPENDENT PRACTICE

Assign any of the following:
1. Exercises, pages 420–421
2. Workbook, *Structure: E–F*, pages 160–161
3. Communication Activities Masters, *Structure: C*, page 79
4. CD-ROM, Disc 4, pages 420–421

Les prépositions avec les noms géographiques

PRESENTATION *(page 422)*

After steps 1–4, have students read the examples aloud. Then ask: *Où est la Tunisie? Où est Shanghaï? Où est la Chine?*

Note In the CD-ROM version, this structure point is presented via an interactive electronic comic strip.

Note You may want to give students the preposition for your state and some nearby states. To say "in" with the name of a state in French, use *dans* before most states preceded by *le* or *l'*, for example: *dans le Connecticut, dans l'Oregon* (exceptions: *au Nouveau-Mexique, au Texas*). Use *en* without the article with states preceded by *la*, for example: *en Virginie*. With Hawaii, use *à: à Hawaii*. Here are the state names: l'Alabama, l'Alaska, l'Arizona, l'Arkansas, la Californie, la Caroline du Nord, la Caroline du Sud, le Colorado, le Connecticut, le Dakota du Nord, le Dakota du Sud, le Delaware, la Floride, la Géorgie, Hawaii, l'Idaho, l'Illinois, l'Indiana, l'Iowa, le Kansas, le Kentucky, la Louisiane, le Maine, le Maryland, le Massachusetts, le Michigan, le Minnesota, le Mississippi, le Missouri, le Montana, le Nebraska, le Nevada, le New Hampshire, le New Jersey, l'état de New York, le Nouveau-Mexique, l'Ohio, l'Oklahoma, l'Oregon, la Pennsylvanie, le Rhode Island, le Tennessee, le Texas, l'Utah, le Vermont, la Virginie, la Virginie Occidentale, l'état de Washington, le Wisconsin, le Wyoming.

Exercices

PRESENTATION *(pages 422–423)*

Exercice A

Use the recorded version of this exercise, if you wish.

ANSWERS

Exercice A

1. En France.
2. En Italie.
3. En Espagne.
4. En France.
5. Au Japon.
6. Aux États-Unis.
7. Au Canada.
8. Au Sénégal.

422

Les prépositions avec les noms géographiques

Identifying Cities, Countries, and Continents

You use the following prepositions to express "in" or "to" with geographical names.

1. *à* with the name of a city

> Le Château de Versailles est bien sûr à Versailles.
> Le Musée du Louvre est à Paris.
> Je vais à New York pour aller au théâtre.

2. *en* with the name of feminine countries and continents. Most countries and continents whose names end in silent *-e* are feminine. *Le Mexique* and *le Zaïre* are two of the common exceptions.

> Henri est en France.
> La France est en Europe.
> Carole va en Tunisie.
> La Tunisie est en Afrique.
> Shanghaï est en Chine.
> La Chine est en Asie.

3. *au* with the name of masculine countries. Most countries whose names do not end in silent *-e* are masculine.

> Il va faire du ski au Canada.
> Cancún est au Mexique.
> Tokyo est au Japon.
> Je passe mes vacances au Maroc.
> Dakar est au Sénégal.

4. *aux* with countries whose name is plural

> Marc fait un voyage aux États-Unis.
> Amsterdam est aux Pays-Bas.

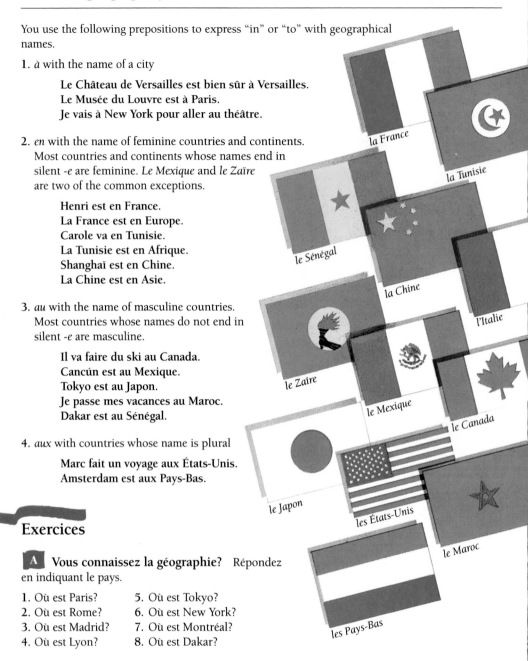

la France
la Tunisie
le Sénégal
la Chine
l'Italie
le Zaïre
le Mexique
le Canada
le Japon
les États-Unis
le Maroc
les Pays-Bas

Exercices

A **Vous connaissez la géographie?** Répondez en indiquant le pays.

1. Où est Paris?
2. Où est Rome?
3. Où est Madrid?
4. Où est Lyon?
5. Où est Tokyo?
6. Où est New York?
7. Où est Montréal?
8. Où est Dakar?

422　CHAPITRE 16

ADDITIONAL PRACTICE

After completing Exercises A–D, designate various areas in the classroom as continents, countries, and cities by taping up signs. Have students move from one place to another while classmates question them on where they or others are going and where they are. For example: *É1: Où vont Luc et Gérard? É2: Ils vont en Afrique. É1: Où sont-ils maintenant? É2: Ils sont à Marseille, en France.*

LEARNING FROM REALIA

1. Have students look at the flags and repeat the names of the countries.
2. Ask students the colors of the flags pictured: *De quelle couleur est le drapeau canadien?*, etc.

B Vous y allez quand? Posez une question d'après le modèle.

Nous allons à Antibes.
Ah oui? Vous allez en France quand?

1. Nous allons à Paris.
2. Nous allons à Cannes.
3. Nous allons à Amsterdam.
4. Nous allons à Barcelone.
5. Nous allons à Québec.
6. Nous allons à Shanghaï.
7. Nous allons à Miami.
8. Nous allons à Casablanca.

C C'est quel continent? Complétez.

1. Le Japon est ___ Asie et la Chine est ___ Asie aussi.
2. L'Italie et l'Espagne sont ___ Europe. Le Portugal est aussi ___ Europe.
3. Le Brésil, le Chili et l'Argentine sont ___ Amérique du Sud.
4. Les États-Unis et le Canada sont ___ Amérique du Nord.
5. Le Sénégal et la Côte-d'Ivoire sont ___ Afrique.

D Les grands musées du monde. Complétez.

1. Le Musée du Prado est ___ Madrid ___ Espagne.
2. Le Musée du Louvre est ___ Paris ___ France.
3. Le Metropolitan Museum est ___ New York ___ États-Unis.
4. Le Musée Britannique est ___ Londres ___ Angleterre, c'est-à-dire ___ Grande-Bretagne.
5. Le Centre Pompidou est ___ Paris ___ France.
6. Le Rijksmuseum est ___ Amsterdam ___ Hollande, c'est-à-dire ___ Pays-Bas.

La Fontaine Stravinski près du Centre Pompidou

PRESENTATION (*continued*)

Extension of *Exercice D*

After completing Exercise D, have students give other famous sites and say where they are.

ANSWERS

Exercice B

1. **Ah oui? Vous allez en France quand?**
2. … **en France quand?**
3. … **aux Pays-Bas quand?**
4. … **en Espagne quand?**
5. … **au Canada quand?**
6. … **en Chine quand?**
7. … **aux États-Unis quand?**
8. … **au Maroc quand?**

Exercice C

1. **en, en**
2. **en, en**
3. **en**
4. **en**
5. **en**

Exercice D

1. **à, en**
2. **à, en**
3. **à, aux**
4. **à, en, en**
5. **à, en**
6. **à, en, aux**

INDEPENDENT PRACTICE

Assign any of the following:
1. Exercises, pages 422–423
2. Workbook, *Structure: G–H,* page 161
3. Communication Activities Masters, *Structure: D,* page 80
4. CD-ROM, Disc 4, pages 422–423

DID YOU KNOW?

Tell students that the whimsical sculptures of the Fontaine Stravinski were created by Nikki de Saint-Phalle in homage to Igor Stravinsky, the Russian-born composer of *The Rite of Spring,* which set off a riot when it was first played in Paris in 1913. The fountain is an integral part of the Beaubourg area around the Pompidou Center, with its perpetual street-fair atmosphere.

Les verbes irréguliers venir, revenir *et* devenir *au présent*

PRESENTATION *(page 424)*

A. Write the forms of *venir* on the board. Have students repeat after you, paying particular attention to the changes in pronunciation. Underline the double *n* in the third person plural form: *ils viennent.*

B. Have students read the forms once again in their book.

C. Then have them read the example sentences.

Exercices

ANSWERS

Exercice A

1. Oui, Claude vient au cinéma avec nous.
2. Oui, il vient avec Martine.
3. Oui, Liliane vient aussi.
4. Oui, elle vient avec sa copine.
5. Oui, elles viennent à vélomoteur.
6. Oui, je viens au cinéma aussi.
7. Oui, je viens avec un copain.
8. Oui, nous venons à pied.

Exercice B

1. Non, il revient cet après-midi.
2. Non, ils reviennent...
3. Non, elle revient...
4. Non, il revient...

Les verbes irréguliers *venir,* revenir *et* devenir au présent

Expressing "to come," "to come back," and "to become"

1. The verb *venir,* "to come," is irregular in the present tense. Study the following forms.

VENIR			
je	viens	nous	venons
tu	viens	vous	venez
il elle on	} vient	ils elles	} viennent

Tu viens ce soir au théâtre?
Beaucoup de touristes viennent en France en été pour visiter ses musées célèbres.
Venez avec nous!

2. Two other verbs conjugated like *venir* are *revenir,* "to come back," and *devenir,* "to become." *Devenir* is seldom used in the present.

Il revient à trois heures.

Exercices

A   Qui vient au cinéma?   Répondez par «oui».

1. Claude vient au cinéma avec nous?
2. Il vient avec Martine?
3. Liliane vient aussi?
4. Elle vient avec sa copine?
5. Elles viennent à vélomoteur?
6. Tu viens au cinéma aussi?
7. Tu viens avec un copain?
8. Ton copain et toi, vous venez à pied?

B   Ils reviennent cet après-midi.   Répondez d'après le modèle.

> Élève 1: Marie est là?
> Élève 2: Non, elle revient cet après-midi.

1. Mon père est là?
2. Mes copains sont là?
3. Sophie est là?
4. Le professeur est là?

La préposition *de* avec les noms géographiques

Telling Where People Come From

You use the following prepositions to express "from" with geographical names.

1. *de* with the name of a city, a feminine country, or a continent

> **Elle est de Bordeaux.**
> **Ses grands-parents viennent d'Italie.**
> **Mes grands-parents viennent d'Amérique du Sud.**

2. *du* with the name of a masculine country

> **Mon amie arrive du Japon ce soir.**
> **Son père revient du Maroc.**

3. *des* with a country whose name is plural

> **Ils arrivent des États-Unis.**

Exercices

A **D'où viennent tous ces touristes?** Répondez d'après le modèle.

> Italie
> *Ces touristes viennent d'Italie.*

1. Espagne
2. Rome
3. Nice
4. France
5. Tokyo
6. Japon
7. Maroc
8. Mexique
9. New York
10. États-Unis

Une rue de Fort-de-France à la Martinique

B **D'où vient ta famille?** Donnez des réponses personnelles.

1. D'où viens-tu?
2. Ta famille et toi, d'où venez-vous?
3. D'où vient ton père?
4. D'où vient ta mère?
5. D'où viennent tes grands-parents?

CHAPITRE 16 **425**

DID YOU KNOW?

Fort-de-France is the capital of the French West Indies island of Martinique. Martinique is a *département* of France and its people are French citizens. See *Le Monde francophone*, pages 113 and 329, for further information on and photos of Martinique. In *À bord*, Chapter 7, students will learn about Martinique in greater detail.

INDEPENDENT PRACTICE

Assign any of the following:

1. Exercises, pages 424–425
2. Workbook, *Structure:* I–J, pages 161–162
3. Communication Activities Masters, *Structure: E–F,* pages 80–81
4. Computer Software, *Structure*
5. CD-ROM, Disc 4, pages 424–425

La préposition *de avec les noms géographiques*

PRESENTATION *(page 425)*

A. Lead students through the explanation of the usage of *de.* Have them read the example sentences aloud in unison.

B. You may wish to ask questions about the example sentences. For example: *D'où arrive ton ami? D'où revient ton père?*

Exercices

PRESENTATION *(page 425)*

Exercice A

You may use the recorded version of this exercise.

Extension of Exercice A

After going over Exercise A, have students make up original sentences using places they know.

ANSWERS

Exercice A

1. Ces touristes viennent d'Espagne.
2. … de Rome.
3. … de Nice.
4. … de France.
5. … de Tokyo.
6. … du Japon.
7. … du Maroc.
8. … du Mexique.
9. … de New York.
10. … des États-Unis.

Exercice B

Answers will vary.

INFORMAL ASSESSMENT

Check comprehension by calling out names of famous people and having students tell where they come from.

THE FRANCOPHONE WORLD

Have students locate the following countries on the map on page 506 or use the Map Transparency: *le Maroc, l'Algérie, la Tunisie.* For views of North African countries, see *Le Monde francophone*, pages 222, 327, 434, and 436.

425

CONVERSATION

PRESENTATION *(page 426)*

A. Tell students they will hear a conversation between David and Carole.

B. Have them close books and watch the Conversation Video or listen as you play Cassette 9B/CD-10. Have them listen a second time with books open.

C. Call on pairs to read the conversation to the class.

D. After doing Exercise A, call on a student to retell the story.

Note In the CD-ROM version, students can play the role of either one of the characters and record the conversation.

ANSWERS

Exercice A

1. Carole est fana de cinéma.
2. Elle aime tous les films.
3. On passe un très bon film espagnol.
4. Non, le film n'est pas doublé. (Non, le film est en version originale avec des sous-titres.)
5. Ils peuvent travailler leur espagnol.

Prononciation

PRESENTATION *(page 426)*

A. Using Pronunciation Transparency P-16, model the key words *une roue* and have students repeat chorally.

B. Now model the other words and sentences in similar fashion.

C. Give students the following *dictée:*

Vous voulez la taille au-dessous? Et tu veux la taille au-dessus? Vous avez vu la roue dans la rue? Tu as vu la statue?

D. For additional practice, use the *Prononciation* section on Cassette 9B/CD-10 and the Student Tape Manual, Teacher's Edition, *Activités J–L,* page 183.

Scènes de la vie   *On va au cinéma*

DAVID: Carole, tu veux aller au cinéma?
CAROLE: Pourquoi pas? C'est une très bonne idée. On passe quel film?
DAVID: On a le choix. Il y a beaucoup de cinémas, tu sais! Tu préfères quels genres de films?
CAROLE: Moi, j'aime tous les films. Je suis fana de cinéma, une vraie cinéphile.
DAVID: Au Rex on passe un très bon film espagnol—en version originale avec des sous-titres, je crois.
CAROLE: Excellente idée! On peut travailler notre espagnol. La prochaine séance est à quelle heure?

A   **Des cinéphiles.**   Répondez d'après la conversation.

1. Qui est fana de cinéma?
2. Elle aime quels genres de films?
3. On passe quel film au Rex?
4. Le film est doublé?
5. Qu'est-ce que les deux amis peuvent faire s'ils voient ce film?

Prononciation   *Les sons /ü/ et /u/*

It is important to make a clear distinction between /ü/ and /u/ since many words differ only in these two sounds. Repeat the following pairs of words.

vous/vu   dessous/dessus   roue/rue   loue/lu   tout/tu

Now repeat the following sentences.

Vous avez vu ces statues?
Tu vas souvent au musée?
Cette comédie musicale est doublée.

une roue

DID YOU KNOW?

French teenagers can go to the movies very often because movie theaters offer discounts to students. Also, since there are fewer TV channels in France, there is less of a selection of programs to watch on TV. In most French theaters there are ushers who show people to their seats. Movie-goers are expected to tip the ushers. Before the film begins, commercials are shown. Movie theaters don't have concession stands. The ushers come down the aisles with trays of candy and ice cream and one buys items from them after the commercials end. Popcorn is not available in French movie theaters!

Activités de communication orale

A **D'où viennent-ils?**   Play this game in small groups. First make a list of as many foreign celebrities as your group can think of (world leaders, actors, athletes, etc.). Next, take turns asking students from another group where these people are from. Then reverse roles. The group with the most correct answers wins.

> Élève 1: D'où viennent les Beatles?
> Élève 2: Ils viennent d'Angleterre. (Je ne sais pas. Je ne sais pas qui c'est.)

B **Où est… ?**   Ask your classmates in the geography class to give you a list of the top 20 tourist sites in the world. (Ask them to include cities, museums, and monuments.) Bring the list to French class and ask your partner where each site is located.

> Élève 1: Où est Montréal?
> Élève 2: C'est au Canada.

C **Je connais bien…**   Think of someone you know well in the class. Using the verbs *savoir* and *connaître*, tell a classmate about this person without saying his or her name. Your partner has to guess who it is you're talking about. Include as much of the following information as you can.

La Place Jacques Cartier à Montréal

1. son adresse et son numéro de téléphone
2. ses cours
3. ce qu'il y a dans sa chambre
4. les membres de sa famille
5. ses activités

> Élève 1: Je sais qu'il aime le football américain et la musique rock. Je connais son frère Bob. Il habite rue Kennedy…
> Élève 2: C'est Andy.

Activités de communication orale

ANSWERS

Activités A and B
  Answers will vary.

Activité C
  Answers will vary but may include the following constructions:

1. Je sais son adresse. Il/Elle habite… Je sais son numéro de téléphone. C'est…
2. Je sais qu'il/elle a le cours de… avec M. (Mme/Mlle…), etc.
3. Je connais bien sa chambre. Il/Elle a… (Je sais qu'il/elle a… dans sa chambre.)
4. Je connais sa sœur… Je sais qu'il y a cinq personnes dans sa famille. Je sais que tu connais sa famille.
5. Je sais qu'il/elle aime (faire)… (jouer au…)

CROSS-CULTURAL COMPARISON

French cinema and theater customs differ from those in the United States. In a French theater or cinema, one tips the usher after being shown a seat. In U.S. theaters, the house lights are dimmed about three times to announce the beginning of the play or its resumption after the intermission. In France this is done with three "knocks." In France, whistling at the end of a play is a sign of disapproval. And never give an actor or actress carnations in France. It means they are fired!

THE FRANCOPHONE WORLD

Students can turn to page 437 in the *Les Arts* section of *Le Monde francophone* for information on African film.

CRITICAL THINKING ACTIVITY

(Thinking skill: making inferences)
  Put the following on the board or on a transparency:
  Beaucoup de personnes aiment aller voir un film au cinéma. Pourquoi, quand il est possible de rester chez soi regarder une vidéo?

Bell Ringer Review

Write the following on the board or use BRR Blackline Master 16-5: What are the English titles of these movies?

1. La Belle et la Bête
2. Hannah et ses Sœurs
3. L'Arme Fatale
4. S.O.S. Fantômes
5. Les Dents de la Mer

Answers: *Beauty and the Beast, Hannah and her Sisters, Lethal Weapon, Ghostbusters,* and *Jaws.*

READING STRATEGIES
(page 428)

Pre-reading

Ask students: Who goes to the movies? How often? Who attends the theater? Is seeing a play better than watching a movie? Why?

Reading

A. Have students open their books to page 428. Read the *Lecture* to them.
B. Call on a student to read three sentences aloud. Ask others questions about what was read before calling on another student to read.

Post-reading

A. Based on the *Lecture*, what differences and similarities do students see between young French people's reading, TV, movie-going, and theater habits and those of young Americans?
B. After going over the *Lecture* in class, assign it to be read for homework.

Note Students may listen to a recorded version of the *Lecture* on the CD-ROM.

Étude de mots

ANSWERS

Exercice A

Answers will vary.

LES LOISIRS CULTURELS EN FRANCE

*I*l est naturellement difficile de décrire[1] un adolescent américain typique. Et il est difficile aussi de décrire un adolescent français typique. Mais généralisons un peu! Disons que Chantal Brichant est une adolescente française typique. Que fait Chantal quand elle a du temps libre? Est-ce qu'elle lit? Oui, elle lit. Elle lit beaucoup? Pas vraiment. On peut dire que les jeunes Français lisent un peu plus que les jeunes Américains, mais ils ne lisent pas énormément. Quand Chantal lit, qu'est-ce qu'elle choisit? Elle choisit des romans[2] et des bandes dessinées[3].

Chantal va au théâtre? Oui, de temps en temps. Dans toutes les grandes villes de France, et surtout à Paris, il y a des théâtres. Chaque année un certain nombre de pièces sont bien accueillies[4] par le public. Mais Chantal, comme la plupart des adolescents «typiques», va plus souvent au cinéma. Les Français voient beaucoup de films français, bien sûr, mais ils voient aussi pas mal de[5] films étrangers. On passe les grands films étrangers en exclusivité[6] dans les grands cinémas. Ces films sont souvent doublés, mais on peut les voir aussi en version originale avec des sous-titres.

Mais quel est le loisir préféré de Chantal et des Français «typiques»? La télévision? Mais oui! La télévision est de loin[7] le loisir culturel préféré des Français. Et les jeunes gens aiment aussi sortir avec leurs copains. Est-ce qu'il y a beaucoup de différences entre les Américains et les Français? Qu'est-ce que tu en penses?

[1] décrire *to describe*
[2] romans *novels*
[3] bandes dessinées *comic strips*
[4] bien accueillies *well-received*
[5] pas mal de *quite a few*
[6] en exclusivité *first run*
[7] de loin *by far*

Étude de mots

A Le français, c'est facile.
Trouvez cinq mots apparentés dans la lecture.

ADDITIONAL PRACTICE

After completing Exercises B and C, ask students the following questions.
1. Est-ce que les adolescents français et américains aiment faire les mêmes choses quand ils ont du temps libre?
2. Comment est-ce qu'on passe les films étrangers en France?
3. Est-ce que les jeunes Français lisent plus que les jeunes Américains?

CRITICAL THINKING ACTIVITY

(Thinking skill: drawing conclusions)
Put the following on the board or on a transparency:
Où veulent habiter les gens qui aiment beaucoup les activités culturelles? Pourquoi?

Compréhension

B **Vous avez compris?** Répondez.

1. Chantal lit quand elle a du temps libre?
2. Elle lit énormément?
3. Quel est le genre littéraire préféré des Français?
4. Il y a des théâtres en France? Où?
5. Chaque année il y a des pièces que le public aime?
6. Où est-ce qu'on passe les films étrangers en exclusivité?
7. Quel est le loisir préféré des Français?

C **Les adolescents.** Il est extrêmement difficile de décrire un adolescent français ou américain typique. Pourquoi?

UNE AVENTURE D'ASTÉRIX LE GAULOIS
les lauriers de CÉSAR

© Albert René, 1996. Goscinny/Uderzo. *Les Lauriers de César*, Dargaud Éditeur.

DÉCOUVERTE CULTURELLE

LES MUSÉES

Les musées en France sont très fréquentés par les Français et par les touristes qui viennent du monde entier— d'Europe, d'Asie, d'Australie, d'Amérique et d'Afrique. À Paris il y a beaucoup de musées. Le Musée d'Orsay est une ancienne gare qui est aujourd'hui un musée extraordinaire où il y a une exposition permanente des peintres impressionnistes. Le Centre Pompidou (ou Beaubourg) a toujours des expositions d'art moderne. Il y a un nouveau Musée Picasso. Et la perle des musées français, c'est le Louvre.

Le dimanche, l'entrée dans les musées nationaux est à demi- tarif. Le dimanche, les gens viennent en foule admirer les peintures et les sculptures des artistes de tous les siècles[1] et de tous les pays du monde.

© Hergé/Casterman

LES BANDES DESSINÉES

La lecture préférée des jeunes de 8 à 18 ans est la bande dessinée. La «B.D.» vient en tête[2] des romans policiers, d'espionnage et de science-fiction. Mais les bandes dessinées ne sont pas seulement pour les enfants. Il est certain que la grande majorité des jeunes Français lisent «Tintin», «Astérix» et «Lucky Luke». Quand ils deviennent adultes, ils continuent d'avoir «leurs» bandes dessinées. Beaucoup de bandes dessinées, comme, par exemple, «Les Frustrés» de la dessinatrice humoristique Claire Bretécher, critiquent la vie moderne.

[1] siècles   *centuries*
[2] vient en tête   *rates above*

Tintin et son chien Milou

CHAPITRE 16   **429**

INDEPENDENT PRACTICE

Assign any of the following:
1. *Étude de mots* and *Compréhension* exercises, pages 428–429
2. Workbook, *Un Peu Plus,* pages 163–164
3. CD-ROM, Disc 4, pages 428–429

Compréhension

ANSWERS

Exercice B

1. Oui, Chantal lit quand elle a du temps libre.
2. Pas vraiment. Elle ne lit pas énormément.
3. Les Français préfèrent les romans et les bandes dessinées.
4. Oui, il y a des théâtres dans toutes les grandes villes de France.
5. Oui, chaque année il y a des pièces que le public aime.
6. On passe les films étrangers en exclusivité dans les grands cinémas.
7. La télévision est le loisir préféré des Français.

Exercice C

Answers will vary but may resemble the following:

Il est difficile—même impossible—parce que chaque personne est différente.

OPTIONAL MATERIAL

Découverte culturelle

PRESENTATION (*page 429*)

A. Have students read the information to get whatever they can from it.
B. You may then let them get together in small groups and tell one another in French something they learned from their reading.

Note Point out to students that there are many sophisticated *bandes dessinées* in France. They are popular with adults as well as with children and adolescents.

Note Students may listen to a recorded version of the *Découverte culturelle* on the CD-ROM.

OPTIONAL MATERIAL

PRESENTATION *(pages 430–431)*

The major objective of this section is to allow students to enjoy the photographs and gain an appreciation of France, its people, and its culture.

A. Ask students to share what they know about the art museums of Paris. Share with them your own knowledge of this topic, showing photographs you may have collected on trips to France or from the library or art department at your school.

B. Call on volunteers to read aloud the captions on page 430.

Note In the CD-ROM version, students can listen to the recorded captions and discover a hidden video behind one of the photos.

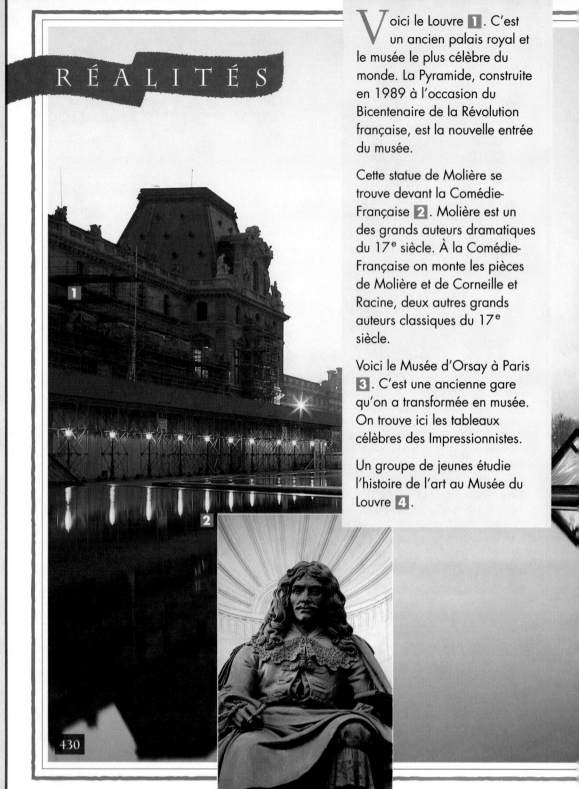

RÉALITÉS

V oici le Louvre **1**. C'est un ancien palais royal et le musée le plus célèbre du monde. La Pyramide, construite en 1989 à l'occasion du Bicentenaire de la Révolution française, est la nouvelle entrée du musée.

Cette statue de Molière se trouve devant la Comédie-Française **2**. Molière est un des grands auteurs dramatiques du 17e siècle. À la Comédie-Française on monte les pièces de Molière et de Corneille et Racine, deux autres grands auteurs classiques du 17e siècle.

Voici le Musée d'Orsay à Paris **3**. C'est une ancienne gare qu'on a transformée en musée. On trouve ici les tableaux célèbres des Impressionnistes.

Un groupe de jeunes étudie l'histoire de l'art au Musée du Louvre **4**.

430

DID YOU KNOW?

In 1680 Louis XIV founded the Comédie-Française by combining several theater companies including that of the actor, director, and dramatist Molière, who had died in 1673.

The present theater has been continuously occupied since 1790. The Comédie-Française has an acting school that prepares future actors for the permanent company. It also offers matinee performances of the classics for school children. The Comédie-Française is subsidized by the French government.

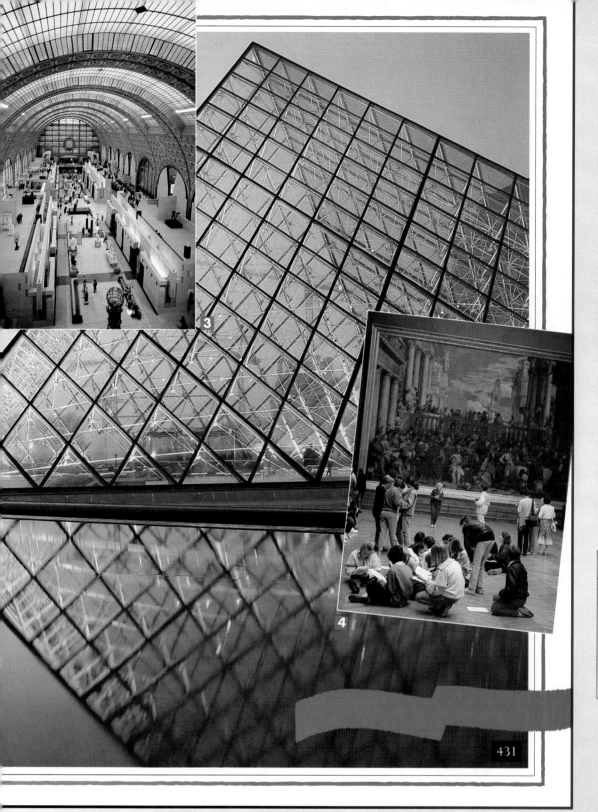

GEOGRAPHY CONNECTION

Vous avez déjà appris qu'il y a beaucoup de musées à Paris. Mais pas tous les musées français sont à Paris. Prenons-en deux exemples. Dans la jolie petite ville d'Albi dans la région d'Armagnac se trouve un formidable musée dans un ancien palais épiscopal. C'est le musée Toulouse-Lautrec. Toulouse-Lautrec est un célèbre peintre du 19ème siècle. Il a peint la vie de Montmartre, mais il n'est pas de Paris. Il est d'Albi, et dans ce musée, le musée Toulouse-Lautrec, il y a même les dessins qu'il a faits quand il était un tout petit enfant.

Pas très loin d'Albi dans la même région d'Armagnac se trouve la petite ville de Castres. À Castres il y a un musée qui a une collection des tableaux du célèbre peintre espagnol Goya. Vous avez entendu parler de Goya? Non? Demandez à un copain ou à une copine qui fait de l'espagnol.

THE FRANCOPHONE WORLD

See *Le Monde francophone*, page 436, for photos of a museum and an art institute in other francophone countries.

431

ADDITIONAL PRACTICE

1. Student Tape Manual, Teacher's Edition, *Deuxième Partie*, pages 184–186
2. Situation Cards, Chapter 16

COOPERATIVE LEARNING

Display Communication Transparency C-16. Have students work in groups to make up as many questions as they can about the illustration. Have groups take turns asking and answering the questions.

CULMINATION

CULMINATION

RECYCLING

The *Activités de communication orale* and *écrite* allow students to use the vocabulary and grammar from this and earlier chapters in open-ended, real-life situations.

INFORMAL ASSESSMENT

Oral Activities A, B, and C provide guided cues and lend themselves to assessing speaking and listening skills. Oral Activity C can also be used to test the skill of reading quickly for information. Use the evaluation criteria given on page 34 of this Teacher's Wraparound Edition.

Activités de communication orale

ANSWERS

Activités A and B

Answers will vary.

Activité C

Answers will vary but may include the following constructions: Tu voudrais voir (*name of movie*) avec moi? On le passe samedi soir au cinéma (*name of movie theater*). Il est doublé/en version originale avec des sous-titres. Je veux voir ce film parce que ma vedette préférée joue dans le film / parce que mon frère m'a dit que c'est très amusant, etc.

Activités de communication orale

A **Dans ta ville.** Since you speak French so well, you've been asked to prepare a radio advertisement to attract French-speaking tourists to a cultural event (real or imaginary) that will take place in your town. Be sure to include:

1. a brief description of the event
2. the date, time, and place
3. how and where to buy tickets
4. the price of the tickets
5. a statement encouraging people to attend

B **La télé.** Divide into small groups and choose a leader. The leader interviews the others to find out how much time they spend watching TV every day and what kinds of shows they like. The leader takes notes and reports to the class.

1. Tu regardes la télé combien d'heures par jour?
2. Quelles sortes de programmes est-ce que tu aimes regarder?

les sports	les clips (vidéos rock)
les comédies	les documentaires
les drames	les dessins animés
le journal télévisé	les séries
les films	

À la classe: Dans mon groupe, tout le monde regarde la télé deux ou trois heures par jour. On préfère les comédies…

C **Tu veux aller au cinéma avec moi?** Look over the ads in this French movie guide. Decide which movie you'd like to see and invite a classmate to see it with you. Tell your partner when and where the movie is playing and whether it's dubbed or in the original language, with subtitles. Discuss whether or not you both want to see the movie or figure out an alternative.

432   CHAPITRE 16

les salles

COMŒDIA
13, avenue Berthelot - Lyon 7e
Tél. 76.58.58.98

ROBIN DES BOIS
(Grand Ecran - Son Dolby Stéréo)
Tlj.: 13h50 - 16h30 - 19h15 - 22h

LA MANIERE FORTE
(Son Dolby Stéréo)
Tlj.: 13h50 - 16h - 18h - 20h15 - 22h15

THELMA ET LOUISE
(Grand Ecran - Son Dolby Stéréo - V.O.)
Tlj.: 14h - 16h45 - 19h30 - 22h

SPARTACUS
(Grand Ecran -Son Dolby Stéréo - V.O.)
Tlj.: 14h30 - 20h15

LES TORTUES NINJA II
Tlj.: 14h - 16h - 18h - 20h - 21h45

UNE EPOQUE FORMIDABLE
+ Court métrage: "Le ridicule tue"
Tlj.: 14h - 16h - 18h - 20h - 22h

FOURMI LAFAYETTE
68, rue P. Corneille angle
cours Lafayette - Tel. 78.60.84.89

BRAZIL
Tlj. (sf. di.): 21h30 - di.: 19h45

SCENES DE MENAGE DANS UN CENTRE COMMERCIAL
Tlj.: 20h

TINTIN ET LE LAC AUX REQUINS
Me., sa., lu.:14h

ASTERIX ET LE COUP DU MENHIR
Me., sa., lu: 14h - di.: 15h30

MAMAN, J'AI RATÉ L'AVION
Me., sa., di., lu.: 15h30

FANTASIA
Me., sa., di., lu.:15h30

ALICE
Sa.: 18h

JACQUOT DE NANTES
Me., sa., lu.: 15h30 - 21h30 - je., ve., ma.: 21h30 - di.: 17h45

FOR THE YOUNGER STUDENT

1. Have students draw and write dialogue balloons for their own *bandes dessinées*.
2. Have students illustrate a poster that advertises a movie in French (real or imaginary), giving the names of the stars, the film genre, and the time and location of the film.

COMMUNITIES

Have students make a poster in French for the school play. Include the following information: title of the play, date, time, location, actors, price of tickets, and a statement encouraging people to attend.

Activité de communication écrite

A **Des renseignements, s'il vous plaît.** You're going to spend a month in the French city of your choice. Write a letter to the tourist office (*le syndicat d'initiative*) asking for information about cultural events during your stay. Be sure to mention your name and age, what kind of cultural activities you like and the dates of your stay.

Réintroduction et recombinaison

A **Je suis malade.** Donnez des réponses personnelles.

1. Tu te sens bien aujourd'hui?
2. Quand tu es malade, tu te couches?
3. Aux États-Unis le médecin vient chez toi?
4. Le médecin te fait une ordonnance? Tu la donnes au pharmacien?
5. Quand le pharmacien te donne des comprimés, tu les prends avec un verre d'eau?
6. Quand tu es malade, tu ouvres un magazine et tu le lis?
7. Tu souffres beaucoup quand tu as la grippe?
8. Tu éternues et tu tousses quand tu es enrhumé(e)?

Vocabulaire

NOMS
le cinéma
le guichet
la séance
la salle de cinéma
l'écran (m.)
l'acteur (m.)
l'actrice (f.)
la vedette
le film
le film policier
le film d'aventures
le film d'horreur
le film de science-fiction
le film d'amour
le film étranger
le dessin animé
le documentaire
le drame

le film en version
    originale (V.O.)
le film doublé
les sous-titres (m.)

le théâtre
la pièce
la scène (*stage*)
le rideau
le décor
le costume
l'acte (m.)
l'entracte (m.)
la scène (*scene*)
le genre
la comédie
la comédie musicale
la tragédie
l'opéra (m.)

le musée
l'exposition (f.)
la peinture
le/la peintre
le tableau
la sculpture
le sculpteur
la statue
l'œuvre (f.)
le nom

ADJECTIFS
chaque
fermé(e)
ouvert(e)

VERBES
connaître
savoir

venir
revenir
devenir
visiter

**AUTRES MOTS
ET EXPRESSIONS**
monter une pièce
passer un film
c'est-à-dire
entre
personnellement
sauf

CHAPITRE 16   **433**

Activité de communication écrite

ANSWERS

Activité A
Answers will vary but may include the following constructions:
1. Je m'appelle ___. J'ai ___ ans.
2. J'aime le cinéma/le théâtre/la peinture /la sculpture/ aller au musée, etc.
3. Je vais être à ___ du 15 au 25 juillet.

OPTIONAL MATERIAL

Réintroduction et recombinaison

PRESENTATION *(page 433)*

Exercice A
This exercise recycles vocabulary related to medicine presented in Chapter 15. It also reincorporates direct object pronouns.

ANSWERS

Exercice A
Answers will vary.

ASSESSMENT RESOURCES

1. Chapter Quizzes
2. Testing Program
3. Situation Cards
4. Communication Transparency C-16
5. Performance Assessment
6. Computer Software: Practice/Test Generator

VIDEO PROGRAM

INTRODUCTION   (49:06)

**QU'EST-CE QU'ON
FAIT CE SOIR?**   (50:16)

Les Arts

PRESENTATION (*pages 434–437*)

This cultural material is presented for students to enjoy and to help them gain an appreciation of the francophone world. Since the material is *optional*, you may wish to have students read it on their own as they look at the colorful photographs that accompany it. They can read it at home or you may wish to give them a few minutes in class to read it.

If you prefer to present some of the information in greater depth, you may follow the suggestions given for other reading selections throughout the book. Students can read aloud, answer questions asked by the teacher, ask questions of one another in small groups and, finally, give a synopsis of the information in their own words in French.

MORE ABOUT THE PHOTOS

Photo 1 Tahar Ben Jelloun was born in Fez, Morocco, in 1944. He is a poet, novelist, essayist, and journalist. He writes in both French and Arabic. In his work, he often presents problems faced by North Africans living and working in France.

Photo 2 Senghor was born in 1906 in Western Senegal. Upon receiving his *baccalauréat* in Dakar, he went to Paris and was admitted to the prestigious Lycée Louis-le-Grand where he was a classmate of Georges Pompidou. He then went on to study at the Sorbonne and was the first African to get the difficult *aggrégation* in France.

During the Second World War he was taken prisoner. Upon his release after the war, he taught at

LES ARTS

Chaque société a sa culture. La culture d'une société s'exprime par sa langue, sa religion et ses arts. La culture est l'ensemble des structures sociales, intellectuelles et artistiques qui caractérisent une société.

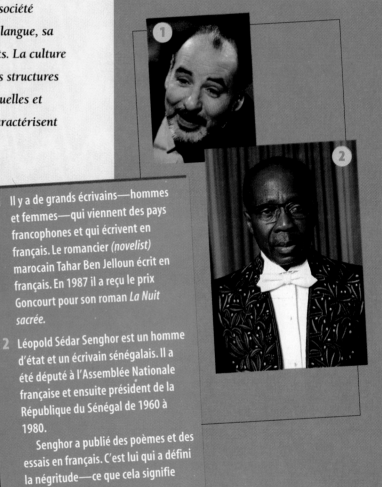

LA LITTÉRATURE

1 Il y a de grands écrivains—hommes et femmes—qui viennent des pays francophones et qui écrivent en français. Le romancier (*novelist*) marocain Tahar Ben Jelloun écrit en français. En 1987 il a reçu le prix Goncourt pour son roman *La Nuit sacrée*.

2 Léopold Sédar Senghor est un homme d'état et un écrivain sénégalais. Il a été député à l'Assemblée Nationale française et ensuite président de la République du Sénégal de 1960 à 1980.
Senghor a publié des poèmes et des essais en français. C'est lui qui a défini la négritude—ce que cela signifie d'être noir.

the École Nationale de la France d'outre-mer. He was elected a representative of Senegal to the French National Assembly, where he served from 1946 to 1958. He contributed to the French constitution on matters concerning French overseas possessions.

With Aimé Césaire, the writer and politician from Martinique, he launched the important magazine, *Présence Africaine*. Senghor held several government posts and was the president of Senegal from 1960 to 1980.

LA PEINTURE

3 L'art naïf est l'art d'autodidactes—c'est-à-dire, de gens qui n'ont pas fait d'études, qui ont appris seuls. À Haïti il y a un grand nombre de peintres naïfs qui ont beaucoup de talent. Le sujet de leurs tableaux sans perspective est souvent une scène de la vie quotidienne, de la vie de tous les jours. Le petit bus aux couleurs vives s'appelle un *tap tap*. Le *tap tap* est le moyen de transport le plus important à Haïti. Chaque *tap tap* a son nom. Le nom est souvent d'origine religieuse. Et ce *tap tap*, «La Divinité», en est un exemple.

4 Gauguin est un initiateur de la peinture moderne. Pendant toute sa carrière il recherche un paradis exotique. Il va de Paris en Bretagne et en Provence. Finalement il va en Polynésie française où il s'installe à Tahiti.

À Tahiti il commence à peindre des sujets exotiques. Mais il veut donner «carte blanche» à son imagination. «Je ferme les yeux pour voir», dit-il. Les yeux fermés, Gauguin voit des rochers rouges, des arbres dorés et des montagnes violettes. Il les peint comme il les «voit». Il aime utiliser des couleurs vives.

LE MONDE FRANCOPHONE

Photo 4 Gauguin was a successful broker and businessman when he began painting as a hobby. At age 33 he left his well-paying job and turned to painting as a career. His paintings did not sell well, and he and his family were reduced to poverty.

Gauguin traveled from place to place looking for an earthly paradise and finally left his estranged wife and children and took off for the South Seas. He settled in Tahiti, where he lived among the Maori people.

In his art, Gauguin was more interested in creating a decorative pattern than a picture that looked real. His paintings have many flat areas of bright colors. His forms look round and solid.

Photo 3 Haitian primitive art (*l'art naïf*) can be found in every little Haitian market. Haitians produce art in great abundance, from simple little paintings done by children to works of art exhibited and sold in prestigious galleries around the world. In the 1940's an American, DeWitt Peters, recognized the beauty and value of Haitian art. He opened the Centre d'Art, a gallery that still exists today in Port-au-Prince, the capital of Haiti.

Most Haitian paintings depict scenes from everyday life or the Bible—particularly Adam and Eve. Note the *tap tap* in the painting seen here. *Tap taps* are often decorated with paintings by rather talented artists. Some of these paintings are very unique.

In addition to paintings, Haitians produce wonderful wood carvings and sculptures. Because of the extreme poverty and lack of supplies in Haiti, the sculptures are often made from the metal of old oil drums.

Photo 6 In 1991, the Israeli architect Moshe Safti built a large modern addition to the Musée des Beaux-Arts in Montreal. The addition was constructed with prefabricated modular units that fit into each other like grape clusters. The units served as models for the construction of affordable housing.

Photo 9 *(page 437) Sango Malo* is "The Village Teacher" in English. The film contrasts two views of education, the traditional rigid "Eurocentric" curriculum and a practical-skills approach to building a self-reliant rural community.

This film (94 minutes, in French with English subtitles) and other francophone African and Caribbean videos are available for rent or purchase from the following source:

California Newsreel
149 9th Street
San Francisco, California 94103
(415) 621-6196

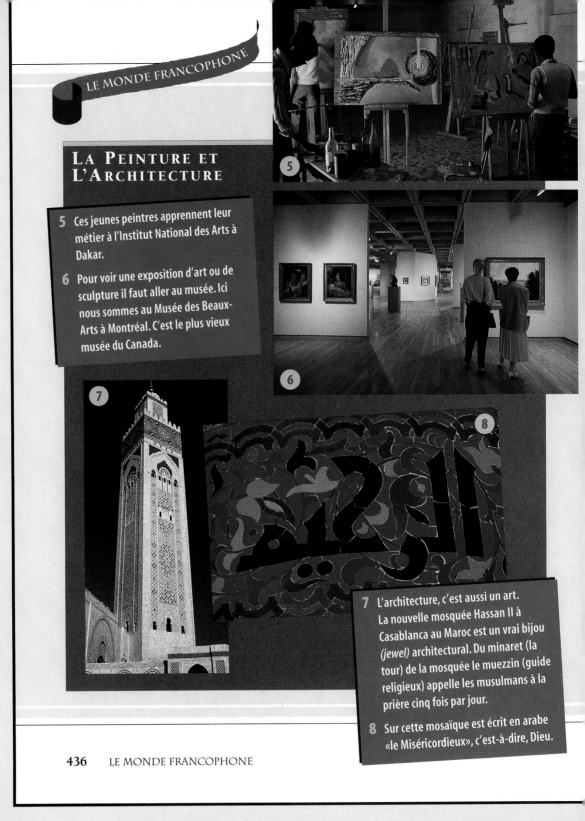

LE MONDE FRANCOPHONE

LA PEINTURE ET L'ARCHITECTURE

5 Ces jeunes peintres apprennent leur métier à l'Institut National des Arts à Dakar.

6 Pour voir une exposition d'art ou de sculpture il faut aller au musée. Ici nous sommes au Musée des Beaux-Arts à Montréal. C'est le plus vieux musée du Canada.

7 L'architecture, c'est aussi un art. La nouvelle mosquée Hassan II à Casablanca au Maroc est un vrai bijou *(jewel)* architectural. Du minaret (la tour) de la mosquée le muezzin (guide religieux) appelle les musulmans à la prière cinq fois par jour.

8 Sur cette mosaïque est écrit en arabe «le Miséricordieux», c'est-à-dire, Dieu.

LE CINÉMA ET LA MUSIQUE

9 En ce moment il y a beaucoup de films produits par des Africains. On peut voir l'Afrique telle que les Africains la voient. Le film *Sango Malo* du Cameroun présente un portrait intime des réalités de la vie dans un petit village africain d'aujourd'hui.

10 Le film *You Africa,* en wolof et en français avec des sous-titres en anglais, raconte le grand succès d'un tour fait par le chanteur Youssou N'Dour dans neuf pays de l'Afrique occidentale. Ce célèbre chanteur est né dans le quartier pauvre de la médina à Dakar. Aujourd'hui N'Dour est le principal interprète de la musique «fusion pop». C'est une fusion de musique africaine traditionnelle avec du reggae, du jazz et du rock.

Son groupe, Super Étoile, est le plus célèbre de toute l'Afrique. Habillés en *boubous* ou en «*baseball jerseys*», ils battent des tambours traditionnels et jouent de la guitare électrique pendant qu'ils dansent aux vifs rythmes africains.

LE MONDE FRANCOPHONE

Photo 10 Music and dance are two extremely interesting aspects of African culture. There are two types of African music: the traditional village music of the bush and modern pop music. Traditional music serves a social purpose. Each social occasion has its own type of music. There are different kinds of music for women, young people, hunters, soldiers, etc. The instruments for traditional music are also different. Pop groups use electric guitars and the like, but instruments for traditional music are hand-made from gourds, animal skins and horns.

One of the most popular forms of African pop music is the modern conga from Zaire and the Congo. African popular music has a Latin sound because it has been heavily influenced by Latin-American music. It is a blend of traditional Latin-American and African-American music with elements of American jazz, rock, and, most recently, reggae.

To purchase recordings of African music, contact:
- African Record Centre Ltd.
  2343 Seventh Ave.
  New York, NY
  (212) 281-2717
  or
- The Kilimanjaro Music Store
  Florida & California Streets, NE
  Washington, D.C.
  (202) 462-8200

OVERVIEW

This section reviews key grammatical structures and vocabulary from Chapters 13–16. The structure topics were first presented on the following pages: object pronouns *me, te, nous, vous*, page 394; direct object pronouns *le, la, les*, page 420; prepositions with geographical names, page 422; *passé composé*, pages 350, 372, and 396; imperative, page 398.

REVIEW RESOURCES

1. Workbook, Self-Test 4, pages 166–169
2. Videocassette/Videodisc, Unit 4
3. Video Activities Booklet, Unit 4: Chapters 13–16, pages 50–63
4. Computer Software, Chapters 13–16
5. Testing Program, Unit Test: Chapters 13–16, pages 102–107
6. Performance Assessment
7. CD-ROM, Disc 4, *Révision:* Chapters 13–16, pages 438–441
8. CD-ROM, Disc 4, Self-Tests 13–16
9. CD-ROM, Disc 4, Game: *Le Labyrinthe*
10. Lesson Plans

Conversation

ANSWERS

Exercice A

1. Non, elles ne le connaissent pas.
2. Oui. Il s'appelle Marc.
3. … dans l'autobus.
4. Il joue au foot(ball).
5. … dans l'équipe du frère…
6. Oui, il est gardien de but.
7. Non, son équipe a perdu parce que l'autre équipe a marqué trois buts.

438

RÉVISION

CHAPITRES 13–16

Conversation   *Le joueur de foot*

CHRISTINE: Tu connais le garçon là-bas?

SABINE: Je sais son nom—c'est Marc. Mais je ne le connais pas.

CHRISTINE: Je le vois tous les jours dans l'autobus.

SABINE: Et tu ne le connais pas!? Tu es trop timide! Je sais qu'il fait du foot tous les mercredis.

CHRISTINE: Comment tu sais ça?

SABINE: Il est dans l'équipe de mon frère. Il est gardien de but.

CHRISTINE: Il joue bien?

SABINE: Pas mal. Mais la semaine dernière, l'autre équipe a marqué trois buts et notre équipe a perdu zero à trois!

A **Trois buts!** Répondez d'après la conversation.

1. Christine et Sabine connaissent le garçon?
2. Sabine sait son nom? Comment s'appelle-t-il?
3. Où est-ce que Christine le voit tous les jours?
4. Il joue à quoi?
5. Il est dans quelle équipe?
6. Il est gardien de but?
7. Est-ce que son équipe a gagné la semaine dernière? Pourquoi?

Structure

Les pronoms d'objet direct et indirect *me, te, nous* et *vous*

The pronouns *me, te, nous,* and *vous* function as both direct and indirect objects of the verb. Remember that *me* and *te* change to *m'* and *t'* before a vowel or silent *h*. Object pronouns always come right before the verb.

Le professeur *te* regarde?	Oui, il *me* regarde.
Le médecin *t'*examine?	Non, il ne *m'*examine pas.
Il va *vous* faire une ordonnance?	Oui, il va *nous* faire une ordonnance.

A **Qu'est-ce qu'on fait?** Répondez en utilisant «me» ou «nous».

1. Quand le médecin t'examine, il t'ausculte?
2. Quand tu as une angine, le médecin te prescrit des antibiotiques?
3. Tes copains te téléphonent quand tu es malade?
4. Tes professeurs vous admirent, toi et tes copains?
5. Ils vous donnent beaucoup de devoirs?
6. Ils vont vous voir l'année prochaine?

COOPERATIVE LEARNING

Have students work in teams of three to make up a conversation about a soccer game and present it to the class.

ADDITIONAL PRACTICE

Have students ask each other as many questions as they can that use the object pronouns *me, te, nous, vous.*

Les pronoms d'objet direct *le, la, les*

Review the direct object pronouns *le, la, les*. Remember that *le* and *la* change to *l'* before a vowel or silent *h*. These pronouns can replace either people or things.

Je vois l'acteur.	Je *le* vois.
J'aime beaucoup cet acteur.	Je *l'*aime beaucoup.
Je vais regarder la télé.	Je vais *la* regarder.
Je n'aime pas les romans.	Je ne *les* aime pas.

B   Qu'est-ce qu'on fait?   Répondez en utilisant «le», «la», «l'» ou «les».

1. Vous connaissez les Impressionnistes?
2. Vous savez l'adresse du Musée d'Orsay?
3. Vous aimez les tableaux des Impressionnistes?
4. Qui aime la sculpture?
5. Tes copains et toi, vous aimez voir les films d'horreur?

C   Non.   Mettez à la forme négative d'après les indications.

1. Je les vois souvent. (ne… jamais)
2. Vous les aimez, ces gens? (ne… pas)
3. La télé, nous la regardons de temps en temps. (ne… jamais)
4. Le ballet? Nous voulons le voir. (ne… pas)

Les prépositions avec les noms géographiques

You use the following prepositions to express "in," "to," and "from" with geographical names.

1. *à* and *de* with cities

   Il habite à Paris.   **Je viens de Rome.**

2. *en/au (aux)* and *de/du (des)* with countries, depending on whether the country is masculine or feminine, singular or plural

	FÉMININ	MASCULIN
to	Je vais en France.	Je vais au Brésil. Je vais aux États-Unis.
from	Je viens de France.	Je viens du Brésil. Je viens des États-Unis.

Remember that, except for *le Mexique* and a few others, countries that end in a silent *e* are feminine.

ADDITIONAL PRACTICE

Give students the following nouns and have them make up questions with *tu vois* and a direct object pronoun. For example: *Le livre? Tu le vois?*

les billets	la photo
la lettre	le stylo
le magazine	le disque
les cassettes	la calculatrice
la vidéo	les cartes postales

PRESENTATION *(page 440)*

Exercice E

This exercise can be done as a paired activity.

ANSWERS

Exercice D

1. de, en
2. de, en
3. à, en
4. au
5. à, en
6. à, aux
7. du, de
8. de, aux

Exercice E

Answers will vary but should include one of the following structures: **en Angleterre, en France, en Belgique, aux Pays-Bas, en Allemagne, au Luxembourg, en Suisse, en Autriche, en Espagne, en Italie.**

Le passé composé des verbes réguliers et irréguliers

PRESENTATION *(page 440)*

A. Have the students repeat the forms of *avoir* after you.
B. Now have students repeat some past participles: *regardé, parlé, joué, gagné, fini, servi, choisi, vendu, attendu, perdu.*
C. Go over steps 1–3 of the explanation in the text.
D. You may wish to ask the following questions: *Hier soir, tu as regardé la télé? Tu as regardé la télé après le dîner? Ta famille a dîné à quelle heure? Tes parents ont regardé la télé aussi? Vous avez regardé la télé dans la salle de séjour?*

D **Quelle ville? Quel pays?** Complétez.

1. Il est ___ Rome. Il habite ___ Italie.
2. Nous venons ___ Londres, mais nous n'habitons pas ___ Angleterre.
3. J'ai un appartement ___ Paris, mais je n'habite pas ___ France.
4. Ils vont tous les ans ___ Mexique.
5. L'Alhambra est ___ Grenade, ___ Espagne.
6. J'ai passé une semaine ___ Amsterdam ___ Pays-Bas.
7. Il vient ___ Maroc. Il est ___ Casablanca.
8. Tu viens ___ New York. Tu habites ___ États-Unis.

E **Dans quel pays?** Regardez la carte à la page 504. Choisissez une ville et répondez d'après le modèle.

> Bruxelles
>
> **Élève 1: Dans quel pays est Bruxelles?**
> **Élève 2: Bruxelles est en Belgique.**

Le passé composé des verbes réguliers et irréguliers

1. The *passé composé* is composed of two parts: the present tense of the verb *avoir* and the past participle of the verb. Review the forms of the *passé composé* of regular verbs.

PARLER	FINIR	VENDRE
j'ai parlé	j'ai fini	j'ai vendu
tu as parlé	tu as fini	tu as vendu
il/elle/on a parlé	il/elle/on a fini	il/elle/on a vendu
nous avons parlé	nous avons fini	nous avons vendu
vous avez parlé	vous avez fini	vous avez vendu
ils/elles ont parlé	ils/elles ont fini	ils/elles ont vendu

2. For the past participles of irregular verbs, see p. 372.

3. Remember that *ne… pas, ne… plus, ne… jamais* go around the verb *avoir*.

Tu n'as pas écouté le prof hier?

ADDITIONAL PRACTICE

Have students complete the following sentence: *Un jour, je voudrais aller (ville) (pays).*

COOPERATIVE LEARNING

Divide the class into four teams. Give students the following topics: *L'hiver; Les sports.* The teams compose as many questions or statements about the topics as they can. One person on each team serves as a secretary and writes down the sentences. After five minutes, collect the sentences from each secretary. The team having the most questions or statements wins.

F Le match de foot. Décrivez un match de foot imaginaire au *passé composé*. Utilisez les verbes et expressions suivants.

regarder	jouer	donner un coup de pied
marquer un but	passer le ballon	arrêter le ballon
égaliser le score	gagner	perdre

G Les achats. Vous avez acheté des vêtements. Décrivez ces vêtements à un copain ou une copine. Utilisez les verbes suivants.

acheter   coûter   prendre   trouver   aimer

L'impératif

Imperative forms are used to give commands or to make suggestions. They are the same as the *tu, nous,* and *vous* forms of the present tense. However, in the case of regular *-er* verbs and *aller,* you drop the final s of the *tu* form.

Travaille!	Attends un peu!	Fais ça!
Travaillons!	Attendons un peu!	Faisons ça!
Travaillez!	Attendez un peu!	Faites ça!

H Le jeu de «Jacques a dit» (*Simon says*). Vous donnez des ordres à vos camarades. Si vous dites d'abord «Jacques a dit», ils le font, mais si vous ne dites pas «Jacques a dit», ils ne le font pas.

(*Jacques a dit*): Levez le bras droit! Fermez les yeux!, etc.

Activité de communication orale

A Enquête sur les saisons. You want to know if your partner prefers summer or winter. On a separate sheet of paper, make a chart like the one below. Fill it out for both seasons. Compare your chart with your partner's and try to guess which season he or she prefers by asking questions about his or her choices.

Élève 1: Tu préfères le ski ou le ski nautique?
Élève 2: Je préfère le ski nautique.
Élève 1: Tu préfères l'été.

	L'HIVER	L'ÉTÉ
Vêtements		
Activités	le ski	le ski nautique
Équipement		
Nourriture		

LETTRES ET
SCIENCES

Microbiologie: Louis Pasteur et L'Institut Pasteur

The three readings in this *Lettres et sciences* section are related topically to material in Chapters 15 and 16. For suggestions on presenting the readings, see page 228 of this Teacher's Wraparound Edition.

Avant la lecture

PRESENTATION *(page 442)*

A. Briefly discuss the *Avant la lecture* topic with the students.
B. Ask students what they know about Louis Pasteur or the Pasteur Institute.
C. Have students scan the reading and pick out the cognates.

Lecture

PRESENTATION *(pages 442–443)*

A. Have students read the selection silently.
B. If you have the students read the selection in class, tell them to look for the following information as they read. Write the questions on the board:
 1. Quel nom Pasteur donne-t-il aux microbes?
 2. D'après Pasteur, qu'est-ce qui cause les maladies?
 3. Pourquoi les savants ne font-ils pas très attention au travail de Pasteur?
 4. Qu'est-ce que Pasteur découvre?
 5. Qu'est-ce que le BCG?
 6. Quel travail le docteur Montagnier a-t-il fait?
C. If you have students read the selection outside of class, give them the following questions in English and have them look for the answers as they read. Have them write the answers (in French or English) and hand them in.

MICROBIOLOGIE:
LOUIS PASTEUR ET L'INSTITUT PASTEUR

Avant la lecture

You have no doubt heard of pasteurized milk. The term comes from the name of the French chemist Louis Pasteur, who invented the method of destroying harmful organisms without altering the milk. Find out how milk and other substances are pasteurized.

Lecture

«*La vaccination de Joseph Meister*»

Louis Pasteur (1822–1895)

Louis Pasteur est né en 1822 dans le Jura. Au collège, il n'est pas très bon élève. Il n'aime pas beaucoup ses cours, mais il aime le dessin. On l'appelle «l'artiste». Il veut devenir professeur et entre à l'École Normale, un institut qui forme les professeurs. Mais maintenant, il est passionné de sciences et passe son temps à faire de la recherche[1]. Il se spécialise en chimie.

En 1854, il commence à étudier ce que nous connaissons sous le nom de «microbes». Pasteur appelle ces microbes «germes» et il fonde une nouvelle science, la microbiologie. En 1873 Pasteur présente à l'Académie de Médecine un rapport qui révolutionne la médecine. Avant ce rapport de Pasteur, on croit que toutes les maladies terribles comme la typhoïde, le choléra et la fièvre jaune sont créées par le corps humain. C'est la théorie de la «génération spontanée». Mais Pasteur a fait des recherches sur les maladies du vin, de la bière et du ver à soie[2]. Il a compris que ces maladies n'arrivent pas toutes seules. Son idée, c'est que toutes les maladies sont causées par des micro-organismes. Ce sont des organismes très, très petits. On les baptise «microbes».

Pour Pasteur, les microbes sont partout. Il dit aux chirurgiens[3] de se laver les mains avant d'opérer, de bien laver aussi leurs instruments, c'est-à-dire de pratiquer l'asepsie. Malheureusement peu de[4] gens l'écoutent. Pourquoi? Parce qu'il n'est pas médecin. Il est chimiste et biologiste. Mais Pasteur ne s'arrête pas là. Il continue ses recherches. Il veut lutter[5] contre les microbes. Ses recherches sur les maladies infectieuses des animaux le conduisent à découvrir la vaccination. En 1885, il réalise le vaccin contre la rage[6]. On vaccine alors pour la première fois un être humain, un petit garçon de neuf ans—Joseph Meister—qui a été mordu[7] par un chien

DID YOU KNOW?

When Louis Pasteur was nine years old, a neighbor girl was bitten on the leg by a wolf. He knew she was in great danger because other people in his town had died of rabies after similar incidents. At the time, no one knew what caused this disease or how to keep animals from contracting it. Later in life, Pasteur developed a vaccine against rabies.

Louis married Marie Laurent in 1849. She became interested in his work and encouraged him in his research. They had five children. In 1859, Pasteur's nine-year-old daughter Jeanne died of typhoid fever. He lost two other daughters to illness within the next few years. These losses spurred him to work harder to try to prevent other children from dying of disease. He eventually proved that heat could kill the microbes that were responsible for some illnesses.

enragé. C'est la victoire, après 40 ans de recherches.

[1] recherche *research*
[2] vin, de la bière et du ver à soie *wine, beer, and the silkworm*
[3] chirurgiens *surgeons*
[4] peu de *few*
[5] lutter *fight*
[6] rage *rabies*
[7] mordu *bitten*

L'Institut Pasteur (1888)

L'enthousiasme est grand, non seulement en France mais dans le monde entier. L'Académie des Sciences reçoit[1] de l'argent de nombreux pays pour la construction d'un centre de recherches en microbiologie.

L'Institut Pasteur est inauguré le 4 novembre 1888. Et qui est son concierge[2]? C'est... Joseph Meister. Les collaborateurs et élèves de Pasteur continuent son travail. En 1891 les docteurs Calmette et Guérin mettent au point[3] le BCG (Bacille de Calmette et Guérin), le vaccin contre la tuberculose. En 1894, le docteur Roux met au point un vaccin contre la diphtérie.

De nos jours, l'Institut Pasteur de Paris est célèbre dans le monde entier. En plus du centre de recherches, il a un hôpital pour les maladies infectieuses et un centre d'enseignement[4]. En 1983, c'est à l'Institut Pasteur que le docteur Montagnier a isolé le virus du SIDA (Syndrome Immuno-Déficitaire Acquis). Aujourd'hui, à l'Institut, on continue à faire des recherches pour trouver une cure ou un vaccin contre cette terrible maladie.

[1] reçoit *receives*
[2] concierge *caretaker, concierge*
[3] mettent au point *come out with*
[4] enseignement *teaching*

Laboratoire de culture cellulaire à l'Institut Pasteur

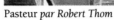

Pasteur *par Robert Thom*

Après la lecture

A **Louis Pasteur.** Copiez ce formulaire (*data sheet*) sur Pasteur et remplissez-le.

NOM
DATES
ÉCOLE
SPÉCIALISATION
SUJET DU RAPPORT EN 1873
DÉCOUVERTE EN 1885

B **Enquête.** Que pensent vos camarades? Quelle est pour eux la plus grande découverte de Pasteur? Pourquoi?

C **Savez-vous que... ?** En France les enfants sont en général vaccinés contre les maladies suivantes: la diphtérie, le tétanos et la poliomyélite (un seul vaccin pour les trois); la tuberculose (le BCG); la coqueluche (*whooping cough*); la rougeole (*measles*); la rubéole (*German measles*) et les oreillons (*mumps*). Les deux premiers vaccins sont obligatoires et les autres sont recommandés. Et dans votre pays? Quels sont les vaccins recommandés?

LETTRES ET SCIENCES 443

---

1. What profession did Pasteur consider before turning to science?
2. What scientific field did Pasteur discover?
3. What vaccine did Pasteur develop?
4. What other vaccines have been developed at the Pasteur Institute?
5. What are the functions of the Pasteur Institute?
6. What virus was first isolated at the Pasteur Institute within the last twenty years?

Après la lecture

PRESENTATION (*page 443*)

You may wish to ask your students the following questions: *Pourquoi est-ce qu'il est important de pasteuriser le lait? D'après vous, est-ce que le SIDA est un grand problème dans votre ville ou dans votre région?*

Vocabulary Expansion

You may wish to have students go through the reading and find words related to the following: **rechercher, une fondation, un malade, une cause, une opération, la lutte, une infection, vacciner, la découverte, construire, collaborer, enseigner.**

ANSWERS

Exercice A

NOM: PASTEUR, Louis
DATES: 1822–1895
ÉCOLE: École Normale
SPÉCIALISATION: Chimie
SUJET DU RAPPORT EN 1873: Les maladies sont causées par des micro-organismes.
DÉCOUVERTE EN 1885: Vaccin contre la rage

Exercice B

Answers will vary.

Exercice C

Tous les vaccins mentionnés dans le paragraphe sont recommandés.

Peinture: Les Impressionnistes
Avant la lecture

PRESENTATION *(page 444)*

A. Go over the *Avant la lecture* activities.

B. Bring in an art book from the library or use Art Transparencies F-7, F-8, and F-9 and show students some paintings by Monet, Renoir, and Degas. Whenever possible, have the students identify the subject of the painting in French.

C. Have students scan the reading for cognates.

Lecture

PRESENTATION *(pages 444–445)*

A. Have students read the selection silently, or break it into parts as suggested in the Cooperative Learning activity below.

B. Tell students to determine what they consider to be the main idea of each section.

PEINTURE: LES IMPRESSIONNISTES

Avant la lecture

1. What does the title of this text refer to?
2. Are any of these paintings familiar to you? Where did you see them?
3. How would you describe them? Realistic? Dreamlike? Colorful?

Lecture

Entre 1870 et 1900, les arts, et en particulier la peinture, commencent à changer. Chaque année, le «Salon» est une grande exposition de peinture. Si les peintres veulent exposer leurs tableaux, ils leur faut être acceptés par un jury.

Nous sommes en 1873. Le jury vient de refuser[1] tout un groupe de jeunes peintres. Ils sont furieux et décident d'avoir leur propre exposition. Elle a lieu[2] en 1874. Le public est scandalisé et crie à la vulgarité: les couleurs sont trop vives, les paysages[3] sont trop «bizarres». Un des tableaux de Monet est intitulé «Impression: soleil levant[4]». De là le terme (péjoratif à l'origine) «les Impressionnistes». Qui sont ces jeunes peintres? En voici trois.

Claude Monet (1840–1926)

Lycéen au Havre, il aime faire les caricatures de ses professeurs sur ses cahiers. Le peintre Eugène Boudin les voit et encourage Monet à faire de la peinture. C'est une révélation pour lui. Il admire les jeux de la lumière[5] sur l'eau, sur tout le paysage. Pour mieux étudier les variations de la forme en fonction de la lumière, il peint le même sujet à différentes heures de la journée. La cathédrale de Rouen est une de ces séries. Il passe la plus grande partie de sa vie dans sa maison de Giverny en Normandie où il reproduit dans son jardin les couleurs de ses tableaux.

Claude Monet: «La Cathédrale de Rouen, le Portail, Harmonie bleue»

COOPERATIVE LEARNING

You may wish to divide the class into four groups. Each group will read one section and report to the other groups about the section they read. The four divisions are: Introduction, Claude Monet, Auguste Renoir, Edgar Degas.

SCIENCES

Auguste Renoir
(1841–1919)
Il commence comme apprenti chez un décorateur de porcelaine à Paris. Il passe ses moments libres au Musée du Louvre où il admire surtout les tableaux du peintre flamand Rubens. Renoir rencontre bientôt Claude Monet, qui l'encourage à peindre avec des couleurs moins sombres. Ils vont ensemble peindre à la campagne. Les Impressionnistes aiment peindre en plein air[6]. Comme tous les Impressionnistes, Renoir reçoit beaucoup de critiques. Il commence à douter, à se demander si les Impressionnistes ont raison[7]. Et pourtant Renoir est le premier Impressionniste reconnu par le public.

Auguste Renoir: «Portrait de Margot»

Edgar Degas (1834–1917)
Son père est un riche banquier qui est amateur d'art. Degas va régulièrement au Louvre où il copie les grands maîtres[8]. Degas aime le théâtre, l'opéra, la vie facile. Il devient ami avec les autres peintres impressionnistes, mais il n'a pas grand-chose en commun avec eux. Il n'aime pas peindre en plein air et il aime peindre des personnages et pas des paysages. On l'appelle souvent «le peintre des danseuses» parce qu'il a peint beaucoup de scènes où on voit des danseuses s'exercer avant le spectacle.

[1] vient de refuser *has just turned down*
[2] a lieu *takes place*
[3] paysages *landscapes*
[4] soleil levant *sunrise*
[5] jeux de la lumière *play of light*
[6] en plein air *outdoors*
[7] ont raison *are right*
[8] maîtres *masters*

Après la lecture

A **Les Impressionnistes.** Dites qui c'est: Monet, Renoir ou Degas.

1. Il aime beaucoup les tableaux de Rubens.
2. Il peint le même sujet à des heures différentes de la journée.
3. Son père est un riche amateur d'art.
4. Il n'aime pas peindre la nature.
5. Il commence par peindre sur de la porcelaine.
6. C'est un de ses tableaux qui leur donne leur nom.
7. Il peint souvent des danseuses.
8. Il aime beaucoup son jardin.

B **Une «Impressionniste» américaine.** Faites un rapport sur la vie et l'œuvre de l'artiste peintre américaine Mary Cassatt (1845–1926).

Edgar Degas: «Dans les coulisses (Danseuses en bleu)»

PRESENTATION (*page 445*)

After going over the *Après la lecture* activities in the textbook, have students tell which artist's paintings they prefer and why.

Vocabulary Expansion

Have students scan the reading and find equivalent expressions for the following:

1. des peintures
2. ne pas accepter
3. enragé
4. les changements
5. personne qui apprend un métier
6. une femme qui danse

ANSWERS
Exercice A

1. Renoir
2. Monet
3. Degas
4. Degas
5. Renoir
6. Monet
7. Degas
8. Monet

Exercice B
Answers will vary.

ADDITIONAL PRACTICE

If any student is particularly interested in art, you may wish to have him/her prepare a short report on one of the other famous French Impressionists or Post-Impressionists: Cézanne, Manet, Pissarro, Renoir, Sisley, Matisse, Toulouse-Lautrec, Gauguin, Seurat, Van Gogh.

Histoire: Trois Explorateurs
Avant la lecture

PRESENTATION *(page 446)*

A. Have students read the *Avant la lecture* information.

B. Have students discuss what they already know from American history about French influence in the United States.

GEOGRAPHY CONNECTION

Have students locate on a map the following places mentioned in the *Lecture*.
France: St-Malo, Rouen.
États-Unis: le Mississippi, le Missouri, les Grands Lacs, l'Illinois, le delta du Mississippi, la Louisiane, Savannah, Saint Louis.
Canada: Terre-Neuve, Québec.

C. Have students look at the map on page 447 and note the routes taken by the three explorers.

Lecture

PRESENTATION *(pages 446–447)*

A. Have students read the *Lecture* or the section assigned to them silently.

B. Ask the following questions about each section:
Section 1 (Cartier): *Où Jacques Cartier est-il né? Quel océan traverse-t-il? Où arrive-t-il? Combien de fois revient-il au Canada?*
Section 2 (La Salle): *Quel est le rêve de La Salle? D'où part son expédition? Quels lacs traversent-ils? Où arrivent-ils?*
Section 3 (Frémont): *Où est-il né? Pourquoi son père vient-il en Amérique? Dans quelle ville Frémont rassemble-t-il ses «voyageurs»? Qui est Kit Carson?*

HISTOIRE: TROIS EXPLORATEURS

Avant la lecture

La Nouvelle-France included territories that covered most of the present-day United States. Although the French presence is not as prevalent as it used to be, it is still very much alive.

Lecture

Jacques Cartier

Robert Cavelier de La Salle

Jacques Cartier

Jacques Cartier est né à Saint-Malo en Bretagne en 1494. C'est une ville de marins[1] qui traversent souvent l'océan Atlantique pour aller pêcher[2]. Jacques Cartier est un marin audacieux, passionné des voyages: de Saint-Malo, il va au Portugal, au Brésil, à Terre-Neuve[3].

En 1534, le roi de France, François 1er, le charge d'une expédition pour découvrir des pays d'Orient où il y a de l'or et des pierres précieuses[4]. Jacques Cartier part avec deux bateaux et 61 marins. Vingt jours après, ils arrivent à Terre-Neuve. C'est un voyage très rapide pour l'époque[5]. Jacques Cartier revient au Canada encore deux fois. La troisième fois, en 1541, il construit un fort qui est devenu une grande ville: Québec.

Robert Cavelier de La Salle

Robert Cavelier de La Salle est le fils d'un riche marchand de Rouen, un grand port de Normandie. La Salle est passionné de l'Amérique et lit tous les rapports des explorateurs qu'il peut trouver. Il rêve[6] de descendre le Mississippi jusqu'au golfe du Mexique. En 1679, il réalise son rêve: il part de Fort Frontenac sur le Saint-Laurent avec six canots qui transportent 23 Français, 18 Indiens, 10 squaws et 3 enfants. Ils traversent les lacs Ontario, Érié, Huron et Michigan. Ils descendent l'Illinois et le Mississippi, et finalement ils arrivent dans le delta du Mississippi en 1682. La Salle prend possession de la région au nom du roi de France et appelle ces nouveaux territoires «La Louisiane» en l'honneur du roi Louis XIV.

John Charles Frémont

John Charles Frémont est né à Savannah en Géorgie en 1813. Son père est un aristocrate français qui est parti en Amérique pendant la Révolution de 1789

COOPERATIVE LEARNING

Divide the class into three groups. Each group reads one part of the *Lecture* and reports to the rest of the class. The three parts of the *Lecture* are: Jacques Cartier, La Salle, and Frémont.

John Charles Frémont

pour échapper à la guillotine. Le jeune Frémont est très intelligent. Il est surtout très bon en mathématiques, mais il aime aussi l'aventure et le danger. Il devient d'abord professeur de maths, mais sur un bateau de guerre[7]. Il devient ensuite l'assistant d'un mathématicien français, Nicolas Nicollet, qui fait le levé topographique[8] des territoires du Nord, entre le Mississippi et le Missouri. Mais à l'époque, c'est la conquête de l'Ouest qui passionne les esprits. Frémont est le candidat idéal pour cette longue route inconnue de plus de 3 500 kilomètres. Frémont rassemble alors à Saint-Louis une équipe de 19 «voyageurs» canadiens qui connaissent bien les fleuves et les forêts. Il est aussi accompagné par un topographe allemand, Preuss, et un guide, Kit Carson. Ils partent en juin 1842. Lorsqu'il revient dans l'Est, il rapporte beaucoup de notes. Sa femme Jessie écrit deux livres d'après ses notes. Les livres sont aussi illustrés de cartes des régions traversées. Ces deux livres font de Frémont et de son guide Kit Carson des héros nationaux et la conquête de l'Ouest est commencée.

[1] marins *sailors*
[2] aller pêcher *to go fishing*
[3] Terre-Neuve *Newfoundland*
[4] de l'or et des pierres précieuses *gold and precious stones*
[5] époque *the times, the age*
[6] rêve *dreams*
[7] guerre *war*
[8] fait le levé topographique *is surveying*

Après la lecture

A **Trois explorateurs.** Vrai ou faux?

1. Jacques Cartier a descendu le Mississippi.
2. Cartier a fondé Québec.
3. Cavelier de La Salle est né en France.
4. Le nom «Louisiane» vient du nom du roi Louis XIV.
5. Le père de Frémont a été guillotiné.
6. Frémont a écrit deux livres.

B **Les voyages des explorateurs.**
Regardez la carte et racontez les voyages des trois explorateurs.

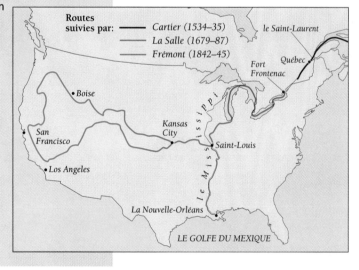

Routes suivies par:
— Cartier (1534–35)
— La Salle (1679–87)
— Frémont (1842–45)

le Saint-Laurent · Québec · Fort Frontenac · Boise · San Francisco · Kansas City · Saint-Louis · Los Angeles · le Mississippi · La Nouvelle-Orléans · LE GOLFE DU MEXIQUE

LETTRES ET SCIENCES   447

CHAPITRE 17

CHAPTER OVERVIEW

In this chapter students will learn to communicate in various types of situations at a hotel. In order to do this they will learn the vocabulary needed to make a reservation, check into a hotel, and check out of a hotel. They will learn the *passé composé* of verbs conjugated with *être* and the indirect object pronouns *lui* and *leur.*

The cultural focus of Chapter 17 is on the many types of hotel accommodations in France.

CHAPTER OBJECTIVES

By the end of this chapter, students will know:

1. vocabulary associated with checking into a hotel, such as requesting different types of accommodations and going through the registration procedure
2. vocabulary associated with checking out of a hotel, as well as hotel features and facilities
3. the formation of the *passé composé* of verbs conjugated with *être*
4. the difference between the use of *avoir* and *être* with certain verbs
5. subject-past participle agreement in the *passé composé* of verbs conjugated with *être*
6. the indirect object pronouns *lui* and *leur*

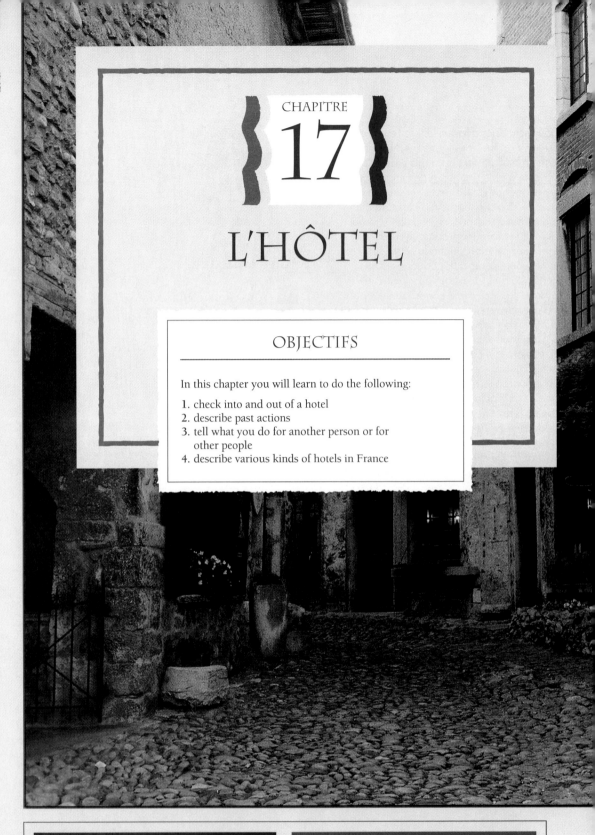

CHAPITRE

17

L'HÔTEL

OBJECTIFS

In this chapter you will learn to do the following:

1. check into and out of a hotel
2. describe past actions
3. tell what you do for another person or for other people
4. describe various kinds of hotels in France

CHAPTER PROJECTS

1. Have students use a Michelin Guide to plan hotel stays in different French cities.
2. Have groups create their own hotel and describe it to the rest of the class, who rate it as to quality, price value, and cuisine.

COMMUNITIES

Go with your class to a local travel agency that specializes in European travel. Have the students listen to a knowledgeable travel agent speak to them about hotels in France and share his/her own (or his/her clients') French hotel experiences. Then have your class compare American and French hotels, based on what they heard.

449

CHAPTER 17 RESOURCES

1. Workbook
2. Student Tape Manual
3. Audio Cassette 10A/CD-11
4. Bell Ringer Review Blackline Masters
5. Vocabulary Transparencies
6. Pronunciation Transparency P-17
7. Grammar Transparencies G-17 (A&B)
8. Communication Transparency C-17
9. Communication Activities Masters
10. Map Transparencies
11. Situation Cards
12. Conversation Video
13. Videocassette/Videodisc, Unit 4
14. Video Activities Booklet, Unit 4
15. Lesson Plans
16. Computer Software: Practice/Test Generator
17. Chapter Quizzes
18. Testing Program
19. Internet Activities Booklet
20. CD-ROM Interactive Textbook

Pacing

This chapter requires eight to ten class sessions. Pacing will vary according to class length and the age and aptitude of the students.

Note The Lesson Plans offer guidelines for 45- and 55-minute classes and **Block Scheduling.**

Exercices vs. *Activités*

All exercises (which provide guided practice) are coded in blue. All communicative activities are coded in red.

INTERNET ACTIVITIES

(optional)

These activities, student worksheets, and related teacher information are in the *Bienvenue* Internet Activities Booklet and on the Glencoe Foreign Language Home Page at: **http://www.glencoe.com/secondary/fl**

DID YOU KNOW?

L'Ostellerie du Vieux-Pérouges, the inn pictured on these pages, is in Pérouges, a perfectly preserved medieval village of crooked, narrow streets, 22 miles from Lyon. The movie of *The Three Musketeers* was filmed in Pérouges. The inn, along with its superb restaurant, is a beautifully restored group of 13th-century timbered buildings.

Bell Ringer Review

Write the following on the board or use BRR Blackline Master 17-1: Think of earlier chapters in your textbook and make a list of places in France you know something about.

PRESENTATION (pages 450–451)

A. Have students close their books. Use Vocabulary Transparencies 17.1 (A & B) to present *Mots 1*. Lead students through the new vocabulary by asking *Qu'est-ce que c'est?* or *Qui est-ce?* and having students repeat the answer. For example: *C'est un hôtel. C'est un escalier. C'est la réceptionniste.*

Teaching Tip You can also use either/or questions to introduce the new vocabulary by contrasting a new item with one known to students. For example: *C'est un ascenseur ou un escalier? (C'est un escalier.)*

B. Now have students open their books and repeat chorally as you model the entire *Mots 1* vocabulary or play Cassette 10A/CD-11.

450

VOCABULAIRE

MOTS 1

À L'HÔTEL

le hall

un escalier

la réception

une porte

la réceptionniste

le réceptionniste

une fiche d'enregistrement

une chambre avec salle de bains

une chambre à un lit

une chambre pour une personne

une chambre qui donne sur la cour

une chambre à deux lits

une chambre pour deux personnes

Lindsay est arrivée à l'hôtel.
Elle est entrée dans le hall.

Elle est allée à la réception.
Elle a montré son passeport à la réceptionniste.
Elle a rempli la fiche d'enregistrement.
La réceptionniste lui a donné la clé.

TOTAL PHYSICAL RESPONSE

(following the Vocabulary presentation)

Getting Ready

Set up places in a hotel, such as *le hall, l'escalier, le couloir, la réception,* and *la chambre.* As props you might use a briefcase as a suitcase, a room key, and a fake passport.

TPR 1

(Student 1) et (Student 2) **venez ici, s'il vous plaît.**
(Student 1), **vous arrivez à l'hôtel.**
(Student 2), **vous êtes le/la réceptionniste.**
(Student 1), **allez à la réception. Demandez une chambre.**
(Student 2), **donnez-lui la fiche d'enregistrement. Demandez son passeport.**
(Student 1), **mettez votre passeport sur le comptoir.**

(continued on next page)

Elle a monté ses bagages.
Elle est montée au troisième étage.
Elle a pris l'ascenseur, pas l'escalier.

Elle a ouvert la porte de sa chambre avec la clé.

Elle est descendue une heure plus tard.

Elle est sortie.

Elle est rentrée à neuf heures du soir.

C. While showing the Vocabulary Transparencies, call on students to read the vocabulary words and sentences in random order. Have other students take turns going to the screen and identifying the appropriate images.
D. Ask *vrai ou faux* questions such as the following: *Le hall est dans le jardin de l'hôtel? La réception est dans le hall? La réceptionniste remplit une fiche d'enregistrement? On peut monter plus vite dans l'ascenseur? Les clients vont à la réception quand ils quittent l'hôtel?*

Vocabulary Expansion

You may wish to give students the following useful expressions they may need at a hotel.
Le petit déjeuner est compris?
Il y a des messages pour moi?
Il y a des lettres pour moi?

TPR (*continued*)
(Student 2), ouvrez son passeport et regardez-le.
(Student 1), signez la fiche d'enregistrement. Donnez la fiche au/à la réceptionniste.
(Student 1), prenez votre passeport. Mettez le passeport dans votre poche.
(Student 2), donnez la clé au client/à la cliente.
(Student 1), prenez vos bagages. Montez l'escalier.

Merci, (Student 1) et (Student 2).

TPR 2
___, venez ici, s'il vous plaît.
Vous êtes touriste. Vous êtes devant la porte de votre chambre dans un hôtel.
Prenez votre clé.
Ouvrez la porte avec la clé.
Prenez vos bagages.
Entrez dans la chambre.

(*continued on next page*)

Exercices

PRESENTATION (pages 452–453)

Extension of *Exercice A*: Speaking

After completing Exercise A, have individual students take turns describing one of the illustrations to the class.

Exercice B

Exercise B prepares students for the *passé composé* with *être*, the grammar topic of this chapter. Note, however, that in the exercise all verb forms are in the third person. Students will learn to manipulate the verbs in the *Structure* section.

Extension of *Exercice B*: Listening

After doing Exercise B as a whole-class activity, focus on the listening skill by having students work in pairs. One partner reads the questions in random order while the other answers with his/her book closed.

Exercice C

You may wish to use the recorded version of this exercise.

ANSWERS

Exercice A

1. C'est un hôtel.
2. C'est la réception.
3. C'est une fiche d'enregistrement.
4. C'est un escalier.
5. C'est une chambre.
6. C'est une chambre à deux lits.
7. C'est une chambre qui donne sur la cour.

Exercice B

1. Oui, Lindsay est arrivée à l'hôtel.
2. Oui, elle est entrée dans le hall.
3. Oui, elle a parlé à la réceptionniste.
4. Oui, elle lui a montré son passeport.
5. Oui, elle a rempli la fiche d'enregistrement.
6. Oui, elle lui a donné la clé.
7. Oui, elle a monté ses bagages.
8. Oui, elle est montée par l'ascenseur.

452

Exercices

A Qu'est-ce que c'est?
Répondez d'après les dessins.

1. C'est un hôtel ou une chambre?

2. C'est la réception ou la réceptionniste?

3. C'est une clé ou une fiche d'enregistrement?

4. C'est un ascenseur ou un escalier?

5. C'est une porte ou une chambre?

6. C'est une chambre à un lit ou à deux lits?

7. C'est une chambre qui donne sur la cour ou sur la rue?

TOTAL PHYSICAL RESPONSE

(continued from page 451)
Mettez vos bagages sur le lit.
Fermez la porte.
Regardez bien la chambre.
Allez dans la salle de bains.
Ouvrez la fenêtre. Regardez dehors.
Indiquez que vous êtes content(e) de votre chambre.
Merci, ____. Vous avez bien fait.

COOPERATIVE LEARNING

Have teams write down a series of events that take place when checking into a hotel. They should be able to mime the events. Each team presents its mime one action at a time. The rest of the class asks them questions to determine what they are doing.

B À l'hôtel. Répondez.

1. Lindsay est arrivée à l'hôtel?
2. Elle est entrée dans le hall?
3. Elle a parlé à la réceptionniste?
4. Elle lui a montré son passeport?
5. Lindsay a rempli la fiche d'enregistrement?
6. La réceptionniste lui a donné la clé?
7. Lindsay a monté ses bagages?
8. Elle est montée par l'ascenseur?
9. La chambre est au troisième étage?
10. C'est une chambre avec salle de bains?
11. Lindsay est descendue une heure plus tard?
12. Elle est sortie?
13. Elle est rentrée à neuf heures du soir?

C Le touriste. Choisissez la bonne réponse.

1. À l'hôtel le touriste remplit ___.
   a. la fiche   **b.** la chambre   **c.** la clé

2. Pour monter dans sa chambre il prend ___.
   a. le lit   **b.** l'ascenseur   **c.** la porte

3. Il ouvre la porte de sa chambre avec ___.
   a. l'escalier   **b.** le lit   **c.** la clé

4. Il prend une douche dans ___.
   a. la salle de bains   **b.** le hall
   c. le petit déjeuner

5. Il dort dans ___.
   a. le lit   **b.** l'escalier
   c. la salle de bains

6. Le matin il se lève et prend ___.
   a. la fiche   **b.** le petit déjeuner
   c. la cour

ALTEA
—— HÔTEL ——

Ne Pas
Déranger

ALTEA
—— HÔTEL ——

PETIT DÉJEUNER
Merci de passer votre commande ce soir.
Bonne nuit.

Le petit déjeuner est servi dans votre chambre de quart d'heure en quart d'heure de 7 heures à 11 heures.
Merci de faire votre choix et suspendre votre fiche à l'extérieur de votre porte.

Chambre N° ____   Signature _____

PETIT DÉJEUNER COMPLET
Jus d'orange, croissant, petit pain, beurre, confiture ou miel, yaourt, fruit ou compote au choix.

❏ THÉ
❏ THÉ CITRON   ❏ DÉCAFÉINÉ
❏ THÉ AU LAIT   ❏ CAFÉ   ❏ CHOCOLAT
                  ❏ CAFÉ AU LAIT ❏ LAIT FROID
                                  ❏ LAIT CHAUD

...us vous suggérons notre petit déjeuner buffet qui vous sera servi au Coffee Shop dès 7 heures 30.

CHAPITRE 17   **453**

9. Oui, la chambre est au troisième étage.
10. Oui, c'est une chambre avec salle de bains.
11. Oui, elle est descendue une heure plus tard.
12. Oui, elle est sortie.
13. Oui, elle est rentrée à neuf heures du soir.

Exercice C

1. a	4. a
2. b	5. a
3. c	6. b

INFORMAL ASSESSMENT
(*Mots 1*)

Check comprehension by mixing true and false statements about the illustrations on pages 450–451. Students respond with «*C'est vrai.*» or «*C'est faux.*»

VOCABULAIRE

MOTS 2

une facture

les frais (m.)

une carte de crédit

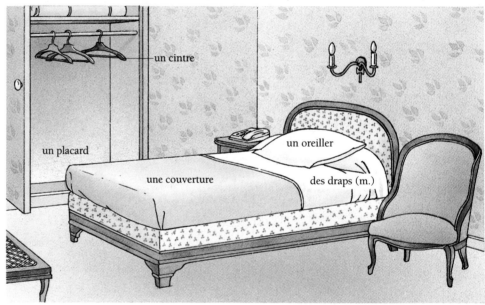

un cintre

un placard

un oreiller

une couverture

des draps (m.)

Vocabulary Teaching Resources

1. Vocabulary Transparencies 17.2 (A & B)
2. Audio Cassette 10A/CD-11
3. Student Tape Manual, Teacher's Edition, *Mots 2: D–F,* pages 189–191
4. Workbook, *Mots 2: D–E,* page 171
5. Communication Activities Masters, *Mots 2: B,* page 82
6. Computer Software, *Vocabulaire*
7. Chapter Quizzes, *Mots 2: Quiz 2,* page 90
8. CD-ROM, Disc 4, *Mots 2:* pages 454–457

Bell Ringer Review

Write the following on the board or use BRR Blackline Master 17-2: Briefly sketch each of the following items: **une clé, un escalier, une fiche d'enregistrement, un lit**

PRESENTATION *(pages 454–455)*

A. Have students close their books Model the *Mots 2* vocabulary using Vocabulary Transparencies 17.2 (A & B) and have students repeat each word or expression twice after you or Cassette 10A/CD-11.

B. Point to the appropriate illustration and ask questions such as: *Qu'est-ce que la cliente lit? Qu'est-ce qu'il y a sur la facture? Avec quoi est-ce que la cliente paie?*

TOTAL PHYSICAL RESPONSE

TPR 1

Getting Ready
Demonstrate the word *expliquer.*
_____, venez ici, s'il vous plaît.
Vous allez quitter l'hôtel.
Allez à la caisse.
Demandez votre facture.
Prenez votre facture.

Regardez et vérifiez les frais.
Il y a quelque chose sur la facture que vous ne comprenez pas. Indiquez le problème au/à la réceptionniste.
Le/La réceptionniste vous l' explique. Vous comprenez. Sortez votre carte de crédit.
Donnez votre carte de crédit au/à la réceptionniste.
Merci, _____. Retournez à votre place.

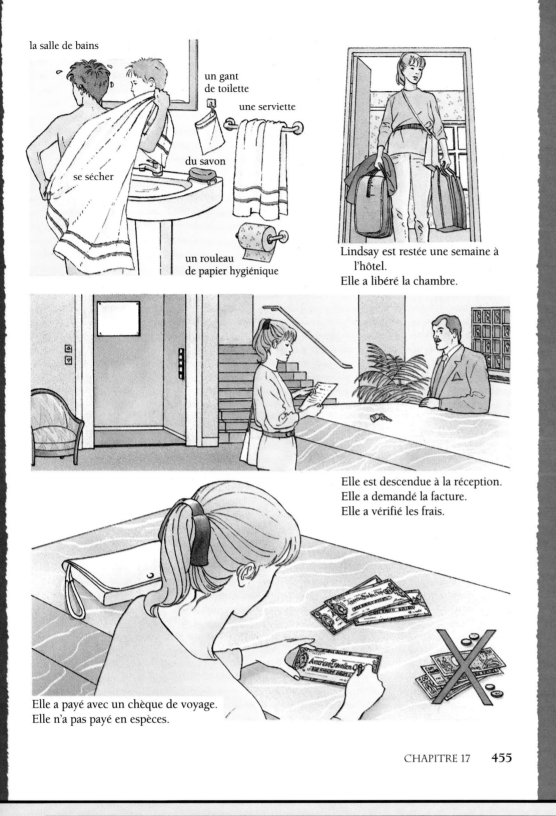

la salle de bains

un gant de toilette

une serviette

du savon

se sécher

un rouleau de papier hygiénique

Lindsay est restée une semaine à l'hôtel.
Elle a libéré la chambre.

Elle est descendue à la réception.
Elle a demandé la facture.
Elle a vérifié les frais.

Elle a payé avec un chèque de voyage.
Elle n'a pas payé en espèces.

C. Using props as cues (a pillow, a wash mitt, soap, a towel, money, etc.), ask students what one needs in order to do various things. For example: *On va prendre une douche. On va prendre un bain. On va se laver la figure. On va se sécher. On va dormir. On va mettre les vêtements dans le placard.*

D. When presenting the sentences on pages 455, ask questions in order to give students the opportunity to use the words. For example: *Lindsay est allée à l'hôtel. Qui est allé à l'hôtel? Où est-elle allée? Elle est restée une semaine à l'hôtel? Combien de temps est-elle restée à l'hôtel? Elle a libéré la chambre? Elle est descendue où? C'est une facture d'hôtel? Qu'est-ce que c'est? Qui a demandé la facture? Elle a demandé la facture à la réception? Où a-t-elle demandé la facture?*

Teaching Tip When asking the questions above, direct the easier questions to the less able students and the more difficult questions to the more able students.

Vocabulary Expansion

You may wish to give students the following useful expressions.
Je voudrais plus de cintres, s'il vous plaît.
Un autre oreiller, s'il vous plaît.
J'ai besoin d'une autre couverture.
Il n'y a pas de savon.
Il n'y a pas de papier hygiénique.

TPR 2
___, venez ici, s'il vous plaît.
Vous êtes dans un hôtel.
Vous êtes dans votre chambre.
Ouvrez la porte du placard.
Prenez un cintre.
Accrochez votre veste.
Mettez-la dans le placard.
Fermez la porte du placard.
Allez à la salle de bains.
Mettez le gant de toilette.
Prenez le savon. Lavez-vous la figure.
Regardez-vous dans la glace.
Prenez une serviette.
Séchez-vous la figure avec la serviette.
Merci, ___. Vous avez très bien fait.
Maintenant retournez à votre place, s'il vous plaît.

PRESENTATION *(page 456)*

Exercice C

🎧 You may wish to use the recorded version of this exercise.

ANSWERS

Exercice A

1. Oui, elle a libéré la chambre.
2. Oui, elle est descendue à la réception.
3. Oui, elle a voulu payer.
4. Oui, elle a demandé la facture.
5. Elle a parlé à la réceptionniste.
6. Oui, elle a vérifié les frais.
7. Non, elle n'a pas payé en espèces.
8. Non, elle n'a pas payé avec une carte de crédit.
9. Elle a payé avec un chèque de voyage.

Exercice B

1. savon, gant de toilette
2. serviette
3. cintres
4. couverture
5. oreillers, oreiller
6. papier hygiénique
7. draps

Exercice C

1. dans la chambre
2. dans le placard
3. à la réception
4. dans la salle de bains
5. à la réception
6. dans la salle de bains
7. dans la chambre
8. dans la chambre
9. dans la salle de bains
10. dans la salle de bains

INFORMAL ASSESSMENT
(Mots 2)

Check for comprehension by having students correct the following statements:
On paie dans la chambre.
Les draps sont dans l'ascenseur.
Il y a un oreiller sur le comptoir.
On se sèche avec du savon.
On vérifie le cintre.
On a libéré le placard.

Exercices

A **Elle a libéré la chambre.** Répondez.

1. Lindsay a libéré la chambre?
2. Elle est descendue à la réception?
3. Elle a voulu payer?
4. Elle a demandé la facture?
5. Elle a parlé au réceptionniste ou à la réceptionniste?
6. Elle a vérifié les frais?
7. Elle a payé en espèces?
8. Elle a payé avec une carte de crédit?
9. Elle a payé la facture comment?

B **J'ai besoin de quoi?** Complétez.

1. Je vais me laver. J'ai besoin de ___ et d'un ___.
2. J'ai pris une douche. Maintenant je vais me sécher. J'ai besoin d'une ___.
3. Je vais mettre ma veste et mon pantalon dans le placard. J'ai besoin de ___.
4. Je vais me coucher mais il fait froid dans la chambre. J'ai besoin d'une autre ___.
5. Je préfère dormir avec deux ___. J'ai besoin d'un autre ___.
6. Ah, zut! J'ai besoin d'un rouleau de ___.
7. La chambre n'est pas prête *(ready)*. Il n'y a pas de ___ sur le lit.

C **À l'hôtel?** Où sont les objets suivants—dans la chambre, dans la salle de bains, dans le placard ou à la réception?

1. l'oreiller
2. le cintre
3. la facture
4. le papier hygiénique
5. la carte de crédit
6. le gant de toilette
7. les draps
8. la couverture
9. le savon
10. la serviette

456 CHAPITRE 17

Activités de communication orale
Mots 1 et 2

L'agent de voyages

A **On prépare un voyage.** You're in a travel agency in Paris to make reservations for a trip you and a friend are planning to take to the Loire Valley. The travel agent is asking you about your preferences.

1. Vous voulez un petit hôtel confortable ou un grand hôtel de luxe?
2. Vous voulez une chambre pour combien de personnes?
3. Vous voulez une chambre avec ou sans salle de bains?
4. Vous allez rester pendant combien de temps? Quelques jours? Une semaine?

B **Comment réserver une chambre.** A family friend has asked you to phone a Montreal hotel to make reservations for her and her husband. You've already jotted down the information you need (see the card below), and now all you have to do is make sure the hotel employee (your partner) gets it right.

C **Quelle catastrophe!** You have just checked into a French hotel that is under new management. When you walk into the room, you find that some things are missing. Call the desk clerk (your partner), give your name and room number, and then tell what's missing and why you need it. He or she will try to resolve the problem. Then reverse roles.

> Élève 1: Bonjour, monsieur (madame). Je m'appelle M. Scott. Je suis dans la chambre 233. Il n'y a pas de draps sur mon lit et je suis très fatigué(e).
> Élève 2: Alors je vous donne des draps tout de suite.

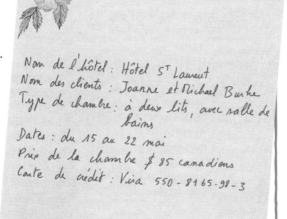

Nom de l'hôtel: Hôtel St Laurent
Nom des clients: Joanne et Michael Burke
Type de chambre: à deux lits, avec salle de bains
Dates: du 15 au 22 mai
Prix de la chambre $85 canadiens
Carte de crédit: Visa 550-8165-98-3

CHAPITRE 17 **457**

Activités de communication orale
Mots 1 et 2

PRESENTATION *(page 457)*

Activité A
In the CD-ROM version, students can interact with an on-screen native speaker.

ANSWERS

Activité A
Answers will vary but may include the following:

1. Je voudrais un petit hôtel confortable (un grand hôtel de luxe).
2. Je voudrais une chambre pour deux personnes.
3. Je voudrais une chambre avec (sans) salle de bains.
4. Nous allons rester (pendant) quelques jours (une semaine, etc.).

Activités B and C
Answers will vary.

Le passé composé avec *être*   *Describing Past Actions*

1. You have already learned that you form the *passé composé* of most verbs with the verb *avoir* and the past participle.

> **Elle a parlé au réceptionniste.**
> **Elle a rempli la fiche.**
> **Elle a demandé la facture.**
> **Elle a vérifié les frais.**

2. With certain verbs, however, you use *être* as the helping verb rather than *avoir.* Many verbs that are conjugated with *être* express motion to or from a place.

arriver	Il est arrivé.	descendre	Il est descendu.
partir	Il est parti.	aller	Il est allé en ville.
entrer	Il est entré.	venir	Il est venu.
sortir	Il est sorti.	revenir	Il est revenu.
monter	Il est monté.	rentrer	Il est rentré.

3. Remember that with the *passé composé* the *ne... pas* goes around the verb *être.*

> **Paul *n*'est *pas* arrivé à l'heure.**
> **Je *ne* suis *pas* sorti.**

4. The past participle of verbs conjugated with *être* must agree with the subject in number (singular or plural) and gender (masculine or feminine). Study the following forms.

MASCULIN	FÉMININ
Je suis sorti.	Je suis sortie.
Tu es sorti.	Tu es sortie.
Il est sorti.	Elle est sortie.
Nous sommes sortis.	Nous sommes sorties.
Vous êtes sorti(s).	Vous êtes sortie(s).
Ils sont sortis.	Elles sont sorties.

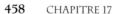

Structure Teaching Resources

1. Workbook, *Structure: A-H,* pages 172–175
2. Student Tape Manual, Teacher's Edition, *Structure: A–B,* pages 191–192
3. Audio Cassette 10A/CD-11
4. Communication Activities Masters, *Structure: A–D,* pages 83-85
5. Computer Software, *Structure*
6. Chapter Quizzes, *Structure:* Quizzes 3–6, pages 91–94
7. CD-ROM, Disc 4, pages 458–465

Bell Ringer Review

Write the following on the board or use BRR Blackline Master 17-4: Complete the following statements.

1. **Sur le lit il y a ___.**
2. **Dans la salle de bains on a besoin ___.**
3. **On peut payer la facture avec ___.**

Le passé composé avec être

PRESENTATION *(page 458)*

A. Have students open their books to page 458. Lead them through steps 1–4. Model the examples and have students repeat chorally.
B. Call on a volunteer to dramatize the verbs listed in step 2.
C. As you write the paradigm in step 4 on the board, you may want to add the endings to the past participle with a different color chalk or underline them for emphasis.

Note: In the CD-ROM version, this structure point is presented via an interactive electronic comic strip.

Exercices

A Un voyage à Avignon. Répondez par «oui».

1. Monique est allée à Avignon?
2. Elle est arrivée à la Gare de Lyon à 10h?
3. Elle est allée sur le quai?
4. Elle est montée en voiture?
5. Le train pour Avignon est parti à l'heure?
6. Le train est arrivé à Avignon à l'heure?
7. Monique est descendue du train à Avignon?
8. Elle est sortie de la gare?
9. Elle est allée à l'hôtel?
10. Elle est entrée dans le hall de l'hôtel?

B À l'école. Donnez des réponses personnelles.

1. Tu es allé(e) à l'école ce matin?
2. Tu es arrivé(e) à l'école à quelle heure?
3. Tu es venu(e) à l'école comment?
4. Tu es entré(e) dans l'école?
5. Tu es allé(e) à ton premier cours?
6. Tu es sorti(e) de l'école à quelle heure hier?
7. Tu es allé(e) manger quelque chose avec tes copains après les cours?
8. Tu es rentré(e) à la maison tout de suite après?

C Au cinéma. Mettez au passé composé.

1. Michel et sa sœur vont au cinéma.
2. Ils partent à l'heure.
3. Ils montent dans le bus.
4. Ils arrivent au cinéma.
5. Ils descendent du bus.
6. Ils vont au guichet.
7. Ils entrent dans le cinéma.
8. Ils sortent du cinéma après le film.
9. Ils vont au café.
10. Ils rentrent chez eux à minuit.

D Qui est sorti? Donnez des réponses personnelles.

1. Le mois dernier, tes copains et toi, vous êtes allés au cinéma?
2. Vous y êtes allés comment? En voiture? En bus?
3. Vous êtes toujours partis à l'heure?
4. Vous êtes arrivés quelquefois en retard?
5. Après le film vous êtes allés manger quelque chose?
6. Vous êtes souvent rentrés chez vous assez tard?

E Un séjour. Complétez au passé composé.

Ce matin Marc ___ (arriver) à Paris avec ses copains. Ils ___ (sortir) de la
                    1   2
gare et ___ (trouver) un taxi. Ils ___ (aller) à l'hôtel. Quand ils ___ (arriver)
          3   4   5
à l'hôtel, ils ___ (entrer) dans le hall. Ils ___ (aller) à la réception et tout
                6   7
le monde ___ (remplir) et ___ (signer) une fiche d'enregistrement. La
           8   9
réceptionniste ___ (donner) les clés à Marc. Marc et ses copains ___ (monter)
                 10   11
au quatrième étage à pied. Ils ___ (prendre) l'escalier. Ils ___ (mettre) leurs
                                 12   13
bagages dans leur chambre et ___ (sortir) tout de suite après.
                               14

Exercices

PRESENTATION (*page 459*)

Exercise C

You may wish to use the recorded version of this exercise.

ANSWERS

Exercice A

Answers are the questions transformed into declarative sentences and preceded by «*oui*».

Exercice B

Answers will vary.

Exercice C

1. Michel et sa sœur sont allés au cinéma.
2. Ils sont partis à l'heure.
3. Ils sont montés dans le bus.
4. Ils sont arrivés au cinéma.
5. Ils sont descendus du bus.
6. Ils sont allés au guichet.
7. Ils sont entrés dans le cinéma.
8. Ils sont sortis du cinéma après le film.
9. Ils sont allés au café.
10. Ils sont rentrés chez eux à minuit.

Exercice D

Answers will vary.

Exercice E

1. est arrivé
2. sont sortis
3. ont trouvé
4. sont allés
5. sont arrivés
6. sont entrés
7. sont allés
8. a rempli
9. a signé
10. a donné
11. sont montés
12. ont pris
13. ont mis
14. sont sortis

F   **Une excursion.**   Mettez au passé composé.

MATHIEU: Tu ___ (aller) en Normandie avec Laure, n'est-ce pas?
THÉRÈSE: Oui, nous y ___ (aller).
MATHIEU: Comment avez-vous trouvé le Mont-Saint-Michel?
THÉRÈSE: C'est vraiment impressionnant. Nous ___ (sortir) de notre petit hôtel à huit heures du matin et nous ___ (arriver) au Mont vers 9h.
MATHIEU: Vous ___ (monter) à la basilique?
THÉRÈSE: Oui, et nous ___ (sortir) sur la terrasse. De là, la vue est superbe.
MATHIEU: Mon frère et moi ___ (aller) au Mont-Saint-Michel l'année dernière et je suis d'accord avec toi—c'est formidable!

Le Mont-Saint-Michel

D'autres verbes avec *être* au passé composé

Describing Past Actions

Although the following verbs do not express motion to or from a place, they are also conjugated with *être*.

rester	Il est resté huit jours.	*He stayed a week.*
tomber	Il est tombé.	*He fell.*
devenir	Il est devenu malade.	*He became sick.*
naître	Elle est née en France.	*She was born in France.*
mourir	Elle est morte en 1991.	*She died in 1991.*

Exercices

A   **Être ou ne pas être.**   Donnez des réponses personnelles.

1. Tu es né(e) quel jour?
2. Tu es né(e) à l'hôpital?
3. Tu es né(e) dans quel hôpital?
4. Ta mère est restée combien de jours à l'hôpital?
5. Où tes parents sont-ils nés?
6. Tu as des grands-parents? Où sont-ils nés?

┌──┐
│ ▉▉▉ **DID YOU KNOW?** │
│   │
│   Ask students to look at the photo on page 460 as you share the following information with them. **On a commencé la construction de l'abbaye de Mont-Saint-Michel au début du 8ème siècle. Les pèlerins (*pilgrims*) sont venus au Mont à toutes les époques. Même aujourd'hui le Mont-Saint-Michel est le site le plus visité de France après Paris et Versailles. L'abbaye est entourée de remparts.** │
│   │
│ **Du haut des remparts il y a une vue splendide sur la baie. Le Mont-Saint-Michel est un îlot, une petite île. Quand la marée (*tide*) est basse, il n'y a pas d'eau dans la baie et on peut aller à pied de la côte jusqu'au Mont. Mais c'est très dangereux à cause des sables mouvants (*quicksand*). Quand la mer monte, elle monte très vite et le Mont-Saint-Michel devient de nouveau un îlot.** │
└──┘

B **Vous êtes maladroit!** Regardez les dessins et dites qui est tombé où.

l'enfant
L'enfant est tombé dans le jardin.

1. tu

2. Michel

3. tes copains

4. nous

5. vous

C **Aux Jeux Olympiques.** Complétez au passé composé.

1. Sophie ___ (aller) à Albertville en France pour participer aux Jeux Olympiques.
2. Elle ___ (rester) quinze jours dans les Alpes.
3. Elle est patineuse. Pendant la compétition elle n'___ pas ___ (tomber).
4. Mais toutes les autres patineuses ___ (tomber).
5. Alors Sophie ___ (gagner) la médaille d'or.
6. Elle ___ (devenir) championne olympique.
7. Après les Jeux elle ___ (rentrer) au Canada où elle ___ (devenir) très célèbre.

CHAPITRE 17 **461**

A. Read the example sentences to the class. After each sentence that has an object, ask: *Qu'est-ce qu'elle a descendu? Quel est l'objet direct? Qu'est-ce que les filles ont monté? Quel est l'objet direct? Qu'est-ce qu'ils ont sorti? Quel est l'objet direct?*

B. Lead students through the explanation on page 462. Use Grammar Transparency G-17(A) to explain more clearly the illustrations on page 462.

C. Now go on to the exercises on page 463.

Le passé composé: *être* ou *avoir*   *Describing Past Actions*

The verbs *descendre, monter, passer, rentrer,* and *sortir* are conjugated with *être* in the *passé composé* when they are not followed by an object. They are conjugated with *avoir*, however, when they are followed by a direct object. Study the following pairs of sentences. Note the differences in meaning.

WITHOUT OBJECT

WITH OBJECT

Elle est descendue.

Elle a descendu *son sac à dos.*

Nous sommes montés au deuxième étage.

Nous avons monté *nos bagages.*

Ils sont sortis hier soir.

Ils ont sorti *leur passeport.*

462   CHAPITRE 17

LEARNING FROM ILLUSTRATIONS

Working in pairs, students write down one question for each illustration on page 462. Then each pair asks their questions of the rest of the class.

Exercices

A **Christine est arrivée.** Répondez par «oui».

1. Christine est arrivée à l'hôtel?
2. Elle est allée à la réception?
3. Elle a sorti son passeport et sa carte de crédit?
4. Elle est montée dans sa chambre?
5. Elle a pris l'escalier?
6. Elle a monté ses bagages?
7. Elle est descendue?
8. Elle est sortie?
9. Elle est allée au musée?
10. Elle est rentrée à l'hôtel à onze heures du soir?

B **En route!** Complétez au passé composé avec «avoir» ou «être».

1. Isabelle et Janine ___ (sortir) de la maison à neuf heures.
2. Elles ___ (sortir) tous leurs bagages sur le trottoir.
3. Elles ___ (attendre) le taxi.
4. Quand le taxi ___(venir), elles ___ (mettre) leurs bagages dans le coffre.
5. Puis les deux filles ___ (monter) dans le taxi.
6. À la gare elles ___ (descendre) du taxi et ___ (descendre) leurs bagages sur le quai.
7. Elles ___ (sortir) leurs billets et ___ (monter) dans le train.

Un hôtel superbe à Tahiti en Polynésie française

CHAPITRE 17   **463**

Exercices

PRESENTATION (*page 463*)

Extension of *Exercice A*

After completing Exercise A, have students do it again, changing the subject in both questions and answers first to *Christine et Chantal* and then to *Ma mère et moi.*

Extension of *Exercice B*: Writing

After completing Exercise B, have students retell the story as a writing assignment.

ANSWERS

Exercice A

1. Oui, elle est arrivée à l'hôtel.
2. Oui, elle est allée à la réception.
3. Oui, elle a sorti son passeport et sa carte de crédit.
4. Oui, elle est montée dans sa chambre.
5. Oui, elle a pris l'escalier.
6. Oui, elle a monté ses bagages.
7. Oui, elle est descendue.
8. Oui, elle est sortie.
9. Oui, elle est allée au musée.
10. Oui, elle est rentrée à onze heures du soir.

Exercice B

1. sont sorties
2. ont sorti
3. ont attendu
4. est venu, ont mis
5. sont montées
6. sont descendues, ont descendu
7. ont sorti, sont montées

THE FRANCOPHONE WORLD

The French artist Paul Gauguin lived and painted in Tahiti in the 1890's. For additional information on French Polynesia and Gauguin, refer students to *Le Monde francophone,* pages 113 and 435.

DID YOU KNOW?

Tahiti, the largest of the islands of French Polynesia, was claimed for France in 1768 by the navigator Bougainville. It became a French *territoire d'outre-mer,* or *T.O.M.,* in 1946. When the HMS *Bounty* visited Tahiti more than 200 years ago, its beauty and its people's hospitality led to the rebellion of the crew: this was the famous mutiny on the *Bounty.*

INDEPENDENT PRACTICE

Assign any of the following:
1. Exercises, page 463
2. Workbook, *Structure: E,* page 173
3. Communication Activities Masters, *Structure: C,* page 85
4. CD-ROM, Disc 4, pages 462–463

Les pronoms lui, leur

PRESENTATION *(pages 464–465)*

A. You may want to write the following sentences on the board. The arrows will help students understand the concept of direct versus indirect objects.

à Gilles.

↑

Il lance → le ballon

à son copain.

↑

Elle donne → l'argent

As students look at these sentences, say: *Remarquez. Il ne lance pas Gilles. Il lance le ballon. Il lance le ballon à qui? Il lance le ballon à Gilles. «Le ballon», c'est l'objet direct. «Gilles», c'est l'objet indirect.*

B. Lead students through steps 1–5 and the accompanying examples on pages 464–465.

Note Be sure students learn that *lui* and *leur* are both masculine and feminine.

C. You may wish to write the example sentences from step 2 on the board and underline the indirect object once and the direct object twice.

D. You may wish to give some additional sentences and have students indicate if the object is direct or indirect. For example: *J'écris une lettre. Une lettre? J'écris à mon ami. Mon ami? Je lis un livre. Un livre? Je lis à mon petit frère. Mon petit frère? J'achète un cadeau. Un cadeau? J'offre le cadeau à ma mère. Ma mère?*

Les pronoms *lui, leur*   *Telling What You Do for Others*

1. *Lui* and *leur* are indirect object pronouns. Observe the difference between a direct object and an indirect object in the following sentences.

Pierre lance *le ballon à Gilles.*

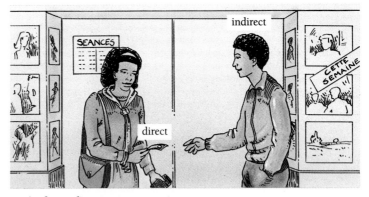

Marie donne *l'argent à son copain.*

In the above sentences, *le ballon* and *l'argent* are direct objects. *Gilles* and *son copain* are indirect objects, introduced by *à*.

2. You use the pronoun *lui* to replace *à* + a person (singular).

Je parle *à Marie.*	Je *lui* parle.
Je parle *à Luc.*	Je *lui* parle.
Il lance le ballon *à l'autre joueur.*	Il *lui* lance le ballon.
Il ne renvoie pas le ballon *à la fille.*	Il ne *lui* renvoie pas le ballon.

3. You use the pronoun *leur* to replace *à* + more than one person.

Je téléphone *à Roger et à Olivier.*	Je *leur* téléphone.
Je téléphone *à Catherine et à Jeanne.*	Je *leur* téléphone.
L'arbitre parle *aux filles.*	L'arbitre *leur* parle.

4. As with other object pronouns, *lui* and *leur* cannot be separated from the verb by a negative word.

Je ne *lui parle* pas.
Il ne *leur téléphone* pas.

5. Remember that in sentences with a verb + infinitive, the pronoun comes right before the infinitive.

Je vais *lui* téléphoner.
Je ne veux pas *leur* offrir de cadeaux.

Exercices

A **Guy offre un cadeau.** Récrivez les phrases d'après le modèle.

Guy offre un cadeau *à sa nouvelle amie française.*
Guy lui offre un cadeau.

1. Guy offre un cadeau *à Danielle.*
2. Il donne le cadeau *à Danielle* au restaurant.
3. Elle est contente. Elle dit «merci» *à Guy.*
4. Elle téléphone *à sa copine Sandrine* pour décrire le cadeau.
5. Danielle dit *à sa copine*: «Guy est sympa, n'est-ce pas?»
6. Sandrine répond *à Danielle*: «Oh, oui, c'est un garçon vraiment chouette!»

B **Un match de foot.** Complétez avec «lui» ou «leur».

1. Il lance le ballon à Gilles?
   Oui, il ___ lance le ballon.
2. Les joueurs parlent à l'arbitre?
   Oui, ils ___ parlent.
3. Et l'arbitre parle aux joueurs?
   Oui, il ___ parle.
4. L'arbitre explique les règles aux joueurs?
   Oui, il ___ explique les règles.
5. L'employée au guichet parle à un spectateur?
   Oui, elle ___ parle.
6. Le spectateur pose une question à l'employée?
   Oui, il ___ pose une question.
7. L'employée vend des billets aux spectateurs?
   Oui, elle ___ vend des billets.

C **Personnellement.** Répondez en utilisant «lui» ou «leur».

1. Tu parles à tes professeurs?
2. Tu dis «bonjour» à ton professeur de français?
3. Tu vas téléphoner à tes copains ce week-end?
4. Tu aimes parler à tes copains au téléphone?
5. Tu parles souvent à tes copains?
6. Tu vas écrire à ta grand-mère?
7. Tu écris souvent à ta grand-mère?

CHAPITRE 17   **465**

CONVERSATION

CONVERSATION

Bell Ringer Review

Write the following on the board or use BRR Blackline Master 17-7: Write these sentences in the passé composé.

1. Martine et Corinne vont au lycée.
2. Elles rencontrent leurs amies.
3. Elles parlent au prof de français.
4. Elles n'arrivent pas à l'heure.

PRESENTATION (page 466)

A. Tell students they will hear a conversation between Linda and a hotel receptionist.

B. Have students open their books to page 466 and watch the Conversation Video, or you may read them the conversation or play Cassette 10A/ CD-11. (Use *Activité D* in the Student Tape Manual to check oral comprehension.)

Note In the CD-ROM version, students can play the role of either one of the characters and record the conversation.

ANSWERS

Exercice A

1. Elle veut une chambre pour deux personnes.
2. Elle parle à la réceptionniste.
3. Oui, elle a réservé une chambre.
4. Elle lui a montré sa confirmation.
5. Elle est au troisième étage.
6. Non, elle donne sur la cour.
7. C'est une chambre à deux lits.
8. Oui, la chambre à une salle de bains privée.
9. C'est 350 francs.
10. Il est compris.

Scènes de la vie   *À la réception de l'hôtel*

LINDA: Bonjour, Madame. J'ai réservé une chambre pour deux personnes.
LA RÉCEPTIONNISTE: C'est à quel nom, s'il vous plaît?
LINDA: Au nom de Collins.
LA RÉCEPTIONNISTE: Vous avez votre confirmation?
LINDA: Oui, je l'ai. La voilà. (*Elle lui montre sa confirmation.*)
LA RÉCEPTIONNISTE: Merci. J'ai une très jolie chambre au troisième qui donne sur la cour.
LINDA: C'est une chambre à deux lits?
LA RÉCEPTIONNISTE: Oui, avec salle de bains.
LINDA: C'est combien, la chambre?
LA RÉCEPTIONNISTE: Trois cent cinquante francs. Et le petit déjeuner est compris. Voilà votre clé.

A **Une jolie chambre d'hôtel.**   Répondez d'après la conversation.

1. Linda veut une chambre pour combien de personnes?
2. Elle parle à qui?
3. Elle a réservé une chambre?
4. Qu'est-ce qu'elle a montré à la réceptionniste?
5. La chambre est à quel étage?
6. Elle donne sur la rue?
7. C'est une chambre à combien de lits?
8. La chambre a une salle de bains privée?
9. C'est combien la chambre?
10. Le petit déjeuner est compris ou pas?

CRITICAL THINKING ACTIVITY

(Thinking skill: evaluating consequences)
Put the following on the board or on a transparency.

1. **Voyager avec beaucoup d'argent en espèces, ce n'est pas une bonne idée. Pourquoi?**
2. **Est-ce qu'il y a des avantages à payer avec une carte de crédit?**

Prononciation   *Les sons /ó/ et /ò/*

It is important to make a clear distinction between the closed sound /ó/ as in *mot* and the open sound /ò/ as in *sort*. Repeat the following pairs of words.

nos / note   mot / mort   dôme / dort   beau / bonne

Now repeat the following sentences.

> Claude ne dort pas beaucoup.
> Paul sort beaucoup trop.
> Il n'y a pas d'eau chaude dans la chambre 14.

Hôtel de Bordeaux

Activités de communication orale

A   **Au voleur!**   Imagine that one of the rooms in your hotel in Paris was burglarized. The house detective (your partner) asks you and all the other guests what you did from the time you left your room this morning until the time you returned this afternoon. Give a full account of your activities.

> Élève 1: À quelle heure est-ce que vous êtes sorti(e) de votre chambre?
> Élève 2: À dix heures et demie.

B   **Qu'est-ce qu'on fait pour toi?**   Think of a friend or family member you like very much. What does this person do for you? What do you do for him or her? Use the following verbs.

acheter	écrire	préparer
apprendre	faire	répondre
dire	parler	servir
donner	poser des questions	téléphoner

> Mon amie Sylvie me téléphone presque tous les soirs… Moi, je lui écris des lettres pendant les vacances…

C   **Une enquête: Tu es né(e) quand?**   Divide into groups and choose a leader. The leader finds out when group members were born and then tells the class who is the oldest and the youngest in the group.

> Élève 1: Judy, tu es née quand?
> Élève 2: Je suis née le 17 août 1985…
> Élève 1 (*à la classe*): Judy est née le 17 août 1985. Meredith est née le 30 janvier 1986. Judy est la plus âgée et Meredith est la plus jeune de notre groupe.

CHAPITRE 17   **467**

INDEPENDENT PRACTICE

1. Exercise and activities, pages 466–467
2. Workbook, *Un Peu Plus,* pages 176–177
3. CD-ROM, Disc 4, pages 466–467

Prononciation

PRESENTATION (*page 467*)

A. Model the key words *Hôtel de Bordeaux* and have students repeat chorally.
B. Now model the other words and sentences similarly.
C. You may wish to give students the following *dictée:*
   Je vais au beau château.
   Beaucoup de mots sont beaux.
   Nous avons reçu nos notes.
   Elle dort sous le dôme.
D. For additional practice, you may use Cassette 10A/CD-11: *Prononciation,* Pronunciation Transparency P-17, and the Student Tape Manual, Teacher's Edition, *Activités E–G,* pages 193–194.

Activités de communication orale

ANSWERS

Activités A, B, and C
Answers will vary.

CROSS-CULTURAL COMPARISON

Bed and breakfast places have become very popular in the United States in recent years. They offer homey accommodations and family-style breakfasts, where the guests (and sometimes the hosts) eat together. Guests are usually lodged in a wing of the hosts' own home, which is often a restored example of vintage architecture. American bed and breakfast places are not cheap, and it is usually less expensive (but also less interesting) to stay in a motel.

The French have had the bed and breakfast idea for centuries in the form of the *pension.* In a *pension,* the guests also often stay in the host's own home and take their meals together. One advantage of the *pension* over the American bed and breakfast is that it offers the same character for much less money.

READING STRATEGIES
(page 468)

Pre-Reading

Have students look at the Michelin Guide hotel rating system on page 471, the hotel ads on page 472, or if possible, bring in any literature you have from French or French-Canadian hotels. Discuss ratings, accommodations, and prices with students.

Reading

Call on individuals to read. After each student has read several sentences, ask comprehension questions before going on.

Post-Reading

Ask students if American towns have any organizations resembling the *syndicat d'initiative*. What are they?

Note Students may listen to a recorded version of the *Lecture* on the CD-ROM.

Étude de mots

ANSWERS

Exercice A

Answers will vary but may include any five of the following: **arrivée, descendues, train, syndicat, initiative, tourisme, touristes, chambre, hôtel, réservé, avance, employée, problème, téléphoné, confortable, minutes, bagages, visiter**

Exercice B

1. c
2. e
3. d
4. b
5. a

468

LECTURE ET CULTURE

L'HÔTEL DE LA GARE

Monique est arrivée avec quelques copines à Nice. Elles sont descendues du train et sont allées tout de suite au syndicat d'initiative. Le syndicat d'initiative est un bureau de tourisme qui se trouve souvent dans les gares ou près des gares. Les touristes vont au syndicat d'initiative pour trouver une chambre d'hôtel dans la ville où ils sont arrivés, s'ils n'ont pas réservé de chambre à l'avance.

Monique a expliqué à l'employée du syndicat d'initiative que ses copines et elle sont étudiantes. Elles ne veulent pas aller dans un hôtel de grand luxe qui coûte très cher. Pas de problème: l'employée a téléphoné à l'Hôtel de la Gare où elle a réservé une chambre pour les filles. L'Hôtel de la Gare est un hôtel confortable mais pas trop cher. Et il est où, l'Hôtel de la Gare? En face de[1] la gare, bien sûr! Il y a un Hôtel de la Gare dans beaucoup de villes en France.

Monique et ses copines sont sorties de la gare, elles ont traversé la rue et sont arrivées à l'hôtel en deux minutes. Elles ont rempli les fiches d'enregistrement et ont monté leurs bagages à la chambre. Elles sont redescendues tout de suite après et sont allées visiter la ville de Nice.

[1] en face de   *across from*

Hôtel - Restaurant de la Gare
Mʳ OBERHAUSSER
Place de la Gare
54120
BACCARAT
☎ 83 75 12 24

Étude de mots

A **Le français, c'est facile.** Trouvez cinq mots apparentés dans la lecture.

B **C'est-à-dire…** Trouvez les mots ou expressions qui correspondent.

1. le syndicat d'initiative
2. réserver
3. expliquer
4. les bagages
5. cher

a. qui coûte beaucoup
b. les sacs à dos, les valises
c. un bureau de tourisme
d. dire
e. louer à l'avance

468   CHAPITRE 17

CRITICAL THINKING ACTIVITY

(Thinking skill: making inferences)

Read the following or write it on the board or on an overhead transparency:

«À Rome il faut vivre comme les Romains.» C'est un proverbe célèbre. Expliquez le proverbe. Qu'est-ce qu'il veut dire? Ensuite, imaginez que vous êtes en France. Dites ce que vous allez faire pour suivre la philosophie de ce proverbe.

468

Compréhension

C Un séjour à Nice. Répondez.

1. Monique et ses copines sont arrivées où?
2. Elles sont allées à Nice comment?
3. Quand elles sont arrivées à la gare, où sont-elles allées?
4. Pourquoi sont-elles allées au syndicat d'initiative?
5. L'employée du syndicat d'initiative a téléphoné à quel hôtel?
6. Où est l'hôtel?
7. Les filles sont allées à l'hôtel?
8. Elles sont allées à l'hôtel à pied, en autobus ou en taxi?
9. Qu'est-ce qu'elles ont fait quand elles sont arrivées à l'hôtel?
10. Qu'est-ce que le syndicat d'initiative?
11. Qu'est-ce que vous avez appris au sujet des hôtels de la Gare?

DÉCOUVERTE CULTURELLE

En France les hôtels sont classés par le Ministère du Tourisme selon leur confort et leur luxe.

★★★★ L	HÔTEL DE GRAND LUXE
★★★★	HÔTEL DE PREMIÈRE CLASSE, TOUT CONFORT
★★★	HÔTEL TRÈS CONFORTABLE
★★	HÔTEL CONFORTABLE
★	HÔTEL AU CONFORT MOYEN, SIMPLE MAIS CONVENABLE[1]

LIGUE FRANÇAISE POUR LES AUBERGES DE LA JEUNESSE
38, Bd RASPAIL 75007 PARIS
TÉL. (1) 45 48 69 84
FAX 45 44 57 47

Quelle catégorie d'hôtel est la plus chère? Et la moins chère?

En France, il y a beaucoup de pensions qui sont souvent très agréables. Une pension est un hôtel simple à caractère familial.

Les jeunes qui voyagent en France aiment aller dans des auberges de jeunesse[2]. Les auberges de jeunesse ont des dortoirs[3] et ne coûtent pas très cher. Beaucoup de randonneurs[4] et cyclistes louent une chambre (ou un lit) dans une de ces auberges, qui se trouvent souvent près des villes. Les jeunes voyageurs les aiment beaucoup parce que dans les auberges de jeunesse ils peuvent faire la connaissance de[5] jeunes gens qui viennent de beaucoup de pays différents.

[1] moyen… convenable *moderately priced, no-frills hotel*
[2] auberges de jeunesse *youth hostels*
[3] dortoirs *dormitories*
[4] randonneurs *hikers*
[5] faire la connaissance de *meet*

Compréhension

ANSWERS

Exercice C

1. Elles sont arrivées à Nice.
2. Elles y sont allées en train.
3. Elles sont allées au syndicat d'initiative.
4. Elles y sont allées pour trouver une chambre d'hôtel.
5. Elle a téléphoné à l'Hôtel de la Gare.
6. Il est en face de la gare.
7. Oui, elles y sont allées.
8. Elles y sont allées à pied.
9. Elles ont rempli les fiches d'enregistrement.
10. C'est un bureau de tourisme.
11. Il y a un Hôtel de la Gare dans beaucoup de villes françaises. Ils sont confortables mais pas trop chers.

OPTIONAL MATERIAL

Découverte culturelle

PRESENTATION *(page 469)*

A. Before reading the selection, focus on the topic by asking students about their own hotel experiences. Can anyone tell about a stay in a foreign hotel? Has anyone ever stayed in a youth hostel, either in the United States or abroad? What are they like?

B. Have students read the information silently.

Note Students may listen to a recorded version of the *Découverte culturelle* on the CD-ROM.

DID YOU KNOW?

French youth hostels used to provide basic comfort at a very moderate price. Most had dormitories with several beds. One could bring a sleeping bag to avoid the cost of sheets. Some hostels provided low-cost meals. Others had kitchens where guests could fix their own meals. Unfortunately, the French government had to close them down in 1996 owing to the increase in drug trafficking in youth hostels.

COOPERATIVE LEARNING

Have students work in groups of three. Tell them: *Chacun d'entre vous a 1 500 dollars et un mois de vacances. Vous allez passer le mois en France. Préparez votre voyage. Ensuite, vous allez comparer vos itinéraires. Décidez qui a préparé le voyage le plus intéressant. Expliquez pourquoi.*

Bell Ringer Review

Write the following on the board or use BRR Blackline Master 17-9: Make up a question about each statement using <u>qui</u> or <u>quoi</u>. For example: *Nous allons <u>chez Jacques</u>. Nous allons chez qui?*

1. Papa parle <u>de nos vacances.</u>
2. On va faire du ski <u>avec nos cousins.</u>
3. Tu vas rester <u>chez ta sœur?</u>
4. Tu viens <u>avec nous?</u>
5. Tu as besoin <u>d'un anorak?</u>

OPTIONAL MATERIAL

PRESENTATION
(pages 470–471)

A. You may have students guess the meaning of the Michelin Guide's hotel categories (Photo 4). (In the English-language Michelin hotel-restaurant guide, *Luxe* is translated as "Luxury in the traditional style;" *Grand confort* = "Top class comfort;" *Très confortable* = "Very comfortable;" *De bon confort* = "Quite comfortable"; and *Simple mais convenable* = "Simple comfort.") As for the restaurant categories, explain to students that *la table* is the way the Guide refers to the food served by the restaurant. It does not mean "the table." Here are the categories with their English equivalents: *La table vaut le voyage* = "Exceptional cuisine, worth a special journey" *La table mérite un détour* = "Excellent cooking, worth a detour" *Une très bonne table* = "A very good restaurant in its category" *Repas soigné à prix modérés* = "Good food at moderate prices."

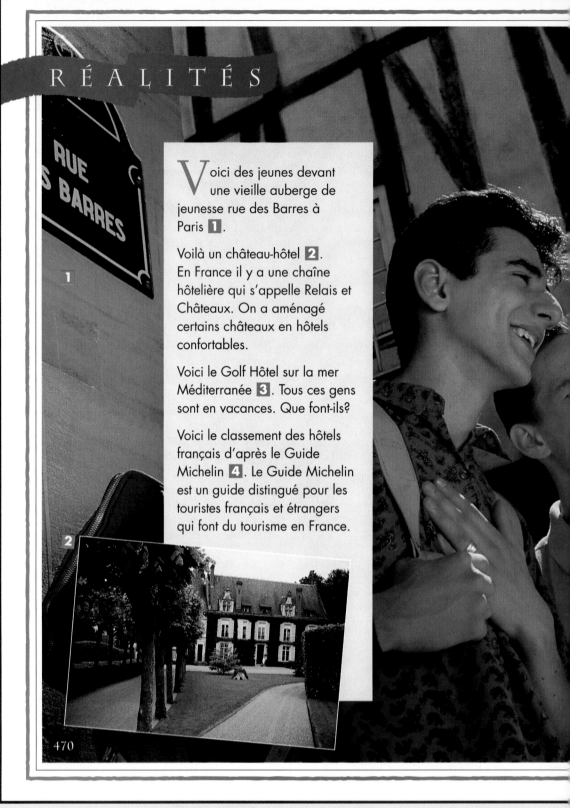

oici des jeunes devant une vieille auberge de jeunesse rue des Barres à Paris **1**.

Voilà un château-hôtel **2**. En France il y a une chaîne hôtelière qui s'appelle Relais et Châteaux. On a aménagé certains châteaux en hôtels confortables.

Voici le Golf Hôtel sur la mer Méditerranée **3**. Tous ces gens sont en vacances. Que font-ils?

Voici le classement des hôtels français d'après le Guide Michelin **4**. Le Guide Michelin est un guide distingué pour les touristes français et étrangers qui font du tourisme en France.

470

DID YOU KNOW?

Usually, breakfast is included in the price of a room in a French hotel. It is a continental breakfast with a choice of hot tea, coffee, or hot chocolate, a croissant, and bread. The breakfast is served in a small room on the ground floor. If the hotel does not have such a room, breakfast is brought up to the room.

LEARNING FROM PHOTOS

Have students look at the hotels on pages 470–471 and decide what rating they think each would receive.

MICHELIN

	Grand luxe	
	Grand confort	
	Très confortable	
	De bon confort	
	Assez confortable	
	Simple mais convenable	

	La table vaut le voyage
	La table mérite un détour
	Une très bonne table
Repas	Repas soigné à prix modérés 100/130
	Petit déjeuner
enf. 55	Menu enfant

471

B. Call on volunteers to read the captions on page 470 and answer any questions students may have about the captions or the photographs.
C. Share with students any photos or memorabilia you may have from your own hotel stays in France.

Note In the CD-ROM version, students can listen to the recorded captions and discover a hidden video behind one of the photos.

COOPERATIVE LEARNING

1. Use Communication Transparency C-17 to review winter weather and ski vocabulary as well as the hotel vocabulary of this chapter.
2. Students work in groups of five to make up the conversations of the people in the bottom illustration.

ADDITIONAL PRACTICE

1. Student Tape Manual, Teacher's Edition, *Deuxième Partie,* pages 195–198
2. Situation Cards, Chapter 17

CULMINATION

RECYCLING

The *Activités de communication orale* and *Activités de communication écrite* afford students the opportunity to further practice the *passé composé* and chapter vocabulary associated with hotels and traveling. Material presented in earlier chapters is recycled.

INFORMAL ASSESSMENT

Both oral activities can be used as a means to assess speaking skills. Oral Activity A offers guided cues for those students who need practice structuring questions and answers. Oral Activity B asks students to synthesize the material offered in the hotel ads into their own personal presentations. To measure speaking ability you may use the evaluation criteria given on page 34 of this Teacher's Wraparound Edition.

Activités de communication orale

ANSWERS

Activité A

Answers will vary but may include the following constructions:

1. Tu es allé(e) où pour tes vacances?
2. Quand est-ce que tu es allé(e)… ?
3. Tu y es allé(e) avec qui?
4. Tu as (Vous avez) fait quelles activités pendant tes (vos) vacances?

Activité B

Answers will vary.

Activités de communication écrite

ANSWERS

Activités A, B, and C

Answers will vary.

Activités de communication orale

A **Des vacances formidables.** Using the following question words and phrases, ask your partner about a great vacation he or she once had. Then reverse roles.

1. où
2. quand
3. avec qui
4. quelles activités

B **Allons en France.** Your partner is planning a trip to France and is going to stay in one of the hotels pictured below. Ask your partner which of the hotels he or she prefers and why. Then reverse roles.

Hôtel de Paris

**34, boulevard d'Alsace
Cannes, Côte d'Azur**

45 chambres de 250 à 580F
Petit déjeuner 35F en salle,
50F en chambre par personne

*Hôtel de grand confort en ville.
Près de la mer. Chambres avec
télé couleurs, radio, salles de
bains. Jardin avec piscine.*

Hôtel Idéal Mont Blanc

**Combloux
Haute-Savoie**

Ouvert: été et hiver
26 chambres de 310 à 365F
Petit déjeuner 37F
Demi-pension 277F
Pension complète 322 F

*Chalet grand confort dans les
Alpes. Séjour idéal pour les
sports d'été ou d'hiver.*

Auberge de Combreux

**Combreux
Val de Loire**

21 chambres de 210 à 350 F
Petit déjeuner 30F
Demi-pension 280F

*Auberge pleine de charme en
forêt, près des châteaux de la
Loire. À l'hôtel vélo, tennis,
piscine, practice de golf.*

Hostellerie du Châteaux d'Agneaux

**Avenue Sainte-Marie
Agneaux, Normandie**

12 chambres de 300 à 600F
Petit déjeuner 37F
Demi-pension 450F
Pension 550F

*Trente km. de la plage. Sur la
route du Mont-St.-Michel.
Confort, calme avec tennis et
sauna.*

Activités de communication écrite

A **Une publicité.** Write an ad for a hotel (real or imaginary) using the ads above as a guide.

FOR THE YOUNGER STUDENT

Have students draw a picture of a hotel. Then have them write a brief description of it.

LEARNING FROM REALIA

Have students look at the hotels in the ads and say as much about each of the hotels as they can. You may also wish to have them pick out one hotel and write a description of it.

B **Mon journal intime.** Write a diary entry describing your activities last weekend.

C **Une vie antérieure.** Imagine you lived in another century. Write a short paragraph telling where and when you were born and died.

Réintroduction et recombinaison

A **Les loisirs culturels.** Donnez des réponses personnelles.

1. Tu es sorti(e) le week-end dernier ou tu es resté(e) à la maison?
2. Si tu es sorti(e), avec qui es-tu sorti(e)?
3. Tu es allé(e) au cinéma le mois dernier?
4. Tu as vu quel film? Avec quels acteurs?
5. Tes copains et toi, avez-vous déjà visité un musée? Quel musée?
6. Vous avez admiré quels peintres ou quels sculpteurs?
7. Tu connais la Statue de la Liberté? Tu sais dans quelle ville des États-Unis elle est?
8. Si tu vas en France qu'est-ce que tu veux visiter?
9. Tu veux voir une pièce à la Comédie-Française? Quel genre de pièce, une comédie ou une tragédie?
10. Si tu vas voir un film étranger, tu préfères le voir doublé ou en version originale avec des sous-titres?

Vocabulaire

NOMS
l'hôtel (m.)
le hall
l'escalier (m.)
la réception
le/la réceptionniste
la personne
la fiche d'enregistrement
la facture
les frais (m.)
la carte de crédit
le chèque de voyage

la chambre
   à un lit
   à deux lits
la porte
le placard
le cintre
les draps (m.)

la couverture
l'oreiller (m.)
la salle de bains
le savon
le gant de toilette
la serviette
le rouleau de papier hygiénique

VERBES
monter
montrer
réserver
tomber
se sécher
mourir
naître

AUTRES MOTS ET EXPRESSIONS
donner sur
libérer la chambre
payer en espèces

Hôtel **★★** NN
BELLEVUE
Françoise et Jean Pierre CHODORGE
RESTAURANT - LOGIS DE FRANCE
Restaurant plein air - Salle de réunion
Repas de groupe - Service traiteur
Fermeture hebdomadaire le mercredi (hors saison)
55120 CLERMONT EN-ARGONNE TÉL. 29 87 41 02

CHAPITRE 17   **473**

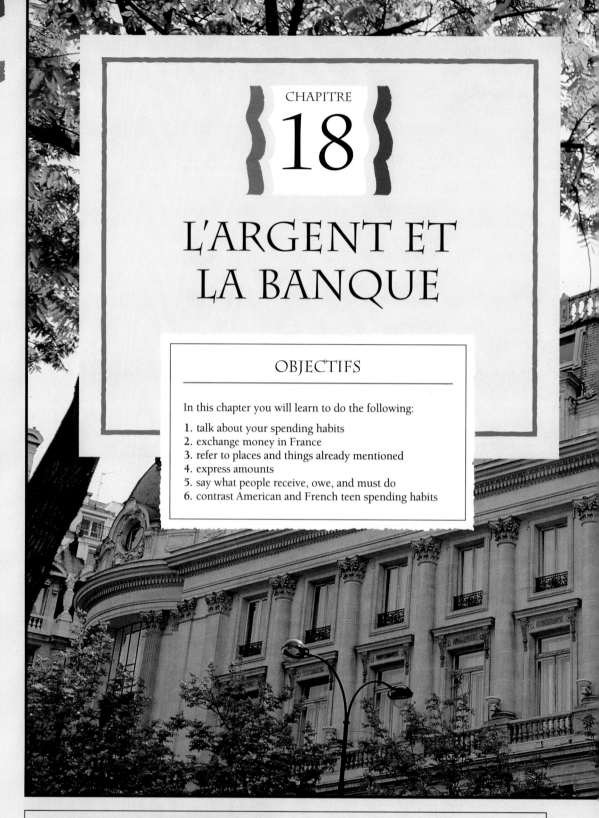

CHAPITRE 18

CHAPITRE

18

L'ARGENT ET LA BANQUE

OBJECTIFS

In this chapter you will learn to do the following:

1. talk about your spending habits
2. exchange money in France
3. refer to places and things already mentioned
4. express amounts
5. say what people receive, owe, and must do
6. contrast American and French teen spending habits

CHAPTER OVERVIEW

In this chapter students will learn to exchange money and carry out simple financial and banking transactions. In order to do this, they will learn vocabulary associated with money and money matters such as currency exchange, savings accounts, and checks. Students will learn the pronouns *y* and *en* and the irregular verbs *devoir* and *recevoir*.

The cultural focus of this chapter is on foreign currencies and French spending habits, particularly those of teens.

CHAPTER OBJECTIVES

By the end of this chapter, students will know:

1. vocabulary associated with making change, exchanging money, opening a savings account, and paying by check
2. vocabulary needed to discuss borrowing and lending money as well as personal budgeting
3. formal and familiar expressions used to talk about money
4. the uses and the position of the pronouns *y* and *en*
5. the differences between *y*, *lui*, and *leur*
6. the present tense and *passé composé* forms of the verbs *recevoir* and *devoir*
7. the meanings of *devoir* and the use of *devoir* with an infinitive

---

CHAPTER PROJECTS

(optional)

1. Check the newspaper for the exchange rates of French francs and those of other countries. Keep track of the rates throughout the chapter.
2. Have students draw up a personal budget and keep a diary of their expenditures while you work on the chapter. At the end of the chapter have them write or tell about what they may have learned about themselves from doing this.
3. If it is available, pass around some real French money or refer students to the photos on pages 9 and 478.

475

CHAPTER 18 RESOURCES

1. Workbook
2. Student Tape Manual
3. Audio Cassette 10B/CD-11
4. Bell Ringer Review
   Blackline Masters
5. Vocabulary Transparencies
6. Pronunciation
   Transparency P-18
7. Communication
   Transparency C-18
8. Communication Activities
   Masters
9. Map Transparencies
10. Situation Cards
11. Conversation Video
12. Videocassette/Videodisc,
    Unit 4
13. Video Activities Booklet,
    Unit 4
14. Lesson Plans
15. Computer Software:
    Practice/Test Generator
16. Chapter Quizzes
17. Testing Program
18. Internet Activities Booklet
19. CD-ROM Interactive
    Textbook

Pacing

This chapter requires eight to ten class sessions. Pacing will vary according to class length and the age and aptitude of the students.

Note The Lesson Plans offer guidelines for 45- and 55-minute classes and **Block Scheduling**.

Exercices vs. *Activités*

All exercises (which provide guided practice) are coded in blue. All communicative activities are coded in red.

INTERNET ACTIVITIES

(optional)
These activities, student worksheets, and related teacher information are in the *Bienvenue* Internet Activities Booklet and on the Glencoe Foreign Language Home Page at: **http://www.glencoe.com/secondary/fl**

DID YOU KNOW?

You may wish to give students the following information: *Le Crédit Lyonnais est une grande banque commerciale française. Le Crédit Lyonnais a des succursales* (branch offices) *aux États-Unis.* Ask: *C'est quel drapeau? De quelles couleurs est-il?*

Bell Ringer Review

Write the following on the board or use BRR Blackline Master 18-1: Write down a suggestion you might make to a friend who is going with you to each of the following places. Use the *nous* form of the imperative.

1. au restaurant   3. au concert
2. en classe   4. à la plage

PRESENTATION *(pages 476–477)*

A. Show Vocabulary Transparencies 18.1 (A & B). Point to each item and have the class repeat after you or Cassette 10B/CD-11.
B. Ask *Qu'est-ce que c'est?* as you point to an item and call on an individual to respond.
C. After going over the vocabulary, have students open their books and read the words and sentences. Ask questions such as: *Sylvie est allée où? Qu'est-ce qu'elle a ouvert? Elle a versé combien d'argent sur son compte?*
D. Show students some French bills and coins or refer them to the photos on pages 9 and 478.

VOCABULAIRE

MOTS 1

de l'argent liquide

un billet

une pièce

de la monnaie

un sac

un portefeuille

un porte-monnaie

Tu as de la monnaie?

Oui, j'en ai.

Tu peux me faire de la monnaie?

Oui, je peux.

une poche

TOTAL PHYSICAL RESPONSE

(following the Vocabulary presentation)

Getting Ready

Set up a mock bank counter. Dramatize the terms *rendre* and *compter.*

TPR 1

___, venez ici, s'il vous plaît.
J'espère que vous avez un peu d'argent sur vous. Vous en avez ou pas? (If the student has no money, lend him/her some.)
Bon. Montrez-moi votre poche (sac).
Sortez votre portefeuille de votre poche (sac).
Montrez-moi un billet.
Montrez-moi une pièce.
Mettez votre argent dans votre portefeuille.
Mettez le portefeuille dans votre poche (sac).
Très bien, ___, et merci. Retournez à votre place, s'il vous plaît.

À LA BANQUE

un chèque (bancaire)

signer un chèque

toucher un chèque

SOCIÉTÉ NATIONALE

--- 39418 ---   3180

SYLVIE VIDAL
75 BOULEVARD DU TEMPLE
75010   PARIS

RELEVÉ DE COMPTE
11345800PT03941
code banque
3003
code guichet
03182
numéro de compte
0048039532

DATE	NATURE DE L'OPÉRATION	DÉBIT	CRÉDIT	VALEUR
2802	VIREMENT ÉPARGNE DECLIC	2802	608,00	010392

* * * * * * * * * * * * * * * * *
* CE RELEVÉ CONCERNE VOTRE *
*   CODEVI   *
* * * * * * * * * * * * * * * * *

NOUVEAU SOLDE   2.618.12

un relevé de compte d'épargne

Sylvie est allée à la banque.
Elle a ouvert un compte d'épargne.
Elle a versé de l'argent sur son compte.

AU BUREAU DE CHANGE

ÉTATS UNIS 5,00 F
ITALIE
ALLEMAGNE
JAPON

le cours du change

la monnaie
française

Steve est allé au bureau de change.
Il y est allé pour changer de l'argent.
Il a changé de l'argent?
Oui, il en a changé.
Il a donné des dollars.
Et il a reçu des francs français.

CHAPITRE 18   477

RETEACHING (*Mots 1*)

After completing the vocabulary presentation, you may wish to call on students to look at the illustrations and say as much as they can about them.

CROSS-CULTURAL COMPARISON

In France there are coins for denominations as high as 20 francs. Since this results in more coins to be carried, it is common for French people— including men—to carry a coin purse rather than carry coins in their pockets.

Vocabulary Expansion

You may wish to give students the following additional vocabulary about money and banking.

un centime
retirer de l'argent de son compte
endosser un chèque
le taux d'intérêt

TPR 2

_____, venez ici, s'il vous plaît.
Hier, vous êtes allé(e) à la banque.
Entrez dans la banque.
Faites la queue devant la caisse.
Signez deux chèques de voyage.
Donnez les chèques au caissier/à la caissière.
Le caissier/La caissière vous donne des francs français.
Prenez-les.

Comptez-les.
Vous voulez de la monnaie. Donnez un billet au caissier/à la caissière.
Il/Elle vous donne des pièces. Comptez les pièces.
Merci, _____. C'est tout. Retournez à votre place, s'il vous plaît.

Exercices

Exercices

PRESENTATION (pages 478–479)

Extension of *Exercice B*

After going over the exercise in class, call on a student to retell the information in his/her own words.

Extension of *Exercice C*

After going over Exercise C, have a student tell about his/her personal money habits.

ANSWERS

Exercice A

1. C'est un chèque bancaire.
2. C'est de l'argent liquide.
3. C'est une pièce.
4. C'est un porte-monnaie.
5. C'est un sac.
6. C'est un bureau de change.
7. Elle touche le chèque.
8. On fait de la monnaie.

A **Qu'est-ce que c'est?** Identifiez.

2. C'est de l'argent liquide ou un chèque de voyage?

1. C'est un chèque bancaire ou une carte de crédit?

4. C'est un portefeuille ou un porte-monnaie?

5. C'est un sac ou une poche?

3. C'est un billet ou une pièce?

7. Elle signe le chèque ou elle touche le chèque?

6. C'est une banque ou un bureau de change?

8. On fait de la monnaie ou on change de l'argent?

ADDITIONAL PRACTICE

1. After completing Exercises A, B, and C, have students make up original sentences dealing with money transactions.
2. Student Tape Manual, Teacher's Edition, *Activités B–C*, page 200.

B **Au bureau de change.** Répondez.

1. Où est-ce que Steve est allé?
2. Il a de la monnaie américaine ou de la monnaie française?
3. Il a changé de l'argent?
4. Il a changé combien de dollars?
5. Quel est le cours du change?
6. Steve a reçu combien de francs pour ses dollars?

C **Mon argent.** Donnez des réponses personnelles.

1. Tu as de l'argent sur toi?
2. Tu as combien d'argent sur toi?
3. Tu mets ton argent dans ton portefeuille?
4. Tu mets des pièces ou des billets dans ton portefeuille?
5. Tu mets les pièces dans un portefeuille, dans un porte-monnaie ou dans ta poche?
6. Ton portefeuille est dans ta poche ou dans ton sac?
7. En général, tu paies en espèces, par chèque ou avec une carte de crédit?
8. Tu as un compte d'épargne?
9. Tu regardes ton relevé de compte chaque mois?
10. Tu verses de l'argent sur ton compte?

VOTRE BANQUE CONFORTABLEMENT CHEZ VOUS

BNP

Tous vos comptes en direct sur Minitel

TELESERVICE BNP

ODYSSEE
LE COMPTE DES 13-18 ANS

LA POSTE
BOUGEZ AVEC LA POSTE

Exercice B

1. Il est allé au bureau de change.
2. Il a de la monnaie américaine.
3. Oui, il a changé de l'argent.
4. Il a changé cinquante dollars.
5. Le dollar est à cinq francs.
6. Il a reçu deux cent cinquante francs.

Exercice C

Answers will vary but may include the following constructions:

1. Oui, j'ai de l'argent. (Non, je n'ai pas d'argent.)
2. J'ai ___ dollars et ___ cents.
3. Oui, je le mets dans mon portefeuille.
4. Je mets des billets dans mon portefeuille.
5. Je les mets dans ma poche (mon portefeuille/porte-monnaie).
6. Il est dans mon sac (ma poche).
7. En général, je paie en espèces (par chèque/avec une carte de crédit).
8. Oui (Non), j'ai un (je n'ai pas de) compte d'épargne.
9. Oui (Non), je (ne) le regarde (pas) chaque mois.
10. Oui (Non), je verse de l'argent (je ne verse pas d'argent) sur mon compte.

RETEACHING *(Mots 1)*

Place props and pictures from the *Mots 1* presentation in a bag. Have students draw one item from the bag and repeat the corresponding word or phrase.

INDEPENDENT PRACTICE

Assign any of the following:
1. Exercises, pages 478–479
2. Workbook, *Mots 1: A–B,* page 179
3. Communication Activities Masters, *Mots 1: A,* pages 86–87
4. CD-ROM, Disc 4, pages 476–479

Bell Ringer Review

Write the following on the board or use BRR Blackline Master 18-2: In French, write at least three different ways you can earn some extra money.

PRESENTATION *(pages 480–481)*

A. Have students close their books. Present the *Mots 2* vocabulary by showing Vocabulary Transparencies 18.2 (A & B) and having students repeat the items chorally after you or Cassette 10B/CD-11.

B. As you present the sentences on page 480, break them into parts. For example: *de côté* (wave your hand to the side); *de l'argent* (as you point to the money in the illustration); *Elle aime mettre* (no comprehension problems since the words are not new). Now put the sentence together. *Elle aime mettre de l'argent de côté.* You may then want to ask: *Qu'est-ce qu'elle met de côté? Qui aime mettre de l'argent de côté?*

VOCABULAIRE

MOTS 2

Voici Lise.
Elle aime mettre de l'argent de côté.
Elle ne dépense pas tout son argent.
Elle fait des économies.

Et voilà Denis.
Denis n'a pas d'argent.
Il est fauché.
Il veut emprunter de l'argent à Lise.

Tu peux me prêter de l'argent?

Oui, je peux te prêter de l'argent.
Tu en veux combien?

480   CHAPITRE 18

TOTAL PHYSICAL RESPONSE

(following the Vocabulary presentation)

Getting Ready

Have students use their own money or give them play money. Demonstrate *vide*.

TPR

(Student 1) et (Student 2), **venez ici, s'il vous plaît.**
(Student 1), **vous êtes fauché(e).**
Montrez vos poches vides à (Student 2).
Demandez-lui de l'argent.
(Student 2), **sortez votre portefeuille.**
Sortez des billets.
Prêtez les billets à (Student 1).
(Student 1), **mettez les billets dans votre poche.**
(Student 1), **vous êtes content(e).**
Dites «merci» à (Student 2).
Serrez-lui la main.

Denis rembourse Lise.
Il lui rend son argent.

Note: Here are some informal words referring to money.

le fric	l'argent
50 balles	50 francs
Il est fauché.	Il n'a pas d'argent.
Il a plein de fric.	Il a beaucoup d'argent.

C. When presenting the vocabulary on page 481, you may wish to have two students (who like to act) present the mini-conversation to the class. They can use a great deal of expression.

CROSS-CULTURAL COMPARISON

The words *fric, balle(s),* and *fauché(e)* are used in everyday informal speech by people of all ages. You may wish to point out to students that many languages have lots of slang expressions for money. Have them think of some in English.

Vocabulary Expansion

You may wish to give students the following popular expressions about money.
Il n'a pas un sou.
Il n'a pas un rond.
Il roule sur l'or.
Il jette son argent par les fenêtres.
Il est près de ses sous.

COOPERATIVE LEARNING

Have students work in groups and make up a skit based on the mini-conversation on page 481.

ADDITIONAL PRACTICE

1. Have students look at pages 480–481. Give them sentences such as the following and have them find the opposite. *Lise dépense tout son argent. Denis a beaucoup d'argent. La jeune fille fait des économies. Denis prête de l'argent à Lise. Il a plein de fric.*
2. Student Tape Manual, Teacher's Edition, *Activité E,* page 202.

PRESENTATION (page 482)

Exercice A

Exercise A gives students practice in receptive comprehension.

Extension of *Exercice B*

After completing the exercise, call on one student to give all the information in his/her own words.

Extension of *Exercice C*

You may wish to have the students dramatize the mini-conversation in Exercise C using the informal language.

Exercice D: **Vocabulary Expansion**

Exercise D gives students practice in developing vocabulary building techniques.

ANSWERS

Exercice A

1. Denis	5. Denis
2. Lise	6. Denis
3. Lise	7. Lise
4. Lise	8. Denis

Exercice B

Answers will vary.

Exercice C

… de l'argent

… de l'argent … je n'ai jamais d'argent

… francs

… beaucoup d'argent

… francs

Exercice D

1. d	5. g
2. f	6. e
3. a	7. c
4. h	8. b

INFORMAL ASSESSMENT
(*Mots 2*)

Check for understanding by making true and false statements about the *Mots 2* vocabulary. Students correct false statements and respond with *«C'est vrai»* for true ones. For example: *Denis a toujours beaucoup d'argent. C'est Lise qui est toujours fauchée. Lise n'a pas d'argent. Lise prête de l'argent à Denis. Denis rembourse Lise.*

Exercices

A **C'est qui?** Décidez si c'est Lise ou Denis.

1. Il/Elle dépense tout son argent.
2. Il/Elle met de l'argent de côté.
3. Il/Elle fait des économies.
4. Il/Elle a un compte d'épargne.
5. Il/Elle est toujours fauché(e).
6. Il/Elle emprunte de l'argent à un(e) ami(e).
7. Il/Elle prête de l'argent.
8. Il/Elle rembourse l'argent qu'il/elle emprunte.

B **L'argent et toi!** Donnez des réponses personnelles.

1. Tu travailles?
2. Tu gagnes de l'argent? Tu as de l'argent de poche?
3. Qu'est-ce que tu fais pour gagner de l'argent? Tu travailles dans le jardin des voisins? Tu laves des voitures? Tu gardes des enfants? Tu aides ton père ou ta mère?
4. Tu dépenses tout ton argent de poche ou tu en mets de côté?
5. Tu as un compte d'épargne? Dans quelle banque?
6. De temps en temps, tu empruntes de l'argent à tes parents?
7. Quand tu dois de l'argent à tes parents, tu les rembourses toujours?
8. Tu leur rends vite l'argent?

C **Un peu d'argot.** Dites la même chose d'une autre manière.

DAVID: Tu as *du fric?*
MARIE: Tu me demandes si j'ai *du fric.* Tu sais bien que *je suis toujours fauchée.*
DAVID: Et tu me dois cinquante *balles.*
MARIE: Oui, je sais. Mais tu n'en as pas besoin. Tu as *plein de fric.*
DAVID: C'est pas la question.
MARIE: D'accord. Je te rends les cinquante *balles* demain.

D **Quel est le nom?** Choisissez le mot qui correspond.

1. épargner	a. le versement
2. économiser	b. le remboursement
3. verser	c. le prêt
4. changer	d. l'épargne
5. dépenser	e. l'emprunt
6. emprunter	f. des économies
7. prêter	g. la dépense
8. rembourser	h. le change

ADDITIONAL PRACTICE

After completing the exercises and activities on pages 482–483, have students role-play exchanging currency. Put some realistic exchange rates on the board for two or three currencies. (These are available in major newspapers.) Have some play money ready in the various currencies or use handwritten cards or pieces of paper. Assign some students to work as "exchange agents" who deal with one kind of currency. Distribute various amounts of play dollars to the rest of the students, who will exchange it for the currency they want. When all the money has been exchanged, have students reverse roles.

Note You may wish to write on the board a few key sentences necessary for the transactions until students become familiar with the language. You can also use slips of paper at the booths as mock exchange receipts, which "customers" must sign.

Activités de communication orale

Mots 1 et 2

A **Ton argent et toi.** The French exchange student at your school, Yves Clemenceau, wants to know about American teens and money. Answer his questions.

Yves Clemenceau

1. Tu travailles pour gagner de l'argent?
2. Tes parents te donnent de l'argent de poche?
3. Qu'est-ce que tu achètes avec ton argent?
4. Tu peux mettre de l'argent de côté?

B **Au bureau de change.** You're at a foreign exchange office in France and want to change 50 dollars into francs. Find out the exchange rate from the teller (your partner). The teller asks you if you have traveler's checks or cash. If you have traveler's checks, you'll have to sign them. You'll also have to show the teller your passport.

C **Quel cours du change!** You and your partner are French tourists visiting the U.S. You'd like to buy a few gifts for your friends and family. Make a list of the items you want and their price in dollars. Your partner will help you figure out how much each of your gifts costs in francs. (The exchange rate is five francs to the dollar.) When you've gone through your list, reverse roles.

> Élève 1: Je voudrais acheter une cassette pour ma sœur. Ça coûte 9 dollars. Ça fait combien en francs?
> Élève 2: Ça fait 45 francs.

D **Un petit problème.** You'd like to buy your mother a birthday present, but you can't afford it at the moment. Your friend (your partner) might be able to help you out. Try to convince your partner to lend you the money.

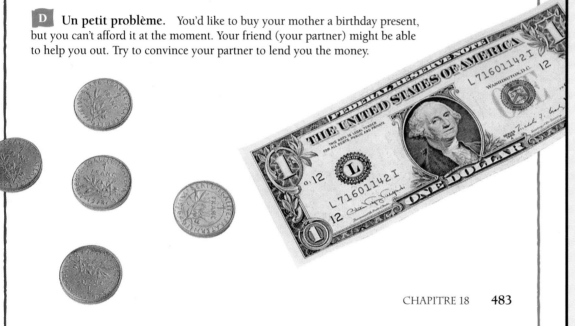

Activités de communication orale

Mots 1 et 2

PRESENTATION *(page 483)*

Activité A

 In the CD-ROM version, students can interact with an on-screen native speaker.

ANSWERS

Activité A

Answers will vary but may include the following:

1. Oui (Non), je (ne) travaille (pas) pour gagner de l'argent.
2. Oui (Non), mes parents me donnent de l'argent (ne me donnent pas d'argent) de poche.
3. J'achète des compact discs (des vêtements, etc.) avec mon argent.
4. Oui (Non), je peux mettre de l'argent (je ne peux pas mettre d'argent) de côté.

Activité B

Answers will vary but may include the following:

É1: Bonjour, Monsieur/Madame, je voudrais changer cinquante dollars en francs français. Quel est le cours du change aujourd'hui?

É2: Le dollar est à cinq francs. Avez-vous de l'argent liquide ou des chèques de voyage?

É1: J'ai des chèques de voyage.

É2: Signez les chèques, s'il vous plaît, et montrez-moi votre passeport.

Activité C

Answers will vary.

Activité D

Answers will vary.

STRUCTURE

STRUCTURE

Structure Teaching Resources

1. Workbook, *Structure: A–G*, pages 180–183
2. Student Tape Manual, Teacher's Edition, *Structure: A–F*, pages 203–205
3. Audio Cassette 10B/CD-11
4. Communication Activities Masters, *Structure: A–F*, pages 89–92
5. Computer Software, *Structure*
6. Chapter Quizzes, *Structure: Quizzes 3–7*, pages 97–101
7. CD-ROM, Disc 4, pages 484–491

Bell Ringer Review

Write the following on the board or use BRR Blackline Master 18-4: List at least five ways you spend money in any given week.

Le pronom y

PRESENTATION *(page 484)*

A. Briefly review the use of the pronoun *y* with *aller*, taught in Chapter 5, page 133.
B. Lead students through steps 1–3 on page 484. In steps 2 and 3, have one student read the questions on the left and another respond with the sentences on the right.
C. You may wish to write example sentences on the board. Underline the expression replaced by *y*. Circle *y* and draw a line to it from the expression it replaces.
D. Now lead students through step 4.

| *Le pronom y* | *Referring to Places Already Mentioned* |

1. You have already used the pronoun *y* with the verb *aller* to refer to a place just mentioned. *Aller* cannot stand alone.

> **Tu vas au restaurant?**
> **Oui, j'y vais.**
> **On y va ensemble?**

2. You also use the pronoun *y* to replace any location introduced by *à* or another preposition.

Tu vas *à Paris*?	**Oui, j'y vais.**
Henri monte *en haut de la Tour Eiffel*?	**Oui, il y monte.**
Il est *à l'Hôtel Racine*?	**Oui, il y est.**
Il veut entrer *dans l'hôtel*?	**Oui, il veut y entrer.**
Tu veux aller *en France*?	**Oui, je veux y aller.**
Ils peuvent dîner *chez leurs amis*?	**Oui, ils peuvent y dîner.**

3. With the *passé composé*, *y* comes before the helping verb.

Ils sont entrés *dans le musée*?	**Oui, ils y sont entrés.**
Elle est montée *au troisième étage*?	**Oui, elle y est montée.**
Elle a vu de beaux tableaux *au musée*?	**Oui, elle y a vu de beaux tableaux.**

4. Note the placement of *y* in negative sentences.

PRÉSENT	**Je n'*y* vais pas.**
VERBE + INFINITIF	**Je ne vais pas y *aller*.**
PASSÉ COMPOSÉ	**Je n'*y* suis pas allé(e).**

La fondation Vasarely à Aix-en-Provence

484   CHAPITRE 18

ADDITIONAL PRACTICE

After completing Exercises A, B, and C, have students tell about a trip they took. They should mention the place by name in the first sentence and use *y* in succeeding ones. For example: *L'année dernière je suis allé à New York. J'y suis allé avec ma famille. Nous y sommes allés en avion. Nous y sommes restés deux semaines,* etc.

DID YOU KNOW?

You may wish to tell students that Vasarely was a 20th-century artist of Hungarian origin who specialized in op art of the type shown in the photo.

Exercices

A **Au gymnase.** Répétez la petite conversation.

BÉATRICE: Tu vas au gymnase?
HÉLÈNE: Oui, j'y vais tous les samedis.
BÉATRICE: Ton copain y va aussi?
HÉLÈNE: Oui, il y va aussi. Il y va souvent.

B **On y va?** Répondez d'après les dessins en utilisant «y».

1. David est allé au bureau de change?
2. Il est allé au bureau de change le matin?
3. Il est allé au bureau de change pour changer de l'argent?
4. Il est arrivé au bureau de change avant l'ouverture?
5. Il a attendu devant le bureau?
6. Il a attendu cinq minutes devant le bureau?
7. Quand le bureau a ouvert, David est entré dans le bureau?
8. Il a fait la queue devant la caisse?

C **À l'école.** Donnez des réponses personnelles en utilisant «y».

1. Tu vas à l'école tous les jours?
2. Tu prépares tes leçons à la maison?
3. Tu parles français au cours de français?
4. Tu parles français au cours d'anglais?
5. Tu attends tes amis dans la cour?
6. Tu mets tes livres dans ton sac à dos?
7. Tu vas à l'école à pied?
8. Tu aimes aller chez tes copains après les cours?
9. Tu veux aller chez eux aujourd'hui?

CHAPITRE 18 **485**

INDEPENDENT PRACTICE

Assign any of the following:
1. Exercises, page 485
2. Workbook, *Structure: A,* page 180
3. Communication Activities Masters, *Structure: A,* page 89
4. CD-ROM, Disc 4, pages 484–485

Exercices
PRESENTATION
Exercice A
You may wish to use the recorded version of this exercise.

ANSWERS
Exercice A
Students repeat the mini-conversation.

Exercice B
1. Oui, il y est allé.
2. Oui, il y est allé le matin.
3. Oui, il y est allé pour changer de l'argent.
4. Oui, il y est arrivé avant l'ouverture.
5. Oui, il y a attendu.
6. Oui, il y a attendu cinq minutes.
7. Oui, quand le bureau a ouvert, il y est entré.
8. Oui, il y a fait la queue.

Exercice C
Answers will vary but may include the following:
1. Non, je n'y vais pas tous les jours.
2. Oui (Non), j'y (je n'y) prépare (pas) mes leçons.
3. Oui, j'y parle français.
4. Non, je n'y parle pas français.
5. Oui (Non), j'y (je n'y) attends (pas) mes amis.
6. Oui (Non), j'y (je n'y) mets (pas) mes livres.
7. Oui (Non), j'y (je n'y) vais (pas) à pied.
8. Oui (Non), j'aime (je n'aime pas) y aller.
9. Oui (Non), je (ne) veux (pas) y aller aujourd'hui.

INFORMAL ASSESSMENT
Check for understanding by asking questions that would elicit a natural negative response. Ask each question three times: once in the present, once in the *passé composé,* and once in the *futur proche.* For example: *Tu vas à l'école en taxi? (Non, je n'y vais pas en taxi.) Tu y es allé(e) en taxi la semaine dernière? (Non, je n'y suis pas allé[e] en taxi la semaine dernière.) Tu vas y aller en taxi demain? (Non, je ne vais pas y aller en taxi demain.)*

Bell Ringer Review

Write the following on the board or use BRR Blackline Master 18-5: Write down several reasons why it is a good idea to have a savings account.

Y, lui *ou leur*

PRESENTATION *(page 486)*

A. Lead students through steps 1 and 2 on page 486.

B. On the board, write original sentences with prepositional phrases or indirect objects with *à*. Call on students to come to the board and rewrite the sentences using the appropriate pronoun.

Exercices

ANSWERS

Exercice A

1. Oui, il y a téléphoné.
2. Oui, il y a répondu.
3. Oui, il y a obéi.
4. Oui, il y a réussi.
5. Oui, il y a participé.

Exercice B

1. y
2. leur
3. y
4. lui
5. leur
6. lui
7. y

Y, *lui* ou *leur*   *Referring to People and Things Already Mentioned*

1. You also use the pronoun *y* to replace *à* + a thing.

Georges répond *à la lettre?*	Oui, il y répond.
Anne a répondu *au téléphone?*	Non, elle n'y a pas répondu.

2. If the preposition *à* is followed by a person, you use *lui* or *leur,* not *y.*

Georges répond *à Marie.*	Il *lui* répond.
Anne a répondu *à ses amis.*	Elle *leur* a répondu.

Exercices

A **Il a téléphoné.** Répondez en utilisant «y».

1. Paul a téléphoné à l'hôtel?
2. Paul a répondu à la question?
3. Il a obéi à la règle?
4. Paul a réussi à l'examen?
5. Paul a participé au match?

B **Y, *lui* ou *leur?*** Complétez.

1. Tu as répondu à la lettre?
   Oui, j'___ ai répondu.
2. Tu as répondu à tes cousins?
   Oui, je ___ ai répondu.
3. Sa sœur a répondu à une petite annonce? Oui, elle ___ a répondu.
4. Elle a répondu à sa mère?
   Oui, elle ___ a répondu.
5. Elle a téléphoné à ses copains?
   Oui, elle ___ a téléphoné.
6. Tes copains et toi, vous avez obéi au professeur? Oui, nous ___ avons obéi.
7. Vous avez obéi aussi aux règles de l'école? Oui, nous ___ avons obéi.

COOPERATIVE LEARNING

Have students form teams of four. Call two members from each team to the board. Dictate a sentence that contains a prepositional phrase with *à* or an indirect object. One team member writes the sentence, and the other rewrites it using *lui, leur,* or *y.* Repeat the procedure with the third and fourth members of each team.

LEARNING FROM PHOTOS

1. The bulletin board has various jobs posted. Ask students to see how many words they can identify.
2. Ask students what Olivier Calendini teaches.

Le pronom *en*

Referring to Things Already Mentioned

1. You use the pronoun *en* to replace a noun that is introduced by *de* or any form of it: *du, de l', de la, des.*

Vous avez *de la monnaie?*	Oui, j'en ai.
	Non, je n'en ai pas.
Richard veut *de l'argent?*	Oui, il en veut.
	Non, il n'en veut pas.
Il va changer *des francs?*	Oui, il va en changer.
	Non, il ne va pas en changer.
Il a besoin *d'argent?*	Oui, il en a besoin.
	Non, il n'en a pas besoin.
Il a parlé *de ses finances?*	Oui, il en a parlé.
	Non, il n'en a pas parlé.
Il est venu *de la banque?*	Oui, il en est venu.
	Non, il n'en est pas venu.
Il y a *des bureaux de change en ville?*	Oui, il y en a.
	Non, il n'y en a pas.

Bell Ringer Review

Write the following on the board or use BRR Blackline Master 18-6: Rewrite the following sentences, replacing the pronoun *y* with a prepositional phrase that makes sense.

1. **Mes amis y vont souvent.**
2. **Nous y restons tous les ans pendant trois semaines.**
3. **Mon père y a fait un voyage.**
4. **Les élèves y apprennent beaucoup.**

Le pronom en

PRESENTATION *(page 487)*

Have students open their books to page 487. Lead them through the explanation. Read the questions on the left and have the students read the response with *en* in unison.

Note In the CD-ROM version, this structure point is presented via an interactive electronic comic strip.

DID YOU KNOW?

French bills are printed in green, brown, blue, purple, and yellow. On them are Saint-Exupéry, the 20th-century author; Berlioz and Debussy, the 19th-century composers; Delacroix, the 19th-century painter; Quentin de La Tour, the 18th-century painter; Voltaire and Montesquieu, the 18th-century authors (the latter is on the 200-franc note shown in the photo), et al.

INDEPENDENT PRACTICE

Assign any of the following:
1. Exercises, page 486
2. Workbook, *Structure: B,* pages 180–181
3. Communication Activities Masters, *Structure: B,* page 89
4. CD-ROM, Disc 4, page 486

Exercices

PRESENTATION *(page 488)*

Exercice A

 You may wish to use the recorded version of this exercise.

Extension of *Exercice A:* Speaking

After completing Exercise A, ask additional questions that name foods not included in the picture. Students respond using *en* in negative sentences.

Extension of *Exercice B:* Speaking/Listening

After completing Exercise B, have pairs ask the questions of other pairs in random order, so *nous* and *vous* forms can be practiced.

ANSWERS

Exercice A

1. Oui, elle en sert.
2. Oui, elle en sert.
3. Oui, elle en sert.
4. Non, elle n'en sert pas.
5. Non, elle n'en sert pas.
6. Non, elle n'en sert pas.
7. Oui, elle en sert.
8. Non, elle n'en sert pas.

Exercice B

1. Oui (Non), j'en (je n'en) ai (pas).
2. Oui (Non), j'en (je n'en) ai (pas).
3. Oui (Non), j'en (je n'en) reviens (pas).
4. Oui (Non), j'en (je n'en) ai (pas).
5. Oui (Non), j'en (je n'en) ai (pas).
6. Oui (Non), j'en (je n'en) ai (pas) besoin.
7. Oui (Non), je (ne) veux (pas) en gagner.
8. Oui (Non), j'en (je n'en) parle (pas).
9. Oui (Non), j'en (je n'en) ai (pas) emprunté à mes parents.
10. Oui (Non), j'en (je n'en) ai (pas) prêté à mes amis.

Exercices

A **La fête de Laurence.** Répondez d'après le dessin.

Laurence sert du coca?
Oui, elle en sert.

1. Elle sert de l'eau minérale?
2. Elle sert des sandwichs?
3. Elle sert de la pizza?
4. Elle sert de la salade?
5. Elle sert du fromage?
6. Elle sert des chocolats?
7. Elle sert de la glace?
8. Elle sert de la mousse au chocolat?

B **Oui, j'en ai.** Donnez des réponses personnelles en utilisant «en».

1. Tu as de l'argent dans ton portefeuille?
2. Tu as de la monnaie dans ta poche?
3. Tu reviens de la banque?
4. Tu as des billets?
5. Tu as des pièces?
6. Tu as besoin d'argent?
7. Tu veux gagner de l'argent?
8. Tu parles de l'argent?
9. Tu as emprunté de l'argent à tes parents?
10. Tu as prêté de l'argent à tes amis?

ADDITIONAL PRACTICE

After completing the exercises on pages 488–489, have students interview a partner on his/her life-style, using questions with *combien.* They should vary the verbs in their questions. Partners respond using *en.* Sample questions are: *Tu écris combien de cartes par an? Tu vois combien de films par mois? Tu manges combien de pizzas par mois? Ta famille a combien de voitures?*

C Dans le réfrigérateur. Répondez d'après le modèle.

du coca

Élève 1: Il y du coca dans ton réfrigérateur?

Élève 2: Oui, il y en a dans mon réfrigérateur. (Non, il n'y en a pas.)

1. de l'eau minérale
2. de la glace
3. des légumes surgelés
4. du jambon
5. des tartes
6. de la viande

Expressing Amounts

D'autres emplois du pronom *en*

1. Note that you also use the pronoun *en* with numbers and expressions of quantity. They cannot stand alone in French. They must be accompanied by *en*.

Tu as combien de magazines?	J'en ai *deux.*
Et tu as beaucoup de livres?	Oui, j'en ai *beaucoup.*

2. Here are some other expressions of quantity. Note the use of *en* with them.

J'en ai *une paire.*
J'en ai *une douzaine.*

J'en ai *très peu.*	*very few, very little*
J'en ai *assez.*	*enough*
J'en ai *quelques-uns (-unes).*	*a few*
J'en ai *plusieurs.*	*several*
J'en ai *trop.*	*too much, too many*

Exercice

A J'en ai assez. Donnez des réponses personnelles en utilisant «en».

1. Tu as combien de paires de chaussures?
2. Tu en as assez?
3. Tu as combien de billets d'un dollar? Tu en as quelques-uns?
4. Tu en as assez pour acheter un coca?
5. Tu as beaucoup d'argent ou peu d'argent dans ton portefeuille?
6. Tu as plusieurs cours aujourd'hui?
7. Tu as trop de devoirs tous les soirs?
8. Tu as beaucoup de cassettes de ton groupe de rock préféré ou tu en as seulement quelques-unes?

CHAPITRE 18   **489**

Exercice C

Answers will vary but É2 answers will use either Oui, il y en a or Non, il n'y en a pas.

D'autres emplois du pronom en

PRESENTATION *(page 489)*

A. Have students open their books. Lead them through steps 1 and 2 on page 489.
B. Call on volunteers to supply true sentences about themselves or people they know using the expressions of quantity in step 2.

ANSWERS

Exercice A

Answers will vary.

Bell Ringer Review

Write the following on the board or use BRR Blackline Master 18-7: Write down three things that can be found in a portefeuille.

Les verbes recevoir et devoir

PRESENTATION *(page 490)*

A. Give students the *ils/elles* forms of *recevoir* and *devoir: ils reçoivent, ils doivent.* Have them drop the final consonant sound to get the sound for all the singular forms.

B. Write all the forms on the board and have students repeat them.

C. Call on a student to read the example sentences in step 1.

D. Lead students through steps 2 and 3.

---

1. Study the following forms of the present tense of the irregular verbs *recevoir,* "to receive," and *devoir,* "to owe."

RECEVOIR	DEVOIR
je reçois	je dois
tu reçois	tu dois
il }	il }
elle } reçoit	elle } doit
on }	on }
nous recevons	nous devons
vous recevez	vous devez
ils } reçoivent	ils } doivent
elles }	elles }

Je reçois beaucoup de cadeaux pour mon anniversaire.
Elle reçoit beaucoup de lettres.

Nous devons de l'argent à la banque.
Mon ami me doit de l'argent.

2. When followed by an infinitive, the verb *devoir* also means "must" or "to have to."

Il m'a prêté de l'argent. Je dois lui rendre son argent.
Elle a un examen difficile demain. Elle doit étudier ce soir.

3. Note the past participles of these verbs.

J'ai *reçu* cent dollars.
J'ai *dû* étudier pour réussir à l'examen.

LEARNING FROM PHOTOS

1. Have students point to the following items: *le sac, le porte-monnaie, le chéquier, les pièces.*
2. Have students describe the *sac, chéquier,* and *porte-monnaie* by giving their size and color.

ADDITIONAL PRACTICE

Student Tape Manual, Teacher's Edition, *Activité E,* page 205.

Exercices

A **Je sais que je lui dois de l'argent.**
Mettez au pluriel d'après le modèle.

> **Je lui dois vingt francs.**
> *Nous lui devons vingt francs.*

1. Je lui dois de l'argent.
2. Je lui dois cent dollars.
3. Si je reçois mon chèque aujourd'hui, je vais le rembourser.
4. Je sais que je dois lui rendre l'argent que je lui dois.

Un distributeur automatique de billets

B **Je dois aller au bureau de change.** Répondez.

1. Si tu as besoin de francs, tu dois aller au bureau de change?
2. Si j'ai besoin de francs, je dois y aller aussi?
3. On doit y aller ensemble?
4. Le dollar est à cinq francs. Si je change vingt dollars, je reçois combien de francs?
5. Si un Français change cent francs, il reçoit combien de dollars?
6. Les Français reçoivent leur salaire en dollars ou en francs?
7. Les Américains reçoivent leur salaire en dollars ou en francs?
8. Tu as déjà reçu un salaire?
9. Tu as reçu combien?

C **On doit faire beaucoup de choses.** Complétez au présent avec «devoir» ou «recevoir».

Dans la vie, on ___ faire beaucoup de choses et ce n'est pas toujours agréable!
1
Moi, tous les matins je ___ me lever à six heures et demie. Je ___ préparer le
2   3
petit déjeuner. Ma sœur Aurélie ___ donner à manger au chien. Nous ___
4   5
quitter la maison à huit heures pour aller à l'école. Le soir nous ___ aider notre
6
mère à préparer le dîner. Après le dîner nous ___ faire nos devoirs. Nous ___
7   8
beaucoup travailler tous les jours! Mais chaque semaine nous ___ de l'argent
9
de poche de nos parents. Tes copains et toi, vous ___ de l'argent de poche de
10
vos parents? Qu'est-ce que vous ___ faire tous les jours pour en avoir? Vous
11
travaillez? Une question de plus! Qu'est-ce que vous faites de l'argent que vous
___? Vous le dépensez ou vous en mettez quelques dollars de côté? Vos parents
12
vous disent que vous ___ faire des économies?
13

CHAPITRE 18 **491**

LEARNING FROM PHOTOS

You may wish to ask the following questions about the photo: *Qu'est-ce que c'est? Qu'est-ce que le garçon a mis (a introduit) dans le distributeur automatique? Qu'est-ce que le distributeur automatique lui a rendu?*

INDEPENDENT PRACTICE

Assign any of the following:
1. Exercises, page 491
2. Workbook, *Structure: F–G*, page 183
3. Communication Activities Masters, *Structure: E–F*, page 92
4. Computer Software, *Structure*
5. CD-ROM, Disc 4, pages 490–491

Exercices

PRESENTATION *(page 491)*

Exercice A

🎧 You may wish to use the recorded version of this exercise.

ANSWERS

Exercice A

1. **Nous lui devons de l'argent.**
2. **Nous lui devons cent dollars.**
3. **Si nous recevons nos chèques aujourd'hui, nous allons le rembourser.**
4. **Nous savons que nous devons lui rendre l'argent que nous lui devons.**

Exercice B

Answers will vary but may include the following:
1. **Oui, je dois y aller.**
2. **Oui, tu dois (vous devez) y aller aussi.**
3. **Oui (Non), on (ne) doit (pas) y aller ensemble.**
4. **Tu reçois (Vous recevez) cent francs.**
5. **Il reçoit vingt dollars.**
6. **Ils le reçoivent en francs.**
7. **Ils le reçoivent en dollars.**
8. **Oui (Non), j'en ai déjà (je n'en ai jamais) reçu un.**
9. **J'ai reçu ___ dollars. (Je n'ai rien reçu.)**

Exercice C

1. doit	8. devons
2. dois	9. recevons
3. dois	10. recevez
4. doit	11. devez
5. devons	12. recevez
6. devons	13. devez
7. devons	

RETEACHING

Have students list the things they have to do each day, using the verb *devoir*. Have them question each other about their lists and do a class summary.

CONVERSATION

CONVERSATION

PRESENTATION *(page 492)*

A. Tell students they will hear a conversation between Robert and a currency exchange teller. Have them close their books and watch the Conversation Video or listen as you read the conversation to them or play Cassette 10B/CD-11. (Use *Activité H* in the Student Tape Manual to check oral comprehension.)

B. Have pairs of students role-play Robert and the teller, repeating their lines after you.

C. Have two students read the conversation to the class.

D. Write a different amount of money exchanged, rate of exchange, and local address for Robert on the board. Then call on pairs to role-play with books open, making the substitutions.

Note In the CD-ROM version, students can play the role of either one of the characters and record the conversation.

Exercices

ANSWERS

Exercice A

1. Il est allé au bureau de change.
2. Il veut changer vingt dollars.
3. Il va changer des chèques de voyage.
4. Il veut changer des dollars en francs français.
5. Le dollar est à 5,80 francs.
6. Oui, il veut le voir.
7. Il est à l'Hôtel Molière.

Exercice B

1. Robert est allé au bureau de change.
2. Il a changé des chèques de voyage.
3. Il a changé vingt dollars.
4. Il a reçu des francs.
5. Le caissier a voulu voir son passeport.

492

Scènes de la vie *Au bureau de change*

ROBERT: Je voudrais changer vingt dollars en francs français, s'il vous plaît.
LE CAISSIER: Vous avez des chèques de voyage ou de l'argent liquide?
ROBERT: Des chèques de voyage. Le dollar est à combien aujourd'hui?
LE CAISSIER: À cinq francs quatre-vingts.
ROBERT: Très bien.
LE CAISSIER: Votre passeport, s'il vous plaît. Et signez votre chèque. Votre adresse à Paris?
ROBERT: Hôtel Molière, rue Molière dans le 1er arrondissement.

A **Des francs, s'il vous plaît.** Répondez d'après la conversation.

1. Où est-ce que Robert est allé?
2. Il veut changer combien de dollars?
3. Il va changer des chèques de voyage ou de l'argent liquide?
4. Il veut changer des dollars en quelle monnaie?
5. Quel est le cours du change?
6. Le caissier veut voir son passeport?
7. Robert est à quel hôtel à Paris?

B **Qu'est-ce qu'il a fait?** Corrigez les phrases.

1. Robert est allé à la banque.
2. Il a changé de l'argent liquide.
3. Il a changé cinquante francs.
4. Il a reçu des dollars.
5. Le caissier a voulu voir sa carte de crédit.

492   CHAPITRE 18

LA POSTE
DCV-01

ACHAT ☐ VENTE ☐ DE BILLETS ETRANG

à M — Johnson, Robert
(nom, prénom) Hôtel Molière
(adresse) Rue Molière
Paris   75001

DEVISE	CODE	MONTANT		COURS	CONTRE-V
USD	03190	20		5,8000	1,

A *Paris*, LE 26/06
SIGNATURE DU CLIENT,

COMMISSION

NET   1

Robert Johnson

Prononciation *Les sons /p/, /t/, /k/*

1. Repeat the following words with the initial French sounds /p/, /t/, and /k/.

   payer   pour   temps   taxi   quand   calme

2. Repeat the following words with the final French sounds /p/, /t/, and /k/.

   nappe   soupe   carte   contente   banque   fric

3. Now repeat the following sentences.

   Philippe a plein de fric à la banque.
   Tes parents vont payer avec une carte de crédit?

payer avec une
carte de crédit

Activités de communication orale

A **Toujours des excuses!** Your friend (your partner) wants your help decorating the gym for a dance, a chore you detest. Each time he or she suggests a day and time, say you have to do something else then.

   Élève 1: Tu peux nous aider jeudi à cinq heures?
   Élève 2: Euh, non, je regrette. Jeudi je dois laver la voiture…

B **Où suis-je?** Think of a place. A classmate has to try and guess which place you're thinking of by asking questions with y. Then reverse roles.

C **Il y en a combien?** Your partner wants to know if there are a lot of the following at your school. Answer with *beaucoup, assez, quelques-un(e)s, très peu,* or *trop.* Then reverse roles.

   bons professeurs
   élèves sportifs ou sportives
   élèves brillant(e)s
   clubs intéressants
   cours intéressants
   examens difficiles

   Élève 1: À ton avis il y a beaucoup d'élèves amusants à l'école?
   Élève 2: À mon avis il y en a quelques-uns.

Prononciation

PRESENTATION *(page 493)*

A. Model the key expression *payer avec une carte de crédit* and have students repeat chorally.
B. Now model the other words and sentences in similar fashion.
C For additional practice, you may wish to use Pronunciation Transparency P-18, Cassette 10B/CD-11: *Prononciation* and the Student Tape Manual, Teacher's Edition, *Activités I–K,* page 207.

Bell Ringer Review

Write the following on the board or use BRR Blackline Master 18-8: You are being interviewed by the school newspaper. Answer the questions with the pronoun *en* and an expression of quantity if necessary.
Tu as…
   des frères?
   des sœurs?
   une voiture?
   des amis?
   du temps libre?
   des devoirs?

Activités de communication orale

ANSWERS

Activités A, B, and *C*
   Answers will vary.

DID YOU KNOW?

There are 100 *centimes* in one franc. The denominations of coins are: 5, 10, 20 *centimes,* and 1/2 franc, 1, 5, 10, and 20 francs. Most French coins have the profile or silhouette of Marianne, a young woman who symbolizes the French Republic.

LECTURE ET CULTURE

LECTURE ET CULTURE

READING STRATEGIES
(*page 494*)

Pre-Reading

Take a survey to see which students receive a weekly allowance, which ones work part-time for spending money, what they use their money for, etc.

Reading

A. Have students read the *Lecture* silently. Allow five minutes. Encourage them to read for the main ideas and important details only, not to use dictionaries, and not to stop each time they have difficulty. Tell them they will have a chance to reread.

B. Call on volunteers to reread the *Lecture* aloud. Stop occasionally to ask questions.

Post-Reading

Call on a more able student to compare his/her money habits with those of Nathalie.

Note Students may listen to a recorded version of the Lecture on the CD-ROM.

Étude de mots

ANSWERS

Exercice A

1. une semaine
2. jeune
3. les parents
4. une façon
5. pas mal de
6. un chanteur
7. faire des économies

LA SEMAINE DES JEUNES FRANÇAIS

Qu'est-ce qu'une semaine? Une période de sept jours? Oui, mais une «semaine» peut être aussi quelque chose d'autre. La semaine peut être de l'argent. La semaine est la somme d'argent qu'un jeune Français ou une jeune Française reçoit de ses parents. C'est de l'argent de poche. Les jeunes Français reçoivent combien d'argent pour leur semaine? On ne peut pas répondre d'une façon générale[1] à cette question. Ça dépend d'abord de la générosité des parents et ensuite de la situation économique de la famille. Nathalie Cassis, par exemple, reçoit 50 francs par semaine de ses parents. Qu'est-ce qu'elle fait avec les 50 francs qu'elle reçoit? Nathalie achète de temps en temps un tee-shirt ou une cassette. Elle achète pas mal de[2] cassettes parce qu'elle aime beaucoup la musique. Elle achète aussi des billets pour les concerts de ses chanteurs favoris. De temps en temps elle va au café prendre un pot[3] avec des copains et bien sûr il faut payer.

Ses parents ont ouvert un compte d'épargne pour Nathalie. Elle aime faire des économies et mettre de l'argent de côté. Quand fait-elle des versements sur son compte? Si elle reçoit de l'argent pour son anniversaire, elle en dépense une partie, pas tout, et met le reste de côté. Quand elle reçoit une très bonne note, ses parents lui donnent aussi un peu d'argent. Souvent elle le dépense mais quelquefois elle le verse sur son compte d'épargne. Tu as une semaine? Tu reçois combien d'argent? Qu'est-ce que tu fais avec ta semaine? Tu fais les mêmes choses que Nathalie?

[1] d'une façon générale   *in a general way*
[2] pas mal de   *a lot of*
[3] prendre un pot   *to have a drink (soda, tea, etc.)*

Étude de mots

A **Des définitions.** Trouvez le mot dans la lecture.

1. une période de sept jours
2. pas vieux
3. le père et la mère
4. une manière
5. beaucoup
6. une personne qui chante
7. ne pas dépenser trop d'argent

CRITICAL THINKING ACTIVITY

(*Thinking skill: supporting statements with reasons*)

Put the following on the board or on a transparency:

1. À votre avis, il est important de mettre de l'argent de côté, de faire des économies? Pourquoi?

2. Il est important ou pas de devenir riche? Pourquoi?

Compréhension

B **Vrai ou faux?** Répondez par «oui» ou «non».

1. Tous les jeunes Français reçoivent de l'argent de leurs parents.
2. Tous les jeunes Français reçoivent la même somme d'argent.
3. Tous les jeunes Français ont un compte d'épargne.
4. Nathalie Cassis a un compte d'épargne.
5. Elle dépense tout son argent.

C **Vous avez compris?** Répondez d'après la lecture.

1. Combien d'argent de poche est-ce que les jeunes Français reçoivent de leurs parents? Ça dépend de quoi?
2. Qu'est-ce que Nathalie achète avec l'argent qu'elle reçoit?
3. Pourquoi achète-t-elle des cassettes?
4. Avec qui va-t-elle au café?
5. Qu'est-ce qu'elle y prend?
6. Qu'est-ce que les parents de Nathalie ont ouvert pour elle?
7. Quand Nathalie fait-elle des versements sur son compte?
8. Quelles sont les deux définitions du mot «semaine»?

DÉCOUVERTE CULTURELLE

*L*a monnaie change d'un pays à l'autre. C'est le dollar aux États-Unis, mais pas en France. Chaque pays a sa monnaie nationale. Les monnaies étrangères s'appellent des «devises». La monnaie française est le franc français. À propos des francs, il y en a plusieurs: le franc belge, le franc suisse, le franc C.F.A. en Afrique et le franc antillais à la Martinique et à la Guadeloupe. Les devises n'ont pas toujours la même valeur. Il y a des fluctuations. Quelquefois le dollar est à dix francs français et quelquefois il tombe à cinq francs. Quand le dollar est à cinq francs,

tout est très cher pour les Américains en France. Et si le dollar est à dix francs, tout est bon marché pour eux. Pour toi, il vaut mieux aller en France quand le dollar est haut ou quand le dollar est bas? Quand est-ce que tu reçois le plus pour le dollar?

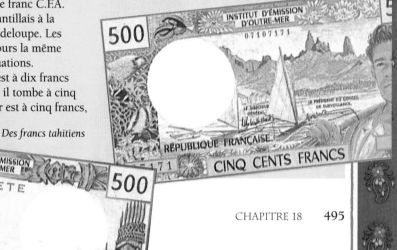

Des francs tahitiens

CHAPITRE 18   **495**

CRITICAL THINKING ACTIVITY

(Thinking skill: problem solving)

Vous êtes en France et vous voyez un tableau, par example, que vous aimez. Vous voulez l'acheter. Il coûte mille francs. Le jour où vous voulez acheter le tableau, le dollar est à 6F. Vous calculez le prix du tableau en dollars. Ça va faire combien? (Answer: $166.) Vous décidez d'acheter le tableau, mais vous ne voulez pas payer en

espèces. Vous le payez avec votre carte de crédit. Quelques jours plus tard, le dollar baisse. Le franc monte. Quand vous payez, le dollar est à 5,5 francs. Combien coûte le tableau maintenant? (Answer: $181.) Vous avez gagné ou perdu de l'argent? Combien?

Compréhension *(page 495)*

ANSWERS

Exercice B

1. Non.   4. Oui.
2. Non.   5. Non.
3. Non.

Exercice C

1. La somme d'argent de poche que les jeunes Français reçoivent de leurs parents dépend de la générosité des parents et de la situation économique de la famille.
2. Nathalie achète des cassettes et des tee-shirts.
3. Elle achète des cassettes parce qu'elle aime beaucoup la musique.
4. Elle y va avec des copains.
5. Elle y prend un pot.
6. Ils ont ouvert un compte d'épargne pour elle.
7. Elle fait des versements sur son compte quand elle reçoit de l'argent.
8. «Une semaine» veut dire (signifie) une période de sept jours et la somme d'argent qu'on reçoit chaque semaine de ses parents.

OPTIONAL MATERIAL

Découverte culturelle

PRESENTATION *(page 495)*

A. Before reading the *Découverte* material, focus on the topic by sharing with students the list of exchange rates taken from a major newspaper. You may wish to photocopy the exchange rates and discuss them with the students.

B. Have students read the information silently.

Note Students may listen to a recorded version of the *Découverte culturelle* on the CD-ROM.

GEOGRAPHY CONNECTION

Have students find *la Belgique, la Suisse, l'Afrique, la Martinique, la Guadeloupe,* and *Tahiti* on the map on page 506.

RÉALITÉS

RÉALITÉS

OPTIONAL MATERIAL

PRESENTATION
(pages 496–497)

The object of this section is to have students enjoy the photographs. However, if you would like to do more with it, you may wish to do the following activities.

A. Ask students what they know about current economic changes taking place in Europe, such as the formation of the European Community.

B. Ask volunteers to read and discuss the captions and photographs on pages 496–497.

Note In the CD-ROM version, students can listen to the recorded captions and discover a hidden video behind one of the photos.

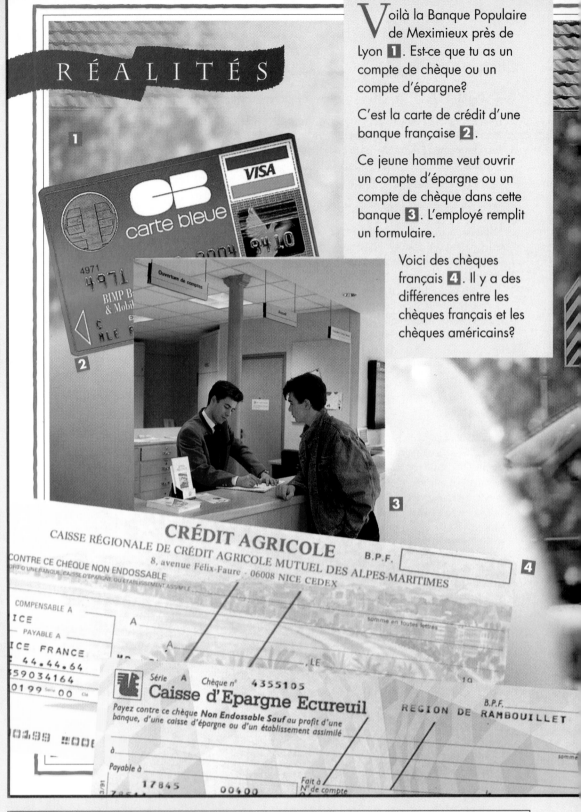

Voilà la Banque Populaire de Meximieux près de Lyon **1**. Est-ce que tu as un compte de chèque ou un compte d'épargne?

C'est la carte de crédit d'une banque française **2**.

Ce jeune homme veut ouvrir un compte d'épargne ou un compte de chèque dans cette banque **3**. L'employé remplit un formulaire.

Voici des chèques français **4**. Il y a des différences entre les chèques français et les chèques américains?

CRITICAL THINKING ACTIVITY

(Thinking skill: supporting statements with reasons)

Discutez: Comment préférez-vous payer —en espèces, avec une carte de crédit, par chèque ou par chèque de voyage? Expliquez pourquoi.

PAIRED ACTIVITY

Have students work in pairs to make up the conversation between the customer and the *caissier* at the exchange office in the illustration of Communication Transparency C-18.

497

LEARNING FROM PHOTOS

You may wish to ask the following questions about the photos:
1. Qu'est-ce qu'une Carte bleue?
2. Quel sont les noms de deux banques
   françaises?
3. Regardez la photo (nº 3) de l'intérieur de
   la banque. Comment dit-on «*new
   accounts*»?

ADDITIONAL PRACTICE

1. Student Tape Manual, Teacher's Edition,
   Deuxième Partie, pages 208–210
2. Situation Cards, Chapter 18

CULMINATION

RECYCLING

The *Activités de communication orale* and *écrite* allow students to apply the vocabulary and grammar of the chapter to open-ended, real-life situations and to re-use the vocabulary and structures from earlier chapters.

INFORMAL ASSESSMENT

Oral Activity A provides guided cues but still allows for free creation of sentences around the given topics. Oral Activity B allows students even freer rein in that they themselves come up with the topics they will discuss in their group. When using these activities for speaking assessment, you may wish to follow the evaluation criteria given on page 34 of this Teacher's Wraparound Edition.

Activités de communication orale
ANSWERS

Activités A and B

Answers will vary.

Activité de communication écrite
ANSWERS

Activité A

Answers will vary.

Activités de communication orale

A **Devinons.** Play this game in small groups. The items listed below are pieces of mail. Copy the names of the items on separate pieces of paper and fold them. Choose an item, and get your team members to guess what you've just received in the mail by giving them clues. You may not say the words on the paper. The first team to guess three items correctly wins.

une facture	une lettre d'amour
une carte postale	un permis de conduire
un billet d'avion	une carte d'anniversaire

Élève 1: Tiens! Mon oncle m'a donné vingt dollars!
Élève 2: Tu as reçu une carte d'anniversaire.

B **Rêves de voyage, voyages de rêve.** Work in small groups. Write down several places you've visited, then exchange papers with the other group members. Tell whether or not you have visited the places mentioned on the paper you've received. If you have visited a place, tell when and with whom. If you have not visited the place, tell whether or not you would like to.

Montréal

Ah, Montréal. Oui, j'y suis allé l'année dernière avec mes grands-parents. (Ah, non, je ne suis jamais allé à Montréal, mais je voudrais y aller.)

Activité de communication écrite

A **Es-tu comme la cigale ou la fourmi?** Are you careless with your money like the grasshopper or careful with it like the ant? Take the test and see what it reveals about you.

TEST

1. **Pour avoir de l'argent de poche...**
   a. je ne fais rien. Mes parents me donnent de l'argent.
   b. je travaille dans un magasin, dans un restaurant, etc.
2. **Quand je vois quelque chose que j'aime beaucoup...**
   a. je l'achète impulsivement.
   b. je réfléchis avant de l'acheter.
3. **Quand je reçois de l'argent comme cadeau...**
   a. je le dépense tout de suite.
   b. j'en mets de côté.
4. **Quand je veux faire ou acheter quelque chose de spéc...**
   a. j'emprunte de l'argent à mes amis ou à mes parents.
   b. je mets de l'argent de côté à l'avance.
5. **Quand j'emprunte de l'argent à mes copains...**
   a. j'oublie souvent de les rembourser.
   b. je les rembourse tout de suite.
6. **Quand un ami a besoin d'argent...**
   a. je ne peux pas l'aider parce que j'ai déjà dépensé tout mon argent.
   b. je peux lui prêter de l'argent parce que j'en ai mis de côté.

SCORE:

Une majorité de a: Tu es une vraie cigale! Tu aimes beaucoup t'amuser dans la vie. Tu dois peut-être essayer de penser un peu plus au futur.

Une majorité de b: Tu es une petite fourmi, responsable et toujours bien organisé(e). Tu es sûr(e) de t'amuser assez dans la vie?

498   CHAPITRE 18

FOR THE YOUNGER STUDENT

Set up a "bank" in the classroom, with students playing the role of tellers at a new accounts window and a currency exchange desk. Distribute play money, photocopied checks, travelers' checks, and any other forms you can get from a local bank. Have other students act as customers engaging in various bank transactions covered in this chapter.

INDEPENDENT PRACTICE

1. Activities and exercises, pages 498–499
2. Communication Activities Masters, pages 86–92
3. CD-ROM, Disc 4, pages 498–499

Réintroduction et recombinaison

A **À l'hôtel.**   Répondez d'après les indications.

1. Où est-ce que Gilbert est allé? (à l'hôtel)
2. À qui a-t-il parlé? (au réceptionniste)
3. Il a demandé quel type de chambre? (pour une personne)
4. Qu'est-ce qu'il a rempli? (une fiche d'enregistrement)
5. À quel étage est la chambre? (au premier)
6. La chambre donne sur la rue ou sur la cour? (sur la cour)
7. Comment Gilbert est-il monté? (par l'escalier)
8. Qu'est-ce qu'il a monté? (ses bagages)

B **Le séjour de Robert.**   Complétez avec «y» ou «en».

L'Hôtel Carlton à Cannes

1. Robert est allé à l'hôtel?
   Oui, il ___ est allé.
2. Il est entré dans le hall?
   Oui, il ___ est entré.
3. Il est dans le hall maintenant?
   Oui, il ___ est.
4. Il va à la réception?
   Oui, il ___ va.
5. Il a des bagages?
   Oui, il ___ a.
6. Il a combien de valises?
   Il ___ a deux.
7. Robert monte dans sa chambre?
   Oui, il ___ monte.
8. Il reste une semaine à l'hôtel?
   Oui, il ___ reste une semaine.

Vocabulaire

NOMS

l'argent de poche (m.)
l'argent liquide (m.)
le billet
la pièce
la monnaie
le chèque (bancaire)
le franc
la balle
le dollar
la banque
le compte d'épargne

le relevé de compte
   (d'épargne)
le bureau de change
le cours du change

la poche
le sac
le portefeuille
le porte-monnaie

VERBES

changer
emprunter
prêter
rembourser
signer
toucher
verser
devoir
recevoir
rendre

AUTRES MOTS ET EXPRESSIONS

avoir plein de fric
être fauché(e)
faire des économies
faire de la monnaie
mettre de l'argent de côté

assez
peu
plusieurs
quelques-un(e)s
trop

CHAPITRE 18   **499**

OPTIONAL MATERIAL

Réintroduction et recombinaison

RECYCLING

Exercise A recycles Chapter 17's hotel vocabulary and asks students to answer questions in the *passé composé* with both *avoir* and *être*. Exercise B has students distinguish between expressions that are replaced by *y* and those that are replaced by *en*.

ANSWERS

Exercice A

1. Gilbert est allé à l'hôtel.
2. Il a parlé au réceptionniste.
3. Il a demandé une chambre pour une personne.
4. Il a rempli une fiche d'enregistrement.
5. Elle est au premier étage.
6. La chambre donne sur la cour.
7. Il est monté par l'escalier.
8. Il a monté ses bagages.

Exercice B

1. y	5. en
2. y	6. en
3. y	7. y
4. y	8. y

ASSESSMENT RESOURCES

1. Chapter Quizzes
2. Testing Program
3. Situation Cards
4. Communication Transparency C-18
5. Computer Software: Practice/Test Generator

VIDEO PROGRAM

INTRODUCTION   (57:38)

BIENVENUE À PARIS,   (58:05)
MEREDITH!

LEARNING FROM PHOTOS

You may wish to ask questions about the photo: *Où est l'hôtel? Cannes est sur la Côte d'Azur? À ton avis, c'est quelle catégorie d'hôtel?*

STUDENT PORTFOLIO

A written assignment which may be included in students' portfolios is the *Mon Autobiographie* section in the Workbook on page 186.

Note Students may create and save both oral and written work using the Electronic Portfolio feature on the CD-ROM.

RÉVISION

CHAPITRES 17–18

OPTIONAL MATERIAL

OVERVIEW

This section reviews key grammatical structures and vocabulary from Chapters 17 and 18. The structure topics were first presented on the following pages: *passé composé* with *être*: page 458; *passé composé* with *être* or *avoir*: page 462; *lui* and *leur*: page 464; the pronoun *y*: page 484; the pronoun *en*: page 487; *recevoir* and *devoir*: page 490.

Conversation

ANSWERS

Exercice A

1. Il s'appelle Michel Boudreau.
2. Il est français.
3. Il doit remplir une fiche.
4. Oui, il est déjà venu plusieurs fois à Montréal.
5. Il est allé au bureau de change où il a changé de l'argent.
6. Il a besoin de monnaie.
7. Il doit prendre un taxi.
8. Non, je ne crois pas qu'il habite au Canada.

500

RÉVISION

CHAPITRES 17–18

Conversation   *L'arrivée à l'hôtel*

M. BOUDREAU: Bonjour, Monsieur. Je m'appelle Michel Boudreau. J'ai réservé une chambre pour ce soir et demain.

L'EMPLOYÉ: Oui, Monsieur. Voilà. Une chambre avec salle de bains pour une personne. Vous êtes de quelle nationalité?

M. BOUDREAU: Je suis français.

L'EMPLOYÉ: Alors, si vous voulez bien remplir cette fiche, s'il vous plaît. *(Il lui donne la fiche.)* C'est votre premier voyage à Montréal?

M. BOUDREAU: Oh non. Je suis déjà venu plusieurs fois.

L'EMPLOYÉ: Si vous voulez changer de l'argent, il y a un bureau de change juste à côté.

M. BOUDREAU: Je sais. J'y suis allé avant de venir ici. Par contre, si vous avez la monnaie de 50 dollars canadiens… Je dois prendre un taxi…

L'EMPLOYÉ: Mais bien sûr, Monsieur.

A   **À l'hôtel.**   Répondez d'après la conversation.

1. Comment s'appelle le client?
2. Il est de quelle nationalité?
3. Qu'est-ce qu'il doit remplir?
4. M. Boudreau est déjà venu à Montréal?
5. Il est allé où avant d'arriver à l'hôtel? Qu'est-ce qu'il y a fait?
6. De quoi est-ce qu'il a besoin?
7. Pour quoi faire?
8. D'après vous, M. Boudreau habite au Canada?

Structure

Le passé composé avec *être*

1. Review the verbs that use *être* as a helping verb in the *passé composé*. Remember that they are mostly verbs of motion.

arriver	sortir	aller	devenir	tomber
partir	monter	venir	rentrer	naître
entrer	descendre	revenir	rester	mourir

2. Remember that the past participle of verbs conjugated with *être* agrees in gender (masculine or feminine) and in number (singular or plural) with the subject of the verb.

Elle est arrivée.   **Nous sommes venus.**

A Un groupe de jeunes en visite à Paris. Répondez d'après le modèle.

> Alain (aller au Louvre)
> *Alain est allé au Louvre.*

1. Caroline et Stéphanie (aller au Musée d'Orsay)
2. Olivier (monter sur la Grande Arche)
3. Bernadette (aller à Versailles)
4. Christian et Marc (descendre à pied du haut de la tour Eiffel)
5. Alain (rester tout l'après-midi au Louvre)

Le passé composé avec *être* ou *avoir*

In the *passé composé*, the verbs *monter, descendre, sortir,* and *rentrer* take either *être* or *avoir.* They take *avoir* when they are followed by a direct object. Otherwise they take *être.*

> Il a monté ses bagages dans sa chambre.
> Il est monté dans sa chambre.

Les Grandes Eaux du Château de Versailles

B Le client et l'employée. M. Delcour est un client de l'hôtel. Mlle Dubois travaille à l'hôtel. Dites qui a fait quoi. (Utilisez le passé composé.)

> monter dans sa chambre   descendre pour changer de l'argent
> descendre les bagages   sortir en ville
> monter le petit déjeuner   sortir sa carte de crédit

Les pronoms d'objet indirect *lui* et *leur*

You use the indirect object pronoun *lui* to replace *à* + a person and the indirect object pronoun *leur* to replace *à* + more than one person. Remember that in negative constructions, the pronoun cannot be separated from the verb by a negative word.

> Je parle *à mon père.*   Je *lui* parle.
> J'écris *à mes parents.*   Je *leur* écris.
> Tu parles souvent *à Marie?*   Je ne *lui* parle jamais!
> Elle va téléphoner *à ses amis?* Non, elle ne va pas *leur* téléphoner.

C Personnellement. Répondez en utilisant «lui» ou «leur».

1. Tu téléphones souvent à tes copains?
2. Tu vas téléphoner à un(e) ami(e) ce soir?
3. Tu aimes parler à tes amis?
4. Tes copains obéissent à leurs parents? Et toi?
5. Tu réponds à ton professeur quand il te pose une question?

Le pronom y

PRESENTATION *(page 502)*

A. Go over steps 1–3 with students.
B. You may wish to have one student read the example sentences in the left-hand column and another student respond with the corresponding sentence with *y*.

Exercices

PRESENTATION *(page 502)*

Exercise E is more difficult than Exercise D because it combines the indirect object pronouns with the pronoun *y*.

ANSWERS

Exercice D

1. Oui (Non), nous (n') y sommes (pas) allés.
2. Oui (Non), nous (n') y allons souvent (pas souvent/jamais).
3. Oui (Non), nous (n') y sommes (pas) montés.
4. Oui (Non), nous (n') y sommes (pas) entrés.
5. Oui (Non), nous (n') y sommes (pas) descendus.
6. Oui (Non), nous (n') y rentron (pas) bientôt.

Exercice E

1. Ils ne leur écrivent jamais.
2. Marie-France y répond.
3. Le professeur leur pose des questions.
4. Les élèves vont y répondre.
5. Vous ne lui obéissez pas toujours.
6. Gilles et Lisa lui disent «Joyeux anniversaire».
7. Michel lui a offert un cadeau.
8. Tu n'y as pas réussi.
9. Carole et Luc n'y ont pas changé 500 francs.
10. Nous y sommes souvent tombés.

Le pronom en

PRESENTATION *(page 502)*

Go over the explanation with students. Have them repeat the example sentences.

Le pronom *y*

1. The pronoun *y* replaces any expression of location introduced by *à* or another preposition (*sur, en, dans, chez, en haut de, en bas de,* etc.).

Tu vas *à Versailles?*	Oui, j'y vais.
Tu es allé *en haut de la tour Eiffel?*	Oui, j'y suis allé.

2. Remember that *y* can also replace *à* + a thing, not referring to a place.

Je vais répondre *à sa lettre.*	Je vais y répondre.
Elle ne fait pas attention *aux autres voitures.*	Elle n'y fait pas attention.

3. In the *passé composé, y* comes before the helping verb.

Il est entré dans l'hôtel?	Oui, il y est entré.
Elle a vu son nom sur la liste?	Non, elle n'y a pas vu son nom.

D **La visite de Paris continue.** Répondez en utilisant «y».

1. Vous êtes allés à Paris?
2. Vous allez souvent en Europe?
3. Vous êtes montés en haut de la tour Eiffel?
4. Vous êtes entrés dans Notre-Dame?
5. Vous êtes descendus dans les Catacombes?
6. Vous rentrez bientôt aux États-Unis?

E ***Y, lui ou leur?*** Remplacez les mots en italique par «y», «lui» ou «leur».

1. Ils n'écrivent jamais *à leurs cousins.*
2. Marie-France répond *au téléphone.*
3. Le professeur pose des questions *aux élèves.*
4. Les élèves vont répondre *aux questions du professeur.*
5. Vous n'obéissez pas toujours *à votre mère.*
6. Gilles et Lisa disent «Joyeux anniversaire» *à Olivier.*
7. Michel a offert un cadeau *à Laurence.*
8. Tu n'as pas réussi *à l'examen.*
9. Carole et Luc n'ont pas changé 500 francs *au bureau de change.*
10. Nous sommes souvent tombés *sur la piste noire.*

Le pronom *en*

Review the object pronoun *en.* It replaces *de (du, de l', de la, des)* + a thing.

Tu as *de l'argent?*	Oui, j'en ai.
Ils ont offert *des boissons?*	Non, ils n'en ont pas offert.

F **On fait un pique-nique.** Répondez d'après le modèle.

Je voudrais du pain. (apporter)
Qui en apporte?

1. Je voudrais du coca. (acheter)
2. Je voudrais des sandwichs. (préparer)
3. Je voudrais de la citronnade. (faire)
4. Je voudrais des chips. (apporter)
5. Je voudrais de la limonade. (acheter)
6. Je voudrais de l'orangeade. (faire)

Les verbes *devoir* et *recevoir*

1. Review the forms of these two irregular verbs.

	DEVOIR	RECEVOIR
PRÉSENT	je dois tu dois il/elle/on doit nous devons vous devez ils/elles doivent	je reçois tu reçois il/elle/on reçoit nous recevons vous recevez ils/elles reçoivent
PARTICIPE PASSÉ	dû	reçu

2. Remember that *devoir* means "must" or "ought to" as well as "to owe."

G **Questions d'argent.** Complétez.

1. Si tu ___ (recevoir) un chèque demain, n'oublie pas de lui rendre l'argent que tu lui ___. (devoir)
2. Vous me ___ (devoir) encore 100 francs.
3. Nous ne voulons pas lui demander de l'argent; nous lui ___ (devoir) déjà 1.000 francs.
4. Vous ___ (recevoir) mon chèque la semaine dernière?
5. Ils ___ (recevoir) de l'argent de leurs parents toutes les semaines.
6. Je ___ (ne… jamais recevoir) votre chèque!

Activité de communication orale

A **Au syndicat d'initiative.** Working with a partner, make up a conversation between a student looking for an inexpensive hotel in Paris and an agent in the *syndicat d'initiative*.

ANSWERS

Exercice F

1. Qui en achète?
2. Qui en prépare?
3. Qui en fait?
4. Qui en apporte?
5. Qui en achète?
6. Qui en fait?

Les verbes devoir et recevoir

PRESENTATION *(page 503)*

A. Have students read the verbs forms aloud.
B. Go over step 2 with them.

ANSWERS

Exercice G

1. reçois, dois
2. devez
3. devons
4. avez reçu
5. reçoivent
6. n'ai jamais reçu

Activité de communication orale

PRESENTATION *(page 503)*

Extension of *Activité A*

After students have completed the activity, call on volunteers to present their conversations to the class.

ANSWERS

Activité A

Answers will vary.

LA FRANCE

La Mer
d'Irlande

L'ANGLETERRE

LES PAYS-BAS

La Mer
du Nord

Amsterdam

L'ALLEMAG

la Tamise Londres

Bruxelles

Calais

Bonn

Lille

LA BELGIQUE

La Manche

Amiens

LE LUXEMBOURG
Luxembourg

Cherbourg

Le Havre

Metz

Les Îles
Anglo-
Normandes

Rouen

Reims

Strasbourg

Caen

la Seine

Nancy

LES VOSGES

Brest

Paris

la Marne

Troyes

Ballon de Guebwiller
1424 m

Rennes

Le Mans

Orléans

Chaumont

Mulhouse

Angers

Tours

la Loire

le Rhin

Dijon

la Seine

Besançon

Nantes

LE JURA

Berne

L'AU

LA SUIS

Poitiers

LA FRANCE

le Lac Léman

La Rochelle

Crêt de la Neige
1723 m

le Rhône

Genève

LES ALPES

L'Océan
Atlantique

Vichy

Chamonix

Limoges

Clermont-
Ferrand

Lyon

Mont Blanc
4807 m

Le puy de Sancy
1886 m

St-Étienne

Grenoble

L'I

la Dordogne

Bordeaux

LE MASSIF
CENTRAL

Rodez

le Rhône

la Garonne

Nîmes

Avignon

Nice

Bayonne

Toulouse

Montpellier

Aix-en-
Provence

Cannes

MONACO

Marseille

LES PYRÉNÉES

Toulon

Vignemale
3298 m

Perpignan

L'ANDORRE

La Mer
Méditerranée

l'Ebro

L'ESPAGNE

504

Aja

Madrid

N

O — E

S

0   100   200

Kilomètres

504

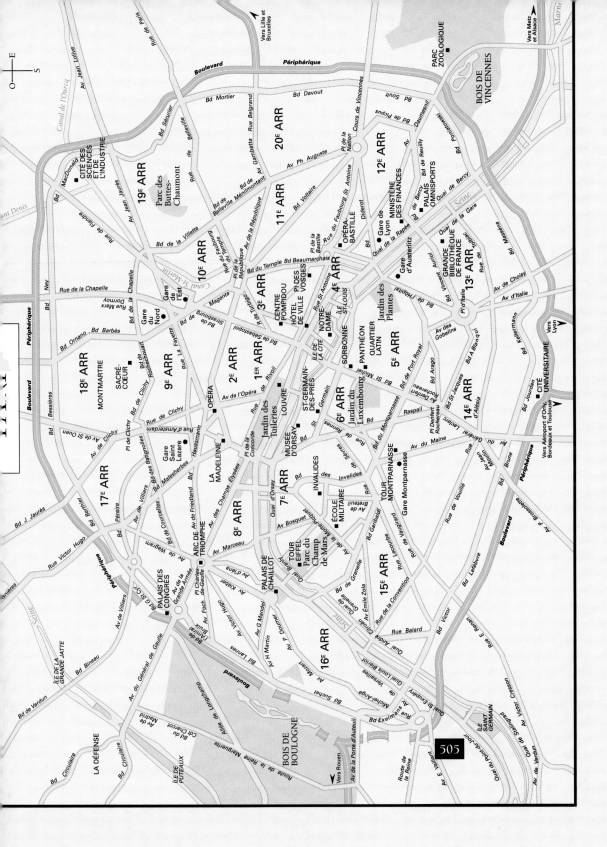

PARIS

Canal de l'Ourcq

Vers Lille et Bruxelles

Boulevard **Périphérique**

Bd Mortier
Bd Davout

CITÉ DES
SCIENCES
ET DE
L'INDUSTRIE
MacDonald

19E ARR

Parc des
Buttes-
Chaumont

20E ARR

Bd de Flandre
Av Jean Jaurès

Canal St-Denis

Bd Ney

Rue de la Chapelle

Bd de la Villette

Gare
de l'Est

10E ARR

Rue de Belleville

Bd de Belleville Ménilmontant

Av de la République

Pl de la Nation
Cours de Vincennes
Av Ph Auguste

12E ARR

PARC
ZOOLOGIQUE

BOIS DE
VINCENNES

Vers Metz
et Alsace

Marne

Bd Soult
Bd de Picpus

MINISTÈRE
DES FINANCES

PALAIS
OMNISPORTS

11E ARR

Bd Voltaire

Rue du Faubourg St Antoine

OPÉRA-
BASTILLE

Gare de
Lyon

Bd Beaumarchais

Pl de la
République
Rue du Temple

Magenta

3E ARR

CENTRE
POMPIDOU

PL DES
VOSGES
HÔTEL
DE VILLE

NOTRE-
DAME

ÎLE
ST-LOUIS

4E ARR

Rue St Antoine
Rue St-Louis

Jardin des
Plantes

Diderot

Seine

Quai de Bercy

GRANDE
BIBLIOTHÈQUE
DE FRANCE

Gare
d'Austerlitz

13E ARR

Av de Choisy

Av d'Italie

Gare
du Nord

Bd Ornano
Bd Barbès

Bd de la Chapelle

Rue Marx Dormoy

Bd de Magenta

18E ARR

MONTMARTRE

SACRÉ-
CŒUR

Bd de Rochechouart

Rue La Fayette

Bd de Sébastopol

2E ARR

1E ARR

Rue de Rivoli

Av de l'Opéra

SORBONNE

QUARTIER
LATIN

PANTHÉON

5E ARR

Bd St Michel

Bd de Port Royal

Av des Gobelins

Bd Arago

Rue de la Glacière

9E ARR

Bd des Batignolles

OPÉRA

LOUVRE

Jardin des
Tuileries

MUSÉE
D'ORSAY

ST-GERMAIN-
DES-PRÉS

6E ARR

Jardin du
Luxembourg

Raspail

Bd du Montparnasse

Bd Raspail

Pl Denfert
Rochereau

14E ARR

d'Alésia

CITÉ
UNIVERSITAIRE

Vers
Lyon

17E ARR

Gare
Saint
Lazare

Hausmann

Bd Malesherbes

LA
MADELEINE

Pl de la
Concorde

ARC DE
TRIOMPHE

Pl Charles
de-Gaulle

Av des Champs Élysées

8E ARR

Quai d'Orsay

INVALIDES
des
Invalides

ÉCOLE
MILITAIRE

7E ARR

Rue de Rennes

Rue de Sèvres

TOUR
MONTPARNASSE
Gare Montparnasse

Av du Maine

PALAIS DES
CONGRÈS

Av de la Grande Armée

Av Foch

TOUR
EIFFEL

Parc du
Champ
de Mars

Av de
Suffren

Av de la Motte-Picquet

Rue du Commerce

Rue de Vaugirard

Rue Lecourbe

15E ARR

Rue de la Convention

Rue Balard

Quai André Citroën

Bd Victor

16E ARR

BOIS DE
BOULOGNE

Boulevard

Bd Suchet

Av Mozart

Bd Exelmans

Vers Rouen

LA DÉFENSE

ÎLE DE
PUTEAUX

Route de la Reine Marguerite

Allée de Longchamp

Route de
la Reine

ÎLE
SAINT
GERMAIN

505

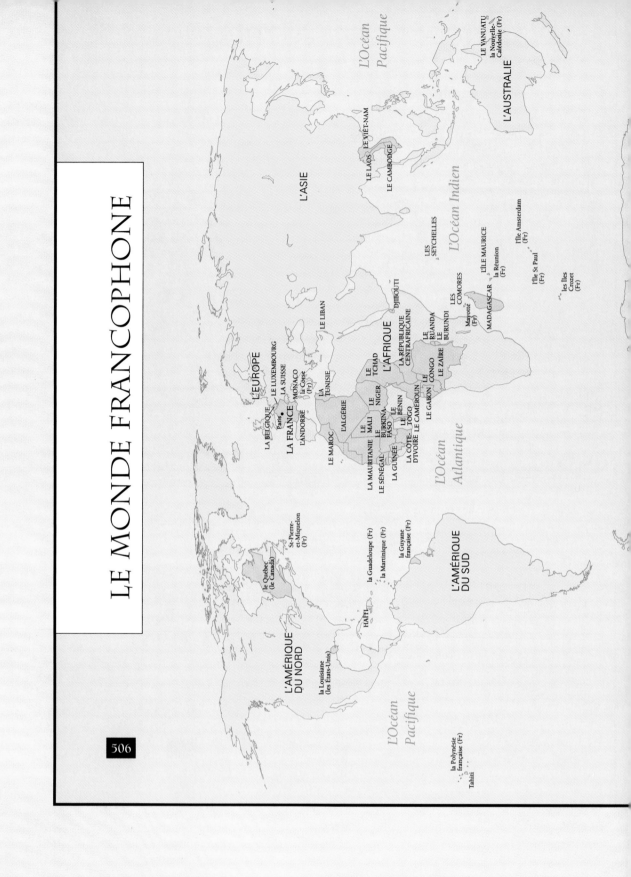

LE MONDE FRANCOPHONE

L'Océan
Pacifique

LE VANUATU
la Nouvelle-
Calédonie (Fr)

L'AUSTRALIE

LE VIÊT-NAM

L'ASIE

LE LAOS
LE CAMBODGE

L'Océan Indien

l'île Amsterdam
(Fr)

LES
SEYCHELLES

l'ÎLE MAURICE

l'île St Paul
(Fr)

LE LIBAN

l'ÎLE MAURICE
la Réunion
(Fr)

L'EUROPE

LE LUXEMBOURG
LA SUISSE

MONACO
la Corse
(Fr)

LES
COMORES

Mayotte
(Fr)

MADAGASCAR

les Îles
Crozet
(Fr)

LA BELGIQUE

Paris

LA FRANCE

L'ANDORRE

LA
TUNISIE

LE
TCHAD

L'AFRIQUE

LA RÉPUBLIQUE
CENTRAFRICAINE

DJIBOUTI

LE
RUANDA
LE
BURUNDI

LE MAROC

L'ALGÉRIE

LE
NIGER

LE
CONGO

LE ZAÏRE

LE
MALI

LA MAURITANIE

LE SÉNÉGAL

LA GUINÉE

BURKINA-
FASO

LE
BÉNIN

LE
TOGO

LA CÔTE-
D'IVOIRE

LE
GABON

LE CAMEROUN

L'Océan
Atlantique

L'AMÉRIQUE
DU NORD

la Louisiane
(les États-Unis)

St-Pierre-
et-Miquelon
(Fr)

le Québec
(le Canada)

HAÏTI

la Guadeloupe (Fr)

la Martinique (Fr)

la Guyane
française (Fr)

L'AMÉRIQUE
DU SUD

L'Océan
Pacifique

la Polynésie
française (Fr)

Tahiti

PRONONCIATION ET ORTHOGRAPHE

I. La transcription phonétique

The following are phonetic symbols used in this book.

[a]	la, là, avec	[ã]	dans, encore, temps
[é]	télé, chez, dîner, les	[õ]	non, regardons
[è]	elle, êtes, frère	[ẽ]	fin, demain
[i]	qui, il, lycée, dîne	[œ̃]	un
[ü]	tu, une		
[u]	vous, où, bonjour	[y]	fille, travailler
[ó]	au, beaucoup, allô		
[ò]	homme, alors	[sh]	chez, Michel
[œ]	deux, veut	[zh]	je, âge
[œ]	heure, sœur	[g]	garder, goûter, Guy

II. L'alphabet français

a b c d e f g h i j k l m n o p q r s t u v w x y z
Voyelles: a e i (y) o u
Consonnes: b c d f g h j k l m n p q r s t v w x z

III. Les accents

There are five written accent marks on French letters. These accents are part of the spelling of the word and cannot be omitted.

1. *L'accent aigu* (´) occurs over the letter *e*.

   le téléphone   élémentaire

2. *L'accent grave* (`) occurs over the letters *a*, *e*, and *u*.

   voilà   frère   où

3. *L'accent circonflexe* (^) occurs over all vowels.

   le château   la fenêtre   le dîner   l'hôtel   août

4. *La cédille* (ç) appears only under the letter *c*. When the letter *c* is followed by an *a*, *o*, or *u* it has a hard /k/ sound as in *ca*ve, *co*ca, *cu*lmination. The cedilla changes the hard /k/ sound to a soft /s/ sound.

   ça   garçon   commençons   reçu

5. *Le tréma* (¨) indicates that two vowels next to each other are pronounced separately.

   Noël   égoïste

VERBES

A. Verbes réguliers

INFINITIF	parler *to speak*	finir *to finish*	répondre *to answer*
PRÉSENT	je parle tu parles il parle nous parlons vous parlez ils parlent	je finis tu finis il finit nous finissons vous finissez ils finissent	je réponds tu réponds il répond nous répondons vous répondez ils répondent
IMPÉRATIF	parle parlons parlez	finis finissons finissez	réponds répondons répondez
PASSÉ COMPOSÉ	j'ai parlé tu as parlé il a parlé nous avons parlé vous avez parlé ils ont parlé	j'ai fini tu as fini il a fini nous avons fini vous avez fini ils ont fini	j'ai répondu tu as répondu il a répondu nous avons répondu vous avez répondu ils ont répondu

B. Verbes avec changements d'orthographe
(*Verbs with spelling changes*)

INFINITIF	acheter[1] *to buy*	appeler *to call*	commencer *to begin*
PRÉSENT	j'achète tu achètes il achète nous achetons vous achetez ils achètent	j'appelle tu appelles il appelle nous appelons vous appelez ils appellent	je commence tu commences il commence nous commençons vous commencez ils commencent
INFINITIF	manger[2] *to eat*	payer[3] *to pay*	préférer[4] *to prefer*
PRÉSENT	je mange tu manges il mange nous mangeons vous mangez ils mangent	je paie tu paies il paie nous payons vous payez ils paient	je préfère tu préfères il préfère nous préférons vous préférez ils préfèrent

[1] Verbes similaires: *se lever, se promener*
[2] Verbes similaires: *nager, voyager*
[3] Verbes similaires: *essayer, renvoyer, employer, envoyer*
[4] Verbes similaires: *célébrer, espérer, suggérer*

C. Verbes irréguliers

INFINITIF	**aller** *to go*	**avoir** *to have*	**conduire** *to drive*
PRÉSENT	je vais tu vas il va nous allons vous allez ils vont	j'ai tu as il a nous avons vous avez ils ont	je conduis tu conduis il conduit nous conduisons vous conduisez ils conduisent
PASSÉ COMPOSÉ	je suis allé(e)	j'ai eu	j'ai conduit
INFINITIF	**connaître** *to know*	**croire** *to believe*	**devoir** *to have to, to owe*
PRÉSENT	je connais tu connais il connaît nous connaissons vous connaissez ils connaissent	je crois tu crois il croit nous croyons vous croyez ils croient	je dois tu dois il doit nous devons vous devez ils doivent
PASSÉ COMPOSÉ	j'ai connu	j'ai cru	j'ai dû
INFINITIF	**dire** *to say*	**dormir** *to sleep*	**écrire** *to write*
PRÉSENT	je dis tu dis il dit nous disons vous dites ils disent	je dors tu dors il dort nous dormons vous dormez ils dorment	j'écris tu écris il écrit nous écrivons vous écrivez ils écrivent
PASSÉ COMPOSÉ	j'ai dit	j'ai dormi	j'ai écrit
INFINITIF	**être** *to be*	**faire** *to do, to make*	**lire** *to read*
PRÉSENT	je suis tu es il est nous sommes vous êtes ils sont	je fais tu fais il fait nous faisons vous faites ils font	je lis tu lis il lit nous lisons vous lisez ils lisent
PASSÉ COMPOSÉ	j'ai été	j'ai fait	j'ai lu

INFINITIF	**mettre** *to put*	**ouvrir**[5] *to open*	**partir** *to leave*
PRÉSENT	je mets tu mets il met nous mettons vous mettez ils mettent	j'ouvre tu ouvres il ouvre nous ouvrons vous ouvrez ils ouvrent	je pars tu pars il part nous partons vous partez ils partent
PASSÉ COMPOSÉ	j'ai mis	j'ai ouvert	je suis parti(e)
INFINITIF	**pouvoir** *to be able to*	**prendre**[6] *to take*	**recevoir** *to receive*
PRÉSENT	je peux tu peux il peut nous pouvons vous pouvez ils peuvent	je prends tu prends il prend nous prenons vous prenez ils prennent	je reçois tu reçois il reçoit nous recevons vous recevez ils reçoivent
PASSÉ COMPOSÉ	j'ai pu	j'ai pris	j'ai reçu
INFINITIF	**savoir** *to know*	**servir** *to serve*	**sortir** *to go out*
PRÉSENT	je sais tu sais il sait nous savons vous savez ils savent	je sers tu sers il sert nous servons vous servez ils servent	je sors tu sors il sort nous sortons vous sortez ils sortent
PASSÉ COMPOSÉ	j'ai su	j'ai servi	je suis sorti(e)
INFINITIF	**venir**[7] *to come*	**voir** *to see*	**vouloir** *to want*
PRÉSENT	je viens tu viens il vient nous venons vous venez ils viennent	je vois tu vois il voit nous voyons vous voyez ils voient	je veux tu veux il veut nous voulons vous voulez ils veulent
PASSÉ COMPOSÉ	je suis venu(e)	j'ai vu	j'ai voulu

[5] Verbes similaires: *couvrir, découvrir, offrir, souffrir*
[6] Verbes similaires: *apprendre, comprendre*
[7] Verbes similaires: *devenir, revenir*

510   VERBES

D. Verbes avec *être* au passé composé

aller *(to go)*	je suis allé(e)
arriver *(to arrive)*	je suis arrivé(e)
descendre *(to go down, to get off)*	je suis descendu(e)
entrer *(to enter)*	je suis entré(e)
monter *(to go up)*	je suis monté(e)
mourir *(to die)*	je suis mort(e)
naître *(to be born)*	je suis né(e)
partir *(to leave)*	je suis parti(e)
passer *(to go by)*	je suis passé(e)
rentrer *(to go home)*	je suis rentré(e)
rester *(to stay)*	je suis resté(e)
retourner *(to return)*	je suis retourné(e)
revenir *(to come back)*	je suis revenu(e)
sortir *(to go out)*	je suis sorti(e)
tomber *(to fall)*	je suis tombé(e)
venir *(to come)*	je suis venu(e)

VOCABULAIRE FRANÇAIS–ANGLAIS

The *Vocabulaire français–anglais* contains all productive and receptive vocabulary from the text.

The numbers following each productive entry indicate the chapter and vocabulary section in which the word is introduced. For example, 2.2 means that the word first appeared in *Chapitre 2, Mots 2.* **BV** refers to the introductory *Bienvenue* chapter.

The following abbreviations are used in this glossary.

abbrev.	abbreviation
adj.	adjective
adv.	adverb
conj.	conjunction
dem. adj.	demonstrative adjective
dem. pron.	demonstrative pronoun
dir. obj.	direct object
f.	feminine
fam.	familiar
form.	formal
ind. obj.	indirect object
inf.	infinitive
inform.	informal
inv.	invariable
m.	masculine
n.	noun
pl.	plural
poss. adj.	possessive adjective
prep.	preposition
pron.	pronoun
sing.	singular
subj.	subject

A

à at, in, to, **3.1**
  à l'avance in advance
  à bord de on board, **7.2**
  à côté next door
  à côté de next to, **5**
  À demain. See you tomorrow., **BV**
  à demi-tarif half-price
  à destination de to (plane, train, etc.), **7.1**
  à domicile to the home
  à droite de to, on the right of, **5**
  à l'étranger abroad, in a foreign country
  à gauche de to, on the left of, **5**
  à l'heure on time, **8.1**; an (per) hour (speed)
  à l'intérieur inside
  à mi-temps part-time, **3.2**
  à la mode in style, "in"
  à mon (ton, son, etc.) avis in my (your, his, etc.) opinion, **10.2**
  à l'origine originally
  à partir de from … on; based on
  à peu près about, approximately
  à pied on foot, **5.2**
  à plein temps full-time, **3.2**
  à point medium-rare (meat), **5.2**
  à propos de concerning, as regards
  à quelle heure? at what time?, **2**
  À tout à l'heure. See you later., **BV**
l' abricot (m.) apricot
absolument absolutely
absorber to absorb
accélérer to speed up, go faster, **12.1**
accepter to accept
l' accessoire (m.) accessory
l' accident (m.) accident, **14.2**
accompagné(e) (de) accompanied (by)
accueilli(e): bien accueilli(e) well-received
l' achat (m.) purchase
  faire des achats to shop, **10.1**

acheter to buy, **6.1**
l' acidité (f.) acidity
l' acte (m.) act, **16.1**
l' acteur (m.) actor (m.), **16.1**
actif, active active, **10**
l' action (f.) action
l' activité (f.) activity
l' actrice (f.) actress, **16.1**
l' addition (f.) check, bill (restaurant), **5.2**
admirer to admire
l' adolescent(e) adolescent, teenager
adopter to adopt
adorable adorable
adorer to love, **3.2**
l' adresse (f.) address
l' adulte (m. et f.) adult
adverse opposing, **13.1**
aérien(ne) air, flight (adj.), **9**
  les tarifs aériens airfares
l' aérogare (f.) terminal with bus to airport, **7.2**
l' aéroport (m.) airport, **7.1**
aérospatial(e) aerospace
les affaires (f. pl.) business; belongings
  l'homme (m.) d'affaires businessman
affolé(e) panic-stricken
s' affronter to collide
africain(e) African
l' âge (m.) age, **4.1**
  Tu as quel âge? How old are you? (fam.), **4.1**
âgé(e) old
l' agenda (m.) appointment book, **2.2**
l' agent (m.) agent (m. and f.), **7.1**
  l'agent de police police officer (m. and f.)
l' agglomération (f.) populated area
agité(e) agitated
agréable pleasant
l' agriculteur (m.) farmer (m. and f.)
aider to help
aimable nice (person), **1.2**
aimer to like, love, **3.2**
l' air (m.) air
  en plein air outdoor(s)
ajouter to add
l' algèbre (f.) algebra, **2.2**
l' aliment (m.) food

alimentaire: le régime
   alimentaire diet
l' alimentation (f.) nutrition, diet
l' Algérie (f.) Algeria
l' Allemagne (f.) Germany, 16
l' allemand (m.) German
   (language)
allemand(e) German
aller to go, 5.1
   aller à la pêche to go fishing,
   9.1
   aller pêcher to go fishing
l' allergie (f.) allergy, 15.1
allergique allergic, 15.1
l' aller-retour (m.) round-trip
   ticket, 8.1
l' aller simple (m.) one-way
   ticket, 8.1
alors so, then, well then
les algues (f. pl.) algae
les Alpes (f. pl.) the Alps
l' alpinisme (m.) mountain
   climbing
l' altitude (f.) altitude
l' amateur (m.): l'amateur d'art
   art lover
aménager to renovate,
   transform
l' Américain(e) American
   (person)
américain(e) American, 1.1
l' Amérique (f.) America, 16
   l'Amérique (f.) du Nord
   North America, 16
   l'Amérique (f.) du Sud
   South America, 16
l' ami(e) friend, 1.2
l' amitié (f.) friendship
ample large, full
amusant(e) funny, 1.1
s' amuser to have fun, 11.2
l' an (m.): avoir... ans to be ...
   years old, 4.1
l' ananas (m.) pineapple
l' anatomie (f.) anatomy
ancien(ne) old, ancient; former
l' angine (f.) throat infection,
   tonsillitis, 15.1
l' anglais (m.) English (language),
   2.2
l' Anglais(e) Englishman
   (woman)
l' Angleterre (f.) England, 16
l' animal (m.) animal
animé(e) lively, animated
l' année (f.) year, 4.1
   l'année dernière last year, 13
l' anniversaire (m.) birthday, 4.1
   Bon (Joyeux) anniversaire!
   Happy birthday!

C'est quand, ton
   anniversaire? When is
   your birthday? (fam.), 4.1
l' annonce (f.) announcement,
   8.1
   la petite annonce classified
   ad
annoncer to announce, 8.1
l' anorak (m.) ski jacket, 14.1
antérieur(e) previous, former
l' anthropologie (f.) anthropology
l' antibiotique (m.) antibiotic,
   15.1
l' anticyclone (m.) high pressure
   area
antillais(e) West Indian
antipathique unpleasant
   (person), 1.2
l' Antiquité (f.) ancient times
anxieux, anxieuse anxious
août (m.) August, 4.1
apparenté: le mot apparenté
   cognate
l' appartement (m.) apartment,
   4.2
appeler to call
s' appeler to be called, be named,
   11.1
applaudir to applaud
apporter to bring
apprendre (à) to learn (to), 9.1
   apprendre à quelqu'un à
   faire quelque chose to
   teach someone to do
   something, 14.1
l' apprenti(e) apprentice
appuyer sur le bouton to push
   the button
après after, 3.2
   d'après according to
l' après-midi (m.) afternoon, 2
l' arbitre (m.) referee, 13.1
l' arbre (m.) tree
l' arche (f.) arch
l' archipel (m.) archipelago
l' architecte (m. et f.) architect
l' architecture (f.) architecture
l' argent (m.) money, 3.2
   l'argent liquide cash, 18.1
   l'argent de poche allowance,
   small change
l' Argentine (f.) Argentina, 16
l' argot (m.) slang
l' aristocrate (m. et f.) aristocrat
l' arme (f.) weapon
l' armée (f.) army
s' arrêter to stop, 12.1
l' arrivée (f.) arrival, 7.2
   la ligne d'arrivée finish line
   le tableau des départs et des

arrivés arrival and
   departure board
arriver to arrive, 3.1; to happen
l' arrondissement (m.) district
   (in Paris)
l' art (m.) art, 2.2
l' article (m.) article
   les articles de luxe luxury
   items
   les articles de sport sporting
   goods
l' artiste peintre (m. et f.) painter
artistique artistic
l' ascenseur (m.) elevator, 4.2
l' asepsie (f.): pratiquer l'asepsie
   to sterilize, disinfect
l' Asie (f.) Asia, 16
aspiré(e) pulled in
l' aspirine (f.) aspirin, 15.1
assez fairly, quite; enough
   assez de (+ nom) enough
   (+ noun), 18
l' assiette (f.) plate, 5.2
   ne pas être dans son assiette
   to be feeling out of sorts,
   15.1
assis(e) seated, 8.2
l' assistant(e) assistant
l' association (f.) association
associer to associate
l' assurance (f.) insurance
l' astronome (m. et f.)
   astronomer
l' atmosphère (f.) atmosphere
attendre to wait (for), 8.1
l' attente (f.): la salle d'attente
   waiting room, 8.1
l' attention (f.) attention
   Attention! Careful! Watch
   out!
   faire attention to pay
   attention, 6; to be careful,
   9.1
atterrir to land, 7.1
l' atterrissage (m.) landing
   (plane)
attirer to attract
attraper un coup de soleil to
   get a sunburn, 9.1
au at the, to the, in the, on the
   (sing.), 5
   au bord de la mer by the
   ocean; seaside, 9.1
   au contraire on the contrary
   au debut at the beginning
   au-dessus (de) above
   au-dessous (de) below
   au fond de at the bottom of
   au moins at least
   au revoir good-bye, BV

au sujet de about

l' **auberge (f.) de jeunesse** youth hostel

audacieux, audacieuse audacious, bold

au-dessous: la taille au-dessous the next smaller size, **10.2**

au-dessus: la taille au-dessus the next larger size, **10.2**

augmenter to increase

aujourd'hui today, **2.2**

ausculter to listen with a stethoscope, **15.2**

aussi also, too, **1.1**; as (comparisons), **10**

l' **Australie (f.)** Australia, **16**

l' **auteur (m.)** author (m. and f.)

l' **autocar (m.)** bus, coach, **7.2**

l' **autodidacte (m. et f.)** self-taught person

l' **auto-école (f.)** driving school, **12.2**

automatique: le distributeur automatique de billets automated teller machine (ATM)

l' **automne (m.)** autumn, **13.2**

l' **autoroute (f.)** highway
l'autoroute à péage toll highway, **12.2**

autour de around

autre other, **BV**
Autre chose? Anything else? (shopping), **6.2**

aux at the, to the, in the, on the (pl.), **5**

l' **avance (f.): à l'avance** in advance
en avance early, ahead of time, **8.1**

avancé(e) advanced

avant before, **7.1**
avant de (+ inf.) before (+ verb)

avant-hier the day before yesterday, **13**

avec with, **5.1**
Avec ça? What else? (shopping), **6.2**

l' **aventure (f.)** adventure

l' **avion (m.)** plane, **7.1**
en avion by plane; plane (adj.), **7.1**

l' **avis (m.)** opinion
à mon avis in my opinion, **10.2**

avoir to have, **4.1**
avoir... ans to be ... years old, **4.1**
avoir besoin de to need, **11.1**

avoir de la chance to be lucky

avoir faim to be hungry, **5.1**

avoir une faim de loup to be very hungry

avoir lieu to take place

avoir mal à to have a(n) ... -ache, to hurt, **15.2**

avoir l'occasion de (+ inf.) to have the opportunity (+ inf.)

avoir raison to be right

avoir soif to be thirsty, **5.1**

avoir tendance à (+ inf.) to tend (+ inf.)

avril (m.) April, **4.1**

B

le **baccalauréat** French high school exam

le **bacon** bacon

bactérien(ne) bacterial, **15.1**

les **bagages (m. pl.)** luggage, **7.1**
les bagages à main carry-on luggage, **7.1**

la **baguette** loaf of French bread, **6.1**

le **bain** bath, **11.1**
prendre un bain to take a bath, **11.1**
le bain de soleil: prendre un bain de soleil to sunbathe, **9.1**

le **balcon** balcony, **4.2**

la **balle** ball (tennis, etc.), **9.2**; franc (slang), **18.2**

le **ballon** ball (soccer, etc.), **13.1**

la **banane** banana, **6.2**

la **bande dessinée** comic strip

la **banlieue** suburbs

la **banque** bank, **18.1**

le **banquier, la banquière** banker

baptiser to christen

Barcelone Barcelona, **16**

bas(se) low, **10**
à talons bas low-heeled (shoes), **10**

la **base: de base** basic

le **base-ball** baseball, **13.2**

le **basket(-ball)** basketball, **13.2**

le **bateau** boat

le **bâtiment** building

le **bâton** ski pole, **14.1**

battre des tambours to beat drums

bavarder to chat, **4.2**

beau (bel) beautiful (m.), handsome, **4**
Il fait beau. It's nice weather., **9.2**

beaucoup a lot, **3.1**
beaucoup de a lot of, many, **10.1**

la **beauté** beauty

les **Beaux-Arts (m. pl.)** fine arts

beige (inv.) beige, **10.2**

le/la **Belge** Belgian (person)
belge Belgian

la **Belgique** Belgium
belle beautiful (f.), **4**

le **béribéri** beriberi

le **besoin** need
avoir besoin de to need, **11.1**

la **bêtise** stupid thing, nonsense

le **beurre** butter, **6.2**

le **bicentenaire** bicentennial

bien fine, well, **BV**
bien accueilli(e) well-received
bien cuit(e) well-done (meat), **5.2**
bien élevé(e) well-mannered
bien sûr of course

bientôt soon

Bienvenue! Welcome!

la **bière** beer

le **bijou** jewel

le **billet** bill (currency), **18.1**; ticket, **7.1**
le billet aller-retour round-trip ticket, **8.1**

la **biologie** biology, **2.2**

le/la **biologiste** biologist

bizarre strange, odd

la **blague: Sans blague!** No kidding!

blanc, blanche white, **10.2**

bleu(e) blue, **10.2**
bleu marine (inv.) navy blue, **10.2**

blond(e) blond, **1.1**

bloquer to block

le **blouson** jacket, **10.1**

le **bœuf** beef, **6.1**

la **boisson** beverage, **5.1**

la **boîte de conserve** can of food, **6.2**

bon(ne) correct; good, **9**

bon marché (inv.) inexpensive, **10.1**

Bonjour. Hello., **BV**

le **bonnet** ski cap, hat, **14.1**
le bonnet de bain bathing cap

le **bord: à bord de** aboard (plane, etc.), **7.2**
au bord de la mer by the ocean, seaside, **9.1**

bordé(e) (de) bordered, lined (with)

le **bordereau** receipt
la **bosse** mogul (ski), **14.2**
la **botanique** botany
la **botte** boot
la **bouche** mouth, **15.1**
la **boucherie** butcher shop, **6.1**
le **bouchon** traffic jam
bouger to move
le **bouillon de poulet** chicken
soup
la **boulangerie-pâtisserie** bakery,
6.1
la **boule de neige** snowball, **14.2**
le/la **bourgeois(e)** burgher;
townsperson
bout (inf. bouillir) boils (verb)
la **bouteille** bottle, **6.2**
la **boutique** shop, boutique
le **bouton** button; bud
la **brasse papillon** butterfly (swim
stroke)
Bravo! Good! Well done!
le **break** station wagon, **12.1**
le **Brésil** Brazil, **16**
la **Bretagne** Brittany
breton(ne) Breton, from
Brittany
la **brioche** sweet roll
bronzé(e) tan
bronzer to tan, **9.1**
se **brosser** to brush, **11.1**
se **brosser les dents (f. pl.)**
to brush one's teeth, **11.1**
le **bruit** noise
brun(e) brunette, **1.1**; brown,
10.2
le **bulletin** card; report
le **bulletin de notes** report
card
le **bulletin météorologique**
weather report
le **bureau** desk, **BV**; office, bureau
le **bureau de change** foreign
exchange office (for foreign
currency), **18.1**
le **bus: en bus** by bus, **5**
le **but** goal, **13.1**
marquer un but to score a
goal, **13.1**

C

ça that (dem. pron.), **BV**
Ça coûte cher. It's (That's)
expensive.
Ça fait combien? How much
is it (that)?, **6.2**
Ça fait... francs. It's (That's)
... francs., **6.2**
Ça fait mal. It (That) hurts.,
15.2

Ça va. Fine., O.K., **BV**
Ça va? How's it going?, How
are you? (inform.), **BV**
la **cabine** cabin (plane), **7.1**
le **cabinet** office (doctor's)
le **cadeau** gift, present, **10.2**
le **café** café; coffee, **5.1**
le **café au lait** coffee with
milk
le **cahier** notebook, **BV**
la **caisse** cash register, checkout
counter, **6.2**
le **caissier,** la **caissière** cashier
le **calcium** calcium
le **calcul** calculation
la **calculatrice** calculator, **BV**
calculer to calculate
calme quiet, calm
calmer: Calmez-vous. Calm
down.
la **calorie** calorie
le/la **camarade** companion, friend
le/la **camarade de classe**
classmate
le **camp** side (in a sport or game),
13.1
le **camp adverse** opponents,
other side, **13.1**
la **campagne** country(side)
la **maison de campagne**
country house
le **Canada** Canada, **16**
canadien(ne) Canadian, **9**
le/la **candidat(e)** candidate
le **canoë** canoe
la **cantine** school restaurant
la **capitale** capital
le **car** bus (coach)
le **caractère: à caractère familial**
family-style
la **caractéristique** characteristic
le **carnet** small book
la **carotte** carrot, **6.2**
carré(e) square
les **carreaux (m. pl.)** tiles
le **carrefour** intersection, **12.2**
la **carrière** career
la **carte** menu, **5.1**; map
la **carte d'anniversaire**
birthday card
la **carte de crédit** credit card,
17.2
la **carte de débarquement**
landing card, **7.2**
la **carte d'embarquement**
boarding pass, **7.1**
la **carte postale** postcard
le **cas** case
en cas d'urgence in an
emergency

en tout cas in any case
le **casque** helmet
le **casse-cou** daredevil
la **cassette** cassette, **3.2**
la **catégorie** category
la **cathédrale** cathedral
le **cauchemar** nightmare
la **cause** cause
causer to cause
ce (cet) (m.) this, that (dem.
adj.), **8**
ce que c'est what it is
Ce n'est rien. You're
welcome., **BV**
la **ceinture de sécurité** seat belt,
12.2
célèbre famous, **1.2**
célibataire single, unmarried
cellulaire cellular
la **cellule** cell
la **cellule nerveuse** nerve cell
cent hundred, **5.2**
les **centaines (f. pl.)** hundreds
le **centre** center, middle
au centre de in the heart of
le **centre commercial**
shopping center
les **céréales (f. pl.)** cereal, grains
la **cérémonie** ceremony
la **cerise** cherry
certainement certainly
certains: pour certains for
some people
ces (m. et f. pl.) these, those
(dem. adj.), **8**
c'est it is, it's, **BV**
c'est-à-dire that is, **1.16**
C'est ça. That's right.
C'est combien? How much is
it?, **BV**
**C'est quand, ton
anniversaire?** When is
your birthday? (fam.), **4.1**
C'est quel jour? What day is
it?, **2.2**
C'est tout? Is that all?, **6.2**
cette (f.) this, that (dem. adj.), **8**
chacun(e) each (one)
la **chaîne** TV channel
la **chaîne hôtelière** hotel
chain
la **chaise** chair, **BV**
le **chalet** chalet
la **chambre** room (in a hotel), **17.1**
la **chambre à coucher**
bedroom, **4.2**
la **chambre à deux lits**
double room, **17.1**
la **chambre à un lit** single
room, **17.1**

libérer la chambre to vacate the room, **17.2**

le **champ** field

  le champ de manœuvres parade ground

le/la **champion(ne)** champion

le **championnat** championship

la **chance** luck

  avoir de la chance to be lucky

  changer (de) to change, **8.2**; to exchange, **18.1**

  chanter to sing, **3.2**

le **chanteur**, la **chanteuse** singer

  chaque each, every, **16.1**

la **charcuterie** deli(catessen), **6.1**

  charger to put in charge

le **chariot** shopping cart

  charmant(e) charming

le **chat** cat, **4.1**

  avoir un chat dans la gorge to have a frog in one's throat, **15.2**

le **château** castle, mansion

  chaud(e) warm, hot

  Il fait chaud. It's hot. (weather), **9.2**

  chauffer to heat

les **chaussettes (f. pl.)** socks, **10.1**

les **chaussons (m. pl.)** slippers

les **chaussures (f. pl.)** shoes, **10.1**

  les chaussures de ski ski boots, **14.1**

  les chaussures de tennis sneakers, tennis shoes, **9.2**

le **chef** head, boss

la **cheminée** chimney

la **chemise** shirt, **10.1**

le **chemisier** blouse, **10.1**

le **chèque (bancaire)** check, **18.1**

  le chèque de voyage traveler's check, **17.2**

  le compte de chèque checking account

  cher, chère dear; expensive, **10**

  Ça coûte cher. It's (That's) expensive.

  chercher to look for, seek, **5.1**

le **cheval (pl. les chevaux)** horse

les **cheveux (m. pl.)** hair, **11.1**

  chez at the home (business) of, **5**

  chez soi home

  chic (inv.) chic, stylish

le **chien** dog, **4.1**

le **chiffre** number

le **Chili** Chile, **16**

la **chimie** chemistry, **2.2**

  chimique chemical

le/la **chimiste** chemist

la **Chine** China, **16**

  chinois(e) Chinese

le **chirurgien** surgeon (m. and f.)

le **chocolat: au chocolat** chocolate (adj.), **5.1**

  choisir to choose, **7.1**

le **choix** choice

le **choléra** cholera

le **cholestérol** cholesterol

la **chose** thing

  Chouette! Great! (inform.), **2.2**

la **chute: faire une chute** to fall, **14.2**

  ciao good-bye (inform.), **BV**

  ci-dessus above

le **ciel** sky, **14.2**

la **cigale** grasshopper, cicada

le **cinéma** movie theater, movies, **16.1**

le/la **cinéphile** movie buff

  cinq five, **BV**

  cinquante fifty, **BV**

le **cintre** hanger, **17.2**

la **circulation** traffic, **12.2**; circulation

  la circulation à double sens two-way traffic

  citer to cite, mention

le **citron pressé** lemonade, **5.1**

le/la **civilisé(e)** civilized person

la **classe** class (people), **2.1**; class (course)

  en classe économique in coach class (plane)

le **classement** classification

  classer to classify

la **clé** key, **12.1**

le/la **client(e)** customer, **10.1**

le **climat** climate

les **clous (m. pl.)** pedestrian crossing, **12.2**

le **club** club

  le club d'art dramatique drama club

  le club de forme health club, **11.2**

le **coca** Coca-Cola, **5.1**

le **cœur** heart

le **coffre** trunk (of car)

le **coin: du coin** neighborhood (adj.)

le **collaborateur**, la **collaboratrice** co-worker, associate

le **collant** pantyhose, **10.1**

le **collège** junior high, middle school

la **colonie de vacances** summer camp

  combattre to combat, fight

  combien (de) how much, how many, **6.2**

  Ça fait combien? How much is it (that)?, **6.2**

  C'est combien? How much is it (that)?, **BV**

  comble packed (stadium), **13.1**

la **comédie** comedy, **16.1**

  la comédie musicale musical comedy, **16.1**

  comique funny, **1.2**

  commander to order, **5.1**

  comme like, as; for

  Et comme dessert? What would you like for dessert?

le **commencement** beginning

  commencer to begin

  comment how, what, **1.2**

  Comment est... ? What is ... like? (description), **1.1**

  Comment t'appelles-tu? What's your name? (fam.), **11.1**

  Comment vas-tu? How are you? (fam.), **BV**

  Comment vous appelez-vous? What's your name? (form.), **11.1**

  commun(e) common

  en commun in common

la **communauté** community

le **compact disc** compact disc, **3.2**

la **compagnie aérienne** airline, **7.1**

le **compartiment** compartment, **7.2**

le **complet** suit (man's), **10.1**

  complet, complète full, complete

  compléter to complete

le **comportement** behavior

  composer to compose

  composter to stamp, validate (a ticket), **8.1**

  comprendre to understand, **9.1**

le **comprimé** pill, **15.2**

  compris(e) included (in the bill)

  Le service est compris. The tip is included., **5.2**

le **compte d'épargne** savings account, **18.1**

le **comptoir** counter, **7.1**

le/la **concierge** concierge, caretaker

le **concours** competition, contest

le **conducteur**, la **conductrice** driver, **12.1**

  conduire to drive, **12.2**

la **conduite: les leçons (f.) de conduite** driving lessons, **12.2**

  confiant(e) confident, **1.1**

le **confort** comfort

  confortable comfortable

De quelle couleur est... ? What color is … ?, **10.2**

de rêve dream (adj.)

De rien. You're welcome. (inform.), **BV**

de temps en temps from time to time, occasionally

le **débarquement** landing, deplaning

débarquer to get off (plane), **7.2**

déborder to overflow

debout standing, **8.2**

le **début** beginning

au début at the beginning

le/la **débutant(e)** beginner, **14.1**

le **décalage horaire** time difference

la **décapotable** convertible (car), **12.1**

décembre (m.) December, **4.1**

le **déchet** waste

décider (de) to decide (to)

déclarer to declare, call

décoller to take off (plane), **7.1**

le **décor** set (for a play), **16.1**

le **décorateur (de porcelaine)** painter (of china)

la **découverte** discovery

découvrir to discover, **15**

décrire to describe

dédié(e) dedicated

défense de doubler no passing (traffic sign)

définir to define

la **définition** definition

le **degré** degree, **14.2**

Il fait... degrés (Celsius). It's … degrees (Celsius)., **14.2**

dehors outside

en dehors de outside (of)

déjà already, **14**

déjeuner to eat lunch, **5.2**

le **déjeuner** lunch

délicieux, délicieuse delicious, **10**

le **delta** delta

demain tomorrow, **2.2**

À demain. See you tomorrow., **BV**

demander to ask (for)

se **demander** to wonder

demi(e) half

et demie half past (time)

le **demi-cercle** semi-circle; top of the key (on a basketball court), **13.2**

le **demi-kilo** half a kilo, 500 grams

le **demi-tarif: à demi-tarif** half-price

la **dent** tooth, **11.1**

avoir mal aux dents to have a toothache, **15**

se brosser les dents to brush one's teeth, **11.1**

le **dentifrice** toothpaste, **11.1**

le **déodorant** deodorant, **11.1**

le **départ** departure, **7.1**

le **département d'outre-mer** French overseas department

dépendre (de) to depend (on)

dépenser to spend (money), **10.1**

la **dépression** low-pressure area (weather)

depuis since, for, **8.2**

dériver to derive

dernier, dernière last, **10**

derrière behind, **BV**

des some, any, **3**; **6**; of the, from the (pl.), **4**

désagréable unpleasant, **1.2**

descendre to get off (train, bus, etc.), **8.2**; to take down, **8**; to go down, **14.1**

la **descente** descent; getting off (bus, etc.)

le **désert** desert

se **déshabiller** to get undressed

désirer to want

Vous désirez? May I help you? (store); What would you like? (café, restaurant)

le **dessert** dessert

desservir to serve, fly to, etc. (transportation)

le **dessin** illustration, drawing

le dessin animé cartoon, **16.1**

la **dessinatrice** illustrator (f.)

dessous: au-dessous smaller (size), **10.2**; below

dessus: au-dessus larger (size), **10.2**; above

la **destruction** destruction

le **détergent** detergent

détester to hate, **3.2**

deux two, **BV**

les deux roues (f. pl.) two-wheeled vehicles

tous (toutes) les deux both

deuxième second, **4.2**

la Deuxième Guerre mondiale World War II

deuxièmement second of all, secondly

devant in front of, **BV**

le **développement** development

devenir to become, **16**

la **devise** currency

le **devoir** homework (assignment), **BV**

faire les devoirs to do homework, **6**

devoir to owe, **18.2**; must, to have to (+ verb), **18**

le **diagnostic: faire un diagnostic** to diagnose, **15.2**

dicter to dictate

la **différence** difference

différent(e) different

difficile difficult, **2.1**

la **difficulté: être en difficulté** to be in trouble

dimanche (m.) Sunday, **2.2**

le **dîner** dinner, **4.2**

dîner to eat dinner, **4.2**

la **diphtérie** diphtheria

diplômé(e): être diplômé(e) to graduate

dire to say, tell, **12.2**

la **direction** direction

diriger to direct

discuter to discuss

disparaître to disappear

disponible available

le **disque** record, **3.2**

la **disquette** diskette (computer)

la **distance** distance

distingué(e) distinguished

le **distributeur automatique de billets** automated teller machine (ATM)

divisé(e) divided

le **divorce** divorce

dix ten, **BV**

dix-huit eighteen, **BV**

dix-neuf nineteen, **BV**

dix-sept seventeen, **BV**

le **docteur** doctor (title)

le **documentaire** documentary, **16.1**

le **dollar** dollar, **3.2**

le **domaine** domain, field

le **domicile: à domicile** to the home

donner to give, **3.2**

donner à manger à to feed

donner un coup de pied to kick, **13.1**

donner une fête to throw a party, **3.2**

donner sur to face, overlook, **17.1**

doré(e) golden

dormir to sleep, **7.2**

le **dortoir** dormitory

le **dos** back (body)

la **douane** customs, **7.2**

passer à la douane to go through customs, 7.2

doublé(e) dubbed (movies), 16.1

la douche shower

prendre une douche to take a shower, 11.1

douloureux, douloureuse painful

le doute: sans aucun doute without a doubt

douter to doubt

la douzaine dozen, 6.2

douze twelve, BV

le drame drama, 16.1

le drap sheet, 17.2

le drapeau flag

dribbler to dribble (basketball), 13.2

droite: à droite de to, on the right of, 5

du of the, from the (sing.), 5; some, any, 6

du coin neighborhood (adj.)

pas du tout not at all

la durée length (of time)

durer to last

E

l' eau (f.) water

l'eau minérale mineral water, 6.2

l' échange (m.) exchange

s' échapper to escape

l' écharpe (f.) scarf, 14.1

l' école (f.) school, 1.2

l' école primaire elementary school

l' école secondaire junior high, high school

l' écolier, l'écolière pupil, schoolchild

l' écologiste (m. et f.) ecologist

les économies (f. pl.): faire des économies to save money, 18.2

économique economical

en classe économique in coach class (plane), 7

écouter to listen (to), 3.1

l' écran (m.) screen, 7.1

l' écrevisse (f.) crawfish

écrire to write, 12.2

l' écrivain (m.) writer (m. and f.)

éducatif, éducative educational

l' éducation (f.): l'éducation civique social studies, 2.2

l'éducation physique physical education

efficace efficient

égaliser to tie (score)

l' électricité (f.) electricity

électrique electric

l' élément (m.) element

l' élève (m. et f.) student, 1.2

élevé(e) high, 15

bien élevé(e) well brought-up

éliminer to eliminate

elle she, it, 1; her (stress pron.), 9

elles they (f.), 2; them (stress pron.), 9

l' embarquement (m.) boarding, leaving

embarquer to board (plane, etc.), 7.2

l' embouteillage (m.) traffic jam

émigrer to emigrate

l' emploi (m.) du temps schedule

l' employé(e) employee (m. and f.)

emprunter to borrow, 18.2

en of it, of them, etc., 18.2; in; as

en avance early, ahead of time, 8.1

en avion plane (adj.), by plane, 7.1

en baisse coming down (in value)

en bas to, at the bottom

en ce moment right now

en classe in class

en commun in common

en dehors de outside (of); besides

en effet in fact

en exclusivité first-run (movie)

en face de across from, opposite

en fait in fact

en fonction de in terms of, in accordance with

en général in general

en hausse going up (in value)

en haut de on, to the top of

en plein(e) (+ nom) right (in, on, etc.) (+ noun)

en plein air outdoor(s)

en plus de besides, in addition

en première (seconde) in first (second) class, 8.1

en provenance de arriving from (flight, train), 7.1

en retard late, 8.2

en solde on sale, 10.2

en tout cas in any case

en version originale original language version, 16.1

en ville in town, in the city

encore still (adv.); another; again

encourager to encourage

s' endormir to fall asleep, 11.1

l' endroit (m.) place

l' énergie (f.) energy

énergique energetic, 1.2

l' enfant (m. et f.) child (m. and f.), 4.1

enfin finally

l' engrais (m.) fertilizer

énormément enormously

l' enquête (f.) survey, opinion poll

enragé(e) rabid, enraged

enrhumé(e): être enrhumé(e) to have a cold, 15.1

l' enseignement (m.) teaching

l' ensemble (m.) body, collection

ensemble together, 5.1

ensuite then (adv.), 11.1

entendre to hear, 8.1

l' enthousiasme (m.) enthusiasm

entier, entière entire, whole, 10

l' entracte (m.) intermission, 16.1

entraîner to carry along

entre between, among, 9.2

l' entrée (f.) entrance, 4.2; admission

entrer to enter, 3.1

l' environnement (m.) environment

envoyer to send, 13.1

l' épargne: le compte d'épargne savings account, 18.1

épicé(e) spicy

l' épicerie (f.) grocery store, 6.1

l' époque (f.) period, times

l' équilibre (m.) balance

équilibré(e) balanced

l' équipe (f.) team, 13.1

l' équipement (m.) equipment

l' érable (m.) maple (tree)

le sirop d'érable maple syrup

l' escalier (m.) staircase, 17.1

l' espace (m.) space

l' Espagne (f.) Spain, 16

l' espagnol (m.) Spanish (language), 2.2

espagnol(e) Spanish

les espèces (f. pl.): payer en espèces to pay cash, 17.2

l' espionnage (m.) spying

l' essence (f.) gas(oline), 12.1

(l'essence) ordinaire regular gas, 12.1

(l'essence) super sans plomb super unleaded gas, 12.1

essentiel(le) essential
essentiellement essentially
l' est (m.) east
estimer to consider
l' estomac (m.) stomach
et and, 1
et toi? and you? (fam.), BV
établir to establish
l' étage (m.) floor (of a building), 4.2
l' étal (m.) (market) stall
l' état (m.) state
l'homme (m.) d'état diplomat, statesman
les États-Unis (m. pl.) United States, 13.2
l' été (m.) summer, 9.1
en été in summer, 9.1
éternuer to sneeze, 15.1
étranger, étrangère foreign, 16.1
à l'étranger abroad, in a foreign country
être to be, 2.1
être à l'heure to be on time, 8.1
être d'accord to agree, 2.1
être en avance to be early, 8.1
être en bonne (mauvaise) santé to be in good (poor) health, 15.1
être en retard to be late, 8.2
être enrhumé(e) to have a cold, 15.1
être vite sur pied to be back on one's feet in no time, 15.2
ne pas être dans son assiette to be feeling out of sorts, 15.2
l' être (m.) humain human being
étroit(e) tight (shoes), narrow, 10.2
l' étudiant(e) (university) student
étudier to study, 3.1
européen(ne) European, 9
eux them (m. pl. stress pron.), 9
s' évaporer to evaporate
éventuellement possibly
évoquer to evoke
l' examen (m.) test, exam, 3.1
passer un examen to take a test, 3.1
réussir à un examen to pass a test, 7
examiner to examine, 15.2
excellent(e) excellent
exceptionnel(le) exceptional
l' exemple (m.) example

par exemple for example
s' exercer to practice
l' expansion (f.) expansion
l' expédition (f.) expedition
expliquer to explain
l' explorateur (m.) explorer
explorer to explore
exposer to exhibit
l' exposition (f.) exhibit, show, 16.2
l' express (m.) espresso, black coffee, 5.1
s' exprimer to express oneself
expulser to expel, banish
exquis(e) exquisite
l' extérieur (m.) exterior, outside
extra terrific (inform.), 2.2
extraordinaire extraordinary
extrêmement extremely

F

fabriqué(e) made
fabriquer to make
fabuleux, fabuleuse fabulous
fâché(e) angry, 12.2
facile easy, 2.1
la façon way, manner
d'une façon générale in a general way
le facteur factor
la facture bill (hotel, etc.), 17.2
facultatif, facultative elective
faire to do, make, 6.1
faire du (+ nombre) to take size (+ number), 10.2
faire des achats to shop, make purchases, 10.1
faire de l'aérobic to do aerobics, 11.2
faire l'annonce to announce, 8
faire attention to pay attention, 6; to be careful, 9.1
faire une chute to fall, take a fall, 14.2
faire la connaissance de to meet
faire les courses to do the grocery shopping, 6.1
faire la cuisine to cook, 6
faire les devoirs to do homework, 6
faire un diagnostic to diagnose, 15.2
faire des économies to save money, 18.2
faire enregistrer to check (luggage), 7.1
faire des études to study, 6

faire de l'exercice to exercise, 11.2
faire du français (des maths, etc.) to study French (math, etc.), 6
faire de la gymnastique to do gymnastics, 11.2
faire du jogging to jog, 11.2
faire le levé topographique to survey (land)
faire de la monnaie to make change, 18.1
faire de la natation to swim, go swimming
faire la navette to go back and forth
faire une ordonnance to write a prescription, 15.2
faire partie de to be a part of
faire du patin to skate, 14.2
faire du patin à glace to ice-skate, 14.2
faire du patin à roulettes to roller-skate
faire peur à to frighten
faire un pique-nique to have a picnic, 6
faire de la planche à voile to go windsurfing, 9.1
faire le plein to fill up (a gas tank), 12.1
faire de la plongée sous-marine to go deep-sea diving, 9.1
faire une promenade to take a walk, 9.1
faire la queue to wait in line, 8.1
faire un régime to go on a diet
faire du ski to ski, 14.1
faire du ski nautique to water-ski, 9.1
faire du sport to play sports
faire du surf to go surfing, 9.1
faire du surf des neiges to go snowboarding
faire sa toilette to wash and groom oneself, 11.1
faire les valises to pack (suitcases), 7.1
faire un voyage to take a trip, 7.1
le fait fact
fait(e) à la main handmade
la famille family, 4.1
la famille à parent unique single-parent family
le/la fana fan

fantaisiste whimsical
fantastique fantastic, 1.2
fatigué(e) tired
fauché(e) broke (slang), 18.2
faut: il faut (+ nom) (noun) is (are) necessary
  il faut (+ inf.) one must, it is necessary to (+ verb), 9.1
la **faute** mistake
faux, fausse false
favori(te) favorite, 10
la **femme** woman, 2.1; wife, 4.1
  la **femme médecin** (woman) doctor
la **fenêtre** window
  côté fenêtre window (seat) (adj.), 7.1
fermé(e) closed, 16.2
la **fertilité** fertility
la **fête** party, 3.2
  donner une fête to throw a party, 3.2
  la **Fête des Mères (Pères)** Mother's (Father's) Day
le **feu** traffic light, 12.2
  le **feu orange** yellow traffic light, 12.2
  le **feu rouge** red traffic light, 12.2
  le **feu vert** green traffic light, 12.2
la **feuille** leaf
  la **feuille de papier** sheet of paper, BV
février (m.) February, 4.1
la **fiche d'enregistrement** registration card (hotel), 17.1
la **fièvre** fever, 15.1
  la **fièvre jaune** yellow fever
  avoir une fièvre de cheval to have a high fever, 15.2
la **figure** face, 11.1
le **filet** net shopping bag, 6.1; net (tennis, etc.), 9.2; rack (train)
la **fille** girl, BV; daughter, 4.1
le **film** film, movie, 16.1
  le **film d'amour** love story, 16.1
  le **film d'aventures** adventure movie, 16.1
  le **film étranger** foreign film, 16.1
  le **film d'horreur** horror film, 16.1
  le **film policier** detective movie, 16.1
  le **film de science-fiction** science-fiction movie, 16.1
le **fils** son, 4.1

fin(e) fine
  aux fines herbes with herbs, 5.1
finalement finally
finir to finish, 7
fixe: à prix fixe at a fixed price
flamand(e) Flemish
flambé(e) flaming
flâner to stroll
le **fleuve** river
flotter to float
la **fluctuation** fluctuation
le **foie** liver
  avoir mal au foie to have indigestion, 15
la **fois** time (in a series)
le **fonctionnement** functioning
fonctionner to function, work
fond: au fond de at the bottom of
le **fondateur,** la **fondatrice** founder
fonder to found
la **fontaine** fountain
le **foot(ball)** soccer, 13.1
  le **football américain** football
la **force** force, power
le **forcing: faire le forcing** to put pressure on
la **forêt** forest
le **forfait-journée** lift ticket (skiing)
la **forme** form, shape
  le **club de forme** health club, 11.2
  être en forme to be in shape, 11.2
  la **forme (physique)** physical fitness
  rester en forme to stay in shape, 11.2
  se mettre en forme to get in shape, 11.2
former to form; to train
le **formulaire** form, data sheet
la **formule** formula
le **fort** fort
fort(e) strong; good
fort (adv.) hard, 9.2
fou, folle crazy
le **foulard** scarf
la **foule: venir en foule** to crowd (into)
la **fourchette** fork, 5.2
la **fourmi** ant
les **frais (m. pl.)** expenses, charges, 17.2
la **fraise** strawberry
le **franc** franc, 18.1
le **français** French (language), 2.2

le/la **Français(e)** Frenchman (woman)
français(e) French, 1.1
la **France** France, 16
franchement frankly
francophone French-speaking
frapper to hit, 9.2
freiner to brake, put on the brakes, 12.1
fréquemment frequently
fréquent(e) frequent
fréquenter to frequent, patronize
le **frère** brother, 1.2
le **fric** money, dough (slang), 18.2
  avoir plein de fric to have lots of money (slang), 18.2
les **frissons (m. pl.)** chills, 15.1
les **frites (f. pl.)** French fries, 5.1
  froid(e) cold, 14.2
  avoir froid to be cold
  Il fait froid. It's cold. (weather), 9.2
le **fromage** cheese, 5.1
le **front** front (weather)
la **frontière** border
le **fruit** fruit, 6.2
  les **fruits de mer** seafood
fumer to smoke
fumeurs (adj. inv.) smoking (section), 7.1
non-fumeurs no smoking (section), 7.1
furieux, furieuse furious
la **fusée** rocket
le **futur** future

G

le/la **gagnant(e)** winner, 13.2
gagner to earn, 3.2; to win, 9.2
la **galaxie** galaxy
le **galet** pebble
le **Gange** Ganges River
le **gant** glove, 14.1
  le **gant de toilette** washcloth, 17.2
le **garage** garage, 4.2
le **garçon** boy, BV
garder to guard
le **gardien de but** goalie, 13.1
la **gare** train station, 8.1
  garer la voiture to park the car, 12.2
  gastronomique gastronomic, gourmet
le **gâteau** cake, 6.1
  gauche: à gauche de to, on the left of, 5
le **gaz** gas
  geler to freeze

Il gèle. It's freezing. (weather), **14.2**
le **gendarme** police officer
le **général** general, **7**
général: en général in general
généralement generally
généraliser to generalize
généraliste: le médecin généraliste general practitioner
généreux, généreuse generous, **10**
la **générosité** generosity
le **genre** type, kind, **16.1**
les **gens (m. pl.)** people
gentil(le) nice (person), **9**
la **géographie** geography, **2.2**
la **géométrie** geometry, **2.2**
géométrique geometric
la **glace** ice cream, **5.1**; mirror, **11.1**; ice, **14.2**
glisser to slip, slide
le **globe** globe
la **glucide** carbohydrate
le **golfe** gulf
la **gorge** throat, **15.1**
avoir un chat dans la gorge to have a frog in one's throat, **15.2**
avoir la gorge qui gratte to have a scratchy throat, **15.1**
avoir mal à la gorge to have a sore throat, **15.1**
gourmand(e) fond of eating
goûter to taste
le **gouvernement** government
grâce à thanks to
le **gradin** bleacher (stadium), **13.1**
la **graisse** fat
la graisse animale animal fat
la **grammaire** grammar
le **gramme** gram, **6.2**
grand(e) tall, big, **1.1**
pas grand-chose not much
le grand couturier clothing designer, **10.1**
le grand magasin department store, **10.1**
de grand standing luxury (adj.)
la Grande-Bretagne Great Britain, **16**
les Grands Lacs (m. pl.) the Great Lakes
grandir to grow (up) (children)
la **grand-mère** grandmother, **4.1**
le **grand-père** grandfather, **4.1**
les **grands-parents (m. pl.)** grandparents, **4.1**
grave serious

la **Grèce** Greece
la **griffe** label
le **grill-express** snack bar (train)
la **grippe** flu, **15.1**
gris(e) gray, **10.2**
grossir to gain weight, **11.2**
la **Guadeloupe** Guadeloupe
la **guerre: la Deuxième Guerre mondiale** World War II
le **guichet** ticket window, **8.1**; box office, **16.1**
le **guide** guidebook, **12.2**
le **gymnase** gym(nasium), **11.2**
la **gymnastique** gymnastics, **2.2**
faire de la gymnastique to do gymnastics, **11.2**

H

habillé(e) dressy, **10.1**
s' **habiller** to get dressed, **11.1**
l' **habitant(e)** resident
habiter to live (in a city, house, etc.), **3.1**
le **hall** lobby, **17.1**
les **haricots (m. pl.) verts** green beans, **6.2**
haut(e) high, **10.2**
avoir... mètres de haut to be ... meters high
du haut de from the top of
en haut de to, at the top of
la haute couture high fashion
à talons hauts high-heeled (shoes)
le **haut-parleur** loudspeaker, **8.1**
le **héros** hero
l' **heure (f.)** time (of day), **2**
à quelle heure? at what time?, **2**
À tout à l'heure. See you later., **BV**
de bonne heure early
être à l'heure to be on time, **8.1**
Il est quelle heure? What time is it?, **2**
heureux, heureuse happy, **10.2**
l' **hexagone (m.)** hexagon
hier yesterday, **13.1**
avant-hier the day before yesterday, **13**
hier matin yesterday morning, **13**
hier soir last night, **13**
l' **histoire (f.)** history, **2.2**
l' **hiver (m.)** winter, **14.1**
en hiver in winter, **14.2**
le **H.L.M.** low-income housing
le **hockey** hockey

le **hockey sur glace** ice hockey
la **Hollande** Holland, the Netherlands, **16**
l' **homme (m.)** man, **2.1**
l'homme d'affaires businessman
l'homme d'état diplomat, statesman
les **honoraires (m. pl.)** fees (doctor)
l' **hôpital (m.)** hospital
l' **horaire (m.)** schedule, timetable, **8.1**
hors des limites out of bounds, **9.2**
l' **hôtel (m.)** hotel, **17.1**
l' **hôtesse (f.) de l'air** flight attendant (f.), **7.2**
huit eight, **BV**
humain(e) human
humide wet, humid
humoristique humorous
l' **hydrate (m.) de carbone** carbohydrate
hystérique hysterical

I

idéal(e) ideal
l' **idée (f.)** idea
identifier to identify
il he, it, **1**
Il est... heure(s). It's ... o'clock., **2**
Il est quelle heure? What time is it?, **2**
il faut (+ nom) (noun) is (are) needed
il faut (+ inf.) one must, it is necessary to (+ verb), **9.1**
Il n'y a pas de quoi. You're welcome., **BV**
il vaut mieux it is better
il y a there is, there are, **4.2**
l' **île (f.)** island
illustré(e) illustrated
ils they (m.), **2**
l' **immeuble (m.)** apartment building, **4.2**
l' **immigration (f.)** immigration, **7.2**
passer à l'immigration to go through immigration (airport), **7.2**
impatient(e) impatient, **1.1**
important(e) important
les **Impressionnistes (m. pl.)** Impressionists (painters)
inauguré(e) inaugurated
inclure to include

inconnu(e) unknown
incroyable incredible
l' **Inde (f.)** India
l' **indication (f.)** cue
indiquer to indicate
industrialisé(e) industrialized
l' **industrie (f.)** industry
infectieux, infectieuse infectious
l' **infection (f.)** infection, 15.1
infiltrer to seep (into)
influencer to influence
l' **informatique (f.)** computer science, 2.2
l' **inondation (f.)** flood
s' **installer** to settle (down), move in
l' **institut (m.)** institute
l' **institution (f.)** institution
les **instructions (f. pl.)** instructions, 9.1
l' **instrument (m.)** instrument
intelligent(e) intelligent, 1.1
interdit(e) forbidden, prohibited
   Il est interdit de stationner. No parking., 12.2
intéressant(e) interesting, 1.1
intéresser to interest
s' **intéresser à** to be interested in
l' **intérieur (m.)** interior, inside
intérieur(e) domestic (flight) (adj.), 7.1
international(e) international, 7.1
intitulé(e) titled
inviter to invite, 3.2
isoler to isolate
l' **Italie (f.)** Italy, 16
italien(ne) Italian, 9

J

jamais ever
   ne... jamais never
le **jambon** ham, 5.1
janvier (m.) January, 4.1
le **Japon** Japan, 16
japonais(e) Japanese
le **jardin** garden, 4.2
jaune yellow, 10.2
je I, 1.2
   Je t'en prie. You're welcome. (fam.), BV
   je voudrais I would like, 5.1
   Je vous en prie. You're welcome. (form.), BV; Please, I beg of you.
le **jean** jeans, 10.1
jeter to throw

le **jeu: les jeux de la lumière** play of light
jeudi (m.) Thursday, 2.2
jeune young, 4.1
la **jeune fille** girl
les **jeunes (m. pl.)** young people
le **jogging: faire du jogging** to jog, 11.2
joli(e) pretty, 4.2
jouer to play, to perform, 16.1
   jouer à (un sport) to play (a sport), 9.2
le **joueur, la joueuse** player, 9.2
le **jour** day, 2.2
   C'est quel jour? What day is it?, 2.2
   de nos jours today, nowadays
   par jour a (per) day, 3
   tous les jours every day
le **journal** newspaper, 8.1
   le journal intime diary
   le journal télévisé newscast
la **journée** day
juillet (m.) July, 4.1
juin (m.) June, 4.1
la **jupe** skirt, 10.1
la **jupette** tennis skirt, 9.2
le **Jura** Jura Mountains
le **jury** selection committee
jusqu'à (up) to, until, 13.2
jusqu'en bas de la piste to the bottom of the trail

K

le **kilo(gramme)** kilogram, 6.2
le **kilomètre** kilometer
le **kiosque** newsstand, 8.1
le **kleenex** tissue, Kleenex, 15.1

L

la the (f.), 1; her, it (dir. obj.), 16
là there
là-bas over there, BV
le **laboratoire** laboratory
le **lac** lake
   les Grands Lacs (m. pl.) the Great Lakes
laisser to leave (something behind), 5.2
   laisser un pourboire to leave a tip, 5.2
le **lait** milk, 6.1
la **laitue** lettuce, 6.2
lancer to throw, 13.2
la **langue** language, 2.2
large loose, wide, 10.2
le **latin** Latin, 2.2
la **latitude** latitude
laver to wash, 11.1

se **laver** to wash oneself, 11.1
   se laver les cheveux (la figure, etc.) to wash one's hair (face, etc.), 11.1
le the (m.), 1; him, it (dir. obj.), 16.1
la **leçon** lesson, 9.1
   la leçon de conduite driving lesson, 12.2
la **lecture** reading
légendaire legendary
la **légende** legend
le **légume** vegetable, 6.2
lent(e) slow
lentement slowly
les the (pl.), 2; them (dir. obj.), 16
leur their (sing. poss. adj.), 5; (to) them (ind. obj.), 17
leurs their (pl. poss. adj.), 5
levant rising
le **levé: faire le levé topographique** to survey
se **lever** to get up, 11.1
le **lexique** vocabulary
   libérer la chambre to vacate the room, 17.2
libre free, 2.2
le **lieu** place
   avoir lieu to take place
la **ligne** line
   les grandes lignes main lines (trains)
   les lignes de banlieue commuter trains
la **limitation de vitesse** speed limit
les **limites (f. pl.)** boundaries (on tennis court), 9.2
   hors des limites out of bounds, 9.2
la **limonade** lemon-lime drink
la **lipide** fat
   lire to read, 12.2
Lisbonne Lisbon
le **lit** bed, 8.2
le **litre** liter, 6.2
littéraire literary
la **littérature** literature, 2.2
la **livre** pound, 6.2
le **livre** book, BV
la **location** rental
   loin de far from, 4.2
les **loisirs (m. pl.)** leisure activities, 16
Londres London
le **long: le long de** along
long(ue) long, 10.2
la **longitude** longitude
longtemps (for) a long time

la **longueur** length
lorsque while
louer to rent
lourd(e) heavy
lui him (m. sing. stress pron.),
9; (to) him, (to) her (ind.
obj.), **17.1**
la **lumière** light
lundi (m.) Monday, **2.2**
les **lunettes** (f. pl.) (ski) goggles,
14.1
les lunettes de soleil
sunglasses, **9.1**
lutter to fight
le **luxe** luxury
luxueux, luxueuse luxurious
le **lycée** high school, **1.2**
le/la **lycéen(ne)** high school student

M

ma my (f. sing. poss. adj.), **4**
Madame (Mme) Mrs., Ms., **BV**
Mademoiselle (Mlle) Miss, Ms.,
BV
le **magasin** store, **3.2**
le **magazine** magazine, **3.2**
magnifique magnificent
mai (m.) May, **4.1**
maigrir to lose weight, **11.2**
le **maillot de bain** bathing suit,
9.1
la **main** hand, **11.1**
fait(e) à la main handmade
maintenant now, **2.1**
mais but, **1**
Mais oui (non)! Of course
(not)!
la **maison** house, **3.1**
le **maître** master
le maître d'hôtel maitre d',
5.2
mal badly
avoir mal à to have a(n) …
-ache, to hurt, **15.1**
Où avez-vous mal? Where
does it hurt?, **15.2**
Pas mal. Not bad., **BV**
le/la **malade** sick person, patient,
15.1
malade sick, **15.1**
la **maladie** illness
malheureusement
unfortunately
la **Manche** English Channel
la **manche** sleeve, **10.1**
à manches longues (courtes)
long- (short-)sleeved, **10.2**
manger to eat
la **mangue** mango
la **manière** manner, way

avoir de bonnes manières to
have good manners
manquer: il en manque deux
two are missing
se **maquiller** to put on make-up,
11.1
le **marathon** marathon
le **marbre** marble
le/la **marchand(e) (de fruits et
légumes)** (produce) seller,
6.2; merchant
la **marchandise** merchandise
le **marché** market, **6.2**
mardi (m.) Tuesday, **2.2**
la **marée** tide
le **mari** husband, **4.1**
le **mariage** marriage
marié(e) married
le **marin** sailor
le **Maroc** Morocco, **16**
la **marque** make (of car), **12.1**
marquer un but to score a goal,
13.1
marron (inv.) brown, **10.2**
mars (m.) March, **4.1**
martiniquais(e) from
Martinique
la **Martinique** Martinique
la **masse** mass
le **match** game, **9.2**
les **mathématiques** (f. pl.)
mathematics
les **maths** (f. pl.) math, **2.2**
la **matière** subject (school), **2.2**;
matter
le **matin** morning, in the
morning, **2**
du matin A.M. (time), **2**
mauvais(e) bad; wrong
Il fait mauvais. It's bad
weather., **9.2**
le **mazout** fuel oil
me (to) me (dir. and ind. obj.),
15.2
la **médaille** medal
le **médecin** doctor (m. and f.),
15.2
chez le médecin at, to the
doctor's, **15.2**
le femme médecin (woman)
doctor
la **médecine** medicine (medical
profession), **15**
médical(e) medical
le **médicament** medicine
(remedy), **15.2**
la **médina** medina (old Arab
section of northwestern
African town)
meilleur(e) better (adj.), **10**

le **membre** member
même same (adj.), **2.1**; even
(adv.)
le/la **mennonite** Mennonite
mental(e) mental
la **menthe: le thé à la menthe**
mint tea
le **menu: le menu touristique**
budget (fixed price) meal
la **mer** sea, **9.1**
la mer des Caraïbes
Caribbean Sea
la mer Méditerranée
Mediterranean Sea
merci thank you, **BV**
mercredi (m.) Wednesday, **2.2**
la **mère** mother, **4.1**
le **méridien** meridian
merveilleux, merveilleuse
marvelous, **10.2**
mes my (pl. poss. adj.), **4**
la **mesure** measurement
sur mesure tailored (to one's
measurements), tailor-made
mesurer to measure
le **métabolisme** metabolism
la **météo** weather forecast
la **météorologie** meteorology, the
study of weather
météorologique meteorological
le **métier** profession
le **mètre** meter
métrique metric
le **métro** subway, **4.2**
en métro by subway, **5.2**
la station de métro subway
station, **4.2**
mettre to put (on), to place,
8.1; to put on (clothes), **10**; to
turn on (appliance), **8**
mettre au point to come out
with, develop
mettre de l'argent de côté to
put money aside, save, **18.2**
mettre le contact to start the
car, **12.1**
mettre le couvert to set the
table, **8**
se **mettre en forme** to get in
shape, **11.1**
le **Mexique** Mexico, **16**
le **microbe** microbe
la **microbiologie** microbiology
le **microscope** microscope
midi (m.) noon, **2.2**
le **militaire** soldier
militaire military
mille (one) thousand, **6.2**
les **milliers** (m. pl.) thousands
le **minéral** mineral

le **ministère** ministry
minuit (m.) midnight, **2.2**
la **mission** mission
la **mi-temps** half (sporting event)
moche terrible, ugly, **2.2**
le **modèle** model
moderne modern
moderniser to modernize
modeste modest, reasonably priced
moi me (sing. stress pron.), **1.2; 9**
moins less
  au moins at least
  Il est une heure moins dix. It's ten to one. (time), **2**
  moins... que less ... than
le **mois** month, **4.1**
le **moment: en ce moment** right now
mon my (m. sing. poss. adj.), **4**
le **monde** world
  beaucoup de monde a lot of people, **13.1**
  tout le monde everyone, everybody, **BV**
le **moniteur**, la **monitrice** instructor, **9.1**; camp counselor
la **monnaie** change; currency, **18.1**
  faire de la monnaie to make change, **18.1**
Monsieur (M.) Mr., sir, **BV**
la **montagne** mountain, **14.1**
  à la montagne in the mountains
monter to go up, get on, get in, **8.2**; to take upstairs, **17.1**
  monter une pièce to put on a play, **16.1**
montrer to show, **17.1**
moral(e) moral
le **morceau de craie** piece of chalk, **BV**
mordu(e) bitten
la **mort** death
  mort(e) dead
  mortel(le) fatal
Moscou Moscow
la **mosquée** mosque
le **mot** word
  le mot apparenté cognate
le **motard** motorcycle cop, **12.2**
le **moteur** engine (car, etc.), **12.1**
la **moto** motorcycle, **12.1**
le **mouchoir** handkerchief, **15.1**
mourir to die, **17**
la **moutarde** mustard, **6.2**
le **mouvement** movement
  mouvementé(e) eventful

moyen(ne) average, intermediate
le **moyen de transport** mode of transportation
municipal(e) municipal
musclé(e) muscular
le **musée** museum, **16.2**
la **musique** music, **2.2**
la **mythologie** mythology

N

nager to swim, **9.1**
  nager la brasse papillon to do the butterfly (swim stroke)
le **nageur**, la **nageuse** swimmer
naître to be born, **17**
la **nappe** tablecloth, **5.2**
la **natation** swimming, **9.1**
la **nation** nation
national(e) national
la **nature** nature
  nature plain (adj.), **5.1**
la **navette: faire la navette** to go back and forth
ne: ne... jamais never, **12**
  ne... pas not, **1.2**
  ne... personne no one, nobody, **12.2**
  ne... rien nothing, **12.2**
né: il est né he was born
nécessaire necessary
négatif, négative negative
la **neige** snow, **14.2**
neige (inf. neiger): Il neige. It's snowing., **14.1**
nerveux, nerveuse nervous
  les cellules nerveuses (f. pl.) nerve cells
n'est-ce pas? isn't it?, doesn't it (he, she, etc.)?, **1.2**
neuf nine, **BV**
neutraliser to neutralize
le **neveu** nephew, **4.1**
le **nez** nose, **15.1**
  avoir le nez qui coule to have a runny nose, **15.1**
ni... ni neither ... nor
la **nièce** niece, **4.1**
le **niveau** level
  vérifier les niveaux to check under the hood, **12.1**
noir(e) black, **10.2**
  le tableau noir blackboard, **3.1**
le **nom** name, **16.2**; noun
le **nombre** number, **5.2**
nombreux, nombreuse numerous
nommer to name, mention

non no
  non-fumeurs no smoking (section), **7.1**
  non seulement not only
le **nord** north
normal(e) normal
normalement normally, usually
nos our (pl. poss. adj.), **5**
la **nostalgie** nostalgia
la **note** bill (currency), **17.2**; grade
notre our (sing. poss. adj.), **5**
nourrir to feed
la **nourriture** food, nutrition
nous we, **2**; us (stress pron.), **9**; (to) us (dir. and ind. obj.), **15**
nouveau (nouvel) new (m.), **4**
nouvelle new (f.), **4**
les **nouvelles (f. pl.)** news
novembre (m.) November, **4.1**
le **nuage** cloud, **9.2**
la **nuit** night
le **numéro** number
  Quel est le numéro de téléphone de... ? What is the phone number of ... ?, **5.2**

O

obéir (à) to obey, **7**
l' **objet (m.)** object
obligatoire mandatory
obliger to oblige
obtenir to obtain
occidental(e) western
occupé(e) busy, **2.2**
occuper to occupy
l' **océan (m.)** ocean
octobre (m.) October, **4.1**
l' **odeur (f.)** scent, smell
l' **œil (m., pl. yeux)** eye
l' **œuf (m.)** egg, **6.2**
  l'œuf sur le plat fried egg
l' **œuvre (f.)** work (of art), **16**
officiel(le) official
offrir to offer, give, **15**
l' **oignon (m.)** onion, **6.2**
l' **omelette (f.)** omelette, **5.1**
  l'omelette aux fines herbes omelette with herbs, **5.1**
  l'omelette nature plain omelette, **5.1**
on we, they, people, **3**
  On y va.(?) Let's go.; Shall we go?, **5**
l' **oncle (m.)** uncle, **4.1**
onze eleven, **BV**
l' **opéra (m.)** opera, **16.1**
opérer to operate
opposer to oppose, **13.1**
l' **or (m.)** gold

l' **orage** (m.) storm
l' **orange** (f.) orange, **6.2**
   orange (inv.) orange (color), **10**
l' **Orangina** (m.) orange soda, **5.1**
   ordinaire regular (gasoline), **12.1**
l' **ordinateur** (m.) computer, **BV**
l' **ordonnance** (f.) prescription, **15.2**
   faire une ordonnance to write a prescription, **15.2**
l' **oreille** (f.) ear, **15.1**
   avoir mal aux oreilles to have an earache, **15**
l' **oreiller** (m.) pillow, **17.2**
les **oreillons** (m. pl.) mumps
   organisé(e) organized
l' **organisme** (m.) organism
   original(e) original
l' **origine** (f.): **à l'origine** originally
   d'origine américaine (française, etc.) from the U.S. (France, etc.)
   orner to decorate
l' **os** (m.) bone
   ôter to take off (clothing)
   ou or, **1.1**
   où where, **BV**
   oublier to forget
l' **ouest** (m.) west
   oui yes, **1**
   ouvert(e) open, **16**
l' **ouverture** (f.) opening
l' **ouvrier, l'ouvrière** worker
   ouvrir to open, **15**
   ovale oval
l' **oxygène** (m.) oxygen

P

le **pain** bread, **6.1**
la **paire** pair, **10**
le **palais** palace
le **panier** basket, **13.2**
le **panneau** backboard (basketball), **13.2**
   le panneau routier road sign
   panoramique panoramic
le **pantalon** pants, **10.1**
la **papeterie** stationery store
le **papier** paper, **6**
   la feuille de papier sheet of paper, **BV**
   le papier hygiénique toilet paper, **17.2**
le **paquet** package, **6.2**
   par by, through
   par dessus over (prep.), **13**
   par exemple for example
   par jour a (per) day, **3**

par semaine a (per) week, **3.2**
le **paradis** paradise, heaven
le **paragraphe** paragraph
le **parallèle** parallel
le **parc** park, **11.2**
   parce que because, **9.1**
   parcourir to travel, go through
   pardon excuse me, pardon me
le **parebrise** windshield, **12**
les **parents** (m. pl.) parents, **4.1**
   parfait(e) perfect
   parisien(ne) Parisian, **9**
le **parking** parking lot
le **parlement** parliament
   parler to speak, talk, **3.1**
   parler au téléphone to talk on the phone, **3.2**
   parmi among
   participer (à) to participate (in)
   particulièrement particularly
la **partie** game, match, **9.2**; part
   faire partie de to be a part of
   la partie en simple (en double) singles (doubles) match (tennis), **9.2**
   partir to leave, **7.1**
   partout everywhere
   pas not
   pas de (+ nom) no (+ noun)
   Pas de quoi. You're welcome. (inform.), **BV**
   pas du tout not at all
   Pas mal. Not bad., **BV**
   pas mal de quite a few
le **passager, la passagère** passenger, **7.1**
le **passé** past
le **passeport** passport, **7.1**
   passer to spend (time), **3**; to pass, go through, **7.2**
   passer à la douane to go through customs, **7.2**
   passer à l'immigration to go through immigration
   passer par le contrôle de sécurité to go through security (airport), **7**
   passer un examen to take an exam, **3.1**
   passer un film to show a movie, **16.1**
   passionné(e) de excited by
   passionner to excite
le **pâté** pâté, **5.1**
   patient(e) patient, **1.1**
le **patin** skate; skating, **14.2**
   faire du patin to skate, **14.2**
   faire du patin à glace to ice-skate, **14.2**

faire du patin à roulettes to roller-skate
   le patin à glace ice skate, **14.2**
le **patinage** skating, **14.2**
le **patineur, la patineuse** skater, **14.2**
la **patinoire** skating rink, **14.2**
le/la **pauvre** poor thing, **15.1**
   pauvre poor, **15.1**
le **pavillon** small house, bungalow
   payer to pay, **6.1**
   payer en espèces to pay cash, **17**
le **pays** country, **7.1**
le **paysage** landscape
les **Pays-Bas** (m. pl.) the Netherlands, **16**
le **péage: l'autoroute** (f.) **à péage** toll road
la **pêche** fishing
   aller à la pêche to go fishing, **9.1**
   faire une belle pêche to catch a lot of fish
   le port de pêche fishing port
le **peigne** comb
se **peigner** to comb (one's hair), **11.1**
   peindre to paint
le/la **peintre** painter, artist, **16.2**
la **peinture** painting, **16.2**
   péjoratif, péjorative pejorative, disparaging
le **penalty** penalty (soccer)
   pendant during, for (time), **3.2**
   pendant que while
la **pénicilline** penicillin, **15.2**
   penser to think, **10.1**
le **penseur** thinker
la **pension** small hotel
   perdre to lose, **8.2**
   perdre des kilos to lose weight
   perdre patience to lose patience, **8.2**
le **père** father, **4.1**
la **périphérie** outskirts
la **perle** pearl
   permettre to permit, allow, **14**
le **permis** license
   le permis de conduire driver's license, **12.2**
le **personnage** character
la **personne** person
   ne... personne no one, nobody, **12.2**
   personnel(le) personal
le **personnel de bord** flight attendants, **7.2**

personnellement personally, 16.2
la **perte** loss
peser to weigh
petit(e) short, small, 1.1
   la **petite annonce** classified ad
   le **petit déjeuner** breakfast, 9
   prendre le petit déjeuner to eat breakfast, 9
la **petite-fille** granddaughter, 4.1
le **petit-fils** grandson, 4.1
le **pétrolier** oil tanker
peu (de) few, little, 18
   un peu (de) a little
la **pharmacie** pharmacy, 15.2
le/la **pharmacien(ne)** pharmacist, 15.2
la **photo** photograph
la **phrase** sentence
la **physique** physics, 2.2
physique physical
   la **forme physique** physical fitness, 13
la **pièce** room, 4.2; play, 16.1; coin, 18.1
le **pied** foot, 13.1
   à pied on foot, 5.2
la **pierre** stone
le/la **piéton(ne)** pedestrian, 12.2
le/la **pilote** pilot
   le/la **pilote de ligne** airline pilot
   piloter to pilot
le **pique-nique: faire un pique-nique** to have a picnic, 6
la **piscine** pool, 9.2
   la **piscine couverte** indoor pool
la **piste** track, 13.2; ski trail, 14.1
pittoresque picturesque
le **placard** closet, 17.2
la **place** seat (plane, train, etc.), 7.1; parking space, 12.2; place
la **plage** beach, 9.1
la **plaine** plain
le **plan** map
la **planche à voile: faire de la planche à voile** to windsurf, 9.1
la **plante** plant
   les **plantes aquatiques** aquatic vegetation
le **plastique: en plastique** plastic (adj.)
le **plat** dish (food)
le **plateau** plateau
plein(e) full, 13.1

avoir plein de fric to have lots of money (slang), 18.2
en pleine zone tempérée right in the temperate zone
faire le plein to fill up (a gas tank), 12.1
pleut (inf. **pleuvoir**): **Il pleut.** It's raining., 9.2
la **plongée sous-marine: faire de la plongée sous-marine** to go deep-sea diving, 9.1
plonger to dive, 9.1
la **pluie** rain
   les **pluies acides** acid rain
la **plupart (des)** most (of), 8.2
le **pluriel** plural
plus more (comparative), 10
   en plus de in addition to
   plus ou moins more or less
   plus tard later
plusieurs several, 18
le **pneu** tire, 12.1
   le **pneu à plat** flat tire, 12.1
la **poche** pocket, 18.1
le **poème** poem
la **poésie** poetry
le **poète** poet (m. and f.)
le **poids** weight
le **point** point; period
   à point medium-rare (meat), 5.2
la **pointure** size (shoes), 10.2
   Vous faites quelle pointure? What (shoe) size do you take?, 10.2
le **poisson** fish, 6.1
la **poissonnerie** fish store, 6.1
le **pôle** pole
la **poliomyélite** polio
polluer to pollute
la **pollution** pollution
la **Polynésie française** French Polynesia
la **pomme** apple, 6.2
la **pomme de terre** potato, 6.2
le/la **pompiste** gas station attendant, 12.1
populaire popular, 1.2
la **porcelaine** porcelaine, china
le **port** port, harbor
   le **port de pêche** fishing port
le **portail** doorway (church)
la **porte** gate (airport), 7.1; door, 17.1
le **portefeuille** wallet, 18.1
le **porte-monnaie** change purse, 18.1
porter to wear, 10.1
le **porteur** porter, 8.1
le **portrait** portrait

le **Portugal** Portugal, 16
   poser une question to ask a question, 3.1
la **possibilité** possibility
le **pot** jar, 6.2
le **pouce** inch, thumb
le **poulet** chicken, 6.1
la **poupée** doll
pour for; in order to, 2
le **pourboire** tip (restaurant), 5.2
   laisser un pourboire to leave a tip, 5.2
le **pourcentage** percentage
pourquoi why, 9.1
pourtant yet, still, nevertheless
pouvoir to be able to, 6
pratiquer un sport to play a sport, 11.2
précieux, précieuse precious
précis(e) precise, exact
   à l'heure précise right on time
préféré(e) favorite
préférer to prefer, 5
le **préfixe** prefix
premier, première first, 4.1
   en première in first class, 8.1
   les **tout (inv.) premiers** (m. pl.) very first
premièrement first of all
prendre to take, 9.1; to buy; to eat (drink) (in café, restaurant, etc.)
   prendre un bain (une douche) to take a bath (shower), 11.1
   prendre un bain de soleil to sunbathe, 9.1
   prendre un billet to buy a ticket, 9
   prendre des kilos to gain weight
   prendre part à to take part in
   prendre le petit déjeuner to eat breakfast, 9
   prendre possession de to take possession of
   prendre un pot to have a drink
   prendre rendez-vous to make an appointment
   prendre le train (l'avion, etc.) to take the train (plane, etc.), 9
préparer to prepare, 4.2
près de near, 4.2
prescrire to prescribe, 15.2
présenter to present, introduce
la **préservation** preservation
presque almost

pressé(e) in a hurry

la **pression artérielle** blood pressure

prêt(e) ready

prêt-à-porter ready-to-wear (adj.), 10

le **rayon prêt-à-porter** ready-to-wear department, 10.1

prêter to lend, 18.2

la **preuve** proof

la **prévision** prediction

prévoir to predict

prie: Je vous en prie. Please, I beg of you., You're welcome., BV

la **prière** prayer

appeler à la prière to call to worship

primaire: l'école (f.) primaire elementary school

principal(e) main, principal

la **principauté** principality

le **printemps** spring, 13.2

pris(e) taken, 5.1

privé(e) private

le **prix** price, cost, 10.1

à prix fixe at a fixed price

probablement probably

le **problème** problem, 11.2

prochain(e) next, 8.2

produire to produce

le **produit** product

le/la **prof** teacher (inform.), 2.1

le **professeur** teacher (m. and f.), 2.1

professionnel(le) professional

profiter de to take advantage of, profit from

profond(e) deep

le **programme** TV program

le **progrès** progress

progressif, progressive progressive

le **projet** project, plan

la **promenade: faire une promenade** to take a walk, 9.1

se **promener** to walk, 11.2

proposer to suggest

propre own (adj.); clean

protéger to protect

la **protéine** protein

provenance: en provenance de arriving from (train, plane, etc.), 7.1

provençal(e) from Provence, the south of France

les **provisions (f. pl.)** groceries

prudemment carefully, 12.2

le **public** public

la **publicité** advertisement

les **puces (f. pl.): le marché aux puces** flea market

puissant(e) powerful

le **pull** sweater, 10.1

punir to punish, 7

pur(e) pure

la **pureté** purity

la **pyramide** pyramid

Q

le **quai** platform (railroad), 8.1

la **qualité** quality

quand when, 3.1

quarante forty, BV

le **quart: et quart** a quarter past (time), 2

moins le quart a quarter to (time), 2

le **quartier** neighborhood, district, 4.2

quatorze fourteen, BV

quatre four, BV

quatre-vingt-dix ninety, 5.2

quatre-vingts eighty, 5.2

quel(le) which, what, 7

Quel est le numéro de téléphone de... ? What is the phone number of ... ?, 5

Quelle est la date aujourd'hui? What is today's date?, 4.1

Quel temps fait-il? What's the weather like?, 9.2

quelque some (sing.)

quelque chose à manger something to eat, 5.1

quelquefois sometimes, 5

quelques some (pl.), 8.2

quelqu'un somebody, someone, 12

Qu'est-ce que c'est? What is it?, BV

Qu'est-ce qu'il a? What's wrong with him?, 15.1

la **question: poser une question** to ask a question, 3.1

la **queue: faire la queue** to wait in line, 8.1

qui who, BV; whom, 11; which, that

Qui ça? Who (do you mean)?, BV

Qui est-ce? Who is it?, BV

quinze fifteen, BV

quitter to leave (a room, etc.), 3.1

quoi what (after prep.), 14

quotidien(ne) daily, everyday

R

raconter to tell (about)

le **racquet(-ball)** racquetball

la **radio** radio, 3.2

radioactif, radioactive radioactive

la **rage** rabies

raide steep, 14.2

la **raison** reason

ralentir to slow down

le **randonneur, la randonneuse** hiker

rapide quick, fast

le **rapport** relationship; report

rapporter to report

la **raquette** racket, 9.2

rare rare

se **raser** to shave, 11.1

le **rasoir** razer, shaver

rassembler to collect, gather together

le **rayon** department (in a store), 10.1

la **réaction** reaction

réaliser to realize (an ambition), achieve

la **réalité** reality

la **réception** front desk (hotel), 17.1

le/la **réceptionniste** desk clerk, 17.1

la **recette** recipe

recevoir to receive, 18.1

la **recherche: faire de la recherche** to do research

rechercher to seek

recommandé(e) recommended

reconnu(e) recognized

la **récréation** recess

récrire to rewrite

récupérer to claim (luggage), 7.2

refléter to reflect

regarder to look at, 3.1

se **regarder** to look at oneself, look at one another

le **régime: faire un régime** to go on a diet

le **régime alimentaire** diet

la **région** region

la **règle** rule

le **règlement** rule

régler to direct (traffic)

regretter to be sorry

régulier, régulière regular

régulièrement regularly

relativement relatively

le **relevé de compte** statement (bank), 18

relié(e) connected

remarquer to notice

rembourser to pay back, reimburse, **18.2**
remplir to fill out, **7.2**
la **rencontre** meeting
rencontrer to meet
le **rendez-vous: prendre rendez-vous** to make an appointment
rendre to give back, **18.2**
les **renseignements (m. pl.)** information
rentrer to go home, **3.1**
renvoyer to return (tennis ball), **9.2**
la **répartition** distribution
le **repas** meal
répéter to repeat
répondre to answer, **8**
la **réponse** answer
se **reposer** to rest
repoussé(e) pushed back
représenter to represent
la **reprise** reshowing
reproduire to reproduce
la **république** republic, democracy
la **réserve** resource, supply
réservé(e) reserved
réserver to reserve
le **réservoir** gas tank, **12.1**
résidentiel(le) residential
la **résistance** resistance
respecter to respect
la **respiration** breathing
respirer (à fond) to breathe (deeply), **15.2**
ressembler à to resemble
ressentir to feel
le **restaurant** restaurant, **5.2**
la **restauration** food service
rester to stay, remain, **17**
rester en forme to stay in shape, **11.1**
le **retard** delay
en retard late, **8.2**
retomber to fall back down
le **retour** return
à votre retour when you return
la **retransmission** rebroadcast
réunir to bring together
réussir (à) to succeed; to pass (exam), **7**
le **rêve** dream
se **réveiller** to wake up, **11.1**
la **révélation** revelation
revenir to come back, **16**
rêver to dream
la **révolution** revolution
révolutionner to revolutionize
le **rez-de-chaussée** ground floor, **4.2**

le **rhume** cold (illness), **15.1**
avoir un rhume to have a cold, **15.1**
riche rich
la **richesse** wealth
le **rideau** curtain, **16.1**
le lever du rideau at curtain time (theatre)
Rien d'autre. Nothing else., **6.2**
rigoler to joke around, **3.2**
Tu veux rigoler! Are you kidding?!
le **rite** rite, ritual
la **rivière** river
le **riz** rice
la **robe** dress, **10.1**; robe
le **rocher** rock
le **roi** king
le **rôle** role
le **roman** novel
le roman policier detective novel, mystery
le **romancier**, la **romancière** novelist
rond(e) round
rose pink, **10.2**
le **rosier** rosebush
la **roue** wheel, **12.1**
la roue de secours spare tire, **12.1**
les deux roues two-wheeled vehicles
rouge red, **10.2**
la **rougeole** measles
le **rouleau de papier hygiénique** roll of toilet paper, **17.2**
rouler (vite) to go, drive (fast), **12.1**
la **route** road, **12.1**
En route! Let's go!
prendre la route to take to the road
la **rubéole** German measles
la **rue** street, **3.1**
le **rugby** rugby
rural(e) rural
le/la **Russe** Russian (person)
le **rythme** rhythm

S

sa his, her (f. sing. poss. adj.), **4**
le **sable** sand, **9.1**
le **sac** bag, **6.1**; pocketbook, purse, **18.1**
le sac à dos backpack, **BV**
saignant(e) rare (meat), **5.2**
la **saison** season
la belle saison summer
la **salade** salad, **5.1**
le **salaire** salary

la **salle** room
la salle à manger dining room, **4.2**
la salle d'attente waiting room, **8.1**
la salle de bains bathroom, **4.2**
la salle de cinéma movie theatre, **16.1**
la salle de classe classroom, **2.1**
la salle de séjour living room, **4.2**
le **Salon** official art show
Salut. Hi., **BV**
samedi (m.) Saturday, **2.2**
le **sandwich** sandwich, **5.1**
sans without, **12.1**
sans aucun doute without a doubt
Sans blague! No kidding!
sans plomb unleaded, **12.1**
la **santé** health, **15.1**
être en bonne (mauvaise) santé to be in good (poor) health, **15.1**
la **saucisse de Francfort** hot dog, **5.1**
le **saucisson** salami, **6.1**
sauf except, **16.2**
sauver to save
le **savant** scientist
savoir to know (information), **16.2**
le **savon** soap, **11.1**
scandalisé(e) scandalized, shocked
la **scène** stage; scene, **16.1**
les **sciences (f. pl.)** science, **2.2**
les sciences humaines social sciences
les sciences naturelles natural sciences
le **scorbut** scurvy
le **score** score, **9.2**
le **sculpteur** sculptor (m. and f.), **16.2**
la **sculpture** sculpture, **16.2**
la **séance** show (movie), **16.1**
sec, sèche dry
se **sécher** to dry (off), **17.2**
la **sécheresse** dryness, drought
secondaire: l'école (f.) secondaire junior high, high school
la **seconde** second (time)
seconde: en seconde in second class, **8.1**
seize sixteen, **BV**
le **séjour** stay

selon according to

la **semaine** week, **2.2**; allowance
    par semaine a (per) week,
    3.2

sembler to seem

le **Sénégal** Senegal, **16**

le **sens** direction; meaning
    sens interdit (m.) wrong way
    (traffic sign)
    sens unique (m.) one way
    (traffic sign)

se **sentir** to feel (well, etc.), **15.1**

séparer to separate

sept seven, **BV**

septembre (m.) September, **4.1**

la **série** series

sérieux, sérieuse serious, **10**

serré(e) tight, **10.2**

le **serveur**, la **serveuse** waiter,
    waitress, **5.1**

le **service** tip; service, **5.2**
    Le service est compris. The
    tip is included., **5.2**

la **serviette** napkin, **5.2**; towel,
    17.2

servir to serve (food), **7.2**; to
    serve (a ball in tennis, etc.),
    9.2

ses his, her (pl. poss. adj.), **5**

seul(e) alone; single; only (adj.)
    tout(e) seul(e) all alone, by
    himself/herself

seulement only (adv.)

la **sève** sap
    tirer la sève to tap (maple
    sugar)

sévère strict

le **sexe** sex

le **shampooing** shampoo

le **short** shorts, **9.2**

si if; yes (after neg. question)

le **SIDA (Syndrome Immuno-
    Déficitaire Acquis)** AIDS

le **siècle** century

le **siège** seat, **7.1**

siffler to (blow a) whistle, **13.1**

le **signal** sign

signer to sign, **18.1**

signifier to mean

s'il te plaît please (fam.), **BV**

s'il vous plaît please (form.),
    BV

simplement simply

sincère sincere, **1.2**

le **sirop: le sirop d'érable** maple
    syrup

situé(e) located

six six, **BV**

le **ski** ski, skiing, **14.1**
    faire du ski to ski, **14.1**

faire du ski nautique to
    water-ski, **9.1**

le **ski alpin** downhill skiing,
    14.1

le **ski de fond** cross-country
    skiing, **14.1**

le **skieur**, la **skieuse** skier, **14.1**

social(e) social

la **société** society

la **sociologie** sociology

la **sœur** sister, **1.2**

soi: chez soi home

la **soie: en soie** silk (adj.)

le **soir** evening, in the evening, **2**
    du soir in the evening, P.M.
    (time), **2**

la **soirée** evening

soit is, exists (subjunctive)

soixante sixty, **BV**

soixante-dix seventy, **5.2**

le **sol** ground, **13.2**

les **soldes (f. pl.)** sale (in a store),
    10.2

le **soleil** sun
    Il fait du soleil. It's sunny.,
    9.2
    le soleil levant rising sun

soluble dans l'eau water-
    soluble

soluble dans la graisse fat-
    soluble

sombre dark

la **somme** sum

le **sommeil** sleep

le **sommet** summit, mountaintop,
    14.1

son his, her (m. sing. poss.
    adj.), **4**

le **sondage** survey, opinion poll

la **sorte** sort, kind

la **sortie** exit, **7.1**

sortir to go out, take out, **7**

souffrir to suffer, **15.2**

la **soupe à l'oignon** onion soup,
    5.1

la **source** source

sous under, **BV**

les **sous-titres (m. pl.)** subtitles,
    16.1

souterrain(e) underground

souvent often, **5**

se **spécialiser** to specialize

le **spectacle** show

le **spectateur** spectator, **13.1**

la **splendeur** splendor

splendide splendid

le **sport: faire du sport** to play
    sports
    pratiquer un sport to play a
    sport

le **sport collectif** team sport

le **sport d'équipe** team sport

les **sports d'hiver** winter
    sports, skiing, **14.1**

sport (inv.) casual (clothes),
    10.1

sportif, sportive athletic

le **stade** stadium, **13.1**

la **station** station; resort
    la station balnéaire seaside
    resort, **9.1**
    la station de métro subway
    station, **4.2**
    la station-service gas station,
    12.1
    la station de sports d'hiver
    ski resort, **14.1**

le **stationnement** parking
    Stationnement interdit No
    parking (traffic sign)

stationner to park, **12.2**
    Il est interdit de stationner.
    No parking. (traffic sign),
    12.2

la **statue** statue

le **steak frites** steak and French
    fries, **5.2**

le **steward** flight attendant (m.),
    7.2

stop stop (traffic sign)

strict(e) strict

le **stylo** (ballpoint) pen, **BV**

se **succéder** to follow one another

le **succès** success

le **sucre** sugar

sucré(e) sweet, with sugar

le **sud** south

le **sud-est** southeast

suffir to suffice, be enough

la **Suisse** Switzerland

suisse Swiss

suivant(e) following

suivre to follow

le **sujet** subject
    super terrific, super, **2.2**; super
    (gasoline), **12.1**

superbe superb

la **superficie** area (geography)

le **supermarché** supermarket, **6.1**

supersonique supersonic

le **supplément** surcharge (train
    fare), **8**
    payer un supplément to pay
    a surcharge

sur on, **BV**

sûr(e) sure

le **surf: faire du surf (des neiges)**
    to go surfing (snowboarding)

la **surface** surface

surgelé(e) frozen, **6.2**

surtout especially, above all
le **surveiller** to watch, **12.2**
le **survêtement** warmup suit, **11.2**
le **swahili** Swahili
le **sweat-shirt** sweatshirt, **10.1**
sympa (inv.) nice (abbrev. for **sympathique**), 1.2
sympathique nice (person), 1.2
le **symptôme** symptom
le **syndicat d'initiative** tourist office
le **synonyme** synonym
le **système** system

T

ta your (f. sing. poss. adj.), **4**
la **table** table, **BV**
le **tableau** blackboard, **BV**; painting, **16.2**
le **tableau des départs et des arrivées** arrival and departure board
la **taille** size (clothes), **10.2**
la **taille au-dessous** next smaller size, **10.2**
la **taille au-dessus** next larger size, **10.2**
Vous faites quelle taille? What size do you take?, **10.2**
le **tailleur** suit (woman's), **10.1**; tailor
le **talon** heel, **10.2**
à talons hauts (bas) high-(low-)heeled (shoes)
le **tambour** drum
la **tante** aunt, **4.1**
tard late
plus tard later
le **tarif** fare
les **tarifs aériens** airfares
la **tarte** pie, tart, **6.1**
la **tarte aux fruits** fruit tart, pie
la **tasse** cup, **5.2**
le **taux** rate, level
le **taxi** taxi, **7.2**
te (to) you (fam.) (dir. and ind. obj.), **15.2**
technique technical
technologiquement technologically
le **tee-shirt** T-shirt, **9.2**
la **télé** TV, **3.2**
à la télé on TV
le **téléphone** telephone
le **télésiège** chairlift, **14.1**
la **température** temperature, **14.1**
le **temps** weather, **9.2**; time

de temps en temps from time to time
Quel temps fait-il? What's the weather like?, **9.2**
la **tendance: avoir tendance à (+ inf.)** to tend (+ inf.)
le **tennis** tennis, **9.2**
les **tennis (f. pl.)** sneakers
le **terrain de football** soccer field, **13.1**
la **terrasse** terrace, **4.2**
la **terrasse d'un café** sidewalk café, **5.1**
la **terre** earth, land
la **Terre** the Earth
la **Terre-Neuve** Newfoundland
terrible terrible; terrific (inform.), **2.2**
le **territoire** territory
le **tétanos** tetanus
la **tête** head, **13.1**
avoir mal à la tête to have a headache, **15.1**
le **thé citron** tea with lemon, **5.1**
le **théâtre** theater, **16.1**
la **théorie** theory
Tiens! Hey!, Well!, Look!, **10.1**
le **tilleul** linden tree
timide timid, shy, **1.2**
le **tissu** fabric
toi you (sing. stress pron.), **9**
la **toilette: faire sa toilette** to wash and groom oneself, **11.1**
les **toilettes (f. pl.)** bathroom, **4.2**
la **tomate** tomato, **6.2**
tomber to fall, **17**
ton your (m. sing. poss. adj.), **4**
la **tonne** ton
le **topographe** topographer (m. and f.)
tôt early
total(e) total
toucher to cash (a check), **18.1**; to touch
toujours always, **5**; still
la **tour** tower
la **tour Eiffel** Eiffel Tower
le **tour: à son tour** in turn
À votre tour. (It's) your turn.
le/la **touriste** tourist
tous, toutes all, every, **7**
tous (toutes) les deux both
tousser to cough
tout(e) the whole, the entire, **7**; all, any
À tout à l'heure. See you later., **BV**
C'est tout? Is that all?, **6.2**
en tout cas in any case

tout autour de all around (prep.)
tout de suite right away, **11.1**
tout le monde everyone, everybody, **BV**
tout(e) seul(e) all alone, all by himself/herself, **5.2**
les **tout (inv.) premiers (m. pl.)** the very first
toxique toxic
la **tragédie** tragedy, **16.1**
le **train** train, **8.1**
le **train à grande vitesse (TGV)** high-speed train, **8**
traiter to treat (illness)
le **trajet** distance
transporter to transport
le **travail** work
travailler to work, **3.1**
travailleur, travailleuse hardworking
traverser to cross, **12.2**
treize thirteen, **BV**
trente thirty, **BV**
très very, **1.2**
le **tricolore** French flag
la **trigonométrie** trigonometry, **2.2**
trois three, **BV**
troisième third, **4.2**
trop too (excessive), **10.2**
trop de too many, too much
le **trophée** trophy
tropical(e) tropical, **9**
le **trottoir** sidewalk, **12.2**
le **trouble digestif** indigestion, upset stomach
trouver to find, **5.1**; to think (opinion), **10.2**
se **trouver** to be located, found
tu you (fam., subj. pron.), **1**
la **tuberculose** tuberculosis
tuer to kill
la **Tunisie** Tunisia, **16**
le **type** guy (inform.)
le **typhoïde** typhoid
typique typical

U

un, une a, one, **BV**
unique: l'enfant unique only child
unir to unite
unisexe unisex
l' **unité (f.)** unit
universitaire university
l' **université (f.)** university
l' **urgence (f.): en cas d'urgence** in an emergency
l' **ustensile (m.)** utensil

utiliser to use

en utilisant using

V

les **vacances (f. pl.)** vacation

en **vacances** on vacation

le **vaccin** vaccination (shot)

la **vaccination** vaccination

vacciner to vaccinate

vachement really (inform.)

la **vague** wave, **9.1**

la **valeur** value

la **valise** suitcase, **7.1**

faire **les valises** to pack, **7.1**

la **vallée** valley, **14.1**

la **vanille: à la vanille** vanilla (adj.), **5.1**

la **vapeur d'eau** water vapor

la **variation** variation

varié(e) varied

varier to vary

la **variété** variety

vaste vast, enormous

vaut: il vaut mieux it's better

la **vedette** star (actor or actress), **16.1**

le **végétal** vegetable, plant

végétarien(ne) vegetarian

le **vélo** bicycle, bike, **13.2**

à **vélo** by bicycle

le **vélo tout terrain (VTT)** mountain bike

le **vélodrome** bicycle racing track

le **vélomoteur** moped, **12.1**

le **vendeur, la vendeuse** salesperson, **10.1**

vendre to sell, **8.1**

vendredi (m.) Friday, **2.2**

venir to come, **16**

venir de (+ inf.) to have just (done something)

venir en tête to rate above

le **vent** wind, **14.2**

Il fait du vent. It's windy., **9.2**

la **vente** sale

le **ventre** abdomen, stomach, **15.1**

avoir mal au ventre to have a stomachache, **15.1**

au ventre de in the depths of

le **ver à soie** silkworm

le **verbe** verb

vérifier to check, verify, **7.1**

vérifier les niveaux (m. pl.) to check under the hood, **12.1**

véritable real

le **verre** glass, **5.2**

vers around (time); towards

le **versement** deposit

verser to deposit; to pour

la **version originale** original language version (of a movie), **16.1**

vert(e) green, **10.2**

vertical(e) vertical

la **veste** (sport) jacket, **10.1**

vestimentaire: les normes vestimentaires (f.) dress code

le **veston** (suit) jacket

les **vêtements (m. pl.)** clothes, **10.1**

la **viande** meat, **6.1**

la **victoire** victory

le **vide** vacuum, space

vide empty

la **vidéo(cassette)** videocassette, **3.2**

la **vie** life

vieille old (f.), **4.1**

vieux (vieil) old (m.), **4.1**

vif, vive bright (color)

vigilant(e) vigilant, watchful

le **vignoble** vineyard

le **village** village, small town

la **ville** city, town

le **vin (rouge, blanc)** (red, white) wine

vingt twenty, **BV**

violent(e) violent

viral(e) viral, **15.1**

la **virgule** comma

le **virus** virus

la **visite** visit

visiter to visit (a place), **16.2**

la **vitamine** vitamin

vite fast (adv.), **12.2**

la **vitrine** (store) window

Vive... ! Long live ... !, Hooray for ... !

vivre to live (exist)

voici here is, here are, **1.1**

la **voie** track (railroad), **8.1**; lane (of a road), **12.1**

voilà there is, there are (emphatic)

voir to see, **10.1**

le/la **voisin(e)** neighbor, **4.2**

la **voiture** car, **4.2**

en voiture by car, **5.2**; "All aboard!", **8**

la **voiture de sport** sports car, **12.1**

monter en voiture to board the train, **8**

la **voiture-lit** sleeping car, **8.2**

la **voiture-restaurant** dining car

le **vol** flight, **7.1**

le **vol intérieur** domestic flight, **7.1**

le **vol international** international flight, **7.1**

le **volley-ball** volleyball, **13.2**

le **volume** volume

vos your (pl. poss. adj.), **5**

votre your (sing. poss. adj.), **5**

voudrais: je voudrais I would like, **5.1**

vouloir to want, **6.1**

vous you (sing. form. and pl.), **2**; you (stress pron.), **9**; (to) you (dir. and ind. obj.), **15**

le **voyage** trip

faire **un voyage** to take a trip, **7.1**

voyager to travel, **8.1**

le **voyageur, la voyageuse** traveler, passenger, **8.1**

vrai(e) true, real

vraiment really, **2.1**

la **vue** view

la **vulgarité** vulgarity

W

le **walkman** Walkman, **3.2**

le **week-end** weekend, **2.2**

Y

y there, **5.2**

le **yaourt** yogurt, **6.1**

les **yeux (m. pl; sing. œil)** eyes, **15.1**

avoir les yeux qui piquent to have stinging eyes, **15.1**

Z

zéro zero, **BV**

la **zone** area, zone, section, **7.1**

en pleine zone tempérée right in the temperate zone

la **zoologie** zoology

Zut! Darn!, **12.2**

VOCABULAIRE ANGLAIS–FRANÇAIS

The *Vocabulaire anglais–français* contains all productive vocabulary from the text.

The numbers following each entry indicate the chapter and vocabulary section in which the word is introduced. For example, **2.2** means that the word first appeared in *Chapitre 2, Mots 2*. **BV** refers to the introductory *Bienvenue* chapter.

The following abbreviations are used in this glossary.

adj.	adjective
adv.	adverb
conj.	conjunction
dem. adj.	demonstrative adjective
dem. pron.	demonstrative pronoun
dir. obj.	direct object
f.	feminine
fam.	familiar
form.	formal
ind. obj.	indirect object
inf.	infinitive
inform.	informal
interrog. adj.	interrogative adjective
inv.	invariable
m.	masculine
n.	noun
pl.	plural
poss. adj.	possessive adjective
prep.	preposition
pron.	pronoun
sing.	singular
subj.	subject

A

a un, une, **1.1**
  a day (week) par jour (semaine), **3.2**
  a lot beaucoup, **3.1**
abdomen le ventre, **15.1**
accident l'accident (m.), **14.2**
act l'acte, (m.), **16.1**
active actif, active, **10**
actor l'acteur, (m.), **16.1**
actress l'actrice, (f.), **16.1**
aerobics: to do aerobics faire de l'aérobic, **11.2**
after après, **3.2**
afternoon l'après-midi (m.), **2**
against contre, **13.1**
age l'âge (m.), **4.1**
agent (m. and f.) l'agent (m.), **7.1**
to **agree** être d'accord, **2.1**
air aérien(ne) (adj.), **9**
air terminal l'aérogare (f.), **7.2**
airline la compagnie aérienne, **7.1**
airplane l'avion (m.), **7.1**
airport l'aéroport (m.), **7.1**
aisle le couloir, **8.2**
  aisle seat (une place) côté couloir, **7.1**
algebra l'algèbre (f.), **2.2**
all tous, toutes, **7**
  all alone tout(e) seul(e), **5.2**
  all right (agreement) d'accord, **3**
  Is that all? C'est tout?, **6.2**
allergic allergique, **15.1**
allergy l'allergie (f.), **15.1**
already déjà, **14**
also aussi, **1.1**
always toujours, **5**
American (adj.) américain(e), **1.1**
among entre, **9.2**
and et, **1**
  and you? et toi? (fam.), **BV**
angry fâché(e), **12.2**
announcement l'annonce, (f.), **8.1**
to **answer** répondre, **8**
antibiotic l'antibiotique (m.), **15.1**
Anything else? Autre chose?, Avec ça?, **6.2**
apartment l'appartement (m.), **4.2**
  apartment building l'immeuble (m.), **4.2**
apple la pomme, **6.2**
appointment: appointment book l'agenda (m.), **2.2**
April avril (m.), **4.1**
arrival l'arrivée (f.), **7.2**

to **arrive** arriver, **3.1**
    arriving from (flight) en provenance de, **7.1**
art l'art (m.), **2.2**
to **ask (for)** demander, **5**
    to ask a question poser une question, **3.1**
aspirin l'aspirine (f.), **15.1**
at à, **3.1**
    at the au, à la, à l', aux, **5**
    at the home (business) of chez, **5**
    at what time? à quelle heure?, **2**
athletic sportif, sportive, **10**
August août, (m.), **4.1**
aunt la tante, **4.1**
autumn l'automne (m.), **13.2**

B

backboard (basketball) le panneau, **13.2**
backpack le sac à dos, **BV**
bacterial bactérien(ne), **15.1**
bag le sac, **6.1**
bakery la boulangerie-pâtisserie, **6.1**
balcony le balcon, **4.2**
ball (tennis, etc.) la balle, **9.2**; **(soccer, etc.)** le ballon, **13.1**
banana la banane, **6.2**
bank la banque, **18.1**
baseball le base-ball, **13.2**
basket le panier, **13.2**
basketball le basket(-ball), **13.2**
bathing suit le maillot (de bain), **9.1**
bathroom la salle de bains, les toilettes (f. pl.), **4.2**
to **be** être, **2.1**
    to be able to pouvoir, **6**
    to be better soon être vite sur pied, **15.2**
    to be born naître, **17**
    to be called s'appeler, **11.1**
    to be careful faire attention, **9.1**
    to be early être en avance, **8.1**
    to be hungry avoir faim, **5.1**
    to be in shape être en forme, **11.2**
    to be late être en retard, **8.2**
    to be on time être à l'heure, **8.1**
    to be out of sorts ne pas être dans son assiette, **15.2**
    to be thirsty avoir soif, **5.2**
    to be … years old avoir… ans, **4.1**
beach la plage, **9.1**
beautiful beau (bel), belle, **4**
because parce que, **9.1**
to **become** devenir, **16**

bed le lit, **8.2**
    to go to bed se coucher, **11.1**
bedroom la chambre à coucher, **4.2**
beef le bœuf, **6.1**
before avant, **7.1**
beginner le/la débutant(e), **14.1**
behind derrière, **BV**
beige beige, **10.2**
to **believe** croire, **10.2**
better meilleur(e) (adj.), **10**
between entre, **9.2**
beverage la boisson, **5.2**
bicycle le vélo, **13.2**
    bicycle racer le coureur cycliste, **13.2**
big grand(e), **1.1**
bill (currency) le billet, **18.1**; **(invoice)** la facture, **17.2**
biology la biologie, **2.2**
birthday l'anniversaire (m.), **4.1**
    When is your birthday? C'est quand, ton anniversaire? (fam.), **4.1**
black noir(e), **10.2**
blackboard le tableau, **BV**
blanket la couverture, **17.2**
bleacher le gradin, **13.1**
blond blond(e), **1.1**
blouse le chemisier, **10.1**
to **blow a whistle** siffler, **13.1**
blue bleu(e), **10.2**
    navy blue bleu marine (inv.), **10.2**
to **board (plane)** embarquer, **7.2**; **(train)** monter, **8.2**
boarding pass la carte d'embarquement, **7.1**
book le livre, **BV**
born: to be born naître, **17**
to **borrow** emprunter, **18.2**
bottle la bouteille, **6.2**
boundaries (on a tennis court) les limites (f. pl.), **9.2**
box office le guichet, **16.1**
boy le garçon, **BV**
to **brake** freiner, **12.2**
bread le pain, **6.1**
    loaf of French bread la baguette, **6.1**
to **breathe (deeply)** respirer (à fond), **15.2**
broke (slang) fauché(e), **18.2**
brother le frère, **1.2**
brown brun(e), marron (inv.), **10.2**
brunette brun(e), **1.1**
to **brush (one's teeth, hair, etc.)** se brosser (les dents, les cheveux, etc.), **11.1**

bunk (on a train) la couchette, **8.2**
bus le bus, **5.2**; l'autocar (m.), **7.2**
    by bus en bus, **5.2**
busy occupé(e), **2.2**
but mais, **1**
butcher shop la boucherie, **6.1**
butter le beurre, **6.2**
to **buy** acheter, **6.1**
    to buy a ticket prendre un billet, **7**

C

cabin (plane) la cabine, **7.1**
café le café, **5.1**
cake le gâteau, **6.1**
calculator la calculatrice, **BV**
can of food la boîte de conserve, **6.2**
Canadian (adj.) canadien(ne), **7**
cap (ski) le bonnet, **14.1**
car la voiture, **4.2**
    by car en voiture, **5.2**
    sports car la voiture de sport, **12.2**
carefully prudemment, **12.2**
carrot la carotte, **6.2**
carry-on luggage les bagages (m. pl.) à main, **7.1**
cartoon le dessin animé, **16.1**
cash l'argent liquide (m.), **18.1**
    cash register la caisse, **6.2**
to **cash (a check)** toucher (un chèque), **18.1**
cassette la cassette, **3.2**
casual (clothes) sport (adj. inv.), **10.1**
cat le chat, **4.1**
chair la chaise, **BV**
chairlift le télésiège, **14.1**
chalk: piece of chalk le morceau de craie, **BV**
change la monnaie, **18.1**
    change purse le porte-monnaie, **18.1**
    to make change faire de la monnaie, **18.1**
to **change** changer (de), **8.2**
to **chat** bavarder, **4.2**
check (in restaurant) l'addition (f.), **5.2**; **(bank)** le chèque (bancaire), **18.1**
    traveler's check le chèque de voyage, **17.2**
to **check** vérifier, **7.1**
    to check (luggage) faire enregistrer, **7.1**
    to check out (of hotel) libérer une chambre, **17.2**

to check under the hood
vérifier les niveaux, **12.2**
checkout counter la caisse, **6.2**
checkroom la consigne, **8.1**
cheese le fromage, **5.1**
chemistry la chimie, **2.2**
chicken le poulet, **6.1**
child l'enfant (m. and f.), **4.1**
chills les frissons (m. pl.), **15.1**
chocolate (adj.) au chocolat, **5.1**
to **choose** choisir, **7.1**
to **claim (luggage)** récupérer, **7.2**
class (people) la classe, **2.1**;
(course) le cours, **2.2**
first (second) class en première
(seconde), **8.1**
classroom la salle de classe, **2.1**
closed fermé(e), **16.2**
closet le placard, **17.2**
clothes les vêtements (m. pl.),
10.1
clothing designer le grand
couturier, **10.1**
cloud le nuage, **9.2**
Coca-Cola le coca, **5.1**
coffee le café, **5.1**
black coffee l'express (m.), **5.1**
coffee with cream (in a café)
le crème, **5.1**
coin la pièce, **18.1**
cold froid(e) (adj.), **14.2**; (illness)
le rhume, **15.1**
It's cold (weather). Il fait froid.,
9.2
to have a cold être enrhumé(e),
15.1
color la couleur, **10.2**
What color is … ? De quelle
couleur est... ?, **10.2**
to **comb (one's hair)** se peigner, **11.1**
to **come** venir, **16**
to come back revenir, **16**
comedy la comédie, **16.1**
musical comedy la comédie
musicale, **16.1**
comic strip la bande dessinée, **16**
compact disc le compact disc, **3.2**
compartment le compartiment,
7.2
computer l'ordinateur (m.), **BV**
computer science
l'informatique (f.), **2.2**
conductor (train) le contrôleur,
8.2
confident confiant(e), **1.1**
convertible (car) la décapotable,
12.2
to **cook** faire la cuisine, **6**
corridor le couloir, **8.2**
costume le costume, **16.1**

to **cough** tousser, **15.1**
counter le comptoir, **7.1**
country le pays, **7.1**
course le cours, **2.2**
courtyard la cour, **4.2**
cousin le/la cousin(e), **4.1**
to **cover** couvrir, **15**
crab le crabe, **6.1**
cream la crème, **6.1**
credit card la carte de crédit, **17.2**
crepe la crêpe, **5.1**
croissant le croissant, **6.1**
to **cross** traverser, **12.2**
crossroads le carrefour, **12.2**
cup la tasse, **5.2**
winner's cup la coupe, **13.2**
currency la monnaie, **18.1**
curtain le rideau, **16.1**
customer le/la client(e), **10.1**
customs la douane, **7.2**
to go through customs passer à
la douane, **7.2**
cycling le cyclisme, **13.2**
cyclist (in race) le coureur
cycliste, **13.2**

D

dairy store la crémerie, **6.1**
to **dance** danser, **3.2**
dark hair brun(e), **1.1**
Darn! Zut!, **12.2**
date la date, **4.1**
What is the date today? Quelle
est la date aujourd'hui?, **4.1**
daughter la fille, **4.1**
day le jour, **2.2**
a (per) day par jour, **3**
What day is it? C'est quel jour?,
2.2
December décembre (m.), **4.1**
degree: It's … degrees Celsius. Il
fait... degrés Celsius., **14.2**
delicatessen la charcuterie, **6.1**
delicious délicieux, délicieuse, **10**
deodorant le déodorant, **11.1**
department store le grand
magasin, **10.1**
departure le départ, **7.1**
to **deposit** verser, **18.1**
to **descend** descendre, **14.1**
desk le bureau, **BV**
desk clerk le/la réceptionniste,
17.1
diagnosis: to make a diagnosis
faire un diagnostic, **15.2**
to **die** mourir, **17**
difficult difficile, **2.1**
dining car la voiture-restaurant,
8.2
dining room la salle à manger, **4.2**

dinner le dîner, **4.2**
to eat dinner dîner, **4.2**
to **discover** découvrir, **15**
district le quartier, **4.2**; (Paris)
l'arrondissement (m.)
to **dive** plonger, **9.1**
diving: to go deep-sea diving faire
de la plongée sous-marine, **9.1**
to **do** faire, **6.1**
to do the shopping faire les
courses, **6.1**
doctor le médecin (m. et f.), **15.2**
documentary le documentaire,
16.1
dog le chien, **4.1**
dollar le dollar, **3.2**
domestic (flight) intérieur(e), **7.1**
door la porte, **17.1**
dozen la douzaine, **6.2**
drama le drame, **16.1**
dress la robe, **10.1**
dressed: to get dressed s'habiller,
11.1
dressy habillé(e), **10.1**
to **dribble (a basketball)** dribbler,
13.2
to **drive** conduire, **12.2**
driver le conducteur, la
conductrice, **12.2**
driver's license le permis de
conduire, **12.2**
driving lesson la leçon de
conduite, **12.2**
driving school l'auto-école (f.),
12.2
to **dry (off)** se sécher, **17.2**
dubbed (movie) doublé(e), **16.1**
during pendant, **3.2**

E

each (adj.) chaque, **16.1**
ear l'oreille (f.), **15.1**
earache: to have an earache avoir
mal aux oreilles, **15.1**
early: to be early être en avance,
8.1
to **earn** gagner, **3.2**
easy facile, **2.1**
to **eat** manger, **5**
to eat breakfast prendre le petit
déjeuner, **7**
to eat dinner dîner, **4.2**
to eat lunch déjeuner, **5.2**
egg l'œuf (m.), **6.2**
eight huit, **BV**
eighteen dix-huit, **BV**
eighty quatre-vingts, **5.2**
elevator l'ascenseur (m.), **4.2**
eleven onze, **BV**
energetic énergique, **1.2**

English (language) l'anglais (m.), 2.2
to **enter** entrer, 3.1
entire entier, entière, 10
entrance l'entrée (f.), 4.2
espresso l'express (m.), 5.1
European (adj.) européen(ne), 7
evening le soir, 2
   in the evening (p.m.) du soir, 2
every tous, toutes, 7; chaque, 16.1
everybody, everyone tout le monde, BV
everywhere partout
exam l'examen (m.), 3.1
   to pass an exam réussir à un examen, 7
   to take an exam passer un examen, 3.1
to **examine** examiner, 15.2
except sauf, 16.2
to **exchange (money)** changer, 18.1
   exchange office (for foreign currency) le bureau de change, 18.1
   exchange rate le cours du change, 18.1
to **exercise** faire de l'exercice, 11.2
exhibit l'exposition (f.), 16.2
exit la sortie, 7.1
expenses les frais (m. pl.), 17.2
expensive cher, chère, 10.1
eye l'œil (m., pl. yeux), 15.1
   to have stinging eyes avoir les yeux qui piquent, 15.1

F

face la figure, 11.1
to **face** donner sur, 17.1
fairly assez, 1.1
fall (season) l'automne (m.), 13.2
to **fall** faire une chute, 14.2; tomber, 17
   to fall asleep s'endormir, 11.1
family la famille, 4.1
famous célèbre, 1.2
fantastic fantastique, 1.2
far from loin de, 4.2
fast vite, 12.2
father le père, 4.1
favorite favori(te), 10
February février (m.), 4.1
to **feel (well, etc.)** se sentir, 15.1
   to feel out of sorts ne pas être dans son assiette, 15.2
fever la fièvre, 15.1
   to have a high fever avoir une fièvre de cheval, 15.2
few peu (de), 18
fifteen quinze, BV
fifty cinquante, BV

to **fill out** remplir, 7.2
to **fill up (gas tank)** faire le plein, 12.2
film le film, 16.1
   adventure film/movie le film d'aventures, 16.1
   detective film/movie le film policier, 16.1
   foreign film le film étranger, 16.1
   horror film/movie le film d'horreur, 16.1
   science fiction film/movie le film de science-fiction, 16.1
finally enfin, 11.1
to **find** trouver, 5.1
fine ça va, bien, BV
to **finish** finir, 7
first premier, première (adj.), 4.2; d'abord (adv.), 11.1
   in first class en première, 8.1
fish le poisson, 6.1
   fish store la poissonnerie, 6.1
fishing: to go fishing aller à la pêche, 9.1
fitness (physical) la forme physique, 11
five cinq, BV
flight le vol, 7.1
   flight attendant l'hôtesse (f.) de l'air, le steward, 7.2
   flight attendants le personnel de bord, 7.2
floor (of a building) l'étage (m.), 4.2
flu la grippe, 15.1
foot le pied, 13.1
   on foot à pied, 5.2
for (time) depuis, 8.2
forbidden interdit(e), 12.2
foreign étranger, étrangère, 16.1
fork la fourchette, 5.2
forty quarante, BV
four quatre, BV
fourteen quatorze, BV
franc le franc, 18.1
France la France, 16
free libre, 2.2
freezing: It's freezing (weather). Il gèle., 14.2
French français(e) (adj.), 1.1; (language) le français, 2.2
   French fries les frites (f. pl.), 5.2
Friday vendredi (m.), 2.2
friend l'ami(e), 1.2; (pal) le copain, la copine, 2.1
from de, 1.1
   from the du, de la, de l', des, 5
frozen surgelé(e), 6.2
fruit le fruit, 6.2

full plein(e), 13.1
full-time à plein temps, 3.2
fun: to have fun s'amuser, 11.2
funny amusant(e), 1.1; comique, 1.2

G

to **gain weight** grossir, 11.2
game le match, 9.2
garage le garage, 4.2
garden le jardin, 4.2
gas(oline) l'essence (f.), 12.1
   regular (gas) (de l'essence) ordinaire, 12.1
   super (gas) (de l'essence) super, 12.1
   unleaded (gas) (de l'essence) sans plomb, 12.1
   gas station la station-service, 12.2
   gas station attendant le/la pompiste, 12.2
   gas tank le réservoir, 12.2
gate (airport) la porte, 7.1
geography la géographie, 2.2
geometry la géometrie, 2.2
to **get** recevoir, 18.1
   to get a sunburn attraper un coup de soleil, 9.1
   to get in shape se mettre en forme, 11.1
   to get off (plane, train, etc.) descendre, 8.2
   to get on (board) monter, 8.2
   to get up se lever, 11.1
gift le cadeau, 10.2
girl la fille, BV
to **give** donner, 3.2
   to give back rendre, 18.2
glass le verre, 5.2
glove le gant, 14.1
to **go** aller, 5.1
   to go (in a car, etc.) rouler, 12.2
   to go deep-sea diving faire de la plongée sous-marine, 9.1
   to go down descendre, 14.1
   to go fast rouler vite, 12.2
   to go fishing aller à la pêche, 9.1
   to go home rentrer, 3.1
   to go out sortir, 7
   to go to bed se coucher, 11.1
   to go through customs passer à la douane, 7.2
   to go up monter, 17.1
   to go windsurfing faire de la planche à voile, 9.1
   Shall we go? On y va?, 5
goal le but, 13.1

goalie le gardien de but, **13.1**
goggles (ski) les lunettes (f. pl.), **14.1**
good bon(ne), **7**
good-bye au revoir, ciao (inform.), **BV**
gram le gramme, **6.2**
granddaughter la petite-fille, **4.1**
grandfather le grand-père, **4.1**
grandmother la grand-mère, **4.1**
grandparents les grands-parents (m. pl.), **4.1**
grandson le petit-fils, **4.1**
gray gris(e), **10.2**
Great! Chouette! (inform.), **2.2**
green vert(e), **10.2**
  green beans les haricots (m. pl.) verts, **6.2**
grilled ham and cheese sandwich le croque-monsieur, **5.1**
grocery store l'épicerie (f.), **6.1**
ground le sol, **13.2**
  ground floor le rez-de-chaussée, **4.2**
guide(book) le guide, **12.2**
gym(nasium) le gymnase, **11.2**
gymnastics la gymnastique, **2.2**
  to do gymnastics faire de la gymnastique, **11.2**

H

hair les cheveux (m. pl.), **11.1**
half demi(e)
  half past (time) et demie, **2**
ham le jambon, **5.1**
hand la main, **11.1**
handkerchief le mouchoir, **15.1**
hanger le cintre, **17.2**
happy content(e), **1.1**; heureux, heureuse, **10.2**
hard (adv.) fort, **9.2**
hat (ski) le bonnet, **14.1**
to **hate** détester, **3.2**
to **have** avoir, **4.1**
  to have a(n) … -ache avoir mal à (aux)… , **15.2**
  to have a cold être enrhumé(e), **15.1**
  to have a picnic faire un pique-nique, **6**
  to have to devoir, **18.2**
he il, **1**
head la tête, **13.1**
headache: to have a headache avoir mal à la tête, **15.1**
health la santé, **15.1**
  to be in good (poor) health être en bonne (mauvaise) santé, **15.1**

health club le club de forme, **11.2**
to **hear** entendre, **8.1**
heel le talon, **10.2**
  high (low)-heeled (shoes) à talons hauts (bas), **10.2**
hello bonjour, **BV**
her elle (stress pron.), **9**; la (dir. obj.), **16**; lui (ind. obj.), **17.1**; sa, son, ses (poss. adj.), **4**
here is, here are voici, **1.1**
hi salut, **BV**
high élevé(e), **15**; haut(e), **10.2**
  high school le lycée, **1.2**
highway l'autoroute (f.), **12**
him le (dir. obj.), **16.1**; lui (stress pron.), **9**; lui (ind. obj.), **17.1**
his sa, son, ses, **4**
history l'histoire (f.), **2.2**
to **hit** frapper, **9.2**
homework (assignment) le devoir, **BV**
  to do homework faire les devoirs, **6**
hot: hot dog la saucisse de Francfort, **5.1**
  It's hot (weather). Il fait chaud., **9.2**
hotel l'hôtel (m.), **17.1**
house la maison, **3.1**
how: How are you? Ça va? (inform.); Comment vas-tu? (fam.); Comment allez-vous? (form.), **BV**
  How beautiful they are! Qu'elles (ils) sont belles (beaux)!
  How much? Combien?, **6.2**
  How much is it? C'est combien?, **BV**
  How much is that? Ça fait combien?, **5.2**
  How's it going? Ça va?, **BV**
hundred cent, **5.2**
to **hurt** avoir mal à, **15.1**
  It hurts. Ça fait mal., **15.2**
  Where does it hurt (you)? Où avez-vous mal?, **15.2**
husband le mari, **4.1**

I

I je, **1**
ice la glace, **14.2**
  ice cream la glace, **5.1**
  ice skate le patin à glace, **14.2**
  (ice) skating le patinage, **14.2**
to **(ice-)skate** faire du patin (à glace), **14.2**
immigration l'immigration (f.), **7.2**

impatient impatient(e), **1.1**
in dans, **BV**; à, **3.1**
  in back of derrière, **BV**
  in first (second) class en première (seconde), **8.1**
  in front of devant, **BV**
inexpensive bon marché (inv.), **10.1**
infection l'infection (f.), **15.1**
instructor le moniteur, la monitrice, **9.1**
intelligent intelligent(e), **1.1**
interesting intéressant(e), **1.1**
intermission l'entracte (m.), **16.1**
international international(e), **7.1**
intersection le croisement, **12.2**
to **invite** inviter, **3.2**
it (dir. obj.) le, la, **16.1**
  it is, it's c'est, **BV**
  It's (That's) expensive. Ça coûte cher., **7.2**
  it is necessary (+ inf.) il faut (+ inf.), **9.1**
Italian (adj.) italien(ne), **7**
Italy l'Italie (f.), **16**

J

jacket le blouson, **10.1**
  (suit) jacket la veste, **10.1**
  ski jacket l'anorak (m.), **14.1**
January janvier (m.), **4.1**
jar le pot, **6.2**
jeans le jean, **10.1**
to **jog** faire du jogging, **11.2**
to **joke around** rigoler, **3.2**
July juillet (m.), **4.1**
June juin (m.), **4.1**

K

key la clé, **12.2**; le demi-cercle (basketball), **13.2**
to **kick** donner un coup de pied, **13.1**
  kilogram le kilo, **6.2**
kind le genre, **16.1**
kitchen la cuisine, **4.2**
kleenex le kleenex, **15.1**
knife le couteau, **5.2**
to **know** connaître (be acquainted with), savoir (information), **16.2**

L

to **land** atterrir, **7.1**
  landing card la carte de débarquement, **7.2**
lane (of a road) la voie, **12.2**
language la langue, **2.2**
last dernier, dernière, **10**
  last night hier soir, **13**

last year l'année (f.) dernière, 13
late: to be late être en retard, 8.2
Latin le latin, 2.2
to learn (to) apprendre (à), 9.1
to leave partir, 7.1
    to leave (a room, etc.) quitter, 3.1
    to leave (something behind) laisser, 5.2
    to leave a tip laisser un pourboire, 5.2
left: to the left of à gauche de, 5
lemonade le citron pressé, 5.1
to lend prêter, 18.2
lesson la leçon, 9.1
lettuce la laitue, 6.2
level le niveau, 12.2
to like aimer, 3.2
    I would like je voudrais, 5.1
line: to wait in line faire la queue, 8.1
to listen (to) écouter, 3.2
    to listen with a stethoscope ausculter, 15.2
liter le litre, 6.2
literature la littérature, 2.2
to live (in a city, house, etc.) habiter, 3.1
living room la salle de séjour, 4.2
lobby le hall, 17.1
locker la consigne automatique, 8.1
long long(ue), 10.2
to look at regarder, 3.1
to look for chercher, 5.1
to lose perdre, 8.2
    to lose patience perdre patience, 8.2
    to lose weight maigrir, 11.2
lot: a lot of beaucoup de, 10.1
    a lot of people beaucoup de monde, 13.1
loudspeaker le haut-parleur, 8.1
to love aimer, adorer, 3.2
love story (movie) le film d'amour, 16.1
low bas(se), 10
luggage les bagages (m. pl.), 7.1
    carry-on luggage les bagages à main, 7.1

M

ma'am madame, BV
magazine le magazine, 3.2
maitre d' le maître d'hôtel, 5.2
make (of car) la marque, 12.2
to make faire, 6.1
man l'homme (m.), 2.1
March mars (m.), 4.1

market le marché, 6.2
marvelous merveilleux, merveilleuse, 10.2
match (singles, doubles) (tennis) la partie (en simple, en double), 9.2
math les maths (f. pl.), 2.2
May mai (m.), 4.1
me me (dir. and ind. obj.), 15.2; moi (stress pron.), 1.2
meat la viande, 6.1
medicine (medical profession) la médecine 15; (remedy) le médicament, 15.2
medium-rare (meat) à point, 5.2
menu la carte, 5.1
merchant le/la marchand(e), 6.2
    produce merchant le/la marchand(e) de fruits et légumes, 6.2
meter maid la contractuelle, 12.2
midnight minuit (m.), 2.2
milk le lait, 6.1
mineral water l'eau (f.) minérale, 6.2
mirror la glace, 11.1
Miss (Ms.) Mademoiselle (Mlle), BV
mogul la bosse, 14.1
Monday lundi (m.), 2.2
money l'argent (m.), 3.2
    to have lots of money avoir plein de fric (slang), 18.2
month le mois, 4.1
moped le vélomoteur, 12.2
morning le matin, 2
    in the morning (A.M.) du matin, 2
Morocco le Maroc, 16
most (of) la plupart (des), 8.2
mother la mère, 4.1
motorcycle la moto, 12.2
    motorcycle cop le motard, 12.2
mountain la montagne, 14.1
mouth la bouche, 15.1
movie le film, 16.1
    movie theater le cinéma, la salle de cinéma, 16.1
Mr. Monsieur (M.), BV
Mrs. (Ms.) Madame (Mme), BV
museum le musée, 16.2
music la musique, 2.2
must devoir, 18.2
mustard la moutarde, 6.2
my ma, mon, mes, 4

N

name le nom, 16.2

What is your name? Tu t'appelles comment? (fam.), 11.1
napkin la serviette, 5.2
narrow étroit(e), 10.2
near près de, 4.2
necessary: it is necessary (+ inf.) il faut (+ inf.), 9.1
to need avoir besoin de, 11.1
neighbor le/la voisin(e), 4.2
neighborhood le quartier, 4.2
nephew le neveu, 4.1
net le filet, 9.2
    net bag le filet, 6.1
never ne... jamais, 12
new nouveau (nouvel), nouvelle, 4
newspaper le journal, 8.1
newsstand le kiosque, 8.1
next prochain(e), 8.2
    next to à côté de, 5
nice (person) aimable, sympathique, 1.2; gentil(le), 9
niece la nièce, 4.1
nine neuf, BV
nineteen dix-neuf, BV
ninety quatre-vingt-dix, 5.2
no non, BV
    no one, nobody ne... personne, 12.2
    No parking. Il est interdit de stationner., 12.2
    no smoking (section) (la zone) non-fumeurs, 7.1
noon midi (m.), 2.2
nose le nez, 15.1
    to have a runny nose avoir le nez qui coule, 15.1
not ne... pas, 1
    not bad pas mal, BV
notebook le cahier, BV
nothing ne... rien, 12.2
    Nothing else. Rien d'autre., 6.2
novel le roman, 16
November novembre (m.), 4.1
now maintenant, 2
number le numéro, 5.2
    What is the phone number of ... ? Quel est le numéro de téléphone de... ?, 5.2

O

to obey obéir (à), 7
o'clock: It's ... o'clock. Il est... heure(s)., 2.2
October octobre (m.), 4.1
of (belonging to) de, 5
    of the du, de la, de l', des, 5
to offer offrir, 15
often souvent, 5

O.K. **(health)** Ça va.; **(agreement)** d'accord, BV
old vieux (vieil), vieille, **4.1**
   How old are you? Tu as quel âge? (fam.), **4.1**
omelette **(with herbs/plain)** l'omelette (f.) (aux fines herbes/nature), **5.1**
on sur, BV
   on board à bord de, **7.2**
   on foot à pied, **5.2**
   on time à l'heure, **8.1**
one un, une, **1**
one-way ticket l'aller simple (m.), **8.1**
onion l'oignon (m.), **6.2**
   onion soup la soupe à l'oignon, **5.1**
open ouvert(e), **16.2**
to open ouvrir, **15.2**
opera l'opéra (m.), **16.1**
opinion: **in my opinion** à mon avis, **10.2**
to oppose opposer, **13.1**
opposing adverse, **13.1**
or ou, **1.1**
orange **(fruit)** l'orange (f.), **6.2**; **(color)** orange (inv.), **10.2**
   orange soda l'Orangina (m.), **5.1**
to order commander, **5.1**
original language version **(of a film)** la version originale, **16.1**
other autre, BV
our notre, nos, **5**
out of bounds hors des limites, **9.2**
over **(prep.)** par dessus, **13.2**
   over there là-bas, BV
overcast **(cloudy)** couvert(e), **14.2**
to overlook donner sur, **17.1**
to owe devoir, **18.2**

P

to pack **(suitcases)** faire les valises, **7.1**
package le paquet, **6.2**
packed **(stadium)** comble, **13.1**
painter le/la peintre, **16.2**
painting la peinture; le tableau, **16.2**
pair la paire, **10.1**
pal le copain, la copine, **2.1**
pancake la crêpe, **5.1**
pants le pantalon, **10.1**
pantyhose le collant, **10.1**
paper: **sheet of paper** la feuille de papier, BV
parents les parents (m. pl.), **4.1**
Parisian **(adj.)** parisien(ne), **7**

park le parc, **11.2**
to park the car garer la voiture, **12.2**
parking: **No parking.** Il est interdit de stationner., **12.2**
part-time à mi-temps, **3.2**
party la fête, **3.2**
   to throw a party donner une fête, **3.2**
to pass passer, **7.2**
   to pass an exam réussir à un examen, **7**
passenger le passager, la passagère, **7.1**; **(train)** le voyageur, la voyageuse, **8**
passport le passeport, **7.1**
pâté le pâté, **5.1**
patient patient(e), **1.1**
to pay payer, **6.1**
   to pay attention faire attention, **6**
   to pay back rembourser, **18.2**
   to pay cash payer en espèces, **17.2**
pedestrian le/la piéton(ne), **12.2**
   pedestrian crossing les clous (m. pl.), **12.2**
pen **(ballpoint)** le stylo, BV
pencil le crayon, BV
penicillin la pénicilline, **15.1**
to perform jouer, **16**
to permit permettre, **14**
person la personne, **17.1**
personally personnellement, **16.2**
pharmacist le/la pharmacien(ne), **15.2**
pharmacy la pharmacie, **15.2**
physical education l'éducation (f.) physique, **2.2**
physics la physique, **2.2**
picture le tableau, **16.1**
pie la tarte, **6.1**
pill le comprimé, **15.2**
pillow l'oreiller (m.), **17.2**
pink rose, **10.2**
to place mettre, **8.1**
plain **(adj.)** nature, **5.1**
plane l'avion (m.), **7.1**
plate l'assiette (f.), **5.2**
platform **(railroad)** le quai, **8.1**
to play **(perform)** jouer, **16**
   to play (a sport) jouer à, **9.2**; pratiquer un sport, **11.2**
play la pièce, **16.1**
   to put on a play monter une pièce, **16.1**
player le joueur, **9.2**
please s'il vous plaît (form.), s'il te plaît (fam.), BV
pocket la poche, **18.1**
pocketbook le sac, **18.1**

pool la piscine, **9.2**
poor pauvre, **15.1**
   poor thing le/la pauvre, **15.1**
popular populaire, **1.2**
porter le porteur, **8.1**
potato la pomme de terre, **6.2**
pound la livre, **6.2**
to prepare préparer, **4.2**
to prescribe prescrire, **15.2**
prescription l'ordonnance (f.), **15.2**
   to write a prescription faire une ordonnance, **15.2**
pretty joli(e), **4.2**
price le prix, **10.1**
problem le problème, **11.2**
to punish punir, **7**
purse le sac, **18.1**
to put (on) mettre, **8.1**
   to put money aside mettre de l'argent de côté, **18.2**
   to put on makeup se maquiller, **11.1**

Q

quarter: **quarter after (time)** et quart, **2**
   quarter to (time) moins le quart, **2**
question: **to ask a question** poser une question, **3.1**

R

race la course, **13.2**
racket la raquette, **9.2**
radio la radio, **3.2**
raining: **It's raining.** Il pleut., **9.2**
rare **(meat)** saignante(e), **5.2**
to read lire, **12.2**
ready-to-wear department le rayon prêt-à-porter, **10.1**
really vraiment, **2.1**
to receive recevoir, **18.1**
reception desk la réception, **17.1**
record le disque, **3.2**
red rouge, **10.2**
referee l'arbitre (m.), **13.1**
registration card **(at hotel desk)** la fiche d'enregistrement, **17.1**
regular **(gasoline)** ordinaire, **12.2**
to reserve réserver, **17**
restaurant le restaurant, **5.2**
to return **(tennis ball, etc.)** renvoyer, **9.2**
right: **to the right of** à droite de, **5**
right away tout de suite, **11.1**
road la route, **12.2**
role le rôle, **16**
room **(in house)** la pièce, **4.2**; **(in hotel)** la chambre, **17.1**

double room la chambre à deux lits, **17.1**

single room la chambre à un lit, **17.1**

to **vacate the room** libérer la chambre, **17.2**

round-trip ticket le billet aller-retour, **8.1**

runner le coureur, **13.2**

S

salad la salade, **5.1**

sales les soldes (f. pl.), **10.2**

salesperson le vendeur, la vendeuse, **10.1**

same même, **2.1**

sand le sable, **9.1**

sandwich le sandwich, **5.1**

grilled ham and cheese sandwich le croque-monsieur, **5.1**

Saturday samedi (m.), **2.2**

sausage le saucisson, **6.1**

to **save money** faire des économies, **18.2**

savings account le compte d'épargne, **18.1**

to **say** dire, **12.2**

scarf l'écharpe (f.), **14.1**

scene la scène, **16.1**

schedule l'horaire (m.), **8.1**

school l'école (f.), **1.2**

high school le lycée, **1.2**

science les sciences (f. pl.), **2.2**

score le score, **9.2**

to **score a goal** marquer un but, **13.1**

screen l'écran (m.), **7.1**

sculptor le sculpteur (m. et f.), **16.2**

sculpture la sculpture, **16.2**

sea la mer, **9.1**

by the sea au bord de la mer, **9.1**

seashore le bord de la mer, **9.1**

seaside resort la station balnéaire, **9.1**

seat le siège, **7.1**

seat (on plane, at movies, etc.) la place, **7.1**

seat belt la ceinture de sécurité, **12.2**

seated assis(e), **8.2**

second (adj.) deuxième, **4.2**

section la zone, **7.1**

smoking (no smoking) section la zone (non-)fumeurs, **7.1**

security (airport) le contrôle de sécurité, **7.1**

to **see** voir, **10.1**

See you later. À tout à l'heure., **BV**

See you tomorrow. À demain., **BV**

to **sell** vendre, **8.1**

to **send (hit)** envoyer, **13.1**

September septembre (m.), **4.1**

to **serve** servir, **7.2**

service le service, **5.2**

service station la station-service, **12.2**

service station attendant le/la pompiste, **12.2**

set (for a play) le décor, **16.1**

to **set the table** mettre le couvert, **8**

seven sept, **BV**

seventeen dix-sept, **BV**

seventy soixante-dix, **5.2**

several plusieurs, **18.2**

Shall we go? On y va?, **5**

to **shave** se raser, **11.1**

she elle, **1**

sheet le drap, **17.2**

sheet of paper la feuille de papier, **BV**

shirt la chemise, **10.1**

shoes les chaussures (f. pl.), **10.1**

shop la boutique, **10.1**

to **shop** faire des achats, **10.1**

short petit(e), **1.1**; court(e), **10.2**

shorts le short, **9.2**

show (movies) la séance, **16.1**

to **show** montrer, **17.1**

to show a movie passer un film, **16.1**

shrimp la crevette, **6.1**

shy timide, **1.2**

sick malade, **15.1**

sick person le/la malade, **15.2**

side (in a sporting event) le camp, **13.1**

sidewalk le trottoir, **12.2**

sidewalk café la terrasse (d'un café), **5.1**

to **sign** signer, **18.1**

since (time) depuis, **8.2**

sincere sincère, **1.2**

to **sing** chanter, **3.2**

sir monsieur, **BV**

sister la sœur, **1.2**

six six, **BV**

sixteen seize, **BV**

sixty soixante, **BV**

size (clothes) la taille; **(shoes)** la pointure, **10.2**

the next larger size la taille au-dessus, **10.2**

the next smaller size la taille au-dessous, **10.2**

to **take size (number)** faire du (nombre), **10.2**

What size do you take? Vous faites quelle pointure (taille)?, **10.2**

skate (ice) le patin à glace, **14.2**

to **skate (ice)** faire du patin (à glace), **14.2**

skater le patineur, la patineuse, **14.2**

skating le patinage, **14.2**

skating rink la patinoire, **14.2**

ski le ski, **14.1**

ski boot la chaussure de ski, **14.1**

ski jacket l'anorak (m.), **14.1**

ski pole le bâton, **14.1**

ski resort la station de sports d'hiver, **14.1**

to **ski** faire du ski, **14.1**

skier le skieur, la skieuse, **14.1**

skiing le ski, **14.1**

cross-country skiing le ski de fond, **14.1**

downhill skiing le ski alpin, **14.1**

skirt la jupe, **10.1**

sky le ciel, **14.2**

to **sleep** dormir, **7.2**

sleeping car la voiture-lit, **8.2**

sleeve la manche, **10.2**

long- (short-)sleeved à manches longues (courtes), **10.2**

small petit(e), **1.1**

smoking (section) (la zone) fumeurs, **7.1**

snack bar (train) le grill-express, **8**

sneakers les chaussures (f. pl.) de tennis, **9.2**

to **sneeze** éternuer, **15.1**

snowball la boule de neige, **14.2**

snowing: It's snowing. Il neige., **14.2**

soap le savon, **11.1**

soccer le foot(ball), **13.1**

soccer field le terrain de football, **13.1**

socks les chaussettes (f. pl.), **10.1**

some quelques (pl.), **8.2**

somebody, someone quelqu'un, **12.2**

something to eat quelque chose à manger, **5.1**

sometimes quelquefois, **5**

son le fils, **4.1**

sore throat: to have a sore throat avoir mal à la gorge, **15.1**

space (parking) la place, **12.2**

Spanish (language) l'espagnol (m.), **2.2**

to speak parler, **3.1**
　　to speak on the telephone parler au téléphone, **3.2**
　　spectator le spectateur, **13.1**
　　speed limit la limitation de vitesse, **12.2**
to speed up accélérer, **12.2**
to spend (money) dépenser, **10.1**
　　spoon la cuillère, **5.2**
　　sporty (clothes) sport (adj. inv.), **10.1**
　　spring (season) le printemps, **13.2**
　　stadium le stade, **13.1**
　　stage la scène, **16.1**
　　staircase l'escalier (m.), **17.1**
to stamp (a ticket) composter, **8.1**
　　standing debout, **8.2**
　　star (actor or actress) la vedette, **16.1**
to start the car mettre le contact, **12.2**
　　station wagon le break, **12.2**
　　statue la statue, **16.2**
to stay in shape rester en forme, **11.1**
　　steak and French fries le steak frites, **5.2**
　　steep raide, **14.1**
　　stomach le ventre, **15.1**
　　stomachache: to have a stomachache avoir mal au ventre, **15.1**
to stop s'arrêter, **12.2**
　　store le magasin, **3.2**
　　street la rue, **3.1**
　　student l'élève (m. et f.), **1.2**
to study étudier, **3.1**; faire des études, **6**
　　to study French (math, etc.) faire du français (des maths, etc.), **6**
　　subject (in school) la matière, **2.2**
　　subtitles les sous-titres (m. pl.), **16.1**
　　subway le métro, **4.2**
　　by subway en métro, **5.2**
　　subway station la station de métro, **4.2**
to succeed réussir (à), **7**
to suffer souffrir, **15.2**
　　suit (men's) le complet; (women's) le tailleur, **10.1**
　　(suit) jacket la veste, **10.1**
　　suitcase la valise, **7.1**
　　summer l'été (m.), **9.1**
　　summit le sommet, **14.1**

to sunbathe prendre un bain de soleil, **9.1**
　　Sunday dimanche (m.), **2.2**
　　sunglasses les lunettes (f. pl.) de soleil, **9.1**
　　sunny: It's sunny. Il fait du soleil., **9.2**
　　suntan lotion la crème solaire, **9.1**
　　super extra, super (inform.), **2.2**
　　super (gasoline) (de l'essence) super, **12.2**
　　supermarket le supermarché, **6.1**
to surf faire du surf, **9.1**
　　sweater le pull, **10.1**
　　sweatshirt le sweat-shirt, **10.1**
　　sweatsuit le survêtement, **11.2**
to swim nager, **9.1**
　　swimming la natation, **9.1**

T

　　table la table, **BV**
　　table setting le couvert, **5.2**
　　to set the table mettre le couvert, **8.2**
　　tablecloth la nappe, **5.2**
to take prendre, **9.1**
　　to take a bath (a shower) prendre un bain (une douche), **11.1**
　　to take an exam passer un examen, **3.1**
　　to take off (plane) décoller, **7.1**
　　to take size (number) faire du (+ nombre), **10.2**
　　to take something upstairs monter, **17.1**
　　to take the train (plane, etc.) prendre le train (l'avion, etc.), **7**
　　to take a trip faire un voyage, **7.1**
　　to take a walk faire une promenade, **9.1**
　　taken pris(e), **5.1**
to talk parler, **3.1**
　　to talk on the phone parler au téléphone, **3.2**
to tan bronzer, **9.1**
　　tart la tarte, **6.1**
　　taxi le taxi, **7.2**
　　tea with lemon le thé citron, **5.1**
to teach someone to do something apprendre à quelqu'un à faire quelque chose, **14.1**
　　teacher le professeur; le/la prof (inform.), **2.1**
　　team l'équipe (f.), **13.1**
　　television la télé, **3.2**
to tell dire, **12.2**
　　temperature la température, **15.1**

　　ten dix, **BV**
　　tennis le tennis, **9.2**
　　tennis court le court de tennis, **9.2**
　　tennis shoes les chaussures (f. pl.) de tennis, **9.2**
　　tennis skirt la jupette, **9.2**
　　terminal (bus to airport) l'aérogare (f.), **7.2**
　　terrace la terrasse, **4.2**
　　terrible terrible, **2.2**
　　terrific super, extra, terrible, **2.2**
　　test l'examen (m.), **3.1**
　　to pass a test réussir à un examen, **7**
　　to take a test passer un examen, **3.1**
　　thank you merci, **BV**
　　that ce (cet), cette (dem. adj.), **8**; ça (pron.), **BV**
　　that is to say c'est-à-dire, **16.1**
　　That's (It's) expensive. Ça coûte cher., **18**
　　the la, le, l', **1**; les, **2**
　　theater le théâtre, **16.1**
　　their leur, leurs, **5**
　　them elles, eux (stress pron.), **9**; les (dir. obj.), **16**; leur (ind. obj.), **17**
　　then (adv.) ensuite, **11.1**
　　there y, **5**
　　there is, there are il y a, **4.2**; voilà (emphatic), **BV**
　　these (dem. adj.) ces (m. and f. pl.), **8**
　　they elles, ils, **2**
to think penser, **10.2**
　　third troisième, **4.2**
　　thirteen treize, **BV**
　　thirty trente, **BV**
　　this (dem. adj.) ce (cet), cette, **8**
　　those (dem. adj.) ces (m. and f. pl.), **8**
　　thousand mille, **6.2**
　　three trois, **BV**
　　throat la gorge, **15.1**
　　to have a frog in one's throat avoir un chat dans la gorge, **15.2**
　　to have a scratchy throat avoir la gorge qui gratte, **15.1**
　　to have a sore throat avoir mal à la gorge, **15.1**
　　to have a throat infection avoir une angine, **18.1**
to throw lancer, **13.2**
　　Thursday jeudi (m.), **2.2**
　　ticket le billet, **7.1**
　　one-way ticket l'aller simple (m.), **8.1**

round-trip ticket le billet aller-retour, **8.1**
ticket window le guichet, **8.1**
traffic ticket la contravention, **12.2**
tie la cravate, **10.1**
tight serré(e); **(shoes)** étroit(e), **10.2**
time (of day) l'heure (f.), **2**
　at what time? à quelle heure?, **2**
　to be on time être à l'heure, **8.1**
　What time is it? Il est quelle heure?, **2**
timid timide, **1.2**
tip (restaurant) le service, le pourboire, **5.2**
　The tip is included. Le service est compris., **5.2**
　to leave a tip laisser un pourboire, **5.2**
tire le pneu, **12.2**
　flat tire le pneu à plat, **12.2**
　spare tire la roue de secours, **12.2**
to à, **3.1**; à destination de (flight, etc.), **7.1**
　to the au, à la, à l', aux, **5**
　to the left of à gauche de, **5**
　to the right of à droite de, **5**
today aujourd'hui, **2.2**
together ensemble, **5.1**
toilet (bathroom) les toilettes (f. pl.), **4.2**
　toilet paper: roll of toilet paper le rouleau de papier hygiénique, **17.2**
toll highway l'autoroute (f.) à péage, **12.2**
tomato la tomate, **6.2**
tomorrow demain, **2.2**
　See you tomorrow. À demain., **BV**
too (also) aussi, **1.1**; (excessively) trop, **10.2**
tooth la dent, **11.1**
　se brosser les dents to brush one's teeth, **11.1**
toothpaste le dentifrice, **11.1**
towel la serviette, **17.2**
track (race) la piste, **13.2**; (train) la voie, **8.1**
traffic la circulation, **12.2**
　traffic light le feu, **12.2**
　green (traffic) light le feu vert, **12.2**
　red (traffic) light le feu rouge, **12.2**
　yellow (traffic) light le feu orange, **12.2**
tragedy la tragédie, **16.1**

trail la piste, **14.1**
　slalom trail la piste de slalom, **14.1**
train le train, **8.1**
　train station la gare, **8.1**
traveler le voyageur, la voyageuse, **8.1**
trigonometry la trigonométrie, **2.2**
T-shirt le tee-shirt, **9.2**
Tuesday mardi (m.), **2.2**
TV la télé, **3.2**
twelve douze, **BV**
twenty vingt, **BV**
two deux, **BV**
type le genre, **16.1**

U

uncle l'oncle (m.), **4.1**
under sous, **BV**
to **understand** comprendre, **9.1**
United States les États-Unis (m. pl.), **9.1**
unleaded sans plomb, **12.2**
unpleasant désagréable, antipathique (person), **1.2**
up to jusqu'à, **13.2**
us nous, **7**

V

to **vacate the room** libérer la chambre, **17.2**
valley la vallée, **14.1**
vanilla (adj.) à la vanille, **5.1**
vegetable le légume, **6.2**
very très, **1.1**
videocassette la vidéo(cassette), **3.2**
viral viral(e), **15.1**
volleyball le volley-ball, **13.2**

W

to **wait (for)** attendre, **8.1**
　to wait in line faire la queue, **8.1**
waiter le serveur, **5.1**
waiting room la salle d'attente, **8.1**
waitress la serveuse, **5.1**
to **wake up** se réveiller, **11.1**
to **walk** se promener, **11.2**
Walkman le walkman, **3.2**
wallet le portefeuille, **18.1**
to **want** vouloir, **6.1**
warm-up suit le survêtement, **11.2**
to **wash (one's face, hair, etc.)** se laver (la figure, les cheveux, etc.), **11.1**
　to wash and groom oneself faire sa toilette, **11.1**

washcloth le gant de toilette, **17.2**
to **watch** surveiller, **12.2**
water l'eau, **6.2**
to **water-ski** faire du ski nautique, **9.1**
wave la vague, **9.1**
we nous, **2**
to **wear** porter, **10.1**
weather le temps, **9.2**
　It's bad weather. Il fait mauvais., **9.2**
　It's nice weather. Il fait beau., **9.2**
　What's the weather like? Quel temps fait-il?, **9.2**
Wednesday mercredi (m.), **2.2**
week la semaine, **2.2**
　a (per) week par semaine, **3.2**
weekend le week-end, **2.2**
weight: to gain weight grossir, **11.2**
　to lose weight maigrir, **11.2**
well bien, **BV**
well-done (meat) bien cuit(e), **5.2**
what quel(le) (interrog. adj.), **7**; qu'est-ce que, **13**; quoi, **14**
　What else? (shopping) Avec ça?, **6.2**
　What is it? Qu'est-ce que c'est?, **BV**
　What is ... like? Comment est... ? (description), **1.1**
wheel la roue, **12.2**
when quand, **3.1**
　When is your birthday? C'est quand, ton anniversaire? (fam.), **4.1**
where où, **BV**
which (interrog. adj.) quel(le), **7**
to **whistle (blow a whistle)** siffler, **13.1**
white blanc, blanche, **10.2**
who qui, **BV**
　Who is it? Qui est-ce?, **BV**
　Who(m) (do you mean)? Qui ça?, **BV**
whole (adj.) tout(e)
whom qui, **14**
why pourquoi, **9.1**
wide large, **10.2**
wife la femme, **4.1**
to **win** gagner, **9.2**
wind le vent, **14.2**
window (seat in plane) (une place) côté fenêtre, **7.1**
to **windsurf** faire de la planche à voile, **9.1**
windy: It's windy. Il fait du vent., **9.2**
winner le/la gagnant(e), **13.2**

winter l'hiver (m.), **14.1**
with avec, **5.1**
without sans, **12.2**
woman la femme, **2.1**
work (art) l'œuvre, **16.2**
to **work** travailler, **3.2**
to **write** écrire, **12.2**
wrong: What's wrong with him?
Qu'est-ce qu'il a?, **15.1**

Y

year l'an (m.), l'année (f.), **4.1**
years: to be ... years old
avoir... ans, **4.1**
yellow jaune, **10.2**

yes oui, **BV**
yesterday hier, **13.1**
the day before yesterday
avant-hier, **13**
yesterday morning hier matin,
13
yogurt le yaourt, **6.1**
you te (dir. and ind. obj.), **15**; toi
(stress pron.), **9**; tu (fam. sing.),
1; vous (sing. form. and pl.), **2**
You're welcome. De rien., Je
t'en prie., Pas de quoi. (fam.);
Ce n'est rien., Il n'y a pas
de quoi., Je vous en prie.
(form.), **BV**

young jeune, **4.1**
your ta, ton, tes (fam.), **4**; votre,
vos (form.), **5**

Z

zero zéro, **BV**